T0368412

An Unconventional *Lifetime* Journey

My 269 Daily E-mail Stories

Bill Faulhaber

AN UNCONVENTIONAL LIFETIME JOURNEY
MY 269 DAILY E-MAIL STORIES

iUniverse books may be ordered through booksellers or by contacting:

iUniverse
1663 Liberty Drive
Bloomington, IN 47403
www.iuniverse.com
1-800-Authors (1-800-288-4677)

ISBN: 978-1-5320-0264-9 (sc)
ISBN: 978-1-5320-0265-6 (e)

Library of Congress Control Number: 2016912707

Print information available on the last page.

iUniverse rev. date: 08/19/2016

CONTENTS

Introduction xiii

Dedication xv

1.   Meeting Bob Hope' Wife 1
2.   Meeting Bob Hope..3
3.   Toney Penna Golf Co...5
4.   Bicentennial Year 1976 7
5.   Toney Penna's Bicentennial Year Promotion 9
6.   The Masters Invitational Golf Tournament 12
7.   I was not Welcome Back to the Masters Golf Tournament 14
8.   Changing Golf Clubs 16
9.   Breaking Down A Golf Course 18
10. A Little More Golf 20
11. Golf and More 22
12. Importance of the Golf Shaft 23
13. Final Golf Shaft Story 25
14. My 3 Wood and Toney Penna 27
15. Long Drive Contests 30
16. Communicating..33
17. A Little Backspin...35
18. More Backspin 38
19. Cousins 41
20. Plow Horses and Beyond..43
21. Back Home, Canton, Ohio 46
22. Canton and Golf..48
23. Golf in My Youth...50
24. Golf in the Forties 52
25. Dad, My Only Golf Teacher 56
26. High School Golf and Dad 58

27. Holes in One..62

28. My Paper Boy Years...65

29. Garage Basketball..68

30. School..71

31. Walking To School...74

32. Why Am I Writing These Stories....................................76

33. High School Basketball..79

34. Learning the German Language.....................................82

35. I Made the Varsity Basketball Team..............................84

36. High School Dance...87

37. My Brother...90

38. Camping Out & Fishing...94

39. Moving To Pittsburgh..98

40. Printers Helper... 101

41. Andy's Loop Café...104

42. United Sates Coast Guard.. 108

43. Coast Guard Conclusion.. 112

44. Back to Andy's Loop Cafe.. 115

45. Fast Pitch Softball and More.. 118

46. Changing Jobs..120

47. Massey Buick..123

48. Duck Pin Bowling..126

49. Ten Pin vs. Duck Pin Bowling.....................................129

50. Bowling Conclusion...132

51. Dangerous Truck Experience..134

52. Mom Called Me a Bum..136

53. Starting a New Life..139

54. Selling Buicks and New Friends...................................141

55. Don't Ever Burn Your Bridges.....................................143

56. How I Met Your Mommy..146

57. Artcraft Mantel Co. 149

58. Getting Married..152

59. Car Accident Conclusion... 155

60. Another Bump in the Road.. 157

61. Selling Vacuum Cleaners... 161

62. More about Vacuum Sales 165
63. Vacuum Sales Continued 169
64. High Pressure Selling 171
65. Leaving the Vacuum Business 174
66. What's next? 177
67. Spalding Hired Me! 179
68. Beginning My Career in Golf 182
69. Some Spalding History 184
70. My Rude Awakening 186
71. I Woke up Fast 188
72. What Was Ahead? 190
73. Getting Accepted 195
74. Spalding Business Problems 197
75. Recognize These Names? 201
76. Sam Snead and West Virginia 205
77. Traveling West Virginia 209
78. More West Virginia 212
79. Ohio 215
80. The Canton Ohio Powell Family 217
81. The Powell Family Part Two 220
82. Learning How To Play Golf 223
83. Golf Tips I Have Received 227
84. Family Insights and More Golf 233
85. Amateur or Professional? 237
86. My New Boss 240
87. Requesting a Career Change 243
88. Close Friend's fatal illness 245
89. Starting My Career Change 248
90. Retail Golf 252
91. A Bigger House 254
92. The Sporting Goods Business 257
93. Baseball Monopoly 260
94. Hotel Sample Rooms 263
95. Bids & Team Equipment 266
96. National Sporting Goods Show 268

97. Duke & Two Districts Salesmen 270
98. The Dinner..273
99. Little League Baseball 276
100. Learning the Sporting Goods Business......................278
101. Relocating...281
102. My New Responsibilities...284
103. The Round Tables 287
104. More Management Duties..291
105. Ohio Incidentals...293
106. Ohio Fun Times 295
107. Classic Golf Matches..299
108. Our New Years Eve Parties.......................................302
109. Family in Ohio 305
110. Good Times in Ohio...308
111. Interesting Incidents 312
112. Public Speaking..316
113. Presenting Football Shoes...320
114. Inventory & Theft Control..323
115. Traveling My District..328
116. Sales Management Realignment.................................331
117. Unpleasant Situations 334
118. Territory Splits 336
119. U. S. Open Golf Tournament 1946 340
120. Golf Balls..344
121. The Top-Flite Golf Ball 347
122. X-Out Golf Balls...350
123. Reclaimed Golf Balls..352
124. My Next Assignment 356
125. Golf Tour Professionals Contracts 359
126. Golf Tour Players Agents..363
127. My Rejection Of a Contract......................................366
128. My Golf Tour Involvements 369
129. My Tour Ball Decision Reaction 372
130. A Couple of Golf Tour Stories 375
131. Missed Contracts 378

132. New England Patriots Game and More 380
133. Back To Business 384
134. Director – Golf and Sales Relations 387
135. My Spalding Resignation 390
136. Looking Forward 392
137. More about Our Move 395
138. Solving a Product Line Problem 398
139. Golf Club Components 401
140. Golf Club Custom Fitting 404
141. Golf Clubs can be Complicated 407
142. Backspin to Ohio 411
143. The Ounce that Counts 413
144. Toney Penna's Friends 416
145. Toney Penna's Hair 418
146. Building a Sales Force 421
147. Growing Pains 423
148. Promoting Penna Drivers on the Golf Tour 426
149. The Old PGA Country Club 429
150. Growing the Penna Co. Business 431
151. Graphite Demonstrators 434
152. Demo Program Outline 436
153. Graphite Demo Results 439
154. Demo Irons? 442
155. Where Do We Go From Here? 444
156. My Thoughts, Etc. 446
157. Almost No Tomorrow 449
158. Conclusion of San Antonio Trip 453
159. Golf Ball Tests 456
160. Golf Ball Tests Inconclusive 458
161. I Am Not Surprised 460
162. Rawlings Golf Co. Conclusion 463
163. What Would I Do? 466
164. What Happened, My Plans Changed 468
165. Welcome Home Letters 471
166. Spalding Customer Trips, Spain First 473

167. Black Leather Coat...476
168. Ireland..479
169. Hurling Match..482
170. Hawaii and More..485
171. Germany, Switzerland & Austria............................488
172. The "Passion" Play in Oberammergau 491
173. A Few More Trips 494
174. Spalding 2nd Time Around...................................497
175. Tomorrow 498
176. The Changing Pro Only Golf Business....................500
177. Pro Only Golf Changed Forever.............................503
178. Pro Only Golf Oversight.......................................505
179. Florida Territory Split..508
180. My Territory Split Plan...510
181. A New Sales Force Is Born 512
182. My New Partners 514
183. Go the Extra Mile 516
184. My Own Warehouse 518
185. What Was I Doing..521
186. Wm. Faulhaber Enterprises, Inc. 523
187. Two New Homes for Spalding 525
188. Spalding's Second New Home................................527
189. My Proposal to Spalding 530
190. Proposal Continued...534
191. Marketing Concept Proposal.................................538
192. More about Wm. Faulhaber Enterprises, Inc. 542
193. Two More Mortgages 545
194. Setting Up a New Business....................................547
195. Faulhaber Enterprises Growth...............................549
196. Upgrading Our Operation 551
197. Expanding Our Operation 552
198. More Service Offerings...554
199. What Does the Future Look Like............................557
200. Our Dock and First Boat 559
201. The Bay Liner..561

202. The Houseboat 563

203. The Houseboat's Condition 565

204. Relocating & Naming the Boat 567

205. The Houseboats Shocking Condition 569

206. Houseboat Repairs 571

207. Houseboat Updates 573

208. Launching the New POS 575

209. Houseboat Survey 577

210. Celebrities Aboard 579

211. POS Sleeps 2 to 4 Adults? 581

212. Our New Pontoon Boat 584

213. A New Boat Lift...586

214. Family Fun on the Pontoon Boat 588

215. Boat Story Conclusion 591

216. Golf, Game of a Lifetime 593

217. More Golf is a Game of Honesty.......................596

218. Caddies and Golf Carts 598

219. Getting Close to Retirement.............................601

220. Old A. G. Spalding & Bros. 603

221. No More Station Wagons 605

222. The Knights of Columbus 607

223. More about the Knights 608

224. What Does Santa Maria Council 4999 Do? 610

225. Family & Community Activities 612

226. Youth & Pro-Life Activities 614

227. My Involvement in the Knights.........................616

228. Join Something, Be Active................................618

229. More Knights Activities...................................620

230. The Treasurers Job 622

231. Treasurers Responsibility 624

232. Bingo 626

233. Bingo Volunteers and More..............................628

234. Bingo Players like Family 629

235. More about Bingo 631

236. Bingo Workers 633

237. Smoke Free Bingo? 635
238. What Happened Next? 637
239. Bingo Story Not Over Yet 639
240. More Bingo Problems...............................641
241. More K of C Experiences 644
242. My Thoughts and Goals............................646
243. Why Have Goals?...................................648
244. More Badges and Goals............................650
245. Added Events 652
246. Knee and Heart Problems 654
247. After Heart Bypass Surgery 656
248. Heart to Heart Club................................658
249. Support Group & Cardiac Rehab...................660
250. Cardiac Rehab......................................662
251. Another K of C Highlight..........................665
252. Our Lady of Bethlehem Icon......................666
253. Father John Mericantante..........................669
254. Pahokee..671
255. Medical and Dental Help and More................673
256. My Monthly Trips..................................675
257. Pahokee Trips Continued 677
258. Miracles at St. Mary's.............................679
259. Is a New Church Possible?........................681
260. The Altar..683
261. The Altars New Look 685
262. More Money Needed 687
263. The New Church Building.........................689
264. The New Church Dedication 693
265. Parting Thoughts about St. Mary's................695
266. DeCesares', the Place for Ribs 697
267. DeCesares Patrons.................................699
268. Rambling Thoughts Continued....................701
269. The Most Important People I've Met, Is You 706

INTRODUCTION

An Unconventional Lifetime Journey
My Daily Email Stories

*H*OW ALL OF THESE EMAIL stories got started was purely accidental. One day I was sending an email to my family and friends and it was about Bob Hope the well known comedian. The thought struck me to write another email that simply started, "Meeting Bob Hope". That is how all of these stories started and one story just led to another. I kept receiving feedback from my children telling me, "Hey dad, I didn't know that about you".

I was sending these stories to about 100 people and I began to hear nice comments from them as well about how much they were enjoying what I had written. And many said they were sending my stories on to others that I didn't even know. Everyone was encouraging me to keep the stories coming which inspired me to do just that. Using the word "Backspin" at times I eventually went back in time to my childhood and started to write stories that I could remember which I thought might be of interest to others as well.

What really surprised me was non family members were constantly letting me know how much they were enjoying my personal history and letting me know they were looking forward to each future story.

For most of my adult life I was employed by Spalding Sports Worldwide and was with that company just short of forty years so my emails were also going to many former employees I have know over those years, and they too were encouraging me to keep the stories coming.

My business life took me and our family to different locations and I enjoyed many different positions within the Spalding Company's sales and sales management divisions. I was mostly involved with the golf business and held several different titles with the higher titles such as Vice President of Sales and Marketing, but never President until I finally gave myself that title when I started my own company, William Faulhaber Enterprises, Inc. My business career was never boring because of all the different positions I became involved with and it enabled me to meet many very interesting and well known people, not only in sports and business world but in the entertainment world as well, plus meeting all the everyday people who are the backbone of this great nation. In other words the most important people I have met in my lifetime are really, you.

Raising a family of four children was a tough job for my wife, Dolores "Dee" because of our frequent relocations in our early years as I was traveling much of the time. Dee has done an outstanding job as mother and wife and without her support I would not have been as successful as I was.

I had so much encouragement from so many to turn all these 269 stories into a book that I have decided to do so. My biggest interest in doing so is that Dee and I have seventeen children, four of our own and they have presented us with eight grandchildren and as of this writing we now have five great grandchildren and that my friends adds up to seventeen. I wanted all of them to have a copy of my book as they might enjoy all of this history I have written about years from now they may never have known in any other way.

And for those of you who may be reading these stories I pray that all of you have a healthy happy and productive life. Be a doer and not a follower and help build a better future leaving this world a better place than you have found it. Have compassion for your fellow human beings and treat people like you like to be treated. God bless you and all of yours, and enjoy the stories.

William H. "Bill" Faulhaber

DEDICATION

*T*HIS BOOK OF DAILY EMAILS sent to my family, friends, Knights of Columbus brothers and many of my Spalding Sports Worldwide fellow employees I dedicate all of this to my mother and father, Helen and Henry Faulhaber. If it hadn't been for them these stories would never have been written. They were outstanding loving and caring parents. And to my older brother Richard who was my protector when we were young kids and he tried his best to keep me in line. RIP my brother and friend.

Also to my wonderful friend and wife Dolores, (Dee), who tried her best to keep me focused? Dee told me from the beginning of our marriage that she would like to have at least six children. Although we fell short of that number Dee presented us with four wonderful children, Diane, Cynthia, James and Linda. And we celebrated our 60th wedding anniversary February 11, 2016.

Also to everyone mentioned by name or otherwise in all these 269 chapters, without you there would have been no stories to tell.

God Bless you all and all of yours.

William Henry "Bill" Faulhaber

Meeting Bob Hope' Wife #1

*W*HAT A NICE, FRIENDLY LADY. This happened when I was still back in Chicopee, Mass., Spalding's home office. I was playing in an Ladies Professional Golf Association Pro Amateur tournament at the Pleasant Valley County Club, Sutton, Mass., which has hosted many men's tour events. Dolores Hope was the hostess for this event. I can't remember the name of the lady professional I was playing with. Everybody played the same distance as the lady professional which was really the men's middle tees, not the lady tees. At the end of the round this lady pro asked me what I thought I shot, and I replied I think I shot 67. She said no, you shot 66. I did play exceptional that day and our team tied for first place.

There was a banquet that evening, and that is when I met Dolores Hope. As the Spalding representative at the event we had donated eight sets of golf clubs for the armature winners of the first and second place positions. Well, I won a set of clubs I donated on behalf of Spalding, which of course I did not need. Footnote, Dolores was a professional singer before she married Bob. I would guess at the time, she was in her early sixties, pretty, and she sang a song or two as well, and pretty darn well. She presented the prizes, and because Spalding donated them, I was expected to say a few words. At the same time of the presentation of the clubs to me, it was my turn at the mike. There was another event at that same course in about two weeks, which was called the "Jimmy Fund", raising funds for cancer research in honor of this young man who passed away. I donated the clubs I won to the Jimmy Fund tournament in the name of Spalding, which went over very well with the audience. No one there knew that I had resigned my job with Spalding and it was my last week with Spalding before moving to Florida and taking a position of Vice President of Sales and Marketing with the Toney Penna Golf Co., located in Jupiter, Florida. I remained with the Penna Co. for three years and then returned to Spalding. My years with Spalding were 1957 through 1974, with Penna 1974 - 1977, and Spalding again, 1977 - 1995, a 38 year span, and then I retired at age 64. (Never burn bridges). That leads me to the rest of the story.

Meeting Bob Hope #2

*B*Y NOW I HAVE RELOCATED to Florida in 1974 having accepted a position with the Toney Penna Golf Co., a small custom club manufacturer. There is a real Toney Penna and I must tell you something about Toney and that will lead me into how I met Bob Hope.

Back in the 1930's, 40's, & 50's even into the early 60's, the Golf Tour was nothing like today. Very few tournaments, a lot of them were more social events. These popular people in the entertainment industry loved to play with those golf professional and a lot of friendships were formed. Toney had many life long friends such as Bob Hope, Bing Crosby, Perry Como and others. Toney Penna was a touring professional in those years, but most all these pros had other jobs, many were head professionals at golf clubs. Toney Penna was a very outgoing well dressed man with a wide grin and he was a very good player who also worked for the MacGregor Golf Co. He eventually was responsible for signing other touring pro's to contracts representing the MacGregor Co., and also ended up as their chief golf club designer.

As a side story, for many years on the tour and up until the metal drivers came into existence, Toney Penna designed woods and irons, first for Macgregor, and then his own Toney Penna Golf Company. Toney's drivers were by far the most popular used on tour. As an example, Greg Norman, when he was on the Spalding touring pro consultant staff, used a MacGregor Toney Penna designed driver. Why was he, a Spalding consultant, allowed to use another club? At one time I was in charge of signing contracts with the men's and ladies' tour players. If a player was playing other equipment, it was difficult for them to change all 14 clubs at one time, and the golf ball as well.

Within a set of 14 golf clubs, the most used are the driver, putter and the wedges, all what we in the golf business call the scoring clubs. It was best to let them continue using the three or four clubs most important to them so the transition wasn't so severe. Spalding at the time required they use no less than 10 clubs to be a Spalding manufacture club.

The golf club Bob Hope was seen with in his shows was made by MacGregor. Bob switched to a Toney Penna club when Toney left Macgregor and started his own company. Bob Hope was loyal to his friends, and when Bob was in this area he would drop in and visit with Toney at his plant which was located in Jupiter, Florida. That is where I met Bob Hope, Bing Crosby, Perry Como and others. They would often drop in to see Toney, which brings me to another story about Toney you might find interesting. Turn the page.

Toney Penna Golf Co. #3

I met Bob Hope through Toney Penna. Toney was a superb Golf Club designer and a wonderful man. However, to work for and with him, everything had to be his idea, or just forget it. So I found out in a hurry as Vice President of Sales and Marketing for the Penna Golf Co. that any idea I had to improve sales and marketing was difficult to convince Toney of those ideas.

The owners of the Penna Co., wanted to increase sales of course. When I arrived all clubs manufactured were not started in production until an order was received. There was no sales force so everything was word of mouth. Orders for clubs were coming from his many friends in the golf business, It was very important that I had to build a sales force by hiring independent reps around the county who were in the golf business. I needed people that were selling golf products other than golf clubs to these golf pros shops.

To support that sales group and increase sales we could not wait to get an order and then make the club. At the time Toney offered three different men's right handed drivers and one left handed driver, in various shaft flexes, all steel at the time. All fairway woods to match were the same design, but were color finished to match the driver in appearance.

How do I increase sales and support the sales group? Clubs take several weeks to produce. You can't call on the Golf shops and ask them to sell a product that won't be delivered for weeks; the product had to be available in a few days. I did some research, and although Toney offered everything as custom made, a very large percent of his sales were for the standard specifications at that time.

So, the key was to convince Toney. He would not listen to anyone else but very close friends. He took the attitude that he was the only one who knew anything about his own world in the golf business. We had to convince him we must build inventory of all models in various quantities so as to support the sales force and meet our sales and profit budgets while keeping the factory workers busy 40 hours a week. All the things needed to run a successful business. The company was not making much profit at the time.

This story is too long now to explain how I got that accomplished, but I did. I planted a lot of little ideas and those ideas stated to grow with a lot of watering. Little things like, Toney, I think what you said makes a lot of sense, and then planted the seed and finally he had a brilliant idea. He would call all his people into his office and stated, "I have a great idea! We're going to build inventory of our most popular clubs."

Mission accomplished. He ended up telling me that that is how to run a business, we needed to build inventory and what the hell was I doing all this time! If you think all of this is patting my own back, well, yes it is!

I have another of Toney's ideas to tell you about. It's our Country's Bicentennial birthday, in 1976.

BICENTENNIAL YEAR 1976 #4

*T*HIS STORY IS ABOUT OUR country's Bicentennial year. What got me started on this was one day I noticed sitting in the corner of Toney's office were a lot of experimental clubs and among them was a driver that had been finished with three colors blending into one another, the colors were red white and blue!

This was in 1975 and I was aware that our great country would be celebrating its 200th birthday in 1976. A little trivia here, Spalding, the oldest sporting goods company in the U.S.A. would be celebrating their 100th birthday on that date as well.

That flash of light in my cranium said that anything Red White and Blue will sell in 1976. Why not a golf club driver, one that could be displayed in someone's officer or den in a home perhaps. Not really to be used but a memento honoring the 200th birthday of the good ol' U.S.A.! Now how do I get that done and make it his idea and not mine?

On top of all this over the years there was a large amount of discarded rejected materials in the warehouse such as persimmon wood heads not useable due to various reasons, mostly cosmetic, sap stains in the wood, bad grain, etc. Those would show up through light stains used to finish the woods. There were all kinds of steel shafts discarded for various reasons, plus all kinds of grips. Everything needed to put a wood club together. All this inventory's cost had been written off over the years so it was just sitting there collecting dust with no cost involved, free materials.

Now if I could just sell this idea to Toney our costs would not involve any materials, only factory costs, labor, generally overhead which goes on anyway, promotional advertising and general costs, but not materials. And I would price those clubs 25 percent above the normal wholesale price for Penna woods. The golf professional could in turn retail them for a higher price a well as a specialty item.

All this worked out and we ran ad's in the golf magazines. It was a very successful promotion, we sold everything, including fairway woods. We actually ran out of written off inventory and had to start using good inventory. That was just fine because out built in wholesale price was 25 percent higher than normal anyway.

We had a very successful year, this was just part of it, but it sure did help. Now how did all of this happen? How did I get Toney to admit he had this idea in the back of his mind all along? Read on.

Toney Penna's Bicentennial Year Promotion #5

*H*ow I convinced Toney Penna to think it was his idea to make a red, white and blue colored golf club.

The year was 1975. To accomplish this, it had to be done the year before 1976. Here is how it happened. Toney and I traveled together to Chicago to promote our products to the tour players who were playing two tournaments back to back in the same city which was very unusual. They were The Western Open and the U. S. Open and we would be there the better part of two weeks. I began to work on him, a little at a time …

We might be anywhere, dinner, on the practice range, if I had his attention for a brief time I started by just saying things like, "Toney, you amaze me that's a great idea you have." And I would just drop it there, saying no more. He just looked at me with a puzzled look, and said nothing. The next day, somewhere, I would drop another one, something like, "Toney, you sly old fox, what a great idea!" And again, say nothing more, his expression again puzzled, Toney said nothing.

After several days of dropping some little tid bits like that Toney finally said to me, "what the hell are you talking about?" Just what I was waiting for! I said, "Well Toney, you know what is going on in this country next year, and what you have in mind is really something." I would say no more, nor did he. He just looked at me puzzled and we went about our business. I did not bring it up again, the seed had been planted. I could just see he was trying to figure out what I was talking about.

Then I dropped another one, "Toney, you know that next year our

Country is celebrating its Bicentennial year." He finally replied, "what the hell is that?"

I replied, "Well Toney, you know our county will be 200 years old, you really are a sly one. You know that anything red, white and blue is going to sell like hot cakes, don't you!" He said nothing, and this was my opening, I said, "Come on, Toney. I saw that red, white and blue driver in the corner of your office. You're planning on bringing that to the market next year in celebration of our County's 200 birthdays aren't you?" Toney said nothing.

I was done, the seeds were planted and watered, they are beginning to grow and the mission is almost complete. Now it is just a matter of waiting for him to act.

It didn't take long. The first day back in the office he called a meeting of all personnel, office, and factory, everybody. We gathered in his office and sitting on his desk was that red, white and blue driver. I had to hide my face I almost broke out in laughter, but held it. He paused for effect, and then said very proudly.

"I have a great idea!" "Do you know what's happening in this Country next year?"

True story but it's not over. The driver he had, the red, white and blue stripes were running in the wrong direction and they did not look right. To explain, when placing the club in a playing position the colored stripes ran towards me, red in the front, white in the middle, and blue towards the back of the club. It did not flow smoothly. If the colors were reversed, the red being on the toe of the club, the furthest point from me, and then the white blended in the middle coming towards me and then the blue on the heel, the part closest to the shaft, it would appear the flow was going in the direction that the club would travel through the swing. As it was, it looked like I was hitting against the direction of the motion of the swing, like a wall.

And that is how it eventually ended up, Toney changed the direction of the colors, because he had another idea, and I don't know where he got that idea! I am not going to tell you either.

Toney did come up with another idea for the club as it needed a decal on the crown. He came up with decal, a soaring eagle. In its claws was an olive branch plus the American flag. Well done, but, in my opinion the decal was way too large. It looked like it covered the top half of the club. Since I won the battle so far, I did not want to lose the war. I did not fight the oversize decal and we proceeded with.

After all that work, I never thought about getting one of those clubs for myself! Not until the last one was gone it dawned on me, but it was too late. I do not have one. I don't have Toney's autograph either. I have another story to tell about Toney and myself which took place at the Masters Golf Tournament and that story will be the next chapter.

THE MASTERS INVITATIONAL
GOLF TOURNAMENT #6

I HAVE BEEN FORTUNATE TO ATTEND six Masters Golf Tournaments. three while with Spalding and three with the Toney Penna Golf Co. There is no other golf tournament like the Masters. The rolling terrain in Augusta, Georgia and the setting of this golf course is breathtaking. I don't have the writing ability to describe it. If you watch on TV you will get some idea, but TV does not pick up the total beauty. TV does not show how much the hills and valleys are sloped nor the atmosphere of being there in person. I'll give you an example of the little things that are done there during the tournament, the concession stands serve everything in the color of green. The cups, straws, napkins and the wrapping paper for sandwiches. Why? If a spectator drops something on the ground it won't see it as it won't show up on your TV picture. The green colors of these items blend right in with the grass and no one seems to drop anything anyway, the people don't seem to litter at the Masters! It seems everyone puts their garbage where it belongs, in the green garbage containers.

The prices they charge for these items, you won't believe. The Masters does not gouge anyone. When I attended years ago, and I have been told even now, the prices they charged have not changed that much. I think my memory is good enough that these prices are pretty darn correct. Soft drinks and water were $1.50. A beer is $2.50 and $1.75 for a southern ham and cheese sandwich, a very large one at that. And parking your car is free!

The attendance is never announced and the waiting list for tickets used to be something like 3 years. Season ticket holders have to die before tickets become available. Spalding had the most tickets of any golf company, because Bobby Jones, one of the cofounders of this club and the tournament itself, was a Vice President of Spalding. I think Spalding had twelve badges.

The Penna Co. had just two badges. No one can get on this course to play without being a quest of a member and the member must play with the quest. The fact that even when Bobby Jones was living, and both the head Golf Professionals at the club were on the Spalding Advisory staff, they could not get us on the course, even Spalding executives.

Back to Toney Penna, I want to tell you about a dinner I had with Toney and two Hall of Fame golfers who were also on TV frequently as commentators and announcers. This will be my next story plus I'll let you know why I was told in writing by Clifford Roberts why I was not welcome to return to the Masters. Clifford was the Chairman of the Augusta National Golf Club and the Masters tournament.

I was not Welcome Back to the
Masters Golf Tournament #7

*W*HY I HAD BEEN TOLD not to come back to the Augusta National Golf Club and the Masters Golf Tournament. I've been thrown out of better places, but can't remember where. It was really Toney's fault, but that story will come later, first things first, a dinner with Toney and two Hall of Fame golfers.

The younger set and non golfers reading this might not have heard about some of these old names I have been coming up with. I assure you, they were real and they were special in their day. In golf circles, they will never be forgotten, especially those in the Hall of Fame as were these two gentlemen I had dinner with.

I have a date for dinner with Toney and his friends and they are none other than Gene Sarazen and Jimmy Demaret. What a delightful evening. I had never met either one of these Hall of Famers before this dinner but they made me feel like we knew each other forever. I can't tell you all about them in this short story but just a quickie about each man. Gene Sarazen is credited with the invention of the Sand Club and Gene also double eagled the par five 15th hole in one Masters tournament and won the tournament. For you non golfers that double eagle was 2 strokes on a par 5 hole is which is 3 under par. That is a much rarer feat than a hole in one, because a hole in one is only 2 under par on a par 3 hole. That shot by Sarazen has been called the shot heard around the world. Dapper Jimmy Demaret wore wild colored clothes, shirt, slacks, shoes and sweaters when he played before any other player ever did. He was also very humorous and could sing too. What a wonderful evening for me personally.

Obviously this was my last Masters, 1977. On the day Toney and

I were leaving to return home, Toney said to me, "Bill, give me your badge, I need it for someone." I said, "Toney, it has my name on it. You can't give it to someone else, it's not allowed, it is for me and only me." Toney's my Boss, right? He says to me, "Bill, give the damn badge to me, nobody knows you." Very reluctantly I gave it to him. About two weeks later I received a letter, the return address was the Augusta National Golf Club, home of the Masters. I'm thinking, what in the world is this, but I knew what it was before I opened it with trembling hands. It was from Clifford Roberts, the main man of the Masters Tournament informing me that my badge was spotted on another person. Spotted by him no less and he informed me it was strictly against the rules to pass a badge on to someone it was not intended for. He made it clear that because I broke the rule, the Masters Tournament was, in so many words, "Out of bounds for me." I was not invited back.

As Toney said, "Nobody knows you, Bill."

I guess I'm in good company. Do you know who Gary McCord is? He is a former tour player with a big handlebar mustache became an on course golf TV announcer. During a telecast at the Masters one year Gary mentioned some minor thing on the air. The Masters people did not like his comments and informed the TV network that Gary was not to set foot on the property again. He was not invited back, either. Another thing about Gary, he was on the tour for many years but Gary never won a golf tournament on the regular tour. His license plate was personalized and it read, "NO-WINS". He finally won a tournament on the Champions Tour, for those fifty years old and older. Had to change his license plate, I don't know what he changed it to but if I had to guess, how about "ONE-WIN".

Changing Golf Clubs #8

*F*OR THOSE OF YOU WHO do not play golf, a lot of this may be a little bit strange, however, I believe you will find this subject understandable and informative, maybe even entertaining. I had mentioned in a previous story about the danger of touring Pros changing clubs. That would apply to anyone. Understand that I have been out of golf now 21 years after retirement. I stopped playing golf too when I was about 70 years young. My friend "Arthur," arthritis, plus bad knees finally got to me. I was still scoring in the mid to low 80's when I stepped away from the game I love. Beyond the physical pain the other pain I was feeling was hitting so many bad shots compared to good ones. Good players will understand that statement. It's hard to enjoy playing when a pretty good player hits more bad shots than good, then the enjoyment of playing tends to disappear. The casual higher scoring golfer is happy by the few good shots he/she hits in a round of golf compared to the bad ones. Those good ones, especially near the end of the round, bring them back. I hope you can understand that reasoning.

Equipment has change dramatically and I have never played with the new tech clubs used today, or the longer golf balls. My woods were persimmon until the last few years when I finally switched from wood to metal. I did hit the ball long and won several long drive contests, one at the age of 50! The distance the ball travels today is ridicules, but things change over time. Golf courses have been lengthened to some degree to try and compensate for the so called longer ball. In this day and age, Tour Pros play par 4 holes with a driver and wedge. As an example let's take a hole of 440 yards in length. They're now hitting drives 300 yards, plus. A 300 yard drive will leave them with 140 yards to the green. That means they only need a little 9 iron or wedge to reach the green, and then its putter time. That's three clubs, driver, wedge and putter. The rules state a maximum of 14 clubs can be used, when do they do use the other 11 clubs in their bag?

Let me explain, when I was playing and if I hit a drive about 260, 270 that left me with 180, 170 yards to the green of a hole that is 440 yards long. That means to reach the green, under windless conditions, I would be hitting a 4 or 5 iron, certainly not a 9 iron or wedge, see the difference? The distance I hit the ball with the driver was pretty close to the average tour player in those days.

As I mentioned before that when dealing with signing Touring Pros to a contract it was best for all concerned to let these players keep their favorite three or four clubs, do not change them for something different. The reason for signing players was for the exposure of a company's equipment to the golfing public. If they change all the clubs, it takes one heck of a long time to get used to new equipment and their game may suffer for quite some time. If that happens you may not see that player in contention. Less exposure due to the fact he won't get much TV time and fewer spectators following his as well. Loss of exposure of our equipment that was intended by singing that player

Normally those clubs I'm talking about are their driver, putter, and one or two wedges. Why those clubs? Those are the so called scoring clubs. Let me explain how I define a golf course which leads to what clubs are the most important to a good player. That takes a little explaining, so that will have to wait until the next chapter.

One last note, it's my opinion that the golf shaft is the most important part of a club. I'll explain that comment later and I think you will find that will be an interesting read. I will also let you in on one of my most embarrassing moments which took place when I was a rookie salesman with Spalding. It happened while talking with the longest driver of the golf ball at that time, Jimmy Thompson. Read on.

Breaking Down A Golf Course #9

*G*OLF COURSES ARE PRETTY MUCH the same when it comes to par. For the non golfers, a golf hole is designed normally with three different configurations. Par is the number of strokes for each hole. Strokes are how many times contact is made with the ball with a golf club. I used this breakdown to figure out which are the most important, or most used clubs of the 14 allowable clubs permitted. That number of clubs can consist of any combination a player is more confident with.

Usually a course has a par of 72. The front nine holes and the second nine holes, each have five par fours, two par fives and two par threes. Par is 36 for each nine holes. This can vary but that is the normal course set up. Now a par 4 it takes two shots to reach the green and 2 putts to get the ball into the hole, that's 4 stokes. On a par 5 hole, three shots to reach the green and 2 putts, that's 5 stokes. A par 3 hole, one shot to reach the green and 2 putts, that's 3 strokes. Bingo, that's 36 strokes. The same on the back nine, so the par is 72, now it get's interesting. As I have stated before there are 14 allowable clubs available to accomplish this goal of scoring as low as possible.

There are 10 par four holes and 4 par five holes that a player can normally hit a driver, that's 14 strokes with one club. There are 18 greens, and 2 putts per green is another 36 strokes. Add those two together you have 50 strokes. On the par fives, the third shot to reach the green for low handicap player would most likely be a wedge and that is 4 more strokes, one for each par five and this ads up to 54 strokes. On the par 3 holes, it would depend on the distance what club is used; it would vary, but would not normally be a driver and usually not a wedge. So now we have 54 strokes so far, 14 driver strokes, 36 putter strokes, 4 wedge strokes. 54 total strokes using just 3 clubs out of 14 available.

That leaves 18 strokes to be played with the remaining 11 clubs not used so far. 72 par or strokes, remember that is how a course is designed. So now you see why we let those pro's keep their 3 or 4 favorite clubs which almost always will be the Driver, Wedge, and Putter. I hope I have been able to make all of this data understandable.

Those other 11 clubs don't get used much do they? The next most used golf club would be the Sand Club, either out of sand traps around the green, or off the fairway or rough, usually within 100 yards of the green. There you have it, the 3 or 4 clubs we have been talking about. And I rest my case.

Before I leave this story today I must to tell a story that happened in the Hospital yesterday. I was in for surgery to get my plumbing fixed. Two very nice nurses were prepping me but I won't get into that part. One told me her name was Dottie, I turned to the other and asked what her name is and she told me, Diane. I looked at both of them and said, double D's. They looked at each other and then they both broke out in uncontrollable laughter. For a second I didn't realize why and then it hit me. While standing up both these ladies can't see their toes! That's right, both nurses were double D's. I doubt very seriously if any hospital room preparing a patient for surgery ever heard such an outbreak of loud laughter.

A Little More Golf #10

*D*O YOU REMEMBER WHEN I said something about the golf shaft being the most important part of a golf club? The same is true of the current exotic shafts and I don't even know what materials there using now. When I retired 21 years ago, I retired! I have not followed the equipment changes and have turned my attention to other things. Why hang on after almost 40 years of what I feel was a successful career.

However some things don't change even though the technology of the shaft and its materials has advanced so much, the shaft is still the most single important part of a club and that will never change.

Golf shafts must be tuned, or fitted, to a persons swing, not visa versa. One should not have to change his swing for a new shaft. It should be fitted to your swing. Simply, the shaft must fit your swing and not the opposite.

I mentioned in the last chapter that one of my most embarrassing moments in my life involved the longest driver of the golf boll in his day. This took place in the 50's. His name was Jimmy Thompson, a touring pro on the Spalding advisory staff. This happened at my very first sales meeting in 1957 and Jimmy was a quest speaker. I have played golf from age 9, my dad was a very good golfer and taught me what little I knew at the time. I played through my High School years, age 17. I was Captain of the golf team and thought I could play. I could hit the ball a long way but sometimes did not know where the ball was going to land. There was not a lot of rough on the courses I played in those days, so it didn't matter where it landed, except out of bounds.

I moved from Canton, Ohio right after High School in 1949 to Pittsburgh, Pa. and I did not play golf again until I got my first interview with Spalding. That is eight long years without touching a club. That's a lot of years where my golf game could have developed quite a bit. I am starting my career with Spalding at the ripe old age of twenty six, married with one child and one baking in the oven. Dee and I eventually became the proud parents of four great kids.

So, here I am talking to a future Hall of Famer, Jimmy Thompson, who was known at that time as the longest driver of the golf ball. I was thinking that I was a long ball hitter as well but rally didn't know much about golf as I thought and less about golf equipment. We are still talking about golf shafts, which at the time I knew nothing about. I thought that if a shaft was really flexible, it would sling the club head into the ball and the ball would take off for a long ride. It would, but with little control as I found out later. So here I am having a conversation with Jimmy and I ask Jimmy what kind of shaft did he use to make the ball go so far, did he use a real flexible shaft?

Jimmy was a real nice guy and he quietly explained to me, so no one else could hear my stupid question, about golf shaft flexes. The shaft flex he used was an extra stiff True Temper. True Temper manufactured the most popular steel golf shafts used in those years. Jimmy explained to me how the shafts worked for the various swings a golfer may have. With a slow and week swing a flexible shaft is best. As a swing increases in speed and strength, the shaft flex should become firmer, to a medium flex, to stiff and then extra stiff for the very faster stronger swing. The shaft is the engine of the club and must be fitted to the proper swing power, or speed, or both, for proper control of where the golf is going to go. I felt rather stupid but Jimmy was great about it and I don't think he ever asked anyone who that stupid kid was.

I will convey to you next what happened to me when I left Spalding and went to work for the Penna Co. as I had to change clubs as well. It was then that it hit me personally about a drastic change in clubs and learned more about golf shafts. Wow, I was aware of the problems that can cause but had never experienced that myself until 1974.

GOLF AND MORE #11

I HAVE TO THANK MY DAD for insisting I take typing when I was in school. He always told me I would find it invaluable throughout my life and he was so right. Sure makes it easy to write these stories. Among other things he always told me that if I wanted to be a good golfer I should always play with better golfers than myself and always have something to play for. No casual golf, I should make bets and that if I loose it hurts the wallet a little bit. Being frugal, that's means cheap and it made me play harder. Dad told me to better myself in what ever I am doing, not just golf.

Another close friend who has just written a book about his life is also receiving these stories is Father John Mericantante and is originally from Boston. I read his book, "The Dangling Urinal", "An Unconventional Catholic Priesthood". I'm serious about the name, not his name, I mean the book. I won't tell you how he came about that book's title as you can find out for yourself if you go online, go to Amazon and type in his name or the name of the book, it is a good read and I think you would enjoy it. Read about a poor little Priest who is now 67 years old. Since retirement he stills says Mass every day using his $260,000.00 Chalice! You read that right, six figures and no cents. I assure you it's a very interesting book.

I wanted to touch on something before I finish my story about golf shafts! I better do that before those shafts become so old and rusted the story might appear like we are back in the hickory wood shaft era. In the next chapter I promise I'll finish at least part of the story ...

Importance of the Golf Shaft #12

*L*ET'S TALK MORE ABOUT GOLF shafts. When I was promoted to regional sales manager I had to relocate from Pittsburgh to the Cleveland, Ohio area. Our office and distribution center was in Solon, we relocated to nearby Chagrin Falls, south east of Cleveland. It was there I ordered a new set of clubs for myself. This was in1964 and little did I know at the time the steel shafts in my new wood clubs would be a part of this story 10 years later. My golf club specifications were not standard and were custom made. I asked John St. Clare our custom club maker at the Spalding plant in Chicopee, Mass., to make up a set of persimmon woods for me, a driver, 3 and 5 wood. It was a custom model so I asked for a light cherry finish so the grain of the wood could be seen. The woods had a black insert in the face of the clubs they had a brass back weight. They were and are to this day, beautiful. I used the standard length of a 43" driver and requested a stiff shaft, but I did not specify which one, not thinking there were several available with the shaft flexes in different areas of the shaft. For instance at that time the True Temper dynamic stiff steel shaft was known to be tip stiff, the part nearest the head of the club. I thought that is what I had in my woods.

That's a different part of the story which I'll try and complete today. Because I was 6 foot 2 inches tall at the time I had my irons 1" longer than standard which worked well for me. I changed my irons from time to time, but not those beautiful woods as they worked very well for me. Once in a while I would try something else but could not find anything that would perform like those woods. "If it ain't broken, don't try and fix it."

I was in Cleveland for 7 years and was promoted again, this time to National Sales Manager Professional Golf Division in Chicopee,

Ma. Spalding's home office, and relocated my family in the suburb of Wilbraham, home of the Friendly Ice-cream Restaurants. Three years later I left Spalding and moved to North Palm Beach, Fl. I took the position of Vice President of Sales and Marketing with the Toney Penna Golf Co. Why both titles? Darn small company. My beautiful woods are still with me. Hold on, I changed Golf Companies, I have to change clubs! Yikes!

Ace Harper was the head man in charge of the Penna manufacturing and was a superb custom club expert. He worked with Toney while they were both with the MacGregor sporting goods company located in Cincinnati, Ohio. Ace made clubs for all of Macgregor's touring and home club golf professionals. I asked Ace to make a set of Penna clubs for me with the same specifications I had been using. Toney Penna was a very good golf iron designer as well as woods, but was generally know for his work with wood clubs. I had absolutely no problem with the irons. But the woods!

I could not hit the driver or the 3 wood at all. As much as I tried to adjust to those clubs I could not control the ball. Great looking clubs, I liked their appearance which is important. Love at first sight is important more ways than one. I did not know the answer to my problem so I called John St. Clare at Spalding, their Custom Club expert who made my favorite woods. I asked John if he remembered my wood's he had made for me some ten years ago and told John about the problems I was having with the Penna woods.

John looked up the specifications and he asked me if I had True Temper Dynamic stiff flex shafts in those Penna woods I was having trouble with. I replied that I do, but I have them in my old woods also, so why am I having all this trouble? John said I have not been using that shaft at all. He went on to tell me the shaft I had been using was an older discontinued model which was heavier than the Dynamic shaft, and the stiff flex point was different and was further up towards the middle of the shaft! Wow! True Temper had stopped making that shaft years ago. John told me he would see if there were any of those old shafts in inventory and if he found any he would send them to me. He did find one but I never used it and still have it in my garage. The reason why I didn't use it will be explained in the next chapter.

FINAL GOLF SHAFT STORY #12-1/2 (13)

*W*E ALL KNOW WHAT NUMBER follows 12, right? I am not superstitious but some of you might so that is why I have numbered this chapter twelve and one half! And I also don't think you can count on this being the final golf shaft story either.

Having this new knowledge about what shaft I had in my 10 year old woods I went directly to Ace Harper, Penna's custom club genius. I asked Ace to pull the shaft out of my beloved Spalding driver and put it into my Penna driver. I put the lonely looking Spalding wood head without a shaft in a safe place and then went out to a golf practice range to try out the Penna club which now had my 10 year old shaft installed. Bingo! It was like nothing changed. The Penna club head looked different but that's all. All this time it was the shaft that was causing my problem and the problem was now solved!

See how the shaft makes such a difference. A golf club is a very temperamental item. While working many years with touring pros, club pros, and single digit handicap players had taught me a great deal about the game and the quirks of the equipment. What I mean by that is these good players find the driver that fits their game and they will always want a back up just like the one that performs well for them in case something happens to their favorite one. It is almost next to impossible to duplicate a club, to look, feel and perform exactly the same, it just does not happen often. That may sound strange, however there are so many variables involved it would take another book to try and explain why. By now you have enough knowledge to go sell clubs! Well, almost. I hope all this explains why it is so difficult for a Tour player, or just darn good players to switch clubs. There are no two clubs exactly alike, just like people.

Maybe this will help explain something most of us don't realize that there are so many differences in the ability of golfers so let's start at the top. A touring professional is called a professional golfer. A head professional at a golf club is called a golf professional. The professional golfer plays for a living and the golf professional teaches others to play, however most of the golf professional are darn good player. Then comes the top armatures and many do play as well as the golf professionals, but very few play as well as the professional golfers. We then look at the good to fair player and the casual golfer. The casual golfer expects less from his game but they truly enjoy being on a course beating the ball around. The big difference between a good player and all the rest is simple in my opinion. Most people playing the game are happy to get the ball airborne and they do not know where it is going to come down consistently. The good player is the opposite. They have no problem getting the ball airborne but he or she knows where the ball is going to come down a good percentage of the time. They will pick a spot where they want the ball to end up and know a high percentage of time the ball will come down where they want it come down. If it doesn't, they get mean and sometimes use funny language while the casual golfer becomes happy and smile a lot. Who is better off? Well, actually all are because no one is bigger than this great game called a four letter word. You pick the word! My choice is golf.

Just one last thing, I have a story about the rest of my Spalding woods. I did not change my Spalding 3 wood when I went to work for the Penna Company and this story again involves Toney Penna himself. I will explain this in the next chapter, tomorrow.

My 3 Wood and Toney Penna #14

I WOULD LIKE TO SWITCH GEARS here a bit. What I am writing about is more than just me and I hope that is coming through to you as you read all of this. My stories are intended to point our events which I was involved with <u>other people</u>. These stories happened with all these <u>other people</u>, I just happened to be there. These other people, certain events and or situations are what really make these stories interesting. Without all the above these pages would be blank.

I have also neglected to recognize my family thus far. I've been thinking about that, wondering how I am going to work that in somewhere and soon.

Now about Toney Penna and my 3 wood problems, but before I get to that something else just popped into my memory banks. The very first time I played golf with Toney it didn't take me long to put one into the trees and undergrowth with my new Penna woods. While searching for the ball I was reaching into and under some palmetto growth. Toney hurriedly comes over to me and said, "Bill stop what your doing." I'm thinking that besides hitting a very bad shot, what the heck did I do now?

"Bill," Toney begins, "You're in Florida! You have to learn certain things. There may be danger in there that you can't see! Never ever put your hands where you can't see them!"

He was so right, and what great advice. That advice should be heeded anywhere, never put your hands where you can't see them. Florida is home to four snakes that are poisonous. They are the rattler, the pigmy rattler, the coral and the water moccasin. As you may know that snakes will not strike if they have a chance to get away. If startled and cornered they may strike. I have been told that the only snake that will actually seek you out is the water moccasin, they are mean critters. There are also scorpions, and of course alligators. Generally speaking you only have to be careful concerning alligators around water. These creatures can be found anywhere there is fresh water. They avoid salt water, but can be found in brackish water which is a mixture of fresh and salt water.

Being brand new to Florida you would think all of those creatures would be enough to scare you half to death. Not so. Those things are nothing like you might think as I am going to tell you about I95. If you don't drive at least 85 mile per hour, you get run over. No, the most dangerous situation I encountered was, get ready for this, driving through the parking lot of shopping centers. It is there that I found different kind of scary creatures. What are they? Old retired people from up north playing a game of, "I saw that parking space first!" That's real fear when they get their automobile rolling and don't look anywhere but at their target and if you don't avoid them you may very well end up as that target.

Are you ready to hear about my all-time favorite golf club, my Spalding 3 wood? I never pulled the shaft out of my 3 wood to put into a Penna club like I did with the driver. The Penna 5 wood worked well for me, so no problem with that. I played quite a lot with Toney which caused a huge problem. I could not use my favorite Spalding 3 wood because he would be upset if he saw me using something other than one of his clubs, naturally.

I never took the head cover off of that club and I was forced to hit the hell out of that 5 wood many times when I really needed to use a 3 wood. He didn't seem to notice as he seldom watched me swing. Most good players don't pay attention and watch swings of the other players in their group. You can pick up bad habits by doing that. What they watch is the ball leaving the club and where it goes but usually not your swing. There were times when Toney was a fair distance away I could sneak that 3 wood out and take the head cover off, hurry up and hit my shot and then without hesitation slap that head cover back on it before he might see it. He never caught me, what a sneaky guy I am.

I'm not done with my 3 wood yet. I also want to clarify something about any comments I have made about how I hit the ball a long way and that I have won long drive contests. What I said could be misleading. I'd like to clear that up a bit ... Tomorrow ... Tomorrow ... ...

LONG DRIVE CONTESTS #15

I HAVE NEVER COMPETED IN AN official long drive contest and I don't want to give the wrong impression. Yes, I was given the gift of being able to hit the ball longer than most, but the so called long drive contests I won were at various tournaments or golf outings such as member guests and charitable events of local tournaments. It is not unusual to have a long drive contest as one of the prizes, or closest to the pin on a par three hole, or a prize like a car for a hole-in-one as well. The golf ball has to be in the fairway to count in a long drive contest. I just happen to be pretty accurate with my trusty old persimmon woods. A lot of guys may hit it longer but I hit it straighter. Brag, brag, brag.

By the way when I left the Penna Co. and returned to Spalding in 1977, I took my trusty heavy old steel shaft out of the Penna driver and put it back into my old custom Spalding persimmon driver. My 3 wood had familiar company again. I used those woods until I was forced to change from wood clubs to metal clubs because that was what we were selling as the wood club market was dead. That was around 1991. My woods were getting close to 30 years old by then and I still have them.

There were a couple of long drives I won that stand out and they both were at Spalding outings. One was in Orlando where Spalding staged a golf outing inviting a number of customers, including some people from other countries who were attending the PGA Show which was held in January. Orlando can be very cold in January and the grass is pretty dormant in the winter as well. To hit a long drive in these conditions I figured the ball would roll a long way on dormant grass. The colder the weather, the less resilient the ball is as well. Many of our salesman were very good players some being golf professionals. Plus several of our quests were golf professionals as well so there was a lot of competition. With the cold weather conditions everybody is wearing a lot of heavy clothing to keep warm which restricts swinging freely at the ball. With the golf balls a little less resilient I figured that if I could keep the ball low and hit that kind of a shot the ball would run a long way, a shot that I could control and keep it in the fairway, I thought I could have a good chance to win. Hey, I was fifty years old at the time. I was trying to outthink those young bombers. I hit the shot I wanted and I won! The young guys couldn't believe it!

Then there was the time we were attending a sales meeting in Lake Tahoe, Nevada. I was a little younger in my mid forties. It was one of those rare times we actually played a round of golf while at a sales meeting. Anyway, the course we played was about 5,000 feet above sea level. At that altitude the air is very thin and the golf ball will travel a lot further in that thin air than normal. The designated long drive hole was a par four with an elevated tee. About 150 yards out the dip in the terrain started to go uphill. The hole was a dog leg to the left and there was a sand trap at the dogleg in the left rough to discourage taking a short cut. The safe shot was to the right of the sand trap. I thought if I could get the ball high enough in that thin air I could carry the ball over that sand trap and land in the fairway beyond. There was a flag near the trap in the fairway indicating the longest drive hit up until now. I decided to hit my 3 wood because I normally hit my driver pretty low. The trick was to get the ball high in the thin air so it would stay in the air longer than my driver would have. This was a hole that would not accept a low running shot, it had to be a shot high in the air.

My 3 wood was really my favorite club and I could hit is almost as long as my driver and just about where I wanted the ball to land most of the time. I hit the ball solid and it cleared the sand trap and landed 15 yards beyond that long drive flag that was out there and I won the contest.

That 3 wood was something special. When my game was on, I could hit that club just about where I wanted the ball to land almost every time. Land the ball on the left side of the fairway, fine, right side or the fairway, again no problem. For a couple of years in Florida I used my 3 wood off the tee more than my driver. I'm a slow learner; it took me a lot of years to finally figure out that it's a lot easier to make pars and birdies from the fairway. Bogies and double bogies are easy out of the rough and the trees.

My lowest handicap was a two and that was in Massachusetts. That handicap didn't stay there very long but I was really happy to have achieved that low of a handicap as I hardly ever played golf more than once a week. Raising a family and working doesn't leave a lot of time to play golf. When we moved to Florida, my handicap jumped to eight! Why? Golf in the south is a different game than I was used to. In the north I hit the ball higher, the ground was a clay base and firmer and the ball rolls better than on sand base fairways here in Florida. The air is thinner in the north and here in Florida we are at sea level. There is less wind in the north and the grass is different.

In Florida the air is thicker, the humidity is higher and air is heavier. The earth is all sand based and softer and the ball will roll less. In south east Florida there is a lot of wind which has an effect on a high flying golf ball. I had to learn how to hit the ball on a lower trajectory. That takes time. The grass is Bermuda which is coarser. The fairways are cut much lower, so the ball sits lower in the grass, tighter lies than I was used to playing on. Bermuda rough is like wire and the ball doesn't sit up as much and it sinks down in the grass. The greens are not bent grass that is used in the north. Florida greens had a lot more grain to them in the nineteen seventies and eighties. The ball also rolled much slower on the greens than I was accustomed to. There are water hazards everywhere. The palm trees gobble up golf balls. You can not hit shots through them like trees in the north. We used to say trees in the north were 80% air. The leaves would not stop a ball, only the limbs. Not so with palm trees. There are more reasons but these should be enough to give you the reasons my handicap shot up to eight.

I had to learn how to adjust to all of these factors. I never got my handicap lower that 4. It kind of settled in at 5 to 6, which means that my highest scores were never over 82. As I got a little older my handicap crept up to 8. I didn't score as low, but I did manage to keep the scores lower than 82, not bad. Enough golf for awhile, let's move on. I said I would write what comes into my cranium as I go. Let's see what tomorrow brings.

COMMUNICATING #16

I KNOW THIS SUBJECT WILL HAVE its supporters and its non supporters. I said I would be writing what comes to mind, pet peeves included. Well this subject comes under the category of included.

I don't even know what all those things everybody seems to have in their ear or in their face everywhere they are going. Cell phones, I Pads, what else? My wife Dee and I just gave up our cell phones which we never used. I don't need a cell phone and only had it for emergencies. If I were still working I would have one of course. The only emergencies I have been having lately are bathroom related. But, that's another story.

Here is where I might loose some of you, communication. Do you really know what that means between you and others around you? I am referring to family, friends, not business related. I am as guilty as anyone because I am on the computer too much. But I rarely go on the internet and search around, and I don't like Face book. I think there is to much personal stuff out there for everyone to see on face book. It doesn't stop with who you send it because messages are sent on to others without your permission. I have also seen some of the worst language by some people responses. My time is spent on emails to family and friends, tracking my personal finances.

When Dee and I go out to dine we sit and talk to each other, really! There's never is a silent moment until the meal is served. When we look around, what do you suppose we see? Most people of all ages are looking into some gadget and not looking or talking to each other. They are more interested in what other people are texting to them than they are interested in each other. Folk's, marriage is much more than that and its tough at its best, every married person knows that. Talk to each other and communicate before it is too late.

When visiting with family or friends at gatherings if you can't put those things down and pay attention to the people you are with, you are heading for danger. Put that thing away and visit, converse and listen to what others have to say. Learn to be a good listener, tune in and communicate, or just leave because you are not really there anyway. I get really upset when I am with people and all of a sudden one of those devices seems more important than who they are with. Unless your a doctor, or waiting for an emergency call, you don't have to answer every darn call. Return the call later, not in front of the people you are with. My family is tired of hearing this, I know. But I will never tire of saying what I think about it.

If the shoe fits, wear it. One last thing to think about, driving an automobile is a full time job! Think about that, again. On top of that, use your darn turn signals! What do you think they are installed in your car for? Did you also know that if you ride a bike that it is the law where ever I have lived that you must stop at stop signs too!

Who me, pet peeves? I'll be calmer, tomorrow …

A Little Backspin #17

I'LL STEP BACK AND CHANGE gears a little and will begin with the present and then I'll go back as far as I can remember. Currently Dee and I have been married 60 years as of February 11, 2016. We also have seventeen children! Let me clarify that number. We have four children, Diane, Cynthia, James and Linda and they have given us eight grand children and so far those grandchildren have produced five great grandchildren and folks that totals seventeen children Dee and I are responsible for thus far.

Backspin time, both sides of my family came to the United States in the 1830's, almost 200 years ago and they settled in western Ohio and were mostly farmers. I remember the outhouses in the 1930's, the little houses with a half moon cut into the door. As a young boy I remember using them, in the middle of winter no less. That is where I was introduced to the Sears & Roebuck Catalog and I didn't use it for reading material.

Western Ohio was home to numerous German families and my mother's family lived in Minster, Ohio. Yes Minster is a German name and there was a brewery in town, the Wooden Shoe Brewery, an appropriate name don't you think? I can remember visiting Minster when I was three or four years old. Mom and her three sisters and they all loved beer so they would go to the local pub and have a pitcher of beer and their favorite snack was the smelliest Limburger cheese you can imagine. German's learn to drink beer at a very young age and mom would give me a little glass of from their pitcher of beer. Mom was born in 1899 and when she was a young girl the Catholic Mass was said in German language. When the World War I started the church had to change to the English language

Mom also had three brothers and she was the oldest of the seven kids. Their mother died at the age of 36 and mom had to quit school while in the 6th grade as she had to help raise her brothers and sisters. I never met my grandmother of course only met mom's dad, my grandfather, three or four times before he passed away in his seventies. Not many people lived to be that old back in the thirties and I remember that he looked like he was 100.

Dad was born in 1898. Funny thing, when he was about 17 the war to end all wars was going on, World War I. Dad joined the Army Air Force and before he was sworn there was a flu epidemic going on and dad caught it. When dad got over the flu the war had ended, thank God. Dad never served and then dad was too old for World War II. The strange thing was, dad never was in an airplane in his life of 76 years. The big reason he never was in an airplane may be that at the age of 19 he went to work for the Pennsylvania Railroad and he traveled everywhere by train, naturally.

Dad's first job was as a male secretary and he was a champion typist with shorthand capabilities. I remember as a young kid watching him type on those really old typewriters; dad had to pound on the keys, and then at the end of the sentence, hit the carriage return bar to put it in place for the next sentence. Dad typing was really fast and I could hardly see his fingers moving and he was timed at better than 120 words a minute! The best I did in high school with better equipment, but not yet electric, was about 58 words per minute. Dad worked his way into the personal claims department ending his career as a Regional Manager for the Claims Department and retired at age 65 with 46 years service with the railroad.

Dad's dad, another grandfather who I never met, was one of six children, five boys and one girl. There were five boys to carry on the Faulhaber name but only one boy was produced which of course was my dad, Henry Albert Faulhaber. He had two sisters, one passed away before she reached adulthood. By the time I came into the picture my dad's mother, my Grandmother, remarried a really nice guy, Oliver Solinger. They lived on a farm in Crestline, Ohio. Crestline was not only a small farm town but also a Railroad town with a car switching yard.

The Pennsylvania RR and the New York Central RR tracks actually crossed each other in Crestline.

I only knew one Grandfather, my mother's dad and one Grandmother, my dad's mother. We lived in Canton, Ohio and did not visit them too often. I did spend some summer school vacations, about two weeks each time on my grandmother's farm. I also spent time on one of my aunt and uncle's farm in Celina, Ohio. My uncle and his kids, my cousins, put me to work doing chores like shoveling you know what and hoeing thistles in the grazing fields. They also had a nice outhouse stocked with the same catalogs my grandmother had. Their supply of water came from a well and there was a pump in the kitchen. Saturday baths were accomplished in a tub.

ACK TO THE FAULHABER FAMILY name and I have already mentioned that my father's father was one of five brothers and the only one who had a son. The family name dropped to one male, my dad, and he had two sons, my brother Richard and me. We now have two males to carry on the family name and my brother had two boys and I have one so there are now three. My brother's boy's Jay and Mark, Jay had one son who has no children and Mark passed away childless at age 51. My son Jim has one son, Chris, and he has one son so we are back to one male to carry on the family name. We are back to one again, just where my dad was. I hope the Faulhaber family name does not die out and my great grandson Faulhaber is not old enough to have children yet. Soon, though, he's three now.

When our recently retired Catholic German Pope was ordained a Priest in Germany, the Bishop who ordained him was Bishop Faulhaber, who later became a Cardinal. Cardinal Faulhaber was very prominent during World War II as he continually had to deal with Hitler. Germany was something like 48% Catholic, 48 % Lutheran and that's most likely the only reason Hitler put up with him. Was I related to him, I have no idea as I have never traced my background?

Back in the 20's and the 40's, Route 30 was the only continuous highway that ran from the Atlantic east coast to the Pacific west coast and it was a two lane road. There were no three or four lane roads back then and it was also named the Lincoln Highway. It ran through Canton, Ohio where we lived and also went through Crestline where my Grandmother lived. We used Rt. 30 when visiting grandma. During World War II did you know that the top speed limit in the entire country on any road was 35 mile per hour? It was a controlled speed to save on gas consumption as gas was rationed. Can you imagine chugging along for hours at that speed? To pass the time my brother and I would count the number of cows in the pastures. We counted their legs and divided by four to get the correct number of the cows out there. Believe that? "Are we there yet, Dad?"

I had no first cousins on my dad's side and luckily my mom's side was more productive. Mom had three brothers, one was a bachelor, one had two girls and one had one boy. Mom's youngest sister Florence, who never married, had a very bad accident when she was in her early twenties in Cincinnati. It was in the winter and she was wearing a long coat. One day Florence was departing from a streetcar and the doors closed on her coat. Her coat was caught in the closed door and the streetcar stated to move. She ran along the car screaming tying to catch the attention of the streetcar operator to no avail. Florence fell and one of her legs was caught under one of the streetcar wheels and run over, she lost that leg.

Florence used a wooden leg painted to match her skin color. Florence was a really fun gal and I remember how she loved having a beer and smoking a cigarette while joking and having fun with her sisters. All four sisters had wonderful attitudes and a really good sense of humor as a matter of fact, they were truly fun to be around.

The next youngest sister was Henrietta who had two daughters, Delma and Helen Ann. Her first husband passed away and Henrietta had a son, Pat, with her second husband. That's three more cousins. Aunt Henrietta and her first husband owned a business which in those days was called a gas station. Connected to that station was a restaurant where they sold beer and hamburgers cooked on a grill. The restaurant had a lunch counter and several booths and there was a "Juke box" that had a selection of records to choose from, plus a dance floor.

I still remember the smell of those burgers frying on the grill, they really tasted good. So did the beer. People not only bought gas there, it was also kind of a local hang out, the dance floor and the Juke Box got a lot of use. It was a busy place and I can still see my cousins dancing to Tommy Dorsey's newest and biggest hit at the time, T. D's Boogie Woogie by Tommy Dorsey. Remember that?

My list of cousins is growing with three of them in California and I only saw them once back in 1946 when mom, along with her next oldest sister Freda, and I went to visit via a train that took three days. I was 15 years old. "Are we there yet, mom?"

Freda and her husband, Albert, were farmers in Celina, Ohio. Next, their five children, my cousins, their farm, another outhouse, a pair of mules and a horse that almost did me in.

COUSINS #19

*A*UNT FREDA AND UNCLE ALBERT were farmers and lived just a mile outside of Celina, Ohio. This story is about their children, my cousins, their farm, the outhouse, a pair of mules and a horse.

Let me set the scene here a little as this takes place in the 30's, depression years. If there were any rich farmers back then my aunt and uncle didn't know them, dirt poor are no truer words. They lived off the land and had nothing but the farm and their family, yet they seem to have had everything. My cousins were Cletus who went by the name Spark, Norma, we called her Sis, and then there was Bob plus the twins, Shirley and Tom. What else would a twin boy be named but, Tom, of course!

There were 13 cousins in our family counting myself and my brother Richard and there are only four of us left, myself, Norma Borgert, who is 88 and lives in Dayton, and as of this writing is not very well. Her sister Shirley Brunswick, age 79 and lives in Maria Stein, Ohio. And Aunt Henrietta's son, Pat Barlage, in his sixties and resides in Botkins, Ohio.

The farm had no indoor plumbing; just a cistern well with a hand pump in the kitchen and a pot belly stove was also used to heat the house in the winter. The outhouse had double seats, two holes, and a good thing with all those kids and family visiting. The Sears catalog and corn cobs were your friend. I spent a couple of weeks there in the summer several times and they put this city slicker through the ropes.

Uncle Al plowed all the fields, planted everything almost by hand and harvested everything with the help of a couple of stubborn mules. Do you know how mules came into existence? They are a mixed breed between a horse and a donkey and they can not reproduce. I guess that is why they are so darn stubborn and mean. Their size is somewhere between a donkey and a horse but they are extremely strong animals. They don't understand English either. How do I know that? Because Uncle Al never used any kind of English I was familiar with when giving them commands, he just used all the swear words ever invented instead. Those donkeys simply would not move if you talked to them nice with a normal tone in your voice. This is where I learned my second language, so I'm by lingual, Ha!

Farmers in those days started work before the sun came up and worked until dark, milking cows, feeding all the animals, all the daily chores that needed done. Planting and harvesting seasons were the toughest. When it came to harvesting the hay, corn, oats, wheat, whatever, all the farmers in the area would come together bringing their equipment with them and they would go from farm to farm until all their farms were harvested. The wives would travel with them and would do all the cooking, breakfast, lunch and suppers for everyone. Dinner was called supper and all the meals looked like supper. Ham, bacon, eggs and potatoes for breakfast and the meals got bigger all day long. What cooperation, it was amazing how well they all worked together. They were all great neighbors and were always there for each other. All the kids pitched in as well.

In addition to the mules, Uncle Al also had two work horses. I haven't gotten to the story about being run over by one of those horses yet. I was about 6 or 7 years old and it was a miracle that my life was not ended at that age. Thank God there are still more tomorrow's for me and you will find out why I said that in the next chapter, tomorrow.

Plow Horses and Beyond #20

MY COUSIN'S LIKED TO RIDE those very large thickly built plow horses around the farm. They were very strong animals and were not built to run, but they could trot. There were no saddles and my cousins rode them bareback using only a bit and bridle to control the animal. I had to hang on to the bridle and the horse's hair on the back of its neck so I would not fall off. The horse would just walk slowly and rarely would they go into a trot. That is until my cousins hoisted me up on one of these giant animals for me to ride.

Picture this, I am 6 or 7 years old on top of this huge animal and I was so small my legs did not wrap around the horse, they just stuck straight out to either side. The horse and I are just doing fine and I am kind of just bouncing up and down a little with each step the horse was taking. And then something must have startled my horse as he started to trot. All of a sudden I'm starting to bounce straight up and down a lot higher. Then my horse started a faster trot and I'm bouncing even higher. The horse is going straight ahead so I'm alright so far. Then he swerved to one side while I'm in the air and as I was coming down there was no horse under me, just space. My little body swung under his neck and I wrapped my arms and legs around his neck the best I could. The horse is running now and his head is going up and down with his mouth hitting my face with every step. I wish someone had brushed his teeth that day.

Finally I lost my grip and I started to fall and at the same time I experienced the longest couple of seconds in my short life. My short life flashed before me before I hit the ground with a loud thud. Then I saw blackness and a lot of stars and heard this loud thunder as this large horse's huge hoof slammed the turf while also clipping my chin and my throat!

I slowly got up off the ground with my head spinning like a top. The first thing I did was put my hand to my mouth and I spit out half of a tooth and there was blood flowing from my chin. My skin on my neck was burning and stinging. When I saw the tooth and then the blood I did what any 6 or 7 year old would do. I started to cry and scream for my mommy.

Why do we always call for mommy when we are hurt and not daddy? I would say the reason is because we lived very closely to our mothers for nine months and then hung on to them for the next year or so. That makes sense to me. No offense dad's, that's just the way it is. Aren't mom's great? Moms are very nice, soft and cuddly. Dads do have a different roll in our life, just as important but in other ways. I think we dad's understand that and are not offended when our kids call for mom first. That's my opinion.

That horse's hoof was a fraction of an inch from crushing my neck and skull. It is said a horse will never step on a person and I sure have to believe that! I was that close to death with no more tomorrows, so maybe that is why I am using the word tomorrow so often.

I will always remember my mom saying to the doctor who was sewing me up with three stitches that she hopes I don't have a scar that will bother me when I am old enough to shave. Old enough to shave! Mom was sure thinking ahead and thank God that eventually I did reach that grand old age and started to shave. My thanks to that horse being so agile for such a huge animal and to the good Lord who created both of us.

Conclusion to this story, it is said when you fall off a bicycle, get back on it or you will never ride one again. I didn't take that advice and I have never been on a horse since that day. Yes I still have that scar and I clip it once in a while when shaving too, which always brings back the memory of that day, a day that could have resulted in no more tomorrow's for me. That incident with the horse may explain why I have been using the word tomorrow so much.

I don't know why but recently I find myself rubbing that darn scar.

So when my hand is at my chin I am not posing like the statue, the Thinker. Heaven forbid I be accused of thinking, I'm just rubbing that 78 year old scar.

I just wished we had more contact over the years as cousins. Unfortunately we just lived all our lives in different places. Not that far away but in those days a trip of a hundred miles was a big deal. Emails have given us the opportunity of keeping in touch as we have reconnected somewhat which is nice.

Let's go back to my home town of Canton, Ohio, also the home of the Professional Football Hall Of Fame. To me it was a great medium size town for kids to grow up. It was a wonderful sports town with a lot of industry, kind of a working mans town back in the 30's and 40's.

Back Home, Canton, Ohio #21

*C*ANTON IS THE HOME OF the Professional Football Hall Of Fame and the professional game was supposed to have started in Canton. The McKinley Monument is also in the same park system and of course the former President of the U.S.A. William McKinley is buried inside.

My birthplace was Crestline, Ohio, not Canton. We actually lived in Ravenna, Ohio the first two years of my life. I have no idea what Mom was doing in Crestline, that's where grandma lived, she must have needed some help. I was late in arriving as the date was supposed to be July 4th and I showed up on the 22nd. I weighed in at nine and one half pounds with the umbilical cord wrapped around my neck and I was blue in color. With a little work they finally got me to the color of pink, I think. I was there but I don't remember. Mom gave me the original doctor's bill for my delivery and it was a whopping $26.00. I still have that original bill and the doctor was a female. Everybody is worth something.

I

Did you ever notice the cycle of life? We come into this world all wrinkled and wetting ourselves and we leave the world the same way, all wrinkled and wetting ourselves

As I have said before, dad worked for the Pennsylvania Railroad, which ran through Canton and he was transferred to Canton in 1933. It was my home from 1933 – 1949. During my time in Canton there were a lot of nationally know companies whose names you might recognize, such as the Timken Roller Bearing Co., the Diebold Safe Co., the Duber Watch Co., Hoover Vacuum Co., and Republic steel, The Pennsylvania RR had a large passenger station in Canton. There was a rather large red light district as well, the oldest business in the world. A very industrious town as I said before.

The area was heavy with clay soil so there were several brick manufacturing companies; one was the Belden Brick Co. Many of the streets in Canton were paved with bricks but most are now covered over with asphalt.

Besides me, a lot of other famous people came from Canton. To name a few, Mother Angelica was one. Dan Dierdorff was a professional football player and is now a TV commentator. Thurman Munson was a New York Yankees catcher who was killed in an airplane accident. Both of these men went to the same High School as I, Lehman high school. Also attending Lehman was Bill Kloss, national marble champion in 1937. When I was a kid all the boys played marbles. Many of you reading this may not even know about that game. It was very competitive many of us carried a bag of marbles tied to our belts which held up the knickers we wore. We would find an area without grass, usually the playground at school and draw a circle in the dirt with a stick. To explain the game would take a chapter in itself. I'm not going there so you may want to look it up on the internet.

We had fun playing together; there were no I-pads and cell phones or TV to distract us. And there was a large amusement park named Meyers Lake Park which had many rides including a roller coaster. Big bands played in the large dance hall where we also had our high school prom. In the 30's and into the start of the 40's we had a minor league baseball team, a Boston Red Sox affiliate named the Canton Terriers. Mom and dad were baseball fans and took my brother Dick and me to the ball park to see them play often. The night games were a challenge as we had to battle the mosquitoes. The smell of Citronella was everywhere and was mixed in with all the cigarette and cigar smoke. Many of the players made it to the Red Sox, such as Whitey Kworoski, I'm sure that spelling is incorrect. Also Tex Houston a pitcher, Matt Batts as catcher and Kirby Farrell a 1st baseman to name a few that I can remember. Matt Batts, what a great name for a baseball player!

Next chapter, Canton continued plus my schools, sports, the depression and more golf stories, tomorrow.

CANTON AND GOLF #22

*Y*ES I REMEMBER THE GREAT Depression in the 30's and until World War II started there was rough times for so many. It is amazing how the American people survived all those years and I think all that suffering maybe made us a better country. I bet it did and maybe it helped our brave boys win that war as they grew up in tough times which in turn helped them through that terrible time. Unfortunately so many didn't make it, all gave some but some gave all. We all need to remember that and never forget those that made the ultimate sacrifice.

Most of our years in Canton we lived in a house located at 1716 Myrtle Dr., N.W. We had three bedrooms and one bathroom with a bath tub and no shower. The rest of the house consisted of a kitchen, dining room, living room, attic and basement. We had a large double car garage about one third as big as the house with basketball court inside. More about that garage later. During the depression years our family was lucky as dad had a job with the Pennsylvania Railroad and he made enough money to pay the rent and put food on the table. Mom handled all the finances and was very good at it. People knocked on the door constantly asking to do any kind of work for a sandwich, really sad. I still remember so many of those desperate faces. I remember my mom handing out a lot of free lunches, some for a little work, and some, just because.

Changing gears here a little as I want to say a few more things about golf. As I have mentioned before my dad was a golfer and a darn good one at that. He didn't start playing until he was 27 and that was in 1925. Dad was not a strong man as he battled stomach ulcers most of his life. Dad drank whole cream back then because there was not a lot they could do ulcers. In the 30's dad was 5'11" and weighed about 135 pounds. He played public golf courses and they did not have watering systems like today. The greens were watered as were the teeing areas but nothing else was watered. When it rained then the fairways would have green grass.

There were weeds were every where and then came the dandelion season. Remember those pretty weeds that had a nice yellow ball sticking straight up. When that little yellow flower became ripe it turned white and the wind would then blow them apart piece by piece. They were like little airplanes that carried the seed through the air. But before they broke up and flew away visualize this. A golf course full of little white flower balls! Finding my little white golf ball in that field of golf balls was not easy. Not having brand new golf balls to play with mine were not really all that white as the dandelions so that made finding my ball a little easier. So there was an advantage of having old golf balls.

Getting back to dad and the rough it really didn't matter if there was any because dad was rarely in the rough anyway. His tee shots were not long because he was not a strong person, but his shots were straight down the fairway. His chipping and putting was something to behold too. When it came to putting he would get upset if he missed 25-30 footers and dad almost always scored in the 70's.

Dad took some old hickory wooden shafted clubs and cut a few inches off the grip end and then re griped them so they were shorter for my brother Dick to use as young kids. We would take these clubs and hit old cut up golf balls around in the local fields and that is how we got started. I was nine years old.

I really didn't start to play on a real golf course until I was about eleven. I can't wait to tell you about the clubs that dad gave me to replace those cut down hickory shafted clubs in tomorrow's chapter.

GOLF IN MY YOUTH #23

*D*AD HAD SOME OLD CLUBS he no longer used so he decided it was time to retire the cut down hickory wood shafted clubs since by brother and I were now a little older and taller. He gave my brother a full set of Kroydon woods and irons which were made by the Northwestern Golf Co. He gave me a Vick Gezzi autographed driver and a Craig Wood autographed 2 wood which was called a Brassie in those days. A 3 wood was called a Cleek but I did not have one and the 4 and 5 woods were not available until a few years later. What irons dad gave me were not matched and not a full set either, they were the 3, 5, 7, 9 irons plus a putter, a total of 7 clubs altogether. The clubs were all normal length for a grown man but still a little long for me and they had smooth leather grips which were slippery. I had to hold on tight or the clubs would be flying through the air along with the ball.

Wow, now I'm ready to play real golf on a real golf course. Dad played at Tam O'Shanter, a public course which had two 18 hole courses. One was named, the Hills and the other was the Dales. The more level course was the Dales and it was pretty much off limits to kids and females until after 3 PM. The Hills was actually a lot more fun anyway with more challenging shots due to the hilly terrain. Even though it was public facility single and family memberships were available. Dad managed some how to pay for a family membership so the three of us could play as much as we wanted. Mom didn't play golf.

Another thing I haven't mentioned about golf clubs is that within a set of fourteen clubs each club is designed, distance wise, to be about 10 to 12 yards apart. So only having seven clubs there is a problem. First of all the driver at 43" is about three and a half feet and my height then was about 5 feet. Get the picture? I had to grip down on those clubs to shorten them and had to find different ways to hit the ball different ways to make up for the distance gaps between clubs

In other words I had to learn how to hit shots that those clubs were not designed for to make up for their length and the absence of seven other clubs. I had to make seven clubs do the job of fourteen. On many shots I either had to hit the heck out of a club or back off somewhat and hit one softer. There were only a few sand traps on the Hills course and when I did get into one I learned to chip out of them as they were shallow and the sand was firm. I didn't have a sand club or a wedge. There was not much sand in them anyway, they were more dirt than sand.

In the summer during the week the golf courses were pretty empty as grown ups were working and darn few kids played golf. There were very few female players in those years in the 40's. When I was 11 it was 1942 and I used to hitch hike with my small bag of clubs to get to the course. Never did I have to wait long for a ride because hitch hiking in those days was common. People stopped asked where I was going and if they were going anywhere near where I was going they were happy to give me a lift. With golf clubs they knew where I was going so getting a ride was a no brainier. I played most of my golf in those days by myself and with hardly anyone on the course I'd play two balls on each hole. That's how I learned to play and hit shots as there was no practice range. So I actually had two scores for 18 holes, I just took my good old time and had fun. There were two water fountains on the course, one on each nine and mom made a sandwich for me so I was set for the day.

The golf professional was and I referred to him as old man Moots, his last name. He was more of a manager than anything else and I don't know if he ever played as I never saw him on the course. Mr. Moots son Mark was a very good player and he became a doctor. The club house was an old converted barn and it had a lunch counter. There was also a men's and ladies locker room, and that was it, not very fancy. When I made the high school golf team that's where we played our matches in 1948 and 1949.

During the war years golf balls were a big problem. Even after the war was over it was about 1947 before real golf balls were available again. It is hard to explain what the golf balls were like in the early and mid 40's but I'll give it a try in tomorrow's chapter.

GOLF IN THE FORTIES #24

*A*s I SAID, GOLF BALLS during the War years were scarce. Rubber was at a premium and regulated like so many other items needed for the war effort. Golf balls normally were made with rubber products and they had a resilient center. The center was then wound with rubber bands. A two piece rubber cover was vulcanized around the wound rubber wrapped ball. The cover material on most balls was called Balata which was a rubber product from a special and fairly rare tree. The top grade balls before the war were the Spalding Dot, theTitleist, the Maxfli, and the U. S. Royal. If I dropped any of those balls from shoulder height onto concrete they would bounce up to my waist. The taller the person the longer the drop but with the same results, it would reach waist high. However, all these rubber materials were not available during the war so synthetics were used and these replacement balls when dropped on concrete would only bounced up to about the middle of my thigh, a very big difference in resiliency indeed.

With the pre war ball a very good drive might be 200 to 210 yards With the war manufactured ball it might only be 175 to 180 yards.

There were no distance markers on golf holes like there are today. The distance given on the scorecard was of a hole was from the middle of the tee to the middle of the green. Today fairway distance is measured from the middle of the green back to the fairway and markers are placed in the ground giving the distance of 100, 150, 200 yards from the middle of the green. With no distance markers like these back then we had to walk the distance off. The scorecard would give us the yardage of a hole from the middle of the tee to the middle of the green as I have mentioned. We would hit our tee shot and walk in steps that were approximately 3 feet apart and count our steps to the ball. If, and

I say if, my ball is in the middle of the fairway and my step count is190 and the hole is 350, then I have approximately 160 to the middle of the green. Then I have to figure out with the naked eye where the pin is located. If it looks like the pin is back a little I then add five yards and I am 165 yards to the pin. That could be off by 10 to 15 yards easily. Today the touring pros are given score cards that are maps. For instance from a certain bush on the left side of the rough it is 162-1/2 yards to the middle. Now on a given day the pin is back left, 13-1/2 yards from the middle, 176 yards from the pin. Oh my goodness, how sweet it is. Plus the equipment is much more precise today. Today's game of golf is so much different than back in the days my dad played and in my early days as well.

A slight miss hit could put a slight crease or a cut into those balata covered golf balls and they went out of round easily as well. Balls were scarce and expensive so I played them with creases and cuts and most of the time that's all i had to play with. When the good balls become really scarce I would guard a good ball like there is no tomorrow. I found a U.S. Nobby one day, and it was made by the U.S. Rubber Company but It was not a top grade ball like the U.S. Royal, however it had a lot of bounce to it. That ball also had a thicker cover than the top grade balata covered balls so it would survive miss hits pretty well. I played with that ball it seemed like forever and refused to loose it. I would search for that ball until I found it. I actually wore the paint off of that ball and it became grey in color. One sad day I hit that little gem into a corn field next to the third hole on the Hills course at Tam O'Shanter. No one was permitted to climb over the fence into that field to search for golf balls. There was even a warning sign in the club house not to go into that field. The farmer who owned that land warned he would shoot anyone with buckshot if the found anyone his field. I was devastated as my favorite ball was lost forever in that field of corn.

I have now entered high school. The Golf team only carried four players with one back up. All the matches were four against four so the back up was there in case one of the players could not make it for whatever reason. When I was a Junior I made the team as the fifth man and the other four were all seniors and all pretty good players. Actually I really didn't know how to play golf then. I thought I could play because I could hit it pretty far. I had never played in any kind of competition before making the team as there weren't any tournaments for kids before high school. What few matches I did get to play, I got my head handed back to me. A leaning process had started!

Speaking of learning the golf game the only teacher I ever had was my dad. He taught me the grip I used all my life, the interlocking grip. The little finger on the right hand interlocks with the index finger on the left hand. Those two fingers do not touch the club at all. This makes your hands work together as opposed to the baseball grip where all ten fingers are independent on the club. The most popular grip by far is the overlapping grip called the Vardon grip named after the famous English golfer Harry Vardon who invented it. The little finger is on top of the left index finger. With this grip, there are nine fingers touching the club. Both grips make it almost impossible for the hands to work against each other, the hands become one unit working together. Got all that?

When my dad first taught me this grip, I though he was crazy. I hit a baseball with all ten fingers on the bat, why not a golf ball? It felt so strange but at his insistence I kept at it until it was a natural feel. It seems when you are first starting to play golf the natural swing is wrong because the game of golf is not a natural game. Golf is also an underhanded game. Think about it. Throwing or hitting a baseball, shooting or passing a basketball, and most all the shots in tennis or throwing a football, even ping pong, is mostly overhand or some kind of a sideway motion. Golf is all underhand much like bowling, which to me is the only sport I know that is similar to golf. Bowling is just me, the ball, the alley and the pins. On a golf course, it is just me, the club and ball and the course. I am all alone with no teammates to bale me out.

I have just mentioned two sports, golf and bowling, that my mental attitude can make or break me fast. I loved to bowl as well as play golf and bowled mostly the duckpin game in Pittsburgh, which is a much different game than Ten Pins and that will be another story later.

One last thing about the golf grip, my dad had the foresight to realize that my small hands were not large enough to use the overlapping grip as a young boy. Later I also found out when as a grown person, why

I could not change from the interlock to the overlap grip as my hands had large palms and short fingers. I guess dad also noticed that as well. My fingers were just not long enough to overlap. I was advised not to change by some wise golf professionals after consulting a few about my grip. Some other guy came along using the interlocking grip that played pretty well, his name is Jack Nicklaus. He has the same kind hands, large palms and short fingers.

The next chapter is about how my dad became smarter as I got older. Tomorrow ...

DAD, MY ONLY GOLF TEACHER #25

*I*T AMAZED ME HOW DAD became smarter as I grew older as he was pretty dumb when I was younger, I knew a lot and he was just an old guy who just didn't understand the new younger generation. All of a sudden dad seemed to catch up and he stated to make sense when he talked to me. We also started to get along a lot better as well.

Now I am about to make the high school golf team and dad purchased a full set of clubs for me. These new clubs were middle grade purchased in a sporting goods store, something dad could afford. We also now belong to a country club, Brookside. Brookside was and is to this day a hidden gem as it was designed by the legendary Donald Ross, a famous golf course designer who I will have more to say about a little later on.

The war is over and I am now in my sophomore year, 1946-47. This set my dad bought for me consisted of a Driver, a 2 and 3 wood and the irons were 2 through a 9 iron and a brand new Spalding "Cash In" putter, one of the best putters ever designed. I had that putter for over 30 years but one day it disappeared from my bag, someone stole it. For many years Spalding always offered a Cash In putter in their club line however the shaft in that original Cash In's were pencil thin towards the bottom which gave it a certain feel that was never duplicated and I never found another like it. At one time the most popular putters used by golf professionals were that original Cash In and the Acushnet Bulls Eye.

New clubs and a new swing, remember I had mentioned before you should not change your swing to adjust to a golf club? A golf club should be fitted to your swing. When I was young I didn't have a choice or that kind of knowledge, I became accustomed to those clubs because they were so much better than the old clubs that I had. I was using different swings with different clubs because those old clubs were all different.

I didn't play with dad that much. When he had a chance to play he was playing with his cronies, naturally. When dad and I did play we seldom finished a round of golf together. A lot of times dad would get so mad at me he would walk off the course, and sometime I did the same. Our relationship was somewhat shaky to say the least. He couldn't understand that if I outhit him on a drive by 50 yards or more, what else did I need to know? Dad would tell me that was a good drive, but. I didn't understand dad was trying to make me better and I was wondering why. Heck, I just outhit him by 50 or 60 yards and he was a good player. Why do I have to change anything and then off dad would go in a huff, or I would.

What he was trying to teach me never really sunk in until years later when I was 26 years old and I had not played for eight years. The reason I didn't play all those years was dad received a promotion and was transferred to Pittsburgh so we moved there after my senior year in 1949. I did not play golf in my new strange surroundings because I didn't know anybody and my life changed big time.

I did not play golf again until I had my first interview with Spalding in 1957 for the position of Golf Professional Salesman. If I was hired I would be calling on golf professionals in the Tri State area consisting of Western Pa, Eastern Ohio and the entire state of West Virginia. I am happy to report I did get that job. Also dad and I got over that period of not getting along, and that happened when I got older and he got smarter, naturally. More about High School golf and some stories about dad's golf as well, next.

HIGH SCHOOL GOLF AND DAD #26

*I*N MY SENIOR YEAR OF high school I was named captain of the golf team. Big deal, I was the only one left from the year before! We had one heck of a time finding three more guys to fill out the team. I don't remember if we won any of our matches, maybe a couple only because other schools had the same problem finding enough kids that played golf to field a team.

I scored in the 80's most of the time but my teammates could hardly break 100. Individually I did pretty well until I came up against guys like Tony Ondrus and his brother Mike, they beat me like an old drum. I don't know what happen to Tony but Mike became a golf professional and was the head professional at Shady Hollow C. C. in Massillon where my brother became a member. Mike actually became one of my customers when I joined Spalding as my most western Ohio territory was Massillon. Then there was Don Keppler who played on the Massillon high school golf team. He showed me a thing or two as well in high school matches. Don also became a golf professional and years later Don ended up here in this area of Florida. For years Don operated his own club repair business, Kepplers Golf Club Repair. He was good and knew what he was doing. A lot of touring pros would come into his shop when they were in this area and have Don do repairs to their golf clubs.

One day I stopped by Don's shop and Ben Crenshaw, a professional tour golfer was there. I knew Ben and at that time he was married to his first wife who was a daughter of a girl that went to my high school, Lehman, back in Canton, Ohio. Small world, here are three of us in golf repair shop in Florida and Don Keppler was from Massillon, Ohio. Ben's wife was from Canton, Ohio and so was I.

Back in Ohio in the forties Don Keppler caddied for my dad a lot at the Brookside County Club. I asked Don what he thought of my dad's game and he assured me my dad was a very good player. News like that coming from Don who really knew the game of golf made me feel good. As I mentioned, Brookside was a hidden gem and it was not that well known just how good that course is. It was designed by the famous golf course architect from Scotland, Donald Ross. I knew nothing about his reputation until years later when I got into the golf business. Donald Ross did most of his golf course designs in the early 1900's. He is quite well known for many really great golf courses and even today his courses are still some of the best ever designed. Donald did all this when there was no earthmoving equipment. He used the natural lay of the land and with the use of horse drawn leveling and shaping equipment. His greens are legendary with most being quite large and they are very to read as to how the ball is going to break because of the various difficult slopes, and his greens are slippery fast. On Brookside's greens the golf ball really rolled two different ways, fast, and faster.

Dad almost always scored in the 70's. Brookside was a long course for those days as well as having very fast greens. A wonderful course that I played round after round and never get bored or tired playing it. As I have stated before my dad did not hit the ball a long way with his driver but boy was he accurate. When approaching the green with his shots dad was rarely left or right of the pin. He approach shots were short or long and not by much. Dad also used an old Spalding Cash In putter exactly like the one I once owned.

With dad's accuracy, I am surprised he only made two holes in ones in his lifetime. His first was in 1933 and his second one 41 years later at age 76. I still have the article that appeared in the paper about that shot. Dad made it on the 17th hole of the Palmetto Pines course, Ellenton, Fl., where he and mom lived in the winter. The paper states that hole was 145 yards and he used a 9 iron. I know that is incorrect as dad could never hit a 9 iron that long, even in his youth. Only if the hole was down hill and a big wind behind him could he do that. I'm sure the hole was 145 yards long but I would bet he was not playing it from that distance, but closer to the front of the tee, probably 115 to

120 yards. At 76 years old that is still a great shot. He was not in very good health at the time either and dad passed away shortly after at the age 76. He was born in 1898 so the year was 1974, the year I moved to Florida. Dad never saw my home here in North Palm Beach as he passed away very shortly after we moved here.

Dad told me about another hole in one he made, but it really wasn't. This happened on a hole with a water hazard in front of the green. Dads first shot went into the water. He could have gone to the spot where his ball entered the water and dropped another ball, the penalty would have been one shot and dad would be hitting his third shot. But he elected to take the penalty and dropped his ball on the tee where he hit his original ball. And then he holed out that shot. That was really his third shot so his score was a three. I would say he made a pretty darn good par.

Although he only made two holes in ones with his accuracy, he did manage to sink quite a few shots from the fairway during his lifetime. The one that amazed me happened in Mass. in 1972, dad was 74. The Golf Professional at the course we played was Danny DiRicco who I played a lot of golf with. Danny said he would like to play with dad and I that day. The first hole had an elevated tee and played down hill. Towards the bottom of the hill the terrain leveled off then went steeply up hill to the green. I hit my tee shot really close to the green and Dad hit his tee shot then his second shot landed about where my tee shot was sitting. I had mentioned to Danny as we walked off the tee how my dad was never a very long hitter but how accurate he was. I said to Danny don't be surprised if he holes a shot somewhere during the round. I had a wedge to the green and dad was probably hitting an eight iron. Because of the elevation we could not see where the cup was, only the top of the flag. I hit my shot then dad hit his. Dads shot went straight at that flag. I said to Danny, remember what I told you. There were three of us playing and when we got to the green we only saw two balls. Where was the third ball? Yes, it was in the hole and it was dad's ball of course! Danny just looked at me in disbelief. Then I three putted and made a bogie 5. Dad made a birdie 3. Yes dad, I'm still learning. Big drives don't mean everything.

One last item about Dad, when he was 71 he shot his age on the

Palmetto Pines course. It was not a long course, but it was all he could handle at his age.

Back in the forties there were very few practice areas and no such thing as range balls. Everyone who practiced at all had their own shag bag full of balls used in previous rounds. If we practiced we hit your own balls then picked them up ourselves, unless we paid a caddy to go fetch them. There is a right way and a wrong way to practice and I never really new how because I did not have a purpose, I just hit balls. I was too young and wanted to play, not practice. So I learned different things on the course that was my practice range. As I said before, I almost always played alone due to the fact there were so few kids that played. Besides the fundamentals my dad taught me I was self taught.

I have to thank dad for introducing me to the world of golf. If he hadn't, who knows what I might have done with my life. Become President of the United States maybe? Dad saved all of you and me from me being elected to that pressure job because of golf.

I made two holes in ones also and I will tell you more about those, plus some more history about basketball inside our garage, in tomorrow's chapter.

HOLES IN ONE #27

I KNOW I SAID I WOULD talk about garage basketball but first I have a couple of other things ahead of that. As long as the ball stays round and holds air, I'll get back to basketball soon.

A hole in one is special, there are so many who play the game who have not had one and may never. Are all holes in ones good shots? Most of them are but even the good shots that go in there is luck involved, lot's of it. It is really difficult to put that little ball into that little hole in the ground from almost any distance, even putting from 30 feet on a green. I have always thought if I ever got one I hope it would be a good solid shot and not some kind of a half hit, half miss that rolled and rolled and accidently fell into the hole.

In all the years that I played golf I never witnessed anyone making a hole in one until I made my first one. I am not sure of the year I made it, there is a certificate around here somewhere, however, I don't know where and I am not going to look for it. I think it was around 1985. That means I was about 54 years old and about 40 years since I began playing golf before that eventful day. We were playing in a golf outing, a local tournament with a lot of prizes. One of the prizes was a brand new automobile for a hole in one. Let me set the scene here a little.

This tournament was played at PGA National Golf Club, Palm Beach Gardens, Fl., on the Champion's Course. This is the same course used for the Honda Classic held in March each year. The event was a best ball of the foursome, plus individual scoring as well. So I played my own ball for my individual score and use the best score in the foursome for the team score. The pace of play at most of these kinds of tournaments is usually very slow. Our foursome knew all four players in the foursome ahead of us. As a matter of fact two of them were customers of mine. They were George Swartout and John Jane and both owned golf retail stores, George here in North Palm Beach, the John in Stuart. This all happened on the 7th hole and we are not playing from the longest tees but the next longest, from the middle length tees. You can watch this very hole on TV during the tournament every March and from the back tees it is over 200 yards. The distance that day was 172 yards to the middle of the green, which is slightly up hill. The pin was slightly back a little from the middle and towards the right side. I would estimate the distance that day to have been just about 180 yards with a slight breeze at our backs. Because he pace of play was slow the group in front of us, after t they finished playing the hole, stood around the green to watch us hit our shots before moving on. I was striking the ball well that day and with the breeze behind me, even if the hole was slightly up hill, I felt a seven iron was the correct club for that distance. I hit the shot pure, really solid. He ball headed straight towards the flag, took a couple of bounces on the green and rolled straight into the cup! Since the hole is elevated somewhat we could not actually see the ball roll in. I knew it was going to be close and all of a sudden those four guys ahead of us at the green started to jump up and down shouting, "You made it, it went in!"

I did it! I finally had a hole in one and it was a good solid shot. About that prize, the one for a car for a hole in one, the prize was only offered on the par three 17th hole, which happens to be a part of the famous bear trap, 16, 17 and 18. I told the committee, I made a 1 on 7. That's adds up to 17 in my book! Give me the darn car. Instead they gave be a golf book written by Jack Nicklaus's long time caddie, Angelo Agureo. Remember him with his long flowing hair and mustache. Angelo was also from Canton, Ohio, believe it or not. Actually he was from Hartville, about 7 miles from Canton and I knew Angelo quite well. Oh, well, no car.

The second one came about two years later while playing the JDM Country Club's north course, also located in Palm Beach Gardens, Fl. JDM was the original PGA complex before they moved to the present PGA National Golf Resort. I was playing with the golf pro, Terry Barrows, Fred Stegbauer, who was another golf pro and owned a Pro

Golf discount store in West Palm Beach, and Don Walker, a retired air lines pilot. It was a calm day and the hole was 155 yards, a solid 8 iron distance for me. I had a brand new set of Spalding Top Flite irons in my bag which I was using for the first time. It was my very first shot with that 8 iron, and I holed it out for a one. I saw this one go in and I do remember it was July 4th.

I knew a person who claimed he had something like holes in ones in his career. His name was Art Wall who was a very successful tour player in the 50, 60, 70's. Can you imagine that? He also used a baseball grip as well, all ten fingers on the grip, very unusual for a professional touring golfer. Bob Rosberg was another who used that grip on tour.

All golfers have had close calls, just missing making a hole in one. One of the misses I will never forget was during a round at the Hudson (Ohio) County Club, near Cleveland. This par 3 green I am referring to it had a pretty good slope from back to front. In the mid 60's the pins were still the old thick metal kind, unlike the current pins, which are very thin and usually made of fiberglass. The thick pins left little room for the ball to go in the hole. I hit my shot which went directly at the hole and took a couple of hops then started to roll very slowly right up to the pin. Our group was watching intently and then we actually heard a soft ping sound. The ball made contact with the metal pin but did not go in the hole and then it started to roll slowly backwards towards the front of the green. Because of the slope the ball never stopped rolling until it was off the green. We all looked at each other in amazement. Not only did I not get my hole in one, it took me three more strokes to hole it out and I made a bogie, one over par, a four! Even with my German temper I couldn't get mad. All I could do was laugh that is what is called the rub of the green.

My Paper Boy Years #28

I WOULD LIKE TO TELL THE story about my years of being a paper delivery boy when I was about 12 years old through the age of 14. The years were 1943, 44 and 45 and I bought my first bike when I was ten. It was a used full size bike with no fenders. At that age I could hardly climb up on it. That old bike cost me $8.00 which was a lot of money to me at that age. I earned that money cutting grass and shoveling snow. The bike was fine if there was no rain because it had no fenders. When it rained the water from the street just rode up on those wheels and with no fenders the water just sprayed all over my back side. If there was any dirt on the road, and there usually was, you can imagine what I looked like. When I got the chance to get a paper route I needed a better bike, one with fenders and lights and I also had to install a huge wire basket on the handle bars to hold the papers. So I purchased a brand new Elgin which cost me $21.00. The lights and basket were added at an extra cost that I do not recall. The entire investment was probably $25.00, but I was in business.

To set the stage again we had a local afternoon paper, the Canton Repository. Almost everyone purchased that paper so the paper boys delivering the Repository had small territories in size, a few city blocks with 50 or 60 customers. A bike was not needed to cover that size area and the delivery boy just needed a big bag slung over his shoulder and walked their route. That was easy work. The paper route that I had was for the morning edition of the Cleveland Plain Dealer. Yes, that was a publication from a city located 60 miles from Canton. It was a good paper that many business men wanted to read before going to work. Because not everyone subscribed for that paper like the Repository, my paper route covered quite a large area which was impossible to walk and a bike was needed to cover the large area. I had to get up at 4:30 to 5:00 AM and go to an automobile service station located about a mile from my house to get my papers which were dropped off for us to deliver. It did not mater what season of the year it was, spring, summer, fall and winter; I had to deliver that paper to my customers. First thing I had to do when I arrived at that service station was get my papers and fold each one a certain way so I could throw them on to house porch. I stuffed all the folded papers into my big bag and put that bag into my very large wire basket. I could hardly balance that big bike to climb up on it. I was like a small ant carrying something three or four times my size.

The way the paper was folded, it could be thrown a long distance and it was like a missile. I never go off the bike and just rode up and down the streets slinging each paper on to the porch of those homes. In those days most homes were very close to the street so the throw was not that long. I just had to be careful not to break a window. Most all of this was done in the dark. When the paper landed on the poach it could be heard. The noise alerted the gentleman inside he had just received his bathroom reading material. Job done, go home and have breakfast, then get my books and ride my bike to school.

Saturday was collection day. I had a large wire ring with held a card for each customer and I recorded on that card what the customer paid and how much. Also strapped to my belt was a coin changer that held quarters, dimes, nickels and pennies. I was making $3.00 a week. Most kids were getting 25 cents a week allowance from their parents if they were lucky. So I was doing pretty well and my parents didn't have to give me an allowance. My mom was very good handling money; she had to be because those were rough depression days. Mom taught me how to save and how to invest. I also sold magazine subscriptions door to door like Collier's. With magazine sales and a paper route plus cutting grass and shoveling snow, the money I made provided all my spending money through high school, and beyond. I also bought War Bonds, as much as I could afford. They cost $17.50 each. If you held them a certain number of years, I think three, and then they were worth $25.00 when redeemed. Cash them in sooner and you just received your original investment back.

I will never forget the day President Franklin D. Roosevelt died in 1945. World War II was still going on and we lost our President. Newspapers put out an EXTRA paper. I stood on the busy corner of 18th St., N.W. and Cleveland Ave. The headline in very large bold print read;

EXTRA! EXTRA!
F.D.R DEAD!

I stood on that corner with tears in my eyes holding the paper high in the air shouting the same thing the headline read. Cars stopped one after the other buying a copy for 5 cents. My papers were gone in no time, tough times.

Who was this guy Truman, the Vice President? Harry S. Truman was his name and all of a sudden he was now our President. He had guts enough to drop an Atomic bomb on Japan, two of them, which saved thousands of our boy's lives by ending World War II. I was 14 years old.

One last thing before we get to garage basketball. I had a lady customer, I use the term lightly, and I had trouble collecting money she owed me for the daily paper delivery. Each week she would come to the door when I knocked and said, "I'm sorry, honey, I only have a hundred dollar bill, do you have change for that?" Are you kidding? That was like a fortune in those days. I don't think I ever saw a hundred dollar bill. I don't remember what she owed me but I think it was like 12 weeks delivery so that would have been a whopping $2.16!

That made my mother so mad she scraped and scraped for weeks and added to what I had saved and finally we came up with $97.84. I don't know what the actual figures were any more, but you get the picture. Mom told me to go and get my money as I now had change for a one hundred dollar bill. When this so called lady came to the door, she said the same thing, and I said, yes, I have change for that one hundred dollar bill right here in my pocket! She was shocked, and then she gave me $2.16 in change. She never had a hundred dollar bill, and we knew it. Aren't mom's great? Thanks mom.

GARAGE BASKETBALL #29

I GET STARTED ON SOMETHING, AND don't you know it, something else pops into my mind. All of a sudden I have to write about that while it is still bouncing around in my cranium. If I don't I loose it. Do you think my age has something to do with that? Before that happens again here we go finally, Garage Basketball.

Next to our modest home on Myrtle Ave. in Canton we had a pretty good size double garage with two big wooden doors with windows and windows on both sides to let in light. The wall opposite the doors was just a solid wall and the floor was concrete. There was electricity in there so we had lights. Dad did not play a lot of sports when he was a kid but he did have very good coordination. When he had time he would throw a baseball around with me and my brother. He loved to use a catcher mitt, could throw and catch very well. Along with his golfing abilities, I could tell he would have been good at other sports as well. Dad recognized that my brother and I were interested in sports, especially me. In basketball season I was always going some where with a basketball to find my friends. We would play ball at playgrounds, but in the fall as the weather became colder and the snow came, playing outside was difficult.

Dad had an idea since our garage had a pitched roof which was pretty high, maybe 14 feet in the middle of the peak dad decided to build a backboard and attach a steel hoop and we could play inside getting out of the cold rain and snow. He installed the steel hoop ten foot off the ground which is the regulation height. There was not much room to shoot the ball without hitting the roof, except at the roof's highest point down the middle. We were small then, so our shots were mostly layups anyway. It was great; all my friends came to my house to play when the weather was bad. We usually played three on three, six at a time. There was no room for two teams of five.

In those days the backboard was used much more than it is in today's game. Almost every shot came off the backboard and we banked the shots off that wood from all angles into the circular hoop. When taking a shot other than a layup we didn't put much height on the ball. We shot the ball on almost a straight line at the backboard hopefully the ball would ricochet back through the hoop. The ball constantly hitting that backboard wasn't exactly quiet, we made a lot of noise. The neighbors put up with it and never complained. I guess they were just happy to see kids having fun and staying out of trouble.

I practiced in there daily teaching myself how to shoot with my left hand as well as my right. I would start by shooting from the left side of the basket close up with my left hand, hundreds of shots, then gradually working further away from the basket. I worked at this until I could make shots with my left hand almost as good as my natural right hand. As I grew, I then learned how to shoot the hook shot with both hands as well. I really became a pretty good shot maker. In high school we still were not permitted to shoot foul shots any other way than the under handed shot using both hands to propel the ball upwards between our legs from the foul line. Remember that shot old folks?

It was after my high school days that we all started shooting those penalty foul shots with our favorite shot, usually the one handed push shot. In practice I could hit eight out of ten right handed and seven out of ten left handed most of the time. I could shoot almost equally as well with either hand which was a big plus. When the jump shot became popular, shooting the ball with different hands became pretty much a thing of the past. Most players only use their dominate hand. Too bad, all those other shots were kind of interesting.

What fun we had in the garage. I made the grade school basketball team in the 7th grade and played two years. Worley was the name of that grade school and I attended all eight years there and our school colors were red and navy blue. The school had a basketball court in the basement with a balcony running around the perimeter above where spectators could watch us play as there were no seats on the floor, just a couple of benches for the players and the coach.

My circle of friends was something else, we loved playing all sports, but I will stick to basketball for now. At Worley there was an outside entrance with steps leading down to the double doors. My friends and accidently found out that those two doors had a security problem as they could be opened by grabbing hold of the door handles and by shaking them. Quite often when the weather was bad we would end up at the school and sneak down those steps, and shake the door open and play basketball. We would relock the doors when we left, no vandalism, we were not into that we just wanted to play ball. One day the janitor was in the building, heard the commotion of us playing and caught us. He was a very well like nice man thank goodness. He asked us how we got in so we told him. You know what he did? Nothing, he knew all of us and just asked us to careful and lock the door when we were done. He trusted us and he never told anyone.

One day we did a little exploring in the school, we went to the principal's office to look around. Our principal was a very large woman by the name of Ms. Ruth Skeels. She was not well liked as she was the one who did all the spankings when any of us were sent to her office for discipline by our teacher. She used wooden paddles for those spankings and she had a collection of them. Her favorite paddle had holes drilled through the wood so it had less air resistance and that's the one she always used on me. It was very long and menacing looking. We thought about hiding them but that would give away the fact someone was entering the school, so we left them alone.

When you make the basketball team you are given a school letter that can be sown on a sweater or sports jacket. Guess what we also found in that store room, boxes full of red and navy blue felt, our school colors. Those materials were used to make our school athletic letter; W. There was some material all cut out and ready to be sown together. She was making them herself rather than purchasing them from a professional supplier. We were shocked, it kind of took the luster off of receiving one of those letters we felt we earned knowing that they were home made by that nasty mean old woman.

SCHOOL #30

I HAD MY PROBLEMS WITH SCHOOL and school had its problems with me. In grade school it seemed like I was always in trouble with the teachers. I got to know the paddle collection our Principal Ms. Ruth Skeels had all to well. In those days spanking kids in school was perfectly alright. On top of that we were given a paper which explained the reason we were disciplined for our parents to read and a signature of a parent was required to confirm the paper got home for them to read and it had to be returned to the school to confirm that. Parents today may not agree with that kind of treatment to their children in today's world. When my parents received those notices it meant I got another spanking when dad came home. Mom saved that job for him, dad was better at it than mom. Dad had a way of making me sweat it out, he would send me upstairs to his bedroom and told me to drop my pants and wait for him. That waiting was sometimes worse than the spanking itself, and he knew it. He made me wait, and wait, and wait, then came the spanking. Bent over his knees my bare butt exposed, he gave it to me with his bare hand and it felt like he had nails imbedded in his palm. He said it was going to hurt him more than me and that's the only time he ever lied to me!

Dad was very careful not to strike my lower back area, just my butt which caused no damage except red welts that lasted about an hour. Dad made sure there was no damage to my back or legs. Parents didn't run to the school complaining about the treatment of their precious kid in those years. They approved of it and I'll tell you how I feel about it after all these years. I deserved I and I would approve of it today. In the long run it was good for me.

My biggest problem in school was that I could not keep my

mouth shut in class. Still have that problem some say, but, that's me. I couldn't sit still either, I was fidgety. None of us are perfect, I know my shortcomings. When I made comments I thought no one could hear, I had a very deep voice even as a young kid, so yes my remarks were heard. Most of the time the kids would giggle, sometimes what I said was funny. The teachers just didn't have a sense of humor, not once did they think I was funny. The teachers would be doing their jobs and sometimes a remark just hit me funny and out it came. I knew I would get a spanking so why would I do it on purpose, I didn't like spankings. I just could not help myself so that's the way it went down, the remarks came out and I paid the price.

By the time I got to high school my reputation was there ahead of me. The teachers were on the look out for me, the trouble maker. My reputation had an effect on my grades. For years I felt my grades were lower than what they should have been.

I did have a couple or problems as a student I was unaware of until many years later. I had a terrible time concentrating on any subject and I had a habit of reversing numbers. I still do. Now there are terms for those problems which were not known back then. I started to think I was stupid, I could not remember my parent's birthdays or anniversary either. What was so important what the heck Cesar did on a certain date back so many years I could not comprehend anyway? What the heck did I care about the past when I was worried about tomorrow?

So the very first year of high school I did not fully advance from freshman to sophomore. I fell behind one half year, not a full year. I started my second year back in the freshman class. When half the school year was over I had enough credits to move up to my normal class. This repeated itself every year. In my 1949 senior class year book my picture was with the junior class group picture. But my individual picture was also in the senior graduating section as well. I had to catch up and get enough credits to graduate with my original class and I accomplished that. If I remember correctly, no one was allowed to take more than four major subjects at a time unless your average grade score was over 90, and mine was not. I think they just wanted to get rid of me because they did let me take two extra subjects to get the credits I needed to graduate regardless of my grade average not meeting those qualifications. I put one heck of an effort into my studies and ended up with an 85 average grade for all six subjects. I am proud of the fact I caught up and graduated with my class. Also during my four years of high school I did keep my grades up high enough to be eligible to play sports.

Our house was located between my grade school and my high school which was very fortunate. There were so many advantages due to our location.

WALKING TO SCHOOL #31

*T*HE ADVANTAGES OF LIVING BETWEEN grade school and high school, I either walked or rode my bike for twelve years and I came home for lunch every as well. We kids got to know each other a lot better walking together too. No school bus for most of us. In the good weather a lot of us stayed around after school and sometimes played marbles on the playground in grade school. The girls jumped rope or played Jax's. We mingled for awhile then headed home to study and have dinner. The kids who had to use a school bus didn't get to do that, they came and went. I have always felt I missed not getting to know those kids better because of that.

In high school, same thing, the high school was about the equal distance for me as the grade school. We would hang around after school awhile and visit, especially if you had a crush on someone. The school buses kept coming and going.

When various sports were in season the teams practiced was after school. Lehman High sat up on a small hill and our official nick name was the polar bears, but we were also called the hill toppers. Most of Canton called us something else, cake eaters. That was because we were located in the more desirable section of town, middle to upper middle class, and the wealthy.

Back to the school sitting on top of that small hill, we also had a football field in front of the school at the bottom of that small hill. Between the field and the school there were long wide concrete steps on that hill side which served as the seats for spectators. Each school in Canton during the early years leading up to the late 30's had their own little football fields. Then the city built Faucet Stadium and all four of the public high schools used that facility for their games.

When Faucet Stadium was built it was the largest high school football stadium in the United States, capacity wise. Before that, Massillon high school had that distinction, only seven miles away. Faucet stadium's bleachers on both sides of the field were concrete structures, one side a little taller than the other all with bench seats. At each end of the stadium behind the goal posts there were the usual metal structured stands you still see today in most small stadiums. Faucet stadium was built in a section of the park system that ran through he entire city. If you watch the Football Hall Of Fame game put on each year by the NFL, the exhibition game between two teams before the regular season begins. That game is played in Faucet stadium and it's capacity is about 30 thousand people.

Our high school had a nice size basketball floor but is a little smaller than most. There was not an official size then, except the basket height of 10 feet and the foul line had to be all the same dimensions but the length and width of the court could, and did vary. The baseball team used a city field. After practice we walked home, parents did not bring their kids to school and then pick them up in those days. If your family had a car, it usually was **a car,** singular. Dad's needed that car for his work and It was really rare if a family had two cars. Besides that, in the early 40's due to the war there were only a handful of 1942 model cars made. There were no 1943, 44, 45 models made during the war. Our car was a 1941 Plymouth. Every one was very careful about the use of those cars during the war, they had to last for a long time. Car production stated again with the 1946 models and there was so much demand it took a couple of years for most people to finally get rid of their late 1930, 1940 and 41 models. Dad's next car was a 1948 Pontiac.

Just how did this series of personal stories get started, and why am I writing these stories?

WHY AM I WRITING THESE STORIES #32

A LITTLE MORE BACKSPIN AS I have to try to explain how this series of personal stories got started, actually it was quite by accident. It all started with a simple email I sent out to my daily email list of about 100 email buddies.

That email featured the great comedian Bob Hope then I followed that up with, I met Bob Hope, and it has just continued from one thing to another. More than once I have questioned myself why am I doing this. These are personal stories about me, things that have happened to me, people I have met. We all have our own personal stories and thoughts and I can understand why my family might be interested my children really are as I get comments like, dad, I didn't know about that! Keep the stories coming dad. The grand kids are chipping in as well letting me know how much they appreciate my past history. Even my dear wife Dee is learning some things that I just have never talked about, mostly business stuff.

Old friends, even old classmates, plus new friends, Brother Knights of Columbus and many former Spalding guys and gals whom I have worked with over the years are receiving these daily emails. For many I suppose these stories bring back some of their own memories. Some are very interested in my golf stories and some don't know a thing about the sport. However I have received word back letting me know they have learned something from those golf stories and have enjoyed them as well. Some have said why not just write about all you have experienced about golf all at one time, don't spread it out. Tell us about all the famous people you know or have met. I don't want it to seem like I am bragging about that, I am not. Meeting famous people just happened in the business I was in. Like meeting the tallest person

I have ever met. That was at a National Sporting Goods Show one year and it was none other than the famous basketball player, Wilt Chamberlain who was 7' 1" tall. Or how about Sam Snead, Arnold Palmer, Bobby Jones, Bob Feller, Oscar Fraley and so many others I know or have met.

I mentioned Oscar Fraley, do you know about him? He was a sports writer who covered a lot of golf tournaments. I had the pleasure of sitting down and chew the fat with Oscar a few times and we were on a first name basis. Do you remember the popular 50's TV series, The Untouchables starring Robert Stack who played the part of Elliot Ness who battled the crime syndicate and Al Capone? Oscar Fraley wrote the entire series!

I know I am bouncing all over the place with these stories but that is because one just leads to something else, nothing has been preplanned. I also feel I have to lead up to some stories with past history first. Things change as we get older, obviously, and I find that although my eyesight may be fading with age, I seem to be seeing a whole lot of things more clearly. With hearing loss I tend to understand some things better as well. Age has a way of improving some things. Some other things, well, been there, done that so won't go there.

One thing that hasn't changed is my patience. You would think with age that would improve. Not everything changes for the better, unfortunately. So, you learn to play the hand you've been dealt. Why am I going to continue writing? It is because so many of you have handed down your various reasons why you are looking forward to receiving these stories each day. I am truly humbled. That is something when you consider the old saying, "he was a legend in his own time," or is it "he was a legend in my **own mind!**"

One last thought for now. I was not a good student and failed a few subjects, one was English. I believe I said before that I don't know a verb from an adjective and always thought nouns were found in the Catholic Church. So, please excuse my grammar, I am not trying to make all of this perfect because I'm not perfect. One of my daughters told me she changed a couple of my stories because of bad grammar before sending them on to others. I tried to explain to her that you do no touch or alter artist paintings. The same goes for what I have written, correct or incorrect, what I write is mine and that is me. It is not for someone else to change. Some things I don't want changed, like old land telephones, I don't own a cell phone.

HIGH SCHOOL BASKETBALL #33

*W*E ALSO PLAYED A LOT of outdoor basketball at the Stark County Home for the aging. Ohio has 88 counties and each county has one of these facilities. The Stark County home was located in Canton and I don't know how many acres that area covered but it was a pretty large piece of property. There were quite a few buildings housing the office, living quarters for the superintendant in charge plus his family. The superintendants last name was Firestone and his son John is a life long friend. There was also a temporary morgue which I went into once but what I saw laying on a slap ended up as my first and only visit.

There was a large barn housing farm equipment, tractors, trucks, harvesting equipment of all kinds. Another big barn was home to horses, some cattle, pigs, a few owls and a flock of sparrows with an abundance of rats. We spent a lot of time shooting at those rats with a 22 caliber riffle. Luckily we didn't kill any of the animals.

This was a home away from home for some of us. There was a basketball backboard and hoop fastened to an 8 x 8 wooden pole at one end of a rather rough cement driveway. When we grew a little older and taller we kind of outgrew my garage, so we played here quite a bit, and we could always bum lunch from the large kitchen.

Most of my basketball buddies were on the grade school team, including my close friends John Firestone and Dick Seiple. We all made the freshman high school basketball team. Next was the reserve team with mostly sophomores and juniors on it and this team was the stepping stone to the varsity team. The varsity consisted of seniors and juniors, and once in a great while, a sophomore but that was rare.

Making the reserve team was tough as a sophomore as most were juniors. I am one who didn't make it that year. A bunch of us wanted to play some sort of organized basketball so we formed our own independent team and named ourselves the **DUKES**. We bought some white tee shirts and had them embroidered with the name **DUKES** in navy blue letters, front and back. No numbers, just the name **DUKES**. We wore navy blues shorts so we looked pretty good like a team should. A couple of guys went as far as getting a small **DUKES** tattoo on their upper left arm. That was not for the three of us, thank goodness we had sense enough not to go that far to identify ourselves.

We became connected with the local Jewish Center, a wonderful facility with a basketball court and a large indoor swimming pool. We played in an independent league and took on all comers. We were pretty good and didn't loose very many games. This helped us gain experience so we could make the high school reserve team and eventually the varsity team, which the three of us finally did accomplish.

As a side note we found out that taking on the name DUKES may have been a mistake as the Canton police became aware of us and thought we might possibly be a new gang in town. We didn't know that they were keeping an eye on our activities to see what we were up to. Eventually a detective made us aware of that and told us they realized what we were all about and we got a clean bill of health. We never got into any kind of trouble so the police backed off and stopped shadowing us.

Since grade school it was always my desire to make that varsity team. Lehman was the smallest high school in Canton as far as attendance. It was a four grade school with about 900 students, yet we were still class A. Back then there were only two classifications, A and B. and unfortunately we just barely made A which meant we were competing in sports with much larger schools. For example McKinley High in Canton had over 1,000 students in their freshman class alone.

Lehman always seem to hold it's own in all sports as we always had winning football and basketball teams. Basketball was probably our best sport with a couple or our teams got to the State Finals over the years. Our school colors were scarlet and grey the same as Ohio State.

A group of girls voted that I had the best looking legs on the basketball team! I think some of the girls were even Jealous. I had hair in those days and as long as I can remember when the hot summer days came, I would get a crew hair cut and get rid of my longer hair style; it was a lot cooler too. When summer was over I let my hair grow longer again. No chance of doing that anymore, the crew bailed out. Now I tell people my haircut style is a reverse Mohawk.

LEARNING THE GERMAN LANGUAGE #34

EFORE I CONCLUDE MY HIGH school basketball career a couple of old memories worked their way into my old cranium. Not good memories really, some still hurt. It was not a requirement to take a class in a second language, however most students did. At that time French seemed to be the language of choice with Spanish a bad third. German was also offered and mom spoke what they called Low German as did all her sisters and brothers. So I thought, why not try and learn the German language so I signed up for the course. The teacher was Ms. Shuster, and old woman and in those days anyone older than 40 seemed old to me but she had to be in her early 60's. For some reason people at that age today do not look nearly as old as they looked back in the 40's. People did look older then, no question about it.

Anyway, I liked the class and thought I was doing really well. I was even helping some of my class mates who were struggling with this harsh language. My test scores were not brilliant by any means, but were all 80 to 85. When the first 6 week report card came out I received a big red 65! Anything under 70 was failing. I could not believe I and asked Ms. Shuster for an explanation since my test scores were what they were. All she said to me was that was the grade I deserved.

I was devastated and I quit the class then and there. Was this a carry over of my reputation from grade school? I don't know. In high school up to that point, I was not in any trouble. Still outspoken at times, but nothing that got me on the hot seat. I felt rebellion building inside me. I think I held that back pretty well, as far as anyone could actually see. But it was there, down deep inside. I wanted to play sports so I tried my best to stay out of anything that would bring attention to me in a bad way. I really felt I was not being treated fairly. That hurt.

Then one day I really screwed up big time, but not intentionally. I was headed to gym class with two others this day. The next class was already in progress and we were a little late descending the stairs which led to the boy's locker room and the gyn. Going down those stair on our right were two bells, not really that close together. One that had a soft ring used for changing classes and, the other was the fire alarm. Don't get ahead of me, I'm telling this horror story!

I was just not paying much attention to the fact they were a lot different in size and I just reached up towards the bell I thought was used for changing class. I pulled back the bells hammer and released it. If I had done that to the bell I thought it was, it would just have been a little ding. You guessed it, wrong bell! All hell broke loose as It was the fire alarm. I activated the whole system throughout the entire school and those bells just rang, and rang, and rang.

If a fire drill test were being done, all the teachers and students would have been forewarned in advance. The bell would go off and all would file out as instructed knowing it was a scheduled test drill. Of course was not a forewarned test and I emptied the school. Thank goodness the weather was mild and no one got hurt, this was a very dangerous situation that I alone created.

Well, there the three of us stood surrounded by noise the bells were making and out of nowhere comes the dean of Canton football coaches, J.R. "Jimmy" Robinson charging towards us. He was also my golf coach or at least supervisor because he didn't play golf. Coach Robinson demanded who had set off the alarm, and I looked at the other two. They looked at me very sadly like this may be the last time they would ever see me.

I confessed that it was me. To conclude this very trying time in my brilliant high school career, I escaped a suspension from school and only a one week suspension from the reserve basketball team. I was a junior at the time. After much interrogation, it was determined that it was just a very stupid mistake. I finally did something wrong and got a break I am not so sure I deserved. I never got into any other trouble the rest of my high school days. That was a very hard story to tell.

I Made the Varsity Basketball Team #35

*W*HEN I WAS IN GRADE school four year older brother was in high school. He would take me to see the high school basketball games, a real treat. Right then and there I wanted to be on that team someday. But when I finally made it, there was something missing. I never did give it my best effort. Why? I am not sure. Deep down inside I think I know.

Why does one want something like making the team mean so much, self satisfaction? Sure. Ego? Yes. Recognition? Absolutely. Get the attention of the girls? Yes, I'm a red blooded young boy. To make your family proud of me? Certainly. But there was something missing, my father. I loved my father and it took years for me to understand him as a person and his personality. You know where I finally got to know him? On the golf course, that is where I finally understood who he was. He was a father who I never remember saying, I love you. He didn't know how to say that. He loved all of us but he just was not able to say it. To this day I'm not much of a hugger myself. If you ever want to know someone, play golf with them and most of the time it takes only one round. The true personalities come out, believe me. My dad was a good man, a loving man who just simply did not know how to let it come out.

Having said that, dad traveled a lot in his job with the railroad and he was not home when we played some of our games. but not all of them. I think he may have seen me play just one time. Not until much later did I come to understand my dad and it was on the golf course. I made the team, but as I said something was missing. It was years later that I finally understood why I didn't give it my all. There is something about hearing approval, a job well done. Well done, son. I finally got the approval I was secretly seeking years later. When and where? On the golf course, dad was at ease there. I finally understand where dad was coming from and he was a good loving father who taught me many values. Thank you again dad. I now know you had been watching me in your own way then, and even now.

I was not on the starting five on the varsity team. My position was a forward and I sometimes played the center position. In the 40's it was really rare to come up against anyone taller than six foot three or six foot four inches tall. I reached my height of 6' 2" when I was sixteen. When I was a seventeen year old senior I was far from having a mature body. As a late developer I was up against much stronger kids. My top weight at that height was 155 pounds. I weigh 100 pounds more than that now. I remember when I was twenty years old I only had to shave twice a week.

I did get a lot of playing time but I became a much better player after high school, playing anywhere I could when we moved to Pittsburgh in the summer of 1949. I even was offered a scholarship to play basketball at Pitt University. That's another story; I don't want to get too far ahead of myself. There were other important moments in my life that happened in high school. Some memories I would like to revisit a little.

I will never forget one practice that I made a shot and got yanked off the court and I was benched and received a strong chewing out from my coach. How in the world can that happen making a two point play? He called it showboating.

Here is how that happened. As I mentioned before I could dribble the ball and shoot the ball almost equally well with both hands. A lot of kids could not do all of that and I could also pass the ball behind my back which the coaches didn't really care for. To them it was not the safe way to pass the ball, so I was not supposed to do that. What happened, I was cutting across the lane in front of the basket going from the left side of the court towards the right, so that my left side was facing the basket. I had the ball and was going to pass it to someone else. I made the mistake of leaving both feet off the court and I was airborne. I did not see any player open that I could pass the ball to so I just flipped the ball behind my back towards the basket, and I made the shot! Then all hell broke loose. I sat on the bench for the rest of the practice. I use to practice that shot when no one was around and I was not surprise that I made that shot. Just everyone else was, it's kind of like winning a battle but loosing the war.

I remember the first date I had. My date and I attended one of our high school dances which were held in the gym, dim lights and all. Big band music, the two step, the box step, and even the jitter bug. I was a terrible dancer, but more about that, tomorrow.

HIGH SCHOOL DANCE #36

$\mathcal{W}$ HAT A TIME IN MY life, my first official date and I had to purchase my very first suit. My favorite clothing colors were browns and tans so I chose a chocolate brown double breasted suit which was the style then. I wore a tie that had a dark brown background with some yellow sprinkled throughout, a white shirt and highly polished dark brown shoes and brown socks and boy did I feel grown up. I didn't have to shave, no sign of whiskers yet, no hair on my chest either but was still very wet between the ears.

I loved big band music and still do. Best music era of all time, swing, jazz, slow romantic tunes. You could understand the words of the songs in the 40's also, but not now. All the songs then seemed to have a message not just a bunch of noise. Dancing was a big challenge for me. I attended dance classes to learn how to do the two step and box step. I got by but not very well. However there was something to be said about me holding a girls right hand with my left and my right hand around her waste dancing cheek to cheek. She smelled good too, a lot better than those guys on the basketball court.

My dad would never let me borrow our car for a date. I had to rely on my friends John Firestone and Dick Seiple and really appreciated that they including me in all the double and triple dating we had together. Dad was afraid if I got in an accident it would jeopardize his job as he needed the car to travel when not using the train to cover rail road personal accident claims.

I had several girl friends during high school but was not going with anyone at the time of the annual Junior/Senior Prom my senior year. I was not going to go until someone suggested that Dolores Fisher did not have a date either. It was suggested that the two of us should team up and go. We did and I bought a large gardenia corsage for her to wear. We double dated with Dick Seiple and his date and the Prom was held at the Meyers Lake ball room. We had a live band with all the trimmings and it was a wonderful dance and evening. Dolores was a very pretty girl who I never had another date with. I got word back that Dolores was wondering why I never asked her out again. I really liked her as a person and friend and we had a really good time together into the wee hours of the morning. But I didn't feel the chemistry between us, its just one of those things that happen, or doesn't happen, and hard to explain.

I just told you a big fib. The real reason why I was not going with anyone and why I didn't ask Dolores Fisher, or anyone else for a date was that I knew we were moving to Pittsburgh that summer. I did not want to get any kind of a romance started and then have to break it off. It was difficult enough to know that at age seventeen my life was going to go through a tremendous change which I had no control over.

My brother was not moving with us, he was now 21 and working for the Ohio Power Co. as an engineer. About my brother Dick, that's what I called him all my life until he got married and his wife insisted on calling him Richard. The name seemed very formal but I got used to it. My brother was three and a half years older than I, and we were four years apart in school. So when I entered high school, he was going to college. That's a pretty good spread for brothers. I can never remember my brother without glasses which he started to wear at the very young age of six. The first thing he did in the morning was reach for them and the last thing he did was take them off when he went to bed. He even wore them when taking a bath. Dick loved sports, but was not to well coordinated. Dick reached the height of 6' 3" and he grew about six inches in one year and that didn't help his coordination. He was thin and gangly and had a little heart problem as well. He had Scarlet Fever which may have contributed to that problem. Richard played golf and was a fair player scoring in the mid 80's while scoring in the high 70' once in a while.

Dick and I were complete opposites as he was on the quite side but we had the same set of values due to our upbringing. I was loud with a very deep voice. Even as a young kid at 6 years old I sounded like a bull horn. When Dick spoke I had a hard time hearing him. He had to say everything twice, his voice just did not project. He was a good student of sorts. He was very intelligent and was only interested in the subjects that interested him which was math, algebra, trig, mechanical drawing. More about my brother, Tomorrow …

My Brother #37

*M*Y BROTHER DICK PASSED AWAY in January, 2000 shortly after tuning 73. He died two months after I underwent my two way bypass surgery. Dick had a massive heart attack, just exactly what I would have happened to me if my problem had not been discovered. I was 69 and lucky, my brother was not. I want to explain how my problem was discovered; a very bad knee saved me. I had been in constant touch with a doctor about a full left knee replacement and I kept putting it off, cluck, cluck as in chicken.

Dee and I went on a seven day Caribbean cruise and my knee hurt so badly I could not sleep. When we stopped at an island for sight seeing and shopping I would get off the ship, but could not walk around with Dee. So I would find a nice comfortable bar near the ship and sit there sipping the native drinks waiting for Dee to return. When we returned from the cruise I went straight to the doctor and told him let's get this operation over with. He said I made the correct decision, leaned over to feel my pulse in my lower left leg and he could hardly find one. Oh, oh, said the doctor, we need to check this out Bill.

I went through a Cath which found artery blockage in my upper leg, and they took care of that. Then I had to take a stress test which I didn't study for very well and I failed it very quickly. I was told to report directly to the hospital at once and was not even allowed to go home to get anything for my hospital stay. They contacted my wife to inform her was happening. It was kind of scary to say the least.

A Cath procedure was done to look inside my arteries leading to my heart. I had two arteries blocked, one 100% and one 99%. How they came up with 1% difference is beyond me. I could have had a massive heart attack at any moment. I shudder to this day thinking I just got off that seven day cruise. If I had had a heart attack on that cruise, I most likely would not be typing this today. Double bypass surgery was performed. My decision to have knee replacement surgery saved me from a very possible massive heart attack.

When I entered high school my brother Dick entered Ohio State University and becoming a Mechanical Engineer was his main goal. He was bored in high school and hardly opened a book. I remember when he was a freshman taking Algebra 1, he was helping a few of the older kids in the neighborhood with their trigonometry. He just had that kind of a mind. He only went to college for about a half a year as he thought he was wasting his time and he dropped out. Dick then took the State of Ohio Exams for an engineer's license and passed! That would not be allowed today as a college diploma is required. Dick knew at the time if he passed that was it, a college diploma was not required in the 40's.

Dick then went to work for the Ohio Light and Power Co., and after a few years he became bored again and decided to get into surveying. So he took the State of Ohio tests for that, passed those tests as well and received his Surveying License. Dick then opened up his own surveying business. He was also into computers when they started to be available for the average person, and learned how to program them himself.

At one point in his life he thought he might want to move to Arizona, I don't know why. Dick went to Arizona and took their State exams for engineering and surveying and he passed both of those tests. He never did move there. While all this is going on I am having problems with simple math. The difference between us was amazing.

My Brother and I were separated in 1949 for the next seventeen years because dad, mom and I moved to Pittsburgh and until I moved back to Ohio we saw very little of each other. After seven years back in Ohio I moved away again, first to Mass., and then to Florida. Again, we saw very little of each other until he decided to move to Florida.

I had a business on the side while working with Spalding in Florida. It didn't take up to much of my time because I had other people running my company, the Wm. Faulhaber Enterprises, Inc. My brother asked if I had a spot for him as he wanted to come to Florida. I did and he did.

I had always admired him as my protector when I was small. Also for all he accomplished without a college education. In turn, he was kind of amazed at what his kid brother accomplished as well. We got a chance to become brothers again.

While I am writing this, the TV is on the Golf Chanel and the long drive contest is being held. These freaks are hitting the golf ball almost 400 yards. That's four football fields long! Watching those guys hitting golf balls just jogged my memory about something that happened one year at the Doral Resort and Country Club in Miami where there was a tour event going on. One day I took my brother with me. I was no longer connected with the tour, but I still knew quite a few of the players. When I attended tournaments, I spent most of my time around the practice green or the practice range so I could make contact with the players. I still had credentials that got me to a lot of places the normal spectator could not go. Like, inside the ropes of the practice range and putting green.

This day my brother and I are at the range watching these players practicing. I spotted Leonard Thompson who was on the Spalding touring staff. Leonard played on the golf team with Lanny Wadkins at Wake Forest, where Arnold Palmer went to college as well. Leonard was a big man, about six foot and a very large strong frame. I knew his swing really well and he did not make a real good body turn due to his muscular build. Leonard relied on his strength to overcome his very short backswing and minimal body turn. I told my brother that I would be right back that I wanted to say hello to my old friend, Leonard, and I ducked under the ropes.

I headed in Leonard's direction and Leonard saw me approaching him. I said something to him when we got closer. Well Leonard dropped his club on the ground, came over to me and gave me one of the biggest bear hugs you could imagine. My brother could not believe what he was seeing that his little brother was being greeted in that manner by a turning golf professional. I spent some time out there saying hello to a few others, then returned to where my brother was standing.

Well, my brother looked at me like who the hell are you and what happened out there? Why did that guy grab and hug you? What did you say to him? I explained to my brother about Leonard's short backswing and minimal body turn. What I said to Leonard was, "old friend, your backswing and body turn is the best that I have ever seen it." It turns out he had been working very hard on just that, a fuller turn and a longer backswing. Leonard was just so happy I recognized the difference that his hard work was paying off and that I could tell the difference. My brother had one heck of a day seeing his little brother being recognized by these famous golfers.

My brother and I were almost the complete opposites. Dick loved to camp out under the stars and he was a little bit of a hermit. I'll expound on those statements, next.

Camping Out & Fishing #38

*Y*ES, DICK AND I WERE very different except for the values our parents taught us. Our thoughts about a lot of issues were pretty much the same. Dick loved the out doors, fishing, camping and was a little bit of a hermit. He used to go to Canada once a year. He had an area where he drove as far as he could. Then with a light canoe loaded with his supplies, he would lift the canoe over his head and hike further north to some out of the way lake where he would pitch his tent and spend a few days fishing and whatever else you do when you camp out, I guess eat and sleep. I'm sorry \but that is not what I call excitement.

My idea of camping out was a nice air conditioned motel with a restaurant, a swimming pool and an active bar.

Dick used to drag me along when he went fishing as kids, because mom told him too. I did not like fishing. I just could not sit there and wait for something to happen and when I did go I never caught any fish anyway. Fish did not like me, and I did not like them. They stink. One day I ate my brother's bait! No, not worms, Dick used raw bacon. I normally like mine crisp but I was hungry and ate it raw. Boy was Dick ever mad at me.

Fishing reminds me of a fish story. We had a Spalding regional sales meeting one year in the Panhandle of Florida. Some of the guys wanted to go deep sea fishing in the Gulf and they rented a charter fishing boat. They talked me into going along and I told them I was interested in the boat ride, the companionship and the two cases of beer. But that I had no interested in fishing as I never could catch any. They scoffed at that and I explained to them how serious I was. Fishing was a waist of time, for some reason the man upstairs would not let the fish go for my bait. Probably because I didn't like them he figured that I didn't deserve to catch them.

So off we go, beer in hand, a nice day and calm water. Two cases of beer should last the four hours we would be on the high seas. An adventure with good friends, there were four fishing chairs and poles to fish with in the stern of the boat and there were six of us. Two of us would have to wait until one of the other four caught a fish, then that person would give up his chair to one of the other two waiting. As each guy caught a fish we changed seats. I was one of the first four in a chair. Now picture this. Four chairs, four poles, and four lines going out side by side into the water next to each other. Those stinky fish could have picked my bait, but they didn't.

We were trawling, meaning we were not standing still in the water but moving slowly. Five guys were catching fish and changing chairs, but not me, I was still the only one without a catch. My friends were starting to believe me. I switched to a different chair which was hot, a lot of catches. I sat there for another half hour or so and did not catch anything while the guys using the chair I had been in were catching fish! I never did catch one and this is a true story. There will be a couple of guys receiving this email who were on that outing and should remember that happening and can verify my story.

For reasons unknown the only time I was ever successful catching some fish was with my son Jim. We went bass fishing one day and I caught the most. Maybe the man upstairs didn't want me to look bad in front of my son.

When we were kids before we moved to Myrtle Ave in Canton, dad was renting a house on 18th street, just across the street from a cemetery. This was during the years the popular movies were the Wolf Man, the Mummy, Vampires and Frankenstein. I could not watch those movies, they scared me half to death, and my dear brother Dick tried his best to finish me off. Living near that cemetery was bad enough and my brother kept telling me these creepy stories about what is going on in that cemetery at night, including all the characters in those movies hanging out in there as well. I guess I was about four or five years old. Dick would hide behind the doors in our house and wait for me to come through. Then from behind the door he would jump out screaming. Wet pants for me became common. I didn't like my brother very well for quite some time. I got over it, I suppose, but I still can not watch any kind of a movie that is somewhat shocking.

One day Dee and I went to see Alfred Hitchcock's movie, Psycho. I did not read anything about that movie before we went and I thought it had something to do with doctors and some kind of mental illness. I walked out during the shower scene, remember that one where the girl was taking a shower and this guy stabs her with a knife, she is screaming and there is blood running down the drain? That was more than enough for me and I waited for Dee in the lounge. My brother Dick fixed me for good with all that scary stuff and I have never really ever gotten over that fear.

My brother eventually bought a house on a lake, seven miles east of Lake Wales, Fl. Like I said, Dick was a little bit of a hermit. His house on that lake was surrounded by citrus trees. He could not see any of his neighbor's houses. He loved being isolated. Dick went to work for a surveying company in Lake Wales. That was after I had to close down my side business, Wm. Faulhaber Enterprises, Inc. We performed punch out work for a large developer, and we also got into the business of Condo Management. My company had an office on the west coast of Florida as well.

My close friend from Chagrin Falls, Ohio, Ed Flaherty, who worked for Ford in a manufacturing plant in Cleveland, eventually moved to Brazil and was working for a division of Ford, Philco. After several years there, he retired and came to Florida to visit me before returning to Ohio. Instead of returning to Ohio he went to work for me along with my brother. Ed and his wife Lorraine moved into the town house I had purchased for investment purposes, which was located in the PGA National complex.

I eventually lost my contract with the developer we were doing most all of our business. I had warned my people we had too many eggs in one basket. I warned everyone if we lost that business without having spread out with a good percentage of our business with other developers; I would close down my business within two weeks. Unfortunately they were not successful in obtaining new customers.

My job with Spalding kept me busy so did not get too involved with the day to day operations with my own company; it was their job to run my operation. As I said before we did loose our contract with our major developer, I had no choice, and I closed down my business in two weeks, It was too late to find new business. I wasn't going to let expenses pile up and cost me a lot of money. It is like looking for a new job while you still have a job. That works a lot better than trying to fine a job when you are out of work.

I ended up with about five of those new computers my brother had programmed for running the business along with loads of office equipment. I did not get burned financially and I had to let everyone go, Ed, Dick, including a son in law who was working for me on the west coast of Florida. So goes business and it was a great experience.

Moving To Pittsburgh #39

A LITTLE BACKSPIN, WHEN IT BECAME closer to the time for our move from Canton to Pittsburgh in September of 1949, fear ran through me. The fear was about beer. How can beer have anything to do with fear? It had something to due with the laws of two different states. I am of German decent and I was allowed to drink a very small amount of beer at a very young age, nothing unusual for German families. As a teenager, dad or mom would drink a beer with my brother and I quite often, it was not a big deal.

Until now! Maybe we shouldn't have but as 16 and 17 year olds my friends and I drank beer all the time. We didn't get drunk, heck; I was used to drinking beer. There were a few bars we could go to and get served even though we were under the legal age to drink. In Ohio the lawful age was 18. We behaved ourselves and even at my young age I looked a little older than I was. If a bartender asked me how old I was I would tell him 19. Everyone under 18 would always say 18. Not I and it worked most of the time. If it didn't I had a fake card saying I was 19. Please don't tell anybody.

Now don't you know it, I was turning the legal age to drink beer in Ohio, July 22nd, I'm 18! We are moving in September, I had a total of six weeks I could drink beer in a bar legally! Then it hit me right between the kidneys. In Pennsylvania the legal age to drink any kind of a drink with alcohol is 21!

Now I am faced with three more years that I would have to tell little white lies! How fair was that? On top of all that the draft age for the service because of the Korean conflict was 18! Come on Man! Go fight for your country, but can't have a beer? What's wrong with this picture?

What was happening to me? I was leaving behind my whole life, all my friends, and a place I knew so well. I was entering a whole new life and did not no what to expect. I was not happy but I had to put everything behind me and actually start over. Meet new people and make new friends. I am out of school with no college plans what so ever and I wasn't even considering going to college. I have to find my way somehow, someway. There I was in my new surroundings and school was in session. All the kids my age were walking around I did not know any of them, and would not get to know them as School is where you meet your peers. I would have been better off if we had moved after my junior year. Then I would have had one year of high school to meet all these kids my age.

I must move on and look for a job and I'm almost broke. As it turns out the first friends I was about to meet were older than I. They will be my new beer drinking buddies and more on that later. Plus the U. S. Coast Guard, another experience coming up.

Putting all that aside for a while, I was moving from an area that had rolling hills to an area where the hills were turning into foothills of small mountains. I was going from a pretty clean small town to a city that at the time had no smoke controls and lots of steel mills. It was just plain dirty. Dad went to work wearing a white shirt and came home wearing a grey shirt.

Dad was already in Pittsburgh when mom and I left Canton. We had to wait for the moving van to load up then we had to drive to Pittsburgh and meet the van at our new residence, 48 Vernon Dr., Mt. Lebanon, a suburb in the south west part of Pittsburgh. We headed east on Route 30 in the family car, a 1948 Pontiac. Went through E. Liverpool Ohio, crossed the Ohio River and into Western Pennsylvania, the rolling hills increasing in size as we worked out way east. We went through the small little town of Imperial, west of Pittsburgh. Little did I know, but 7 years later I would marry Dolores, "Dee", my first and last wife, who was raised in, yes, Imperial. There was a large service station and auto repair shop on a curve of the main street in Imperial, which was Route 30, that I remembered seeing. That station was owned and operated by none other than Dee's Aunt and Uncle. Her cousins still operate that service station to this day, small world.

Entering this smog filled area the skies were as grey as my disposition. I saw for the first time steep hills with cobble stone paved streets. Why cobble stones? Before automobiles, the cobble stones help horses get a foothold to help them to travel up those steep slopes. I won't even get into the winter, driving in that town was crazy. On the main streets, there were streetcar tracks running through the center of the streets, two tracks, one coming and one going.

Our house was on Vernon Dr. in Mt. Lebanon, which was an upper middle class very nice residential suburb and it was the nicest house we ever lived in. All our homes had been wooden frame construction up until now. Our new home was brick and stone with a slate roof. Not real large, it had the usual three bedrooms, one and one half bathrooms, a shower in the main bath, our first shower ever. A living and dinning room, kitchen and kitchenette for daily meals, and a basement with a one car garage with an entrance from the rear with a sloping driveway from street level to basement level. This will be my home until I go from being single to double. (Married)

There was an ad by the Fuller Box and Label Co. in the newspaper and they were looking for a printer's helper which sounded interesting to me.

The only job I ever had before, besides paper boy and selling magazines door to door, cutting grass and shoveling snow, was between my Junior and senior year in high school. Our coach Jimmy Robinson got some of us jobs for the summer at Republic Steel working in the mason department. Hot work, not only because it was summer but working in and around those open hearth furnaces that were lined with special fire resistant bricks. The bricks had to be replaced periodically. After the furnace was shut down for a couple of days to cool off, those furnaces were still very hot. We went into the furnace with picks and crow bars which we used to knock those bricks off the walls. New bricks were then installed then the furnaces ready to be used again to melt scrap metal into molting steel.

I was making .59 cents and hour. I thought that was great, I was making almost one cent a minuet, unheard of for kids in those days. Now I am applying for the printer's helper job. I'll let you know how I made out, next.

Printers Helper #40

*T*HIS WAS QUITE AN EXPERIENCE. I answered the ad for the Fuller Label & Box Co., and I was hired. There was one problem, I had no car and this place of business was on the east side of Pittsburgh, I lived on the south side. If I was working the day shift I had to be there at 8 AM. That meant a trip by bus and streetcars. If I remember correctly it took almost an hour and one half. But at that time of the morning the bus service was not available. I had to walk with my lunch pail to the center of Mt. Lebanon where the street car ended, or started, because it was the end of the line and there was a loop where the streetcar turned around and began its run in the opposite direction. I would take that streetcar into Pittsburgh and then transfer to another streetcar to my designation. At the end of the shift the trip would be reversed, two streetcars and a bus ride in the late afternoon. If I was working the late shift, 4 PM to midnight, I could catch a bus from my house going, but coming home I would have to walk about a mile and one half. It became a very long day. It was also at this streetcar loop that I found a new bunch of friends. There was a little bar there named Andy's Loop Cafe. It became my second home and more on that story later.

This printing company had many well know customers and they were experts in their work, printing labels for containers such as boxes, cans and bottles. Some of their customers are Famous names such as I.W.Harper, a well know bourbon. The jelly people, Smucker's from Orville, Ohio fame, and the H. J. Heinz Co. As a printer's helper my first job was working on a large two color printing press. The toughest job was setting up a job so that all the printing plates were aligned correctly in the bed of the press, so the two colors being printed at the same time would be exactly where they should be. It is a little complicated to explain so I won't try.

I had to bend over in a position that my upper body was horizontal over the job. One day I must have been in that position for a least a half an hour and when I started to straighten up, I couldn't. I was frozen in that position, a disc in my back slipped slightly out of position. I was 18 years old and suffered for almost 40 years with that bad disc. On and off, my back would go out and many times I could not even walk. I finally had surgery to remove the disc in 1988 at age 57.

Fuller Label and Box Co. was a union shop so I had to join the Printers Union. After only a few months I got the chance to run a press of my own and I became a Printers Union card carrying printer at the age of 19. Wow, and I'm a Republican! The press was a one color Miehle horizontal made in Germany, most of the presses in the shop were manufactured in Germany.

A point of interest printing labels was tricky especially if printing on foil paper. Foil paper attracted electricity going through the press and was very hard to handle. To combat that I had foil tinsel hanging all over the press, the same tinsel used to decorate Christmas trees. The tinsel would attract the electricity in the air so the foil paper could pass through the printer smoothly.

Another problem was the color of gold as there was no gold ink. To achieve the gold color we used a light colored yellow/tan ink. As the paper came through the press with that fresh wet ink, there was an extension on the press that the paper passed through. That extension had a shaker attached above the paper and it shook a gold dust onto the wet ink. That is how gold color printing was done and that gold dust in the air caused another problem.

Anybody in the area was exposed to that gold dust flying in the air and we were breathing that bad air. The men I am working with are a bunch of older tough guys who wouldn't wear masks. Instead they chewed tobacco to combat the dust. How that would work, I'll never know. But being the new guy on the bloc, they expected me to do the same. They gave me a big slug of tobacco and I inserted it between my cheek and teeth like they did. I tried my best to be a man but I was a young kid who made the mistake of accidently swallowing some of that terrible tobacco juice. Sick? You bet I was. It was like that horse I fell off of when I was six; I never rode a horse again and I only tried chewing tobacco one time that was enough.

I finally talked my dad into letting me buy a car so I didn't have to keep making that long trip to work. I bought a 1937 Studebaker with the gear shift on the floor and I paid $90.00 for that thing. It ran pretty good but the car had a problem, it burned more oil than gas because the piston rings were bad. When I put the car in gear there was a trail of blue grey smoke trailing behind as we moved down the street. I carried extra cans of oil in the trunk and every time I got gas in the tank I had to add oil to the engine as well. At least the car got me to work and back to Andy's Loop Cafe, where the cold beer hung out. Next I will talk a little more about Andy's Loop Cafe plus the U. S. Coast Guard tomorrow.

ANDY'S LOOP CAFÉ #41

REMEMBER WHAT I WAS SAYING upon driving into Pittsburgh with my mother. I was starting a new life. It turns out that I spent seventeen wonderful years in Pittsburgh. I witnessed the City's transformation from a dirty smoky steel industrial area into one of the cleanest most beautiful cities anywhere in the world. During that same period of time I witnessed myself being transformed into adulthood and there was a whole new life ahead for me. I went from knowing no one to where I felt like I knew everyone. The different jobs I had and my activities were, I thought, very interesting.

Before I get into my Andy's Loop Cafe stories where I met many life long friends, the U. S. Coast Guard played a very important part in my life as well. I was a member of the U. S. Coast Guard Active Reserve for nine years beginning in 1950 and ending in 1960. When I became 18 I was eligible for the draft out of Canton, Ohio where I registered in 1949. In 1950 the trouble with North Korea was brewing. The government started to draft young men into the Army. In Pittsburgh they were drafting 19 and 20 year olds to start with, but in Canton the age was 18 and 19. Since I was registered in Ohio I figured my number was going to come up soon. I hurt my back working on a printing press and have two bad knees. I didn't want to go into the Army and have a 90 pound pack on my back while marching for miles. I went to the Navy recruiting office to join up but I failed their physical due to a curvature in my spine, so they told me. Great, there were no 90 pound backpacks in the Navy and I was sure the Army would take me; I didn't think the Army physicals were going to be a strict as the Navy.

As luck would have it, someone told me they heard the Coast Guard was just starting to form a reserve. In peace time the Coast Guard is not part of the Military Service. The Coast Guard is our country's first military unit and has always reported to the Treasury Department and up until now never had an organized reserve. In time of war the Coast Guard becomes an arm of the military. I went to see them and passed their physical and I became a member or the United States Coast Guard Active Reserve.

My enlistment was for three years and I had to attend a meeting once a week which was held on Thursday evenings, plus two weeks active duty every year was required. Now the Korean conflict was in progress but I would not be called to active duty unless a war was declared. That never happened because the Korean problem was called a conflict and war was never declared. I was required to attend 90% of the meetings and that means we could only miss five out of 52 meetings. Miss 6 meetings or more and I would be transferred to active duty for a period of two years automatically. To avoid active duty a strong commitment had to be made by making all those meetings. The reserve was not a casual deal; I trained hard and learned all the rules of being a part of a military service. I learned to march and how to take apart weapons like the M1 rifle and the 45 automatic revolvers, strip them down blindfolded and put them back together and how to use them at a nearby military firing range. During our two week active duty each year I learned how to handle small boats and became well trained in seamanship. If I was ever called to active duty I was ready.

I made quite a few lifelong friends in this unit, some of them from my own neighborhood. One was my very close friend of 64 years Don Haus, who passed away this past June. He was almost two years older than I. His family still lives in Daytona Beach, Florida. Another was Jim Drizos, a big gentle man of who is also deceased. There were six of us who lived in the same general area who became beer drinking buddies after the meetings. I have to set the stage for the next story about my buddies.

Pittsburgh was a blue collar town where there is not lot of guys wearing those cute navy uniforms because it is not a Navy town. We wore white uniform in the warmer months and dark blue in the winter.

The white uniforms had normal pants but the blues as that uniform was called had pants that had a flap in front and 13 buttons and those buttons represented the original 13 colonies. The white uniforms had the usual white cap, same as the navy but the blues had that cute little blue hat with the U.S. Coast Guard in gold letters across the front. We were a peaceful group and always avoided trouble. After meetings we has a couple of beers and never got tipsy. We went to local bars near the meeting place which was not in a very good neighborhood. A lot of rough looking guys frequented these bars.

Visualize this picture, six guys in these funny uniforms walking into bars like that. We never ever had a problem. As a matter of fact more times than not we drank for free. These tough looking men bought us our beer many times. The reason why we never had a problem was probably because the six of us were all 6'2" to 6'4" tall and looked pretty impressive with all six of us walking into a bar together.

There is an old saying about the Coast Guard. It was said to be in the Coast Guard you had to be over 6' tall just in case the boat sank you were able to walk to the shore!

After my first three years enlistment was up I could have dropped out and become an inactive reservist because the Korean conflict was over but I reenlisted for three more years, twice. Some of us who were in this unit together for a number of years became a very close group and most of our officers became close friends as well. Bert Flister was a Chief Warrant Officer in his early sixties and he owned and operated a watch repair shop. Our commanding officer was Dave Ellis who held the rank of Commander. Bert and Dave in our later years in the Reserve would join us for a couple of beers. We all knew our place and after the meetings we were off duty. We were just friends wearing uniforms at that point. I finally reached the rate of Second Class Petty Office and it took a long time as advancement in rank was very slow in the Reserve. Commander Dave Ellis wanted me to consider going to officer's school because he thought I would make an excellent officer. I was the senior enlisted man in our Reserve unit at the time. I asked him if I did that and became an officer, would I then be on recall for the rest of my life. He said, yes. I told Dave no thanks, nine years of active reserve was enough and I didn't want to be tied to the military for life because I had a wife and children.

I said I was going to talk about Andy's Loop Cafe but that will have to wait, more about the Coast Guard is on my mind.

United Sates Coast Guard #42

A FACT ABOUT THE COAST GUARD, a sad one, during World War II the Coast Guard suffered percentage wise the greatest number of casualties of any service. I believe that is a true fact, and it was due to its smaller size in the number of men and women. The Coast Guard did not just guard our coast's either, the Guard was everywhere our military was. Almost all the landing craft carrying our men and equipment to the shores during the invasions were manned by the Coast Guard as those sailors were experts at handling smaller vessels.

There is another saying that when ships come to port because the sea becomes to rough, that is when the Coast Guard goes out. Sea and Rescue, "when the going gets tough, the tough get going."

Where did I go for two weeks active duty all those years? The first year we were sent to Cape May located on the southern tip of New Jersey. That was the Coast Guards boot camp. Our group was put through the ropes and the two weeks spent there was really some rough training. The things I remember most that year were the mosquitoes as Cape May was located in a very swampy area. I never saw such big ones mosquitoes. I think I could have put a small saddle on them and rode them.

Some other two week active duty locations were Norfolk, Va. and twice in New Orleans. Once I served on the East River in New York. That's five. Three times in Pittsburgh, believe it or not. I seem to be missing one but that gives a pretty good idea and I would like to comment on a few of the above before we leave the Coast Guard stories.

First, another fact you may not be aware of The Coast Guard patrols all of America's coasts and our countries possessions, such as Porte Rico and the Virgin Islands. However that is just a little bit of their territory.

The Coast Guard is responsible for every body of water in the U.S. that can be navigated. The Guard is responsible for all channel markers, buoys, everything. One huge responsibilities and the Guard is also constantly on the lookout for smugglers, drugs and humans.

One of the things that stands out about my Norfolk duty was an assignment to cover a race regatta in the northern end of the Chesapeake Bay. We left Norfolk in a "forty footer" which is a dual engine 40 foot long patrol boat. The numeral markings on Coast Guard boats indicate the length of that particular boat. In other words, the first two numbers on that "forty footer" is 40! So if you spot a Coast Guard boat look at the numbers on the bow and they will tell you the length of that boat. Aren't you glad you know that? Now you can impress your friends with that kind of knowledge.

There is hardly any cover from bad weather on these small crafts and if the weather becomes rough things are going to get wet and all of a sudden a storm did came upon us when we were only half way to our destination. It was a very large thunder storm that lasted for quite some time; we could not see anything past the bow so we were using our compass to guide us. By the time we arrive at our destination we were completely soaked with no change of cloths. My belt buckle which was brass, turned green and a couple of the crew became sea sick. What a day that turned out to be but the race went on and we did our job and returned to our home port and dried off with a few beers.

The only time I became sea sick was on my two week duty on the East River in New York City, and we were docked! We were on a fairly large cutter and I was below deck scraping old paint and repainting in fairly close quarters. The veneration was not real good and our cutter was tied up sideways to the river. The boat traffic was pretty steady and the wake caused by these passing boats was rocking our cutter side to side. With that rocking motion and the smell of paint, all of a sudden a couple of us looked at each other and all I saw were green faces. We all bolted topside at the same time. The water level of the East River became a little higher that day. One night we also had the job of pulling a body out of that river. Felt sick again, but not sea sick. Let's move on.

New Orleans was my best and worse tour of duties. The first tour of duty was 1952 and the Commander of the base was one tough guy who ran the place like a boot camp. He wasn't real friendly towards Reservists and showed it. The Coast Guard Station was located on Lake Poncatrain, a very large salt water lake connected to the Gulf of Mexico. There was no air-conditioning in those years, except in the best hotels. It was also in July in one of the hottest summers in New Orleans history. During the two weeks we were there it was reported in the news papers that 123 people had died from the heat! Most were in the real poor sections where conditions were very poor and most of these unfortunate people were elderly.

Our daily work uniform was the usual white hat, a white undershirt and a chambray long sleeve work shirt and blue jeans. We wore white socks and black shoes and over those shoes we had to wear a pair of buttoned up canvas leggings. During Reveille in the morning, we stood at attention facing the sun while our United States Flag was raised. Then we had breakfast before our work day started. Dressed like that we were soaking wet all day long. At night we lay on the top of our mattress and mine became soaked with sweat. I would be lying on my side and my ear would fill up with sweat. I turned over to let the sweat run out of one ear then the other ear would fill up. Darn little sleep with that oven like condition and the exhaust fan at the end of the barracks did little good. It was tough and darn uncomfortable and it felt like I was wet the entire fourteen days.

During breakfast one morning I had a little problem. There was a big sign on the wall which read, "Take What You Want, But Eat What You Take". I preach that saying to my kids and grandkids to this day, I hate to see food uneaten and thrown away. As I was going through the chow line that morning I spotted what I thought was hot cream of wheat cereal and I filled up a bowl of it and added milk and sugar and sat down to eat. I took one spoon full and almost threw up. It wasn't cream of wheat at all, it was grits which is a very popular southern dish and salt is added, not sugar and milk. It tasted awful and then my eyes drifted toward that darn sign. There was no way I could eat those grits and I could not go through the line to rinse off our plates and hide that bowl, or dump it without being seen doing so. What in the heck was I going to do? No one around me was willing to help me by eating my bowl of grits. Hard to believe what I did with it but since I was already soaking wet with sweat and my socks were beginning to get soaked with sweat, what the heck I'm going to be soaked all day anyway so I poured that bowl of grits down inside my leggings! I made funny squishing sounds walking around all day long and that's how I got rid of those dreaded grits. That's my story and my socks and I are slipping to it. My United State Coast Guard story conclusions are next.

Coast Guard Conclusion #43

At the end of our first grueling week at the base in New Orleans we received weekend liberty. Our liberty started Saturday morning and we did not have to report back to the base until 6 PM on Sunday. We had to wear our white uniforms, no civilian clothes allowed. If we wanted, we could have gone back to the base Saturday night to sleep but I wanted to let that wet mattress dry out. My buddies and I never went to bed Saturday night at all and Bourbon Street was open 24 hours a day so we never stopped partying. In the 50's New Orleans and Bourbon Street and the French Quarters were just absolutely great. Everywhere you went there were great restaurants and all the bars had live Dixie land music. There were no strip joints and the crap they have in the French Quarters now. New Orleans is nothing like it was then. I have been to New Orleans a total of five times and unfortunately I have no desire to go back the way it is now.

Anyway, that weekend we drank one heck of a lot of beer and ate a lot of really great food and the big plus was listening to all that wonderful jazz and Dixieland music. Sunday morning we stopped bar hopping long enough to have breakfast. We found this small quiet restaurant and I ordered bacon and eggs and what I thought was coffee. I drank my coffee with cream and sugar back then and as I added cream to it the color didn't change, it was still black. I added some more, it was still black and then poured a little coffee out to make room for more cream and the color changed slightly to tan. I took one sip of that coffee and not only was it strong enough to stand up on its own this so called coffee tasted like there was sand in it. It turns out it was chicory coffee which I never had before, and never again. I just pushed it away and ordered another beer, goes good with breakfast don't you know?

When we reported back to the base, we sure were a sorry looking bunch. Unshaven, same clothes except they were not exactly white anymore. We all agreed if we had the opportunity to repeat a weekend leave like that we would do it again. I finished my two weeks and home never looked better. My next two week tour of duty in New Orleans was about two years later with different commander and an entirely different enjoyable two weeks, not near as hot and no cream of wheat.

My nine years in the reserve covered a period of about five or six different jobs, a marriage and two of our four children. The last three years I was now working for Spalding as a Golf Professional Salesman. I had a problem with two weeks active duty now because they were always in the summer and I actually had about five months off during the winter time as all my golf course accounts were closed for the winter. Because of that I could not take two more weeks off in the summer. Being the senior enlisted petty officer in the unit and the friendship I had with my officers we were able to work a deal where I did not have to go with our unit for two weeks. The Coast Guard had a station on the Ohio River in Sewickley, Pa., a suburb of Pittsburgh because there are three rivers running through Pittsburgh, actually two rivers, the Allegheny and the Monongahela Rivers meet at the "point" in Pittsburgh and form the beginning of the Ohio River. There is heavy traffic on those three rivers which the Coast Guard is responsible for. We worked it out that I could put my two weeks in for the next couple of years, in January so I would not loose any time during my busy golf season.

Unfortunately I did have a serious problem in 1958. I was sleeping on a not so clean mattress at this station and I had a scratch on my left wrist that became infected, and a small boil was starting to form. The Coast Guard does not have a medical unit so they use the Public Health Service. The infection was like a hard little ball where a head was just starting to appear. The doctor at this facility looked at it and decided to lance it before it was really ready to drain. He gave me a shot of penicillin and sent me on my way. My infection went from bad to worse and it turned into a "Staff" infection, a super germ that loves penicillin. I got another boil under my left upper elbow, and then a third under my lower left elbow, three places now and my arm swelled up like a balloon. They sent me to a larger Public Health Service hospital, get this, located in Baltimore, Md. I flew to Baltimore on a Connie, the Constellation aircraft with the three fins on the tail, a popular four engine plane in the fifties.

I was assigned a bed in a ward that had 8 beds! Baltimore has a port with access to the Atlantic Ocean so my 7 bedmates were all young men who were sailors on cargo ships from all over the world and none of them spoke English, Each one had some sort of skin disorder, including gonorrhea and more. I watched a lot of TV while I was given about 20 to 25 pills each day as they were trying to find some kind of combination to knock out the staff infection and I was there two weeks.

It was there that I first saw Candle Stick bowling on TV. More on bowling later, but I will explain this game if you are not familiar with it. The bowling alley is the same as used in Ten Pin bowling. These Candle Stick pins are set up in the same configuration as the Ten Pins. Candle Stick pins are round thin and tall and the ball used is much smaller with no finger holes, about the size of a good size cantaloupe melon. Keeping score is a little different because three balls a frame are allowed if needed, not the usual two balls per frame. If all ten pins go down with the first ball, it is a strike. When there are pins still standing there remains two chances to knock over the remaining pins. A spare is scored with the second or third ball, either one. Its very hard to score over 100 out of a possible perfect score of 300. There are two more bowling games I will touch on later as well, Duck Pins and Rubber Band Duck Pins. In Pittsburgh the Rubber Band Duck Pins were very popular.

I was sent home with some pretty strict instructions. I am going home to my wife Dee, and two very small children and I am not to have any body contact with anyone, plus all my clothes, bedding, towels, everything must be boiled to kill germs. This went on for two weeks and poor Dee was really busy with all that. I finally get over the infection but I was not very happy about the health care provided by the Coast Guard and decided that I would not re enlist at the end of my current three year term ending nine years of service.

Back to Andy's Loop Café where the beer is cold and the friendship is warm.

BACK TO ANDY'S LOOP CAFE #44

REMEMBER I AM ONLY 18 years old when we moved to Pittsburgh and when I got off the streetcar after a shift at the Fuller Label and Box Co., I still had work clothes on and went into Andy's for the first time. I was asked my age by the bartender, who turned out to be Andy. I stood up to the bar, all 6' 2" with my deep baritone voice and said, "Sir, I am 22!" I got my draft beer, drank it then had a second one and left. I assumed he thought I was a young working man and he believed that I was 22 years old. Noticed I did not say 21 as most everyone under age would say. That is too automatic for someone underage and stating I was 22 years old I thought was more convincing and that seemed to work for me.

I started to drop in to have a beer on a regular basis. I started to recognize the regulars and they turned out to be quite a group who knew each other and appeared to be pretty close friends. The range in age was from the late 20's into the 60's, married men, single, divorced and widowed, the whole nine yards. If there was ever an original Cheers it was Andy's Loop Cafe. Andy's did lack one thing, ladies. Very seldom were there any female customers.

Most of these guys could be found at Andy's after work. Some had a couple of beers and went home and some stayed for hours. Watching sports was a big thing on Saturdays and I found out that almost any time in the afternoon and evening there would always be a few regulars there to socialize with. I was being accepted and they really knew darn well I was not 21. I never got drunk, maybe a little tipsy at times but was always in control. They were one bunch of nice guys whom I learned a lot from. The price of a draft beer was, hold on to your hat, 10 cents for an eight ounce glass. Not hard to figure what a dollar would buy.

We played a lot of different games with the loser buying a round of beer. Sometimes it would cost next to nothing if you're winning, but sometimes it was the other way around. Some times you're the pigeon and some times you're the statue. There were about four different games we played; some are a little difficult to explain, so I won't try. Well, one is pretty easy to explain. The cooler behind the bar against the wall under the mirror had a bottle cap remover. The loose caps would fall into a container attached to the cooler. We would take turns pitching peanuts into the container. These guys were really good at this and the first guy who missed had to buy a round of beer for everyone. They were very active guys with something always going on like that, a lot of fun to be with and they were my very first group of new friends.

A couple of the younger guys in there thirties played fast pitch softball and wanted to start a team of their own. One was a pretty darn good pitcher, just what you have to have to be able to compete as scores are usually low in fast pitch softball games because the pitchers dominated the game with the speed they generate pitching that ball with a very big underhand motion. They really whip that ball and curve it as well.

I played a lot of baseball when I was a kid and during my high school years. I didn't go out for the high school team because it was a spring sport as was golf and I could only play one spring sport so I choose golf. I played a lot of sandlot ball in the summer. My main position was a pitcher and when not pitching I played first base and sometimes filled in as a catcher. Was I any good? Not bad, maybe better than average. When we were in grade school in the summer we played everyday all day.

This was way before Little League started. Thank goodness we didn't have to worry about all those frustrated fathers pushing their kids to play ball and relive what they could or couldn't do as kids themselves. We just had fun and we were our own umpires calling our own strikes and balls.

I damaged my elbow a bit because I pitched all day, every day. I only had a couple of pitches, a pretty good fast ball, a slider and a curve that didn't curve much. I messed around with a knuckle ball a little as well. I was a fair pull hitter, everything to the left side of the field and a below average fielder of ground balls. We played on rough fields which produced many strange bounces. I didn't like getting hit in the face as. it was too pretty to mess up. Ha!

My baseball cap was navy blue with a red bill, the same as the Cleveland Indians, the team we rooted for. Except my mom, she was a Cincinnati Reds fan having grown up in the south western part of Ohio. My whole life as an athlete was easy to explain. In all the sports that I played, baseball, basketball, bowling, ping pong, golf. I was better than average, a jack of all trades and master of none. Golf was my best, tennis, which I didn't play until I was in my thirties, was my worst sport.

I must explain myself a little about my athletic abilities. Why not, this is my story. I was not a natural and I was not strong as a kid, I was thin and on the tall side. I could not run fast, which I blame on my very short toes. But I was, and am a competitor. If it was a team sport, I wanted to beat your team. In individual sports I wanted to beat the other guy. I liked individual sports best. Why? Because if I lost I only had myself to blame and there was no finger pointing, except at myself.

To give you an idea of how slow I was we had no fences on those baseball fields. If I hit a long ball past the outfielder, I just ran as hard and as fast as I could. It's a home run if I beat the ball thrown back by the outfielder. I remember one day I hit a very long ball way over the outfielders head. Any one else would have trotted around the bases for a home run. I got thrown out at third base and that is how I originally hurt my right knee too.

Back to fast pitch softball, we put a team together and our sponsor was none other than Andy's Loop Cafe. I was the first baseman and we played in an independent league. We were pretty good too. Our highlight or at least it was mine is when we went to prison! We got there because one of our beer buddies, Vince Johnson, was a reporter for the Pittsburgh Press newspaper. Vince had connections with the Western Pennsylvania State Federal Prison. He told us our softball team should consider playing inside the Prison against their all star team for moral purposes. We agreed. The prison had six teams and they used their best players from all teams to make one all star team to play us, the outsiders, the enemy. We played in prison a total of three different times. I will let you know who won, tomorrow.

Fast Pitch Softball and More #45

*F*AST PITCH SOFTBALL IS A pitcher and catcher's game. To explain that statement, scores for a seven inning game were usually 1 to 0, 2 to 1. The pitcher is very close to the batter with the distance much closer than baseball. Some of these pitchers have a ball speed of around 80 miles and hour, some faster. As a batter it seems like I started my swing at the ball before the pitcher releases it and hope my bat is somewhere near the ball. If I didn't the ball is in the catcher's mitt before I finished my swing. Most balls that are hit are grounders, very few leave the infield. Because of this the most active of the players is the pitcher, catcher, and first baseman. Being a first baseman I saw a fair amount of action. I don't know how the outfielders kept from falling asleep!

Not only were those pitchers throwing very fast pitches, most of those fast balls would have a drop or a curve and sliders as well, and the ball didn't just come in on a straight line. Our pitcher did not process a really good fast ball but he did have very good control with a lot of stuff on the ball that did not create a lot of strikeouts like most pitchers, but a lot of ground balls to the infielders, and he rarely walked anyone one.

We had a pretty good team and were we ready to play in prison? How would we react to being inside a Federal Prison housing the hardest of criminals? What do you say to them? How do they feel about outsiders coming into their domain? We talked about that before going there and decided the best thing we could do was be ourselves. Be friendly, say hello and go about our business of playing ball and treat this as just another ball game. However we really felt it best if we didn't win. We were sure they would not like to be beaten, especially since we were playing their best players picked from six teams.

Turns out we didn't have to worry about that, they beat us pretty good. One of the reasons was a very short right field. Prison is a little short of space for a ball field. In right field there was a very high security wall, there was not much room between the infield and that wall. The right fielder looked like he was a backup infielder. They had a local rule due to the wall being in play. Any ball hit off that wall was played as it would be in any large ball park; get as many bases as you can. Most were held to just a single because it was so close to the infield. Any ball hit over that wall was ruled a ground rule double, the batter advances to second base with all runners already on base moving ahead two bases.

Those guys had it down to a science of how to use a very short swing making contact with the ball and getting it in the air like a pop up to right, but it was enough to carry over that darn wall. They doubled us to death and they laughed, and laughed to the point it wasn't funny. We had to make the best of it. We laughed with them. Hey, the plate umpire was a prisoner doing life for murder. All the umpires were prisoners, do you think they were bias? We didn't have a chance to win, which was exactly what we really wanted anyway. After the game we all had lunch together under very heavy guard. We did this three times and the prisoners seemed glad to see us the second and third time around. We had a reasonably good time together playing ball and having lunch with them. That was quite an experience.

Changing Jobs #46

*I*T HAS BEEN 65 YEARS ago that I left my job as a Union card holding pressman. I got tired of driving to the other side of Pittsburgh and working some crazy nighttime shifts. That cut into my budding night life and I wanted something closer to home. At this point in my life I had no idea what I wanted to do for my future; I was just living it up day by day, or was that night by night.

I was meeting and making more friends and playing basketball at the local high school gym in a local league. I was playing softball and I had my new Coast Guard buddies, and of course there was always Andy's Loop Cafe. I was flipping through the want ads one day and spotted something close to home. The Massey Buick auto dealership on Liberty Ave in Dormont, Pa., another suburb next door to where I lived in Mt. Lebanon was looking for a young man to work as grease monkey, no experience required. I applied for the job and I was hired.

In the 50's the automobile's moving joints had to be greased and the oil and oil filter had to be changed every 3,000 miles. On most Buicks there were about a dozen joints that had little nipples where I applied a grease gun replenishing the area with new lubricant. The car was put on a lift and hoisted into the air about 6 feet. Then the areas to lubricate were easy to get at and the oil pan plug could be removed to drain the old oil into a container. This was a very busy garage so I was working two lifts at the same time. I would go out to the parking lot and find a car with the work order on it and drive it into the garage, put it on the lift and press the button to activate the lift. While that car was going up I retrieve the next car putting it on the other lift. While it was going up I was working on the other car. When I was done with that car as it was coming down I was working on the other car. When I was done with the second car as the lift was descending I would drive the other car out to the lot and get another car placing that car on the lift and then drive the other car to the lot, and kept repeating this all day long. I was doing all this on a couple hours sleep and half a beer hangover. How good was I at this job? As usual better than the average as in sports and I knew how to work.

Laying down a grey smoke screen with my 1937 Studebaker was not seen as something that an employee of a Buick Garage I should be driving. Joe Evanko, our master body shop foreman had a car he bought that had a little body damage which he was repairing for resell. I He offered to sell it to me for $275.00. This was in 1951 and the car was a 1941 Buick Super two door club coop, a sleek looking design. It had a long hood with a straight eight cylinder engine and a small back and a sloping roof towards the back with a long trunk lid. It was painted black with white side wall tires, a really good looking automobile. Goodbye grey smoke screen, you served me well for a $90.00 investment. I was moving up in the world.

Within a year another car became available that I couldn't resist. Remember the movie The Rain Man staring Tom Hanks and Dustan Hoffman who played the part of a young man with Autism and he had a mathematical genius mind? In the movie the car they were seen driving was a light yellow 1948 Buick Road Master Convertible. This car was a very large long automobile with a back seat that actually had a lot of leg room. When I saw that movie and that car I could not believe it, it was exactly like the convertible I had many years ago, I thought my old car resurfaced!

When I bought that 1948 convertible it was actually a very light blue which was fading. I am not particular fond of light blue for a car and the interior leather upholstery was all black and the convertible top was also black and other interior appointments were black and silver. I decided to paint it a very pretty pale yellow, a perfect fit with the other colors. That was a beautiful car for such a good looking single guy! Ha! Ha!

The car was a heavy load and built like a tank. It was with the brand new automatic Fluid drive transmission. That new transmission was very sluggish and It took forever to get up any speed. When it got going it was ok, but oh boy what a gas burner. The gas mileage around town was only eight miles per gallon and on the open road I only got twelve or thirteen miles per gallon. That car was a very expensive car to drive and maintain but I had a lot of fun driving it around and the girls liked it. There's more about Massey Buick coming up.

Massey Buick #47

I was enjoying working for Massey Buick and besides the people working in the garage I was getting to know all the other employees, the salesmen and office personnel. Massey Buick had a company bowling team which I have been invited to join. There are several teams that bowl against each other one night a week and then have a banquet at the end of the bowling season. I bowled a little back in Canton, Ten Pin bowling. This bowling game is different and new to me. It is called Rubber Band Duck Pins and was very popular in Pittsburgh and in the east. Not everyone reading this will be familiar with the game, there are several different bowling games and I will try and explain the difference.

All these games have one thing in common, the bowling alley is standard but the pins and the balls are different. Ten Pin bowling is known everywhere, with the large pins and large ball with two or three finger holes for controlling the ball. The perfect score for all games is the same as well, 300.

I have already touched on the game called Candle Pins using three balls per frame as it is very difficult to get these pins to fall and very hard to score above 100. Duck pins are short and squat and there are two different games; the regular Duck Pin game is played mostly in the east and is also is played with three balls like Candle Pins. Rubber Band Duck Pins is the game played in Pittsburgh. The belly of these pins have a rubber strip wrapped around it which softens the action of how the pins react after being struck by the ball. The Candle Pins and Duck Pins have nothing around the pins and are just solid wood and they fly all over the place. While the rubber band pins tend to bump into each other more softly they do not fly over the other pins. Two balls are used in this game just like the Ten Pin game. I don't know how to explain it any better than that.

Bowling is not an easy game, there are many factors involved when it comes to serious, or good bowlers. The highest average scores are achieved with Ten Pin's because of the large ball and pins. I will eliminate the Candle Pin and Duck Pin games using three balls for the rest of my talk about bowling.

When I was bowling in Pittsburgh it was prior to the time of the bowling craze period when all those new big glitzy bowling lane establishments were being built. When I bowled Duck Pins it was on old alleys, nothing elaborate. While Ten Pin bowling alleys had automatic pin setters Duck Pin bowling alleys did not have automatic pin setting devices. Young boys hired to reset the pins and they were located in the pit area at the end of the alley where the pins ended up after being struck by the ball. The pin setters had to avoid being hit by the flying pins and the ball. They did this by sitting on a shelf against the back wall and raising their legs each time the ball and pins care flying into the pit.

Many Ten Pin bowlers have their own personal ball. Only one ball is used by a Ten Pin bowler and after the first ball is used the bowler then waits until that ball is returned. Then they use that same ball for their second roll if they did not get a strike on their first attempt. All this results in a much slower game than Duck Pin bowling because balls used for Duck pins come in matching pairs. There is no waiting for the first ball to come back, the second ball is used so there is no waiting time in-between. After the frame is over both balls are returned at the same time resulting in a much faster game.

Resetting the pins by the pin boy was a real art. There are 10 metal pins set under the floor forming the triangle that the pins are set. At the end of the alley in the pit, there is a metal bar the pinsetter puts his foot on which raises these imbedded pins so the pinsetter can then reset the pins on top of these metal pins. He then takes his foot off the metal bar which retracts those devices and away we go! Not an easy job, those kids work their tails off.

The Duck Pin balls are about the size of a large cantaloupe melon with no finger holes. There is three ways to roll these balls down the alley. For most beginners the ball is placed with the hand under the ball like pitching a softball. Taking three or four steps towards the foul line, the ball is delivered under hand, usually with a fair amount of speed. With this type of delivery there isn't much spin or action on the ball. By that I mean it just has an over spin and does not curve or spin from one side to the other. This type of delivery gets the poorest results as the ball has little action when contacting the pins. The pins just fly over each other rather than spin into each other causing others to fall.

The next type of grip is holding the ball in your hand while your hand is in a natural hanging position to your side. The thumb is on the left side of the ball while the other four fingers are on the right side of the ball. Again approaching the foul line the ball is released with a more twisting motion, the hand rotating from right to left. This creates a side spin and gives the ball a slight curve from the right side of the alley towards the left side contacting the head pin on the right side between the head pin and the number 3 pin. This ball action has a good amount of action and pushes the pins back into each other. Too much speed is not good as it causes pins to jump over each other. You don't want that, you want to get those pins staying close to the floor spinning and pushing each other into the rest of the pins. Have I completely confused you by now?

By the way I touched on speed. A very slow ball will not get the job done nor will a ball going to fast. Novice bowlers think they have to hit the pins fast and hard to knock them over. That is wrong as it creates little action between the pins and causes the pins to jump over one another as well. The speed has to be moderate so the ball can be controlled with the proper amount of spin on it to create the action desired for the pins to contact each other, hence, knocking each other down. The ultimate delivery of the ball is the back hand method, I'll explain that, tomorrow.

Duck Pin Bowling #48

*F*IRST LET ME TRY AND explain the difference in difficulty between Ten Pin and Duck Pin bowling. If a person averages around 150 in Duck Pins, it would compare to about 180 averages in Ten Pins. 30 pins per game is quite a difference but both of those averages indicate very good bowlers. My averages in Duck Pins were in the range of 165 on home alleys. In the traveling league on strange alleys it was around 160.

When I bowled Ten Pins, which I did very little, I would bet anyone that I would score better than 170 anytime and almost always won that bet. Ten Pin bowling is so much easier because most of the time just being off a little bit of the head pin would produce a nine pin hit leaving only one pin left standing. To make that spare in Ten Pins with the size of the ball and the lone pin I have half the size of the alley to make it. Visualize one big pin in the middle of the alley, then visualize the size of the ball on either side of the pin I have half the size of the alley to make that one pin. Not so in Duck pins with much smaller pins and smaller ball. Get the picture, on the first ball in Ten pins if I don't strike, more pins go down on an average than I would get down in Duck's. Duck pins produced a lot of funny hits. A side duce hit if I miss the head pin slightly then the small ball can and does quite often, go right through on the left side taking out the #2 and the #8 pins, or on the right side, the #3 and the #9, leaving a very tough spare shot to take down the reaming eight pins. There is also the un makeable center split. The ball hits the head pin straight on and takes out the head pin then the #5 pin behind it, goes on through leaving 8 pins standing. This is an un makeable spare. Below is how the 10 pins are set up. This should help you understand what I am attempting to explain.

7 8 9 10

4 5 6

2 3

1

Back to the back hand delivery that I learned how to use because this method produces the best action when striking the pins. Facing the target the back of the right hand is facing the pins. All five fingers are placed holding the ball in that position, but the palm of my hand should touch the ball ever so slightly. Taking a three or four step delivery approach, I used the 3 step delivery due to my height, my arm swings back at the start and half way through the approach my arm is swinging towards my target with the back of the hand facing the target as well. Upon delivery I lift the hand up slightly for the start of the release, my wrist cocks upward as the ball is released giving the ball backspin. Using moderate speed, the ball travels towards the intended target. About 3 to 4 feet from the pins the ball stops its backspin rotation and slides into the pocket between the 1 and 3 pins, this pushes the front pins against each other moving all the pins against each other. The action of the rubber band around the pins is soft and the pins don't jump up and over each other, and they also have a tendency to spin. The pins push against each other and there you have it, another strike.

I never looked at the pins when approaching the foul line while releasing the ball! Most good bowlers spot bowl. Once familiar with how the alley is rolling spot bowlers pick a spot in the alley which they want the ball to roll over. When the ball reaches that spot that is when i raise my eyes towards the pins to see the final results, and not until then. Looking at the pins only while making my approach tends to create negative thoughts and this can create small adjustments in my delivery, which is never the way to bowl. When approaching the foul line I should be committed to the intended thought process about what I intended to do. Attempting a last second adjustment hardly ever works out well. I have to believe in my swing, so to speak. The same thing applies in golf.

I have mentioned how the alley was rolling, meaning how the ball is rolling. There are many variables involved in this game people may not realize. These differences are recognized by good serious bowlers. Most bowling alleys in those days were old and they became worn and all alleys roll a little differently. After a couple of practice balls I would get the feel of how the ball is reacting to that alley. Another factor besides wear is the top dressing of the alley. Alleys need to be cleaned at least once a day. In those years a large wide push mop was used with a cloth wrapped around it that had an oil substance applied to it. This not only cleaned up any dirt it also put a light coat of oil on the alley and that not only made it shine it also aided the ball to roll with less resistance, or less friction. The real problem with this is the amount of oil left on the surface of the alley affects how the ball is going to roll as it can cause the ball to spin more or spin less, or will the ball curve more or curve less. All that has to be taken into consideration and again a few practice balls will tell you what to expect. It is up to me then, to adjust to the conditions. Good bowlers are able to adapt to these conditions rather quickly. When an alley has too much oil applied to the surface scores are generally not as high. The action of the ball may not be exactly as I want it; some of my corrections just will not overcome some conditions. The ball also may be picking up oil from the alley. Checking for that is important too, I have to wipe that excess oil off the ball or it will become slippery.

Easy game, right? It is more complicated then most people realize. When bowling on strange alleys all these factors come into play. When I was involved in a traveling league I would have maybe six different alleys to bowl that I was not used to and my average score will be lower than my home alley average. Mine was about five pins lower as my averages on our home alley were about 165 and on strange alleys my average was around158 to 160.

According to what records that were kept in those days, there had never been anyone who averaged over 200 in a traveling league in Duck Pins. Until Norm Henning did it one year, in the league that I was a member as a matter of fact. His average was, I believe 203. I had the pleasure of bowling against him several times, he was something special. Norm was a nice guy as well. What a smooth backhand delivery he had and I never saw him come close to missing the head pin. I have more bowling stories to tell, flip over to the next chapter.

TEN PIN VS. DUCK PIN BOWLING #49

*T*HERE WAS ONE BOWLING ALLEY were I bowled in the traveling league that had 20 alleys. It had 10 alleys on each side, with the snack bar in the middle separating them. The unique thing was that one side the 10 alleys were for Ten Pin the other side 10 alleys were for Duck Pins. The night we bowled there, there was always the same guys bowling Ten's. We got to know each other pretty well and they started to kid us about bowling with those small balls and pins indicating we weren't bowling a man's game.

Remember I said I would bet anyone that I could bowl a Ten Pin game and score no lower than 170? I was not a Ten Pin bowler and here is the catch. Usually a Ten Pin bowler did not bowl Duck's, so they don't know how difficult the game is. But most Duck Pin bowlers have bowled Ten's before they took up the Duck pin game. We were getting a little tired of their remarks about our sissy game compared to their man's game so we decided to offer a challenge which we knew we would win.

A Duck Pin bowler can bowl a decent game of Ten's but a Ten pin bowler could not bowl a decent game of Duck's and we knew that. We wanted to prove that to these guys and beat them at their own game. We challenged them to bowl two games of Ten's and two games of Duck's and the total scores of all four games would determine the winner. The losers had to buy cocktails and dinner for the winners. We offered to bowl Ten's first, knowing they would have a better score than us but not as bad as they might think. We also knew we would blow them away in Duck's, which is exactly what happened. We beat them badly winning the bet going away. They accepted their defeat in style and we all had a good time together over cocktails and dinner. We never heard another peep out of them after that about our sissy game and we made our point about who was bowling a man's game.

When I was still single I bowled in the Massey Buick group and joined another local bowling league where I met a lot of new friends and that led to the traveling league as well. I also bowled pot games on Sunday afternoons, for money of course. Everybody threw a dollar in the pot. There were 10 lanes where we were bowling and we used five of them for the pot games. The number of guys bowling pot games was usually 12 to 16. We used the alleys 6 through 10 all at the same time. In other words the first frame would start on 5 then each bowler would continue on 6 and finish his 5th frame on 10, five straight frames. By the time the first 5 frames were finished it was time to start the last five frames using the same rotation. It was quite a fete to keep the score for all those guys bowling at the same time. When not bowling all helped each other keep score; one guy would keep score and we would help by keeping him up on who was doing what.

Everything was very fast and there were always two matching balls on each rack that each of us used, no waiting for balls to be returned. It was very competitive to say the least. We would bowl all afternoon, maybe 12 games and that's a lot of bowling. The cold beer sure tasted good when we were done at our local hang out bar in Dormont.

I'm getting ahead of myself a little with this next story but it has to do with bowling. When this happened I was married and we had two small kids and we had just purchased our first house. I was kind of in between jobs also and I took a job selling vacuum cleaners door to door hoping for a better job to come along. I did not like selling vacuums and will expound on that later. Things were very tough financially.

One evening I was a sales meeting to teach us how to sell vacuums and to pump up a couple of the new salesman and I was one of them. After the meeting our sales manager, Milan Trittica, suggested we all go Duck Pin bowling and he was suggested if there was enough interest why not bowl a pot game or two as there were eight of us. My ears perked up, sounded good to me. As I found out to my surprise a lot of these guys were fairly good bowlers. Even so I found very quickly I had a bunch of pigeons on the hook. They all were pretty good, but I was having a good night.

We were bowling for a dollar a man and I was winning most of the games, but that did not discourage them as they just kept on saying one more game. I was going to stay there as long as they wanted to bowl and It was in the wee hours of the morning when I finally got home. Dee was pretty darn mad and who could blame her. She was in the process of chewing me out and I just started to pull one dollar bills out of each pocket dropping them on the bed. She calmed down when they started to pile up to winnings of about $100.00. That was like a thousand to us at that time and it took almost the whole night to win that much money. How many games would that be to win $100.00 from seven other guys. It would take about 15 games if I won every one of them, which I didn't. We must have bowled 20 or more games. I was shot, but thankfully not by Dee.

My old buddy from Spalding days Frank Karr recently told me, "Never let the truth stand in the way of a good story Bill." All these stories are true, folks, I don't know how to write fiction. Every time I try and tell a little white lie my nose gets bigger. It's big enough now so I don't dare tell anything but the truth and I promise to conclude my bowling stories soon and that's the truth.

Bowling Conclusion #50

*I*NDIRECTLY, DUCK PIN BOWLING IS what led to my interview with Spalding for the position of sales for their Golf Professional sales division, more about that later. There is so much more that happened between this story and when that occurred.

I never bowled a perfect game of 300, which are 12 strikes in a row. For those that do not know how anybody could have 12 strikes as there are only 10 frames. a strike in the 10th frame and that person will receive two bonus balls to accomplish that total amount of strikes.

I once had 15 consecutive strikes. Unfortunately this was done in two separate games as I finished one game with seven in a row and the very next game I started with eight. Once I held the high score for the whole year in two different bowling alleys! One score was 263, and the other was 279. The latter was 11 strikes, a nine pin hit, and I made the spare. One pin standing cost 21 points because that spare was in the middle of the game.

One of those two high scores I rolled that year was at an alley that was owned and operated by Howard Grubbs, who also was in the trucking business. Howard only had one truck and it was a short double. Picture the truck this way, first the engine in front with a rather long hood, then the cabin and then an open flat bed behind the cabin. Attached to this rig was another flat bed unit which was attached to the main truck like two railroad cars are attached, the locking device plus all kinds of hose's that housed the tail lights, turn signal lights and the braking system for the wheels on this second unit. The truck had a separate breaking system, it was not connected to the main trucks breaking system. The truck had a break peddle, of course, however the brakes on the second unit operated by a separate leaver which had to be operated manually by hand.

This rig can not be stopped by just using the brakes on the main flat bed truck only, the trailing flat bed would jackknife, or may just jump up and into the flat bed in front of it because of it's momentum. Both had to be braked at the same time and that takes a lot of coordination. We aren't talking about an automatic transmission back then in the 50's. I believe this truck had five or six forward gears which were manual. There was a lot to do to get the truck in motion. Turning corners was tricky, but slowing down and stopping was both gearing down the transmission and braking two independent units at the same time.

Howard hauled all kinds of freight, anything that the elements would not damage since there was no cover over the flat beds. One day Howard approached me and asked it I would like to accompany him on a weekend run to Cincinnati and back. I thought why not, it would be an interesting experience. It was indeed, and I almost got us and a car full of people with kids injured, or even worse.

Dangerous Truck Experience #51

We DELIVERED OUR LOAD AND started our return trip back to Pittsburgh from Cincinnati without a return load, the flat beds were empty. This was a roundtrip without staying overnight and Howard did all the driving up to this point, I was observing how he handled all the complexities. The braking system was the hardest part as the rear flat bed had its own separate braking system. Coordinating the slowing down and stopping was indeed a difficult task.

When we cleared city traffic Howard asked me if I would like to drive. While in the Coast Guard I had acquired a special driver's license to drive heavy duty trucks, which was required in the service as a normal driver's license was not good enough to handle heavy equipment. I had some prior experience so I said I'd give it a try, but the dual braking system bothered me. Howard said he would take over the braking system for the second flat bed when slowing down and stopping and that made me feel more confident.

We are going along nicely for an hour on open country highway and I am becoming more comfortable with how the controls reacted. We were on a four lane road, not to many of those around in the 50's, and there was a car in the right lane going along at a fair speed, but under the speed limit. Howard said we should take the left lane and pass. As I started the slow process of easing into the left lane that car started to do the same and cut in front of me with the intent of making a left hand turn at a small turn around.

I was gaining speed at the same time for us to be able to pass as he cut in front of me, I started to apply the brake to slow down and head for the right lane but I was still gaining on that vehicle. I had to turn rather sharply to the right to avoid contact, a reaction I had to make. I actually clipped that cars bumper on the right rear with the left front bumper of our truck. My reaction was to turn more sharply towards the right lane hoping to avoid any further contact, which I accomplished. However that move was almost enough to tip the truck over. Rather than react and start a turn back towards the left, I spotted a very narrow dirt road coming up on my right. I wanted to avoid another sharp turn which could have flipped the rig so I made a decision to continue straight on to that small road going completely off the main highway. We are both working the brakes to bring the truck to a stop. About a half mile later, there we were standing still on this little dirt road leading to a farm house with no turn around room available to accommodate this big, long truck.

We looked at each other and let out a big sigh of relief. Howard congratulated me on how I handled the whole situation and stated that turning into that road was the right thing to do. Howard had to back that rig all the way out to the highway. A short double was not made for going backwards and backing up about one half mile was quite a job. But Howard did it and then we wanted to know if that car I clipped was OK. As far as we could tell there were two adults and three or four kids in that car and It was gone, no where in sight. Thank God I only slightly clipped its bumper and they were able continued on their journey not knowing how close we all came to a possible disaster. Unlike my horse incident where I never got back on one after falling off, Howard left the drivers seat and walked around to the passengers side and told me take over. I got back behind the wheel and we completed our round trip without further incident.

Back home again safe and sound. My poor mom was really having a hard time dealing with my late hours. A sound sleeper, dad never heard me come home late, or I should say, early. Early was towards morning, as in the middle of the night. Well, maybe 1 to 2 AM. Mom was a light sleeper and she always knew when I came home, but never told dad because he would have blown his top which mom wanted to avoid. However, mom was becoming very upset with my late habits. One morning after dad had left for work my mom looked at me and said, "Bill, your nothing but a bum!"

What was my reaction?

Mom Called Me a Bum #52

ONE MORNING, I RECEIVED THE shock of my life. My mom looked at me with a look I had never seen before. She put her hands on her hips and said.

"Bill, your nothing but a bum!"

How could my mother say that to me? I was going to church with her every Sunday! All kidding aside, I was not only shocked, I never felt so bad in my life. My mom was the best mom in the world, as I am sure yours was/is also. She was smart, funny, loving and caring. Mom only had a sixth grade education due to the fact her own mother died at the age of 36, leaving my mother who was the oldest of seven kids, Mom had a heavy load doing her best to take her mothers place as much as she could and helping the family through really tough times. She had a rough life as a young girl and now she is unhappy with me.

She shocked me and she was absolutely correct. I had no idea of what my future was, or what I was going to become. What career path was I taking? None! I guess deep down inside I still resented the fact I had to leave all my friends back in Canton and move to this strange new place. I sat down and started to analyze why she was called me a bum. I was making new friends, good people too. None of my new friends were anything but good people. I was not associating with any questionable individuals. They all seemed to have goals, where were mine? Mom had just told me to grow up and become a responsible person, didn't she? Thank you mom for waking me up and what do I do next?

One of the salesmen at Massey Buick seemed to take a special interest in me. All the new car sales guys were really a good bunch and

I considered all of them friends. We bowled together and had a few beers together as well. I was spending a lot of time with them, and for some reason, they with me, a young kid, a grease monkey. The salesman who was taking a special interest in me was about 50 years old. A lot of my friends were a lot older than I, which turned out to be good, I'm learning a lot from more mature people. His name was Charles, "Charlie" Michaels. He must have sensed something was going through my thoughts because it was only a couple of days after my mom put me down, or lifted me up, he said something to me about what I was planning for my future.

After bowling one night Charlie and I were having a beer and he says to me, "Bill, what are your future plans? You can't continue on as a grease monkey!" I replied I was struggling with that and did not really know wanted to do since I only had a high school education and I had no particular skills. He said, "Bill, yes you do. You know how to get along with people. You're outgoing and friendly." Charlie went on about my personality that kind of surprised me.

"Bill, I am going to give you a piece of advice. This is what I want you to do. Ask the old man (Harry Massey) for a new car sales position!"

That hit me like a ton of bricks. I hadn't thought about it, I did have sales ability. I sold newspapers, interfaced with all kinds of people while making my collections. I sold magazines door to door. I sold my self in order to get lawn and snow shoveling jobs. I have an "A" personality. I got along with my classmates, my team mates, my coaches, even my opponents in Golf and other sports.

I finally realized my goal, sales. A career I could get into without a college education, a career that if successful I could make a pretty darn good, better than average living. A sales career is not a dead end job, the sky is the limit.

I called Mr. Massey's secretary and made an appointment to see him. He was a very distinguished looking portly man who was about 60 years old. Not unfriendly, but he kind of kept his distance from his employees. He and his wife did not have any children. They were horse people, raised show horses and attended quite a few cities showing their horses in competition. I was asked what I wanted see him about and I said that I had a question to ask and would prefer not to disclose that question until I was able to be with him in person.

I am now the legal age to drink, I'm 21 years young. My appointment was for 10 AM on a Saturday and I put on my one and only suit and wore a tie. I entered his office where he greeted me with a warm handshake and asked me what I had on my mind. I said, "Mr. Massey, I would appreciate it if you would consider giving me a chance to become a member of your new car sales staff."

He was silent for what seemed to be an eternity. He said, "Bill, I am impressed with your approach. You have been a very good employee in our repair shop and our people like you. I will give you that chance. You can start your training just as soon as we find a replacement for you in the shop." He shook my hand and wished me good luck. I believe that is the only time I had ever had any kind of a conversation with him, other than just the usual hello's as he wandered around the place once in a great while.

I went straight to Andy's Loop Cafe for a beer and to let all my friends know of my career change. Then I went home and told my mom and dad. They were both extremely happy upon hearing that news. Mom and dad must have thought I might make something of myself after all.

Starting a New Life #53

$\mathcal{B}$OY, CLEAN HANDS! NO MORE printers ink or grease under my finger nails and embedded in my skin. Had to go to the men's store and get myself another suit and a couple of sport coats and slacks, new shoes, dress shirts and more ties. Cost me a small fortune to upgrade my wardrobe. What a change, I am now a Massey Buick new car salesman! The other salesman welcomed me with open arms and could not do enough to get me started by teaching me what I had to know about the product, how to qualify a potential customer, how to present the product properly to fit the customers desires and needs.

The biggest problem about becoming a new auto salesman is I have no past customer base. I wouldn't have to rely on potential customers coming through the showroom door for the first time if I had been around long enough to build a following of past customers. Most auto buyers if happy with the product will usually seek out the same brand when replacing the old one and they will usually ask for that same salesperson. I did not have that going for me. I am like a new born and must start from scratch.

A really good salesman will be in constant touch with his customers on a regular basis. Back in the 50's that were done through phone calls and post cards. He will know when his old customers are ready to buy again. Contacting customers today would still be by the telephone, but most of the post card system would most likely be replaced with email communication. You must have constant communication with your customer base, plus, working on some sort of a program with them so they will recommend their friends and relatives to come see you as well.

Without that customer base I have to rely on potential customers walking through the door. Every salesman on duty alternates who will get the first walk in that day and who is second, and so on. This sales job is straight commission but the company set up a draw payment system for me and I was given a small salary, which is really a loan. As i start selling a few cars the commission on those sales is applied to the draw until it is finally paid off, then I'm back on the straight commission compensation.

There are other perks you receive like becoming eligible for a retirement program, health insurance and group life insurance programs. One big thing is a demo automobile. Once you are past a trial period and when you have completed that trial period successfully, I will then receive a brand new demo automobile to drive for my personal use as well as for business. That is really a big perk, eliminating the expense of buying your own car and paying all the Insurance and maintenance that goes with car ownership.

Now picture this. Since I moved to Pittsburgh in 1949 I went from having no car to a 1937 oil burning Studebaker, to the sleek looking 1941 Buick Super 2 door sedan, and then the beautiful 1948 Buick Roadmaster convertible. Now I will be driving a band new 1952 Buick Special 4 door sedan, all in four years time. I brought the new car home and parked it next my dad's 1951 Oldsmobile. I'm not sure my dad liked getting upstaged like that, I had a newer car than dad but I had no money. The small salary I was on was less than I was making as a grease monkey. Sometimes you have to take two steps back before going one step forward.

Selling Buicks and New Friends #54

BEFORE GETTING INTO THE SUBJECT title above, I was thinking of my mom. Some little things came to mind she taught me I never forgot. A couple just crept into my mind. I can't resist passing these gems along. Things like insisting I hang my pants on a hanger and never leaving any clothing lying around. Put everything in its place. I can't remember how many times I hung my pants up in total darkness after coming home late at night, or, early in the morning after a few beers, it was quite a balancing act sometimes.

Also before putting the milk bottle back in the refrigerator wipe off any excess milk running down the side of the bottle so there would be no milk on the shelf to go sour creating a bad odor. How to eat crackers without dropping crumbs all over the place after taking a bite, mom told me to suck in air when removing the other half from my mouth which prevents loose crumbs falling all over the place. If I can't stand the smell of limburger cheese I should take my index finger and thumb of my other hand and pinch my nose tightly.

Last and most certainly not to be overlooked, this one is a gem. Mom told me that when I was on the golf course and with no outhouse available, when relieving myself behind some trees, do not head into the wind. Little things like that. I have never forgotten those great pieces of advice my mom was constantly teaching me. Aren't moms just great?

There are two other guys my age working at Massey Buick, Regis Burke and Russ Ahlers. We bowl together and pal around together. Russ moved to Mt. Lebanon with his parent's right out of High School just like I did. He was from New Jersey and a really good athlete. As a matter of fact he was all state in two different sports, half back in football, a guard in basketball and was also on the baseball team. He was also on our Andy's Loop fast pitch softball team with me. Russ was my best man in our wedding in 1956 and he passed away in May of 2014, age 83.

Regis Burke was 6' 4" tall and was a salesman in the used car department. Regis was six days younger than I and was also in our wedding party. He lost his life in an automobile accident at the very young age of 30 leaving a wife and young child behind. His was the second funeral I had ever attended. The first funeral was an Andy's Loop Cafe friend by the name of Carl Singhouser who was a bachelor and 35 years old. A good looking really nice guy who had a mole on his leg that turned into Melanoma Cancer which killed him really fast. He was the very first person I had ever seen in a casket. I think I was 21 and when I left that wake I got into my car and sat there for at least a half an hour, I could not stop crying. I started to realize how delicate life is. Carl was only 35 and Regis 30!

It did not take me long to realize that selling cars was not going to be my life long career. While I was learning a lot and enjoying my new job, there was something about it that I did not like. One thing I found is that I was not use to the slow pace of work. I was never a clock watcher in any job I ever had and I arrived early and left late. Waiting for something to happen in an automobile showroom was really not for me. One day I was so jittery I did not know what was going on within me, I had to get out of there. I left the showroom and went for a brisk walk. That did it, that walk calmed me down. I needed to keep busy somehow or tension would build up inside me and that made me realize this job was temporary.

I didn't make a move right away. My sales were picking up and I was no longer on a draw and I was holding my own. So, what did I end up doing? I learned not to burn bridges behind me.

Don't Ever Burn Your Bridges #55

ONE THING I NOW KNEW is my goal was to be a success in sales. That was now my career goal, but not automobiles. I just did not like sitting on the phone trying to drum up business. In my whole career, I have never liked talking to customers on the phone. I like the personal contact Appointments, I want to be face to face with my clients. That feeling started with my first sales job, I'd rather knock on doors than use the phone. It is hard to explain why I wanted a change I just knew a career in automobile sales was not for me.

My memory is a little cloudy of how this change came about. The next sales position I tried was selling residential chain link fences. When I made this decision I approached my sales manager at Massey Buick and sat down with him to expressed my feelings. I told him I was uncomfortable, there was something troubling me and I thought it was best if I tried something else. I just needed a change to see how I would react. All the while I made sure that he and the Massey Buick people knew how much I appreciated the opportunity presented to me. I gave all of my files and all information of anything pending and my list of customers to my sales manager. I gave them two week notice and asked that if things didn't work out for me could I possibly return. I just had to take a period of time away from car sales. I had to find myself.

The sales manager understood my position and he accepted my, as he put it, leave of absence approach. They were happy with my progress and he assured me that if things didn't work out I would be welcomed back. Can you imagine? Don't ever burn your bridges you just never know when you might want the opportunity to do what I did. And I did go back to Massey Buick after a short period of time selling fences.

I'd like to touch on that my short career of selling fences as it was interesting. I had to buy a car and I purchased a 1952 Buick Super 4 door sedan at a very good price. No sports car or convertible as I am attempting to become a professional business man and didn't want anything flashy.

The name of my new company was the Anchor Fence Co. Specializing in chain link fences and believe it or not they are not all the same. This in not what you might call a romantic product either. Chain link fences to me mean confinement as a matter of fact. Keeping something confined like pets, or a statement that says stay out and leave me alone That is what it says to me and there is nothing romantic about that.

The Anchor fence product was more expensive than its competition for a couple of reasons. When I have a more expensive product and it appears at first to be the same as my competition, I have a real selling job on my hands. I'm dealing with something more than just the best price. A potential customer has to be convinced of why they should spend more money with my fence than the other guys. All things being equal then Mr. Salesman, why do you want more money than everybody else? Darn good question. Are my answers going to tip the scales in my favor? Sometimes, but not all the time as price is sometimes difficult to over come, especially in a blue collar town like Pittsburgh.

The big difference was Anchor fence had its own patented way of installing the posts into the ground. Cement was not used to place the posts in position; their method was using two anchors attached to the bottom of the post which crossed over each other under the ground. Because of the length of these anchors the post would not work loose over time as posts set in concrete will do due to changes in temperature such as thawing and freezing conditions.

At every gate or a turn or bend in the direction of the fence and at the corners a larger post is required. The supporting posts are spaced every ten feet are smaller in diameter. These end and gate posts are heavy duty and the end and gate posts used by the Anchor fence people were not round, they were square posts. They frames of the gates were square as well. These square posts were stronger and made a better appearance, but were also more expensive.

Price was not easy to overcome. To some people galvanized steel was galvanized steel, round or square. Concrete sounds strong as opposed to two metal anchors. Price is important in blue collar towns as I have stated and money is tight for these hard working people.

I'm sounding somewhat negative as there is a lot to overcome. On top of all that, Pittsburgh was not a residential fence town. Many areas are, like Florida. Build a house, up goes a fence and if that house has a pool it has to be fenced as a safety requirement. Pittsburgh is very hilly and I though every house should have a fence, but few do.

I was also misled about how many prospects I would be receiving. Most leads came from people calling the fence companies for free estimates. This is not a product you just go knocking on doors, so these leads were very important. I tried selling fences for about six months. There were just not enough leads to make this worthwhile and I returned to Massey Buick with my tail between my legs. Because of my uncertainty my sales manger and I agreed that I was not to get a demo car for a period of time. I could use the other demos available for potential customers. In a few months we would then discuss what my long term intentions were.

Being single and living at home helped financially. I did not live there free, I paid rent, but that included meals and everything else that goes with a roof over your head. The price was right and the people I was sharing living space with were pretty nice.

Andy's Loop was still getting some of my business. The Coast Guard kept me busy one evening a week. I bowled a lot, ran around with my friends to parties and bars. I was a busy guy and I never even thought about golf and none of my friends played golf. It would be eight years after my high school days before I played another round of golf.

Another job opportunity came up within a couple of months and I took it? I left Massey again, this time for good, but on good terms. But wait, before I talk about my new opportunity it's about time I bring Dee into the picture, so tomorrow it's "hey kids, how I met your mommy".

How I Met Your Mommy #56

I'M CHANGING JOBS ONCE AGAIN. I'm not sure I met Dolores (Dee) before this career change or just after. I was dating a lot of different girls and was not going steady with anyone. One of the girls I had about three or four dates with was Peggy Walsh who was sharing an apartment at the time with Dee. Peggy was a very nice girl, very pretty and she reminded me of a thin Elizabeth Taylor. I never met Dee at their apartment when I was calling on Peggy but I spoke to Dee on the phone several times when I called Peggy for a date. When Dee answered the phone we said hello to each other, but little else. She had a difficult time with my name. When Dee answered the phone she would call out to Peggy something like; Bill Ferbhaver is on the phone. I believe to this day I think Dee still has a problem with my name. When she is upset with me what she calls me sure doesn't sound like Faulhaber! Someday she will get it right.

I need to bring my friend Russ Ahlers, back into the picture as he was a part of my meeting Dee. Russ and I sometimes double dated and we would go to parties together. There were a lot of single people around, and a lot of parties. Some parties we took dates and there were others that everyone went stag. We all just mingled, had few drinks and socialized.

The guys always brought whatever they wanted to drink with them, so the people throwing the party did not have that expense. Russ and I drank bourbon and soda and we came together in the same car. We had decided that both of us should not drink at the same time so we took turns driving and the one driving would not drink that night. By doing this we would always have a sober driver, not two guys half in the bag. It was really a very smart move on our part and it worked out really well, we never had a problem.

But, the night I met Dee at a party Russ was the driver. As it turned out I needed the car that evening, so read on. This is what happened. There Dee was, standing across the room. She had black hair and a black dress, a very pretty young woman. I believe we were 23 years old at the time. Dee was a very modest person and she never wore anything tight or revealing, she was and is a class act. I also found out her favorite word was, no. But that's another story, later.

Someone pointed out to Dee who I was, the guy with the funny last name who had dated her roommate, Peggy. We were looking at each other from across the room and I went over and introduced myself and started a conversation. We have been together ever since. Well not quite, there was the courting period. It turns out Dee was no longer sharing the apartment with Peggy, Dee moved in with her mother and step father above the bar in Millvale.

Dee actually grew up in Imperial. Remember the small town west of Pittsburgh on Route 30 that I drove through on me way from Canton? She went to grammar school there. Anyway, I asked her if I could take her home that evening. She was hesitating, but finally agreed after I released my very tight hold on her arm. After she agreed I almost had a fist fight with Russ to let me have the car. Being the understanding good friend that he was, he finally gave me the keys and said he would find a way home with one of our other friends, which happened to be a girl. Darn kind of him, he was already planning on splitting anyway.

I only had a couple of drinks so I was OK to drive. After that evening we started dating and that eventually led to her agreeing to marry me, but again not until I loosened my grip on her arm. This is for our four kids; did you ever stop to think how you arrived on this planet? If your mom or I skipped that party you would not be here. Now if you are happy with that, Dee and I will both take the credit. Think about it. Twists and turns in life are interesting to say the least. It is a lot of what ifs? I suppose we are all who we are because of, what should we call it, fate?

Now, my new opportunity, I was working at my new sales job with the Artcraft Mantel Co., also located on Liberty Ave, and can't seem to get away from that street. I bowled there, went to bars there, the streetcars ran up and down that street as well. Even my church, St. Bernard's, was located on Liberty Ave. Liberty Ave also went directly into Pittsburgh going through what was called the Liberty Tubes, a pair of tunnels cut through some very high mountain foothills.

My sales position with the Artcraft Mantel Co., was selling all kinds of fireplaces. This was a unique product created by a unique person, Joe Bliss. Joe was a big portly man who had little formal education. Joe was rough around the edges but was a really smart creative person and a very good business man. Before I get into explaining the product I'll give you and idea of how creative he was. He installed a TV in his 1954 Cadillac which was unheard of back then in those days. More about Joe's great products is next.

Artcraft Mantel Co. #57

I was still single when I started my next career path with Artcraft Mantel. As I said Joe Bliss the owner was a very unique man and his product was as well. Most of the fire places were false cast concrete made to look like elongated stones mostly grey with a touch of coloring, light brown, light red scattered but not in any particular pattern. This is hard to describe, but I assure you these fireplaces were beautiful. The front of the building housing this company looked like one of those fireplaces and the hearth was the entrance. It was really attractive and unique and it was an advertisement for the product, like a big billboard. The shop to creating all these units was in the back and Joe and his wife lived in a beautiful apartment on the second floor.

Not everything was of a false nature as Artcraft installed all sorts of wood and gas burning fireplaces. Most all of their business was remodeling, or just adding a fake fireplace where there was none. As long as there was a chimney with flu then any kind of a wood burning or gas burning fireplace could be installed, including Colonial, which is usually a white wood and dark marble combination with mirrors on top of the mantel. Where there was no chimney then a false fireplace could be installed and electric lighted logs were available and they looked like real logs burning.

The focal point of any living room, especially up north, is a fireplace. It makes all the difference of how a room looks. A salesman's dream, a product when delivered and installed received a 99% approval rating from the customers. Selling with confidence is a great feeling. Joe only had one salesman before adding me, Les Caufiel. The business was growing and there were too many leads for one man to handle, what a great problem to fix. The leads came from newspaper advertising plus word of mouth. When people saw this beautiful product in a friend or relatives house, many of them wanted one also.

This product was the easiest product I ever had to sell. We had a beautiful catalog, plus Joe put together a device popular in those days, a slide picture viewer. A device that was hand held and looked like binoculars. Insert a slide with a picture in it, turn on the battery operated light and the customers feels like they are in their own living room viewing all the various choices of fireplaces to choose from. The customer could see exactly what their choice would look like in their home. That was a wonderful sales aid.

I went through a sales training period, I traveled with Les Caufiel for about two weeks and he was a great teacher and a wonderful low key sales person. He was raised on a farm and a high school education and he was a really down to earth person. I leaned a great deal from him. Such as, when you think you're done for the day or night as the case may be, make one more call. He carried with him a log of not only customers he sold he also had a list of people he presented the product to who did not buy. Here is what Les would do. After completing a sales call if there was someone in the neighborhood that he did not sell on his first call, he would stop and knock on the door and reintroduce himself. Les would then ask them if they had reconsidered or had any questions. Many times when he made that extra call he got another sale. Many people just won't buy on the first sales presentation. But many times that little push, that extra call, does the trick.

Selling is an art. What a good salesman attempts to accomplish is simply present his product in a professional manner while asking as many questions as possible where the prospect answer is going to be a yes. If a person has a need for that product, put that person in a position that he/she wants to buy your product. I'm not selling anything, just making a presentation so that person wants to buy because they have a need or a desire to have that product. If there is no need or desire there will be no purchase and you will not get a sale, simple as that. No high pressure. After my presentation and if I feel I have done a good job and have answered all their questions that has satisfied my prospect, and then I ask for the order. Example. "We will be able to install your unit in 10 days Mr. & Mrs. Jones. What day is best for you?"

The only drawback was a lot of late nights. When I have a situation where two people need to make a decision, I try to avoid two different presentations. It is important I present my product only once with both of those people being present.

The exception to that is selling vacuum cleaners door to door, most of the time it takes two presentations. More about vacuum cleaner sales later, but first it's time to go from being single to being, double. Getting married is next.

Getting Married #58

*I*SN'T THIS IRONIC? I DIDN'T plan this! This chapter is the exact number of years Dee and I have been married when I wrote this! 58! Kind of spooky isn't it? No, not being married that long, I meant, well, what the heck, say no more.

Dee said yes! The bruises on her arms are no longer visible. We were both working I was doing well selling fireplaces so we thought we were in pretty good shape, even though we did not have much money saved. We felt we could start a life together, both being employed. In February of 1956 we tied the knot, a nice Catholic Church wedding in Millvale. We were both 24 1/2 years old. Most of our friends got married much younger than that. We had a small reception which included our families and our close friends. Peggy Walsh, Dee's former roommate whom I had dated a few times, was the Bridegroom. Russ Ahlers was my best man. Others, including my friend Regis Burke, were part of the wedding party. Dee and I paid all the expense of the luncheon reception. The weather for February was unusual; the temperature was in the fifties and raining. That is very warm for that time of the year in Pittsburgh. We only had a week for our honey moon so we decided to go to Atlantic City. Why there? We didn't have the time or the money to head south for better weather.

By the time we broke away from the reception it was late afternoon and still raining It was a happy but gloomy looking day. We headed for the Pa. Turnpike. Dee and I first though we would drive for a couple of hours than stop overnight somewhere. As we approached the Turnpike entrance it was already getting pretty dark and still raining and we were tired. We decided we needed to get some rest and get a fresh start the next day.

Near the entrance to the turnpike was Conley's Motel and we pulled in there. Conley's Motel was not what you would call the Plaza by any means. It was neat and clean looking but not exactly what we might have expected for our wedding night, but it's not a perfect world and we had no other choice. When we got to the room I sat on the end of the bed, and it collapsed! Honest. Dee and I still laugh about that. Why not, no one believes that anyway.

We planned to spend a couple of days in Atlantic City and the weather was still holding steady with the daytime temperatures in the fifties and the rain stopped. The weather was really pretty good and we wandered up and down the boardwalk and around town. When we left Atlantic City we to stop for a night in Gettysburg, see the sights and take in some Civil War history. I remember the movie we watched that night in our motel room. It was The Man with the Golden Arm, starring Frank Sinatra. Remember that movie? If you don't I am not going to tell you what it was about, you do not need to know it had to do with drugs and all that, so I won't bother telling you all about it.

We headed home to Pittsburgh and the weather was turning back to winter. Snow flurries started to fall but not bad. When we retuned home we had $30.00 in cash and about one hundred in our checking account and that was it. We knew we could make the marriage successful, who needs a lot of money?

We rented an apartment in Mr. Lebanon, just one block from, yes; you guessed it, Andy's Loop Cafe! The apartment was unfurnished and we had a table with two chairs in the kitchen, a couch, a 10" TV, and a brand new huge bedroom set with a double chest and a triple dresser. We had an extra long mattress so my feet wouldn't stick out of the end, a head board with two end tables, all in a dark mahogany. It was so large the bed reached from one wall to the door, which we could not close. That really didn't matter since no one was there but us. The reasons why we had so little cash was the reception, the honey moon and the $1,000.00 we paid for that bedroom suit. Back in the 50's, one grand was a small fortune. We still have that bedroom furniture but not the same mattress, yikes. Turns out it was a pretty good purchase after all. When we bought it we did not want to buy something cheap. Dee and

I wanted something built well that would last for years, something that would not collapse when sitting on the end of the bed!

Things were going pretty smooth, but there were a few bumps in the road ahead. The first bump was when I totaled my 1952 Buick in an accident on a sunny clear day around noon. I was traveling along the Ohio River in Sewickley, a suburb of Pittsburgh, while making a call for Artcraft Mantel. Traffic was light and as I approached a small incline, I noticed some smoke ahead of me. I reached the crest of the hill and the smoke didn't look to be too thick but upon entering the smoke, almost immediately all hell broke loose. I was going about 50 miles per hour and collided with an object hidden in that cloud of smoke. Thank God that Buick was built like a tank. The front seat of my car broke loose sending me into the steering wheel and the windshield. I actually put two dents in the dash board with my chins and I broke the windshield with my left wrist and watch. My body was being thrown forward, and my face broke the steering wheel!

My car then veered right after colliding with what I found out later was a stalled car in that smoke, I hit a guardrail preventing me and the car from going down a steep hill onto some railroad tracks. I later got billed for the repair of that guard rail, would you believe? The state billed me for the damage.

Stunned and bleeding, I pushed the seat back so I could get out of the car, still in surrounding smoke. The smoke was beginning to clear and I saw a man standing in the middle of the road. It turns out that he was the owner of the car I hit. He was not in the car when I struck it I learned later. He came over to me and asked if I was alright? While we were waiting for the police to arrive he told me he had just gotten the car out of the repair shop because he was having some problems. He said that as he was driving along he noticed his car was producing smoke and he stopped the car, he got out and went to the middle of the road. That is when I hit his car. It is a wonder he didn't get hit by another car, or by mine, but as I said, traffic was light.

CAR ACCIDENT CONCLUSION #59

*T*HE POLICE ARRIVED AND STARTED taking the usual information and our statements, separately. I think the other man's name was Bloom or something like that. Both cars were totaled and had to be towed away leaving us without transportation. The police dropped me off at the local hospital as I needed stitches inside and outside of my mouth and chin. When my face hit the steering wheel, my bottom teeth actually went through the skin of my chin, half way between my bottom lip and my chin. My nose took a beating, bending the inner cartilage, the piece that runs between the nostrils and it never did straighten out. I needed stitches under the inside of my upper lip, up under the nose area.

I was a mess I was. I had on a suit and tie which were a little bloody. I had a bandage on my chin and my upper lip was badly swollen. My wrist was all scraped up and my watch was broken and my legs hurt like heck from hitting the dash board. I felt like I just lost the heavy weight championship to Joe Louis, or was that Rocky Marciano who hit me? The only way to get home was via streetcar. I received directions to the nearest streetcar stop and walked there a few block from the hospital and waited about half an hour I got on the streetcar which would take me to downtown Pittsburgh where I could catch another that would take me to Mt. Lebanon and would drop me off at the end of the line, right at Andy's Loop Cafe's front door, a block away from our apartment. You can imagine the looks I received from all those people on those streetcars. They must have thought I was some kind of a brawler who lost the fight.

By the time I got off the streetcar it was about four in the afternoon so I staggered into Andy's, had three or four classes of draft beer and explaining to Andy and his customers what had happened to me. Then

I went to the apartment and called Artcraft to let them know what happened, sat down on the couch, exhausted. I waited for Dee to come home from work. Dee opened the door, saw me sitting there, and screamed!

When my insurance rep contacted me the whole story was of what happened, changed. Mr. Bloom, or whatever his name was, changed his story. What he told the police and his insurance company what not what he had told me? He claimed he was driving along and I came out of nowhere and slammed into the back of his car. Of course he was not hurt because he was not in his car, would you think the insurance company would question that! My insurance company was telling me that I was at fault because I hit him from behind. I did not get a ticket from the police, so maybe they didn't think so. The police report confirmed his story. So why did the police not give me a ticket for being at fault? I told my insurance man there was no break marks of on the road because I never had the chance to hit the break. To make a long story short, I got nailed. My insurance company cancelled my policy and I had to find another company. My rates went sky high and had to buy another car, a real setback. But life went on and so shall my story.

One of my older beer buddies at Andy's was Art Bourne. He was old enough to be my father and it turned out his son Tom and his wife, Marietta, was living in the same apartment building as Dee and I. Small world. We became friends and spent quite a bit of time together as couple's playing cards and having a beer or three. Marietta was going to have a baby so they were in the process of buying a Ryan built home. It was not long after that Dee was going to have a baby as well, so we started looking for a place of our own.

ANOTHER BUMP IN THE ROAD #60

*W*ONDERFUL, WE'RE GOING TO HAVE a baby! Dee has now left her job because the baby will soon be here. I was doing pretty well selling fireplaces. Business was good I had a new Ford after I wrecked my 52 Buick. I could not afford another Buick, darn. Our friends were all buying brand new homes, including our friends Tom and Marietta Bourn. The hottest selling homes were those very popular priced Ryan homes. I did not like that Idea as I did not want to go into debt that deep. Those homes were selling for $19,900.00 to $21,000. They were frame constructed houses; they had a one car garage, living and dining room, kitchen, three bed rooms, all small. The third bedroom had about enough room for a crib and a chest for clothes. They also had one and one half baths and a basement. The buyer had to put in their own lawn, buy storm doors and storm windows, screens doors and screens. The floors were bare wood and there were no window treatments, like blinds or drapes. All costs for these items were in addition to the purchase price of the home.

I felt there has to be a better way, something I can afford. I did not want to get behind the eight ball by jumping into something like that. Remember now this was in the mid 50's and middle class incomes were around $5,000.00 yearly. My dad was probably making less than $10,000.00 and he was a district claim agent with nearly 40 years service with the Pennsylvania R.R.

We made the best decision of our lives when we found a one and one half story brick constructed bungalow home in nearby Dormont. The first floor consisted of a living room, one bed room, dinning room, a fair size kitchen with room for a table and four chairs, and one bathroom. The second floor had one large room with a patrician creating two bedrooms. There was also had a double car garage. Half of the basement was converted into a game room with a small horseshoe shaped bar no less. The house was fully carpeted, had drapes and blinds in the widows, storm doors and widows and screen doors and windows as well. It was about 15 years old and just down the street was a huge park with a little league ball field and a huge swimming pool which looked like a very large cemented lake. This was a very good location.

The price we paid? **$12,500.00!** We came up with the 10% down payment and signed a contract. Were we ahead of the game, you bet! Then another bump in the road, just before we were to close on the purchase of this property, all the Artcraft Mantel factory workers who made the fireplaces, plus the installers, voted to join a Union. The owner, Joe Bliss, would have none of that. Everyone went on strike and walked off the job. Joe had plenty of money, he didn't need the income, and flatly told all these men he would close the business before he would let a Union come into his place of business. He closed down the business and didn't open it up again until about a year later, with no Union. I couldn't wait to see when and if he was ever going to open again, I had to move on.

Just like that I had no income. What I did have was a wife, a small baby and no place to live if I didn't close the deal on the house because our apartment lease was up. What did we do? We went to the bank as if nothing had changed and closed the sale on the house. They did not know I was out of work. Somehow we would make this work, but how? We had enough money to last two to three months. We had house payments, car payments, insurance payments, utility payments, and we had to eat. There was no going back to Massey Buick, even if I wanted. I don't think three times is a charm in this case. I had to find some kind of work.

I scoured the want ads and there was an ad looking for salesmen to sell an electric product of some kind, the ad didn't say what the product was. I answered the ad and found out the electric product had an electrical cord and a plug. On the other end of the cord was a vacuum cleaner! When I answered the ad, I was told to come to their address at a certain time. I did and there were about 15 guys that showed up at the same time. That is when the fun began.

We sat down in a couple of rows of chairs in an empty room. We were about to see a demonstration of how to get people fired up. The name of the product was Filter Queen, a tank style vacuum. but more about the product later. The way it was presented, it made all other vacuum cleaners look obsolete. These guys were actually throwing other vacuums against the wall. Smash! Bam! Bang! It was quite a show.

At this point of my story, I need to explain what kind of professional door to door vacuum cleaner sales people are. They are aggressive individuals, very talented high pressure sales people. There were several there who have been doing this for years, they love it and make a very good living. Milan Trittica was the head of this operation and he was a heavy set man with good personality and one hell of a salesman and his nickname was Trit. There was three other gentlemen assisting Trit and all four of these men have been in this business for years, all very talented high pressure sales people.

The turn over of new so called salesman is very high and Trit knows very well what to expect from these new guys looking for work. They may last one to six weeks and what kind of sales do these guys get in that amount of time? They sell a few units to their family members and friends, and their career as a door to door salesman ends. Trit just kept hiring enough guys every two weeks and every once in a while he finds someone who stays for a longer period of time, like me. This is an amazing time in my selling career. I did not like it, but I sure did learn plenty about people, selling and how you can bend and twist them into buying something they did not think they were going to buy. I learned how to close sales.

As I said, I didn't like this business at all, but I sure did like the Filter Queen. We are still using one. It is now almost 60 years old and more about the product, tomorrow.

Before I sign off today an unrelated story just hit me. Do you remember the long running TV western, Bonanza? A rerun was just on TV and reminded me of this story. Remember Lorne Green who played the role of Ben Cartwright, the father of three sons. Dee and

I were traveling to Hawaii, I think it was 1972, and It was a Spalding sponsored customer trip. We were transferring from one flight to another at the Los Angeles airport. We were on a shuttle car and having a good time with some of our customers. There was a gentleman sitting in a seat facing us and he spoke to us and said, "You sure are having a good time. Where are you headed?" I replied we were Hawaii bound and this was a customer trip sponsored by my company, Spalding. Then I took a good look at him and asked, "Aren't you Loren Green?" He replied, "Yes I am." He was a very nice outgoing and friendly man and he jumped right into our conversation just like an old friend.

There's more to the story. Do you remember one of the sons in Bonanza, Hoss? Dan Blocker played that part and he had a brother, Chris Blocker, who played on the PGA Golf Tour a few years back in the sixties. I spoke with Chris a few times and Chris was a well built nice looking blond, not quite as big as his brother. Not many people know that, but now you do!

Just a little trivia I had to throw in while I thought about it.

SELLING VACUUM CLEANERS #61

*B*EFORE WE START SELLING THIS electrical product, a story my Dad told me long time ago popped out of my memory bank. My dad made two birdies on the same hole on the same day. And he only played that hole one time. How is that possible? His tee shot hit a small bird in flight killing that poor bird. He also made a score of three on that par four hole, another birdie! True story, my dad never lied to me. I just had to tell you that before I forgot about it again for another seventy years. Back to selling vacuums before I forget.

I needed income. I needed something, anything, to pay our bills, until a better opportunity comes along and maybe going back to Artcraft Mantel if and when the Union issue ever gets solved. Until then I have to make a living. I was convinced from the demonstration I witnessed that the Filter Queen was a superior product. First, I'll try to explain the product and then how I had to go door to door to sell it. There was no salary involved, it was a straight commission job and I had to pay all my own expenses. There were no benefits either. I was not being hired as an employee, I was hired as an independent contractor.

The Filter Queen was a Healthmor Inc. product and their home office was located in the Chicago area. It was a round tank with a wheel attachment for easy mobility. There was no bag to hold objects vacuumed. The Filter Queen has two parts, the bottom with four wheels that was also the container holding the dirt. The top part was fastened to the bottom with two clips. The hose was attached by a device that fit over the housing of the intake hole in the bottom tank. The upper part housed the motor and the air exhaust. If air goes in it has to have an outlet for the air to pass through. There were vents all around the upper part with another opening on the top with a cap. When the cap is removed it was also part of the exhaust, and the hose could be attached for use as a blower. Sounds complicated? It is hard to explain without actually seeing the unit and I hope my explanation is understandable.

On the inside of the top where the motor is was shaped like a cone with its tip pointing downward. Over this cone the filter is placed. As the air comes into the unit at the bottom sucking in the items picked up by its tremendous suction, the air passes through the filter and exits out of the vents, but the dirt and dust is trapped by the filter which is a paper like material that would not permit anything to penetrate it but the filtered air. That means the unit could be actually used as a hair dryer as an example, the air was that clean.

The carpet cleaning unit also had another device that could be attached for cleaning all types of floors not carpeted. This device was covered with a felt like material that would slide over smooth surfaces easily. There was also a round brush that could be attached at the end for cleaning cob webs and spider webs from the corners of ceilings or hard to reach places, also venetian blinds. There were several other upholstery tools. There was also a spray can unit, and I could spray paint small jobs with it.

The Filter Queen had everything. It could be used to clean the air by running it without any attachments. Place it in the middle of a room, turn it on, and let it run for an hour or so. Eventually all the air in that room would pass through the unit, filtered. There was also a small felt pad in the top cap where a few drops of a pine scent liquid would expel a very nice clean refreshing odor throughout the room.

The air we breathe everyday is not pure. I remember as a kid watching the sun coming through the window forming a stream of light which exposed dust particles floating in the air. Do you remember seeing that? Part of our training was to create the same situation in a home. As part of our sales aids, we were given a portable powerful light with a solid shade that would only let the light from its high intensity bulb shine in one direction. The brightness was like the stream of light the sun made shining through the window. I still have that light in the garage somewhere. The point was we wanted to show how much dust was in the air in their home.

One part of our demonstration was to prove that the present vacuum being used in their home was part of the problem of why they had so much dust collecting on their furniture and shelves, all the things that the housewife had to dust all the time. Most all vacuums do spread the dirt and dust from the floor back into the air but that is not visible under normal lighting.

If my prospective customer was using an upright vacuum with a bag attached I take that unit and turn it on. Then I would take that special light and while holding it close to the bag of the vacuum while it was running, they could see dust particles coming out of that bag. The same thing could be done with floor units like the Electrolux. To make a bigger impression, I would tap the bag, and dust flew all over the place. Then I would make a comment. "Can you see what happens when you are cleaning and you bump the bag against that table over there? Your vacuum is the culprit that is placing all that dust on your furniture isn't it?"

Did you notice I made a statement and I asked a question, and the only answer would have to be a yes? She had to agreed with what I said. These kind of questions used throughout the presentation are designed to produce yes answers. When it is time to close the sale using this method, the customer is already saying yes many times. That's important when it is time to close the sale by asking for the order.

Again I am ahead of myself because I have not explained how I got into their house in the first place. After we learn all about the product knowledge and the weakness of our completion, the next step is on the spot training. We are assigned to go on calls with a seasoned salesman. Their compensation for training you is they receive an override commission of any sales that you make after you are on your own. Our commission was $50.00 per unit sold, not bad. The sale price was around $179.00 as I remember. That was a lot of money in those days. (I believe the cost of a Filter Queen today is around fifteen hundred dollars!) I think the override commission for the salesman that trained me was about $10.00 a unit, so the more guys a salesman trained the more money he could make in addition to your own sales. A veteran salesperson had the opportunity to build his own sales group. He could actually sit back and train more guys and live off of their sales. As you can see the potential to make good money was there. That appealed to me. But first, how do we get into the house to demonstrate the Filter Queen?

More about Vacuum Sales #62

I JUST RECEIVED A CALL FROM my daughter Diane. She lives in Spring Hill, Tenn. with husband Bobby. She told me that after reading my #61 story this morning, they went out and bought a Filter Queen! Said the sun light was shining through their window and the dust in the air was visible falling on a table that she had just dusted a day or so ago. Diane said it was a rebuilt 2001 model and she paid $350.00. New ones cost about $1,500.00. Boy, what a vacuum salesman I am. I got shut out of my commission however. Enjoy your new Filter Queen Diane, thanks for the call. Hope everyone enjoys this extra part of my Vacuum story.

To make a sale the product must be demonstrated as that means I have to get into a persons house. Again, People in the 50's were a lot more trustworthy then today and most didn't even lock their doors in those days, some of us even left their keys in the car. So asking a lady if you could have just a few moments of her time was a lot more acceptable back then. One or our seasoned veterans used this little gem a lot. He would ring the bell while holding the electrical cord and plug of the unit in his hand. When the lady of the house opened the door, he would say, "Good afternoon lady is there a place I could plug this in?" It was amazing How that worked for him.

It was amazing how that worked for him but it was easy to be invited in. This is just the beginning of some very interesting sales presentations and the last thing you want to do is embarrass the lady of the house. One thing that works well is to complement her about her housekeeping by letting her know how nice and clean everything looks even if it didn't. I want a friend, not an enemy. It was rare a sale is made without her husband being involved, and I have to set everything up so I am able to come back when he is home. I need that lady to be on my side, my friend. The following is some of the things that I did to solve so that invitation happened.

Once inside a little small talk is needed to get a little bit acquainted while putting the lady at ease. Complementing her is the best way to start because you are going to eventually show her she has a very dirty house after all. Not her fault though, it's the fault of the old vacuum she is using. She may have already said something to her husband that she could use a new one, but he most likely has told her to make the old one last. That may not be the case at all, but i planted the seed of something she may not have even thought of, but she is now, because I put that thought in her mind.

Now I have to go to work and I am not there to clean her house but I want to show her a lot of dirt in a very short period of time. I don't care how clean a house looks and I know where to find dirt, in the busy areas. All those other vacuums don't have the power the Filter Queen has and they will pick up surface dirt but will not pull up dirt that works its way deeper into the carpet over a period of time. So again I keep repeating that I'm probably wasting my time because she has such a clean looking house. Then I go to where the most dirt will be, in the heavily traveled areas right in front of the doors. I work the area very slowly, moving the unit so it will have its maximum pulling power. If I go fast, the dirt will not have time to come out of its deep hiding place, give it a chance.

I must back up a bit. When showing her the unit I make sure I open it up and show the nice clean filter and explain how it traps everything in the tank. I would turn the unit on while the top and the motor are separated from the bottom and the power of the motor is very impressive, but becomes very quite when it is put back into the round holding tank and the two clips are locked. Remember, the last thing she saw was a very bright white clean filter.

After I clean a very small area, and I mean small, what I have done becomes very impressive that I have found so much dirt in such a small area. I then turn the Filter Queen off and I am about to open the unit, and again I complement her by saying something like, "Mrs. Jones, I think I am wasting my time here, as you really have such a clean looking home."

The next thing she is going to see is a mountain of dirt and I am going to have a very surprised lady to deal with. Remember what the top of this unit housing the motor looked like? A large cone shaped structure holding the filter. The clips holding the unit together are released and I remove the top unit with the cone. Now I have the round tank sitting there with the bright white filter exposed. The dirt is out of sight under the filter and now I turn the whole bottom over on to the carpet and remove the tank. Now I have the filter sitting there pointing to the sky all blackened with dirt and loose fuzz from the carpet. It looks like a mountain of dirt, but for the most part it is the size of the filter that makes it look worse than it really is. The less dirt I find the more fuss I would make about it.

About 100% of the time the lady of the house is in complete shock. Now is the time I make a friend who will be on my side when I have the opportunity to come back and go all through this again for her husband, who by the way is usually ready to shoot me on the spot for getting into his home in the first place. That is something I will have to deal with when I return.

But before that I have to deal with a lady who is feeling uncomfortable. I ask to see her vacuum because I must act like I am also surprised about all the dirt I have found. It has to be her vacuum that is at fault, not she is what I tell her. Then I explain to her that the vacuum she has is not doing the job. She is starting to be on my side now because she is thinking it's not her fault at all; it's that damn old thing over there.

Now she knows that her husband is not going to be very happy about what has happened during the day. He has not seen what his wife has witnessed, so he is not going to be very receptive of letting me back in the house. I will need her help and to make it easier I leave the Filter Queen in the house. 99 times out of 100 I will be asked in and have a good opportunity to explain to the husband what a wonderful housekeeper his wife is but she has a problem keeping his home as clean as he wants it because of that damn thing sitting over there may be looking good, but it's not earning its keep. I have to convince them that it is the real enemy dressed up to look like their friend.

When I am making calls I do not just take one Filter Queen, I take four or five with me. When making a sale I do not want the customer to wait for one to be delivered, it's too easy for them to cancel later. I deliver the Filter Queen on the spot. Besides, on a good day and evening, I may be demonstrating the Filter Queen multiple times so I don't want to run out of the product I am selling.

Vacuum Sales Continued #63

*N*OW THE HUSBAND IS HOME and I am now entering the twilight zone. My most important function now is to protect the lady of the house. The husband has seen the dirt we left on the carpet and he may be thinking his wife is not doing her job. As a matter of fact he may be very angry with me and his wife for her letting which cause this on going situation. I don't know what he is thinking or what has been said but I do know I have to take her off the hook and try and keep her on my side. She has to like this new unit from what she has seen so far and she now knows her vacuum in insufficient and it's the reason why there is dirt in her home. Maybe she has been cleaning, maybe she hasn't and that makes no difference as the man of the house is my challenge now.

I explain to him what the problem is and that I found myself in a very clean looking home and his wife and I were both completely surprised at what i found, dirt, lots of it. I make sure he understands his wife is not a fault and I proceed to demonstrate my Filter Queen and prove to him how their vacuum is not doing the job and that it is actually spreading dirt from the floor rearranging it onto their furniture. She is now off the hook and i have convinced him their old vacuum, or even a new one like it, can not do what the Filter Queen can accomplish.

Most of the time this is enough to make the sale and I explain the cost of their new Filter Queen. I now refer to it as theirs as the one I have in their home hopefully will become theirs. I explain there is no waiting for days or weeks for delivery and explain our easy payment plan and no waiting time for credit clearance. This payment plan is backed by our parent company Health MOR, Inc. as the company takes the risk for no credit check. We are only dealing with a couple hundred bucks, a tidy sum in those days, but a minimum risk for the company.

Ask for the order. "Mr. Jones, I have explained your payment options. Do you wish to pay for it all now, or would you rather take the easy time payment option? Sign right here, Mr. Jones. Look at your wife over there, your sure making her happy, she's all smiles!" Mrs. Jones face tells the story; she really wants this beautiful new Filter Queen. Mr. Jones signs the order.

"Do you want us to dispose of this worthless vacuum?" I will take there old vacuum with me if at all possible. Then they have nothing to fall back on and the sale is really complete.

There was a lot of work involved making this sale, which turned out to be fairly easy. Mr. Jones was a reasonable man and recognized his wife's desire and the fact that they did need to upgrade their equipment for all the reasons I presented. There vacuum was not that bad. It just proves most vacuums don't have the ability to clean as well as the Filter Queen. At least I proved that.

As a salesperson, having a proven quality product that outperforms its competition is a salesman's dream. I am not pushing a bad product and can present my product with confidence. I'm not really selling as I am presenting an opportunity for someone to buy my product. All I have to do is present to the prospect with enough reasons to buy. There are buying, I'm not really selling. That is what real selling is about, except with this type of a product it is a very high pressure type of presenting. It is high pressure selling.

When I run into heavy resistance from a potential customer, then I would change my presentation. Many sales are not as easy as the one I just described. I have personally used some very high pressure methods and some I have seen other salesman use that I would not. This really gets interesting and reveals why I was not, and am not, a high pressure sales person. I did not like what I was doing even though I was dealing with and excellent product. I would like to explain, next.

High Pressure Selling #64

*W*E ARE IN OUR NEW house for awhile now and I have been selling Filter Queen vacuums for several months and the bills are being paid. I am not going to do this all my life either. Until some other opportunity happens, I am going to do the best I can. I now have the experience needed to train new hires. As a matter of fact I am now assisting with running the ads and taking part in the presentation of our product to new potential salesmen. Plus I am also taking new men with me on sales calls training them. When they sell on their own I will be earning an override commission on what they sell.

I will never forget some sales and a few really stand out as different. Remember I stated before that the Filter Queen could help filter the air in a room. I got the chance to prove that on a call one day. I had a trainee with me and we were down to one unit as I had already made a couple of sales. Sometimes i demonstrated the strength of the hoses to impress people how well the Filter Queen was constructed which I did on this next call.

This house had little carpet so I used the hand held powerful light at one point to show the people how much their air was polluted, and theirs was really pretty bad. I also got to the part about the strength of the hose. I used a little trickery here. With the hoes lying on the floor I would take my foot and stomp on the hose to show it would take a blow like that. The trick was to make sure that most of the force of the heel of my shoe made contact with the floor and not the hose. This time I misjudged where my heel was supposed to hit the floor and struck the hose instead, and I flattened the hose.

My trainee must have thought he was with a brand new guy at this job. He gave me this big unbelievable look. But I showed him a thing or three, I sold the unit as an air purifier first and a cleaning unit second. I got the sale and delivered a new hose the next day.

A sales presentation is positioned so that we I am asking my prospect questions that are designed to produce a yes answer, very important. The more yes's I get, the easier it is for the prospect to say yes when I ask for the order. I use questions like, "Mrs. Jones, do you like how this cleans?" "Mrs. Jones, would you like to have one of these Filter Queens to help you with your work?" "Mr. Jones, do you like how this performs?" "Mr. Jones, do you think your wife would like to have a Filter Queen to help her with her work around the house?" Do you think he is going to say no to that question? If he does, I had better leave that home, quick.

After those kinds of questions, I ask for the order.

If I come across a tough guy who is still on the fence, we were taught several different approaches of how to put him on the spot that will make him look bad in his wife's eyes. If his wife is not number one with him, he is in trouble. One such closer I used effectively was this. I It is designed so that his only answer has to be a yes, or he may never see their bedroom together again, or he could end up cooking his own meals and doing the laundry for himself. It could also get me shot if I don't do it right.

Assuming I am dealing with a working man he has to have lunch. Now he may be brown bagging it, taking his own lunch to work, or he could be eating in a restaurant. It doesn't matter, because there question leave him with only the answers I am looking for, or he is going to have one ticked off wife. I hope I explain this well enough for you to realize what a delicate position I am placing him, and me also.

"Mr. Jones, by choosing the easy payment plan, it will only cost you about .25 cents a day. When you have lunch at work, you go to a restaurant, right?" Without waiting for an answer, "You are waited on by a waitress, correct. She probably spends just a few minuets taking your order and serving you and for her service you leave her a tip, right?" Again, not waiting for an answer, "What do you leave for a tip, maybe .25 cents?" Continue on with the conclusion. "Now Mr. Jones, your wife waits on you more than a few minuets a day doesn't she? Don't you think your wife is worth more than .25 cents a day in comparison with that waitress?

Now, you wait for an answer, at the same time put the unsigned contract and pen in front of him. His wife is waiting for his answer! He may not even go to a restaurant for lunch. He is in a corner he can't indicate his wife is not worth .25 cents a day! He sings the contract without saying a word.

I will only relate one more unreal strong close that I once witnessed Milan 'Trit" Trittica. He had a really tough couple, both were resisting buying. Here is what he did, which is hard to believe. He unplugged the unit and he had the upholstery tool without the brush connected to the hose and he headed for the stairs and asked them which bedroom was theirs? Both were kind of taken back but they led him to that room upstairs. He plugged the unit in and was explaining to them that the human being sheds dead skin on a daily basis which at night penetrates the sheets and ends up in the mattress. He told them that mattresses needed to be cleaned periodically like anything else. With that, he pulls the covers and sheets off the bed! They just stared at Trit in disbelief, as did I.

Trit was prepared for this. He reaches into his coat pocket and removes a bunch of black colored filters about eight inches in diameter. He unplugs the hose from the air intake and places one of these black filters over the intake, attachés the hose, takes a few swipes over the mattress, removes the black filter which now has an area the size of the intake covered with grey matter. He places this on the bed, and repeats doing this about a dozen times. He only worked on one side of the mattress and places these filters on the side he just cleaned and says, "All that grey matter is dead skin. I only cleaned one side of the mattress." He then looks at the lady and says to her, "Mrs. Smith, which side of the bed are you going to sleep on tonight?"

It Mr. Smith wants a clean side he is going to have clean it, but with what? He is getting a look from his wife that he had better come up with the right answer. He bought the Filter Queen. "Trit" had more brass than a 21 piece band. I never, ever even thought about ever using that method of closing a sale.

Before leaving the vacuum business, I have one final vacuum story to tell. It made me decide I have to get out of this business as fast as I can. I had a lady of the house in tears, and I had three trainees with me. Next ... ...

Leaving the Vacuum Business #65

*U*NFORTUNATELY I HAD A LADY in tears because of the dirt I found in her home, or the dirt I didn't find! It was a call that was unusual in a couple of ways. First of all I had three new trainees with me and it was best if there are no more than two. Secondly I could not find any dirt! I was trying to make a point with my trainees that I make more fuss when I find less dirt. It there is a lot of dirt, that speaks for itself.

I was trying to impress these new guys. I have never seen a cleaner carpet, unless it was brand new which this one was not. After the first try when I dumped the container upside down to expose the large cone like filter and the dirt appeared larger than what it really was, there was no dirt, only a few pieces of fuzz! I tried this twice more in different areas where the traffic is heavy, same results. Each time, the dirt was invisible, there wasn't any!

I was so involved I was not paying much attention to the lady. When I did turned to her, she was standing there with tears running down her cheeks. I was shocked. I asked her what was wrong. She said her husband would not be very happy with her because the house was dirty! She was actually scared.

I felt like a bully. I was making a huge mistake which I had to correct right then and there. There was no way there was any need to come back when her husband was home and try to sell them anything. I didn't even know what kind of vacuum she was using. I did know she didn't need any further harassment, period. I asked the trainees to pack everything up while I talked to her.

I sat her down and explained that I was making a mistake about finding any dirt. I showed her it was only carpet fuzz I found, but no dirt. I assured her she had the cleanest carpet I had ever seen and whatever she was doing her husband should be very proud of her housekeeping. I concluded with the fact she did not need a new vacuum, and I apologized for my behavior. She accepted my explanation and was satisfied she had nothing to be ashamed of, that she had every right to be proud. I got the job done.

I knew all along this business was not my future. This call made me realize I needed to pursue a possible interview with Spalding. Just about a week before when I was at the local bar down the street that we frequented after bowling, there was a man I became acquainted with as he seemed to was always there when we were. We got to know each other, his name was Lester Lonergan. Les always joined in our conversations and knew of my love for the game of golf because I would often mention how much I enjoyed playing when I was younger and in high school and hoped to get back playing again someday.

It turn out that Les was with Spalding as their dealer salesman covering sporting goods stores and other related business involving all sports Spalding was involved in, including golf equipment. Let me explain here what the two different type salesman positions Spalding had at the time. One was called a dealer salesman as they dealt with what I have explained above. The other was the professional golf sales division and their title was pro golf salesman and they sold a line of golf clubs and Balls only available to the golf professionals located at golf courses.

Les said that there may be an opening for a new salesman in this area soon. It turned out Spalding was considering early retirement for their current salesman, Eddie Orin, who was turning 62 and had been with the company 40 years! Les asked me if I would be interested in applying for that position. He told me he thought I would have a good chance of being hired because of my golf background. I told Les I would think about it.

I was a little hesitant and I was thinking, wow, Albert G. Spalding & Bros. was a well know giant in the sporting goods and golf business. Would I be considered seriously for a job like that with my limited education and sales background? My confidence level was not very high at that time.

A few days after my upsetting contact with the lady in tears, I talked to Les and told him I was definitely interested and asked him if he really thought I would have a chance. He said he had a lot of influence because of his success with Spalding over the years. He felt Spalding would take his recommendation seriously.

Meanwhile I had to continue doing what I had to do to pay the bills. I had no choice but to keep my options open and do the best I can do no matter what happens. We were happy in our new home and we were also very fortunate to have a terrific couple living across the street as well, Dick and Doris Flynn. Dick was about 7 years older than I, a very wise 34 year old.

They both became God parents for two of our kids. Dick also convinced me that I should discontinue playing basketball and softball. He made me aware that my responsibilities of caring for my family were on what I made in commissions on what I sell. He made the point that if I got hurt and couldn't work, how would I be able to support my family? I had not really thought about that and he made a lot of sense. I could not afford to get hurt and be out of work so that was when I ended my active participation in team sports, sadly. Now what is happening next since I told Les I was interested in an interview with Spalding.

WHAT'S NEXT? #66

*D*EE AND I SPENT A lot of time with our neighbors from across the street, the Flynn's. They played bridge as I did. My mom taught my brother and I the game when we were kids. Dee was just learning how to play. With both our families having young children, it gave us a chance to socialize at each others house. We played cards, drank a few beers, had a few snacks and had a lot of good laughs and conversations. Dick resembled Dennis Morgan, a movie star in the fifties and sixties. Dick really had a good down to earth handle on life in general. He would give some pretty good advice. As an example he would say, if there are two ways of doing something, take the toughest way to do it as opposed to the easy way. Then you are sure you did it the right way. The easy way is not always the correct way.

Dick was in the beer distributor business. In Pennsylvania back then liquor was only sold through State run liquor stores. Beer and wine could be purchased in grocery stores, or you could buy beer by the case from distributors. Their price was competitive and it could either be picked up at their place of business, or they would deliver beer by the case to your home.

Beer in those days was sold mostly in glass bottles and was a deposit of a few cents on each bottle. Buying in stores was troublesome as I had to take my empty bottles back to redeem my deposit. It was easier with the distributor, once i paid for the first case, all I had to do was trade that case of empty bottles for a new case and the deposit was taken care of with the trade.

I finally got word that the Spalding national sales manager Harold Cross, and the district sales manager, Paul Jones, Sr., were coming to Pittsburgh and wanted to interview me. Paul Jones conducted most of the interview which was quite informal. Harold Cross asked a few questions also and they were easy to talk to, both had a knack of putting a person at ease. They made me feel like we had known each other for years. Both were very understanding of my background and were impressed with what products I had been selling. They were impressed to that I was married with one child and another one on the way and that we were buying a house and we were just twenty six years old.

The fact that I had not played golf for eight years was not a factor as Paul explained they were not hiring a person to play golf, but to sell golf products. Paul and Harold were in town to interview at least two others. One was Andy Borkovich who was head golf professional at a golf club in the area. The other was an assistant professional working for the President of the Tri State Section of the PGA, Paul Erath. In addition to the interviews they had the unpleasant task of meeting with their salesman Ed Orin to convince Ed that he should consider accepting early retirement. I found out later they had been unhappy with his performance for several years. Ed was with the company for many years and was approaching sixty two years old the age that he would eligible for early retirement. Ed could retire early with his pension and end his career with grace and dignity. However Ed would not reach that age for several months so a decision would not be made immediately.

Spalding Hired Me! #67

*B*EFORE ENTERING THIS PART OF my stories I have often wondered what it would have been like to have had only one, two or three positions in my working lifetime. By that I mean I never had a position, or job, that was the same day after day longer than six years even though I ended up working for Spalding 35 years over a span of 38 years, 1957-1974, and 1977-199. I held seven different positions of responsibilities during those years.

I never came close to being bored by doing the same thing year after year in my entire working years. There were always new challenges with every job since I was a paper boy. It was a very interesting ride to say the least. Many of those miles were over very bumpy unpaved roads but no one ever said it would be easy. How true that was. At the final destination of that ride, I have absolutely no regrets. I am just thankful everything worked out as it did. I worked very hard to help make that happen and I believe The Good Lord helps those who help themselves as well, I know I had his help.

I have had my first interview and I had no idea what kind of an impression I made on those two gentlemen. When I asked Les Lonergan if he knew anything he said what he should have said, no. I also asked Les what he thought I could do to improve my position. He told me to read about everything in the sports page everyday. Not just golf, learn what's going on in the world of sports.

After the interview I knew I wanted that job. In the meantime I had no choice but to continue selling vacuum cleaners. After not hearing anything from the Spalding people for a couple of weeks I was becoming very anxious and I called Paul Jones. I asked if he had made a decision and Paul told me it might be a while as it was several months before Ed Orin's 62nd birthday.

I didn't know if that was a put off or not. Les kept telling me he knew of no decision and to be patient. I called Paul again and told him I wanted that job and I began calling him once a week. A squeaky wheel gets oiled.

Paul finally did get back to me with the news that a decision had been made. They decided to hire me! It turns out the two big reasons I was hired I was the only candidate interviewed who kept calling them about wanting the job, the squeaky wheel. The other reason I found out later was that Harold Cross was leaning towards someone else, and he was Paul's boss. Harold and Paul were pretty close friends but Paul insisted I was the one he wanted, and that I would be working for him, not Harold. And Harold finally agreed I was their guy.

The compensation was set up as a salary and bonus plan. A quota is established each year and a bonus is paid when certain goals are met. The company rented a fleet of automobiles for the sales people and I received a station wagon and all expenses were paid by the company. In addition our family was covered by a health and accident plan. A retirement plan would not kick in until after five years of employment. The starting salary was a whopping $4,500.00 a year. I believe the maximum bonus was around $1,500.00, I don't remember because the first two years I never made any bonus, more about why that later.

If it weren't for the car and expenses, I would never have made it those first two years. Talk about bumps in the road, some turned out to be mountains, and I am not talking about West Virginia. By the way my territory was Western Pa., Eastern Ohio and West Virginia.

My official title was Golf Professional Salesman and job was to call on all the golf facilities in my territory selling Spalding's line of golf clubs, balls, bags and accessories to the golf professional. In those days the golf pro's owned and operated the golf shop at their clubs. It was his shop to stock with merchandise, pay any of the help, an assistant pro usually, and any other personnel in the shop. The pro made all the profit and most pro's received some sort of salary as well. They also gained more income from fees charged for golf lessons.

They sold everything from golf tees, shoes, clothing, umbrellas, club, balls, hats, everything a golfer needed. Most golf professionals in those days were ex caddies who became good players and worked their way up to bag boy, club cleaner, assistant professional and then hopefully landed their own head pro job. All this while working towards becoming a member of the Professional Golfers Association, and most had no more than a high school education. Many turned out to be very good businessmen, many did not.

Ed Orin still had several months to go, so it was decided that I would travel with him and he could show me the ropes while introducing me to my new customers. What a big mistake that was, traveling with Ed lasted about two weeks. I am about to begin my education in the golf business, the hard way. What happened? Turn the page, please.

BEGINNING MY CAREER IN GOLF #68

*F*IRST, A HUMAN INTEREST STORY I have been holding back until I finished other subjects. I waited until now to tell you about a golf professional customer of mine in Pittsburgh. He was the head professional at the Edgewood Country Club when I started my career with Spalding in 1957. That was 58 years ago. His name is Gus Andreone. Did you notice I said Is, not was? I was 26 years old then and Gus was 45 years old. Yes, Gus is still with us, he is now 103 years old as I write this.

A couple of years ago an old grade school and high school buddy, Dick Seiple, called me from his winter residence in Venice, Fl. Dick said, "Bill, I just had lunch with someone you know. He told me he was from Pittsburgh, a retired golf pro. I asked him if he knew you. He said he did remember you and to say hello. Bill, do you remember Gus Andreone?" I replied, "of course!" Dick said, "Well, he lives here in Venice and he is 101 years old! And he is still playing golf several times a week." I said, "Wow, that is really great, please give him my best. Dick, did you know Gus hit the Pa. Lottery one year? There was an option, lump sum of one million dollars, or one thousand dollars a week for life! He took the option of $1,000.00 a week for life. Obviously he is still collecting that amount each week. Want to try and figure that out what he has collected so far!"

There is more, how can I leave a short story when discussing a person who is one hundred and three years old now? Gus Andreone now holds the distinction of being the oldest living member of the Professional Golfers Association of America. Gus just reached that platitude in late 2014. That record had been held by a man named Errie Ball, he was102 years old and I also knew him. Erie lived right here in this area for years and was a frequent visitor at the Toney Penna Golf Co. v I had lunch a few times with Errie and Toney and played golf with him a couple of times. Errie was born in England and he was still playing golf and giving lessons until his death in 2014.

The Gus Andreone story is not over. He made news around the world when he became the oldest person in the world at the age of 103 to have recorded a hole in one and was still playing golf three times a week. A short note to my Spalding friends reading this, yes I added Gus to the Spalding Home Pro Consultant Staff shortly after I started calling on him. He was only the 3rd Pro in the area playing our equipment. The Pittsburgh area was all Wilson and MacGregor back then. Spalding was not much of a factor until I changed that somewhat.

To Gus Andreone, your life long dedication to the golf business and to the many you have touched these many years, is second to none. You are, and always have been, a true gentleman. God bless you my friend. "May the wind be always at your back."

Unfortunately for me, my early days with Spalding, the wind always seem directly in my face. I had to put my head down and fight through some pretty rough storms. Some of that Spalding history is next.

SOME SPALDING HISTORY #69

Back to some Spalding history, the original
name of the company was ...
Albert G. Spalding & Bros., then A. G. Spalding
& Bros, then shortened to just,
Spalding
Its most recent name was,
Spalding Sports Worldwide

*T*HE COMPANY WAS FOUNDED IN the year of this great county's
Centennial year, 1876, by Albert G. Spalding who was a baseball
pitcher for a team in Chicago. In those days Albert pitched every day, I
believe he was the first player to use some kind of a fielder's glove. The
company started with baseball products, and then expanded into other
sports.

Spalding was this countries first Sporting Goods Co., and was the
first company to bring a strange game played in Scotland to this country,
golf. An executive with Spalding was visiting Scotland witnessed the
game being played and purchased some clubs and balls and he brought
them back with him. Spalding then introduced the game here in North
America in the late1800's.

Spalding was never on the Stock Market as it had always been
family owned until the Spalding family finally sold the company in the
early sixties. Over the years Spalding was under the ownership of a few
different Investment firms. Unfortunately Spalding as a company no
longer exists. Bankruptcy was filed at the turn of this century and the
company was split up. The sporting goods division was purchased by
the Russell Southern Co., a uniform company. The Golf Division was

purchased by Calloway Golf Co. as they needed Spalding's Golf Ball technology so they could compete in the golf ball business.

In my humble opinion, Spalding should never have gotten into a bad financial position to force it into bankruptcy. The profit made on the Top Flite golf balls alone was enough to make the company profitable. Again, my opinion, bad management, plus blood sucking owners are what did the company in. I may get some arguments on my opinion, but that was going on long before I retired in 1995. What a shame. If management would have asked me, I could have saved the company. But, they didn't ask, so no one can prove me wrong can they?

Moving on to my humble beginning with one of the greatest companies ever when I was hired it was sales meeting time. There were two different sales meetings because there were two different businesses with two different sales forces. I was invited to attend both sales meetings so that I could be more acquainted with all the products the company offered. In my early years the sales meetings were always at the company headquarters in Chicopee, Mass.

Tours of the factory were very informative seeing firsthand how most of these products were made was valuable knowledge. It was at this very first meeting that I had the privilege of meeting and talking to the great Bobby Jones who was a Vice President of the Company. He attended the sales meeting every year until his health did not permit him to travel. When I first met Bobby he walked without help. As time went on Bobby's health problem began destroying his body and then he used a cane, then a walker, then a wheelchair. Eventually he could no longer attend, sad.

The new 1958 line of golf products was presented along with all the programs and time payment plans. It was the salesman job to travel his entire territory in the late summer and fall months presenting this new line to the golf professionals so they could make their purchases to stock their shops for the next season. That is when I started to travel with Ed Orin and I drove his car for him on this trip.

As I said before, this arrangement was one big mistake. What happened and the start of my rude awakening, is next.

My Rude Awakening #70

BEFORE WE START ON THAT fall sales trip with the retiring Ed Orin, let's set the stage a little. I have the station wagon loaded with samples and when arriving for an appointment, the first thing to do is let the customer know I have arrived. Then I ask him to give me about fifteen minuets so I can get the samples ready to be shown. I placed several strips of canvas along side the car and place the clubs and putters on the canvas leaning them against the side of the wagon and all the bags side by side. I place as many accessories as possible on the tail gate. That's my outdoor showroom golf fans. Then I go fetch the golf pro and show him the line and explain the spring shipment and payment plan available.

I know he is going to buy golf balls so I never brought that subject up until last. With some customers if presented first, he might just say that's all he wants and you may not even have the opportunity to present the entire product line to him. So I always started with the clubs and putters, then the bags and head covers and the accessories, golf gloves, hats, windbreakers, umbrellas, what ever. When all this is done I would then deal with golf balls.

That is a lot to go over. About the maximum calls that could be made in a day if everything went smoothly was about four. I am getting ahead of myself again. Ed Orin is a little guy with small glasses and does not look like a sports oriented person. He doesn't even play golf and I don't know it he ever did play the game. He was not overly friendly which did not bother me because I thought he was probably not real happy about his early retirement. Or, so I thought.

Ed explained that we would start our fall trip on the road because we had to get the trip in before fall and winter set in and it would be best to get the out of town territory covered and then the Pittsburgh area last. Made sense to me, I guess. We headed towards the Youngstown, Ohio area. We would arrive at a club and let the golf pro know we had arrived. Ed would introduce me and then ask me to go out to the parking lot and set up the samples and they would be out in a few minutes.

What normally would happen since the season was coming to a close, these orders would normally be shipped in December through April with terms for payment as late as late June. If the customer wanted his order right away the terms would be 2% discount 10 days or 30 days net, but since winter was coming this merchandise was really not needed until spring. I hope you get the picture because there was some strange ordering going on before I realized what was happening.

I would go set the samples around the wagon and shortly Ed and the pro would arrive. Ed would casually show the Pro the clubs and I was to write down what was ordered. I did not have any records of what these customer ordered last year, so I did not know what to expect. The first couple of calls were almost exactly the same. The pro would order one set of Top Flite clubs, a couple of Cash-In putters, 6 or 12 dozen Spalding Dot golf balls. And then the customer said rather than ship in the spring ship at once. This was still Ed's territory until the first of the year and January 1st is when the new quotas started. Anything shipped before that time did not carry the spring dating plan, and Ed would get credit for the sale. I would have nothing being shipped in my sales year from these customers.

What was going on? I found out, and you will also, tomorrow. I woke up fast!

I Woke up Fast #71

*H*ERE IS WHAT WAS GOING on. When we were making our last call of the day I set up the samples around the wagon and was waiting for Ed Orin and the golf pro to come out to the parking lot for quite some time. I went looking for them and as I was walking down a hallway beside the pro shop I overheard Ed talking to the pro. I stopped and I was out of their sight and I listened to Ed's conversation. Ed was telling this golf pro how Spalding had forced him to retire. Then he was saying they were replacing him with this kid, when they should have hired some assistant pro. I didn't hear everything that was said, but I heard enough to know what he had been doing and saying on every call. He was telling them that whatever they ordered he would get credit for the sale and receive the commission if they would have the merchandise shipped at once and not in the spring, that would help his retirement.

It wouldn't because he was put on salary only while training me, and only until he reached his birthday. He was not being truthful about how he was being treated by Spalding after his years of service, and he was hurting me badly.

No wonder why these guys were giving me the cold shoulder. They were giving Ed a token order and shipping it now instead of the spring. I would not get credit for any of these sales. Wow. We went to the motel, freshened up a bit and headed for dinner. What was I going to do? I knew what I had to do. I had to put a stop to all this nonsense right now. I am green as hell to this business, but I have the keys to the station wagon and I have a brain.

So we ordered dinner in the motel's small restaurant and when the salad was served I looked at Ed and said, "Ed, I have something to discuss with you and now is as good a time as any. I know what you have been saying to every customer we have called on so far. I overheard you on our last call today. Why are you doing this to me?"

He looked at me and then started to pick at his salad with trembling fingers. I'll never forget that. Then he blurted out Spalding should not have pushed him into retirement and they should not have hired a young kid like me who was not in the golf business. There were a few other Pro's and assistant Pro's who wanted the job, one of them should have gotten the job, not an unknown like me. He got that off his chest, good, now I know.

He was pretty upset but not as upset as he was going to be. Then I flat out told him to pack his bags and that we were leaving for Pittsburgh the first thing in the morning and this trip was over. I told him I would not be making any more calls with him and that I was taking him home and I would continue this fall trip on my own. I had control of the station wagon so Ed had no choice. I told him I did not want to hear another word out of his mouth all the way back to Pittsburgh. "Utter one word and you may find yourself taking a bus back home."

I called the District Office in Philadelphia where my boss Paul Jones, Sr., was located. I related the whole story to Paul and I asked him if he would approve of my going it along. I said I would have to learn as I go. He did approve. I asked him make sure the station wagon, which was rented be turned over to me with all the proper paper work and insurance in place, which we got done with two days. I was on my own.

This was only the beginning of what I was up against. When I started making calls in the Pittsburgh area, I encountered much more resistance. The Tri State Section of the PGA was a tightly knit group. However, as I found out later, a fair group, but that was some time later.

After one heck of a rough start it is hard to put into words and describe what went on but I'll give it a shot.

Sometimes, waking us is hard to do but I had trouble sleeping. What was ahead?

WHAT WAS AHEAD? #72

$\mathcal{B}$ACKSPIN, BEFORE GOING AHEAD, IT occurred to me I have to go back. Realizing the overall age group receiving these stories, almost everyone is younger than I, naturally. Even the Spalding people receiving this story most of them are twelve to fifteen years younger than me. That can make a big difference in how they view their careers as opposed to what the golf business was all about 12 to 20 years before their start in this business. Twelve years is the amount of time I started first grade and graduate from high school! You think many things have not changed in all that time? Perspective … hard to imagine!

We all have a tendency to think of things going on in our lifetime. It is hard to visualize "Back then." When I started my career with Spalding the golf business was very small. Baseball was by far Spalding's biggest business. It was the national pastime and there wasn't a close second and minor league teams were everywhere. The adopted baseballs in both the National and American leagues were made by Spalding. All the minor league teams used these same baseballs as well and the trickle down effect on sales was very large. Pro football teams were still playing in baseball stadiums. Pro basketball just got started in the early fifties. Tennis was probably as big as or bigger than the golf business. It didn't cost much to play tennis like it did in golf. The LPGA just got underway and golf was not even on TV, maybe a major tournament or two. Shell's Wonderful World of Golf, hosted by Gene Sarazen and Jimmy Demaret was just getting started. Golf was a very small part of Spalding's business; it was baseball, before the Japanese started to poke their nose into the business with very large gloves. During that time period Spalding owned Rawlings Sporting Goods. Those two companies dominated the baseball business then our government stepped in and ruled that Spalding had a monopoly on the baseball business. Spalding was ordered by law to sell off Rawlings because of the governments ruling concerning the Monopoly law.

The point of all this is, why would Spalding wait so long to discover any golf salesman was performing satisfactorily? All the sales mangers were not golf orientated, most knew little if anything about the golf industry. They were all busy taking care of the large sales numbers generated by the other sports. The golf business was so small it was easy to overlook underachievement, which is what management finally realized of Ed Orin's performance.

Golf was just starting to grow and would become the most important part of Spalding's business in later years, but not now. My quota the first two years was only $145,000.00! Most other territories were not a great deal larger. The first salesman to reach $500,000.00 in one year was Bob McLain in Detroit in the mid to late sixties.

To put things into perspective in the late fifties golf was not a popular sport, it was for the affluent. Arnold Palmer and a President by the name of Eisenhower stated to change all that. Looking back Ed Orin's output was not a big deal back then. In time I forgave Ed Orin for his actions. I'm not sure how I would have reacted if I were in his shoes.

I hope I have made what I am writing about a little clearer. We all have a starting point of what we see is happening in our time, while not having much interest or knowledge of the "Old days." It is hard to compare without some explanation. Maybe this helps the younger people understand a little better about what I am writing about.

Its time to move ahead but before I do I have to get one more thing off my mind. I need to clarify my remark about being a "Green kid." Yes, I was a green kid as far as the golf business but hardly was I really a green kid. I played a lot of team sports, baseball and basketball I competed individually as well, high school golf. I won money bowling when things were tough financially, another individual achievement. When I got over the shock of moving at that young age, I had seven different jobs before joining Spalding. As a Printers Union card holding pressman, a grease monkey at an automobile dealership, car sales, twice, and then chain link fence sales, fireplace sales and then as a door to door vacuum cleaner salesman. I got married, bought a house while out of work with a baby and one on the way. I was mixing it up with the human race, there were multiple type sales and multiple type people and situations I was dealing with. Joining Spalding I was not a "Green kid." I learned early on when you get knocked down six times, get up seven. That is a whole lot of experience dealing with all sorts of individuals. There was no backing down in me, not anymore. I didn't know what exactly was ahead, but I was prepared for it at that young age of twenty six. These golf pros put on their pants the same was as I did. I think I had a lot of common sense and I was a seasoned salesperson, I was no rookie and I was ready to move ahead. I enjoyed a fair fight, so bring it on. That was a lot to get off my mind, so now I am ready to move ahead.

Back in the fifties there were no gated golf communities that are so common today. When I was making calls all I had to do was drive into the parking lot and go directly to the golf pro shop and ninety five percent of the golf pros accepted these unannounced calls. If they were to busy to see me, then I just waited until they could see me, or I moved on and would call back another time. The only time an appointment was needed was during the important fall selling trip when presenting all the equipment.

I met a few of the Pittsburgh area golf Professionals before Ed Orin and I started on our disastrous road trip, just briefly. I did sense some at arm length during introductions at those brief meetings but didn't think much about it. Now on my own, I thought the best place to start would be calling on several of the local golf professional's and hit the road later; I had to get some things cleared up. I did not present the new line of equipment as I just wanted to get acquainted. I though the best place to start would be to call on the President of the PGA Section, Paul Erath. In a way, it was. And in a way, it was not. I bit the bullet and I found out where I stood with him and what I was up against real fast.

I tried to be as diplomatic as possible. As I introduced myself and I presented my new business card with my left hand and extended my right hand to shake his hand while stating, "Mr. Erath, please except my card so you will know where to get in touch with me." He looked at me and said, "I know where to get in touch with Spalding if I need anything." With that said he bid me good day, turned and walked away without shaking my hand or taking my card! The President of the PGA Section no less. Nice start! I found out later that it was one of his assistant pro's who was in the running for the position I finally ended up with.

Most all golf clubs are closed on Mondays, the only day most golf pro's don't work during the golf season. Do you think they stay home on their day off? No, they play golf. Almost every Monday there is a tournament, either a Pro/Armature or a Pro/Pro. The Pro will bring three armatures, usually their members for the Pro/Pro event. These events were mostly held in the afternoon so it was lunch first then golf. After golf everyone headed for the bar to socialize and a lot of the guys would play Gin Rummy and a fair amount of money changed hands.

All the local golf sales reps would show up because many of their customers were in the same place at one time. It was good time to take orders from anyone who may need something. The reps also ran the tournaments by acting as starters and also took care of the scoreboard. I jumped at the opportunity to join in with all the other sales reps as it was a great way to get to know everyone. This was a pretty close group and all the sales reps were very friendly to with other, at least face to face.

It was a long hard fall trip trying to find all the golf facilities on my own. I got through it is about all I can say. Now came winter, the snow began to fall and all the courses closed until spring. There was nothing for me to do but study the equipment, study each account and make notes of what they had been buying. I would make notes on each account of what items they were not buying. That way I set goals to increase sales by adding one or two new items to their inventory if at all possible.

The time off also gave me the opportunity to fix up the house, make small repairs and a lot of repainting was needed. Dee and I also hosted our first of many New Years Eve parties. We had a very nice party room in our basement, horseshoe shaped bar and all. There will be more about New Years Eve parties later.

I could not wait for spring. Starting in March, the weather was beginning to break away from winter a little. The golf pro's were starting to restock their shops so there were people to call on again. The more they saw me coming in the door, the more they would be used to having me as their new salesman, at least that's what I figured. So I made as many calls as I could.

GETTING ACCEPTED #73

$\mathscr{B}$ACK IN THE FIFTIES IN the golf business there was the "Big Three." As far as golf clubs were concerned, the big three companies who dominated the club market were Wilson, Spalding and MacGregor. The golf ball market was dominated by Titleist, followed by the Dunlop "Maxfli" nicknamed "Old Red Eye" because of its red circle marking, and the Spalding Dot. At one time in the early 40's the Dot was the number one ball but was overtaken by Titleist, manufactured by the Acushnet Co. There is a lot that I want to talk about golf balls but that's another story another time.

I found out in a hurry there was no big three in clubs in my territory. It was the big two, Wilson and MacGregor. There were several reasons for that. Wilson had a very large showroom and warehouse in Pittsburgh. MacGregor's home was in Ohio and was a very popular product. The other problem was the absence of an aggressive salesman. Ed Orin was happy with an order for a set of clubs, a couple of putters and 6 to 24 dozen Dot's and he didn't even try to sell anything else. He also only had two or three Golf Pro's signed to his "Home Pro Consultant Staff" to push Spalding products to their members.

These Spading "Staff" pro's were provided every year with a complete set of woods and irons, a large staff golf bag which was Red with the name Spalding in white letters on both sides of the bag plus the pro's name in big white letters. The Pro also received no charge 24 dozen Dot's for his personal use. For all this he was expected to push the Spalding products for sale in his shop. There was Wilson and MacGregor all over the place, plus some Walter Hagen, H & B Power Bilt, and Dunlop. Titleist had many of the Pro's tied up with golf ball contracts. At that time, Titleist did not have a golf club line, just golf balls and their popular "Bulls Eye" putter and they had golf gloves were also very popular.

Spalding was not represented very well in the entire territory! What a hole to dig out of. The good part about that, it would be hard for sales to get much worse. Unfortunately that didn't happen, partly because of that first fall trip and the resistance to a new kid on the block. The Western Pa. area was a disaster. The rest of the territory was a lot better, just because they never did not see their Spalding salesman much I was accepted rather quickly, other than the short trip with Ed Orin to the Youngstown area where he had already bad mouth Spalding and me.

I tried to soften things up a bit the more a pro gave me the cold shoulder, the more I called on him. I was in Paul Erath shop almost as much as he was. I eventually wore these guys down. Being 6' 2" with a deep voice helped as well. The guy I thought might be the most difficult was Andy Borkovich because Andy was interviewed for the Spalding sales job as well. I was in for a pleasant surprise as Andy was unbelievable friendly. He accepted me from the start. He was a big, nice looking, very nice man. We eventually became pretty good friends. I know Andy helped break the ice for me with a few of his fellow pro's ane here are the names of some of them. His brother Paul Borkovich, cousin Tony Barkovich, Red Blaskovich, Eli Marovich, plus Ray Grabowski, and Frank Melageri. All of these pros were former caddies and all were very good players and nice guys.

Things were looking up for my second year, then something else happened, both company problems. Spalding and I had to overcome some very serious unexpected business situations, unreal. Something new called a computer was one. Remember, this is 1958 and the other problem was a faulty product and both problems will take some time to explain so I'll talk about all that, tomorrow.

Spalding Business Problems #74

$\mathcal{B}$EFORE WE GET INTO MY second year with Spalding and the continuing problems Spalding and I were having, I wish to make something clear. I don't want you to think every sales job I have had up to this point, and including my first year with Spalding, was bad. Not every thing was negative, not at all. I learned so much with each position I have had thus far. What I have been learning is not taught in school. In all reality I was going to school and its name is the "School of hard knocks." I was becoming "Street smart."

There is not one thing, not one job that I have had so far that I would trade for one so called soft or easy job. No thank you. I look back on all I've been through so far, what a great experience. I did not get to college however I've earned degrees by doing, by practical knowledge. What I have learned is not being taught in school. No one can convince me that I have not earned at least a Masters Degree in sales and sales management. I can, and did run a business as well. I proved that with Wm. Faulhaber Enterprises, Inc. It was a successful business, but more about that when I get to Florida.

Spalding's problems and what a difference a year makes. There is no more animosity towards me by any of my customers that I can tell. I will spend the next six years working in this territory before I move on to another position with Spalding. During those six years there were lots of good times and I met a lot of interesting people. I'll talk about some of those interesting episodes and people later. But first I have an obligation to pay attention to the title above and here is what occurred.

The first one was called a computer. In my second year Spalding installed that new fandangle device, something really new in the year 1958. Up until then all invoices were created by real people. At our fall sales meeting that year we were given a tour of a large room that housed this monster computer and it was huge. The room temperature must have been around 50 degrees as this thing had to be kept cool. But a cool computer it was not. All it could do was spit out mistakes as we salesmen found out.

The other problem was with our wooden clubs that in those years were made with a solid piece of persimmon. We did not use laminated woods until a few years later. Persimmon had to be cured before use for several years. During World War II everything got backed up, or put on hold. Eventually the cured wood ran out and what we were receiving was wood that was not cured and all of a sudden our woods were splitting. The higher lofted woods were the ones splitting as they were smaller than the driver and had less strength. All woods had to be weighted and balanced so the specifications matched. First the wood is shaped then an insert is placed in the face, an aluminum plate is screwed into the sole (Bottom) of the driver. A brass sole plate is used for the fairway woods since they are smaller they needed the extra weight of brass. Under these plates a round piece of lead was inserted, the size depended on the weight needed so all woods are the weight required to produce a matching set. The wood not being cured properly would pick up moisture and start to swell up, and then break. A lot of these woods were flying father than the ball! At first we were just replacing the broken wood one for one. But it got so bad, if one wood broke in a set, we would replace the entire set of four woods. That was really expensive.

To combat this problem, Spalding was really busy installing a new "Hydroseal" system designed to solve the problem. The blocks of persimmon wood were placed in a large vat which held a liquid chemical. Then under pressure this liquid was forced into the wood sealing the pours which would eliminate moisture penetration. The Hydroseal system also made the wood heavier so less lead was needed under the sole plate for counter balancing. This wood problem was eventually solved, but not until we suffered a big loss of sales. We had to prove ourselves all over that our woods were again a safe and sound product,

All I was doing on my calls was handling complaints. Many invoices were incorrect and I was taking them with me so I could talk to our accountants and get them corrected. I was also hauling woods with me to send back to the factory as well. About all the orders I was writing was for golf ball reorders, little else. Business was really bad.

One of the big reasons why I won my customers over was that I did what I said I was going to do. If they had a question I could not answer, I told them I would find the answer and get back to them. I did just that. I also took care of all the invoicing and defective wood problems. A salesman is not going to be successful unless he gains the respect and trust of his customer.

Another thing, I was never late for an appointment. There is no excuse for being late and I always anticipated what might happen, a bridge opening, or that long freight train blocking the road, or the traffic accident. I always tried to be 15 to 30 minuets early. Most of the time the customer could work with me right away, so that gave me more time to get to the next appointment. I was not only accepted I was getting the feeling my customers were glad to see me. What a difference from my first year. I felt pretty good, and gained more self confidence in myself as well.

The first two years I did not hit quota, so no bonus. As I said my income was $4,500.00 a year for two years. That is about $86.50 a week. Out of that I paid our mortgage and everything else that goes with buying a home and raising a family. Dee and I learned how to live within our means. We never bought anything that we could not pay for in cash. In other words, we would not buy something now and pay for it when the bonus money came in, no way. We learned to live within whatever salary I made. Any commission or bonus money was put into the bank and I would pay extra on the mortgage whenever I could. I hate being broke, been there more than once and I did not like it. So we did something about it, something called sacrifice. Peace of mind is better than wondering how to make ends meet. We learned never to buy anything on time that we could not pay cash for, except a home or automobile. We would buy things on time, pay a couple of monthly payments to establish credit, and then pay it off. To this day we have never paid one cent interest on a credit card. Why should I give them my money? If I can't pay off my credit card debt in full each month, I have no business charging or buying anything. That's how we got ahead of the game. When you're ahead stay there, I call it winning.

You might recognize some of my customer's names. Let me introduce a few to you, next.

RECOGNIZE THESE NAMES? #75

*H*ERMAN KEISER, MIKE SOUCHAK, ED Furgol, "Wee" Bobby Cruickshank, Lou Worsham, Sam Snead, Pete Snead, Deacon Palmer, and Tom Strange? These men were a few of my customers. Here is a short Bio on each, except maybe a little longer one on Sam Snead.

Herman Keiser was in the Akron, Ohio area. Herman had eight PGA Tour wins, including one Major tournament, the Masters.

Mike Souchak, 15 PGA Tour wins. No Majors. Mike played college football and I believe a native of Pittsburgh.

"Wee" Bobby Cruickshank, all 5 foot 5 inches, and born in Scotland. Bobby fought in World War I, was captured by the Germans and escaped. Bobby played in the twenties and thirties with the likes of Bobby Jones, Walter Hagan and Gene Sarazen. He had 29 total wins world wide and 17 tour wins. When I called on Bobby he looked more l like 5 foot 3 inches. Bobby was a great little guy and all man.

Ed Furgol was in the Pittsburgh area. Ed injured his left arm as a child and it never healed properly. His left arm was shorter than his right arm and it was fixed in a crooked position, Ed could not straighten it but overcame that handicap to win 6 PGA Tournaments, including one Major, the US Open in 1954.

Lou Worsham had 6 PGA Tour wins to his credit including one Major, the US Open in 1947 beating Sam Snead in an 18 hole playoff. Lou was the professional at Oakmont Country Club for many years. His brother Herman was also head golf professional in the Pittsburgh area. Lou and Herman had a brother and he was a college classmate of Arnold Palmer's and was Arnold's best friend and he was killed in an automobile accident while in college.

Tom Strange worked as an Assistant Pro for Sam Snead at the

Greenbrier Resort in White Sulphur Springs, W. Va. He was the father of Curtis Strange who won back to back US Open's and many more PGA Tour tournaments. Tom ended up with a head pro position in the state of N.Y. I saw Tom again at a New York PGA sectional meeting when I was National Sales manger right before he died of a brain tumor. I believe he was only 43, very sad. Did you know his son Curtis has an identical twin brother?

Deacon "Deak" Palmer was Arnold Palmer's father and only golf instructor. Deak was head professional and the golf course superintendent as well at Latrobe, PA. Country Club. Most of the time when I called on him I had to walk out on the golf course in my Foot Joy loafer shoes to find Deak mowing fairways on that old tractor you may have seen Arnold use for Pennzoil ads on TV. Deak was a good guy, tough, but fair. One late afternoon I was calling on Deak and it was about 4 PM, cocktail hour, and Arnie was home that day. Deak asked me if I would join them and have a beer. It was my last call of the day so I said sure. He said he would meet me and Arnold in the men's locker room. He went to the bar and got three beers, brought them into the locker room, then opened a locker and took a bottle of booze off the shelf. Deak then proceeded to get three shot glasses and filled them up. Deak, Arnold and I tossed those down and drank the beer for a chaser. In the Pittsburgh area that's called a "Boiler maker." The reason why Arnold is the way he is, is because of his father and Arnold will be the first one to tell you that. Deak knew his place as well. He was not a member of the club, he was an employee. That is why we had that drink in the locker room and not the club's lounge. I politely turned down a second drink as I had to drive back to Pittsburgh and one of those boiler makers was enough.

Pete Snead was Sam's brother and the head professional at The Pittsburgh Field Club. Pete was a very friendly nice man who I watched hit balls on the range one day. Pete's swing looked just like his brother Sam. He never played in any of the local tournaments and I wondered why. I asked another pro in the area, Russ Sherba, why Pete didn't play any tournaments. Russ told me he was playing with Pete a few years previous and Russ said Pete had the putting "Yips" so bad that on one hole while over a putt, Pete couldn't pull the putter back to start his putting stroke, his hands started to shake so bad, the putter actually fell out of his hands. Russ said he happened to be the one who played the last round Pete played up to that time. Pete would hit balls, but would not go out on the course.

Sam Snead was the head golf professional at the Greenbrier Resort, White Sulphur Springs, West Virginia and a customer of mine also. Sam won 165 tournaments world wide, 86 official PGA Tour victories, including seven Major tournaments spanning 5 decades. He won 17 W.Va. Opens too. His last official win was when he was 53 years old. His official PGA Tour lifetime money winnings were less than $800,000.00! A single win today is worth more than one million dollars!

Just a couple of other things about my personal relationship with Sam, he didn't do the buying of merchandise for his pro shop at the Greenbrier, Gary Nixon, his assistant pro did. When I made my calls there, Sam was usually around the shop between rounds of golf he played with the well healed guests at the hotel. He always spoke to me and loved to say, "You're the guy with that other company." He was a staff member of the Wilson company all of his life, so he was referring to that "Other" company, Spalding. Sam told me that before Wilson had a ball good enough to play on tour he played the Spalding Dot. That was back in the late 40's early 50's when the Dot was king before the Titlleist became the popular ball. Besides Bobby Jones, Sam Snead was, and still is, my all time favorite golfer, followed closely by Arnold Palmer.

The Greenbrier was my most southern call in W. Va., a very long state from north to south. By the time I worked my way down there I would stay overnight at the Old White Motel. I would hang out at the pro shop and maybe play a round of golf on one of their three courses.

A few times I had the pleasure of watching Sam warm up on the practice range. He would use his own practice balls and have his caddy go out on the range and catch each ball on the second or third bounce. That was something to watch, Sam would start with the wedge and the caddy would take a position about 100 yards out. Sam would hit about five or six wedges shots and his caddy only had to move one step, if any, to catch the ball on the first bounce. Sam would reach for the next club, the 9 iron. His caddy would move back about 15 yards, and catch the balls again. That was repeated for every club in Sam's bag, three or four shots with each club. It was amazing, his caddy never had to move more than four steps as that was how consistent and accurate Sam was with his shots.

On one of my trips Gary Nixon asked me if I was staying over night and I said yes I was. He said that on that particular night he, Sam and a few other local musicians got together for a little "Jam session" at a local speakeasy. He asked me if I would like to join them. Gary played the clarinet and Sam played the trumpet. I said I would be delighted to join them. W. Va. was a dry state and only 3.2 alcohol beer was legal. There were no bars so beer was sold mostly in restaurants. Gary gave me directions, he said to take this certain road out of town, g go about a mile then slow down and start looking for a single light bulb in the trees on the left side of the road. At that light bulb there was a narrow path that a car could pass through the heavy brush. Gary told me to follow that path a short distance and I would come to a white house. Gary said they would be there at 10 PM.

I found the house without a problem and there were several cars already parked there. I rang the bell and a gentleman opened a little opening in the door and I told him I was a quest of Gary and Sam and he let me in. The first floor was converted into a fairly large room with a bar, tables and chairs and a small band stand. Gary and Sam were sitting at a table, they saw me enter and motioned for me to come over and sit with them.

Three or four musicians showed up and these guys did this about once a week, they played for their own enjoyment and were pretty good. They played some Dixie Land music and other types of jazz. Sam was not a drinker, he would drink beer and two was his limit. That was a very nice memorable evening. There's more about Sam and West Virginia coming next.

Sam Snead and West Virginia #76

*S*AM MAY HAVE NOT MADE a fortune by winning all those tournaments but what he made from endorsements and his income from the Golf Shop at the Greenbrier and playing with the Hotel quests are stories by themselves.

Sam was a member of the Wilson advisory staffs his entire golf career. I don't have any idea what Wilson paid Sam to use his name on a line of golf clubs; they were the "Sam Snead Blue Ridge". Sam's clubs were sold in retail outlets, sporting goods stores, Department stores, anywhere golf equipment was sold. Sam received a royalty, maybe 2% to 5%, for each set sold. Over the years, that had to mean millions of dollars of income for Sam.

On most days at the Greenbrier he would play 18 holes in the morning and 18 holes in the afternoon with three hotel guests. These guests would stand in line to play a round of golf with the famous Sam Snead. And they would pay through the nose to do so. Here's the deal, they would sign up for a "Playing lesson." Every day six quests would do this. I don't know what Sam's fee was for his playing lesson, perhaps around $200.00, quite a large sum back in the fifties and sixties. That fee was added to the guest hotel bill. Maybe Sam would give them a tip or two during the round of golf for the so called fee they paid, and maybe not. It was also made known that each of these quests would be playing a match with Sam as well. I think it would be up to the quest of how much they would be playing for. One thing I am almost sure of, I think the minimum was a $10.00 Nassau.

To explain that to non golfers, a Nassau bet means you are playing for $10.00 on the front nine holes and $10.00 on the back nine and $10.00 for the eighteen holes. That is a minimum of $30.00. However there are "Presses" involved. Anytime a person is two holes down there is an additional bet called a "Press", which means for the remaining holes of that nine, you are playing for an additional $10.00. The back nine is also "Pressed," which means the bet increases to $20.00. I will stop there because this can become somewhat complicated if not already. The point I am making is, on a minimum $10.00 Nassau it could easily add up to $100.00. And with Sam these so called "Presses"" were automatic and all those bets can come to a considerable amount of cash.

To top this all off Sam was unbeatable. Why? I'll attempt to explain the handicap system. Sam would give these "Pigeons" shots so as to even up their chances of beating him. If, for example, a quest had a 20 handicap, which in theory his average score for eighteen holes would be no lower than a 92 average on a par 72 course. Sam would never give the full handicap, he would give 80% of that handicap, that would be 16 strokes, eight per each 9 holes. I won't go into all the details of how this works, but there is more.

That handicap is figured by even par, lets again say 72. Sam never shot worse than 72. His average score on the Old White course, the best course of the three at the Greenbrier, was something like 66 or 67! So, figuring the 20% cut meant to a 20 handicapper, that is 4 strokes and Sam's under par average of five to six strokes, that's a real difference of 9 to 10 stokes in Sam's favor. I witnessed three guys one day shelling out all kinds of cash to Sam after a round. I wonder if the IRS ever got their cut. Those well healed quests didn't mind what it cost just so they could brag, "I played a round of golf with Sam Snead!"

There were all kinds of stories about Sam having all his money buried in cans in his back yard, that he was cheap. A reputation something like the comedian Jack Benny had. Sam really wasn't. His employees at the pro shop told some stories about things Sam would do for people in need. He was very good that way and only people close to him knew about that.

One last story about Sam, I was attending the West Virginia Open which was being played at the Mountain View County Club, located on Cheat Lake, in Morgantown, W. Va. Mike Krak was the Professional there at the time. This was a fairly new course carved out of heavy trees on the side of a mountain overlooking Cheat Lake. It was very difficult to keep the ball in these narrow fairways because this was not level ground. If a fairway was high on the right side and sloping to the left, a fade (A shot from left to right) was needed. For the opposite, slopping from left to right, a draw (A shot from right to left) was required. Mike Krak was a very good player who played the tour on a limited basis. He held the course record at the time, which I think was 70, two under par.

This tournament was 36 holes and Sam shot a pair of sixty sevens! I don't remember how many shots he won by but it was a walk in the park for Sam. I was following him one day and witnessed one of the best shots I have ever seen. This happened on a par four hole and Sam hit his tee shot into the woods on the right. He had a clear lie, in other words he could take a full swing. It appeared there was no place to go except sideways back out to the fairway. He kept looking towards the direction of the green. In front of him there was a very small opening in the branches of the trees, I mean, small. Then he would walk out to the fairway and look at where his ball was, and then at the green and the flag. Then up at the tops of the trees. I'm thinking no way, he has to play this safe and chip it out to the fairway. He came back to his ball, took out a seven iron and looked up at that opening. Sam took his stance, addressed the ball then took his usual smooth powerful swing and hit that ball right through that small opening. The ball landed on the green and was about 15 feet from the hole. He made the putt for a birdie! He could have made a six or seven it he didn't pull that one off. I could have put my ball in that spot and if I tried to hit a ball through that opening I might still be there. What an experience seeing this great golfer hit a shot like that. It is pretty obvious I never forgot it.

Sam could be fun to be around as he had a great sense of humor. With his kind of talent and money, even I might be fun to be around. But that's a different story, isn't it? Sam had a reputation of being very curt as times as well. Overall, from my experience with Sam, he was really a good guy.

Traveling West Virginia out of Pittsburgh was not easy. I never considered the North West panhandle of W. Va., really W. Va. Located in this panhandle, the most northern city was Weirton with Wheeling to the south, both between the Pennsylvania line and the Ohio River. Those two cities were more like Ohio and Pa. cities. The rest of the state was really different from the panhandle. I need another chapter to tell you some of my experiences traveling West Virginia.

As I have always said, W. Va. was a great state to work in. When I got tired, I could always lean up against it! There is a reason they call it the Mountain State.

Traveling West Virginia #77

$\mathcal{W}$ ITH THE EXCEPTION OF THE northwestern panhandle where the Cities of Wheeling and Weirton were located, the rest to the state was not easy to travel. Remember that I am talking about the years 1957-1966. Wheeling and Weirton weren't that far from Pittsburgh, so I sometimes went there and back in one day.

The only four lane road in those years was between Huntington, which is on the Ohio River, and Charleston, which is due east of Huntington in the middle of the state. The West Virginia Turnpike began at South Charleston and ran south to Princeton. But it was only a two lane turnpike, with an extra third passing lane once in a while and that was called the suicide lane. The road was concrete and very bumpy. The turn pike was only about 60 miles long and it cost .90 cents from one end to the other. That was expensive in those days. The rest of the roads were two lanes and narrow, winding through the Mountains. The speed limit on those state roads was 50 miles per hour, but, most of the time it was to dangerous to drive that fast. On many sharp curves I could not see what was coming around the bend. It was a lot of pressure driving and not getting anywhere very fast.

I only made two trips a year into W. Va. The all important fall trip, then early summer to keep in touch and see it I could pick up any additional business. I was told by many who I called on they hardly ever saw any other salesman from the other companies. I did get more accessories business because I was calling on them and other salesmen was not. My customers were all really nice people to deal with. I also realized that the golf clothing we wore in those years was a little different than what was worn by my customers. So I wore modest shirts and slacks, nothing fancy as I did not want to stick out like a sore thumb.

This is an extremely poor state. For years West Virginia lost population because the young people had little future, and I think they still are loosing population. Working in the mines did not appeal to the young. On one trip to Huntington at the end of the day I entered a restaurant to get a beer as there were no bars as we know them. There were three service men sitting at a table having a beer, each one was a member of a different service, the Navy, Army and the Air Force, which I thought was odd. Being an active Coast Guard reservist I went over to them and introduced myself. They asked me to join them and I found that they were recruiters for their respective services. I mentioned that since the young men in West Virginia had a tough time finding work, that their job of filling their quotas must be pretty easy as I assumed those W. Va. young boys must be looking to join the service for a couple of years to get some sort of training and income. The recruiters all told me the same thing, many of these young folks wanted to join but the sad thing is that most of them could not pass the simple tests required as their education was so bad so they had a tough time filling their quotas.

When traveling W. Va. I didn't make any motel reservations in advance because I simply did not know where I would be. I did not work on appointments either because of that as well. I would always I head south down the west side of the state along the Ohio River and work my way to Parkersburg, Clarksburg, and then to Huntington. From Huntington I would head east to Charleston. From there I headed south eventually arriving in White Sulpher Springs where the Greenbrier was located. Then I headed north and worked myself towards Morgantown which is located near the Pa. border and then back home to Pittsburgh.

Spalding provided sales figures for my W. Va. territory and they were quite a bit lower average wise per account than the rest of my territory. So my first trip there I was determined to call on every account I was given. As far as Spalding was concerned if their records said County Club, Golf Club, or Golf Course, then those accounts should be like all other facilities. Why so little sales? I found out why as many of these so called golf courses were nine hole pastures. Some even had sand greens, not grass, but oiled sand that was rolled with water filled heavy roller to smooth them so they could be putted. At one such facility the little gravel road leading to it went through a sallow creek with water up to my hub caps!

There were hardly any golf pros or pro shops. I found lunch counters with a few dozen balls sitting on one end of the counter. Some of these so called "Country Clubs" bought as little as 6 dozen Spalding balls for the year! Trying to explain all of what I found to my company would be a waist of time, so I informed the person in charge at these places that I was closing their account for lack of activity. I told them that if they were buying less than $250.00 the company could not afford to keep them as an account. So I closed about a dozen such places. All the other small accounts which had a half decent golf course and building with a ligament business, I tried to sell them more items to increase sales, which I accomplished.

MORE WEST VIRGINIA #78

*M*ANY YEARS AGO THE GREENBRIER held an invitational tournament named the Sam Snead Festival. This event was not an official PGA Tour tournament But It was a promotional tool the Hotel used to promote business. I was spending the night there so I had some time on my hands and I attended the tournament as a spectator. I liked to spend time around the practice facilities watching these great golfers hitting shots. I wandered over to a practice area where there was a sand trap and a green, I noticed this very young man hitting sand shots to a pin on the green. Shot after shot was within 2 to 3 feet of the hole, with a couple of balls going into the hole. What a show this young man was putting on. Turns out he was a nineteen year old from South Africa, Gary Player was his name! I thought at the time, what a career Gary had in front of him. He is now in the Hall Of Fame.

When traveling I always left on a Monday and returned no later than a Thursday because I was still in the Active Reserve of the Coast Guard. As I have stated before, we had to attend one meeting every week. Because of this, there was one trip that I did not stay over night in White Super as I usually do. I was running behind schedule. I had to get back for one of those Thursday Coast Guard meetings. So late one Wednesday afternoon I headed north. I wanted to get as far as I could so I could get a couple of more calls in on Thursday and still get to that meeting. I had no idea where I was going to stay overnight and there is not much population on the northern route I was taking. It was getting dark, about 7 or 8 PM and I am looking for any kind of a hotel or motel to spend the night. It was almost 9 PM when I spotted a very small sign that said motel. I don't know exactly where I was. I pulled into the parking lot, went to this very small building that said office. Rang the bell, an old lady came out, said she had a room, so I said OK.

That's what it was, a room with an old iron poster bed, one little chest of drawers, a single dim light bulb hanging from the ceiling with a chain, a small bathroom and tub. No TV, only a small radio plus an alarm clock. It was awful, but, where else could I go. I slept on top of the covers with one eye open, with the light on. In the morning I shaved, brushed my teeth, washed my self as best I could, I was not going into that tub, there was no shower. I went to the office to pay my bill, it was for $2.00. Motels back then charged about $7.00 to $10.00 a night, but, $2.00! The company paid our expenses; we had to turn in receipts. How could present a receipt for $2.00? My boss would wonder what the hell was I doing. I asked the lady to make the receipt out for $5.00 and I would give her $4.00. I might not get questioned about a $5.00 motel charge. So she did, and I made a buck on the deal. That made my trip! Talk about padding an expense account.

As I stated before, I traveled W. Va. six years covering the golf professional accounts and three years covering the dealer accounts, and more about that later, that's another story!

There are many memories of those years, I'll stop after just two more that I remember so well.

One spring I was calling on the Logan County Club, a nine hole course owned and operated by the local coal company. Glenn Thompson was the golf pro who was a really nice man and he was also the Postmaster for this small town, Logan. There are two stories here. I asked Glen a question, I said, "Glen, I noticed there are about a dozen kids hanging around the cart barn. School is in session, why aren't they in school?" Glen said, "Bill, to go to school in here in Logan, those boys must wear shoes and these kids don't have shoes! I keep them around here to caddy and give them odd jobs to keep them out of trouble."

I was really taken back about that. What kind of chance do these kids have and what kind of a rule is that for a school? I had tears in my eyes thinking about that as I drove out of that parking lot.

The other story is, Glenn, who was about 5' 8" tall, had a son named Barney who was about 6' 4" tall. Barney made it to the PGA tour for several years, and I could never figure the difference in their height. I never met Mrs. Thompson. She must have been very tall?

The final story today, one day I was traveling and ran into a Detour. I forget exactly where that was, but it was not near Morgantown. I mention that town for a reason which will be explained later. It was raining like cats and dogs. I am following a Cadillac, a rare car in these parts. Visibility was poor and I'm following that Cadillac and the detour signs, or at least I thought I was. We are on a very muddy road and I'm starting to think this is a unusually long detour. Since the Cadillac was still in front of me I just keep following it, and then we started to ascend down a pretty steep slope. I'm thinking, what is going on? The road is slippery and now a hill appears very close to my left and a drop off on my right. We finally level off, the Cadillac stops, I stop.

A man gets out and I recognize him! It is Ward Christopher who I met at the Mountain View CC at Cheat Lake, Morgantown. We are not near Morgantown, what is he doing here in front of me? Ward was a good looking man in his early forties who I knew owned coal mines. I get out and he recognizes me. He asks, "Do you know where you are?" "No," I replied. "I was just following your car after I saw that Detour sign. What are you doing here and where are we?" Ward answered, "You missed a sign; you are in one of my strip mines!"

You could have knocked my over with coal dust. So we exchange greetings and Ward tells me to be very careful going back up that muddy narrow path. He told me if I got stuck or started to slide, just sit there, a truck would come along before too long and it would help me up that uphill grade by giving me a push.

Luckily I made it out OK on my own and found my way back to the detour and finally to my destination. What a small world. There is a sad ending to this as it was not six months later Ward was killed in an automobile accident in that very same Cadillac.

Back to civilization, Ohio, next,

OHIO #79

I WAS REALLY HAPPY THAT PART of my territory took me back to my home town of Canton. Before talking about some memories from there, I have to take another detour. Its about what I learned very quickly writing orders on a preprinted order form.

On my first fall trip I would write the order on a preprinted form which had a carbon copy for the customer. On the top of this order form was a "Sold to, Deliver to" heading, shipping dates, and more information taking up a lot of space. It was also in a horizontal format, not vertical, so the spaces for writing items ordered were not very generous, only about eight spaces.

I noticed a couple of times when writing orders for clubs and balls, the spaces were used up very quickly. When I reached for another order form several times my customers would just say, "That's all I need." That ended any chance of selling any more items. I quickly realized the limited spaces on the order form were the problem. My customer thought he was buying a lot more than he really was when I reached into my briefcase for that second order form.

After that happened a few times I stopped using them altogether. I used a folder which had a legal size paper tablet. I just kept on scribbling the order on this and never turned over to another page. I just informed the customer that I would rewrite the order that evening and mail a copy. They didn't seem to mind that at all, problem solved. A little thing like that was really a big thing for me. What a difference that made in the number of items they purchased. I never used a preprinted order form again. I always used a folder like that, or a small note book on my follow up calls my entire selling career. To be able to do that, the customer had to trust that I would not "Pad" the order with something he really didn't order. Some sales people would do that, then if questioned would simply say that was a mistake of the shipping department, or some other excuse, if he did indeed get caught. Many times, those little added items go undetected. But if you're caught just once, you have lost that customers trust. I never did that, ever. My customers trusted me and I never gave them a reason not to.

As a matter of fact after a couple of years, I wrote abut 85% of my customer's orders before I even presented the new line. How did I do that? I will explain, later.

Traveling Ohio was fun. After my first couple of days with the retiring Ed Orin, I had no problem with anyone. They hardly ever saw Ed, so I was accepted as their new kid on the block. I don't recall any really unusual things that happened during my six years calling on the golf professionals in Ohio, except for one black family who owned and operated a golf course in East Canton. This is quite a story about an outstanding family. This story will take another chapter or two of its own. Learn more about them in Chapter 80.

The Canton Ohio Powell Family #80

*B*ILL POWELL, A BLACK MAN, started caddying at the age of nine, that's how he got into the game of golf. He was a good athlete, a halfback and the captain on his Minerva, Ohio High School football team, also was on their golf team. I don't quiet understand that because this took place before World War II. Back then, black people could not get on very many golf courses to play golf, only to work. I don't know where their team would have been allowed to play, especially the "Away" matches. Why do I say this? Because Bill himself said that when he returned home from England where he served our country during the war, he was a Sergeant in the Air force, he was not allowed to play on the area courses around the Canton area. Blacks were called "Colored" people in those years. I remember very clearly all those signs at the public water fountains and restrooms were clearly marked "White" and "Colored." Public bus transportation had a sign, "Colored seating in back of the bus."

Bill went to college, I don't know if he graduated. He married his high school sweetheart, Marcella, who was really a sweetheart and one of the nicest people I have ever known. They had three children, Bill Jr., Renee and Larry. Bill Sr. worked as a security guard for the Timken Roller Bearing Co. and he was a bitter man. He told me once he was treated better in England than he was upon his return home having served our country in the service during the war. I think I could understand his feelings.

Bill Powell had a dream, he wanted to buy a small farm and build his own golf course, but could not obtain a loan anywhere. Two friends came to the rescue, both black doctors. Plus Bill's his brother took a second mortgage on his home. With that financial help in 1946, Bill purchased a small farm of 78 acres in East Canton, located on Rout 30. There's that highway again! Bill and Marcella moved into the farmhouse Bill started to fulfill his dream of building his own golf course.

Bill Powell was the first black man that designed, constructed, owned and operated his own public golf course, "Open to everybody." Bill once said, **"The only color that matters is the color of the greens!"**

He continued working for Timken and on his golf course every day in his spare time. Working eighteen hours a day to accomplish his goal was not uncommon. Bill built his course without earth moving equipment, using his imagination; he worked the land as it was. He opened the first nine holes in 1948. Bill eventually built an additional nine holes and how he built his course without earth moving equipment is beyond me. Bill named his eighteen hole dream golf course, Clearview Public Golf Course. I played his course several times and my impression; it was a nice friendly course with very large excellent greens.

My personal involvement with my eventual friend and his family began in 1958. My first meetings with Bill were not all that friendly. Bill was standoffish, I was not a surprise knowing his background and the discrimination factor he had experienced throughout his life. I tried to understand where he was coming from. He did not know me, and he did not trust me. That was nothing personal, Bill was black, and I am white, understandable.

As I have stated Bill and Marcella moved into the farm house and they converted the first floor into a Golf Shop with a lunch counter and rest rooms. Marcella was in charge of these operations and I never had to prove myself to her. At least I don't think so and she was, so nice to deal with, Marcella had a lot of class with a wonderful personality and she was a pretty lady with a great smile.

But with Bill I could sense when he was buying he was giving me the impression he was not getting the best price. He indicated that to me more than once. After my third or fourth call I finally said to him, "Bill, I have a strong feeling you don't trust me. You give me the impression I am not being honest with you." Bill said, "I know there are better prices that you and other companies give to others."

We really didn't have quantity pricing at that time. We did have discontinued merchandise available from time to time, but no quantity pricing. We also had x-out "Dot" balls in limited quantities also. X-out's were balls with imperfect stamping or paint imperfections, or they did not meet the United States Golf Association specifications. The X's were stamped over the name of the ball. These items were never offered to Bill in the past, but he knew they existed. No wonder he had little trust.

It was time for me to take action. I looked Bill in the eye and stated, "Bill, I am your Spalding salesman. I will be calling on you as long as you let me come through your door. You are not a one time sales call and hopefully I will be calling on you for years to come. I promise you one thing; if we are to become partners in business then we have to trust each other. I will always give you our best price and best program available. I will always make special sales items available for you to purchase if you so desire. If we can't trust each other, we will never get along and there is no reason for me to call on you again."

That did it, I broke the ice and our relationship became a close one! I eventually signed Bill to a contract to join our Home Professional Consultant Staff. For this he received a new set of clubs and a Spalding Consultant staff golf bag with his name on it, just like the touring professionals, and twenty four dozen golf balls for his personal use each year of the contract. For this, he was expected to feature Spalding products in his golf shop as his main line of golf equipment, which he did.

One day when I was calling on Bill, he told me his young daughter, Renee, was becoming a very good player. He asked me to watch her hit some balls. Well, that's another story in itself about the Powell family.

The Powell Family Part Two #81

BILL POWELL WANTED ME TO watch his young daughter Renee his some golf shots. It was not a very nice day, a light drizzle was falling and it was chilly. I think Renee was about 12 years old at the time. We headed to the course and Bill had his driver and a shag bag full of balls. I asked Bill where were Renee's clubs. Bill just gave me a little grin and said Renee was going to use his driver. I had that driver made for Bill; it was not a standard golf club as Bill was a very strong man. His driver was ½ inch longer than standard, had an extra stiff shaft with oversize grips to accommodate his large hands. When the grip is larger than normal it lightens the swing weight, the weight that is measured for balance and proper weight distribution. In other words, a larger grip makes the head of the club lighter so extra weight has to be added to the head of the club to offset the oversize grip. Because of all this the total weight of the club is quite heavy. It is a club only a very strong man can swing with enough power to activate that extra stiff shaft and propels the head of the club through the ball.

We have a little girl here who was hardly big enough to use women's clubs! I simply said to Bill, "You got to be kidding. I couldn't swing that club!" He replied, "Bill just watch what she can do with my driver."

Renee, a very polite girl with a big smile, a very articulate skinny little thing takes a couple of practice swings. She had a very long back swing which took the club way past parallel. Very smooth with power coming through the area where the ball would be. I thought to myself, Hmmm! She tees up the first ball and takes that big long swing with that huge driver; she pushes the ball way to the right. She did not get the head of the club square at impact as the face was open. I thought, well, what do you expect with a club so long and heavy?

Renee tees up a second ball, takes that big long back swing and hits the ball way to the left. She overcorrected! Wow! The next "Wow" is even bigger. She calmly stripes the third ball straight down the middle and it's long. "Wow!" Renee hits about six more balls and they are all the same, perfect. She had this enormous talent that enabled her to adjust to that big war club.

I told Bill how impressed I was. He told me Renee wanted to play professionally someday. At that point in time, the Ladies Professional Golf Association, (LPGA) was only about 10 years old. The LPGA was formed in 1950 by Patty Berg (Wilson staff), Louise Suggs, (MacGregor staff), Betty Jamison, (Spalding staff). These three spearheaded the LPGA. Others, such as Marilyn Smith, (Spalding staff), were part of this organization in the beginning. I had the pleasure of knowing all of these ladies. Over the years I attended many of their tournaments while in my various capacities with Spalding. That's another story later.

Renee had her goals at a very young age. Now that I had Bill on the Spalding Home Professional Staff, I figured Spalding would have a very good chance Renee would play Spalding equipment as well, which she started to do. If Renee reached the potential of playing professionally, Spalding would have the inside track of signing her to a contract.

Fast forward. In 1967, I was now a District Sales Manager in the Cleveland, Ohio. Spalding had a distribution warehouse and sales office in nearby Solon, Ohio, just south east of Cleveland. One day I received a call from Bill Powell. He asked it he and Renee could pay me a visit as he wanted to have a conversation with me and needed some advice for Renee. Renee was now 21 years old and wanted to join the LPGA golf tour. I said I would be more than happy to and looked forward to their visit. We met in my office and had a nice discussion. Bill wanted me to let Renee know what she might expect and what to be on the lookout for. I will not go into all of the advice I offered, but one thing I told Renee, she would become the second black woman to play that tour. The other was the famous tennis great, Althea Gibson. I won't go any further with our discussion as it was private. Bill thanked me for being upfront about what Renee might not have expected.

One of my big disappointments, Renee signed a contract to play

Wilson equipment! For several years I kept our people responsible for singing contracts with both the men's and ladies tour players to consider signing Renee. They never contacted her, and never gave me a reason why. I have nothing more to say about that, but, I never forgot it.

When I stopped calling on the Powell's in 1963, it was because of a change in my job within Spalding. Over the years when I was in the Canton area I made it a point to drop in on the Powell's for a visit. One of those visits Bill grabbed a couple of bottles of beer and we headed outside for a chat under a shad tree. Bill looked me in the eye and said, "Over the years we have developed a good friendship, haven't we?" We tapped each others bottle and I replied, "We sure have, my friend." Then we had another beer.

Bill eventually was recognized by the Golf Hall Of Fame for all of his accomplishments. Bill Jr. died a tragic death in his late twenties. Bill Sr. died in 2009 at the age of 93. Marcella passed away about 15 years earlier. To this day Renee and her brother Larry still operate the Clearview Golf Club. Renee now in her mid sixties runs the operation up front and Larry takes care of the course. They feel the same way as their mom and dad, "The only color that matters is the color of the greens."

In my opinion, the Powell family gave more than they have received.

It's backspin time, back to Pittsburgh, the late fifties and early sixties. I won't get back to Ohio for more stories there until the mid sixties. My first six years as a Golf Professional salesman continues.

Learning How To Play Golf #82

*B*ACK TO PITTSBURGH AND 1957. The clubs I played with in high school are now 11-12 years old. They were not top grade clubs and the shafts as I found out were not firm enough for me and were second grade quality. Nothing like the new set of Spalding Top Flite clubs I just received. Wow! What a difference. It has now been eight years since I last played, I don't even have a pair of golf shoes. I really didn't have any "Golf clothing" either. In those days golfers dressed quite a bit differently than your normal casual clothing.

In the golf business I found out there are many perks that did save me a lot of money for many years. Most golf professionals will offer items in his inventory at his cost, the wholesale price. Also, if he invites me to play a round of golf as his guest, that will cost nothing as well, unless there is a caddy involved, then I pick up the cost for that. Nice perks!

After I got to know the clothing sales reps I was able to buy direct from their companies through them. For almost 40 years I purchased all my cloths, shoes, socks, slacks, shirts, sweaters, sport coats, jackets, rain gear, even dress shirts at wholesale prices. I didn't buy ties as I received enough of those as gifts for Christmas. I only had to by underwear at retail prices. No wonder over the years I did not like to go shopping, I didn't have too. At least now I looked like a well dressed golfer with my old underwear, but nobody new that.

My own company offered clothing from time to time as well. As a matter of fact when I first started we offered a dress shirt line. They were excellent button down collars', long sleeve and short sleeve in white and light blue. The material was an Oxford cloth which did not wear out easily. From time to time Spalding kept trying to break into the clothing market. In my opinion you're either a hard goods sales person or a soft goods salesman. There were very few that I ever knew over the years that were good at both. Clothing takes up a lot of time to present compared to hard goods. Tying to sell both to golf pro was next to impossible, they would not give you that much time, and frankly there was not enough time available to cover all of the accounts we had selling both the golf club line and a clothing line. They are quite simply, two different businesses. That is my humble opinion.

Another thing I learned, the golf pros never wore shorts on the golf course no matter how hot it was. Wearing shorts was just not professional. Since I was now in the business I never did either, not until I got to Florida. Even then for a number of years I wore slacks. All my playing partners wore shorts and they finally convinced me I did not impress them by wearing slacks. I was also a "Sweater." My dark slacks were showing salt stains and I finally gave in.

What has all this have to do with learning how to play golf? Nothing, I just like detours. Here we go, please visualize this. As a kid in high school I thought I was pretty good. Captain of the team! As I look back, the others on the team could not play a lick. So, being Captain of what? I could not help them either so there was no ship to command. I didn't realize that then so that brings me to this point.

From the age of 18 through 26, that is the eight years that I did not play the game. Those years are development years. Most tour professional don't make it to the tour until their mid twenties. It takes time, and talent, to become good enough to make it to the tour. Could I have been that good if I had played all those years? No way. I think I could have become a much better player and I have seen what it takes to make it to the tour as I have worked with golf professionals and professional's golfers for years. I simply didn't have enough killer instinct or talent to play professionally on the tour level.

Let me explain something you may not realize about golf professionals. To me, there are two different kinds. One is a **"Golf professional"** who works at golf courses, running the golf operation, the golf shop, and teaching the game. He usually is a very good accomplished player as well. The other is a **"Professional golfer"** who plays golf for a living, period.

Forward spin, now I have a quality set of golf clubs with the correct stiff shaft flex which will give me more control of where my ball is going. Being really rusty I am almost back to the beginner stage and will soon be playing golf with some of me customers, golf professionals! How in the world am I going to do that without embarrassing myself? My game at this point is mostly a fade, with a big old slice thrown in! I figure they don't expect me to be a good player anyway, plus they are use to playing with their members and most are not good players anyway. They see bad shots all the time. I just might surprise them, let the chips fall were they may.

As I mentioned somewhere, the PGA Tri State Section was active with Monday Pro-Pro and Pro-Am tournaments. The local sales reps always attended these events because where else can they see so many of their customers in one spot in one day? In addition we ran the tournament for them by acting as starters and recording all the scores hole by hole on the scoreboard. After all of them were off the first tee we had some time on our hands waiting for the first group to finish their round. A few of us would get our clubs and play nine holes. That was a learning curve for me as well. Some of these guys were former professionals, or just good players with a burning desire to knock my socks off and win a few dollars. I took a few beatings before I learned my way around. I was improving pretty fast. **If you really want to learn how to play golf, you must play with better players than yourself and you must be playing for something.** My dad told me that many years ago. The amount of money is not important; the competition of competing is the key that opens the door of becoming a better player. It didn't take too long for me to hold my own with these guys. My scores at first were in the high eighties but dropped rapidly to the mid to low eighties, finally breaking eighty getting into the high seventies and eventually into the mid seventies.

Another thing I learned very quickly. When calling on my customers they would often ask if I would like to play their course. During the week most courses were not that busy, so they didn't mind if I wanted to play a round of golf. That became one big temptation I didn't need. I needed to make calls and do the job I was hired to do and make a living for my family. So I decided not to carry my clubs with me during the week. Even that didn't stop some of them offering me a set of clubs when I told them I didn't have mine with me. Then I would say I didn't have my shoes with me. Would you believe, some of these guys were so nice, more than once I was offered a free pair of shoes! I finally had to take the honest way out and simply tell them I would love to play their course some day but not today. I really can't, I'm running behind in my calls, I have to keep moving. "Thanks pro. Another time, I really appreciate your offer."

I have seen salesman who have lost their jobs for just that reason. A person is hired to work. not to play. Once in a great while is acceptable, making a habit of it can be terminal. When I entered management, I had to deal with this problem more than once. Most ended in a sad situation. I might write about that later.

I have never had a formal golf lesson. Most of what I knew starting out was taught to me by my father. Getting a few tips along the way playing with some of my customers was a big help, but I never had a complete formal lesson. Some of these "Tips" are interesting and worth passing on.

Golf Tips I Have Received #83

I WAS BASICALLY A ONCE A week golfer and never learned how to practice correctly. I hardly ever went to a range to practice and hit balls. I was always learning on the course. If I went to a practice range, which was rare, it would be for the purpose of getting warmed up by hitting several shots before a round of golf. My usual way I started a round was three or four practice swings on the first tee, tee it up, and let it fly!

The best golf tip I ever received changed my game from fair to pretty good. I had a little bit of a bad habit of sweeping the ball off the grass with my irons. Taking a good divot was hard for me to do, and I didn't know why. Because of this I really didn't get a lot out of my iron shots, not near the control or distance compared to my woods, which requires more of a sweeping motion through the hitting area. The tip I received not only helped my iron game, it improved my wood play as well.

Dave McCormick, a golf professional in the Pittsburgh area, and I were playing one day. Dave was a really nice guy and I really liked him. Dave had a problem with his left foot and he wore a brace. Without the brace his foot would just "Flop." The brace made his foot stable so he could walk properly. The fact that he could play golf as well as he did with this handicap was amazing. Dave didn't say anything to me about my swing until about the sixth hole. He asked me if I would mind if he gave me a little advice about my swing. I said, of course not, please do, I can use a little help. Dave simply told me, "Bill, you are using your right hand too much. You are "Scooping" the ball with your right hand through the hitting area tying to help get the ball into the air. You are not taking a divot." A "Divot" for you non golfers, is a hunk of turf, grass and dirt beneath the ball, is what is seen flying in the air after those guys on TV hit the ball with their irons. I also call a hair piece some guy wear covering their bald spot, a "Divot."

Dave continued, "Bill, let the loft of the iron do what it is designed to do. Think of this, when your iron is coming into contact with the ball, get the feeling that you're hitting the ball with the back of your left hand. This will help you make contact with the ball by using a descending blow. Your iron will continue downward through the ball, the ball will ride up on the clubface and the loft of the club will project the ball on the proper path and the groves in the face of your iron will provide the proper spin. Your iron will continue down through the shot giving you more control and power. That in turn will produce a divot after the ball leaves the club face."

Understand? Dave didn't say that to me. I am asking you. It made a lot of sense to me as I never had that explained to me before. What a difference it made. So many of us are tying to "Lift" the ball in the air by swinging up, scooping the ball off the grass. Actually, the ball will go up if you swing down on it, letting the loft of the club propel the ball airborne.

I changed the way I was swinging my woods as well. My backswing was a little long at the top of my swing. My tee shots were pretty long, but a little wild with to much fade. I started to concentrate on a little shorter backswing for better control giving me much better contact with the ball. I began swinging my woods with the back of my left hand leading into the ball, not hitting down on the ball with my driver like irons shot, but sweeping through the hitting area with more left hand into the shot using my right hand as a guide and releasing my right hand when making contact with the ball at the bottom of the swing through the hitting area.

My scores dropped significantly. I started hitting more fairways and greens in regulation. My shots were much closer to the hole which took the pressure off three putting from long distances. What a difference. Boy was it easier to make pars and birdies having the ball in the fairway as opposed to the rough and the trees! Shorter putts made birdie possibilities more often and pars became a lot easier also. My scores started to descend into the mid seventies with my bad rounds being no higher than 82 and I became much more consistent in my scoring.

The second best tip I received which made me a better player. This one was given to me by Russ Sherba, the head golf professional at the Mt. Lebanon, Pa., County Club. Russ was a rules freak, he knew them all. I should not call him a freak; I should use the words, rules expert. That he was, as you will find out from a couple of things he and I were involved with. I played a lot of golf with Russ, social rounds and also as a partner in Pro Am tournaments. Russ was a very good player and teacher and was highly respected by his peers.

I have to set the stage again. In most of the north when spring has sprung the course conditions can be quite soggy due to thawing and spring showers. Many times the grass can not be cut as the mowers would damage the course due to these very wet conditions. The basic rules of golf states the ball is to be played from where it lies. It is not permitted to touch the ball after it is hit off the tee until the ball is on the green. Then, and only then and after marking the location of the ball with a marker, usually a penny or a dime, then the ball can be lifted and cleaned. Then it can be replaced on the green where it had been marked with the coin when it is your turn to putt.

Under normal conditions a ball in the fairway will be sitting nicely on top of the grass. Early spring weather causes mud to stick on the ball and some very poor lies because the grass is just starting to grow. Because of this, there are "Winter" rules used in the north. These rules are usually posted for all to see before starting. Winter rules allow moving the ball in the fairway using only the head of your golf club, not your hand. You can only use your hand if the rule states you may lift, clean and replace the ball no nearer the hole. Otherwise, the ball is to be rolled over with the club head, no nearer the hole, for a better lie.

Some more terminology for you non golfers, when a ball is on the ground, the ball is lying there. The term "Lie" is used. That is where the ball "Lie's." Which can mean it is a good lie or a bad lie. It is not the same as telling a little white lie. This is confusing enough and I hope this helps you understand what I am attempting to explain.

The second tip from my friend Russ Sherba, the rules expert. We were partners in a Pro Am when this happened. It was in the spring, and the conditions were like I was explaining above, soggy and winter rules were posted. Russ was a different guy as I think you will find out as I relay to you what happened, not one story but three. This is the first. It seemed like he had his own set of rules sometimes. We are playing pretty well, no bad lies for a few holes, so I didn't move my ball up to this point. Then it happened, I had a bad lie in the fairway. I was about to move my ball out of this bad lie with my club. Russ sees me about to do so, rushes over to me and says, "What are you going to do?" I said, "I was going to move my ball out of this bad lie, we are playing winter rules, are we not?" Russ looks at me and very sternly says, "Bill, do you want to learn how to play this game? Never under any circumstances move your ball for a better lie even if all the others may be doing so? Play the ball as it lies, learn how to hit out of bad lies because one day when you have a bad lie and we are not playing winter rules you won't be allowed to move the ball, you will be better prepared to cope with it." He spoke to me later after the round about why he feels that way. Bad lies never bothered him, they are just part of the game. In other words, take the bad bounces with the good ones. It all evens out and the bad ones will not seem so bad, don't let them upset you and ruin your day its just part of the game. Great advice.

Balls will roll into an unrepaired divot occasionally and the ball has to be played as it lies. This is a good example of what Russ was teaching me really pays off. You learn how to hit those shots. Funny things can and do happen to a ball coming out of bad lies, most times as you really don't know exactly how the ball is going to react. Experience will tell you what to expect with certain lies, so you do your best to anticipate and compensate. All this helps make a person a better player, adversity is a good teacher.

The next episode Russ and I are again playing together in a Pro Am. While playing a par five hole, I pushed my drive into the rough on the right side of the fairway. My ball is sitting up nicely, so much so I could use my three wood which would give me a chance to reach the green in two shots, a good chance for an eagle or a birdie. There are players on the green so we have to wait until they move on. About six feet behind my ball there was a burned out cigarette ash about two inches long. No filters in those days, so it was all ash. It was a long wait so to pass the time away I went over to that ash and gently tapped on it three times with my 3 wood and the ash disappeared. Russ came over to me and said, "Bill, you now lay four and you're hitting five!" With a look of bewilderment I said, "Russ, what the hell are you talking about? I am laying one and my next shot will be two." "No your not," he said. You just grounded your club three times behind your ball." I replied, "Russ, I was at least six feet away from the ball when I tapped my club on that cigarette ash, what are you talking about?" Russ said, "Bill, look back at the tee. See those guys waiting to hit. What do they see from that distance? It may look to them like you are tapping down the rough and improving your lie. That is a one stroke penalty for each time you grounded your club." "Russ," I replied, "I'm your partner, you know that is not what I was doing!" "Bill," Russ replies, "It doesn't matter, it is what they think you might be doing. Hit your shot and let's move on and that's the way I rule it." Can you imagine? I scored a nice fat eight.

The next story is not a golf tip it is just an interesting round of golf that I was fortunate to be a part of as a witness. It was the best ball striking18 holes of golf I have ever seen anyone play. Who was it? Russ Sherba, the rules guy! This was not in a tournament; I wish it would have been. We were playing a social round and again we were playing partners. We had a Nassau bet with the other two in our foursome. Russ made 11 birdies and 7 pars and scored a sixty one (61)! Of those 7 pars, his so called misses, were all within 6 to 15 feet of the hole and all were very makeable putts. Russ had one heck of a chance to break the magic mark of 60 and shoot a score in the fifties. That round happened on Russ's home course, the Mt. Lebanon CC, which was a very good golf course, far from being a pushover. What an experience. He asked my after the round why I didn't help him as a partner on the 7 holes he didn't birdie. I told him I was just trying to keep out of his way. He was right, I didn't help our team one shot, our best ball was 61, his score. As I recall, I made three birdies myself on holes that Russ birdied as well. Not easy to help a guy playing that well is it?

The terrain in Pittsburgh is hilly and there are very few level lies.

Most lies are either down hill, up hill, or side hill. The ball is above or below the level of your feet. A lot of adjustments have to be made in your stance when hitting those kinds of shots. In Florida and many other parts of the country, about 90% of the time you're dealing with a level lie. Those hills make it interesting, as most golfers playing in those conditons are well aware of.

FAMILY INSIGHTS AND MORE GOLF #84

I FORGOT TO MENTION WHEN I was making all that money for the first couple of years with Spalding, $4,500.00 a year, or $375.00 a month. I was married with two kids and a mortgage. That income was before the IRS and Social Security got their cut. Moving on beyond all that luxury.

But before moving on it was just today I was going through some old papers and I came across my father's entire history of employment with the Pennsylvania Rail Road. Here I am feeling sorry for myself about my income. The same years I am referring to, 1957/58, my dad as a Regional Claim Agent with 38 years of service was only making $11.130.00 a year! Dad started his career with PRR in 1920 as a male stenographer making $1,162.20 a year!

Dad was a champion typist with shorthand capabilities. He worked his way into the Claim Department in 1924 making $1,670.40 a year as a Clerk. The year I was born, 1931 he was now a Claim Agent making $2,700.00. His salary was cut 10% in 1932 and 1933, back to $2,430.00 because the depression hit, but thank God he was never out of work. Through the years Dad kept getting promoted, from Claim Agent, to District Claim Agent in 1940 then to Special Claim Agent in 1944. The year I graduated from High School, 1949, dad was promoted to Assistant Chief Claim Agent and we had to relocate to Pittsburgh. His salary was now $9,000. When Dee and I married in 1956 dad was again promoted to Regional Claim Agent and he and mom had to relocate to Buffalo, N.Y., he was making $10,600. Dad retired in 1963 with 43 years of service, his final salary was $13,275.00.

I just thought I would pass that history along for a comparison. In1962 and 1963 combining my income, a company car and expense account I was pretty close to what my dad was making after 43 years! Go figure. OK, I'll get back to my above subject; this was just another one of my detours. I just thought that history was interesting.

My wife Dee became quite a salesperson. Between all the choirs a housewife has plus eventually raising four kids, she became my Spalding answering service. I got a lot of calls from my customers about various things. I was never home in the daytime so Dee had to drop anything she was doing, except the dirty diapers, and answer those calls with a "Smile." She would write down the message, or an order for merchandise, or a complaint. She was very good at all of this, the customers told me they were very comfortable talking to her. As a matter of fact, a lot of them said they would rather talk to Dee than me! Dee was, and still is, a wonderful asset to me, not only in the business world but also with our long running friendship which now spans some 62 years, 60 of them as a married couple. That friendship is still running strong I am happy to report. (More points if she read this!)

Thanks for all your help Dee! You did one heck of a job raising our four children, Diane, Cindy, Jim and Linda, plus one dog, Kola, who used to play the piano, but that's another story. The kids were two years apart, not exactly in age but in school years. One year they would be in the odd number grades, 1,3,5,7 and then 2,4,6,8. Sure made it easy to remember what grades they were in.

For a married man to be successful he must have the support and backing of an understanding partner. I had all of the above. I could not have accomplished what I did without you and your support Dee. You're my best friend! (More points?)

We will spend seven years in our first house and we are starting to outgrow it as we only have three bedrooms and one bath. Four kids, three girls and one boy mean one bedroom has to be shared by one girl and one boy. That is OK at a very young age but they grow up fast, so it won't be long before we need a larger home. Before that happened, another change in my career with Spalding was forthcoming. Before I get to that, there are a few other interesting things that occurred.

As I mentioned before, the number one selling top grade ball was the Titleist with the Dunlop Maxli, "Ol' Red Eye" second while the

Spalding Dot was a bad third. The Dot needed to be upgraded in quality and performance. Spalding was working very hard to come up with such an improved product. With great secrecy a new improved Dot ball was ready. The sales force had no idea of what was coming and Spalding pulled off one of the greatest promotions I have ever witnessed to this day. I thought when this event happened some competitive company had just come out with one heck of a new ball. We salesmen in the field had no idea whose ball this was. Here is how the promotion unfolded.

Every one of my accounts received a package with a postmark indicating it was mailed from Ft. Knox, Kentucky. Inside this package was a round tube and inside the tube was one golf ball that had no markings on it. Included with the ball was all the individual parts used to manufacture that ball. In other words, there was a small liquid pellet, the liquid center of the ball common in those days, and two pieces of a rubber like material that had a cavity the liquid pellet would fit into. These two pieces interlocked together around the liquid pellet. Then there was a substantial amount of rubber threads which would be wound tightly around this center and these threads, or bands, are two different thicknesses. Then two pieces of the outer cover would be molded around this round bunch of rubber bands. The cover material was made from a special rubber like substance called balata. This is how liquid center wound balls were made before the introduction of two and three piece solid balls were introduced which I will write about later.

This unmarked ball with all the parts that went into the creation of this unmarked ball and we also find inside this tube a piece of heavy duty paper strip when unfolded was a 3 foot long yardstick. There was also some reading material which had a picture of a very small red bird holding the ball in its claws flying away with the ball. This bird I found out later is actually an African Wren, a tiny little red feathered bird and the picture was showing the actual size of this very small bird.

The statement read, "10 to 15 yards farther on the fly!" That's a very strong statement indeed, significant longer yardage in the air, ten to fifteen yards longer than its competition. The mailing created a lot of excitement, interest and suspense. A brilliant promotion some company is putting on. What company was doing this?

On my next calls after my customers received the mailing my customers were showing me the ball and the packaging. I was receiving remarks like, "Boy are you and Spalding in trouble. I played with this ball and it's great!" Remember, none of the Spalding field personnel knew it was out new Dot!

We later referred to this ball and the mailing as the "Ft. Knox Dot." Had it been mailed from our factory in Chicopee, Mass., it would have been a dead giveaway with no impact. Spalding wanted an unbiased opinion from the golf pros; this was the way to obtain that kind of information.

"The Bird on the Ball" became quite a buzz within the industry, who's ball was it?

When Spalding finally let the cat out of the bag our sales rose sharply and surpassed the number two ball, the Dunlop Maxfli and became a strong second to the number one selling ball, Titliest.

Detour. A new unrelated problem popped up as several of my customers were telling me that I should not be playing in these local tournaments as an armature since I am making my living selling golf equipment for a living just like they are. Has my amateur status changed? Am I now considered a professional, or a non amateur? This interesting question led me to writing to the United States Golf Association for a ruling as these guys were really giving me a hard time.

The question and the results, am I an amateur or a professional because of my job making a living in the golf business?

AMATEUR OR PROFESSIONAL? #85

*B*EFORE I GET INTO THE subject matter, I would like to make something about my golfing abilities more transparent. If I have given you the impression I was an accomplished, a very good golfer, I was not. My abilities as a good player could be overstated. Do I feel that I was a good player? For the amount I played, yes.

If you found me on a practice range, it would be like finding that needle in the haystack people have been trying to find for centuries. I did not know how to practice, nor did I find the time to do so. All my years in the north there were only about 7 to 8 months one could play. If, I say if, I played once a week that would amount to approximately 28 to 32 rounds of golf for the year! Touring Professional play about 6 rounds in a week and that would be 168 to 192 rounds in the same period of time that I am playing 30 rounds.

Those numbers tell me I did just fine. No one was aware that I was known for my playing abilities, my name was never in the paper or anything like that, which brings me to the subject title.

This happened in 1962, I am now a veteran of five years calling on golf professionals. My golf game has gotten better. I have been playing in Pro Am tournaments with various local Pro's as their partner. After one such tournament while we were having cocktails before dinner, one pro brought up a question. He stated that I should not be playing golf as an amateur since I made my living in the golf business, just like they did. My income and theirs came from the game of golf. Several others chipped in and agreed. If this were true, then I could not play as an amateur or in any professional run event either because I was not, or could not be a member of the PGA.

They were telling me the United States Golf Association (USGA) rules states that I would not be eligible to play in tournaments except tournaments that had "Open" status. All this means they thought I had no status, pro or amateur.

I was really starting to get a lot of flack about this, so I decided to write to the USGA for their ruling. The USGA replied to my letter and asked for what purpose I was hired, who my superior was and how to get in touch with him. The head of the professional golf sales division was Harold Cross. They wanted to know if I was hired because I was well known for my golfing abilities which might influence sales because of a celebrity status. After several letters of correspondence back and forth between Mr. Cross and the USGA, I received the following letter, which I still have and carried in my golf bag for years in case that question came up while I was playing in some event.

UNITED STATES GOLF ASSOCIATION
"GOLF HOUSE"
40 EAST 38TH STREET
NEW YORK 16, N.Y.

April 4. 1962

Mr. Wm. H. Faulhaber
3033 Annapolis Avenue
Pittsburgh 16, Pa
Dear Mr. Faulhaber:

Our Amateur Status and Conduct Committee has considerer the statements made by you and by Mr. Harold S. Cross of A. G. Spalding & Bros. and it is the decision of the Committee that you did not violate the Rules of Amateur Status by accepting a position as salesman with A. G. Spalding.

Sincerely,
(Signed)
P. J. Boatwright, Jr.

Assistant Director

CC: Mr. Harold S. Cross

I had to go through all of that to quiet these guys down. We all got a big kick out of it. By now, most all of these golf pros are friends as well as customers. They were a great group who enjoyed getting together to compete, not only golf, also some very lively gin card games and cocktails after a great afternoon of golf. All the local salesmen were welcome as a part of their group. We salesmen all got along well together, at least face to face. I had to watch my back with some of them and you have to expect that with some competitors. Unfortunately there are two faced people everywhere. I did not let if bother me, I minded my own business and never talked about my competition. When you do that you are only hurting yourself, not them.

Around this time I was getting a new District Sales Manager. Paul Jones, Sr. who hired me had moved on to our home office in Chicopee, Mass. His replacement was another salesperson out or the "Dealer" sales division, the guys who sold all the other sports equipment, baseball, football, etc. His name was Bob Ferrera, and he was a great guy. On his first visit with me, we were both invited to play in a Pro Am. Poor Bob. Why do I say that? You'll know soon.

My New Boss #86

*H*IS NAME WAS BOB FERRERA, a really nice man. Bob was built like a fireplug, about 5'6" tall and wide. His sales career with Spalding was in the "Dealer" division selling all of our other products. The Dealer salesmen did not have a lot of knowledge about the golf business but these were the men who were always promoted to sales management positions, not guys from our professional golf division. Why, more about the reason later and why I asked for a job change.

Bob did not play a lot of golf, but tried. When I asked him what sports he played, he said football and baseball. He told me his position in baseball was first base! Now wait a minute, first base? I was a first baseman and I was 6'2" tall. If you never noticed first basemen were usually on the tall side so they had more reach to catch errant throws. They were also usually left handed because it was a more natural position for throwing a ground ball to second base if there was a runner on first to start a double play and they only had to pivot to throw to the catcher. I, as a right hander, had to pivot to throw the ball to all of the infielders except the catcher. The left hander was faster than the right hander delivering the ball to the others. Who ever heard of a short right handed first baseman? I told Bob he must have been one heck of a hitter that couldn't play any other position. He had a good sense of humor so he didn't fire me!

This was Bob's first visit to the Pittsburgh area and I had informed my customers in advance that my new boss was coming to town. There was a Pro Am scheduled the day he was to arrive and Ted Luther, the professional at the South Hills County Club holding the event, invited both of us to tee it up and play. I told Bob about it and he accepted the invitation. Ted paired us up with a professional partner and he had

240

Bob going off the first tee in the very first foursome because Bob was a visiting Spalding executive so to speak; Ted wanted to introduce Bob to all the golfers who were waiting their turn to play.

So there were quite a few people around the first tee and one would think it was a tour event without spectator ropes. With that many people watching anyone not used to that has to be nervous. Bob was used to playing baseball in front of people, and that was as part of a team. Golf is a lonely sport in some ways as it is just you, not a team. So Ted announces Bob and what his title is when it was his turn to hit. Poor Bob.

We did not go to the practice range and warm up so Bob is taking a few practice swings on the first tee. I am watching those swings and saying to myself, I hope he gets the ball airborne, as his practice swings were not pretty. Poor Bob. You could see he was nervous as he teed up his ball his hand was a little shaky. Poor Bob. All of a sudden there was complete quiet as Bob approached the ball. He aligned himself up, took a little waggle with his driver, looked down the fairway, back at his ball, took a mighty swing and completely missed the ball. Poor Bob. He darn near fell down. There was dead silence. Poor Bob, I could feel his embarrassment myself. What a guy though as he just started laughing at himself which broke the silence and everyone joined in with laughter and shouts of encouragement. He set up again, swung the club and probably hit the best drive of his life. What an ovation he received. That incident made him a very popular guy at cocktail hour. Everyone wanted to meet him personally and shake his hand. Poor Bob came away that day with a lot of new friends and respect as a stout man of 5'6" who could hit and play first base. He hit a grand slam home run that day with how he handled a very embarrassing moment.

Bob Ferrera won a lot of heats that day. He actually helped me and Spalding with his almost instant respect he was receiving from my customers. It got back to me some of them were thinking those guys from Spalding are OK. They were getting a different view of our company and our people. I could not overcome the fact that Wilson had a sales office and distribution warehouse in Pittsburgh with a pretty well liked salesman, Smiley Mcgee. MacGregor had a good following as well, but I was making inroads, as my sales began to climb so did my income. I was inching up to around $8,500.00 yearly. By the time I would change jobs within the company, at the six year mark, I was approaching the $10,000.00 number. Dee and I were used to getting along on a low income, so we didn't start spending a lot more, some yes but most of our bonus money went right into paying down on our mortgage. We knew it would not be long before we would have to find a larger house; our family was now up to four kids. And I was about to ask management a rather strange question for them to consider about my future with the company, a new venture.

REQUESTING A CAREER CHANGE #87

I AM ENJOYING THIS JOB, NO doubt about that. It has been a challenge, no doubt about that either. Fortunately many problems have been overcome but here are a couple of drawbacks to this job. Number one, from mid November to mid March, about four and one half months I am idle. There is no one to call on during the winter months. The rooms in our house are becoming smaller from all the coats of paint I have been applying in my spare time. I have also come to realize the structure of the Spalding sales management, all the District Sales Managers and the National Sales Manger that have been promoted from a sales position to sales management, have all been "Dealer" salesman. I have an itch, I wanted their jobs.

I also realize why the promotions came from the dealer salesforce. Up until now, the early sixties, golf equipment sales volume is no where near the volume of all the other sports Spalding is involved in. Baseball is number one of course. Baseballs, gloves, bats, catcher's equipment, shoes, hats, little league equipment and softball. Then there is all the football equipment, the popular J5-V ball, helmets, shoulder pads, all the protective pads, shoes, a full line of retail leather and rubber balls, kids equipment, b basketball, the popular leather Top Flite 100 ball used by the NBA exclusively to this day, a full line of leather and rubber balls, the "SS" basketball shoes. A full line of soccer balls, volleyballs, tennis balls, shoes and racquets. Then there is the retail golf club and ball line, a full range of price from junior clubs, ladies, left hand, starter sets, about four different price points, same for golf balls. And more that I can't think of.

It is no wonder sales managers are promoted from within that sales force and not the pro golf sales force. They have a complete knowledge of all of the products being offered by Spalding. They are also calling on many different types of customers. Sporting goods stores, Department stores, Jobbers, and others. At one time, I even called on K-Mart when there were only three stores, all in the Detroit area. I was a District sales manager then. I even remember the name of the man who had the golf club concession for those three stores, Bob Smallsreid. The dealer sales managers didn't know a thing about the professional golf business but would learn a little as they worked with their pro golf salesmen. The pro golf salesman just does not have the knowledge to be promoted as a sales manager whose job it was to manage both sales divisions and make as much contact as possible with retail and golf professional buyers, all this while dodging upper management demands.

I guess I am not one to sit still. If I have any chance of advancing with Spalding I decided I must consider changing sales jobs. I love a challenge, just like playing golf or any sport. So I approached management by requesting that they consider transferring me to a dealer sales territory. Well, you would think the world was coming to an end. My request started a rumble all the way to the top. Why would I want to do that, was the feedback when most dealer salesmen would love to have a soft job like the golf pro salesmen had, or so they thought. It was not as easy a job as they thought, but that is beside the point. I simply stated if I had any chance at all for advancement into sales management I had to learn about all the sporting goods business, not just golf.

At least I was making management aware I was interested in moving forward. That request made management aware of Bill Faulhaber as they never had been up until now as I was just another guy in the field sales force. Now they were taking notice, here is a guy who is not satisfied standing still.

There were a total of eight district sales manager positions in the country, that's not many opportunities as most did not leave those positions until they retired. Soon to be added was another district sales manager added along with a warehouse and sales office which would be located in Cleveland (Solon, Ohio). And Jim Shea would be promoted to that new position. There also was a small warehouse in Detroit with a showroom that would become the responsibility of the Cleveland district, and mine eventually.

CLOSE FRIEND'S FATAL ILLNESS #88

*N*OW THAT I HAVE MANE it known I wanted to change my career path by leaving the Golf Professional sales group to join the Dealer sales group, I discussed this with wife Dee that we might have to move to a different location if an opportunity presented itself. If I was not willing to do that then Spalding would loose interest in my request. Dee was more than cooperative full well knowing we have to go where the opportunity is. I also told my superiors I was in no hurry, however if the right situation should come available for both myself and Spalding I was ready to talk about it. Until that happens, business as usual. The year was 1961.

My good friend and neighbor Dick Flynn was going through a serious medical problem. He was seeking help from the doctors and trying to find out why he had no energy and he was loosing weight. Unfortunately, he was diagnosed with a very rare blood disorder. I don't remember what it was called but it was not something that could be treated, there was no cure. It was some kind of an iron buildup in his blood that had to be removed so his blood had to changed every so often and that kept Dick going for awhile.

Dick got to the point he couldn't work and I made it a point to get him out of the house once in awhile by taking him with me while I was making local calls. One day as we passed a cemetery he looked over and muttered under his breath, just loud enough that I could hear, "I'll be in there soon." I didn't know what to say, I don't know of any words I could have used in reply to his remark. I acted like I did not hear him and it became a little hard for me to see the road. There was not one damn thing I could think of to respond, so I didn't. Soon after, Dick passed away. He was 38 years old leaving behind a wonderful young wife and two young children. Dick, his wife Doris, Dee and I got together at least once a week for a little card playing, bridge. We drank our share of beer, Dick and I. It there was a shortage of cheese and crackers back then, blame Dick and me.

Life is so fragile. I just never imagined I would loose three close friends at my age, and their young age in the span of about six years. First, Carl Singhouse was 36, cancer, then Regis Burke 30, car accident, and Dick Flynn. Regis was 6 days younger than me. They were so young, so very young. Sure makes one look at life differently. We have to accept what Gods plan was for all of us.

I am now nearing six years with Spalding. My income is inching towards $10,000.00 for my sixth year. I received a call from my superiors, they wanted to come to Pittsburgh and talk to me about a possible move into the Dealer sales division. That's all I knew, no word where or when, until they arrived. "They" were my District Sales Manger and the National Sales Manager. I was in for a shock. I was informed that this meeting was to be kept between the three of us due to the fact they were going to replace the salesman in my area, Pittsburgh! The very man that led me to the job I have! Was I shocked? Yes and no. Unfortunately the man asked to accept retirement, had a serious drinking problem I was well aware of. It had been going on for years. When I passed by a certain bar on Liberty Ave in Dormont, where I lived, I would see his station wagon parked there in the morning and it was still there in the late afternoon as well. Every day, he was making his calls via the pay phone in the bar. These bars were drinking establishments that by law had to serve some type of food, but did not have to be a restaurant. As long as they served snacks, like Andy's Loop Café offered a plate of swiss cheese, or a plate of sliced ham, some pickled hard boiled eggs, chips and pretzels, that is all they had to do. I don't know any bar's like that around here any more. The only bar's I know of are now located in restaurants.

My superiors were in town to meet with him and I think he probably new what was coming. Until all of that was settled, he had many years with Spalding and was fully vested in the retirement program, so he was not being let go without some kind of income. Until that was completed,

I was not to talk to anyone. I was chosen to replace him. My request was being fulfilled and we didn't even have to relocate! However this new opportunity did not come without pain. The man I was replacing was a friend who was instrumental in my gaining employment with this so well known company, A. G. Spalding & Bros.

I was not happy about how I entered into my new position as I felt badly about how it all came about. There was nothing I could have done to prevent my friend's demise as he brought it all on himself. It's too bad he could not have gotten some help along the way. So I am starting a new venture.

STARTING MY CAREER CHANGE #89

*I*N A BIG HOLE! BEFORE we get to that, I wanted to make this transaction as easy on management as I could, because they also had to replace me. I had someone in mind in advance and in confidence I talked to this person about the fact that I may be changing jobs sometime in the future. I wanted to know if he would be interested, and he was. I had to caution him that I did not have the say so of who would be my replacement. I could only guarantee that he would be interviewed and I would very strongly recommend him for the position. There was a problem, he was fifty years old! That's not old my today's standards but 55 years ago it was. His name was Tony Joy. Tony was of Italian decent, was a golf professional and was an independent rep selling a line of golf accessories on a straight commission basis and paying his own expenses. He was not getting rich, that's for sure. Tony had been an excellent player back in the days when there really wasn't a tour as we know it. He played back in the thirties and forties, depression and war years. Tony played with the likes of Sam Snead, who he knew very well. Tony couldn't make a living playing professionally. Hardly anyone could in those years. Life was not easy for Tony, a very likeable good looking individual.

When the time came management had no one in mind for my replacement and was open to suggestions. When I recommended Tony Joy and told them his background and age, they almost flipped. I knew how hard Tony worked and how well the golf pros liked and respected Tony. I convinced management that they would be hiring a winner, a man who I guaranteed would make more calls than any young person. I witnessed that for a number of years. I told management they could expect fifteen solid years out of Tony. He was in great shape and did not look his age either. I asked management how many salesmen lasted fifteen years, not many. What did they have to loose by giving Tony a chance. Tony was hired and he did exactly what I had predicted. Tony came to me and asked me how many calls did I generally make in a day, because he didn't want me to look bad when he turned in his daily reports! I told Tony if he could make more calls than I did, there must be thirty hours in a day. I told Tony to do his thing and not worry about something like that as I was no loafer. Tony did work for fifteen years and was a complete success retiring at age 65 with a Spalding pension. End to a good story, now, back to mine.

I was starting my new venture as I said, in a big hole! This was not a promotion, it was a career change of my choosing, no increase in compensation. I actually would be taking a loss for a whileuntil I can rebuild this run down territory! Of course it was my decision so I could learn more about our companies business, giving me a chance for further advancement into possible management opportunities. I had to look at this change as my college education so to speak, another learning curve was before me. I was nearing the ten thousand dollar income level in the position of golf professional salesman and now I was looking at drop in income my first year in this territory.

My first project I encountered was with Dave Lando, the owner of the largest sporting goods retail store and team equipment dealer in Pittsburgh. Our departing salesman sold his samples, everything he had to Dave after finding out he was being replaced. Dave said his warehouse personnel could not figure out what they received versa what they were invoiced for those samples. Salesman receives samples of almost every item offered for sale and these samples are billed to the salesman at 25% off the wholesale price. When the salesman is finished covering his territory showing a majority of these samples, some items no longer appear brand new. So this discount makes it easier to sell them to a customer. It's a good deal for the customer as most of these items can be sold as brand new. The slightly worn samples would be slightly discounted at retail as not brand new but as a little "Shop worn".

I had to take an inventory of these samples to figure out what the problem was. The weather was early winter and their warehouse was not heated. I was freezing. After recording every item I started to cross check these items against the invoice. What I found was a number of very old baseball gloves and protective equipment along with other old items no longer in our present line. Some of this stuff had to be up to ten years old and some items were worthless goods. I finally got this problem resolved. Not the best way to start a new job. It was difficult because I was not familiar with these products or the code numbers but somehow I got the job done.

Dave Lando was a very hard person for our management to get along with. He was very demanding and never believed he was getting the best price available from us. Kind of like the problem I had with Bill Powell, the black man who owned a golf course back in Canton, Ohio. I would say it was around six months when I had a similar conversation with Dave that I had years ago with Bill Powell. Dave became more receptive to me and Spalding as I earned his trust over time. Dave and I became pretty close eventually. Our sales improved dramatically with him and my management wanted to know what I did that they could not accomplish with Dave. I said I was honest with him and convinced him he would not be ignored any longer, he should not concern himself about not getting the best price. I simply showed him our quantity pricing and he would be a preferred customer as far as any special pricing was being offered and would also be given the opportunity of purchasing any discontinued merchandise available at discounted price. I made sure all of these promises were kept.

My new territory was almost the same as my old one so I still traveled to my old home town, Canton. I had no problems meeting my new customers. They welcomed me with open arms as they had not seen too much of their Spalding salesman in person very often. When meeting each one I asked them for their help! When you ask someone for their help, they are usually pretty interested in what you have to say and are eager to help if the request is honest and reasonable. My general approach was, "Mr. Jones, I know nothing about your business. At this point I don't even know my own line of equipment. I have a lot to learn and I would appreciate your helping me by being patient with me. I do know something about golf as I have been involved with our professional golf division for six years. If you need help with your golf department and sales people I know I can help you with that."

Most people are flattered when they are asked for their help. This approach seemed to work very well. In sort time I learned enough to get along until I really learned the business. It can be complicated at first as there are a number of different type businesses to call on. For example there are the general retail sporting goods stores, and then there are some who also specialize in team equipment sales. Then I have to deal with department stores, wholesalers and jobbers who buy and resell to various retail stores that only carry a small about of sports equipment. When I first got into this area of the business there were no K-Marts. No big box stores and operations like Sears were national accounts.

There were no golf only specialty stores either, they came later. The golf products sold to these retailers was different than the professional only line. I'll explain the retailer's golf business and the difference in the products first, and then get into some other interesting facts about my new venture and the retail golf business.

*T*HERE WERE TWO DIFFERENT GOLF club and ball offerings by all the companies. The golf professional line sold only to on course golf shops and the "Retail" line which was different and sold to Sporting goods stores, Department stores, Jobbers and national chain stores such as Sears. The national stores were handled by the national accounts people so I will not be commenting on that part of the business.

Our top of the line clubs and balls were the Robert T. Jones, Jr. registered men's clubs and our ladies clubs were the Marylyn Smith line and the golf balls were the Air-Flite and Kro-Flite brands. These items were sold to all the accounts mentioned above. When it came to the middle of the line clubs, this became a little confusing when there were mutable stores in a close proximity. For instance, there were three department stores in Pittsburgh which competed with one another, Horne's, Gimbels and Kaufmanns. When it came to the middle of the line autograph clubs, we offered each store a different name that we would not sell to anyone else in the Pittsburgh area. Some of the available autograph names we offered were Dave Stockton, Al Geiberger, Don January, Chi Chi Rodriguez, Jerry Barber, Johnny Pott, Dave Ragan and ladies Peggy Kirk Bell, Sandra Haynie, Betty Jamison, Wiffy Smith, and Mary Lena Faulk. Each department store would have a different name and I offered the same programs to the various large sorting goods stores clustered close to each other. Each individual business had different name clubs which eliminated a price war to compete with each other with the same player's name.

The retail golf business was a small part of the overall sporting goods business. Remember this was in the early sixties and up to now there was not much golf on TV. Arnold Palmer was a big factor making the sport more popular, including the blue collar set, the working man. Then three others came into the picture to make it more exciting for the public. They were Jack Nicklaus, Gary Player and Billy Casper. Why in the era it was the big three and not the big four is anyone's guess. Billy Casper, who shared the same birthday as my wife Dee, June 24, 1931, was one of the most underrated players of all time. Billy just passed away in February 2015. So was Hubert Green underrated, ever heard of him? I was sitting with Hubert having a chat one day at the Firestone County Club in Akron, Ohio. Hubert was pretty outspoken sometimes and I suppose for a reason. It may have been because of what he told me that day. He said that he felt he was not getting the recognition he deserved because at that time he had won 19 times, including 2 major tournaments. There are only a handful of players who had won as much as Hubert Green. I personally liked Hubert, we got along well and I felt he was absolutely correct. At that time the big three were in full swing and "Hubbie", as his friends called him, was really left out.

I will always remember the first time I saw Jack Nicklaus, he was playing in the Western Open, a fifth major back then. This tournament was always held in the Chicago area, except the year I am writing about, it was held at the Pittsburgh Field Club in the late fifties, I don't remember the year, and I am not going to look it up. I also have no idea why it was held outside of Chicago that year. Let's see, Jack just turned 75, he was still going to Ohio State and an amateur at the time he was 19, so that would have been 1958 or 1959. Jack was "Chubby" then and his blonde hair style was a crew cut. The clothing Jack always seemed to wear was a white shirt and kaki slacks, really dull looking in those days when golf clothing was rather loud.

Where am I going with all of this? I mentioned that TV golf coverage being very small. That started to change and was getting better as the game of golf began to grow, and golf equipment sales were growing as well. Enough about the retail golf business for now. I will be getting back into more golf in the near future, but now my focus is on the sporting goods industry, my new venture for the next three years in Pittsburgh. But now its time to look for larger living quarters, a bigger house, and our family is growing also.

A Bigger House #91

I HAVE TO STEP AWAY FROM the sporting goods business for awhile as Dee and I have to find a larger house for our growing family. The four kids are getting older and our small one story and a half bungalow is getting cramped, plus the fact that two of our youngest, one girl and one boy are sharing a bedroom. That's alright when they are still in diapers but they are getting the point in age where they need their privacy. Although I was not making a lot of money I had been putting most of my bonus income towards our present mortgage and paying all bills when I received them well before the due dates. We have established good credit and we were way ahead of our payments on our present home, so we had very good equity built up. We owned more of our house that we owed and felt our financial situation was sound enough to purchase a more expensive and larger home.

We liked our neighborhood and it was an affordable community for us plus the schools were acceptable as well. Everything was convenient, a grocery store only a couple of blocks away, Dee did not have a driver's license at this time either. We didn't have to look far; just two blocks away we found our next home. I have to describe the area and the home, both were unique. I don't remember how old this house was. It was located on Earlsmere drive on a corner lot. The house faced the south. On the west side was Dormont Ave. There was an alley in back of the house, the north side. Earlsmere was not a level street it went up hill from the west to the east and Dormont Ave went up hill from north to south, which means the front of the house the ground sloped towards the west. In other words, the back of the house the basement level was exposed and the garage was in the basement, located on the same level as the alley.

The home was originally built as a model home. It was a dark colored brick construction with a slate roof. On the first floor was the main entrance, then the living and dining room, the kitchen and dinette and half a bathroom. Second floor were three bedrooms and a full bathroom. On the third floor, yes, I said third floor, there were two more bedrooms and a full bathroom! There were five bedrooms and two and one half bathrooms. The house in back looked like a hotel. There were four floors and the top floor the roof came to a peak, which was about 6 feet above the top of the window. From the concrete driveway looking up there was the garage, first floor, second floor and third floor. That's four sections plus the distance to the tallest part of the roof. And the wood trim at the very top needed painted! That is a real story to write about and scary too.

The house also had internal built in vacuum system and it was steam heated. There were cast iron radiators in each room. The house had it all except a nice kitchen. We paid $21,000.00 and had the kitchen totally remolded for $3,000.00. We now have a total investment of $24,000.00. Shortly before we bought the house, my mom and dad were visiting and they were still living in Buffalo, Orchard Park, NY actually. We told them we were thinking about buying this larger house. I asked my dad if I could borrow a thousand dollars for a short period of time to help with the down payment. Dad said, "Bill, you don't need a bigger house." That was his way of saying no. That was also his way of telling me to be my own man. I said, "OK dad, we are buying that house without your help. When you visit, we might even find a guest room for you and mom". Just kidding him a little bit.

Other than the kitchen, the house was in good shape. Most rooms needed repainted but that was not a problem as I was taught how to hold a brush properly and how to paint by dad. I painted our original home inside and out and that is another story for tomorrow.

One more thing, directly across the street from our new home was a little league baseball field which was part of a very large park. Just a little further towards the north in the park was the Dormont swimming pool for residence of the community. It was huge and in the winter it was not drained but was frozen over and was used as an ice skating rink.

I didn't ice skate but Dee and the kids started to skate. I did watch a lot of little league baseball however. And more when my son Jim came of age to play, but that was after we moved again. We would only be in this house about two and one half years but during that time I was learning the sporting goods business.

THE SPORTING GOODS BUSINESS #92

I THINK IT IS INTERESTING TO note that many products were produced by companies for other companies. That may sound confusing, I will attempt to explain. For instance, at one time Spalding made baseballs for Rawlings and other companies and Rawlings made baseball gloves for Spalding plus protective equipment, both baseball and football. Spalding baseball bats were made by the Louisville Slugger people, Hillerich & Bradsby. Wilson made the Spalding golf bag line and Spalding made all the tennis rackets for Wilson. The Wilson Jack Kramer racket was the top seller by far. The Spalding Poncho Gonzales racket was the same as the Kramer with different markings however its sales were not even close. Wilson did a much better job promoting tennis than Spalding, that's a fact. Spalding eventually built its own golf bag plant in Ava, Mo.

This goes much deeper but this gives you a fair idea. For many years Spalding had the baseball contract with the National League, Spalding #1 and the American League, the Reach #0, the Reach Wright & Ditson name was owned by Spalding. These balls were the same except the stitching; one had all red stitching and the other a blue and red combination. Spalding made all baseballs and softballs in Chicopee for years. All baseballs and softballs are still hand stitched. Explaining how they were stitched is difficult but I'll give it a try. All I saw were ladies doing this, ladies I would not want to meet in a dark alley. What they had to do eight hours a day is hard to imagine and they were paid on a piece basis, not by the hour.

Try and picture these ladies sitting on a stool with a high small table holding a wooden vice in front of them that which held a baseball ready for its cover to be sewn on. These two piece covers are placed

around the ball and the stitching begins. In each hand these ladies hold
a large half round curved needle with a very long thread attached. The
covers have very small holes punched in them where the thread is to go
through. Once the first stitch is placed through the cover, one with each
needle, the motion is to pull the thread straight up pulling the thread
through, then swings the arms outward and down towards the floor
so the thread follows the motion of the needles. Then the two curved
needles are place in the next two holes, pulled through and the same
motions are repeated, all the while the ladies turn the ball in the vice
as needed so the next holes are exposed until the entire ball is sewn. I
forget the total number of stitches required. Not only are these "Girls"
arms built up, there are other certain parts of their body that are built
up as well. Get the whole picture? If I got into a fight, I would want
them on my side, believe me. Unfortunately it became to expensive to
continue manufacturing baseballs and softballs in the U.S., and all these
jobs went overseas.

The Spalding contract was a loosing proposition with the major
leagues as most of the balls were given to them under the cost to make
them. Since our balls were the adopted ball of the major leagues, all
minor leagues used them as well, but at the normal wholesale price.
The filter down effect was that most baseball leagues, colleges, and
high schools used the Spalding baseballs and that is where Spalding
made its profit. Albert G. Spalding was a famous pitcher in Chicago in
the 1980's and his founding of the company In 1876 was first making
baseballs which were used exclusively until sometime in the 1960's, then
Rawlings took over the contract. The minor leagues were becoming
fewer and fewer, independent leagues were disappearing. Spalding
actually asked there salesmen to vote it they thought it would hurt our
baseball business with their customers if we dropped our agreement
with the major leagues. The salesmen voted to drop it and move on.

Also around that time Spading purchased the Rawlings Sporting
Goods Co., Spalding was into baseball in a big way and so was Rawlings.
Remember I said Rawlings made the Spalding gloves. Between the two
companies the government finally stepped in with their monopoly laws
claiming we had indeed created such a situation in the baseball business.

Spalding was ordered by the courts to divest itself of the Rawlings Company. What a shame, Rawlings was and is a very good quality company. I personally thought we should have fought that ruling. On what grounds you might ask? You may ask and I'll tell you my thoughts on this subject, wrong or right, about the baseball monopoly ruling in my next chapter.

BASEBALL MONOPOLY #93

*W*HY DO I THINK SPALDING should have challenged our Government's decision that the Spalding/Rawlings merger had created a baseball monopoly situation? Because when all this was happening the Japanese were entering the baseball business in the United States in a big way and their baseball gloves were about twice as big as the gloves we were manufacturing at that time. These Japanese gloves were much bigger and better with a wholesale price much lower as well. The Japanese gloves killed our business, and there was no way we had a monopoly at that point. The American made baseball gloves could not compete, the glove business changed in a rising sun beat. We had to start acquiring our gloves made in Japan as well or drop out of the business. The majority of the baseball business had gone overseas. Can you imagine how many U.S. jobs were lost? Have things changed much since then? Look at almost anything you pick up, you see China and other countries on almost everything. How often do you see "Made in the U.S.A.?"

Did you know that footballs were made inside and out? The guys in the factory making footballs had arms on them that could match the ladies stitching baseballs, but not the other parts. Anyway, footballs were stitched inside out; they were put on a wooden dowel and worked by hand to turn itself back through the area of the lacing, which was only about one quarter the size of the ball. Watching this operation there was no way i would want to shake hands with them. Chicopee was filled with a lot of people who looked like Popeye. I won't touch the subject of Olive Oil.

While we are on the subject of footballs, during my years in the business the most popular footballs were Wilson, its ball is the official ball used by the National Football League, and the Spalding J5V. Both balls are the most popular in college and high schools. On the other hand in the world of basketball the Spalding "100" is the official ball of the National Basketball Association, and used heavily by Colleges and high schools.

Spalding was not in the uniform business, other than offering football shoes and the popular "SS" basketball shoe, the sole of which had two S's in its design, and tennis shoes. The tennis business as far as I was concerned was an afterthought for us. We did little to promote our tennis line of products as far as I could see. I felt we never put much money and push to gain market share in the tennis business. And we were making about 95% of the rackets made in the U.S. at one time but we let everyone else outsell us because, in my opinion, they spent much more money on promotion and advertising and signing top players. Hey, not everything is rosy with the company you work for. You just suck it up and do the best you can with what you're given.

Salesman sales are only as good as the pull through of the product the salesman places on the retailer's shelf! That's a salesman's job. Making the public aware of that product is the marketing department's job, which can only do so much as well. It has to have the backing of top management and the company owners who handle the purse strings, the money and man power to get the job done. Proper advertising and promotion to generate pull through of the product is what makes a salesman look good and a company successful. That is really the only way to meet sales quotas given to the salesman as long as that salesman gets the product on the shelf. Spoken like a true salesman. Sales management does not like to hear salesman say that. They have enough to do being the buffer between the sales force and top management, especially when top management is maybe not top management, again my opinion.

Getting back to my new responsibilities, I had to learn how to cover my territory. The golf professional salesmen have only one major selling trip to make with one product line, golf. Dealer salesmen had the fall line, football, basketball, soccer included. The spring line of golf, tennis, baseball, softball, tennis and so on. Two important trips around the territory are needed, the fall line was presented in the spring and the spring line is presented in the fall. Both required sample room set ups in major areas of the territory. At least in this business in the north, unlike golf when winter set in we were idle until spring, we could work twelve months of the year.

How were two major selling trips accomplished? One big undertaking about which I will attempt to paint a picture for your viewing, hotel sample rooms coming up.

Hotel Sample Rooms #94

*F*IRST THERE IS ONE HECK of a lot of planning. What samples am I going to be able to stuff into my station wagon? Packing samples became an art and the front seat was for my suitcase, briefcase and customer files with past history and what goals I have set for presentation to each customer this trip. Samples were packed to the ceiling so a very good pair of side view mirrors was a must. The other rear view mirror would only reveal my samples. Motels in those days were limited. Hotels had special rooms that were used with ample room for displaying products and most were a combination of a bed, bathroom, display space and a desk. I stayed in my sample room which helped cut expenses. This trip was by appointment only and customers had to be contacted days in advance and each given enough time to cover the items most important to that customer. Not every appointment had the same time frame. I had to know my customers needs and their personality as well. Some like to linger, others were very fast and had to be slowed down sometimes. This you don't know on your first trip, its something you pick up as quickly as you can.

Depending on the driving time, the first trip day is getting there, checking into the hotel, getting the bell boys with enough carts to transport everything in the wagon into my sample room, including all the display holders. Then displaying the samples on tables covered with white sheets. Besides the samples I had to pack display items, such as ball holders. These items stacked one on top if the other so they did not take up too much space. We had one holder that could be used for baseball gloves, footballs, basketballs and other assorted items, so it was very versatile. Before setting up it was time to sit down and call every customer I have made an appointment with letting them know I have arrived and confirm the appointment. The phone call is a reminder of their appointment and if there is a problem we can resolve it before it becomes a bigger problem.

Again, I never used an order form to write down what was being ordered. I learned my lesson years ago and my method worked for me. I would use my tablet and rewrite the order later and mail the customer his copy later. I never had a problem with any of my customers doing this. When you use a sample room like this, the hours are extremely long. It is not an 8 to 5 day. Appointments are scheduled early in the morning and into the evening as well. I have a small bar set up for the cocktail hour. Some appointments are for lunch and some for dinner. The few free minuets are used to prepare for the next customer and rewriting my orders. That can go on until I have to finally hit the sack for some much needed sleep, usually around midnight.

When finished with one area I pack up and get the bell boys help. I have to repack my wagon and move on to the next location. When I was in my home base of Pittsburgh, because of the large base of different kinds of customers, I was in the sample room for more than a week. I slept in the sample room most of the time because of the late appointments and the need to finish the heavy paper work. Not every night, I had to see Dee and the kids too. These sample rooms twice a year would make or break the year. So it was very important to put in the time needed to be successful.

Another thing to remember is that there were no calculators in those days, I did it all the old way, pencil and paper, adding, subtracting, multiply by the old hand and mind method. No computers, we used the mail to send in our orders except something a customer was in need of at once I would use the phone. Yes, we had phones back then. Hey, what I am writing about was only 50 some years ago!

Another thing happened to me along the way; I lost any feel for penmanship. Since I started with Spalding all the orders I wrote destroyed any ability I had to write longhand. To this day I print everything. All those order forms had a least three copies and two sheets of carbon paper to make the copies. Of the three copies, one was the original, then the customer copy and the salesman's copy. I had to press hard to get a clear third copy through 5 pieces of paper. I used single letters and printed them in upper case. To his day, I print everything. I have not tried to write long hand for sixty years, except my signature, which is almost a complete straight line since my friend Arthur started to help me with my usual daily routine. Isn't it funny how one can form habits like going to the bathroom and brushing your teeth, not necessarily in that order either?

When I was in a highly populated area large enough to have more than one sporting goods store, those stores would feature one company's equipment. Some stores are more team equipment minded than others, dealing in outfitting teams with protective gear and uniforms as well. One might feature Wilson, another MacGregor, another Riddell, Spalding, or Rawlings. When it comes to public schools, purchasing large amount of equipment is done by bids and I think how that was done is interesting

Bids & Team Equipment #95

*S*PALDING WAS NOT BEEN MUCH of a factor in supplying very much protective football equipment purchased by schools through the bidding system in the Pittsburgh area, except for the very popular J5V football. We also did well with the Spalding 100 basketball but we were not known very well for our football protective equipment since we did not make any of it ourselves. Most was made for us by Rawlings and the Riddell company was very big with their equipment, especially their helmets. Wilson was a heavy hitter as well.

I had no team equipment dealer pushing, or bidding Spalding, except balls. There was a small sporting goods store near where I lived run by the Sodini brothers, a couple of nice guys who did feature Spalding, but they were not into the team equipment business. I approached them on the idea of getting involved but they were not very interested in all the work involved, and the very small profit that bids usually created. I ask them if I did all the work, would they be willing to go along with it as I needed to get some of that business and they agreed.

There was a lot of research to do. I had to go to the purchasing office for the public schools and ask for a copy of the lasts bids which are public record, so I could get a feel for not only what the equipment was up for bid and the prices all the other team equipment dealers bid. Except for balls, there were no Spalding items on these bids. The bids were asking for certain brand names and or equivalents, which opened the door. If it was Rawlings it was easy to figure out what our matching item was because ours was similar to theirs. Others I had to figure out as closely as I could. Do you know all shoulder pads are not the same design and size? The largest by size are used by the linemen. Different positions use different pads depending on how much running, catching and what certain defensive players are required to do. Some positions need smaller and lighter pads. The smallest shoulder pads are used by quarterbacks because they need extra movement of their arms and shoulders to be able to throw the ball.

I was somewhat successful as we did win some bids on several items. That got the Spalding name on the next bids so other team dealers started to bid on some of those items in the next round of bids. There is much more to this business but what I have touched on is enough for now. I think I am painting the picture of how much different the dealer business versus the pro golf business and why sales management positions are filled from the ranks of the general sporting goods business. As a matter of fact, about the first year I entered this new venture, a new district was created which included my territory and eventually my future as well. I would no longer be working out of the Philadelphia district. To create the new district Spalding took my area from the Philadelphia district and from the Chicago Midwest District Spalding used Michigan, Indiana, Ohio, Kentucky and Western Pa. That left the Chicago District with Illinois, Wisconsin, Minnesota, North and South Dakota, and Nebraska.

The new district was being planned for several years. Jim Shea, who was from the east and a dealer salesman was transferred to the Cleveland area to work in that territory for a couple of years and then was appointed the new District Sales Manager after the new warehouse, offices and showroom was constructed in Solon, Ohio, which was about fifteen miles south east of Cleveland. That area would become my home in a few years. I now have a new boss, more about all that later.

There are national trade shows in both the golf professional and sporting goods business. I never attended the PGA Show while a salesman in Pittsburgh. In those years the show was not very large and there was no need for a guy in Pittsburgh to be in attendance. The sporting goods business was quite different; the National Sporting Goods Association hosted its show in Chicago during the middle of winter when the weather is nice and balmy! So my first show was an eye opener.

NATIONAL SPORTING GOODS SHOW #96

I WOULD ATTEND THIS SHOW EVERY year for the next six years. We did not stay at the Palmer House where the show was held. We stayed in another hotel and I can not remember the name at the moment. It was about three blocks away and the blocks in Chicago are like most cities, they are very large. It seemed like it was a half a mile from our hotel to the Palmer House. We took a cab if possible because the weather in Chicago is brutal and it is always windy. Most of the time we walked the distance in our street shoes, overcoat and dress hat which were popular in those days.

One year the temperature did not reach zero degrees during the week we were there. The windows in the hotel had thick frost on the inside. The wake up call would be around 6 AM and this is what I heard when I answered. "It's six o'clock and it is minus 18 degrees!" Every morning, "It's minus 21 degrees!" I have never been so cold in my life. We could not get a cab and I could not walk those three blocks without ducking into another building along the way for a few minuets to catch my breath. The first time I did this I was wearing horn rim classes, the style then. As I went out the door and headed into the wind in two minuets my glasses fell off my face. The cold temperature spread the arms of the glasses outward and they just dropped to the ground. After that I put my glasses in my coat pocket until I arrived at the Palmer House. I didn't know anything about Florida in those days, having never been there. Boy, do I look back on those days now. I know this is cruel, but now I don't know why anyone would live in the north if they didn't have too.

Back inside the Palmer House I don't think the temperature ever got over 70 degrees either. The show was very large and I did have many of my customers attending but for the most part they did not come to buy from me because my fall sample show rooms provided for their needs. We would offer specials at the show so additional sales were generated, plus any odds and ends that needed to be taken care of was finalized. We hosted cocktail parties for invited customers so it was a great time to entertain my accounts. The show was more social than business for me because I have already taken care of my customers with my sample room appointments.

Most companies had famous athletes that were on their consultant staffs in attendance as well. I can't begin to remember all that we had there over the years. These celebrities would roam around and visit other company's displays so we would meet more than just the ones we had in attendance. We had people like Poncho Gonzales the tennis great, basketball players Rick Berry, Jerry Lucas, Wilt Chamberlain, Gail Goodrich, baseball players Whitey Ford, Roger Maris, Jim Palmer, various football personalities as well. Those are just a few names to give you an idea. The one that impressed me the most was Wilt Chamberlain, all 7' 2"! I was 6" 2" and I almost broke my neck looking up, and up, and up. On TV he looked really thin, but in person he was just a very large individual. I have never seen anyone that tall and big. He was a really nice guy, very friendly and good conversationalist. Actually almost all of them were really good down to earth guys. We had a good staff of guys we could be proud of.

We also had a man whose name was Duke Zilber and he headed up our promotional department. Also our district and the Chicago district salesman mixed together very well and we enjoyed getting together with them. I'll write about both of the above next

DUKE & TWO DISTRICTS SALESMEN #97

*D*UKE ZILBER WAS ONE HECK of a guy and he and I became close friends over the years. He grew up in baseball as a businessman who at one time headed up a minor league operation for the Cleveland Indian organization. He provided me with a pass that would get me into any major league baseball game no charge, both the American and National league. He was known by everyone in every sport. You hear about a person who seems to know everyone, but Duke not only was in that category, everyone who was anyone in sports knew Duke. That is a big difference, people knowing who you are as opposed to you knowing who they are. See the difference? Duke was in charge of our promotional Department and responsible for signing athletes to contracts in every sport except golf. Our overall consultant staff in all sports needed an overhaul and when Duke came aboard all that changed as Duke did a wonderful job of singing many great athletes to Spalding contracts.

One of my highlights with Duke was when he called me and asked me if I wanted to attend the final World Series game between the New York Yankees and the Pittsburgh Pirates being played in Pittsburgh in 1960. Of course I jumped at that opportunity.

The series was tied and this was the final game and Duke promptly informed me that Pittsburgh had no chance against the power house Yankees. I answered him and said, "Duke, if you don't think the Pirates have a chance, then why is this series tied at three games apiece?" I continued to give him a hard time as I loved to kid him, "Duke, this Pirate team has been making comebacks all year long and I'll just bet you five bucks they win the series'. He accepted the bet and there we were sitting side my side, Duke pulling for the Yankees and I keep telling him to pay me the five bucks even before the game is over. Then we get to the bottom of the ninth inning and the game was tied. I turned to Duke and said, "I hate to take your money. This game is over the Pirates are going to win it in this inning."

He was getting a little flustered and a little nervous as well. Then it happened, you sports fans may remember this. Bill Mazeroski, the second baseman for the Pirates was at the bat and 'Wham' he hits a home run. Game over, the Pirates win the World Series over the mighty Yankees! What a day and I got to witness one of the most famous home runs of all time. Got a free seat and five bucks too! Love you Duke, I know you're in baseball heaven, remember that home run my friend?

When Jim Shea was promoted to District Manager he hired Jack Stanton to take his place as the dealer salesman in Cleveland and northern Ohio. Jack was a very funny guy, not by telling jokes; he was just off the cuff humorous. When he presented items to the customer I don't think they knew what the hell he was talking about, they just purchased what he suggested and that was it. They all left laughing, most with tears in their eyes.

I'll give you an example. When the large baseball gloves came on the market the fielder's gloves had a slit in the back of the glove that a player could put their index finger through. The purpose was getting the index finger out of the pocket area where the ball would slam into it, so the index finger was protected better with the extra thickness. Jack would show the glove to his customer, put his left hand into the glove with his index finger through the slit in the back of the glove and pounded his right fist into the pocket and then lift the glove to his face and pretend to pick his nose. Jack explained that is what the slit in the glove was crated for.

You had to be there, the way Jack did that was funny, really funny and not offensive at all. Jack was a stocky guy and a pretty good athlete and he could throw a football 60 yards. He was a really good guy and I hope he is up there keeping Duke laughing.

For the next two years I worked with Jim Shea as my boss. When we went to the show in Chicago, our sales district's guys and the Chicago district guys got together during the show and in the evenings for the cocktail parties and beyond, most of us hung out together and just had a lot of good clean fun. I won't go into all the names of all the guys but one salesman from Indiana name was Jack Julian. Now we have two Jacks with equally funny humor. When these two got together all hell broke loose. They should have been on TV. Nothing was planned, their humor was spontaneous off the cuff, quick and funny as any two guys you have ever seen. When I came home from being with these two guys, which was at least a five year run, my stomach hurt so much from laughter it took several days for the pain to finally settle down,

I try and tell another story that also happened in Chicago when the two Jacks, Jim Shea and I went to dinner one evening. This is one of the funniest things I have ever been a part of and will take some time to tell it, so I will attempt to recreate that evening. I only hope I can paint this picture the way it played out it won't be easy to do. I'll give it my best shot in chapter, "The Dinner # 98".

The Dinner #98

*W*E WERE AT A TRADE show and with a District Sales Manager who had an expense account larger than ours so you know it was a very good restaurant as he was going to pick up the check. There were four of us, myself, Jim Shea the DM, Jack Stanton and Jack Julian, who was wearing a pair of sun glasses. It was evening so I have no idea why he would be wearing dark sunglasses. He didn't have an eye problem so maybe he just forgot to take them off as it turned dark. I'm glad he didn't because those glasses got us past a long line of people standing behind a rope waiting for an empty table. This place did not take reservations and there was a pretty long wait.

I will try and paint a picture of this event for you. I'll use last names now since their first name is the same. Julian is acting a little odd with those dark glasses and we are not being loud, just talking with one another while standing in line and the head waiter assumed on his own that Julian was blind! The head waiter spoke to the people in front of us and asked them if they minded it he sat our group ahead of them because he explained one had a serious handicap.

Julian didn't say a word, reached over and took hold of Stanton's arm as a blind person would do for assistance and away we went to the front of the line and to a table. Well that set the stage and there was no turning back, Julian was blind and Stanton was his guide. What next? Unbelievable, sometimes funny, sometimes not and at one point it almost got dangerous.

These two clowns started to put on a show. Jim Shea and I were straight men just keeping out of their way. We were all in our early to mid thirties, this was about 1963 or 64 and we were all dressed in coat and ties. The tables were very close together, almost touching elbows.

The people around us watched as we were being seated and Julian fumbled around a bit getting into his chair, as a blind person might, so the people around us thought he must be blind. His actions at the table convinced them as he would gingerly reach for the glass of water, tough it gently before picking it up for a sip. Everyone smoked cigarettes in those days and Stanton made it a point of lighting Julian's cigarette and taking his hand to let him know where the ash tray was.

We received our cocktails and the show continued. Stanton placed Julian's drink in his hand and said something like he was getting tired of doing everything for him, loud enough for the people around us could hear, and it seemed they were really paying attention to our table, unfortunately.

One nice looking lady whose elbow was close to Julian's said hello and asked Julian if everything was alright, as Stanton was starting to put on an act of being a little rude to this blind guy. Julian said everything was fine that he and his friend like to kid each other. She said something about she was sorry about his problem and Julian cut her off a bit with something like being blind helped activate many of his other senses, like hearing, and touch. Now get this one, he knew she was wearing a sweater as Chicago is cold. It looked like cashmere which was very popular then and the sweater sleeve came down to her elbow. So he said to her that he could tell fabrics by touching them and she is sitting with a gentleman and another couple. That didn't stop Julian as he said to her, "I'll bet you're wearing a sweater tonight as it is really cold." She said yes she was. Julian continued, "I can tell you what different clothing material is by touching the fabric," This lady says to Julian that she is wearing a sweater and extended her arm in such a manner that Julian could only touch her sweater at her elbow. So up her arm he went with his fingers, her male companion watching all of this closely. Julian reached her sweater, pinched and rolled the sweater fabric for a few tantalizing moments in his fingers and announced that he thought it was cashmere. "Yes, you're correct," she said. "That's really amazing!"

Now come on, cashmere looks like cashmere and has a distinctive feel. A blind man could do that easily. Anyway, Julian has sense enough to recognize her gentleman friend is not really enjoying what is going on, so Julian backs off saying it was nice talking to her and turned his attention to his tormentor, Stanton. They have quite an audience now and the two Jacks become a little louder while appearing they are becoming a little agitated with each other.

All of a sudden Stanton tells Julian he is tired of his BS or something like that, takes his lighted cigarette and grinds it out on one of Julian's dark sun glass lenses. Julian does not flinch one bit as the hot ashes are falling down on his trousers. Julian never moves, I don't know how he could just sit there, but he did. Up to that moment things were really funny. That was also, but not to the people around us. Several started to get up and looked like they were going to come to the aid of this poor blind man. Jim Shea, who is about 6' tall and I stood up and quieted every one down, saying everything is OK and we would take care of it.

Stanton apologized and put out any hot ashes on Julian's pants with his napkin then the two of them gave each other a hug to calm things down before something unpleasant was about to happen. Hard to believe what went on and even harder to try and paint that picture!

All in all, it was one of the funniest things these guys ever did, but they did get out of hand somewhat. I don't remember if we ever did eat dinner. I did the best I could telling this story but you had to be there to really see how funny and how good Julian was acting his part of a blind person. There is not much more I can tell you about these two and all the good times we had at this trade show so will move on.

Backspin time again, to our new house and we will go from there. I was watching a lot of little league baseball across the street from our house, play ball!

LITTLE LEAGUE BASEBALL #99

I HAD MENTIONED BEFORE THERE WAS a little league baseball field right across the street from our second house which was located within a very large park. I played a lot of baseball as a kid way before little league was even thought of and loved to watch the game being played by kids. Many times after dinner I could not resist going over and watching those young boys growing up and playing ball. That is exactly what is happening, playing ball is helping their development and learning how to get along with other kids, how to play as a team and how to compete early in life itself. When I was that age we played all day long, sometimes on a ball field and most of the time just on an open field. We used anything lying around for bases, even dried up cow paddies. Never try sliding into the other kind.

One of the best things about being our own umpires was learning how to play and be fair and honest. We didn't have to put up with adults either, those pushy dad's trying to replay their own youth through their kids. I'm not sorry I said that, it's just how I see it and how I feel about it. I don't see kids doing that today, playing ball anywhere. I see empty ball fields. I see kids looking at hand held idiot boxes. They are not learning the basics, my friends. Got that off my chest and I know not all will agree with it. You don't have to read these stories if you disagree, write your own.

It would be a few years before my son Jim would be old enough to play ball if he so chooses to do so. I believe in not pushing kids into anything. Just open the door, give them the opportunity and the encouragement then let them decide if that is what they want to do. I'll talk more about that when my kids get a little older which will be when we move to the Cleveland area.

There was this one young boy I was fascinated with and he was a pitcher. He was the coolest kid I have ever seen on the pitchers mound at that young age. He looked like he was a seasoned big league player. He was not a show off or anything like that, he showed little emotion and he knew how to pitch. He even had a slider and a pretty good curve ball. Those kinds of pitches at such a young age are rare and can be a strain on a young arm. His motion was so smooth you could not tell what pitch he was going to throw, every motions was the same for all his different pitches. He would not waste any time, toe the rubber, look at the catcher for some sort of sign, which I don't think meant anything, and smoothly throw the pitch where he wanted the ball to be. What control, he hardly ever walked a batter and I never saw him loose a game. I really enjoyed those evenings. My young ones went with me most of the time as well. Peasant summer evenings with the kids watching other kids having fun. Good times.

I remember when we were playing all those pickup games as a kid, I played two main positions, pitcher and while I was not pitching I played first base. Once in a great while I would fill in as the catcher. Dad had a catcher's mitt and back then it was a small glove with a pocket the size of the baseball. The glove was very stiff, not much flex at all and was hard to use but I learned how to catch with my dad's catcher's mitt. It was fun behind the plate, a lot of action.

I had one big fault which I had a hard time correcting. When waiting for a pitch you have to wait for the ball to come to you, thus you hold the glove close to your body. I had a tendency to reach for the ball which is what I was used to doing playing first base, stretch my arm out as far as I could and reach for the ball. I did not do that often behind the plate as the catcher but when I did and the batter swung at the ball, many times the bat would hit the back of my hand. Not only was that interference with the batter, he got to advance to first base, my hand hurt something terrible, as did my embarrassment as I had to walk out to the pitchers mound to retrieve my glove. That is where it usually ended up after the batter blasted the back of my hand. Ouch! I was very lucky my hand never was broken.

Forward spin, I am really enjoying my new job so will get back to that and learning the sporting goods business.

Learning the Sporting Goods Business #100

I AM COMING UP ON THREE years experience working in the world of sporting goods equipment. Its 1964 and we are still in Pittsburgh. I am having a little problem moving on with moving on! Here is a town, I call Pittsburgh a town rather than a city because over the years my opinion of a "Big town" has gone from, what in the heck am I doing here (1949), to why in heck do I want to leave? During my time here I witnessed a dirty filthy smoky very hilly area change completely to a clean smoke free beautiful downtown, the three rivers forming the breathtaking "Point" which is framed by large tall buildings. I have fallen in love with the people as well. Down to earth hard working sports loving culture loving caring people. I arrived here knowing no one. Through all my various "Jobs" I have met hundreds and hundreds of nice people.

When I got into the sporting goods business, first golf then all the other sports It got to the point there was hardly a day no matter what I was doing or where I was I ran into people I know or have met before, somewhere. I met my wife here and we have been given by the grace of God four really wonderful children. All this happened in Pittsburgh and I am doing better financially as I am again approaching earnings of about $10,000.00 a year. Not getting rich, no where near that is going to happen with this job but all bills are paid and we are making extra payments on the mortgage. We live in a very nice large house located in a very nice area. Why would I want to change all of this?

Because I don't believe a person should stand still. If I stand still long enough I am going to start going backwards as others pass me by. So move on I must. We will soon be leaving the Pittsburgh area and my present position with Spalding. I am not leaving Spalding, just changing responsibilities and our location. A promotion is coming shortly with many added responsibilities. Sink or swim.

My present boss is my District Sales Manager Jim Shea. This talented young man had been groomed for his present position, first by being transferred to the Cleveland area as a dealer salesman who also had experience in the professional golf division as well and because the company was planning on forming a new district sales office and distribution center in this area. That happened and Jim was appointed to that position. Now the home office was making another move as the national pro golf sales manager position was open and Jim was approached about filling that position. Jim was happy in Cleveland and had just moved into a new house he just had built in Chagrin Falls, a suburb of Cleveland located about 15 miles south east and only two or three miles from the district offices located in Solon, Ohio.

Jim had indicated to me previously if upper management actually offered him this promotion he wanted to know my level of interest in replacing him if he moved on. He told me I was his choice to replace him and if I were interested he would recommend that the company appoint me to his vacated position of District Sales Manager. His biggest concern was he just moved into his dream home. It was located on the outskirts of Chagrin Falls, the home of Tim Conway of the Carol Burnett show. The area where his new home was named Twilea Park and his home was built on one and one half acres which was loaded with many trees.

There can be problems relocating a family of six. Number one, Dee was born and raised in the Pittsburgh area. Number two, uprooting four young children. Number three, did I want to relocate again and did I want that kind of responsibility, middle management with no college education. Was I capable? Was I scared of the pressure? Was this really the right move for me and my family?

The answer to number one was Dee and I had already discussed this possibility before and she was in agreement within reason, and this was. Number two our four children are very young, the oldest about 8.

At those ages they adapt very quickly and make new friends. Number three. Yes to all of those questions.

Next, how I helped Jim Shea make the decision to accept the position offered to him and move on. What could I possibly have done to accomplish this and what did it mean to me and my family? Another new house for us and what have I stepped into? A whole lot of new things were about to happen, relocating was one of them.

RELOCATING #101

$\mathcal{H}$ow did I help Jim Shea make the decision to accept the promotion offered to him as National Sales Manger of Professional Golf? He had to sell the brand new home he had just built and moved into, then relocate his family where Spalding's corporate office was located, Chicopee, Mass. It was all agreed if Jim accepted I would be replacing him as the District Sales Manger in Cleveland. Jim and I were discussing all of this and I said to Jim, "I have to relocate my family which means I have to sell my house and look for a new one also. How would you like the idea if I bought your house Jim?"

Jim replied, "Bill, I like that idea. Then I would know my dream house would be occupied by someone I know who would enjoy what I was looking forward to. Let's work out a deal!" We did, he moved on and so did our family and I was going back to my home state of Ohio. This two story white frame home was built on a one and one half acre wooded lot. It was covered with trees, mostly in the rear of the property with 90 to 120 foot high maple trees. It was located in a sub division of Chagrin Falls with a total of 21 very nice homes, all with the same size lots. Across the road behind my property was the Tanglewood Country Club sub division which hosted the Cleveland Open Golf Tournament one year.

Entering this house through the front door was a foyer with steps leading to the second floor that had four large bedrooms and two full bathrooms. There was also a half bath room located downstairs. Downstairs to the right was the dining room entrance with another entrance towards the rear of the house leading to the kitchen area. On the left was the living room also with an entrance to the rear of the house leading to the very large family room which ran from left to right, the right side was a dinette area and the large kitchen. There was a wood burning fire place in the living room which was back to back with a wood burning fire place in the family room. A double sliding glass door in the middle of the family room led to the back patio and a small forest of trees, which supplied all the fire wood we could use. Facing the house, the drive way from the street was on the right and turned left into a paved area leading to a two car garage which was part of the house. The drive way went all the way though the property exiting onto Route 306. The garage also housed a "Mud room" used for removing winter coats and all those ugly things we wore on our feet used for getting through all the darn snow we had in the winter. A second room in that area was the laundry room.

We sold our home in Pittsburgh for a modest profit and bought our new home for $40,000.00. All we had to do was put in a lawn in the front. Grass would not grow in the back because of the density of the trees. Jim Shea had already installed a basket ball backboard and hoop in the driveway area, thank goodness. I forgot to mention I had a backboard and hoop with our other two houses and I had one at my parent's home in Mt. Lebanon as well. I didn't play golf for eight years but I never stopped shooting baskets, it was fun and good exercise.

There were kids all over Twilea Park was a very productive area. Our next door neighbors Chic and Rita Porter had seven and our other next door neighbors the Turley's only had two but the Sullivan's down the street also had seven. There were more kids of course, so our four had a lot of playmates which helped them adjust to their new surroundings with out missing a beat. It was not too long before we added a new member to our family. One day the kids came home with a little puppy which they said was ours if we wanted to keep it. This cute little girl puppy came from a littler from nearby. How could Dee and I refuse such a cute puppy and the anxious expressions on our kid's faces waiting for an answer? We had a lot of room for a dog, inside and outside, so why not. She was a mix of a Golden Retriever and we think, Collie. A very pretty dog, it there are such things. There are, God made them too. Made some ugly ones too, but this dog was far from one of those. Those were the days when dogs ran loose all over the neighborhood, no walking behind them with a spoon and plastic bag. I would never ever do that. Let the dogs fertilize the area.

We burned wood in our family room fireplace almost every night in the fall and winter. There was all kinds of wood available from all the trees we had. A few had died so I eventually cut them all up and built three stacks of firewood about six feet high and ten feet long. There were large limbs that would come down on a regular basis I used as well. In the seven years there we never ran out of firewood. The fireplace was very romantic, nice to sit in front of a wood fire with a cocktail before dinner, and so on, whatever that means?

Moving on and accepting a promotion with enormous responsibilities was a huge decision. You would think the compensation package was huge also, right? Wrong, you will have a hard time believing what I am about to reveal next, my new responsibilities.

My New Responsibilities #102

*H*ERE IS HOW MY COMPENSATION plan stacked up against rather large responsibilities. In Pittsburgh my income had finally gotten close to the $10,000.00 yearly level. I had a company car as well. Dee did not have a driver's license as she really had no desire to drive. Moving to a rural area changed all that. She learned how to drive and got her license. Now she needed a car when I was out of town with my car, which was no longer a company car but my own.

There was no company car provided for the District Sales Managers, just travel expense. Up until now we did not own a car. Now, I had to buy two cars. My starting salary was a whopping, hold on to your hat, $10,000.00! Of course there was bonus clauses involved tied to the performance of my sales force. Think about this, all a salesman has to do to earn his bonus level is reach them on his own. They don't have to rely on others to get their bonus. As a sales manager I have to rely on about nine salesmen to obtain theirs for me to obtain mine.

So here is where I start, move my family, loose my company car, buy a house twice the price of the one I left and I may make less money. To make less I have taken on the following responsibilities. I must be crazy. Just because I don't want to stand still and go forward? Funny way to go forward, I'm going backwards financially, temporally I hope.

Besides the sales force I am also responsible for two distribution centers, both with showrooms and office personnel. One is in Cleveland and one in Birmingham (Detroit) Mich. Each has a "Branch manager" who doesn't report to me, they report to someone in the Chicopee Distribution Department. However, I am responsible for the operating budget of these two facilities. Each facility has an inside sales person to handle customer phone calls and walk in customers. There are two office girls in Cleveland, one a clerk and one my secretary, and one in Detroit who is a combination of both.

As the District Sales Manger I am responsible for both the pro golf salesmen and the dealer salesmen. I have two sales quotas given to me for the entire district which I have to massage and reassign to each salesman then they must be approved by management. I have to wear two hats when calling on customers with my salesmen. In total number I was responsible for were four pro and five dealer salesmen covering Western Pa., West Virginia, Ohio and Michigan, plus the two inside salesmen. There is no training program for me other than long distance advice from my superiors and from the salesmen as well. The salesmen have to bring me up to date on what goes on in their territories and what problems they have that needed to be resolved. No big deal, that's why I am being paid the big bucks. Actually, my compensation plan would end up paying me 13 to 15 thousand dollars. I really don't remember exactly what those figures were anymore.

The saying its "Lonely at the top" will become a reality for me. I am not really all the way to the top, but in my district I am. Basically down deep, everyone likes to be "Liked." That just doesn't happen in real life. I found out soon enough not everyone it going to like me. Being promoted and becoming the "Boss" of a number of people, especially salesmen who are/were my peers, my friends, or what I though were my friends came to a sudden change. If I were promoted and sent to another part of the country where I didn't know the salesmen it would have been much easier. I don't think my personality or out look changed any. I am now their boss, the very guys I worked with. Not in all cases, but some of their attitudes changed. There are reasons I suppose, maybe I changed somewhat without realizing it and maybe in some cases there was envoy or jealously involved. One thing is certain, not everyone is now my friend. I must find a way for all of us to work as a team.

As a manager I have people reporting to me. Unfortunately I have learned I can not afford to make close friends with anyone because someday I may have to fire them. You just can't get to close personally. Things smoothed out soon enough but it was a learning process for all concerned. I had to learn something about myself as well. I had to become a little more distant and at the same time be understanding of their needs and concerns. I am now in the middle as well, my people below me and management above. I also learned there are some people who got promoted that forgot where the heck they came from. I never wanted to be one of those and I worked hard to protect my people defending them if something came up management had concerns about. That's if they deserved to be defended. Some times I had to go the other way.

One of the first things I did when traveling with my guys was to have dinner with my salesman and there wives. I didn't know many of their wives because Spalding never held any meetings which included wives, which I think was wrong. Wives are very important to a man's success and many times to their failure. I wanted to get to know what was behind each of my men. Most sales people are pretty good readers of personalities and I prided myself at being very good at that. What makes this guy tick and the other one doesn't? It is his wife? Many times it is. She may not be causing the problem it there is one, it may be him. Sometimes you can see that. The more you know about a couple the better chances you have to deal fairly with them.

When I hired new salesman there was no way I would make a decision without having met his wife. Most of the time it was over dinner and there were times when the wife got her husband the job and sometimes when they didn't. I also want a guy who wanted my job eventually. As a sales manager, or any kind of a "Boss" you are only as good as the people you have working for you. Never be afraid for your job by having sharp individuals working for you, if their promotable and your doing your job you and the company will find a place for them somewhere else. There always seems to be a place for productive energetic people.

I have now become a member of the "Round table." That has two meanings really, I'll explain that remark, tomorrow.

The Round Tables #103

*T*HE FIRST ROUND TABLE IS comprised of all the District Sales Managers. With the addition of the Cleveland District there were now nine. Middle management is what we were. As the youngest and newest DM the others took me under their wing so to speak offering their advice when asked. They did not push themselves on me at all. They gave me an open invitation, "Bill, if you need help just call." This job can be rough because you really are in the middle. There are a lot that happens and is passed down from above that sometimes we at the lower level find some subjects or decisions difficult to understand or to communicate, and visa versa. Caught in the middle and I am going to leave it at that. One of my favorite sayings is;

> If you understand this, no explanation is necessary ...
> If you don't understand this, no explanation is possible.

The second round table is simply when I held any kind of a meeting in my district, no matter how many people were involved I did not want a long table and sit at the head of it. I wanted a large round or square table so there was no beginning and no end with the seating arrangements. Everyone would be sitting in an equal position. Have I explained this clearly? Does this concept make sense to you? If not, revert to the paragraph above.

If I try to explain everything I might well be writing 300 "Stories." I'm already up to 103 and I just moved to Cleveland in 1964, it will be 10 more years before I move to Florida and 51 years until we get to 2015. Hang in there I might be doing this for quite sometime, the Good Lord willing. There are now two trade show I will be attending as a DM.

Adding to the Sporting Goods National show wilt is the Professional Golf Association (PGA) show held in January in Florida. Living in Cleveland the January show will be a treat, for sure. I better get used to the PGA show as I will be attending 31 of them in one capacity or another during my sometimes scattered career. The PGA show started in the fifties in Dunedin Florida in a parking lot with equipment displayed on card tables. That was before my time. My first show was in one single tent, expanded to three large circus tents in Palm Beach Gardens and finally to the Orange County Convention Center in Orlando. The show grew so large I don't think you can walk all the isles and view all the displays in one day and not stopping at any of them.

I remember one show being held in those tents when a very large thunder storm with high winds kicked up. Our display was right near one of the large main poles holding up the tent. A couple of us were standing next to that pole when a gust of wind hit. That pole lifted off the ground ever so slightly and it change positions by moving about two feet from its original position. We looked at each other and without a word we moved away from the center of the tent towards an open flap entrance way. We were getting wet there as the wind was blowing the rain through that opening but that didn't matter. We were sure that tent was going to collapse and we got ourselves in a position to escape a possible disaster. Thank God that didn't happen. We were fearful people were going to get hurt, or worse. I believe that was the last year for the tents.

Backspin to some of my other new responsibilities, I was required to attend any men's or women's professional golf tour tournaments held in my district as well. We did that as salesman in our territories also. If the national people responsible for communicating with our Consultant Staff Members could not attend we would fill the void. At every tournament we provided golf balls they needed. It was usually three dozen per player. This was back in the days of the wound golf balls. Solid two or three piece balls were not introduced as yet and would not be for some years later. These balata rubber covers were very thin and subject to scuffing and cutting very easily. The players would also rotate a ball every three holes as wound balls would not be perfectly round after being hit after a couple of tee shots. The rubber windings inside would move slightly but with time to rest would have a tendency to return to their original position. That is why the ball was taken out of play to give it just a little time to restore itself back so as not to be a little lopsided, something very few people would be able to detect.

We were there to take care of any other needs or concerns the players had. Many were always ordering a new club to replace something they didn't like. Over the years I was getting to know not only our staff members but many of the others players as well. We spent a lot of time during practice rounds Monday through Wednesday on the practice tee or putting greens with them. We were given the same credentials the players had identifying us as someone who was entitled to enter the grounds, clubhouse, everywhere the players themselves were able to go. It was usually a money clip with the PGA emblem and the year it was issued clearly embossed on it. We had to get a new one each year. If someone stopped me for any reason all I had to do was show this money clip and that got me to where I wanted to go.

To give you an example about unusual situations working with tour players, I was attending one of the Ladies Professional Golf Association (LPGA) tournaments near Cincinnati one year. Marilyn Smith, who was a longtime staff consultant with Spalding came to me and asked if I would join her, she was an absolute baseball nut, and attend a Cincinnati Reds game that evening as she had been invited to put on a little clinic to promote the nearby LPGA tournament. I said I would be delighted to carry her Spalding Staff golf bag into the stadium for her, kidding of course, but that is what I did. So there we were before the game in the Reds dugout meeting the manager and all the players before the game. That is when I met their future Hall of Fame 19 year old catcher Johnny Bench. The thing I remember most about Johnny was the size of his hands. When we shook hands his hand almost wrapped around mine.

After infield practice and shortly before the game was to start the stadium was pretty full of fans. Out to the batters box we went, with me carrying Marilyn's big red golf bag with Spalding in big white letters on the each side of the bag, along with a gentleman who was going to introduce us. Yes, I said us. He introduced Marilyn and mentioned the golf tournament she was playing in, and Marilyn as a Spalding Consultant and me as a Spalding executive. Can you imagine? Marilyn spoke to the fans about attending the tournament and then said she would hit a few shots with her eight iron as a demonstration of how the ladies played the game. We stood on the grass next to the batters box the distance to the center field wall is not far by golf standards. To hit one out of the park, a golf ball I mean, all she needed was the eight iron as she could hit the ball about 125 yards with that club, or 375 feet, more than enough for an easy home run. She received a lot of Oh's and Ah's along with a lot of applause. Not only did the tournament get a lot of publicity but Spalding did as well.

That's kind of the unpleasant things we had to go through. Ha! It was fun and it is a good example of how companies use their Consultant Staff members to publicize the company and its products. By the way, there were no fans in the area where those golf balls were landing, in case you were wondering. Marilyn Smith was one of the founding members of the LPGA. She was from Kansas but lived in Jupiter, Florida for many years now resides somewhere in Texas. She was a wonderful ambassador for the LPGA tour, always wore a skirt which hung just below her knees, a nice looking top and a sweater. She also wore a short pearl necklace with matching earrings. She was a very good looking lady who would always mingle with the fans, something like Arnold Palmer would do.

More Management Duties #104

*T*HERE ARE A LOT OF little things to keep one busy but like someone said, "Someone has to do it!" The salesmen are required to fill out a daily sales report indicating who he called on and how much he generated in sales for each individual account, what the daily sales total were and the sales for the week. They also had to make out their expense report. All gas receipts are required with the odometer mileage reading written on the receipt. A receipt was required for any expenditure over $25.00 as required by the IRS. Receipts for tolls, parking, bell boys, small stuff was not required. Lodging receipts of course but no receipt is needed for meals except if you are entertaining a customer, then the receipt has to have the customer's name also.

These reports have to me mailed every Saturday so they arrive in the District office on Monday or Tuesday so that I, as their sales manager, can process and approve their expense and generated a reimbursement check to go out in the mail the same day. I also have to review their sales reports and determine if all is going well. Both of these reports can be very interesting and revealing too. Sometimes you look at an expense report and you see a number that may seem a little strange. Like one old veteran once told me, "Try and find my new sport coat in there somewhere!" A little of that goes on, but again, I don't like to point a finger at anyone because while I am doing that there are several of those fingers pointing back at me and my new sport coat. So, we will move on, just a little better dressed.

Most sales people have "A" personalities and when you get a lot of "A's" together their personalities can clash. Working with all those "A's" all the time can become a challenge. Sometimes it's just best to step back and let some conversations pass rather than contest everything all the time. No one wins. Anyone can win a battle and end up loosing the war. No one gains so you learn to sidestep a lot of issues, especially ones involving some decisions coming down from upper management. Too many things put the middle management in, yes, in the middle. That works the other way as well. I am not the best diplomat in the world and I know I have ruffled a lot of feathers in my time. It is not a perfect world and you just do the best you can for everyone involved and hope things work out for all involved.

Coming up, Ohio Incidentals.

OHIO INCIDENTALS #105

*B*EFORE I GET BACK TO business with some of its rewards and some not so good situations I'll sidetrack here a bit and peek into some old memories of the good times we had during our seven years living in Twilea Park in Chagrin Falls, Ohio. The first thing Dee did when we moved was to get the family registered in St. Joan of Arc Catholic church. It was not long before we saw a familiar face it was Tim Conway who was a regular guest appearing on the Carol Burnette TV show. Tim was from Chagrin and his mother still lived there. It was not uncommon to see him as he visited as often as he could. What a funny guy. I knew he was on the small size and seeing him in person confirmed Tim was a very small man with a very large sense of humor. I never had the pleasure of meeting him.

The next person we saw was a couple of familiar faces from Pittsburgh. It was Irene Michaels and her husband Cliff. We knew them fairly well and were at several gatherings together and also attended the same church in Pittsburgh and we were casual friends. Small world isn't it. Irene became involved in the real estate business in Ohio with much success. Unfortunately Cliff passed away a few years later. Would you believe how really small this world is, jumping ahead, maybe 10 years we would again meet Irene by accident, in North Palm Beach, Florida! For years in Florida we saw a lot of Irene and sadly she just passed away about six months ago at the age of 92.

There will be another couple we will meet shortly. And that is Ed and Loraine Flaherty who lived across the street from us in the Tanglewood Country Club development. They were originally from the Detroit area and Ed worked for the Ford Motor Company. Ed was transferred to a Cleveland assembly plant. Years later he would again become a neighbor in Florida after he retired and Ed ended up actually working for the Wm. Faulhaber Enterprises Corp. But that is another story about 15 years from now. Can you wait for that episode to present itself? I'll tell you all about that later.

And before I forget, when Jim Shea left Cleveland and we bought his house, I inherited a pair of Cleveland Browns football season tickets from him. There were priceless because there were none available. He purchased them under the name of Spalding so I had no trouble keeping these two tickets for the seven years we were in Cleveland. In those days the Brown's games were all sell outs except general admission tickets and the attendance was always announced at right around 82,000 people. In those years the Browns played in the old Riverfront Cleveland Indians baseball stadium. You remember me telling you how cold Chicago was? Riverfront Stadium didn't get that name by being inland, no sir. It was smack on Lake Erie with the open end of that stadium facing the lake. You talk about cold games in November and December. The wind would blow in from off that frozen lake through that open area of the stadium and it acted like a wind tunnel. To help keep us warm we would take a thermos bottle full of Manhattan's, no ice, please, just straight up. There might have been two thermos bottles depending who was with me. When I took any of the kids the bottle was left at home. We got so bundled up it was hard to move our arms. However we could move just enough to wet our lips.

Now this was not in the days of Otto Graham, Marion Motley, Alex Groza, Mac Speedy, Horace Gilliam, Dante Lavelle and those guys but it was the last year Jim Brown played. After Jim it was fun watching Leroy Kelly run the ball. There were two quarter backs who played while I had those tickets, the first was Frank Ryan and he was replaced by my soon to become friend and golfing buddy, Bill Nelsen. More about Bill and some more of my friends, including our popular New Year's Eve parties which we continued to have after so many good ones in Pittsburgh, fun times.

OHIO FUN TIMES #106

$\mathcal{B}$USINESS ASIDE, OUR FAMILY HAD a very good seven years in Chagrin Falls. We lived in a very nice small development with only 21 homes and everyone got along just fine. Our immediate neighbors, the Porter's and the Turley's were really great. I have to say that because the Porter's receive my daily emails! Seriously, if they weren't what I am saying about them they would not be on my list.

Our kids still talk about their seven years in Ohio. Our dog, Kola, became famous while there also. This was back in the day dogs were on their own, we didn't walk them and pick up after them as everyone does today. If I had to do that, I would not have had a dog. Unfortunately, Kola was a roomer, she went everywhere. The dog catcher in the area would call about every two weeks for us to come pick her up at the dog pound in Chardon, a small community nearby. The dog catcher really liked Kola. He would pick her up and instead of putting her in the cage in the back of his truck with other dogs, he would put her in the front seat and sometimes rather than take her to the dog pound and call us, he would just drive to our place and drop her off, asking us why don't we tie her up?" No way, I didn't believe in tying dogs up it they were harmless. How did she become famous? She was a National TV star the year the Cleveland Open golf tournament was being played across the road at Tanglewood CC. Unbeknownst to us, she was mingling with the players on the course. The TV cameras at one point put her on the air. When we found that out, we did contain her for the rest of the tournament. She looked good on TV as she was pretty dog. Dee eventually taught her to play the piano for our quests as well, but that is another story.

Halloween was fun in the neighbor hood also. For the kids and adults as well because after the kids were done trick and treating it was the adults turn. Going door to door with an empty shot glass was my costume. Knock, knock, trick or treat? It was safe because I didn't have to drive home. No, I didn't get that shot glass filled at all 21 homes, if I had I would probably still be there somewhere in the bushes.

One of the local golf professionals we became very close friends was Jim Chapman and his wife Sharon. Jim was the head pro at Chagrin Valley Country Club. He got there by the way of Scotland, to the Detroit area and finally ended up in Chagrin. His accent was not to bad, just certain words. Jim was about six year younger than I, so he was a head professional at a very young age. The membership liked Jim and Sharon so much that he spent his whole life at that very nice club. When Jim retired the members voted to give Jim and Sharon life membership to the club dues free. They are still very active and Sharon became an accomplished player herself and won the ladies championship quite a few times. I believe Jim is still playing gin rummy in the men's lounge drinking his scotch with milk since he has stomach ulcers. Probably got those ulcers playing all that golf with me.

I played a lot of golf at that club as a guest of Jim's. Jim's assistant professional at the time was a young man by the name of Mike Limback. Mike was a very good player and we played together as partners in many local Pro Amateur tournaments. Mike was also an excellent Ten Pin bowler whose average was over 200. He bowled a little professionally but never really hit the big time. Mike later became a head professional at a club in Evansville, Indiana.

My own golf game kept getting better. Chagrin CC was a very nice rolling tree lined course. To play that course well you had to learn how to hit the drive off the tee in the fairway or the ball would have a lot of bark marks on it. Good course, very pretty and very fast bent grass greens. Jim and I ended up playing a lot of golf with another pro, Bob Hamrich, and the Cleveland Browns quarterback, Bill Nelsen. Bob was a good player, he and Jim played about equal and so did Bill and I. Bill had a good golf swing but as big and strong as he was, he did not hit the ball a long way and that was due to his very bad football knees. He could not put a lot of pressure on his left side due to those bad knees, but he was very accurate and had a good short game. Bill was continually having his knees drained between games and sometimes had a hard time walking let alone play and throw a football. Joe Namath had nothing on Bill when it came to bad knees, you just heard about Joe's more because he played in New York. Bill may not be that well known as a quarterback but he led the Browns for about five years as I recall, maybe more. Bill had a big ego but was a really nice guy and fun to be around. I have found almost all successful athletes have rather large egos that are part of what sets them apart from being mediocre. Bill was a leader and you could see him take complete charge of the team on the playing field.

The real interesting thing about Bill is, at least I think so, he was not the starting quarter back in college. Bill played at USC under coach John McKay who eventually ended up as head coach for the Tampa Bay Buccaneers professional football team, a team Bill Nelsen also joined at one time as it's quarter back coach. Pete Brethard was the starting QB in college and Bill was his backup, so having not been a first string starting QB in college and still making it as a starting QB in the NFL I think is pretty unique. Bill also had another talent in college as he married Sue who was the college football queen one year.

Another interesting thing about Bill Nelsen and me is the last year Dee and I lived in Pittsburgh Bill was drafted by the Steelers. I moved to Cleveland and Bill was traded to the Browns. I moved to Mass, and Bill became the QB coach for the New England Patriots in Mass. I moved to Florida and Bill told me at the time maybe he would continue to follow me and end up in Miami with the Dolphins. He came pretty close as he did come to Florida and ended up with the Tampa Bay Buccaneers. Then we became separated when he left Tampa to become QB coach for the Detroit Lions football team for Monty Clark, the new coach and teammate of Bill with the Browns. When that happened I talked to Bill and bid him farewell, we were done following each other around the country at that point. I spent enough time in Detroit as a sales manager and that was it. Good by Bill Nelsen, but not really, Bill now resides in Orlando.

We played matches against each other once in a while, Bill Nelsen and Bob Hamrick against Jim Chapman and me. We played often but there were two big ones each year that were classics and even hit the sports page, but that's something you have to wait to hear about, our classic golf matches.

CLASSIC GOLF MATCHES #107

*M*AY 7, 1971 IN THE sports page of the Cleveland Plain Dealer, Tom Place, the Golf writer in his column "ON THE TEE" wrote;

Bob Hamrich, Head Pro at Mayfield, and quarterback Bill Nelsen of the Browns will be featured on TV-3's "Golf with the Pros" show at 5:30 p.m., Sunday. Incidentally, one of the fieriest rivalries in the district matches Hamrich and Nelsen against Jim Chapman of Chagrin Valley and Spalding's Bill Faulhaber several times a year. The losers buy the dinners. There are no "gimmes" in this one.

I still have that newspaper clipping and it is so old and brown I can hardly read it. Tom Place became a close friend as well and he along with Hamrich, Nelsen, Chapman and wives always attended our News Years Eve Parties. Tom Place went on to head up the PGA Golf Tour's press room for years, so even when I left Cleveland I would always see Tom at the various tour events I attended over the years. We were always able to keep in touch through those tournaments. Tom is now retired, in his late eighties and lives with his wife in Ponte Verde, Fl., near Jacksonville.

Back to those matches, what Tom wrote about that dinner wasn't all that was involved. We only played for a $2.00 Nassau bet but money on the course was not the issue. Bragging rights was the real battle. There was not much money lost or won on these bets because most of these matches were very close. Not only did the losers have to buy dinner for all eight, our wives were a big part of this, but the winners had to buy cocktails before dinner and during dinner as well. The cocktails were way more expensive than the dinners. So the losers paying for dinner, and whatever they lost on the golf course were really the winner's money wise as it cost the winners more than it did the losers! But then again, as I said, the whole thing was about bragging rights.

But that's not all that happened. Can you imagine eight of us, four loud big mouths, Nelsen was louder than me believe it or not, sitting at one table in nice restaurants with more than a few down the hatch bragging how two beat hell out of the other two? The girls were well behaved but the guys were pretty noticeable. There was more than one restaurant that indicated pretty strongly as we were leaving we should take our business elsewhere. We were pretty rowdy no question about that, especially one outing at Stouffer's restaurant.

On our way out of Stouffer's, there was a very large stuffed race horse in the lobby and its back had to be at least six feet high. We all had a tendency to pick on Bob Hamrich, and the three of us looked at each other and without a word we knew what we were about to do. All three of us went straight to Bob, picked him up and deposited him on top of that horse, and we all walked away leaving him there. Bob was not a big guy with short legs, he needed help getting down but we didn't help him for what seemed a very long time but it was only about a minute. Yes, we got the same suggestion from Stouffer's as well. A lot of their customers thought it was kind of funny but the head waiter didn't. Over the years we really had a good time together.

Bill Nelsen was also involved in one of my strange nine hole scores. Late one afternoon after work he and I went to Chargin valley to get in a fast nine holes before dark. It was early spring and a pretty warm day but very wet. We had to walk, no carts allowed. We had a $2.00 bet with automatic presses when a person was 2 down in the match. Golf is a strange game as I made six birdies, two pars and one bogie and shot 31, five under par. I wish it didn't get dark, it would have been interesting had I been able to play all 18 and see what I would have scored. Who knows, I might have made 9 bogies. Anyway I think I won eight bucks from Bill. I felt good to have that Browns money in my pocket. Speaking of money, Bill's salary as the starting QB in those days, I am pretty darn sure about this, was $30,000.00! Boy how things have changed.

I had another strange 9 holes one day in Warren, Ohio at the Trumble County Club. I was playing with the golf pro Irv Kleinelder who was 6' 6" tall, a first class guy, and two other sales reps. Irv and his club hosted the Youngstown Kitchens Open, an LPGA event each year for a number of years. We sales reps used to work the scoreboard for that tournament; our pay was all our meals and an open bar. This nine hole venture, or maybe I should say adventure, happened after the final round of one of those tournaments. The four of us wanted to unwind, so off we go and I scored a one over par 37 and didn't score a par on any of the nine holes. Talk about feast or famine; I had four birdies and five bogies.

Irv was a wonderful merchandiser who had the best looking golf pro shop I have ever seen. When calling on him he would insist that I would be his last call of the day because he insisted on taking me to dinner. A salesman is supposed to entertain his customers however Irv would have none of that, it was he entertaining me. We always went to nearby Ravenna where Cherry's Steak House was located. Best steakhouse I have ever been, I have never had better steaks anywhere. Funny thing about Ravenna, I lived there my first two years of my life, but for some reason I don't remember much about my first two years on this earth. Do you? But I do remember our New Years Eve parties.

Our New Years Eve Parties #108

$\mathcal{D}$EE AND I STARTED HOSTING these parties back in our first house in Pittsburgh in our finished basement with the horseshoe bar, I think the first one was in 1958. The format was established way back then, invitees bring what they want to drink we would furnish the place, the mixes for the drinks and the late night food. There were two things we changed because this first party turned out to be a learning curve.

Number one, although the party was a success it could have been better because not everyone invited knew each other. The invitees could have mingled with each other a little better rather than getting into a few separate groups. We decided we would use name tags for everyone in the future. We did that and even though we knew everyone we wore a name tag as well. That prevented any resistance from anyone saying why they should wear a name tag when we weren't. That worked out so very well over the years, people mingle when they see the name of the person rather than avoid them because of not knowing their name. It works, folks, it works and at any type of gathering as a matter of fact.

Number two and without doubt the best thing we ever did. Don't bring out the food after midnight because the quests are consuming alcohol for several hours on an empty stomach! Not good. We didn't have a real problem with the first party but it was obvious that pretzels and chips do not do the job. Some guests were not in good shape. Since that party, beside all the snacks all around the place, the dining room table was loaded with food from the time the first guest arrived. Our guests had food available for them when anyone felt a need to eat something. Our biggest concern was our guests driving home. Was there a lot of drinking at our parties'? I would say controlled was more like it, I don't remember anyone getting out of line and just plain drunk.

A few may have gotten a little warm and fuzzy, but not drunk. Most all of our neighbors at the parties in Ohio were there as well, they walked to our house and I assume they got home the same way, walking hopefully.

Our house in Chargin Falls was ideal for a good size group. The family room really quite large with the dinette area and kitchen at one end, it was accessible from the dinning room and living room as well, so the flow of people around those three areas was ideal. We always had a large group with eighty eight attending one year. That's a lot of bodies, almost ran out of name tags, had twelve left. Should have been eleven, I forgot to put a name tag on our dog, Kola.

We had many guest over the years that claimed they did not go out on New Years Eve, but came to ours once to see how things went, and always returned. In Cleveland a good example of that was most of that famous foursome, Bob Hamrich, Bill Nelsen, and the golf writer for the Cleveland Pain Dealer, Tom Place. They all said they hardly ever went out that night, but showed up at every one of ours. What was the attraction? It was just good fun with nice people mixing and talking to each other with a lot of laughter. No cell phones or any of those other gadgets to interrupt good conversation in those days. We always had some interesting guests and it just seemed like everyone clicked with each other.

Remember I told you that Jim Chapman, my partner in those famous matches against Bob Hamrich and Bill Nelsen, Jim was from Scotland, the great country that provide us with that wonderful medicine, "Scotch?" After one New Years Eve party, which by the way I never got to bed until 3 or 4 AM due to the party lasting until the wee hours as the Scots may have said. Well, on this particular morning about 8:30 AM the doorbell rings and their stands Jim holding a piece of charcoal in one hand and a bottle of Scotch in the other. I'm thinking my partner has lost it, not his golf ball, his mind. Jim explained to me that this was a custom in his native country that he was expressing the fact we were to have a swig of Scotch along with the charcoal gift was indicating we would remain close friends for life.

I was very touched by this and told him if he ever woke me up again after such a party he was not much of a friend. No, I did not say that, I really was touched, especially by that swig of Scotch with only a couple hours of sleep, made me warm and fuzzy all over again rather quickly. I know what happened to the Scotch but I'll be darn it I can remember what I did with that piece of charcoal. I never heard of that tradition before or since and always wondered it he just made that up, Jim had a great sense of humor that was kind of wrapped around a tree like a bad 2 iron shot, which I did once while playing a round of golf with Jim. The 2 iron didn't really wrap around the tree, the shaft snapped when it hit the tree, just like my temper. That really did happen one day, but it really wasn't anger, strangely enough, I just got the urge to do break that 2 iron and did it. I felt really good after expressing my self, kind of like going to the bathroom.

I conclude my New Years Eve party story with the fact they did not continue much past the Pittsburgh/Cleveland era. I think we may have had one small one in Mass., but I don't remember. I don't remember much about my time in Mass. but that is another story, later. In Florida we tried two parties but found most of the people we invited wanted to come and go. Stop in and then go to another party or parties. We were not used to that, we did not intend for our invitation to be like an open house, stop, have on drink and move on. That is not what Dee and I wanted so we discontinued the parties. In Florida the people we became acquainted with were all from different parts of the County and every area have different customs, I suppose. The great big New Years Eve parties for us came to an end. But the memories of those good ones will remain forever. Good memories always do. Who wants to remember bad ones anyway?

FAMILY IN OHIO #109

*D*EE PASSES HER DRIVERS TEST and now has her Ohio driver's license! Look out world. Although born and raised in Pennsylvania she can never be accused of being a Pennsylvania driver. Actually; I found that Pa. drivers were very good. The real reason Dee was not anxious to drive was that when Dee was 13 years old she was involved in an accident. She was hit by a drunken driver and spent the next year in the hospital. Dee became a little gun shy, who could blame her for that. I have to give credit where credit is due, Dee became a very good driver. That remark should be good for at least 5 points. It seems like every time I earn 5 points I find a way to loose 10. I suppose that's another way to use the term, "Backspin."

Diane and Cindy were becoming familiar with their new school. They, along with Linda and Jim, were making new friends with all the kids in the neighbor hood. Everyone was very friendly and made our family feel welcome. That is how Midwestern people are, openly friendly much like the people in Pittsburgh are as well. Being an old "Buckeye" I felt like I had never left Ohio, I felt very much at home.

Son Jim is getting on in age, about six now and about time he learned how to play catch and throw a ball. It turns out Jim is left handed so a good prospect to be a pitcher and a right handed golfer. Speaking of golf, Dee is now starting to play. Got her some clubs at a good price and paid wholesale price for her shoes, paid zero for golf balls. Dee joined a ladies nine hole league playing at the public course in nearby Chardon. She began to take Jim along and while she played nine holes Jim spent all that time on the practice green, putting and putting and putting. The very first time I took Jim to play nine holes, I believe he was about 10 or 11 years old, it was across the street at Tanglewood. The greens on

Tanglewood were very large and undulating and very fast. It took a lot of shots for Jim to get his ball onto the greens and surprisingly he got down in two putts on all nine greens! Amazing, Jim really leaned how to putt while Dee was playing those nine holes each week.

Back to son Jim, I taught my left handed son to play with right handed golf clubs. There were several reasons for that. First of all there were no left handed clubs for kids in those days. Even it there were I would have given him right handed clubs simply because even adult left handed clubs were not up to par with right handed clubs. Even if they were my choice for Jim would have been to go righty anyway because the leading arm for right hander's is the left arm. So Jim's dominate arm is his left which is an advantage in that respect. Bob Charles of New Zealand was the best left handed golfer ever in his time on the tour. Bob was a natural right hander as is Phil Mickelson, another lefty on the course. The most left handed golfers in any country is Canada. Most all are natural right hander's too. Why? Hockey is the national sport in Canada and did you notice how most hockey players hold the hockey stick? Their right hand is on top and their left is half way down the stick on the left and they swing the sick from their left side towards the puck. Left handed, so when they take up golf it is natural for them to play left handed just like Mike Weir, the golfer in Canada who have been playing the tour for years. Back to son Jim and learning how to play catch.

I took Jim out back with a small soft rubber play ball. We started with that just a little at a time. Then got him a small glove and gradually graduated to a baseball. I did not push him, just kind of introduced him to playing catch. When he got a little older he started asking me to play catch with him. That is what I wanted, him to ask me, means he wanted to do it, not me wanting him to do it. Big difference, he took up the sport because he wanted to, not me pushing him because I wanted him to, but of course I did.

Before Little League there was Pee Wee baseball. This was before Tee Ball came along. An adult would pitch underhand to the kids from up close. One of these vey first sessions Jim had the pitcher and me in stitches. Jim took his stance left handed, swung at the first pitch, missed, looked at the pitcher and slowly moved to the other side of the batters box and tried it right handed, missed again and kept switching sides with every pitch. You had to be there to fully appreciate the determined look he had on his face.

One day I noticed something was missing from the fireplace mantel in our family room. Then it struck me, a baseball was placed there and it was gone! It was autographed with the famous New York Yankee players who had won a World Series, I can't remember which one. However, there were names on that ball even non baseball fans would recognize, like Joe DiMaggio. It was not there. It turns out son Jim wanted to play catch with some neighborhood kids because they didn't have a ball!. I asked him if he took that ball and he handed it over to me. Guess where they played catch? On the street in front of our house, the autographs were no longer visible on this very valuable ball, ruined. I know Jim will not be happy I have written about this, but it wasn't his fault you see. If I hadn't taught Jim how to play catch this would never have happened. It was my fault. Jim was really too young at the time to realize the ball had value, to him, it was just a baseball. That's ok Jim; it was just part of your inheritance that you will miss some day.

When Jim got to Little League age he became a pitcher. After a couple of years he was becoming pretty dominating because he had a very good fast ball. The kids were taught back then that is all they should attempt to throw because trying to throw curves and other type pitches could hurt their elbow and shoulder. Just throw straight pitchers, and his was faster than most. He was a pretty good ball player and then one day he and other kids were swinging on some vines like Tarzan when Jim dislocated his left shoulder. After that his fast ball was never the same, lost some of its zip. Jim continued to play baseball but turned to hockey when we moved to Mass. That's another story for later. Jim had a lot of athletic ability and a lot more coordination than I ever had.

As far as athletics concerning the girls, our youngest, Linda, was the best of the three sisters. She would become a very good diver in high school in Florida. She also at one time had a full size motorcycle, one that Jim had and passed on down to his sister when he upgraded to a more expensive model. Those kids never gave me and their mom any worries! Am I kidding? You bet I am!

GOOD TIMES IN OHIO #110

*T*HE SO CALLED SNOWBELT BEGINS on the East side of Cleveland and continues up through Erie, Pa. which is located on Lake Erie and onward through Buffalo, N.Y, That weather pattern comes over Lake Erie and does not effect the West side of Cleveland all that much. Chagrin Falls is on the edge of that snow belt so there was hardly any time that there was not some snow on the ground. Twilea Park with all its trees was very pretty when snow covered everything, except the drive way and the streets, ugh. Christmas Eve most of the neighborhood created a Luminary which was simply a lot of little brown paper bags with a small amount of sand in them with a lighted candle placed in the sand inside the bag. These bags were placed about 10 feet apart up and down both sides of the driveways and the streets. With snow on the ground the glowing candle lights in those bags was really impressive. What a nice warm feeling, it was beautiful. I have never liked snow very much but have to admit sometimes it sure is pretty. Other times it just pretty, bad. There were a few eggnogs glowing around the neighborhood as well. The Luminary and the eggnogs were a real treat without the trick! Good times.

There were a few other neat things in the area like the little private club nearby named the Trout Club, which I guess was for fishing, also horse riding and dinning. I don't know about the fishing and I was not a member so I don't know. There were horse stables with real live horses that our daughters, Diane and Cindy, somehow worked their way in and were helping groom the horses. Their payment was they got to ride these horses bareback. The girls really had a ball doing that. Riding horses bareback brings back a not so good memory for me but good ones for the girls. Good times.

A gentleman by the name of Don Lybarger had a dream about a private club and he finally did create it. He named it the Chagrin Racket Club. Don converted a large farm house into a clubhouse with a very nice dinning room and bar. He built tennis courts and then built an indoor tennis facility as well. For swimming he built a fairly large lake with a concrete bottom, when frozen over in the winter it was used for ice skating. It was a family friendly facility and our family joined. I couldn't play golf in the winter so I took up tennis. My ability in sports was that I was better than average in most sports I played but master of none. Tennis by far was my worst sport but I enjoyed playing in the winter. I hardly played at all in the summer because tennis is a overhand and side hand game as opposed to golf being an under handed game. Playing both sports in the same season was not a good mix for me. Tennis affected my golf swing if I played both, so that is why I only played indoors in the winter. The food was excellent also, the kids and Dee enjoyed swimming and ice skating and they played a little tennis too.

Chagrin also had a very nice ten pin bowling alley that also had a very nice little restaurant. We did a little bowling in a mixed league and the kids liked the restaurant, good cheeseburgers. I had to travel quite a bit with my salesmen so I was on the road a lot. Dee suggested that when the kids have a birthday I should take that child out to dinner, just the two of us so I could spend some quality time alone with them on their special day, which I really enjoyed doing. Guess where they wanted to go? The bowling alley restaurant! Over the years those dinners kind of slipped out of my memory bank until recently I was reminded of them by my kids. Until they jogged my memory, I did not realize how much they enjoyed those dinners, something they obviously haven't forgotten. Good quality times.

We are now going to cross over Route 306; the road behind our property that separates us from Tanglewood CC. There, running parallel to the road is a long par 5 golf hole and it runs down hill from tee to the green and has a small creek crosses the fairway in front of the green. In the winter the kids and adults as well use that par five for sledding, snow boarding and even ski down that hill. It was just perfect, that is if you stopped before going into that creek. Sometimes that creek was not frozen over so you had to put the brakes on. Many people in the area also had snowmobiles which were becoming quite popular at that time. There were a lot of open fields with rolling hills in the area where snowmobiles could be used safely. A lot of adults were having more fun in the snow than the kids. Good times.

Dee and I became very good friends with Ed and Lorraine Flaherty who lived in Tanglewood with their two children, Ed Jr., and Patricia. Patricia now lives around the Ft. Pearce, Fl. area and is on my email list, so she will receive this one as well. Many evenings we, or they, trudged back and forth through snow drifts and across Rt. 306 for an evening fun, we had a lot of laughs and we tipped a few together, just to keep ourselves warm of course. The Flaherty's will become our neighbors again in the 70's in Florida and will not only end up renting a town house that I will own in the PGA complex, but he will also help me with my Wm. Faulhaber Enterprises, Inc. business as well. Good Times.

I also had a ping pong table set up in the garage. There were a lot of competitive games played on that table when Dee didn't have the laundry piled up on it. In good weather the basket ball hoop got a lot of use too. Hey, when you're young, you can do all these things. Good times.

There were other neighbors we spent a lot of time with besides the Porters and Turley's, our immediate neighbors. The Griffiths, Jim and Peggy and the Long's, Jack and Edie were quite active. Jim Griffiths loved tennis and played as often as he could. He also loved his Shaffer's, a New York bottled beer that had to be almost frozen or he wouldn't drink it. He would pour a little at a time in a small champagne glass so it would not get warm. Jim's dad was a Preacher, I don't know what religion, and as a small kid Jim learned how to play church music on the piano. He had a very active rocking right hand on the ivories, very lively gospel tunes. Jim loved to play at parties, including our house as we had, and still do, have that piano that our dog, Kola, played also. There were many fun times with great neighbors and good friends. Good times.

Our kids leaned over the years how to sleep through all these parties as we entertained a lot. Or so we thought the kids were sleeping. It was years later they finally told us they were sitting at the top of the steps just listing to all that was going on. The kids said they were good times! I am happy to write that these good times continued.

INTERESTING INCIDENTS #111

*F*OR ALMOST A DOZEN YEARS now I have been involved with the golf business which has taken me too many men's and ladies professional golf tournaments. I'm getting to know quite a few of these professional touring people pretty well while dealing with them on behalf of Spalding, delivering golf balls and clubs they had ordered or taking down information and specifications for clubs they need. There are darn few "Standard" clubs being used out here on the tour. As an example, Lanny Wadkins irons have to be made 4 degrees flat lie which was about the maximum a forged iron could be bent. Lanny is a short man and he held his hands very low and very close to his body creating a very flat swing. With a normal lie the heel of the club would be touching the ground the toe of the club would be high off the ground. Hitting a ball with a club in that position would cause the heel to dig into the turf. There are a lot of opposites in golf as an upright stance such as Al Geiberger who is tall with an upright swing, the toe would be touching the ground and the heel of the club would be off the ground and that would cause the toe to dig in. Al's irons needed to be bent 1 to 2 degrees upright.

When bending a forged iron flat or upright that changes the loft of the iron so more bending is required to get the desired loft back to where it should be. A cast iron club can only be bent about one degree. In addition to that for years forged clubs were preferred by good players because they had a softer feel than cast iron simply because they were a softer metal. Also these players grew up with forging so they were reluctant to change, most were feel players and worked the ball in different directions. Younger players began growing up playing cast irons so their feel was different, plus the game became more power than finesse. The players today don't work the ball in different directions as much as players did in the past.

Talk about detours, but this one will lead us back on the correct route to good times. Dave Stockton, a touring Golf Pro and a Spalding staff consultant, and our Cleveland salesman John Plumb became friends so when Dave was in the area, Dave, John and their wives would get together for dinner. One day John arranged a game with him and Dave as partners against Jim Chapman and myself. We played at Jim's course, Chagrin Valley CC. We had a $5.00 Nassau bet going. Dave over the years is well known for his short game, especially his putting ability. As a matter of fact Dave and his two sons run a golf school in California, Bakersfield I believe, featuring the short game, mainly chipping and putting. Many tour pros seek them out for advice when having problems to this day.

Back to our match, we are having a good time and the match is all tied when I had about a twenty foot putt that I drained for a birdie. Dave was about 18 feet away, he smiled and congratulated me on my birdie putt, and confidently said, "Nice putt Bill, you just tied us," and he promptly sank his for the tie, another birdie. Jim and I ended up loosing, no thanks to John Plumb, we just could not handle Dave by himself and I believe he shot 66. If I remember correctly Jim had 74 or 75 and I scored 77 and no score for John. Good times.

Homero Blancas, born in Texas and of Mexican decent, and I became good friends. Dee and I had a fun filled dinner one evening with "Homer," as he liked to be called, along with Homer's wife Noel, who was a blonde girl originally from Chicago. The four of us hit it off really well and had a great evening together. They had two boys who Homer called seek and destroy. Homer had a successful career while playing the Tour. He was not exceptionally long off the tee as he was not a big person but had great ability to hit any kind of a shot. I was watching him one time at a tournament while playing a par 5. His second shot was about 50 yards short of the green which had a big sand trap in front guarding against any kind of a run up shot. The pin was pretty close to the front of the green which did not leave much room between the trap and the pin to pitch the ball. I fully expected him to use his sand wedge, his most lofted club, and hit a high soft shot over the trap to get the ball close to the hole. All of a sudden I see Homer's ball on a very low trajectory sailing past the pin, and he spun that ball back about 20 feet with the ball ending up tap in distance for a birdie. I had never seen a shot like that before, or since. Backing up a ball that distance is no big deal for these guys but that shot was so low over the trap I thought he was going to catch the top of the trap with his ball.

Homero was a nice looking guy with a great smile and a small beer belly who loved to joke around and have a good time and he liked to tip a couple of beers also. The year the Cleveland Open was played across the street from our house at the Tanglewood CC, Homers wife Noel was not with him on this trip. It's a lonely life sometimes staying in motels. Dee and I invited Homer to dinner on Saturday after the third round of the tournament. He was off the course about 3 in the afternoon and together we went to my house for a couple of beers before dinner. Homer was only one shot behind the leader with a very good chance of winning so we are entertaining the possible next Cleveland Open winner. Homer spots my basketball hoop and wants to shoot baskets and play a little one on one game with me. I had no problem with that for myself but after warming up, running around shooting the ball, before we started to play one on one I asked Homero, "Hey Homer, your only one shot out of the lead. You could sprain and ankle or hurt yourself in some way doing this. You ever think of that?" He replies, "Bill, I got to take my mind off all of that, let's play." And we did. Homer was a pretty good little player but my height advantage did him in, then we had another beer and dinner. Good Times.

Cleveland weather in the summer can be fickle because of the Lake Erie effect. Many clouds are created and come off the lake which makes Cleveland the second least sunny city in the US. I guess Seattle is number one with the least amount of sun shine.

Backspin, when we first moved into the area, I came home from work one day and I find Dee in the kitchen standing at the sink looking out the window with tears running down her cheeks. To my alarm I wondered what the heck I did now, and I was freighted to asked, but I did. I said, "Dee, my darling" as gently as my deep loud voice would let me, "What's the matter?" She turns towards me with this forlorn look and says "I haven't seen the sun in the seven weeks we have been here, it is so depressing." Well I was relieved it wasn't me she was crying about but that was a cause for concern. It was something we had to get used to, and eventually we did. So this detour brings me back to the final round of this tournament.

It's Sunday and the day turned ugly, overcast, a slight drizzle falling as was the temperature, the low sixties, damp and chilly for a typical summer Cleveland day. Dee and I attend an early Mass and by the time I got to the golf course I see all these people and the players under umbrellas and wearing sweaters or rain gear to ward off the chill. Not a good day for golf and especially for my hot weather friend from Texas. By the time I catch up to him I find him with no protection to ward off the cold drizzly rain. He is only wearing his golf shirt, no sweater and his arms are bare. Homer spots me in the gallery and between shots comes over to acknowledge my presence. I said "Homer, why aren't you wearing something to keep you warm, you really look cold?" He replied, "I can't stand to have something covering my arms it affects my golf swing. The hotter the better for me, this weather I can't handle. I'll just have to do the best I can." Not good times today.

Gardner Dickinson won the tournament and Homer finished three shots back. I didn't know Gardner very well but would get to know him very well later when I moved to Florida. He was a close friend of Toney Penna, more about those memories later on.

PUBLIC SPEAKING #112

I DID NOT TAKE PUBLIC SPEAKING courses in school, I wish I had because now that I am a District Manager I am about to be shocked with the news I have been given the assignment or presenting the basketball line of products at our upcoming sales meeting. Normally the product personnel who work with the development and improvement of products do the presenting. But not all as management for some reason want some presentations done by sales people to their peers. As a salesman I have presented many different products but that has been mostly a one on one situation. Some presentations may have been before a few people like families or small district sales meetings with my own group and mostly informal around a table.

But not from a podium in front of top management, factory personnel, product and marketing people and last but not least, my peers. If you have never done this, you have no idea of how scared you can become. I have found over the years when giving a speech or presentation to a group who does not know anything about what you are presenting and you make a mistake, they don't even know it. Only you do so you learn to ignore mistakes and keep on going. But when you are presenting or talking about a subject to a group who may very well have more knowledge about the product or subject than you do, you can be in real trouble. Any mistake you make does not go unnoticed and they stick out like a sore thumb. And stage fright is a very unnerving feeling, I know, I've gone through it more than once and it is not fun. It's worse than the yips in a putting stroke.

When I received my assignment via mail from Howard Nannen our Vice President of Sales, it stated my presentation was scheduled for an hour. I thought, an hour, what the heck can you say about a round object for an hour? So I called Howard and said something about that to him as he brushed me off with some very good advice, he simply said, "Bill you can do it!" End of conversation. Well, I didn't think so, and I looked up the previous year's agenda. The same presentation for basketballs was for one half our and there were three names as presenters, one sales person and one person from manufacturing and one product guy. Three presenters for one half hour was simply a dog and pony show, not a one man one hour execution. I called Howard with my newly found information. There was a short silence and I knew what was coming. I am one hard headed German confronting another hard headed German who was my boss's boss.

Who do you think is going to come out on top with this? Howard broke the silence with a deeper voice than normal, "Bill the schedule is set and I am not going to change it. Sleep on it, you'll figure a way to do it." Funny he said sleep on it because it always seemed when something was on my mind that was troubling me or needed a solution I did sleep on it. I dreamed about those kinds of issues and almost always I would eventually come up with some answers in my sleep, waking up in the middle of the night muttering my decisions. Dee thought I was having nightmares tossing, turning and talking to myself. I was having discussions with myself trying to solve issues. They were nightmares until I was able to put those troubling issues aside and solve them.

I made up my mind I was not going to let that nasty German get the best of me, nine, no way. This could be the most boring presentation ever given. Take one round object and make a mountain out of a basketball. So I have to get to work and I though of several things and one was that for many years basketballs were not really round at all, so I was going to talk about the entire history of a circle, basketball, which was not a circle at all. Not until our own very company Spalding came up with a ball that no longer needed laces so a rubber bladder could be inserted inside the ball to hold the air. Yes, I said laces on a basketball, do you remember that? Basketballs were made just like footballs at one time, the leather panels were sewn together, a rubber bladder placed inside and the ball was closed using leather laces. Weight, size, circumference and resiliency were hard to control and there were probably not two balls exactly the same.

There was no way I could talk for an hour about the different balls we had to offer and what the wholesale price was on each and what our quantity pricing programs were and the dating terms. Very dull stuff indeed. We had several different leather balls with the Top Flite 100 the top of the line for leather indoor balls and are currently the adopted ball used by the National Basketball Association. We had about six more balls at different price points for outdoor and indoor use plus a junior size ball. All this information could be completed in less than 15 minuets.

Anyone familiar with the history of basketball would know where the game was invented and by whom plus the original basket used was a peach basket. So I put all that old stuff on them. Of course it was Dr. James Naismith in the year of 1891 in Springfield, Mass., now the home of the Basketball Hall of Fame. There were 13 original rules and I went over some of them, killing time of course. At first it was a game with nine on each side and the peach basket had a bottom the ball had to be retrieved with a ladder until a hole was cut into the bottom so a stick could be used to pop the ball out. A soccer type ball was used until 1906 when Spalding introduced the first basketball. The first professional league was formed in 1946, the Basketball Association of America (BAA) and the National Basketball Association (NBA) was formed the year I graduated from high school, 1949.

I was scared to death but got through it. I found out later a lot of information I used to kill time ended up educating many of the salesmen who really didn't know all that history. If I were to grade my presentation I would say it was a C. I have no idea what management thought because the feedback I received were polite, such as, "Nice job Bill." I never did know what people actually thought, and maybe that was good.

Incidentally, while on the subject of basketball, do you remember the name of Julius Irving who was given the nickname of Dr. J.? This comes under the category of famous people I have met. He was one of the greatest basketball players of all time; maybe the greatest until

Michael Jordan came along. He attended a sales meeting one year when it was held in the Carolinas and I ended up having dinner with Dr. J and his wife, lovely people. He was and is a class act and he was hooked on the game of golf. Both were very nice to converse with, I was very impressed with his golf knowledge as well. Julius and his wife were an interesting couple and it was a wonderful evening.

What do you think happened at next years sales meeting? Howard Nannen gave me another assignment, this time presenting the football shoe line! Would you believe football shoes! Pardon me while I go back to sleep and I'll let you know how that nightmare turned out.

PRESENTING FOOTBALL SHOES #113

*N*ow Howard Nannen gave me the job of presenting football shoes at the next national sales meeting. I don't know if that is a complement for doing a good job with the basketball presentation or a penalty for doing a bad job. I didn't want to ask either. I went back to bed trying to find a way to present a product that our salesmen hardly ever took orders for, I had to sleep on it. Football equipment was not Spalding's strength, game balls of all sports was what we were known for, baseballs, softballs, golf balls, footballs, basketballs, volleyballs, soccer balls, tennis balls, even high bounce balls, but not football shoes. We didn't manufacture any kind of protective equipment and now all of a sudden this product is one of the highlighted product presentations at the sales meeting? I started to question the mentality of our management, but not out loud.

I'm beginning to wonder if I made that nasty German mad and he is punishing me with this assignment. I'm only kidding about that, Howard was a great guy who started working for Spalding in the warehouse in Philadelphia and worked his way up to inside salesman, then married the boss's secretary and eventually went on the road as a salesman. Howard kept getting promoted through the ranks of sales managers to the very top of the sales organization as Vice President of Sales for all products. Spalding had a history of promoting people within their ranks if at all possible which I thought was a great way to let others know they had the same chance for advancement. Up until now there were no sales managers hired from outside of the company; they all came from within our own organization.

Back to my assignment, the only football product we were really known for is the very popular Spalding J5V high performance football used extensively in College's and High Schools. Presenting a product is one thing but at the conclusion of the presentation a powerful meaningful closing. Something is needed to hold the audiences attention and interest, leaving them with positive thoughts. One night in my sleep the subject pops into my subconscious mind and all of a sudden I sit up in bed and blurted out, "I've got it!" This wakes Dee up and she shouts, "You've got what?" No Dee, let me explain.

In my sleep it came to me what I should attempt to do for my conclusion of the presentation. To paint a picture of this romantic product I have to revert back to the year 1965 when this was happening. Football shoes were all black then and they were all high tops with long black plastic spikes. We didn't even offer low cut shoes in those years. Ugly looking things and now it's my time for my presentation; I was next on the agenda. I'm already sweating and nervous as all get out and frankly I had a bad case of stage freight. Here I am again about to make myself look foolish talking to a bunch of sales guys who have had a lot more experience with this product than I have. So I pick up a shoe with shaky hands and almost drop it while starting to point out its features and how well it is constructed and all that garbage. I then present the pricing structure, the quantity pricing program and the payment terms with early payment discounts. Exciting as all get out, and I am wishing I was getting out.

The conclusion that I dreamt about was something like this. "I would like to leave you with this thought. We are all concerned with selling the J5V football. Think about this, it only takes one football to play a game. The wholesale price of that ball is $18.00. There are eleven men on a team and each team dresses four teams so that is forty four for each team. That totals eighty eight players and each of those players have two feet. That equals 176 feet! That means all those 176 feet have a football shoe on them. Two feet per player equals 88 pairs of football shoes with a wholesale price of $18.00 a pair. While we are spending all of our time attempting to get a sale for one football worth $18.00, if you spent the same amount of time selling 88 pairs of shoes, we are now talking about a sale that would total $1,584.00!" "Now I want all of you to figure out what your commission would be for each sale, $18.00 or $1,584.00 and figure out what your time is worth." "Smart selling gentlemen, your choice," and then I walked away from the Podium. Or was that a "Stagger"? I can tell you it was not a "Swagger."

Good dream or a bad dream? I don't know. What do you think?

Inventory & Theft Control #114

*A*s I mentioned before why we as sales mangers had the additional responsibilities involved with distribution facilities was beyond me. That will change but for now I have to do what was expected and now it is inventory time which is taken twice a year. We counted everything except the pencils. It is impossible to have more of an item than you are supposed to have in inventory but it sure is common to have less, it is called "Shrinkage". The most desirable item to disappear is golf balls as they are the easy to resell anywhere. For that reason all golf ball inventory is kept inside a wire cage under lock and key and only unlocked when filling orders.

I took it upon myself that I would be the only person allowed inside that cage and take the inventory, fill out the inventory cards and then lock them up within the cage for safe keeping. It was always possible if one of our people was stealing golf balls and allowed in that cage to take inventory the count could be falsified and would not be detected for another six months. We were in pretty good shape with no large amount of missing product for the few years that I was involved. Small shrinkage can and does happen sometimes by small mistakes filling orders and sometimes by carless paperwork. So if the amount missing was small it was not a big deal. For one thing I made sure that any of the people working for me that played golf was provided with free golf balls through my promotional donation account. I did not want my people to even pay wholesale I wanted them to pay nothing. In that way I felt if there was temptation for anyone to take some it would be eliminated and they would appreciate receiving free golf balls. You have to take care of your own.

Of course I had the distribution facility in Detroit to worry about as well but I could not be in two places at the same time so I put the responsibility on two of my salesman in that area. They did not have to borrow any golf balls because they had more than ample promotional balls at their disposal. Plus I trusted them so things went pretty well in Detroit too. However there were a few incidents I had to deal with and was lucky enough to spot and stop. Another thing I had to be careful about our Cleveland warehouse personnel belonged to a Union, I won't mention which one. They had to be treated with kid gloves or there could be big problems if there was a reason to accuse a Union man of anything, like even loafing on the job. Our main man in the warehouse was also the, I forgot what his so called title was, the go to guy between the company and the Union. Steward I think was the term.

There were two thefts or attempted thefts that I uncovered myself I thought were quite interesting. During the Christmas holidays we always had an "Office party" starting at noon on December 24th. We had food brought in for lunch and had a bar setup. We also had a gift exchange by picking someone's name out of the hat, which we did about a week before the party. We concluded the party in mid afternoon and everyone went home early to their families sober as we controlled the drinking.

I was the last one there to secure the building so I checked all the doors and I also checked the dumpster when locking up just to see what was is there. We had double doors at our loading dock where trucks backed up to deliver merchandise to us and to pick up merchandise for delivery. There was a drop off from the shipping platform to the driveway where the dumpster was sitting. I opened the shipping door and looked into the dumpster. Well, what do you know; there are six unopened cartons of baseball gloves, six gloves to a carton, in the dumpster. Now why would anyone want to steal baseball gloves, one box was catcher's mitts to boot. Where can you get rid them? Taking baseballs would make more sense than stealing gloves.

OK, so someone is going to come back for these items, but when. We had lights that illuminated the parking lot and they came on when it got dark. There was a timer for these lights so I decided to check it to see if anything had been changed. It had, the timer was set for the lights to go on at dusk but the time had been changed for when they would normally be turned off at daybreak. The timer was changed so the lights would turn off at midnight. So the thief was coming back at that time or shortly thereafter.

I called the Solon police and explained to them what I had discovered. I asked if they would cover the place at about that time and catch the thief red handed. You know what they told me? I almost didn't believe what I heard. I was reminded that it was Christmas Eve and that it would be a very busy time for them and they could not spare anyone to catch a thief in action! They could not spare any officers to stake out our warehouse.

I had no choice but to removed the six boxes and put them in the closet in my office. Dee and I were going to midnight mass that evening and I told her about the situation and told her after Mass I was going to drive over to the warehouse and check things out. It just so happened that a light snow was falling. Perfect, I wanted to see if there would be any car tracks in the snow leading to the dumpster. I did that and there were. One set of car tire tracks going straight to the dumpster, a pair of foot prints also visible and then the car tracks led out to the street. I know for sure we have a thief working for us and it had to be someone in the warehouse. We had three Union employees, the head man and two others one of which had only been with us a short time. What do I do, I am not certain who it was and of course I had no proof but I would bet anything it was the new man. To accuse a Union employee, or any one for that matter without proof, is a no, no.

I didn't tell any of our employees about this and decided to pull a bluff on this guy. Whoever put those cartons in the dumpster had to be nervous as heck knowing they were discovered and removed. I did not want a problem with the Union, that's the last thing I wanted but I knew what I was going to do and I was pretty sure I could pull it off. You know where I got the idea? In my sleep, of course! The next working day I asked this guy to step into my office without the other two warehouse employees seeing me ask him. As we approached my office I could see he was nervous so I knew I had the right guy. I didn't say a word to him as I opened the closet door and pointed to the six cartons in there. I looked at him and said, "I'm going to tell you what I am going to do. I am not going to call the police if you walk out of this building right now and do not come back. If you don't walk out of here right this minuet then I am going to call the police and have you arrested for theft." I could hardly finish my sentence and he was gone. My bluff worked.

I went to the warehouse after he left and approached our head man and told him I don't know what happened or why but your man just came to me and said he quit and walked out the door. That was the end of it and I never told anyone anything about that whole situation except Bob Hudkins who was our inside salesman at the time. There was no reason to tell anyone as I did not want to take a chance that the Union people got wind of it. It was over as far as I was concerned.

Another time I caught a guy stealing and we were paying the cost of shipping the stolen goods as well. I was nosing around the shipping department desk and leafing through the UPS record of shipments to customers when I spotted a name that was not familiar to me. I became curious and leafed back through the records and found the same name about five times. It looked to me like the address was a private residence. To make a short story short after some checking on that person we found out it was a cousin of one of our newer shipping clerks. This guy was packaging items and making shipping labels to that address and we were shipping the goods out the door to his cousin. And we were paying the shipping costs as well. Our head guy was embarrassed that one of his Union shipping clerks was doing this behind his back. He was really upset that he had been had because it was his responsibility and his alone to make out the proper paper work for anything being shipped so he fired this guy and there was no Union problem.

There was one other that I discovered but it was small and I don't recall the details. I won't write about anything concerning the Detroit operation except one problem which was really sad. I had a young man working for us as an inside salesman in Cleveland. He was also married and was really not the sales type and he knew that sales was not in his future but maybe becoming a distribution facility manager would be a better job for him.

It just so happened we had such a need in our Detroit operation and we gave him a shot at it. He moved to Detroit and for about a year everything seems to be going well then one inventory we had more shortages than usual. Our inside salesman there had some suspicions but didn't tell me until they had proof our manager was indeed stealing, as it turned out, to pay for his addiction to alcohol. We didn't know it but he was an alcoholic out of control. He would enter the facility at night and take things. My guys set a trap by going into the warehouse after closing when our suspect was gone for the day. They acquired a very soft invisible thread like yarn material and strung it across several isles in the warehouse about six inches above the floor. Then the next day the two of them went back early in the morning before anyone else arrived to check on the threads and found them broken. Someone had been in the ware house during the night. The threads were so soft and easily broken without that person knowing he had broken them. They knew who it was and informed me of what evidence they had. He had not been caught in the act so it was another ticklish situation.

My guys suggested we confront him with this evidence and see what his reaction would be. We made the arrangements that I would meet them about a half hour at the facility before the normal opening time. In other words all three of us would be there, me as a surprise, when he arrived because I had to drive there from Cleveland very early in the morning. So I got up in the middle of the night and drove to Detroit and arrived about an hour before the opening time. When he arrived he was very surprised to see the three of us, especially me, and became very nervous and started to sweat. We simply said "I guess you know why we are all here early to see you." He confessed that he was having a bad time and admitted what was going on. He resigned and moved back to Cleveland. We lost track of him and of course we did not push the issue with the police, or the company. He left us and it was over, done with. Sad, very sad indeed.

Those are times when I just wished I was not in the position I was. All I wanted to be was a sales manager, not a detective and prosecutor. It's lonely at the top.

Traveling My District #115

*A*LTHOUGH I COULD HAVE USED the airlines to travel within my District I rarely used them because the distance and time to drive within this area was more convenient for me. By the time I drove to the Cleveland airport which was on the west side of Cleveland, parked the car, check in and waited for the plane to take off, land in Detroit or Pittsburgh or Columbus or Cincinnati retrieve my overnight bag and meet my salesman I could be there by driving and have everything I need and more in my car. Hang my sport coats on the hook in the car; take my clubs if needed, briefcase and overnight bag made it easy. The longest trip was Cincinnati; I could get to Pittsburgh and Detroit in a little less time. All this would change when an alignment of duties and territory after about 2 or 3 years of being a District Manager. That will be happening soon.

I think I mentioned once before that I called on K-Mart when they had just three stores, all in the Detroit area. Dick Lockwood was our salesman and K-Mart was his account before it became a national account. Dick was very helpful to me when I became a dealer salesman and I always appreciated that. Detroit was a large and important market for us and Dick did a very good job.

I spent quite a lot of time there because of the importance of the business and because of the distribution facility as well. Several of our salesman started their careers as an inside salesman in that facilities showroom. To name a few, John Plumb who became our northern Ohio pro salesman, Frank Karr became a very successful sporting goods salesman for so many years. And Ron Gurziel was also promoted to the pro golf sales force. Both Frank and Ron are of Polish decent and came from a Polish area in Detroit and both changed their last names somewhat because they resembled the alphabet.

All these guys I am about to write about became successful and at this point I have a little side story about Ronnie Gurziel. Ron had a little problem using proper English and even needed a little help in reading a menu. He was a very determined young man and one heck of a salesman. When a customer came into the showroom to pick up an item he had ordered that customer hardly ever walked out with just that item. Ron was like a little bull dog, when he got a hold on someone he didn't let go very easily, those customers walked out with a lot of additional product. Ron just kept suggesting other items until he sold something else to them. When a territory opened I gave Ron his chance and he did very well. I told management he was my diamond in the rough and I just knew he would find the fairway one day. He was well liked and he, like Frank Karr, was very intelligent, both knew how to treat people and how to work. Ron Gurziel ended up owning a Pro Golf Discount store! His store and his success were in the fairway grass I had predicted, he did find his way out of the rough grass.

There were times when upper management would be critical of some we hired. As a matter of fact at one point we were told we must strongly consider hiring only people that had a college education. Of course that bothered me more than I let on because I didn't go to college; my degree was on the job training. Did that mean they made a mistake hiring me? I read so many resume's that were so badly written by college graduates I wondered what they were taught. I hired who I thought would get the job done, some with a college education and some without. Every one of the people I hired but one was successful, thank you very much. The one that was not I had a funny feeling that I didn't quite trust him. There will be no story about him and his name is not in this story either. I relied on my judgment of people.

In Cleveland the first one I promoted was Bob Hudkins, my friend after all these years. The other following him was Bob Near. Another side story, after we closed the district office after work hours some of us would go play a few holes of golf down the street at a public course, and after have a cocktail or two and then head home. John Plumb would join us sometimes and it was just John and me who really played much golf, the others were learning and of course John and I were giving them tips. I always made sure everyone had new golf balls so it didn't cost them anything. I won't use the names but one day on the first tee a couple of my people went to the ball washer and started to wash dirty used balls before teeing off. I almost fainted. I said "No one working for Spalding should ever use anything but a new ball on the first tee! Put those dirty balls out of sight! What do you think other people might think?" Or something to that effect, the language might have been a little different.

I also had to let a few men go during my seven years as a District and then Regional sales manager. Very unpleasant memories and something I hoped I would never have to do. Sometimes people give you no choice and I had to do my job. I'll be touching on that subject soon and I need to explain why and how these unpleasant incidents happened.

It is also time to move on to my next management change, from two years as District Sales Manager to Regional Sales Manager for the next four years. How were these two positions different? Sales Management Realignment was a big change and a welcome one.

SALES MANAGEMENT REALIGNMENT #116

OUR OVERALL BUSINESS WAS CHANGING and the game of golf was growing. Arnold Palmer had a lot to do with that, along with the popularity of President General Dwight D. Eisenhower. Both had their fans, "Arnie" appealed to the blue color worker. Golf was no longer looked at as just a rich man's game. And "Ike" loved golf; he played a great deal and had his admirers as well. TV coverage of Golf was growing and so were our sales of golf equipment. I always had the feeling the dealer salesmen looked down a bit at the pro golf salesmen and felt they were somewhat superior. The difference between total sales volume dollars between the two divisions was changing rapidly; golf was no longer the step child and the golf division was starting to look like the beauty queen.

Most of the District Sales Managers were, for the most part, not golf oriented and their knowledge of the other sports was their strength. That was probably one of the reasons for the realignment. Finally, the company started to realize they needed golf oriented sales managers to manage the Pro Golf Division and its sales force. Again, most sales managers were really not qualified because they did not know the quirks of this quirky golf business and the people we had to deal with. The golf business quite simply was much different than most businesses. There was a lot of friendship involved as well. We were dealing with a lot of ex caddies. We were dealing with human beings not educated in business. They were good golfers trying to learn how to be business men.

And what the heck were sales manager being shackled with responsibilities for inventories and distribution problems anyway? Release them from those duties so they can spend more time managing their salesmen and customer problems. Let the dealer guys do what they know best and the same for the golf pro division. It's important to know the game of golf and gain the respect of the people your dealing with. Those golf pros spot people in a second if they know anything about golf.

IA good salesman and sales manager becomes his customer's partner. Make his business important to you, not just the sales generated. Sales will come with the respect you gain from your customer, and you have to show outright respect for your customer as well. To me, the customer comes first, then my company. My home life of course is number one, business is there to support my family so a balance in needed to do both well.

How did this realignment of sales area affect me? First, the word district will disappear and be replaced with the word regional. No more responsibilities for anything to do with the distribution facilities in Cleveland, Detroit and Chicago, because now my region has been extended to include what I already have, Western Pennsylvania, West Virginia, Ohio, Michigan, and the following states of Indiana, Iowa, Illinois, Wisconsin, Minnesota, North Dakota, South Dakota and Nebraska. That is eleven and one half states. My counter part will be the Regional Dealer Sales Manger with offices in Chicago. I will cover my region out of the Cleveland (Solon) office. Hurray, just golf and no more inventories or thefts to worry about. No more basketball and football shoes presentations to sweat over. Now I have to worry about Indians with bow and arrows in the Dakotas! Do they play golf I wonder, or just shoot golfers?

I have inherited nine salesmen to look over plus two inside sales people. A few of these are some really great seasoned senior veteran salespersons. They are Tony Joy in Pittsburgh, Bob McLaren in Detroit, Carey Spicer in Indiana, Ted Horvath in Minnesota/Wisconsin. As I write this the date is 3/24/15 and the Kentucky basketball team has a record of 36 wins and 0 loses, undefeated so far. The reason why I bring this up is because of past history. Kentucky years ago had a coach by the name of Adolph Rupp whose teams are legendary. Rupp produced many All American players and his very first one was our very own Carey Spicer, our salesman in Indiana!

Working with these guys is easy as I really speak their language having been in their shoes for six plus years. We were all on the same page knowing the personalities of our customers and their ways. In those days there were no retail golf stores selling pro only golf equipment. Sporting goods stores, department stores and the up and coming K-Mart stores sold golf equipment but a different retail line of clubs and balls so the only competition the golf pros had was other golf pros. Most pretty much held the line on pricing so there was not much infighting between them. The business was pretty clean and our main concern was our competition, the other golf companies. We had to fight them for better distribution of our products and better position of our clubs and balls in their shops. We needed to build up our consultant staff of professionals playing our equipment and featuring Spalding products in their shops. Of course all the other companies are doing the same thing so it is very competitive. That is why friendship is so important. Plus we needed strong advertising and marketing strength so the consumer was aware of our products and were inclined to ask for what we were advertising. It all goes hand in hand, the chicken and egg story, marketing people and sales people are into that scenario pretty deeply.

My travel habits have now changed drastically as well. To cover my newly acquired mid western states I am going to have to take to the air quite a bit. It seemed like I spent half my time in the Chicago O'Hare Field airport. To get anywhere in the mid west all connecting flights went through Chicago, or at least it seemed like they did.

Not all was peaches and cream with the salesmen as I had and some problems came up from time to time. Unpleasant situations ... ...
Next ... ...

Unpleasant Situations #117

I WROTE THIS STORY AND I deleted the entire chapter as it was about several situations where I was forced, or rather I had to let some of my sales personnel go. I don't see how writing about these unpleasant situations can do anything to make my stories better. Some things are just as well forgotten as writing about them can't make interesting reading in my opinion. And some of those situations still hurt after all these years. I hope my readers don't find this the most interesting chapter because I deleted it!

However I feel I must explain that "Firing" someone is not a simple matter of just telling someone they are terminated. It is a much more complicated situation then most people realize. First of all every one of these unpleasant situations I was involved with I tried to save that person from being terminated. I had my reason for possible termination. If I felt that person was worth saving or not, I must present to he or she my reasons, in writing, of what I feel is wrong and give my direction of what changes have to be made. That person must have a copy of this in writing and must sign that correspondence if that person agrees. Assuming it is agreed a time limit is set for the corrections to be resolved. After that time period I must reevaluate and again in writing make my findings.

If the problem(s) are not resolved then this second correspondence is a final warning and again I must outline what solutions I expect. Then that person must sign again agreeing to what is expected of them with another time limit assigned. When that time period has expired and if the problems have not been resolved that is when the termination is concluded, in writing. The person has been given the opportunity of avoiding termination and if they have not met what was agreed upon that person has no recourse and the possibility of their bringing a lawsuit has pretty much been eliminated. I have to protect myself and my company by following the correct procedures. I believe I did that and my conscious is clear because I gave it my best trying to help these people from being terminated.

Concluding this unpleasant chapter, over the years almost every one of these people remained in the golf or sporting goods business. And I crossed paths with most of them and there was only one who did not thank me for, as they put it, waking them up, and that they were doing well and have corrected their ways of doing the things I suggested in the first place. Those conversations help ease the unpleasant memories of going through all of those incidents, but it still hurts.

TERRITORY SPLITS #118

*W*HEN YOU'RE INVOLVED IN SALES one thing is just as certain as death and taxes, and that is healthy sales quotas. Every year we can expect an increase in our quotas of 10 to 12 percent at least. No matter the business conditions we are expected to reach our quotas and our income is tied directly to those quotas as is our performance reviews. An individual salesman only has to worry about his own quota and I as a sales manager need for the better part of my sales force to reach and exceed theirs so I can expect to reach my quota and earn my bonus money. When we are given a quota there is no negotiation, it's mine and mine to keep and meet. No excuses, no weather reports that my region is going through more rain days than normal for the year and rounds of golf played are down considerably. No, no, that won't work. If business is bad in general then I am expected to not only match last years sales which would be good but I am expected to take away business from my competitors to reach my goals. Management won't listen to the fact that that is exactly what our competitors are telling their sales managers and salesmen!

In a way the message from the top is that I had to be better than my competition. And then they will tell me because business conditions are bad they are cutting down on advertisement money, fewer ads that help expose and pull through our products the salesmen place in their customer's shops and on their shelves. If that inventory is not shrinking then there are no reorders which you need to meet and exceed all these quotas, as top management sees it, as obtainable. It almost comes to the point where I started to feel sorry for top management because their boss's, the owners of the company are breathing down their necks. And so it goes. Middle management is just exactly what the word "Middle" means. I am right in the middle of the people above and the people reporting to me. I am right in the middle of everything and just have to "Take the bullet!" Sound like a double edge sword to you? Sometimes it seems like a no win situation. But you are expected to win and take no prisoners. It's a war I must win.

I predicted long ago that middle management would cease to exist some day and when I was approached to consider becoming a regional manager again later in my career as a salesman in Florida and move back to the mid west, I said no, I was not about to get into that rat race again. I was back as an individual salesman with no other reasonability's and that is where I wanted to stay.

Territory splits was one way of increasing sales, not a bunch but a little. I created two territory splits increasing the salesmen reporting to me from 9 to 11 in my remaining four years as a Regional Manager before I really got my butt in a jam by accepting another promotion. Later on that subject also, got to finish this part of my life first. Even though I am a native of Ohio the only reason I know there are 88 counties is because of the maps I bought for mapping out a new territory. Along with maps of other states which also game me population figures to work with. Do you know how many counties in the state you reside? If you live in Ohio don't answer that you are eliminated. Come to think of it I am in my 41st year in Florida and I have no idea how many counties there are.

I have already touched on the subject of creating a new territory in southern Ohio/West Virginia which turned out very well. The other one was in the very western part of my region. In the 60's the population of N. Dakota was 500,000, S. Dakota was 750,000 and Nebraska 1,500,000. That is not a lot of people, 2,750,000 in three states which included the Indian population. I won't go into all the details but coverage there was very thin as you might imagine so I realigned a couple of territories and created three adding one more salesman which also worked out well. Both of these splits required a lot of backup information involving population, number of customers including total sales figures needed to support additional salesmen plus what effect would these splits have on the original territories making certain they would not suffer great losses that might be difficult to overcome for the salesmen who had their territories cut. All this had to be presented to upper management for their approval. Adjustments of quotas and income potential so those salesmen whose territory was cut did not suffer income decline. The territory cut always grew back to and exceeded sales totals within two years due to better coverage of the remaining accounts and the new territories had first year increases of over 20 percent because of better coverage as well. A win, win situation and another battle won.

Enough about this dull story but before I move on while going over this in my mind reminded me of an embarrassing call I made with Ted Horvath in Wisconsin. We were visiting one of his really good customers who was on our home pro consultant Staff. This professional had just received his new Spalding Staff consultant golf bag. He was so proud to show it to us. Being my first trip to the area with my salesman and being a new rookie sales manger I had to make a good impression, right?

We had just recently had our national sales meeting and one of the items presented to us was new zippers on our upscale bag line including of course our staff bag. Up until now metal zippers were used and because bags often got wet from rain these zippers would tend to become a little hard to open and close easily. It was explained to us by our Product Manager for golf bags, Bob Friese, of the virtues of this plastic zipper being problem free from the elements, PLUS, they were self healing. In other words unlike metal zipper if they were damaged and separated they were not repairable. So Bob in his demonstration to the sales force took a pencil and jammed it into one of the large zippers separating the two sides. He then took the little thing a ma jig used to open and close the zipper. He ran it one way over the open zipper and then back and the zipper was back together again as if nothing happen to it. It was indeed self healing as we all saw that demonstration. So I am going to show my knowledge of the newly designed self healing zipper to this valuable customer.

So I took his band new bag and jammed a pencil into the zipper as I had seen demonstrated and promptly ruined his new bag. I destroyed that zipper completely. Well, my face tuned as red as that bag. You can not imagine how embarrassed I felt. My salesman Ted looked at me in disgust and our customer was holding back what I think was laughter. Of course I apologized the best way I could. I informed him a new bag would be on the way post haste. I tried to explain that Ted and I both witnessed that demonstration and I expressed the fact I could not wait to confront our Product Manger Bob Friese that he must have used trickery and mislead us with that demonstration. He really didn't I just used too much force. Actually, that little episode turned out well as that customer realized I was human and not some young stiff shirt executive. He was very forgiving about it and bought our lunch including a glass of wine. Made my day! Ted Horvath was a really class guy and very well liked by his customers and he was kind enough to never let me forget what I had done that day. Oh well, I made a mistake once, but I may have been mistaken about that! Let's be honest, if you have never made a mistake then you have never done anything in your life.

U. S. OPEN GOLF TOURNAMENT 1946 #119

*M*Y VERY FIRST EXPOSURE TO a golf tournament was the U. S. Open. It was in 1946, the first open played since 1941 because of World War II. My dad took my brother and me, I was 15 years old, to the Canterbury County Club in Cleveland, the site of the tournament which was won by Lloyd Mangrum. Lloyd appeared to be a chain smoker, wore a white cap and had a mustache. He was a pretty dapper looking guy, funny how you remember things like that. Something else I remember that had nothing to do with golf but with a couple of spectators, I saw two of the tallest guys walking together who appeared to be over seven feet tall. In those days even the tallest basketball players were not near that tall. Maybe the circus was in town. A sight I never forgot, obviously.

Canterbury was and still is one of the best golf courses in the world and when I arrived in Cleveland in the mid sixties as a sales manager with Spalding I finally got a chance to play that great golf course. What a thrill after first being there twenty years before.

During my seven years covering the Midwest there were numerous men's and ladies professional golf tournaments and I attended most of them representing our company. I delivered golf balls to our Spalding staff members and taking care of their needs was part of my responsibilities. One of the best tour stops each year was played at the Firestone County Clubs south course in Akron. Another great course and one of the longest courses played on tour in those days. It was not a fancy tricked up course as It was long with tree lined fairways that required great control or you would never get a sun tan looking for your golf ball. One of the best run tournaments I've ever attended as well.

Firestone had one of the best deals for people like me who had PGA credentials. We received a fifty percent discount on all beverages and meals just by showing those credentials. Pretty darn nice and I don't recall any other tournament I attended that did that.

Another thing I remember was for years there was a group of golf loving guys from the Chagrin Falls area that I knew that would attend this tournament at Firestone every year. Right next to the course there was a wooded area that they somehow got permission to park a large motor home during the tournament. There were about 12 of these guys involved. The motor home was stocked to the ceiling with food and beverage and they had another truck loaded with tables and chairs that they set up under the trees so everyone could sit, play cards, just visit with their cocktails and of course consume nice big thick charcoal grilled steaks. I was one of their invited guests along with a few of the tour players.

After watching the action, these guys returned to the motor home, it was cocktail hour. About the time the charcoal was ready for grilling the steaks, Julius Boros, the famous touring pro and winner of many tournaments showed up after his round of golf to have a couple of beers and cook the steaks. He loved to do that and he was just one of the guys. Guests could not pay a dime towards the expense of the food and beverage, great hospitality, good times.

My involvement with these tour events got to be extensive. When I was working a tournament my routine was to arrive Monday or Tuesday and leave on Thursday the first day of the tournament. I rarely went out on the course to watch golf that was not my job. I spent almost all my time meeting the players and talking to them on the practice range, putting green and locker room. I would wander from the first tee to the 9th green and the tenth tee to the 18th green and watch the players there. I would meet and converse with the golf writers and got to know them and just about anybody of importance connected with the golf tour and the golf industry.

I met all the executives and writers of many newspapers and Golf magazines. I also got to know many of the executives of competing companies as well. One big family on the tour circuit, we were all on a first name basis. Making friends or at least friendly conversations with as many people in the golfing world was important. You never know when you need a favor, or being asked for one. I treated my competitors with respect and I received respect in return.

I also became acquainted with many of the agent/managers representing the touring pros which turned out to be helpful later when I would arrive on the national level in a couple of years from now. I am now approaching 14 years in the sporting goods business with most of those years working within the professional golf world. The important thing was that I could honestly say not only was I on a first name basis with these people they were on a first name basis with me. It's more important that they know me rather then saying I know them. Understand the difference?

This was a people business as far as I was concerned. By the time I was promoted to the national level I already new a lot about part of the responsibilities I would be assuming. I knew the executives of the True Temper golf shaft manufacture, the two major golf grip companies, the golf cap people, the clothing people involved in golf, the shoe company people and the other major golf companies. I would not get to know all these people by going out on the course and watching these guys play. I would scout prospects for our consultant staff on the practice tee and practice green and face to face conversation. And the better I knew their agent/managers the better chance I would have in dealing with them and visa versa.

One of the most important phrases I learned **not to use** while dealing with all these men and lady golf touring professionals was a parting remark that it seems like almost everyone uses to this day. If you watch golf on TV you will know at once what it is. The parting remark after an interview on TV is simply this, **"Play well!"** Or, **"Good luck."**

Just what the heck does that mean to a player? Nothing, everyone says that all the time. A player can play well and come up empty. Just a so, so round, no putts are going in or hit the ball really well and nothing happened. "I **played well** but did not **score well.**" That last sentence is where I came up with a word I used speaking with these great players, **Score.**

So I decided to use a different phrase I never heard anyone else use and it was simply, **"Score well!"** The heck with saying "Play well" I did use the **"Score well"** phrase for years. When I first stated to say that I can not count how many times a player would start to turn away and go about his business, stop in their tracks, do a double take after hearing me say that and ask, "What did you say?" **"Score well"** I would repeat. I got a lot of smiles, a lot of thank you, and a lot more of these people seemed to say hello to me before I had a chance to say hello to them. Many players really took notice to that remark and to me personally. So my friends **"Score well"** in everything you do.

GOLF BALLS #120

A LITTLE INFORMATION ABOUT THE MODERN era golf balls going back to the sixties and seventies. I guess that the sixties is not really modern is it? Going back to the early days is like having a dinosaur for a pet, so I am not going there. My subject is about the evolution of the wound balls with a liquid center and a balata rubber cover and two piece solid golf balls. Spalding was not the first to introduce a ball made with solid materials it was the Faultless Rubber Co. Located in Ohio, they first introduced a one piece ball in the early sixties and it was not very good. But for the high handicapper it was welcomed because it would not cut when it was miss hit like the thin covered wound balls. It was also shorter in distance but not all that much for the type golfer using it. With a good $1.25 wound ball one bad swing that ball would be unplayable. So this type ball had a very large potential since the average golfer does not break 100. The marketing and R & D people in the golf ball division knew this and began working on our own solid golf ball project headed up by the VP of R & D, Bob Molitor.

Just a little back ground about Bob Molitor. He was responsible for the present day under listing of tennis grips, he also helped develop the present day basketball that no longer needed a rubber bladder inside the ball to hold air and the outdoor rubber basketballs became the rage. Bob was involved with many other product improvements as well but that gives you an idea who was behind the two piece Top-Flite ball which became the favorite ball of the majority of average to high handicapped golfers for many years.

The Top-Flite ball didn't start out that way however, it had a rather long rocky road to success. There were two prototypes prior to the Top-Flite was finally introduced in 1971. First Spalding introduced a two piece range ball and at the time the U. S. Rubber Co. owned the range ball business. Spalding was starting to make some inroads with this new two piece ball range ball. Then Spalding introduced a new ball and named it Executive. This was an upgrade of the two piece range ball and there was not much fanfare with its introduction because Spalding needed to test this product and get player feedback.

If the Executive ball proved bad people would remember that name, so the Top-Flite name was not used on these early prototype balls. After much field testing and many improvements then Spalding finally introduced the ball as the Top-Flite. Clever, if the Top-Flite name was used from the beginning it may never have been accepted. Good move.

First came the range ball, it was not very long and it flew very low but it would not cut and people hitting balls at public driving ranges were usually higher handicappers so they did not notice those little things as much as a more skilled golfer might. This is what happened in the north in the fall and spring. Many ranges were lighted and at the end of the evening the balls weren't picked up until the next morning. There was a small amount of these new two piece balls breaking, but it was not an alarming situation, until all of a sudden, many were breaking like glass. Customers were bringing these broken balls back to us for replacement or credit. We recognized the problem and did replace them, one new ball for each broken half that was over fifty percent in size. Some of these operators were trying to get a new ball for each piece, large and small. We are not dumb but we are fair, replace the big half, not the small half.

Why were these balls breaking? Because they were lying in the open field overnight in the fall and spring when it became quite cold and the balls were picking up frost. The next day when the balls still had frost they would just break when struck. The Executive was having small breaking problems as well. R & D and Bob Molitor figured out a new formula adding a secret chemicals that eliminated this very big problem. Once that was solved Spalding did become a major supplier of range balls. However the Top-Flite story was a lot more complicated than that.

While all this new technology of these solid one and two piece golf balls had been going on the sales of the "Dot" ball were dropping and we were not keeping up with our competition. Remember the Bird on The Ball promotion I talked about back when we introduced a new and improved Dot ball, 15 yards farther on the fly, the "Fort Knox Dot" we called it because of the mailing of an unmarked ball from Fort Knox Kentucky some years ago? Our sales shot up from third place to a good solid second place behind the Titliest ball. In my opinion it seems we stood still with that product or maybe even slipped a little quality wise as our competitions kept improving their product. The Dot is again back in third place. I am also hearing some of our Tour players grumbling about how the Dot was under performing.

We were spending all our R & D efforts on this new two piece product in high hopes it would replace the wound ball as the ball of the future. Which of course in time the two and three piece solid balls have done just that, but that didn't happen overnight, it took years. In the meantime Spalding was leading the industry by far in the new technology of non wound golf balls, but loosing credibility with the Dot ball.

THE TOP-FLITE GOLF BALL #121

*B*EFORE I GET TOO DEEP into the subject of golf balls I would like for you to remember that the years I am writing about are in the sixties and early seventies. I am also not going to get into deep technical information that may be very boring especially for the non golfers reading this. Keep in mind also of the time period I am and will be writing about golf equipment will be up to July of 1995 when at the age of 64 I retired. Although I still follow golf I have not kept up on equipment changes and improvements simply because I had to for almost 40 years as it was important for my career to do so, and now I don't have to. When I retired I retired and moved on to different things.

The official introduction of the Top-Flite ball was in 1971 and it was a very low flying ball off the driver, it did not stay airborne as long as the wound balls. The ball was inconsistent distance wise because it depended on ground conditions and weather as well. I won't go into all the different variables about the problems hitting this ball with the wood clubs, except I personally found out I could get better results while using my three wood off the tee because loft of the three wood was sixteen degrees compared to eleven degrees the loft of the driver. Getting that ball in the air was the key of a better performing ball with the first low flying Top-Flite ball, and that was true for most of its history.

I am going to abbreviate the name from now and indentify the ball as TF for typing purposes. Off the irons the TF was a lot longer by comparison to the distance achieved by the wound balls. There are several reasons for these characteristics and some of it had to do with spin, the spin of the ball, or the lack of it. I am not going to get too technical, I don't know if I even have all the knowledge anyway, but I have enough to try and explain some things the non golfer can understand.

When a ball is compressed by striking it with a golf club the ball leaves the club and is spinning backwards, not forwards. The dimple pattern in the cover gives the ball lift something like the air flowing under the wings of an airplane lifting it into the air. A ball with no spin will knuckle ball and drop out of the air very quickly. The TF ball had less spin than wound balls for several reasons. It could not be compressed as much as a wound ball so if the dimple pattern on both balls are the same the spin will be less, meaning less distance in the air. Because of less spin it will fly straighter however because it is not rotating one way or the other much either having less spin. So this is good for the high handicapper as they normally slice the ball badly to the right and even the better shots will not be off line as much with less spin. So this TF is better for the average to high handicapper because it will go farther with less compression for the "Soft" hitters and go straighter. In addition the ball lasted longer because it was impossible to cut into the cover like softer wound balls. What more can an average golfer ask?

It was not a ball for the better player who likes to "Work" the ball either right to left or left to right and the TF won't spin enough to let that happen. It won't stop on the greens very well either, with minimum spin it will roll forward. It was said that Sam Snead was asked a question from a high handicapper about spinning the ball on the green, that he had a hard time doing that. Sam asked him how often he hit the green with his shots or was he always short of the green. The man replied he was always short. Sam said, "Then why do you want the ball to spin and stop?"

That's why the TF was good for some and not good for others. The trick was to make the TF better so it might be played by the better golfer as well. Keep in mind that I and other fairly good to good players working for Spalding were encouraged to play this new ball and when we no longer offered the Dot we had no other Spalding ball to play but the TF. Did it hurt our game some what? If it did, and I am not going to say it did, we had to find ways to play a little differently to compensate for the difference in how this ball reacted. But if we were all that good to overcome all those little things we should have been on the tour. However, we were not hired to play we were hired to sell. Over the years I had seen some of our guys playing a completive ball and I frankly told my guys when I was a sales manager, if they ever did that and I found out about it they could go to that other company and ask for a job because they were going to need one.

Another thing that started to disappear was how to read compression of a golf ball. With wound balls that could be done and balls came in three different compressions. For the very fast hard swings it was best to use a 100 (Harder) compression ball. The 90 compression was the most used for the good to average player and the 80 compression was ideal for the softer slower swings by seniors and most ladies. The hard two piece solid non wound balls could not be measured for compassion because of its hardness. A whole different animal so to speak and that is enough about that subject. Except that all the different compressions and all the different companies competing for shelf space it was an inventory headache for the buyer. Most of the time he could or would not stock all three compressions of the three or four most popular brands and that is where friendship with your customer comes into the picture.

With the headway Spalding was making and share of the total golf ball market was improving dramatically for us our competitors were not sitting still. We had one big advantage since Spalding was the front runner in creating and constantly improving the two piece golf ball every new development we applied for Patents for all of those changes. So other companies had to work around our patents which made it more difficult for them to catch up. While that was going on the TF kept getting better and was appealing more and more to more golfers. That's a lot of mores' but more is better is it not?

X-Out Golf Balls #122

*H*ERE IS SOME GOOD INFORMATION for you golfers, all of you. I can't really say this about what is on the market today but I would expect what I am about to relate to you would still apply today because over the years as technology and manufacturing continues to improve. Golfers are all aware of x-out golf balls. How this product got started was years ago when all balls were wound with softer covers there were many things that could go wrong during the manufacturing of a ball.

There were various imperfections. The ball use to have three coats of paint, one primer, one normal then the decals and whatever was printed on the ball was applied and then a final clear coat paint to seal all of those markings so they would not wear off. The paint may have runs or the stamping might be off. These balls were downgraded and then the name of the ball would be stamped over with xxxxx. If the ball was rejected before the name was stamped on it, the ball would be downgraded to a medium price ball that did not have to conform to the United States Golf Associations specifications rules of golf indicating what a "Legal" golf ball had to meet to be eligible for tournament play.

Basically the USGA rules state a ball can not exceed a certain speed per second measured by a device to measure that speed. I won't explain how that was done as it would be too complicated. Actually the ball was shot out of cannon into a steel plate and all of this was measured by cameras. Do you believe that? I told you I wasn't going to explain that and I probably didn't. Moving on to the other basic rules, a ball could only be so small in circumference but it could be larger. The weight of the ball could only be so heavy but it could be lighter. That's enough to give you an idea. If the ball did not conform to those rules it would not be a legal ball to play in any USGA event that followed those rules. Those balls were rejected and xxxxx-out.

The xxxx-outs were packaged or sold in bulk at a reduced price. This became a very large market as many bought them knowing it was a good buy and they were not going to be played in any tournament but for casual play. The retail price for an x-out was usually $.90 to $1.00 instead of $1.25 a savings of 25 to 35 cents. Doesn't sound like much? Hey, you could by a gallon of gas for around that amount back then! It all adds up and those balls were easy to cut. However, if someone was using an x-out in a match that I was involved I would not permit it because it was not a legal ball and could very well be an advantage for that player. That x-out could be smaller which would travel father and the wind would not affect it as much. The same is true it if was heavier. Also it could exceed the foot per second rule. All advantages and that is why it is not allowed in tournament play so why should I let someone use one against me in a match?

Moving on to my advice as the two piece ball became a much improved product so did the manufacturing process. The technology became so precise that 99% of the balls coming off the line all met the USGA specifications plus they no longer needed painted as the color was now in the cover itself. The stamping had to be applied and a clear coat applied over the stamping so there were only a few true x-outs. This created another problem because there was a very large market for x-outs as it became a very important price point. Many of those x-out buyers would not purchase a higher price ball, period. The industry created a price point and had to deal with it. How did we make everyone happy?

By xxxxing out perfectly good balls, the profit structure was very healthy so that was not a problem. We had to supply and be involved with that very important price point in the market place.

So my advice at that time to many was why buy anything but x-outs for casual play, there was nothing wrong with the ball and if tested would most likely be legal. Just don't play it in a tournament or against me in a match!

I would think the same would apply in today's market but to honest I don't know. Many have told me I am out of touch, and some may say I never was!

RECLAIMED GOLF BALLS #123

*M*ORE GOLF BALL COMPETITORS WERE popping up and they were cutting into the market share. These competitors were divers. Divers? Yes, with fins and oxygen tanks and nets and buckets. These divers were contracting with golf courses for the right to dive into their water hazards to retrieve lost golf balls. This became a very large business. One of the first to get into this business and was recognized as the king, the one who really spearheaded this business became a customer and a good friend of mine in Florida when I eventually moved there. Forward spin a little, his name was Jerry Gunderson and he and his wife Judy, his business partner as well, ran this water ball business. They also started with one golf equipment store in Delray Beach, Fl., and eventually owned I believe six stores, one in Hilton Head in the Carolina's.

Jerry set up his own separate facility for processing these reclaimed "Water balls". He washed and cleaned them with a solution that did not damage or bleach the markings in anyway and graded the top grade balls. Many were like they came out of the package brand new, and these he also separated by brand and repackaged them by the dozen. Others he would sell in bulk. He was even selling range balls because more players than you can imagine were pocketing a few at their range and used them on water holes. This was a serious loss for the range operators.

Jerry was selling and shipping balls all over the country, that's how large his water ball business became. And it got bigger as hundreds of these business started to follow what Jerry was doing. Spalding was very aware that our own "Used" balls were our competition. These reclaimed balls looked brand new and the ones that didn't and were sold for less and were competing with our x-out business. There was nothing that could be done to stop it as balls that were sold then lost and found were no longer our property, "Finders, keepers". There was some discussion at Spalding of developing a new outer ball cover that would start to break down when submerged in water for a couple of days but that never happened. I told Jerry about that one day just kind of kidding him. He was not very thrilled to hear something like that, for sure.

The USGA implemented another rule, I did not lookup the date but I think it was in the eighties. Up until this rule came into being a player could start his round of golf with a brand of ball of choice and change the brand anytime as long as it was not in the middle of a hole, but when starting a new hole. This was quite common and didn't seem to be a big problem because it had been done since the game began. But the Top-Flite ball may have been the real reason that rule was changed, a player can not change the brand ball used on the first tee. It could be interchanged between holes with exactly the same identical ball but not a different ball even if that ball was made by the same company.

In other words if a player teed up a Spalding Dot on the first hole it could not be changed to a Spalding Top-Flite during that round. Same brand, Spalding, but it is a different ball. The TF as it improved was a desirable ball in the a side wind or head wind because it did not spin as much as other balls. It did not tend to balloon high into a head wind or get blown off its line of flight caused by a side wind. Many tour players had discovered this and had a couple in their golf bag which they were using on long par three holes when the wind conditions mentioned were present. The TF was also a least one club longer off irons than wound balls as well. In other words a player might have an advantage of at least two clubs because under Normal conditions the TF was longer and into the wind because of less spin it would bore into that wind so is would travel that much further as well. The down side of all this is it would make it difficult to judge how far the TF was going to travel, but all in all it would be more predictable than the wound ball in those wind conditions. Confused yet? You think the game of golf and its equipment isn't complicated? One more thing makes it more complicated, the human mind! But that's a whole different story; I'm not going to get into the "Head game," because there is enough about the game of golf that can get to you if you let it.

Having said all of this there were many complaints about ball switching during rounds and eventually it was outlawed. The exact year really doesn't matter as far as this story is concerned. No more changing to different balls during an eighteen round. But a ball could be taken out of play anytime if deemed unplayable by damage to it as long as the others playing with that player inspected the ball and agreed as long as it was not in a hazard.

The two piece balls rolled much truer when putting as they did not go out of round after being hit as a wound ball actually did. One can not actually see if a ball is not perfectly round but most wound balls took a little time for the rubber windings inside to return to their normal position, true story. Many players in those days would carry a ball ring with them, this is interesting. I did also but for different reasons. A ball ring (I still have two of them) is a round metal object with a hole in the middle. That hole is machined so its size is very accurate. It will tell me a ball is too small or too large or if it is indeed out of round and how much. A ball is inserted into the hole and if it is of legal size the ball will not drop straight through the hole, it will hang up a little and by rotating the ball it will pass through. If it drops straight through without hanging up a little then the ball is to small and not legal. If a ball will not go through at all or it is difficult when rotating the ball and kind of forcing it through it is either out of round or larger than normal or both. Lager is not illegal, to small is. Out of round speaks for itself. For years with the wound balls most players before starting a round of golf would go thr ough the three dozen or so balls given to them by their respected affiliated companies and select the balls that would go through that ball ring easy. They would not use the balls that would not pass through the ring easily in tournaments but might in practice rounds.

I think that is enough about golf balls and ball rings. Another small detour before I move on. This is about a series of putters Spalding was successful promoting which I think is interesting because of their name and how that came about and who designed them. I have forgotten the exact number of different models we had. I used the model 12 for years, but we didn't have 12 models, maybe eight including one left handed one which was the opposite of the model 12 that was an offset goose neck design. These putters were known as **TPM's**. Their official name was Touring Pro Models. The heads of the putter were made with a special metal and were gun blue in color, very dark blue and looked black. If not taken care of properly they would rust easily. Here is the kicker, these putters were designed by a southern gentleman who was a Post Master in a small southern town in, I believe, Alabama. His name was ...

Truit **P.** Mills ---- **TPM** ---- Touring Pro Model

Now you know the rest of, oh well, time to move on and that is what I am about to do, to my next assignment.

My Next Assignment #124

*T*HERE HAD BEEN A MANAGEMENT change in our home office in Chicopee, Mass. we had a new Vice President of Marketing and the sales division reported to him. His name was Bob Miller. Bob was probably in the job for about six months to a year, I really don't remember exactly, and he paid me a visit in Cleveland. He wanted to visit with me but I did not have any idea what about other than to just get to know his Regional Mangers better and visit with a few key customers. He spent most of the time asking me a lot of questions and revisiting my background, my previous 12 or 13 years with Spalding. We talked about family with Dee and me over dinner one evening. It was then I started to think there was something on his mind more than just a normal visit between upper management and middle management. Bob then laid a bomb on me.

I had no indication of any discord in the sales department in the home office as he laid out what his intentions were. He wanted to make a major change and bring me into the home office as the Spalding National Professional Golf Sales Manager! Wow!

Obviously this offer was a shock, I never expected that. Maybe a few years from now but this never really crossed my mind, I was enjoying my present position and the challenge it presented and also what I had accomplished up until now as well. I felt I belonged at the level I was at and I was no longer a greenhorn in the sales management business with seven years of experience behind me. My sales group was doing well with no major problems that I could see. My family loved our home and the area. We have made a lot of new friends over the past seven years and of course the kids had all of their friends as well. Every thing was just fine. Why would I want to change all this. I needed to sit down with Dee and have some very deep conversations.

There were a lot of questions in my mind as well and I don't remember them all. Was I ready for this? Was I capable? I am 39 years old, no kid anymore but still a young man. I have had a varied sales career so I have a lot of sales experience and some as a manager. I know one thing is almost certain, turn down an opportunity like this it is doubtful if there would ever be a second chance for promotion. In the end it would be like standing still and in a sense going backwards while Spalding and the world passes right by me.

Was Dee willing to relocate? How will if effect the kids? I had my own experience moving after graduating from high school. It would have been better in some ways had I had a year or two of school left in my new surroundings to meet new friends my age. So in that regard I knew the kids would be able to adjust and meet new friends in school. In a short time they would be fine. After much discussion we decided to accept. We were going to relocate to the Springfield Mass. area and that would eventually be Wilbraham, the home of Friendly's Ice Cream restaurants.

My responsibilities in addition of overseeing nine Regional Sales Managers were interacting with the Marketing Department and all of their MBA's, including being involved in final decisions on advertising. I would also be sitting in on meetings with the R&D people and manufacturing people on product development. The Vice President of Manufacturing was a gentleman by the name of Jim Long. Jim was so knowledgeable it was scary. A wonderful helpful individual who started his career with Spading as a teenager and did not retire until he had sixty, yes, I said 60 years with the company. Can you imagine?

I was also responsible for the men's and ladies golf professional tour players. Including making decisions of who we wanted to sign to a Staff Consultant contract and dealing with the player or their manager or both. I had to be the go between these players for their equipment needs using special specifications to create golf clubs for each individual and work with the custom club department headed up by John St. Clare. I also had to schedule appearances of our trick shot artist, Paul Bumann,

The Clown Prince of Golf who would be performing many exhibitions for us.

My entire National Sales Department consisted of myself and my secretary, Mary Jagodowski. She was my right and left hand lady and she was good. We had to do it all including creating sales and expense budgets, breaking these dollar budgets down from one big number and spreading these dollars down to the Regional Sales manager who then dolled the budget out to their salesmen. Also work with the Marketing Department on all the details for the National Sales Meeting and the PGA National Golf Show in Florida as well. I am sure there was more but that is roughly my duties, plus trying to get along with everyone, which is next to impossible.

So we sold our house, gave my two season tickets to the Browns games to the next Regional Manager, Jack Rubins. We moved everything including our dog Kola and her piano to a new house in Wilbraham. At about the same time my friend and now retired quarterback of the Cleveland Browns, Bill Nelsen, was himself moving to the Boston area as he accepted the job of Quarterbacks coach and would have a lot to do with the development of quarterback Jim Plunkett with the New England Patriots. Bill keeps following me around, from Pittsburgh to Cleveland and now to Mass., and later to Florida.

Golf Tour Professionals Contracts #125

"*S*core well." That is a carry over term I have now used for a couple of years when ending a conversation with golfers about to start their round of golf. As far as I can determine I was the only one saying that as I have never heard it said by anyone up to this day. I wonder why, it just made more sense to me than saying "Play well," or a couple of "Good lucks." I have already explained my reasons for that in a previous "Story."

There were times I could not attend certain tournaments so John St. Clare who was our expert club maker and headed up our custom club department attended as our representative. We were both going to the same tournament one week but John would be arriving a day before me so I asked him if he would get in touch with Dan Sikes, one of our staff consultants and inform he we would be terminating his contract. At the time I thought John would be the person dealing with the players helping to take the load off me. When I arrived I asked John if he had talked to Dan and he said no. Right then I realized I should not have asked John, a very nice low key person, to be the one passing on such unpleasant news like that. I told John I am glad he didn't talk to Dan Sikes because that kind of information should come from me. Dan Sikes was a winner on tour but he was on the down slope of that hill. He was not the easiest guy to talk to as well. While attending tournaments as a Regional Manager I spoke to Dan many times but he was very standoffish. Down deep though, Dan was a good guy, you just had to know him, and visa versa.

I went looking for Dan and found him on the practice tee. This was on a Tuesday; I would never talk to players on the days of a tournament, only practice days as you never want to disturb their tournament concentration. I approached Dan and after some small talk I informed him I needed to sit down and talk to him about his contract and we made arrangements to have dinner that evening. Dan was very friendly, which caught me a little off guard. We had a cocktail or two before dinner and he informed me that my predecessors were never up front with him and avoided him, or so it seemed to him. I was new at this job and he congratulated me and said for almost the last year he knew his contract date was coming to an end and several times tried to talk to our people about future plans. Dan said he hated getting the run around. I looked at Dan in the eye and said, "Dan, I appreciate the information. I will not treat you that way and leave you hanging. Dan, we appreciate your loyalty to Spalding all these years. Having said that, I have a budget problem and we can not continue with your contract. I am sorry but it will not be renewed."

We sat there in silence for a few long seconds, but to me it seemed like minuets. He looked at me and said, "Bill, I appreciate your honesty and thank you for not beating around the bush." As he was saying that he was extending his right hand to shake mine in a friendly manner. He was not upset; we had another cocktail and a very nice dinner with lively conversation. We went our separate ways and every time our paths crossed at tournaments he went out of his way to come over to me and greet me with a very friendly hello and a good man to man handshake. He was friendlier while not being on our staff than he was while being on it. Imagine?

That meeting was part of my realizing we had a big problem that I felt had to be corrected somehow and as fast as possible. It had to do with our overall dollar budget covering all of our touring Consultants playing the tour and some who had already retired from active participation but were still staff members still under contract and collecting money further depleting the budget. Here is the problem, as players get older their talents begin to decline and eventually leave the tour. They had to be replaced with new young talent and the only way to get money to sign new players was to discontinue resigning the older staff members because there was not enough money to continue paying them as well.

We were creating enemies out of those being cut off when they should become life long friends and supporters of Spalding. In those years many leaving the tour were not independently wealthy like today's players are because of the enormous amount of money most of them make now. These retiring Tour Pros needed to work and many became head professionals at golf clubs and if they remained loyal to Spalding would feature our products. How we were treated them in the end by discontinuing there contracts, they became upset and would feature our competitors products and they became bitter towards us. Understandable, but how can I overcome this unfair situation? That was something I had to correct.

In other words, how do we continue a good relationship and finally get some return from these long time members of our consultant staff after their playing days are over. We need them supporting our products when they become in a position to do so, not be mad at us. We have been doing just the opposite with our methods. Our system had to be overhauled and I sought out one of the MBA's in our marketing department for some advice and help. I had an idea but I needed help in putting it all together, why not use some of these educated business men who held Masters Degrees in Business. I knew that were good for something. Only kidding of course, or am I?

I felt that a player in decline should cut himself somehow. We should not be the bad guy because his talent is declining; it should not fall on us to tell him he is at a crossroads in the career he chose for himself. A person should be rewarded for his production and not for the lack of it and he should understand that. So, here is my thought that I needed help in putting it together.

Think of a tall hill that one needs to climb to succeed. Starting at the bottom we climb slowly to the top and then we descend a little faster on the downside. Continuing the original goal of climbing the hill we continue our journey of descending and eventually reach the bottom and a successful journey has been completed.

In other words, sign a player to a minimum dollar contract and then he has to prove he can climb that hill. We shouldn't have to pay a person for something he has not produced. As he climbs that hill to a successful career his contract money increases as his production increases. At the top he is paid for reaching that on a scale to be determined. As he starts his decent down the other side of the hill along with his declining talent his production also declines as does his sliding income. He cuts himself! He remains your friend as it should be.

Where I needed help was working out that formula within the total players under contract and the budget. I won't use the name of the MBA who helped me with this. I bounced this idea off a couple of player's agents who I will not name as well and received thumbs up. My pitch to them is that I didn't think it was fair for them to try and sign untested players to contracts that deemed them super stars before they proved anything. I told these agents if they thought their player was going to become a superstar then they should not have a problem with this contract. The money would be there if they performed the same any of us get paid, me, the player and his agent. The agents would rather have money up front but they had to admit I had a justifiable argument.

This system worked out and was used for a few years with most players. But there are always exceptions depending on a player's reputation some contracts were different. However, overall this method did work much better and most players remained friends of Spalding long after their playing days were over. I felt I good about that.

GOLF TOUR PLAYERS AGENTS #126

*T*HE DAYS OF DEALING DIRECTLY with touring professional golfers are gone because they all hired agents to do their bargaining for them. Arnold Palmer teamed up with a young lawyer from Cleveland, Mark McCormack, as his agent and business manager. Mark was putting together all sorts of deals using Arnold's enormous popularity, paying them huge royalties. Mark started to build an organization that became the biggest in the business and although Mark is no longer with us his organization is still handling all sorts of sports personalities. Marks dealings with Arnold stated a trend and many agents started to show up. At one time Mark McCormack represented the Big Three all at one time, Arnold, Jack Nicklaus and Gary Player. The latter two did go in another direction and left Marks stable. I could no longer begin to discuss contracts or business in general directly with a staff member or potential staff member.

I now had to go through their agent and many of them were not very realistic. Naturally they made their money collecting a minimum of 10% of anything they earned for their client. So many agents wanted as much as they could get up front, regardless it their client had proved his worth on the tour or not. I did not like the idea of paying anything until that player started to show by his performance they were worth it. Don't we all get paid on what we produce after we produce, not before?

One of the Agents I worked well with was Marvin "Vinnie" Giles. Vinnie was a lawyer and a great player in his own right, winning the U. S. Amateur and the British Amateur along with many other amateur tournaments and Vinnie never turned professional. Vinnie was one of the agents I talked to about my sliding scale contract I was working on. He like the idea but the McCormack group did not. Of course

McCormack felt his group was superior and they wanted everything done their way. I had a big problem with them as they had signed a couple of our staff members and when their contracts came up I had a difficult time in dealing with them on their terms. I simply did not have the budgets to work out contracts and I lost several players and that did not make me very happy. I like to win too.

McCormack grew his business very fast and to talk to him directly was almost impossible, I had to deal with others working for Mark. One of those was Hughes Norton who must have been assigned to me and Spalding. I liked Hughes personally; he was a good guy and he was following the guidelines that were set for him. He was a little green to the golf business at first. As a matter of fact at one tournament he was looking for me and I happened to be out on the course that day, which was rare for me. Lo and behold I see this guy from a distance walking towards me, he was dressed in a suit and tie, and he was carrying a briefcase! It was none other than Hughes Norton! I looked him up and down, looked him in the eye and said "Hughes, do you know how silly you look?" He said why? So I explained why. I replied, "Hughes my friend can I give you a little advice?" I don't want to offend you."

Hughes was just new to the world of golf so he just didn't know he should join the rest of us in this business and dress casually while attending tournaments. And leave the briefcase in your car Hughes. He was not offended and thanked me for the advice. After all I was a customer of his so what else could he say.

It turned out I could not do business with the McCormack Agency and every time Hughes came to be with a prospective player to sign a contract I simply told him I was not interested in that player as long as his company would not consider our contract. I refused to deal with them. I couldn't afford them with the budget restrictions I had. We had a nice staff as it was I just didn't need another body. Then it happened, the crowning blow. Lanny Wadkins was one of our staff consultants and he signed a contract with McCormack as his agent.

As the golf business was growing so were our promotional budgets so my sliding scale contract was being used with our staff members, but not exclusively. We were in a position to offer more lucrative contracts to players we felt were more valuable to us because it may be pretty obvious certain players were indeed something special. One such individual was Lanny who in his first two years on the tour he was named rookie of the year and then sophomore of the year. So now I will present the contract we had worked up to present to his agent, Mark McCormack himself. He got the word that I was not working well with his people so I guess he decided Lanny was a very valuable commodity and he would negotiate with me rather than have Hughes Norton work with me. I'm getting the reputation of being tough to deal with? Good. So let's see if I score well.

My Rejection Of a Contract #127

*J*ERRY LANSTON (LANNY) WADKINS WOULD eventually become a member of the Golf Hall Of Fame. Lanny won the U.S. Amateur in 1971 and joined the tour in 1972 and won his first PGA Tour tournament. He won a couple of times in 1973. Lanny signed a contract with Spalding when he joined the tour mainly because he was using Spalding equipment throughout his college years. His two year contract was coming to an end in 1974 setting up my meeting with Mark McCormack. I was to meet Mark in New York as we were both traveling on Thursday at 10 AM June 20, 1974. No my memory is not that good. I am a pack rat of sorts as I still have that contract negotiations for Lanny Wadkins! It also states that I was to have a review about that meeting back in Chicopee on Tuesday July 2, 1974 and a second session with Mark McCormack on Friday July 5th.

Fast forward. There were a couple of problems with that as I had turned in my resignation with Spalding to be effective June 30, 1974. Mark McCormack did not know that I was leaving Spalding and I did not tell him. I was still on the job so I went ahead with our meeting; I was still doing what I was being paid to do. That's why I was getting the big bucks! Ha!

Lanny's first contract was not on the performance sliding scale I outlined previously because it was decided with his record in college and having won the U.S. Amateur he would be rewarded differently. We also had put his name on a golf club and golf ball to be sold in retail stores for which he was paid a royalty on sales as part of his contract. The new contract proposal was to be for three years 1975, 76, 77. The dollar amount escalated each year with a minimum of $46,000., $50,500., $55,000. This was tied into International royalties. Remember those last two words as all of our contracts with our stall members were world wide. After Mark and I met and concluded the usual greetings we got down to business. Mark started talking first and kept using the words "Super star" and started to throw some ridicules figures around including the fact that Mark wanted to discuss creating a separate contract for every country in the world that had a golf course! What?

I finally stoped him when I said, "Mark, who the hell are you talking about? I am here to talk to you about Lanny Wadkins who is not a super star**, yet**. He has not won a major tournament on tour **yet.** He may become a super star but he is **not one now.** Our contracts also are only world wide and I cannot consider what you are proposing so we are both wasting our time. I will relay our conversation to my superiors for their evaluation. It was an interesting meeting Mark, hope to see you down the road." And I got up and left, I never left the copy of our contract negotiations, those are the ones I still have.

Spalding did not resign Lanny, although Lanny again rejoined Spalding after this new deal did not pan out as Mark had planned. He signed Lanny to a lesser know company who was making inroads and the contract was tied to this companies stock. That company did survive but its stock really didn't grow so Lanny was not happy. Lanny would also go on to win 21 times including one major the PGA in 1977 and was inducted into the Golf Hall Of Fame; indeed he reached super star status. He climbed that hill and **scored well.**

I am jumping ahead a little bit but I want to complete my Lanny Wadkins involvement. As I left Spalding and was starting my new position with the Toney Penna Golf Company my son Jim and our dog Kola were driving to Florida. I had made arrangements to meet Toney Penna where the 1974 PGA Championship was being played August 8-11th near Winston-Salem, Tanglewood C. C., in nearby Clemens, N.C.

Ironically Toney had made arrangements to play golf prior to the tournament with a pair of brothers who lived in the area. Their names were Bobby and Lanny Wadkins! I kid you not. Lanny was still under contract with Spalding and was carrying the bag and playing Spalding clubs. I knew Lanny and Bobby pretty well and we had a really good time but Lanny was somewhat upset that I hadn't talked to him about his contract. I had to explain that sports agents would not permit companies dealing directly with their clients, so I could not. He did not want to leave Spalding, but did. And he did return after a few years. That is my story with Mark McCormack and Lanny Wadkins, interesting memories.

My Golf Tour Involvements #128

*D*URING MY INVOLVEMENT WITH THE men's and ladies professional golf tour, meeting all the many media people, both writers of newspapers and magazines, plus some TV personalities along with top executives with other golf companies was very interesting. All this was happening starting in 1957 but primarily 1964 though 1977. I could not possibly mention every one I met simply because I can't remember all of them. It also sounds like I am name dropping. But in actuality it did happen, and I still sometimes can't believe that skinny kid from Canton rubbed elbows and tipped a few with people most of us just don't ever get the opportunity to meet.

In high school one of my hero's was Sam Snead. He even won the Masters in 1949 the year I graduated. A few years later I find myself calling on him as one of my customers. I even had a couple of beers with Sam in a small speakeasy in W. Va. Go figure! At first it can be a little overwhelming and unreal but it did not take long to feel comfortable as most of these celebrities are not much different than you or I. They are just unlucky in some ways; most can not go anywhere and not be noticed. They find themselves always under the microscope all the time. No real privacy.

It was not all fun and games standing on the practice range with all those players like long lost friends. Had to listen to a lot of complaints about their golf clubs not being exactly like they wanted or expected them to look or perform. There are no two clubs alike, especially drivers. Most players are constantly searching for a back up driver they can depend on it something happens to their favorite. Back in those years it was more difficult than perhaps it is today with all the technology advancements to accomplish.

The biggest problem I had was the golf ball. While we were busy creation the solid two piece Top-Flite ball the old reliable "Dot" was not being looked after as well as it should have been and our tour players were complaining that it was not up to tour standards. Some were not playing the ball at all but said they were. There was a company that took surveys at all tournaments. It was run by a family by the name of Darrell. The Darrell Survey Co., Very nice people who job it was to look into the bags of each player and write down exactly what clubs they were using. Was the Wilson guy using Wilson and if not how many clubs were Wilson and what were the other clubs. The Darrell's made their living by contracting with the golf companies as the golf companies wanted to know what clubs and balls their consultants were using. The golf ball count was really important. The players were asked by the Darrell's what they were using before they teed off. There was a problem with that as back then there was no one ball rule. A player could switch between holes and some would play the first and maybe a couple of holes with the ball they were being paid to use and then switch. I knew it and they knew I knew it. I had a hard time convincing our management this was going on and our ball was not as good as our competition.

I did not go out on the course that often but once in a while I did. I did like to watch Dave Stockton because of his short game was just something to behold. Dave was a really good guy who was not afraid to tell you what he thought. His best friend on tour was Al Geiberger, Mr. 59, the first man to ever score below 60. Al was the most likeable human being you would ever want to meet. Both Dave and Al were Spalding Staff players, Dave spotted me one day after he hit his second shot on a par four holes, he came towards me and about twenty yards away Dave threw a ball towards me and said some unpleasant things about it. Before I could pick it up about a dozen people rushed over to take a look to see what ball it was. It was a Dot of course and I didn't want anyone to see it but I could not pick it up fast enough.

I was not too happy with Dave and I told him so after the round. "Dave, don't ever do that again. Come to me quietly and tell me what is on your mind". Don't embarrass the Spalding name, and so on. He apologized and told me everything he thought was wrong with the ball and claimed it was costing him a shot or two every round. That is serious stuff. A shot a round is four a tournament and he stated he could not afford to let that happen. It could be the difference between winning and placing well up the leader board and could cost him a great amount of prize money. Understandable to me, but as you will find out later, not to management.

Dave's complaints were that he felt it was shorter in distance than other balls and it was not holding its shape very well. I asked nice guy Al Geiberger about the ball and he would just say it was ok, but didn't mean it. He would not bad mouth anything. Other staff members had the same complaints as Stockton. I carried a ball ring with me at all tournaments and the balls I was given by the players were not very round. I had a difficult time forcing them thought the ring. Many of our staff members were not playing the ball all the time. I made a deal with them at one time. I told them I was not questioning them if they were playing the Dot but I wanted them to promise to use the Dot during Pro Am day so their amateur partners would see them using the Dot and not a competitor's ball.

Finally I made a decision at a tournament and told our staff players they no longer had to play the Dot and I was removing that statement from their contract. That was a very big decision to make on my own, but I felt it was the right thing to do on behalf of our tour staff players. They were openly not happy and I was convinced they were right, the ball was not up to tour quality standards regardless of what some back at the factory might think. Some of the greatest players in the world were not playing the Dot and I respected their opinion. Plus I could see for myself by using the ball ring the ball was not what it should be.

I had many happy staff members shaking my hand and even giving me a hug when I informed them of my decision. Could I expect the same reaction back in Chicopee? Well, when I reported what I had decided during a meeting with the President, the V.P. of Marketing and all my superiors can you predict their response? Yes? No? Or maybe?

MY TOUR BALL DECISION REACTION #129

AFTER I MADE THE DECISION while at a tournament about our Tour Staff Consultants no longer were under contract to play the Dot ball because I agreed with the players the Dot was not up to tour play standards due to several factors. Its length was being questioned and being out of round after being struck a couple of times by the drive was another. Many were claiming the ball was inconsistent in its performance. They did not trust the ball. Most of the players were not playing the ball anyway and felt guilty about that. I did not think that was fair to them to feel that way because it was not their fault. They really didn't want to cheat on their contract by playing a competitors ball.

I have always felt that if you're in management and are responsible for something I have the right to make a decision. Hopefully those decisions turn out to be the correct ones. I felt I had been given enough proof by the players who are talented enough to know when a ball is not what it is suppose to be. In management part of my job is to listen! Collect enough information, weight the facts and make a decision. I made one that was not to popular with my superiors who were not golf orientated. I don't think some of them even played golf. If they did, they did not play or know the game I and the professionals know.

I am not going to use any names of the management team. No, my decision was not taken to well. One of the reasons a company spends money on athletes is for exposure of that company's product. The rub off is that consumers will take notice of what a payer is using and buy that product for their use. It is important to have our players in contention to win as they are in the final groups of the golf course so the many spectators see them, what caps they are wearing and seeing that big red bag with Spalding in big white letters. Being in contention means more TV exposure which is free advertising if your players are in those last groups, the contenders.

I attempted to defend my decision by restating those facts and if our ball is holding our players back by costing them shots then they will not be in contention and we will not get the exposure we are looking for. If they are in contention fans can not see what ball they are playing, except if the TV cameras zoom in on the ball for some reason. Otherwise people will notice that big red Spalding bag and the Spalding logo hats most of them wear. Isn't that what we are after, why we spend money to sign good players?

The President and the Vice President of Marketing, who was new and had replaced Bob Miller. who had hired me, were not happy. It was very hard to get manufacturing to admit that the ball was not equal to competition, who wants to admit that? Their focus was on the development of the Top-Flite ball, the ball of the future. Rightly so, the TF ball was gaining in sales and popularity while the sales volume and profit looked very promising. Our TF ball sales were picking up speed while our Dot ball sales were fading fast.

I guess in the long run I was right because it was not too long before the Dot disappeared. A Tour Edition ball was developed in hopes of replacing the Dot ball for the low handicap players and the tour players. It was also a two piece ball but with a much softer cover material. The TF was very hard, the Tour Edition very soft, too soft which caused it to spin too much at times. A few of our tour consultants were testing the Tour Edition in tournaments; Greg Norman was one of them. He claimed to like the ball very much but I remember one tournament I was watching on TV, I think it was a major tournament and can't remember much except it was a par three. I do remember this, Greg was using the Tour Edition ball and was either the leader or one shot out of first, his shot hit the green a few feet past the pin, the ball backed up all the way off the green into some heavy rough. Instead of a possible tap in birdie two, Greg made a four, a two shot swing and he did not win the tournament. I really thought that ball cost him the tournament. He stopped using the ball shortly there after. Maybe I was right, maybe not. I don't know as I never got the chance to ask Greg about it.

Now it is backspin time again. Back to the period of 1971-74, a few more tour stories and then back to business at the home office.

A Couple of Golf Tour Stories #130

REMEMBER STEVE MELNYK? STEVE HAD an outstanding amateur record winning just about everything. When he turned professional he joined the Spalding staff. Steve is one of the nicest guys I have ever met. After his days on tour Steve worked as an on course announcer on TV. Steve had moderate success on tour but never reached the potential that was expected of him. Paul Bumann, the Clown Prince of Golf, the trick shot artist, knew Steve very well. One day Paul told me the reason he thought Steve didn't make it big on tour was his physical build, his own body kept him from being a big winner. Steve was a large man with a very big chest. Paul claimed that Steve's problem was that he had no neck. No neck? He really didn't, it appeared that Steves head sat right on top of his shoulders and that big chest of his. Paul said that during Steve's backswing he could not keep his head steady over the ball as his shoulders turned taking the club back was causing his head to turn with his shoulders which took his eyes off the ball. Paul said that was the reason he did not become the player he was when he was younger and a little slimmer. He could not help it his body was what it was, a very short neck. I watched Steve swing after that and I could see what Paul Bumann was talking about.

My personal story with Steve was during my visit to a tour event in Texas in March one year. I had not hit a golf ball since maybe November, about four or five months. I'm on the practice tee with Steve watching him hit shots and just talking. One thing I learned a long time ago is that you never touch a players clubs. Look into his bag fine, but never touch a players clubs without asking permission. I'm dying to hit a golf shot and we were almost alone on that practice range. I said to Steve, do you mind if I look at your five iron? Steve said no, go right ahead. I took it out of his bag put it into my hands, griped it and Steve is watching me closely.

He said to me, "Bill, that's a pretty good looking grip, you look like you want to hit a shot." I told Steve I really would since I have not hit a ball since last fall. I asked Steve if he would mind if I did and he rolled a ball over to me and said, "Go ahead hit it, let's see what you got!" I'm standing there in my Foot Joy loafers with very slippery leather soles. I said, "Steve, with these shoes and how stiff I am I will most likely miss the ball completely." He said, "No one around but you and me so ahead." I took a couple of practice swings, set up over the ball with a fairly narrow stance since I did not want my feet to slip, took a three quarter backswing, came through the ball and hit the most beautiful shot of my life. I just striped it straight down the range with a very slight draw at the end. Steve could not believe it. He said, "Let me see you do that again," and he rolled another ball over to me. I was still in shock and did not say anything and I repeated what I had done, slightly narrow stance for balance, took the same backswing and again hit the identical shot. Steve about went nuts, rolled another ball over to me and I calmly cleaned the dirt off the club and put it back in his bag. I am not an odds maker but I can tell you I know when to quit while I was ahead. I said, "Thanks Steve, I just had to hit a ball or two. That sure felt good." We both had a good laugh and I told him it was pure luck. He said, no, it wasn't. Why would I want to argue with a touring professional? I think because the shoes were so slippery I made it a point not to over swing, I used a very controlled swing. That should tell me something about hitting a golf ball!

There were three players I missed signing to contracts that has always bugged me somewhat. Their names were Tom Kite, Laura Baugh and Pat Bradley who is Keegan Bradley's aunt. Keegan for you non golfers is currently playing on the PGA Tour and is doing quite well.

I am not going into any details but many good college teams used Spalding equipment. When these players turned professional after leaving college many of them were playing with Spalding clubs and they leaned towards signing contracts with Spalding because they were used to using Spalding clubs. Tom Kite looked like a very good prospect and

I wanted to talk to him. Again, I sent someone (I won't use his name) to a tournament a day before I could get there and asked that he seek Tom out and let Tom know I wanted to talk to him about discussing a contract with Spalding. I knew he was a hot item and did not want another company to speak to him if they had not already.

Tom Kite was very friendly and very approachable and as luck would have it as I arrived at the tournament site before I even had a chance to meet with my man the first person I ran into was Tom Kite! I had met Tom before and I approached him and reintroduced myself. We shook hands and I asked Tom if my man had spoken to him yesterday and he said he had not. I started to tell Tom what I had in mind. He interrupted me and said, "Bill, I am sorry I didn't know that. I just signed a contract with Wilson this morning. I didn't know Spalding was interested." That convinced me that my front man had to be me. It's a hard way to learn something I had known for a long time, if I wanted something done, than I had better do it myself. Then I would have no one to blame but myself.

About Pat Bradley and Laura Baugh's missed contracts, next page.

$\mathcal{P}$AT BRADLEY WAS A NEW England girl who won everything in college and looked like a shoe in to be the next LPGA superstar. She did achieve that status and was also elected to their Hall of Fame. We really didn't have much of a chance to sign her but I gave it my best. I was working with her brother Tom who was also her business agent. She never played Spalding so I had a set made up for her to her specifications for her to try out. I still have the letter from Tom written May 9, 1974 informing me of their decision. Below is a part of that letterTom wrote to me. Tom also spelled Spalding with a U.

"Pat received the Spaulding clubs and played some practice rounds with them. She was very happy with the way they responded to her style of play. However we have decided to accept the offer made by the Colgate-Palmolive Co."

I won't retype the entire letter but just a few more lines of interest.

"The deciding factor was in the possibility of television advertising of Colgate consumer products. Five per cent of Colgate's total advertising budget for 1974 is involved with women's golf and I want Pat to be a part of that movement."

"I am writing to you now as I have just gotten off the line with Pat after making the decision. From the beginning at the show in Florida you have dealt with us in a sincere and honest manner not demonstrated by some of your more will known competitors. It has been a pleasure to work with you and I hope we can meet

again in the future (for we did not sign a lifetime contract)."
Signed,

Sincerely Thomas K. Bradley

I sent a copy of that letter to my superiors and noted on it, "What can I say?"

The next one I missed was Laura Baugh a very pretty young lady from Southern Californian who was on the cover of all the Golf Magazines not only for her very talented golf game as an amateur and what she accomplished during her college career. Laura was a pin up, a very attractive girl next door type. She was just really cute, something the LPGA tour could be proud of, and was. She drew a lot of attention. She did not play Spalding but I was going to give signing her my best shot. I even gambled and had a staff bag made up with her name on it, just in case she did sign with us, she would have it.

When we met face to face with Laura and her agent I had that bag with me but out of sight. She was very nice as was her agent and they decided it was best for her to sign a really lucrative contract with the company of the clubs she had always played, Wilson. They thanked me and Spalding for our interest and said they were very sorry it could not have been a deal with Spalding. I told them we appreciated the opportunity to discuss a contract with them and that I understood how much confidence a person has in a certain product and how hard it is to change. I looked at Laura and with a big grin I said I had a surprise for her. I said in anticipation of a possible deal I had this made up for you and I presented the bag to for her to see. Laura looked at me and said, "Bill, that's a great looking bag, can I have it anyway? I would love to have it in my den."

Laura never won a tournament on the ladies tour but she sure attracted a lot of attention and had numerous contracts with all sorts of companies who featured her smiling pretty face. She later married and had six children. You win some and you lose some. There may be some more stories about the tour when I get to Florida so I am going to wrap up this part for now; the New England Patriots Game is just starting.

New England Patriots Game and More #132

MY OLD FRIEND AND FORMER Quarterback for the Cleveland Browns is now the Quarterback coach for the New England Patriots. He has invited Dee and I to be his quest for a game and this was in 1972 or 73. Dee and I get on the Mass. Turnpike and drove across the state to meet Bill and attend the game.

After the game we meet a few players and coaches and then have dinner with Bill and his wife Sue. It was great being with these two friends again. We had a lot to talk about, really enjoyable. Time to go home, back across the state on the Turn Pike, darkness has now fallen. I am driving a Chevrolet Caprice four door sedan, their largest model, a very good heavy car.

Not a good trip, we were involved in an accident and could have been injured or worse. We were so lucky we didn't get hurt at all except for a couple of bumps and bruises. Here is what happened. We are in the left lane behind maybe three cars, all of us passing slow traffic on our right. I don't know what our speed was, maybe seventy. We did not know this of course until later but what was going on ahead there was a pickup truck and pulling a flat bed trailer. The bed of this trailer was just about the height my headlights. The idiot driving this rig for some reason decided he wanted to turn around so he pulled his vehicle off the left lane onto the grass medium but his flat bed trailer was still sticking out into the left lane of the Pike. We had no idea of this however; it is what we found out later.

All of a sudden we see debris flying towards us and then we hit something, the flat bed. The two cars in front of me hit it first and we were the third car to hit it. I avoided hitting the two cars in front of me somehow. When I hit that trailer he impact tore through my left front head light, fender and damaged my left front wheel and tire and I somehow controlled the car and moved towards the right lane bringing the car to a stop just right of the right lane off the road. I think there was a fourth car hit that damn trailer right behind me. No cars that hit that trailer hit each other or any other cars and I don't know how that was possible. And no one was hurt either, a small miracle, or maybe a very large miracle. The left front of my car was almost ripped off and the left front wheel was destroyed. Tow truck time.

We were about two thirds of the way home so after all is said and done, the police and all the reports and then tow truck finally arriving, we got to ride all the way back to Wilbraham in the front seat of the tow truck with the driver. Nice guy, he was kind enough to drop us off at our house and then took the car to the Chevy dealership. What a trip. That was the only game we went to while in Mass.

Moving to a happier subject, the kids are getting acclimated as is our dog Kola, the roamer. This part is not happy, the darn dog must not be happy in our new environment as she takes off and when she returns she has found the dirtiest stinky stuff to roll her neck in. I don't know why she does that as she hates baths and we have to give her one almost every day. Remember, dogs ran free back in those dark ages. We didn't take them for walks with a plastic bag and scooper. If I had to do that, there would be no dog.

Son Jim discovered he could still play baseball but found out the sport of choice in New England is Ice Hockey. While in Cleveland Jim only ice skated a few times with soft fitting ice skates which means he was more on the inside of his ankles. He was not good but he had not skated much. So he saw all those kids who started skating as soon as they could walk playing hockey. Jim went out for the team and of course got cut right away. Fast forward and you see Jim going anywhere he could find ice on the ground or small ponds, anywhere and he was skating and skating. The next year he went out for the team and others who had been skating for years got cut, and Jim made it! I have always thought it I had the athletic ability as my son I would have made it to the NBA and the golf tour. He really could play anything he took up, but never really stuck to any one sport. His mind was and is, other places, the future is tomorrow every day with him. Which is good, he is resourceful. He is probably not going to be too happy about my saying this when he reads it. True story tho ...

The ice rinks in the Springfield area are going night and day so it was common that these kids were playing scheduled games during the middle of the night. No kidding, I mean like 2 AM, 6 AM., all kinds of early hours so we had to either stay up late or get up early. Go to bed when you can, some nights were like that. Jim wasn't first team right away but he got a lot of playing time and did just fine with the little bit of experience he had. Nice job, Jim.

I really don't remember to many things about our two and one half years in Mass. I'll explain that later if I can but in the meantime I joined Hampden Country Club in Wilbraham. It was a new club with only nine holes open for play which was constructed in a valley on pretty level ground. The other nine holes were under construction and would open soon. This nine was being built on the side of a hill, so each nine holes were very different. All good golf holes, this was a very good and difficult course. The hill side nine was the most difficult because of sloping fairways which were tree lined as well.

I began playing a lot of evening to let off steam after work, mostly nine hole rounds with the Golf Pro Danny DiRico. Danny was a good player and we had a lot of really hot contested rounds trying to beat the heck out of each other and I was holding my own. He stopped giving me handicap strokes; we played even as I was playing the best golf of my life for some reason. I even set the course record of par 72 that is how tough the course was. I did that right before leaving the area for Florida, in July of 1974 and I was playing with Danny when I shot that round. That score held up as the course record for both Pro and Amateur for several years. There were many local tournaments held there, Professionals included but no one broke that record until someone sent me the following article while I was in Florida several years later. The article read as follows;

**DiRico Breaks
Hampden Mark**

HAMPDEN- Home Pro Danny DiRico sharpened up for his trip to the National Club Professional Championship Tournament by breaking the course record Saturday at the Hampden Country Club. DiRico's 34-35-69 shattered the old mark of 72 set by amateur Bill Faulhaber in July 1974.

My claim to fame, Score Well!

Strange thing about June and July of 1974, the last week of June, my last week with Spalding back then, I went through the Lanny Wadkins contract deal, and then in July I was getting ready to move to Florida. When I set that course record of 72 playing with Danny DiRico, it was the last round I played at Hampden Country Club. And the next round of golf I played was with Toney Penna, Lanny and Bobby Wadkins on my way to Florida. Strange things happen, don't they?

BACK TO BUSINESS #133

I AM NOT GOING TO SPEND a lot of time writing about my three years in Chicopee Mass., Spalding's headquarters. That was a very busy three years and frankly I do not have a clear memory of everything simply because I was not really very happy there. My wife Dee will not like me saying that because it has to do with memory. She says if you keep saying your memory is bad, it will become just that. While that may be true I believe I just plain shut out the things I didn't want to remember. I will comment on a few things however because they tie in with my departure.

As the National Professional Golf Sales Manager the company appointed me to represent Spalding as a board member of the National Golf Foundation. The NGF was totally funded by the various Golf Manufactures and I attended their annual meeting. There was also the Golf Club Manufactures Association and I attended their meetings as well.

So I was rubbing elbows with all these other executives representing their companies. Between the Golf Tours, the PGA Shows and these kinds of meetings there were not many important people in the golf business I didn't know. You never know when these kinds of associations become important in various ways. It was at one of these meetings in Puerto Rico while playing golf at the Dorado Golf Club. As I had mentioned in the past for some reason I played, or I should say, scored well on very good golf courses. This particular day I shot 71, which impressed Evan Baker who was in our foursome. Evan was an executive of a company that owned the Toney Penna Golf Company and also Rawlings Sporting Goods, and some other companies in the sporting goods business, including Fred Perry Tennis apparel.

Evan started talking to me about the fact he was thinking about changing the way Toney Penna Golf Company was doing business and he wanted to talk to me about what he was thinking. He wanted my advice. He was picking my brain somewhat but then later his thoughts went beyond that. He wanted to know if I would be interested in making a career change. I told him I didn't think so but I didn't want to close the door on that entirely and I asked Evan what his time table was concerning his changes and what these changes involved. He said he was not in a rush but wanted me to think about it and we could talk more seriously if I might be interested. He wanted to keep in touch with me which I said was fine with me. Actually I was thinking of making a change but did not want to make that known to anyone at that time.

There were a few things happening I was uncomfortable with. I did not see eye to eye with top management and some of the MBA's in our Marketing Department. None of these people were knowledgeable golf people. Business, yes, no doubt, that's what they learned in college. They knew how to sell soap. As far as I was concerned they did not take the time to learn what was really going on in the trenches of the professional golf business. I am not going to get into a long discussion about all that because it would be debatable and of course I could be wrong. So let's just say we were not seeing eye to eye and let it go at that. Of course in a situation like that I am going to loose. I know that my decision of telling our touring staff pros they no longer had to play our Dot ball did not go over well. That was only one thing. Another thing, I can be pretty stubborn. That is part of being a good salesman. There is never a "No" in a good salesman's vocabulary. However I do use that word "No" when I disagree with something.

I guess the real question in my own mind is should I have been in this position in the first place. Was I ready for this kind of responsibility? Was I really capable? Those kinds of questions are hard to answer. If anyone would ask me any of those questions now my answer would be a very firm yes. No doubt in my mind and I can now run a business which I might not have been capable of way back then. But that's history and I am going to be moving forward in my education of life and business.

Remember, standing still is actually moving backwards. Also a moving target is harder to hit.

Part of that movement was management realigning the structure of the sales management team and what that amounted to I was given a lateral move in my responsibilities. I didn't get fired but I might as well have. With all of this going on I ended up with bleeding ulcers and a new title, which was,

Director – Golf and Sales Relations.

DIRECTOR – GOLF AND SALES RELATIONS #134

*I*MPRESSIVE SOUNDING ISN'T IT? A brand new title accompanied by bleeding ulcers. My frustrated wife finally convinced me to take a one week vacation. Dee rented a cabin some where, I don't even remember where it was, I think it was on the Cape. I had not taken a vacation for several years. A few days here and there and some long weekends but not an actual vacation and I was eligible for three weeks a year with my 17 years of service.

It was during this time that I was still dealing with the tour players and going to all those association's meetings, like the one in Puerto Rico. So yes, I really was thinking very strongly about moving on. I just knew that the two top Spalding executives would not last. The company directors who put them into those positions would see the light and take them out. I also knew that my bleeding ulcers were a sign I could not wait for that to happen. I finally decided to look elsewhere. If and when those two executives are gone where does that leave me anyway? I have to look out for myself and my family. I am not going to fail my family so I put some feelers out in addition to my conversations with Evan Baker and the Toney Penna Co.

I had a couple of small west coast companies interested in talking to me but I was not interested in moving to California and I took them out of the picture without any conversations whatsoever. I was traveling covering my responsibilities with Spalding and interviewing with people on weekends. I met twice with another company located in Miami, met with them in New York, once on my own and once with Dee. They were looking for a National Sales Manager. This was primarily a soft goods operation. I have had some experience in clothing but primarily I am a hard goods man. I explained my concerns about that but was told being a sales manager was the same regardless of the product. Salesmen are salesmen and need supervision and guidance. That did not seem to be a problem with them. That is true to some extent, but will leave it at that.

One of the products was the Foot Joy shoe line and I met with Dick Tarlow the CEO of Foot Joy. He wanted me to be involved with the Rep firm handling his product. I once played golf with Dick in the Tampa area during one of those association meetings I have mentioned. Again, I shot a good round, this one on one leg. The night before I woke up in the middle of the night with a cramp in my left calf and the cramp swelled up about the size of a tennis ball. It hurt so bad I started pounding on it with my fist. Dee thought I had lost it. After seeing a Doctor a couple of days later told me I had, Phlebitis. I caused that because I pounded on it so hard I did a lot of damages and caused bleeding in the muscles, Anyway I could not even lace up my left shoe and shot 76 on the Copperhead Course. I knew Dick Tarlow for a number of years but that was the first time I had spent any amount of time with him. The best place in the world to get to know people and do business is during a round of golf. Dick relayed to the head man of this rep. organization that he was recommending that I be hired.

After several interviews I was offered the job but I could not pin down just exactly what my compensation plan was. There was a salary figure but beyond that it was a grey area. I was informed that if I did alright and they did alright then I would do alright monetarily as well. I was not comfortable with several things and two were what I have just described and the other was Miami. I loved the idea of moving to Florida but not Miami. A beautiful city but really not for me as I found out later I was right. When I traveled to Miami for business I did not hear much English spoken. I felt like I needed my passport! If I moved there I would have to learn the Spanish language. Not for me and Dee agreed. I thanked them for the opportunity and informed them I didn't feel like I was the right person they were looking for and declined.

Of course all during these interviews I was having several with the Toney Penna Co. and was making my own suggestions which coincided with what Evan Baker had in mind. There was no sales force selling the

Penna line of "Custom clubs." Almost all sales were coming from club professionals familiar with Toney and his wood clubs. There was also a more than modest amount of clubs being shipped to Japan. Evan Baker wanted to establish a sales force to call on the golf professional trade and he needed someone to do that plus create advertising through a local ad agency to promote interest. So that person was to act as the marketing arm of the company as well. The position was the Vice President of Sales and Marketing, but I did not use that title when I took the position; it was just Vice President of Sales with marketing responsibilities. The complete compensation program was spelled out including a car and a Country Club membership. The location of the Penna Company was Jupiter Florida which is part of the Palm Beaches, A wonderful Florida location, north of Miami and Fr. Lauderdale, Paradise.

After Dee visited the area we agreed we should accept this opportunity. We were given all the time we needed to sell our house in Wilbraham Mass. and look for a new home. All the travel and moving costs were paid for. In 1974, there was not much in Jupiter so we eventually ended up purchasing a home in North Palm Beach, more about all of this later.

My Spalding Resignation #135

ONE THING YOU SHOULD NEVER do is burn bridges when leaving the people and company you have been working with and for. I did the best I could by giving my resignation, a copy I still have. It is as below;

June 13, 1974

Mr. X X

Dear X:

After seventeen years service with Spalding, during which time Spalding has treated me well, and in turn I feel I have more than given my personal dedication and energy to Spalding, I find myself at an impasse. I find myself in a position of total frustration observing changes that are being made or that are about to be made in many areas of the company which I am very close and sensitive to.

Since I have never written a letter of this type before, and with my length of time with Spalding, it is very difficult to express my feelings of seventeen years in one short letter. My feelings for Spalding run very deep and Spalding is, and always will be, a part of me.

However, I find many things about the company, and the way it views my skills and my future, unacceptable:

1. **Considering personnel to fill top Sales Management positions –**

   a. **Who do not have the qualifications I possess.**
   b. **I am being completely passed over without consideration.**

2. My present job leads nowhere –

    a. My career with Spalding is at a standstill, at best.

3. The climate at Spalding is no longer conducive to my personal growth.

I feel it is very unfortunate that I must ask you to accept this communication as my formal resignation. I wish Spalding well as it is, and will continue to be, a great company.

I would also like to say that I have enjoyed working with you. I feel that it has been a period of time that both of us have learned a great deal from each other.

I would like to suggest that my last working day be June 28th.

Regretfully yours,
Wm. H. Faulhaber

What is that song, leaving is hard to do? Or is that a song. Whatever, this was really tough, seventeen years is a long time with a company I loved. To leave didn't break my heart, it just made me more determined to be successful, for me personally and for my family. I owed them the best I could be. One can only try and I have always believed giving 110 percent. There is no clock watching in my makeup, and no quite either. The history of Spalding is so great that even people I think were hurting it, can't. There are too many loyal employees within Spalding that will pick it back up and they would do that with or without me.

It is said "Don't look back." In some ways that may be true however how do you not look back on seventeen mostly great years?

I started to work for Spalding on July 1, 1957 so that is seventeen years exactly. I will rejoin Spalding on July 1, 1977, exactly three years to the day of my resignation. I then retired on July 1, 1995 giving me 35 years service over a period of 38 years. Guess doing things in complete years is my thing.

Looking Forward #136

O F COURSE WE HAD TO sell our home and it sold very quickly. Dee and I had made the decision to move forward probably two months before I turned in my resignation and we had been house hunting. We did not consider moving to Jupiter where the Toney Penna business was because back in 1974 there was hardly anything there. Florida had a Turn Pike but there was no Interstate I95 that reached into Palm Beach County then. All the four, six and 8 lane roads we have now were all two lane roads back then. Where I95 runs now west of it there was wilderness, swamps, snakes, alligators, mosquitoes, you name it.

We found that North Palm Beach was a very nice area and was a 20 minute drive to Jupiter. Being in the golf business and the fact there were quite a few golf course development home sites available one might think we would relocate in one of those gated developments. There were going to be a lot more golf course developments but only so much water front property was available and would not expand as much as golf course lots. We chose to buy on water and found a great home on the Earman River in North Palm Beach. It was a custom built home and did not look like the usual Florida white stucco homes. A two story home with a brick front, a large sloping Shake Shingle roof, four bedrooms, one on the second floor and a walk in attic, a winding staircase with no handrails leading up to the second floor onto a balcony overlooking the entrance and a high ceiling with a chandelier hanging over a little pond at the bottom of the staircase. Three full bathrooms, a sunken living room and t dining room at the front of the house then a dinette and kitchen with sliding windows and lunch counter overlooked a very large screened in porch. The family room with sliding glass doors also leading to the porch and a very deep pool, 11 foot at the deep end with a diving board and 5 foot deed in the shallow end with steps leading into the pool and a slide. This pool is not screened in. A double car garage is part of the house as well. The lot is 100 feet wide and 300 feet deep to the back fence, beyond the fence is an easement about 60 feet in length and then the Earman River which leads to the intra coastal water way which is a few blocks away and that leads to the Atlantic Ocean. As the pelican flies the Ocean is about one and one half to two miles away.

South East Florida is very flat but our property sits 14 feet above sea level. Due to this elevation we were not required to purchase flood insurance. The Earman River is not a canal. Man made canal's have a sea wall but rivers do not, so we do not have a sea wall. We did have a dock built after a couple of years. The Earman River is a mixture of salt water and fresh water, brackish, and the tide rises and falls about 4 feet. No alligators here as they do not like salt water, but most living things in the Ocean can be found in this river at high tide, but we have never seen a shark, Dolphins rarely, Manatees all the time, Sting Rays yes, all kinds of fish and blue crabs also.

The person who built this house was a custom home builder originally from Shaker Heights, Ohio. He built three houses like this one in North Palm Beach. He built ours in 1972 and moved into it himself. Then he sold it to us in 1974 for $130,000.00! I almost chocked to death on that amount of money, back then that was huge. And the mortgage rates were high then, ours was 9 and ¾ percent. Moving our children again was not so easy; so we felt we had to make this as enjoyable as possible, and we jumped into this purchase with both feet. The best deal I ever made though, we are now in our 41st year in this home, and we have a beautiful back yard including a water fall and a beautiful humongous tree with a patio and a table and chairs under the shade of that tree. We sit there on the hottest days, there is always a breeze, and watch boats go by our dock.

We also purchased the land beyond the fence which is still an easement but we own the land all the way to the rivers mean, or average tide. We built a dock around 1978; it has a ramp leading down to a large T shaped dock with concrete pilings, not wood. Its equipped with electric, two large lights, and fresh water. If I remember correctly the dock cost me around $10,000. Then we added a boat lift in 2001. A house next door never had a dock but our new neighbor is going to have one built and I have heard it is going to cost him nearly $60,000.00! The pilings are not concrete either and do not include a boat lift. That is how much prices have gone up since we had ours installed.

We are also on our third roof. Two shake shingle roofs was enough for me, their life span is 12 to 15 years and Raccoons' like to dig holes in the shake shingles looking for a place to have childbirth. We had to reinforce the whole structure when re roofing with concrete barrow tile because of the added weight of the tiles. Another unique thing is this home; it has an outside door in every room except the bedroom up stairs. Even the three bathrooms have outside doors, two of them leading on to the porch. I think the kids liked the idea of having an outside door in their bedrooms, but I have not idea why. They thought we were deaf and blind. I had our home appraised recently and it is now worth one million dollars. We made the correct decision of buying on water and not golf course property.

More about Our Move #137

*D*EE AND OUR THREE GIRLS drove to Florida ahead of son Jim, our dog Kola and I. We had to wait for the van to pack up all of our belongings. After the van left we headed south and as I stated before we were to meet Toney Penna and then attend the PGA Championship tournament in North Carolina. In the meantime Dee and kids checked into a motel on Singer Island which was located on the beach of the Atlantic Ocean not far from our new home in North Palm Beach. We had to wait for the van to reach us and I believe we all occupied that motel for around 10 days, hard to take but we survived. The kids loved the beach, the Ocean and the house. We finally moved in and we are still here. As a matter of fact as I write this we are having a new complete kitchen installed, everything new except the tile floor. This is our second update of the kitchen, hey, the house is now 43 years young and it looks great. The kids loved our pool and our youngest, Linda, became very good on the diving board and eventually became a member of the high school swimming team as a diver.

While on the subject of swimming and water, our first winter in Florida we went to the beach and entered the ocean waters, and we used our pool all winter long as well. Moving from the north to a semi tropical area that was no problem, the temperature of the water, even though it got a lot colder in the winter, did not bother us. The body changes and adapts to the new climate and the very next winter we could not get into our pool or the Ocean because the water was now to cold for us.

Now I am ready to start my new position with the Toney Penna Co. and all the people working there are not strangers. The inside sales person is none other than Bernie Fishesser who I have know for a number of years. Bernie was a sales rep who worked for many years in Indiana and I also know his brother Don is a golf professional. A really good guy, Bernie's total knowledge of golf clubs was second to none, the most knowledgeable salesman I had ever known. Bernie was about 10 years older than I and had been working for Penna for two years. This was somewhat of a touchy situation as I realized that maybe Bernie may have thought he should have gotten the job instead of me. Regardless, Bernie seemed very happy that if he was not considered someone he knew came aboard. Bernie and wife Barbara were very nice to us and we had dinner together the first week we were on the job. Bernie and I worked together very well and as a couple we spent a lot of time socializing as well. Bernie had a way of handling Toney Penna as well; he was a very good people's people. Bernie could get along with anybody, I really liked him and I miss him to this day. RIP Bernie.

I started immediately to make myself familiar with the operation and the product line. In charge of manufacturing was Ace Harper, a very knowledge custom club man that Toney brought with him when both left the Macgregor Golf Co. Ace and wife Betty became friends as well. Penna's business up to now was all "Custom" made woods and irons. Toney was best known for his wood designs and never received credit for being one heck of a designer of irons as well. His Penna "Super Blade" irons are a separate story. The main thing I had to do was create a national sales force and to do that I had to have a product line for them to sell. Up until now all clubs only went into production when there was a firm order. That created a lot of problems as it took about six to eight weeks to deliver a new wood and there was not always enough orders to keep the factory busy eight hours a day, another problem to solve.

Toney had a line of different drivers but all the fairway woods were the same design. There was nothing in stock except the raw materials. In other words if I had a sales force and we received an order we could not deliver that item for at least six weeks! That does not work when a club is a standard club, that cusotmer wants it now. If an order is for a special club, that customer will wait a reasonable amount of time.

How do I correct all of this and make it Toney's idea as well? That is how things have to be done, everything has to be done through Toney. Toney no longer owns his company, but he holds the title of President. We need to work together of solving a product problem, easier said than done.

Solving a Product Line Problem #138

I discussed my thoughts with Bernie and Ace as I wanted to create a team that worked together. I did not want to come in as a one man show and make decisions without my key people being a part of a team. I also needed to pick their brains and learn everything I could about the Penna Co., how it functioned, how they functioned, how they worked for and with Toney himself. This is not Spalding, it is a small golf club manufacturing plant with no sales force or marketing arm, no advertising in place and doing business because Toney's reputation. There was a fourth person in the office besides three girls. A comptroller whose name escapes me and who we confided with on money matters, I included him in on all of our discussions. I wanted a complete team leaving no one out. The girls were also included when anything pertained to their part of the operation. Golf is an individual sport but running a business is a team effort.

I had no problem with Bernie but Ace and I did not know each other. Ace was very loyal to Toney which I appreciated so I had to get to know Ace better, so I wanted Ace to know my background. Both being from Ohio made it easier. Ace was a little standoffish at first but we started to hit it off quickly and he finally joined the team. I did not want to create friction or go around Toney in any way. This has got to be a team effort and we have to include Toney, but I have to do some work and get some facts together before approaching Toney.

To give you and idea about Toney's reputation as a club designer, he was with Macgregor as their chief club designer for years and also was responsible for singing all of their tour staff players. Toney recognized talent and he had a very good staff of top players. A tour player's most important clubs are his putter and his driver followed closely by their wedges. The overwhelming choice of drivers on the tour was Macgregor drivers designed by Toney and also his own Toney Penna drivers. I would guess as high as 75 percent were those two Penna designed drivers being used on the tour back then. That is pretty darn impressive and I am dealing with a legend, Toney Penna. Walk softly Bill, very softly.

It is a simple fact that before I create a sales force I have to have a product line for them to sell that can be shipped within a few days, not weeks. The owners of Penna know and understand that and know this can not be done overnight but they want results and a return on their investment. I have got to get going and deliver on what I was hired to do.

With the help of Bernie, Ace and the office staff we researched about a years worth of past orders to find out what were the most popular specifications of all these "Custom" clubs. It turned out what I expected; the overwhelming specifications for drivers were standard stock specifications. Penna had been manufacturing "Standard specification custom built clubs!" Standard specifications in those days for a driver were men's medium shaft 43 inch length with a standard size grip and a swing weight of D-1 or D-2. A men's stiff shaft the same length and grip size with swing weights of D-2, D-3 or D-4.

"A golf club can be and is a very delicate destructive instrument That not used properly can be harmful to your mental health."

With the information collected we can now move ahead and plan how many different model drivers we needed to produce with these "Standard" specifications. We could also manufacture the fairway woods for stock as there was only one design. We did not have to completely finish all of them, just build them up to the point that all there was left to do was apply the correct final finish on them as needed, only a couple of days to complete that task. The three of us, Bernie, Ace and me came up with a plan to presented to Toney in such a way he would have thought he planned it himself.

It was explaining to Toney that these "Stock" custom clubs would begin to support a sales force yet to be developed. It would also keep all the factory people busy with little down time making this part of the company more efficient. Most of the items needed to start this production was already in inventory so we could get started manufacturing slowly and as sales picked up so could production. Up until now the orders from Japan kept this business alive. If the Japan business ceased the Penna Company would most likely have a hard time surviving. Thus the reason the parent company decision to move ahead with creating a sales force and building a good solid profitable business.

Just solving a product problem was just the beginning; I have a lot of work before me, so I will attempt to explain more abut golf clubs as a part of my work load.

Golf Club Components #139

REALIZING THESE "STORIES" ARE BEING received by many non golfers I do not intend to bore you. I have been told by so many non golfers throughout the years, how can anyone hit a non moving little round white object then chase after it, can be any fun and consider it a sport. I think I can keep you interested while not boring you with information designed to explain golf and golf equipment so it will be interesting to you as well. Golf is one of the most complicated games ever devised by man.

I am not an expert who knows everything about golf clubs but, I know more than most. I will start off by alerting all you fathers and grand fathers out there who are about to take an old set of clubs and shorten them for your kids or grandkids. By cutting off the top part of the shaft to make them shorter you will be defeating the purpose of the golf shaft, which incidentally is the most single important part of a club. It is the engine that drives the car so to speak. The shaft is designed to propel the golf ball. A more flexible shaft is designed to help the ladies, the weaker or older and kids get the ball in the air due to the shafts action in the swing. By cutting a shaft sorter the shaft becomes very stiff and ridged. Think of a bull whip, it has to be thin and flexible, if it were made out of a stiffer material it would not work. Creating a shorter club takes the flex out of the shaft which helps whip the head of the club creating speed at impact resulting in propelling the ball into the air. The shafts must also have a certain amount of "Torque" a twisting of the shaft. I will not try and explain all of that.

That cut down shaft with no flex will only make learning the game more difficult as that child will be trying to hit the ball when the club cannot do the job it was designed for. Go out and buy a set of junior size clubs, please. Then that child has a chance to do what you yourself think you are trying to accomplish. Does that make sense? You bet it does.

Golf clubs are complicated. When golf was first invented it was not even close to being the game it is today. Our dad started my brother and I playing with cut down shafts but they were hickory wood shafts, not steel. They still had a little flex and clubs were not so complicated back in the thirties and forties either, but one heck of a lot better than the 1800's. Remember I am still talking about equipment dating back to when I was still active working and playing myself, 20 to 50 years ago. I started working for Spalding 58 years ago and started playing at age 9 or 10, 75 years ago. I am not talking present day equipment. My knowledge of metal wood woods is not really up to date, although I did use them for a few years. My knowledge and what I am talking about are "Wood" woods. But I am sure the principals are still the same.

Why are there "Grooves" cut into the face of golf clubs? Simply to create spin for golf ball control, when the ball is struck it rolls up on the club face spinning backwards so the dimples lift the ball into the air. If that spin is not exactly straight towards the intended target, spinning off to one side or the other, the ball will either go to the right, a fade or "Slice," and to the left, a draw or a "Hook." Did you know that there are groves on the driver but they are not needed? Drivers are not built with a straight face. There are two terms defining this non straight face, roll and bulge. I will not discuss degrees of either as they can differ however the roll is form the toe to the heel and bulge is from the bottom to the top. The curvature of the face of the driver creates the spin on the ball and that spin depends on where the impact is on the face or the club. Usually hitting the ball towards the heel will spin the ball so it will fade or slice to the right and the opposite, hitting the ball on the toe will send the ball to the left producing a draw or a hook. Hitting the ball low on the club will normally produce a low flying ball while hitting the ball on top the ball will tend to fly very high. That brings up the subject of how high you place the ball on the wooded tee. Think about that, it should be teed up for normal shots in the middle of the face of the driver. An accomplished golfer can tee it lower or higher depending on what type of ball flight he may be attempting to hit.

There are rules about how wide, how deep and the angle of the grooves as well. There are many reasons for those rules but I will not bore you with all of that, except that those rules do not apply to the driver or fairway woods until we come to the higher lofted woods, the 5, 6, 7 and so on. These high lofted woods begin to perform like irons as they have flat faces the grooves grab the ball like the irons.

The lofts of the metal woods are much different than what they were on the "Wood" woods because the weight distribution is so much different and the center of gravity of the club has been lowered, that causes the ball to fly higher, so the lofts are now much less. For instance, the standard loft of a wooden driver is 10 or 11 degrees whereas the metal driver is in the single digits. With all the new club and ball technology the distance off all clubs has increased to ridiculous lengths. The tour players today are hitting there drivers more than 50 yards longer than with the wooden woods. The length off a driver in the past, 250 to 275 yards was considered pretty darn good then. The lady professionals hit the ball that far now.

I say ridiculous for several reasons and the big one is. most golf course are not long enough now. Only the brand new courses are designed for those kinds of distances. The older designs are outdated. New courses are much more expensive as they take up many more acres of expensive land and the upkeep becomes more expensive as well. There are a lot of reasons of why distance should be curtailed and even scaled back somewhat. I am not going to write about that though, I'll never conclude these stories.

GOLF CLUB CUSTOM FITTING #140

MOST PEOPLE CAN START OUT using standard clubs. As their game improves then a change may very well be the next step to better golf. That all depends on the person's gender, build and strength, taller people may need clubs that the lie of the clubs may need to be a little more upright, the swing is usually upright and the club length possibly a little longer, and a firmer shaft may be needed as well. The longer the club the more flexible the shaft becomes. A shorter person may need a flatter lie due to a flatter swing. The better the player becomes the possibility of needing "Custom" fitting of equipment increases. The correct equipment will help that person to become even a better player. One very important thing a person starting to play golf is to get a series of professional lessons from a golf professional, get started correctly before forming any bad habits that become hard to get rid of.

The golf swing is really a series of opposites. What feels right to a beginner is usually 99% wrong. The right way does not feel natural simply because the correct golf swing is not natural but it does not take long to feel natural after some practice. The grip is the first most important thing; the club is not a baseball bat. The correct grip could be three different types of grips. The most natural is the 10 finger grip, a "Baseball grip." This is the least used of the three because with all ten fingers on the club the hands are not connected with each other and have a tendency to act independently. There have been some very successful tour players using the baseball grip but not many, Bob Rosburg and Art Wall come to mind and both had very successful careers. First of all with any of the three grips they are all "Finger" grips as the palms should never touch the grips. The club is held in the crooks of the fingers only.

When Arnold Palmer first gripped a golf club his dad, Deacon

"Deak" Palmer, placed his sons hands on the club and told him "Don't you ever dare change that grip!" He placed those big strong young hands in the proper position which did not feel natural. First the left hand on the club with the thumb on top of the grip, right hand next with the little finger overlapping the little finger on the left hand, the right thumb on top of the shaft almost touches the right index finger. Are you running to get the broom to try this out? It's to thick, get something smaller in diameter. This is the most popular grip and is called the "Vardon grip" named after Englishman Harry Vardon, the man who first used it back in the early 1900's.

The interlocking is the third grip and is the same as the Vardon except instead of overlapping the two little fingers one goes between the other. This is the grip that my father taught me to use. I felt for years I should be using the Vardon overlapping grip but every time I tried to change it was a disaster, I could not change. I did not know why the interlocking grip worked for me until one day I was reading an article in a golf magazine. Jack Nicklaus was explaining why he used the interlocking grip. He explained that his hands were different; he had short fingers and large palms which prevented him from overlapping due to his short fingers. I immediately took a good look at my hands, they looked exactly like Jack described. Very short fingers and large palms I finally knew why that grip was the correct one for me. I was in pretty good company. Again, my dad must have known what he was doing because he used the Vardon grip. Dad sure got smarter as he got older.

All this about the grip is not about golf clubs is it? Well it really is because that club means nothing without knowing how to caress the club properly. That is the very beginning of how to play this very difficult complicated game. You just do not hit a little white round object and chase after it. As a beginner without some proper instruction your chase after hitting that white ball may only be a couple of steps, not 200 plus yards. Your choice, there is a saying I have always appreciated. **"If it's worth doing then it's worth doing well."** Another saying about the proper golf grip--**"Grip it and rip it!"**

I have witnessed many very good athletes in other sports who are almost helpless when it comes to playing golf. From my observation the athletes that have the hardest time are football players. I would never laugh at any 6' 5" 300 pound guy trying his best to hit that little round white stationary object and finds out he can't hit it past a 5' 6" 125 pound guy. First of all he might pound me into the ground and not with a golf club, just the club on the end of his arm, his fist. Secondly, I really feel sorry for them, most are just too big and too strong. Talk about frustration when they see that small person hitting the ball longer than they can.

Proper equipment is a big part of that. The small guy could not take a big strong mans club and hit the ball anywhere near what he can do with his own clubs which have the correct flex shaft, grip and swing weight for him. The big man may be able to hit the small mans club but would have no control of where the ball is going.

GOLF CLUBS CAN BE COMPLICATED #141

$\mathcal{A}$ GAIN I REPEAT MYSELF, THE most single important part of a golf club is the proper shaft and its flex. It is the "Engine" that runs the golf swing. A little trivia first, Spalding was the only company for many years using the reverse thread method of applying the shaft into the neck (Hozel) of the iron. The female hozel had reverse threads and the male end of the shaft was threaded. No pins or screws penetrating through the hozel and shaft and there was no epoxy glue used either. When the head of the club struck the ground and ball the reverse threads tightened themselves. Very clean and easy way to assemble the shaft to the head of the iron, or "Blade" as Toney Penna called an iron head. Blade, that's a term I will be using during my discussions about Toney Penna Irons.

Another short detour, I just came back from my 1 PM Cardiac Rehab session, I go for an hour three times a week. As I was about to get my departing blood pressure taken a new "Patient" just came in and sat down next to me looking a little grim. I said "How are you doing?" He replied, "I'm doing." The way he looked and that remark alerted me to the fact I have another scared person beginning rehab after heart surgery. Not unusual, I see it all the time. So I said to him, "We are all doing." He said, "I guess we are all in the same boat." I replied, I have been doing this rehab for fifteen years and what you have to do is get in that boat and row it. He looked at me and his expression changed, he said "You have, 15 years? I guess this is a second chance?" I replied, "Exactly, I had my open heart surgery fifteen years ago so look at it this way, that second chance has given me he opportunity to look forward to a long and happy productive life. Just work on it and don't get depressed. Thank God and your medical team for all you have to look forward to." His attitude changed immediately. That made my day. I know it made his as I could see I helped take the fear and the unknown out of him. Depression is very common with heart patients and the best encouragement can come from someone who has already been through what he has. There are more important things than golf clubs, are there not?

But as long as there is the unknown, I'm talking about golf clubs again, I am here to write about it, and your there to read about it, I will continue, thanks for putting up with my detour. I just thought it was an interesting day you may find interesting yourself. You know if you sit back, look around, and find something to be thankful for I'll bet your day will be a little better as well. No matter how things may look there are so many others with far worse problems than I have.

There were many problems for golfers years ago as well. Think about this, before golf clubs became a matched set of clubs, standard lengths with matching flex shafts and all weighted so each club in a set feel and react the same. Before this was accomplished golfers were using all sorts of clubs that didn't come close to being matched. The very best golfers had to learn how to swing each club differently to get the best results. In other words golfers matched their swings to the different clubs as opposed to the proper fitting of a set of golf clubs to match the swing. A complete reversible situation but you know something else. Those guys were shot makers; they had to learn how to hit all sorts of different shot with those unmatched clubs. There were no sand clubs and various lofted wedges or high lofted woods let alone all the hybrids being used today.

The lofts on woods and irons are all designed so the yardage a ball travels off each club is uniform as far as how much distance is between clubs. In other words, let's go back to the wooden woods era. The Driver was 11 degrees, 2 wood 13, a 3 wood 16 and so on. Using a good player's ability the distance he would hit the ball with each wood would be approximately 15 yards. The irons the distance between clubs is approximately 10 to 12 yards. Using myself as the subject, since I was a single digit handicap player which is considered a good player, I could hit the ball off the tee as long as most tour players. So using my distances per club is pretty close to what a good player hits the ball for each club. And I had a big problem as I was never a good wedge player, and that is where you **score well**. I never had the time to practice that short game so got by with what I had. I'll show you where and why I was a week player. I hit the tee shot usually 255 to 270 yards which is not bad with the old wooden woods. Forgetting that, let's look at the iron play.

My distance was, give or take a couple of yards each way; I am going to use a 10 yard difference between clubs with a normal swing, 3 iron 200, 4 iron 190, 5 – 180, 6 - 170., 7 – 160, 8 – 150, 9 – 140 and wedge 110, Sand Club from grass, 60. Can you see my weakness? I could not hit a wedge very far and the sand club I hardly ever used off grass because I hit it badly. Between 140 and 110 yards I had trouble, that's 30 large yards. I started to use a 10 iron a long time ago, which was just a strong wedge and that helped somewhat but that still left me 15 yards a club difference between the 9 and wedge. From the wedge to the hole of about 90 yards I had to improvise the best I could. Most tour players have a problem with that range as well. How many time have you watched them on TV and the announcer says so and so will most likely lay up short of the green about 120 yards away so he can hit a full shot, usually a soft wedge or a sand club. 100 yards to the green and the hole is a very delicate distance.

There are three basic shots, or swings, used per each club. There are many ways to hit each club and that gets too complicated. I can explain all of that but it would take another book. So back to the three, lets use the 8 iron for terminology, a normal 8 iron swing, a hard 8 and a soft or ¾ 8. They can all be hit low, normal or high, a fade hit low, normal or high, and a draw hit low, normal or high. Follow this, hitting a ball with a "Normal" swing the trajectory can be normal, high or low (3), or a "Fade," normal, high or low (3) or a "Hook or draw" normal, high or low (3) that is 9 different ways to hit one club with a normal speed swing. So if a hard swing is used there are 9 different ways that the ball can be hit also, and the same for a "Soft" swing, another 9 which means I have just explained how one club can be hit 27 different ways, have I not? The game of golf is a lot more than what most people think it is Lets shift gears for a while, there are more than one of those also.

The actual date I am writing this is April 25, 2015. Dee and I just came back from seeing our fourth great grand child, a boy, who was born on the 21st. We have a fifth great grand child, a girl, due in June. While visiting, my son Jim and my daughter Linda were there and they reminded me of a couple of stories that I have not written about that took place back in Chagrin Falls Ohio and Wilbraham Mass so it's backspin time again. It is impossible to write about everything but they assured me I should not forget about what will be next, a short break from golf clubs, next, backspin to Ohio ...

BACKSPIN TO OHIO #142

I NORMALLY DON'T DO REQUESTS BUT how do you turn your own kids down? So back to Chagrin Falls Ohio we go. In the mid sixties Linda and Jim are reminding me about a walk in club house that was built back in the woods behind our house. It needed repairs and upgraded so I installed a new door, put in Plexiglas windows and a new roof. Our daughter Diane, who became a graphic artist, painted a large star in red white and blue on the inside back wall. Why do I bring this up after all these years? Because Jim, Linda along with Chrissy, Linda's daughter and our Grand Daughter made a trip back to Chagrin in 2007 and they visited the old neighborhood and our old house. They rang the doorbell and when no one answered they went out back and saw that the old club house was still there. They opened the door and it was the same as it was 40 years ago, the star on the wall. Can you imagine?

Jim also brought up the time when I was coaching little league basketball. When it was time for all the coaches to pick kids for their team, all the coaches first pick was their own sons, except me. Watching Little League baseball for years I got tired of seeing all of these fathers picking their sons and then watching all the favoritism. I did not want to do that. I wanted Jim to make a team on his own ability. I'm there to help kids learn how to work and play together as a team. I did not want them to see my son being treated any different then they were. No favorites. It took Jim years to get over that and understand why, but he did. He is his own man.

If you think any of the above reminds you of the Twilight Zone, get a load of this. When we were moving from Ohio to Wilbraham Mass we were looking at a home on **Porter** Drive. At the same time we were looking a house that we bought on Porter Drive there was a family living across the street on **Porter** Drive by the name of Jarvie. At the same time the Jarvie's were house hunting in Ohio. Get set to enter the Twilight Zone. They were looking at a house, which they bought, **and it was ours**, in Chagrin Falls! **They bought our house!** We almost bought theirs! We did not know each other and had never met until after they bought our house. And guess who their new next door neighbors were going to be in Chagrin Falls, Chic and Rita **Porter**. Can you imagine?

It doesn't end there. Years later when we moved to Florida our daughter Cindy was attending the University of South Florida near Tampa. One day she turned a corner and bumped into a young man. They opened a conversation and I think it went this way. Cindy asked him where he was from. He said originally Wilbraham Mass. Cindy said she lived there once also. He said he now lived in Chagrin Falls Ohio. Cindy said so did I? Now you know the rest of the story, right. Yes, it was a Jarvie boy living in our old house in Chagrin Falls, Ohio. Can you imagine?

We now exit the Twilight Zone and reenter the unbelievable Golf Club stories.

The Ounce that Counts #143

*D*ETOUR. YESTERDAY I WROTE ABOUT a backspin story "Back to Ohio." I have receive a number of positive responses concerning my story about my being a basketball coach for young little league age kids and not choosing my own son for the team I was coaching and I was doing my best to explain why. Thank you all for understanding although I am sure there are some who would not agree with that decision. The important thing to me is that later in life my son Jim did agree, or at least understood my decision. One response that I received was from a friend and Brother Knight's of Columbus who was involved with baseball Little League as President here in Florida for many years. His name is Rubin "Skip" Hill and I thank you for your support Skip, it is as follows;

"I liked your attitude about not selecting your son for your team. I think he grew as a person from that move. It reminds me of one of my best Little League speeches."

"Prepare the child for the path.
Not the path for the child."

I believe Skip's quote was **exactly** what I was attempting. Even though I struggled with that decision for years I knew deep down inside I did what I thought was the best thing for me to do. I guess you could call it, **"Tough Love."** Jim and his sisters, Diane, Cindy and Linda, heard more **no's** than yes's from their mother and father growing up they did not get everything hey asked for just because their friends had things they didn't.

As I said before Toney was better know for his design of woods than irons. His irons were excellent golf clubs. His last iron design was what he called his "Super Blades." Toney used the term "Blade" when referring to the head of an iron. These were cast iron clubs and the big difference was a very short hozel, the neck of the iron where the shaft was inserted. The tips of the steel shafts he used had to be made about an inch longer because of this short hozel. What this accomplished it eliminated some total weight of the club so Toney added that weight to the head of the iron placing most of it behind the sweet spot. Simply put, you don't contact the ball with the hozel or shaft, so the extra weight removed from the hozel was redistributed which gave those irons more punch. They were really a solid feeling iron and I found out myself that I hit the ball about five yards longer with each of those irons compared with other clubs with the same loft.

While I was working with a local ad agency we came up with an advertisement promoting the Super Blades. In the ad in large bold print we made a statement ...

"THE OUNCE THAT COUNTS"

We thought that statement was something that would grab the attention of the consumer so they would read the ad which went on to explain what that meant, what it did for the playability of those Super Blade irons. I'm getting a little ahead of myself as I have not put a sales force together yet but while on this subject of advertising I would like to bring up the name of a very well know touring professional who was a huge fan of Ben Hogan and wore a white cap just like Hogan wore when he played. He admired Toney Penna as well, his name was Gardner Dickinson. Remember my story back in the sixties when he edged out my friend Homero Blancas and won the Cleveland Open? That's the one and only Gardner Dickinson.

Gardner lived in North Palm Beach and was in the Penna plant so often I thought he worked there. Gardner was not on any company's consultant staff and he loved Toney Penna clubs so he played them and carried a Toney Penna staff bag on Tour. He did not ask for one cent for doing so. When Gardner told me we could his name in any advertising and he would continue to carry the bag and play the clubs for no compensation, I told Gardner we would have to draw up a contract anyway because we had to do this legally. So I made a deal with Gardner, drew up the contract agreeing to pay him $1.00 a year.

Toney had a lot of very good loyal friends. Many of Toney's friends were in show business. Way back in the thirties and forties there really wasn't a tour as we know it. There were not too many tournaments and the "Touring Pros" of that era had other jobs to support themselves. Show business people loved to play golf with those pros. That is how Toney got to know so many of them. Toney was a very engaging young man who had a great big grin, plus his own hair then. He was also a very dapper dresser. Off course you would never ever see Toney not wearing a jacket. He would never think of going to lunch without a jacket. And show business people loved him.

Toney Penna's Friends #144

$\mathcal{B}$EFORE I GET INTO THE title here I would like to touch on how good Gardner and Toney were as "Teachers." They were both exactly the same in their approach. The only time they really got into the art of the golf swing and it's fundamentals, they would only give their advice when someone they knew would ask. In other words, they did not make their livings teaching the game but they were excellent teachers and both strongly believed in not rebuilding anyone's swing. They did not work with beginners, usually only with better players who already had developed their own personal swing. Toney and Gardner would only work with those swings eliminating a few bad habits or just correcting the swing that was already there. Both were of the opinion there is not a perfect golf swing and never will be so play with what you have, just fine tune it, so to speak. But never do a complete change or rebuild someone's swing.

Does that ring a bell? So many players today don't even practice by themselves. They have to have their swing coaches with them almost every minute. Redoing and rebuilding, changing everything. Do you think a guy by the nickname of Tiger falls under that category? He is now on his fifth teacher. His father Earl was his first when he came on tour and I think that may have been his best swing. Now into his fifth teacher he is trying to go back to his original swing somewhat. I am not naming names with this comment but I think some players need to go back into their own brain, that's where it all began. A mental game it is, things get twisted and can get too complicated. My favorite saying is when some people have long term swing problems they might just be the host of a bunch of "Head worms."

I never saw Sam Snead, Byron Nelson, Ben Hogan, Billy Casper,

Arnold Palmer, Gary Player, Lee Trevino, Tom Weiskoff, Lanny Wadkins, Greg Norman have swing coaches around them. They figured out any of their problems on the course. I was not a great player but one thing I learned early on was not to read golf instruction articles in the Golf Magazines. They messed me up. I would read something and the next time I was playing somewhere during a round right in the middle of my backswing something in the last article I read would pop into my mind and mess me up. I stopped reading anything pertaining to swing instructions, what the heck, I didn't play golf for a living and I played pretty good for the amount of rounds I played. As I said I never had a formal lesson, just what my dad taught me and some tips along the way. I love golf magazines like Golf World and Golf Weekly. These publications do not feature instruction articles, just good golf reporting.

You have got to trust your own swing and boy is that a hard thing to do. I have some personal thoughts about that and how hard it is to play golf. Bowling is a game that comes closest to golf that I know. Hey, that is another story I'll touch on another time, and I will throw in Tennis and Ping Pong into the discussion as well, all individual sports vs. team sports. But for now, let's get back to Toney's friends.

TONEY PENNA'S HAIR #145

I WAS INFORMED THAT AT LEAST one of Toney's famous friends backed him in some way to get his golf manufacturing business started, probably financially. I think I know who they were but it doesn't matter, what does matter is what friends are for? I remember some who dropped by to visit Toney, Bing Crosby, and Bob Hope, to name a couple. Perry Como was a frequent visitor as he lived right next to the Jupiter Inlet and the Light house. Perry and Toney would have lunch together and play a round of golf often. I had many conversations with Perry, a really nice guy. All of those guys were. I believe I am repeating this, if you remember Bob Hope during his shows, especially the shows he put on for the troops, he always had a golf club in his hands. I am not sure what the make of his first club was but when Toney was with Macgregor it was a Toney Penna designed club and later a Toney Penna manufactured club. Bob played Toneys clubs, all those friends did.

Toney's business was located on Toney Penna Drive in Jupiter. Next to his building there was a large piece of land we used to demonstrate clubs. There was a green about 180 yards at the back end of this property we could hit irons to it, but we could not hit woods, just not enough length for that. Once in a while Toney would be visited by a gentleman from New York who would fly in on his private helicopter and land next to our plant on that piece of land. On one of those occasions the pilot asked Bernie Fischesser and I if we would be interested in taking a ride over the ocean to see all the sharks swimming off shore. We jumped at the opportunity and climbed aboard.

Several times a year thousands of sharks show up along the shore line. When in the water myself I can not see what is swimming next to me but if you are above the water like we were in that helicopter looking straight down you can see everything in the water. Seeing for myself hundreds and hundreds of sharks that close to the shore was awesome and down right scary.

Many people were in waist high water and there were sharks all around them which they could not see. We were flying pretty low and hovering over all these people so Bernie and I were hanging waving our arms urging the people to get out of the water. They just waved back at us! They thought we were waving at them. So much for that, actually those people were safe, the water was very clear. Sharks don't attack humans and when that does happen it usually a mistake like in murky water when the visibility is bad. My first helicopter ride was quite an experience.

During the winter in Florida, golf professionals from the mid west to the east coast and the south would stop in and not only say hello but would order clubs for their shops, or for themselves. Bernie Fischesser took care of their needs. I knew many of these pros also; it was like old home week. Business was really good during the season but with out a sales force Toneys business was small and seasonal. So that brings me back to what my job was, it's now the time build a sales force.

But before that another story popped into my memory bank I don't want to forget so here it goes. As I mentioned Toney was a dapper dresser and was pretty vain about how he looked. I also mentioned something about when Toney had hair. He always had hair but there was a time it was not his own. Toney wore a wig and his was the best I have ever seen. I can normally spot a hair piece right away and from a pretty good distance but I have to admit Toney's was hard to detect. He must have spent a fortune on it. As a matter of fact his "Hair people" were located in Miami. When he needed a "Trim" he didn't go to a barber he went to his people in Miami. I like to refer to a wig as a divot, as they reminded me of a big chunk of grass flying thought the air after a well his iron shot.

I was with Toney in Miami attending a tournament at Doral, I was driving and Toney asked to take him to see his "Hair" people. They removed Toney's divot in my presence which kind of surprised me as I didn't think Toney wanted anyone to see his head naked. His people did their thing, trimmed his hair so it blended perfectly with his hair piece, a piece of art.

The next thing I know his people have me in a chair, Toney wanted them to "Fit" a hair piece on me. He wanted me to see how I would look by covering up my thinning hair line. At that time I was mostly balding at the back of my head and still had a fair amount in the front, so when I looked in the mirror I really didn't looked bald from the front. The divot they put on me looked ridicules as far as I was concerned. I hated hair pieces on other people so why would I consider one on my own. To make a long story short I said to Toney if they were done with him, let's get on the road. He tried his best to get me to wear a divot. I have always thought people should let nature takes its course they are only kidding them selves about looking younger, they aren't fooling anyone else. To this day I do have hair on the top of my head but it is very thin. I have my barber shave it off the top of my skull every time I see him. I can't stand the comb over look with thin hair. My hair style is a reverse Mohawk, let it go at that. I don't have to carry a comb anymore either.

Building a Sales Force #146

OW THAT WE HAVE A system in place so that we can build a modest inventory of "Standard" specification line of Toney Penna woods and iron models, the next thing we did was create a modest catalog and wholesale price brochure to be mailed to the golf professionals who have done business with us in the past. These catalogs and price lists would be used by our sales people when they are in place. As with anything new, you have to crawl before you walk.

Building a national sales force all at once would not be a good idea as we have no idea how much volume would be created so building slowly was the only way find out how much we could handle. We did not know if we were going to be successful or not, so this was the prudent way to go. Having more sales than can be delivered would be a nice problem but we would rather be able to deliver. On the other hand, if we didn't generate enough volume to support what we have in place that would not be acceptable either.

First of all we are not in a position to build our own sales force; we must use existing sales people already out there calling on the golf professional trade, "Independent Reps." I will be looking for Reps who have other non competing lines of golf equipment, selling golf clothing, golf bags, and shoes, anything but golf clubs. Independent reps pay all their own expenses and are responsible for their own pensions. They pay their own taxes and social security and any insurance they may need. All we are responsible for is to pay them a certain percentage for the sales they generate. There are certain other qualifications but you get the general idea without spelling out everything. We do need to know what type of Insurance they have for our own protection; they must be bonded and insured. We are only interested in well established reps and their compensation would be a 10% commission, which is pretty standard in the golf industry.

There are many independent rep organizations out there. In other words, there may be one man who has four of five states and he has various lines of goods that only he has the right to sell in that area. He may have two or three working for him as his "Sub Reps" and he pays a portion of his commission, say 8% and he is making 2% off what they sell. All that can vary; he may be getting up to 20% on some goods. There are a few rep organizations that cover the entire United States but that is not what I are looking for at this time. So that is the background of what I am looking for.

The first people I contacted were former Spalding salesmen who had left the company and were now independent reps. There were several who did not have a golf club line and they did come on board. There were also a few small rep organizations covering several states who I knew as well. It did not take me long to put together a fairly large amount of reps covering about 50% of the country. A sales meeting is out of the question so I personally traveled and met with all of my new people and set them up as legal representatives of the Toney Penna Co.

A bit of trivia here, this has to do with World War II. I hired a rep organization covering the Pacific Northwest. One of the salesmen who I met and talked to at several PGA Golf Shows was a member of the famous "Merrill's Marauders." I will not use his name either. You may have heard of the Merrill's Marauders, they fought behind the lines against the Japanese in Burma, China and India. Jungle warfare and they became quite famous. You older people may remember there was a movie made in the sixties about their exploits with Jeff Chandler playing the part of Merrill. The person I am writing about was a very nice quiet soft spoken middle age man. When I talked with him and looked into his eyes I could not help wondering what kind of personal hell he must have gone through to survive. Hand to hand fighting was not unusual for these wonderful heroes, and this man was one of them. Jungle warfare, can you imagine?

GROWING PAINS #147

$\mathcal{W}$E NOW HAVE ENOUGH SALES reps selling Penna clubs and the next step is to see what the results were going to be. That is going to take some time and the next event coming up was the National PGA Show in January. This was the first PGA show I would be attending after 15 years in a Spalding booth; I would be in a different location with a different company. It was pretty well published in the Golf magazines that I had left Spalding and joined the Toney Penna Co., so most people were aware of that. There was a public address system through out the show and I could have someone paged over that loud speaker system. When someone was paged it would be something like this. "Paging Bill Faulhaber, Toney Penna Company." It would be repeated twice. The person being paged was to pick up one of the many phones available and answer the page.

So crafty Bill thought this would be a good way to remind people of who and where I was and get the Penna name blasting all over the place, constantly. I had lined up several guys to have me paged about every forty five minuets the first day and about every sixty minuets the second day. I cut it off the following two days as it was getting pretty obvious what I was doing. A lot of people showed up and said they either didn't know I had changed companies or just kind of forgot and were glad they were reminded. It worked pretty darn well and I got away with it, it brought in quite a bit of business. Don't fool with old people! Actually I was only 43 but aging quickly and balding faster!

Our sales were increasing nicely; the manufacturing hours were picking up keeping everyone pretty busy. As sales increased over the first two years we were getting pretty close to capacity. Now I am looking at another problem. How do I increase sales dollars to meet sales quotas handed down by management if we reach capacity without expanding and I have heard of no plans to do that. We were not quite at capacity but I could see it coming. I did not expand the sales reps as the major golf areas were covered.

What can we do to increase dollar sales and profitability to meet our goals set by management? Several things but they are short term fixes as far as I could see. Before I get into that there was one thing that was bothering me, it was the expense of attending the PGA Show itself. For such a small company as we were the expense was very high for the amount of sales we could generate. I was still a member of the Golf Manufactures Association which worked closely with the PGA of America whose show it was. The show at that time started Monday and ended at noon on Thursday. Three and one half days.

Here is the problem which I presented to the board. Set up days were Saturday and Sunday. We have a designated spot for our display, but to move the displays and equipment to their proper booth area we had to use the convention centers labor force. This had to be accomplished on Saturday and Sunday at a cost of time and one half as It is a weekend. Setting up a show takes time, tearing it down after the show on Thursday only takes a couple of hours at an hourly cost, not time and one half. The only things we need to ship back are whatever displays we use. All the merchandise samples are pre sold to a customer at a discounted price, usually 25 to 30 percent off the wholesale prices. So the person who buys the merchandise is responsible for removing it.

I informed the board it was too expensive for small companies like Penna and that the show should be reversed. My proposal was to start the show on Thursday and end it at noon of Sunday. By doing that we would have to pay the hourly rate on Tuesday and Wednesday. If that was changed the show would run into the weekend and would attract more people because the show as it was only ran during the week. The cost of the tear down on Sunday would be minimal. That would only be a few hours, not two days of time and one half. Every company would benefit. I should have worked out a deal with all the manufactures of receiving a small percentage of what they would save over the years by the change, which did happen. The two associations took my proposal and did exactly what I thought should be done. All companies saved a ton of money over the years. There are some things we all do that we never get credit for, like being good parents. Oh well, I "Done" good and I know it, so self satisfaction was my reward. That is payment enough.

Promoting Penna Drivers
on the Golf Tour #148

ONE OF THE THINGS WE needed to keep doing was promote Penna Drivers on the golf tour. As I have already mentioned Penna designed drivers were the most popular by far back in the sixties and seventies. Macgregor drivers designed by Toney and his own Penna drivers. Our travel expense budgets were moderate as you can imagine being such a small company so we did not attend many tournaments. We focused on the Florida tournaments which were more affordable and some Majors such as The Masters. Sometimes we might attend the U.S. Open or the PGA tournaments if the travel was not too distant.

We did not have one single touring pro under contract to play the Penna clubs and carry the bag as that was not possible, again because of being a small business. Gardner Dickinson was the only Penna bag on tour and it was his choice to do so. We also did not give the Penna clubs to any tour player who wanted to play a Penna club, mainly the driver. These guys received almost everything free, clubs, balls, bags, shoes, socks, gloves, shirts, pants, sweaters, rain gear, umbrellas, hats, sunglasses, pills, meals, drinks, courtesy cars, sometimes lodging, you name it, but not underwear or Penna drivers, maybe the two most important things they needed.

If they found a driver they liked they were happy to dip into their own pocket, I never had a problem with that. I don't recall any touring pro that hinted he should get one no charge. We charged them the wholesale price. They did not mind paying for specialty clubs such as a driver, putter or wedges. Those were the clubs I would concede our Spalding tour consultants to use that might not be Spalding when I was in charge of Spalding's tour players. I asked them to play a minimum of 10 clubs out of the maximum of 14 allowed.

Sometimes I would go alone to tournaments but some I would travel with Bernie Fischesser or Ace Harper our custom club man. Toney would go to some tournaments and do his thing talking to old friends and was very approachable by the players he did not know. But he did not participate working the practice area, he let us do that. We would have a bag full of various drivers with different lengths, shaft flexes and swing weights and a few fairway woods along with a set of standard stiff shafted irons. About thirty clubs in all and during practice rounds it was permissible with the correct credentials to go through the ropes protecting the practice range. I would place that bag at the very end of the range and then let the players come to me. It is not kosher to go to them. I would always have some duplicate drivers in my car to replace any that were sold so I could keep things going and not run out of product.

A couple of encounters with players come to mind, both very different. That is why I remember them I suppose. Both very different personalities and golf swings, both very well known and the first was at a tournament at Doral. This young man who was approaching me I knew what his name was, a highly touted rookie and he beat me to the punch. Before I could speak his name he stuck out his hand to shake mine and said "I'm Fuzzy Zeller, could I look at some of your Penna drivers?" I replied, "Fuzzy, I know who you are and welcome to the tour. Of course you can. Do you want to try a few and see it there is anything you like?" Which he did, Fuzzy was a very friendly polite young man who appreciated the invitation to hit some balls with a few different drivers. I don't remember if he bought one but I do remember his unusual golf swing which is the same today as it was way back then. Fuzzy was medium height and held his hands very low and close to his body, something like Lanny Wadkins. When addressing the ball he hardly touched the ground with the head of the driver and due to his hands being so low the heel of the club almost touched but the toe of the club was way off the ground. That is how he positioned the club through out his career. He really needed the club to have the flattest lie possible. Back then we could bend irons up to about four degrees but wood woods there was a maximum of about two degrees of change. The thin wood neck of the club would not permit drilling the hole for the shaft more than that. We had a very nice visit with him and he always came by and said hello when he saw us at tournaments.

Next up, Tom Weiskoff, runner up at the Masters many times but he never won it. Trivia, Tom played golf for Ohio State; his mother was from my home town of Canton, Ohio. Her maiden name was Eva Shorb and there is a street in Canton named after their family. This meeting took place at the Firestone CC in Akron, Ohio. Tom was on the Macgregor staff and was playing a Toney Penna designed Macgregor driver. He approached Bernie and me on the practice tee after he just finished a practice round. Tom was about six foot two inches tall and unlike Fuzzy's flat set up, Tom's was just the opposite, very upright, his swing was about as pretty as a golf swing could be. He was a very talented player who many golf experts felt that Tom never really reached his potential. He did have a very successfully career and I agree he could have achieved much more. I have my own opinion of why, but I will keep that opinion to myself. If we ever talk person to person, then and only then will I offer my opinion.

Anyway, Tom asked Bernie and me if he could hit a few shots. I kid you not; about an hour later he thanks us for letting him practice with our Penna clubs, all of them. He hit everything and talked to us between shots like long lost friends. Tom kept complementing us on how great the clubs felt and how they performed. Kept telling us how much he admired Toney. Actually Toney signed Tom to his Macgregor contract before leaving to start his own company. Here is the kicker to this story. The next day Bernie and I are walking towards the club house and here comes Tom walking towards us. We both said something like "Hi Tom," He didn't even acknowledge our being right there in front of him, just walked right passed us! Not one word, not even a glance. Can you imagine? Yes, I have an opinion.

The Old PGA Country Club #149

*A*NOTHER SHORT DETOUR! PART of my compensation plan was a Country Club membership and I choose, at Toney's suggestion, the old PGA Country club. I believe there is an interesting story here; some of you old Spalding guys receiving this may know this story. Actually when I became a member in 1974 the name had just changed from PGA to JDM Country Club. There were three courses, the East, North and South courses, 54 holes and not one bad hole. The reason the name was changed is that the PGA was asked to leave this great complex owned by John D. MacArthur. JDM, John was the owner of a very large insurance company located in Chicago and John became very wealthy and at one time owned most of Palm Beach County. No kidding. I'm not sure when he started to purchase all the land he owned, most likely back in the fifties. There was little here then and land was cheap, he just started buying anything he could. He also owned the Colonnades Hotel on Singer Island and his office was in that hotel, it was a table in the corner of the coffee shop. No kidding, but he did have another office in a small building at the corner of Park Ave and 10th Street in Lake Park, right next door to North Palm Beach where I live.

John D. entered into an agreement with the PGA which was really a good deal for the PGA and its thousands of Members. The PGA did not have any ownership but by lending their name is was an excellent tool for John D. to sell memberships and lots as it was to become a very large housing development as well. PGA members could join for a very low fee, most of them coming from the cold north and they also were given a special cart fee as well. John D. was using the PGA name as a draw, good deal for both. The Director of Golf was Lou Strong, a former PGA President.

After a period of years, John D. wanted to raise the membership fee and cart fees by a very few dollars due to inflation and rising costs of running a business but the PGA officers asked John D. to not raise the membership and cart fees to the PGA members, they wanted John D. to freeze, not raise those fees for several years. John D. showed them the door. He then changed the name to JDM. Years later after his death the club was sold to the members and renamed, it is now named Balen Isles C. C.

Next, the PGA made a deal with Lloyd Eckelstone, another developer. The Florida Turnpike runs just west of JDM and directly on the other side of the Turn Pike is where the new PGA development was built. The PGA would not have any ownership for the use of their name but were given a large piece of land on location and a rather large building was built and still is the PGA's National Headquarters. Their name was being used to sell memberships and home sights and the PGA had no ownership of the complex or the golf courses at all and did not participate in any percentage of the income their PGA name created. By the way, my daughter Diane (Pobiak) worked for the PGA for 10 years as a graphic artist. Years later the PGA built their own courses in Port St. Lucie, Fl., but their headquarters are still in Palm Beach Gardens.

I could never understand why the PGA with its thousands of members did not set up a separate corporation and build their own complex by offering stock to their members. I think that would have been very successful. They could have structured a membership of non PGA members and PGA member stockholders. The PGA should have never given up their name to a developer who was the only one who really benefitted, what is one building and a piece of land for the right of someone else to use your organizations name? That of course is my opinion and I could be wrong.

I joined JDM in 1974 and remained a member for 19 years. Never got tired of playing those three courses, they were exceptional. What has all this to do with growing pains you ask? I told you I like detours, I can see all the hills and valleys that way. Next we will touch on the subject of the beginning of the graphite shaft era and how they played a part of the Penna Companies growing pains.

Growing the Penna Co. Business #150

$\mathcal{B}$USINESS IS GOING ALONG NICELY and we are nearing manufacturing capacity; after all we are a very small company. Here is the total number of people employed, Toney as President, myself, Bernie, Joe Werstak the controller and three girls in the office. That's six people. In the plant we have Ace and I believe seven other people so that is a total of fourteen people. That is pretty darn small to be competing with all the big boys. We are a specialty company, our product is first class and our profit structure is very good, we are making money. There is no standing still in business, so moving forward is a given. There are several ways to increase sales dollars, obviously more sales and we are not at our maximum manufacturing capacity yet. But when we get to capacity, there are things we must do to increase sales and profit. One, we must consider raising prices somewhat to offset raising costs and to help reach our sales dollar and profit goals. Expanding is an option that may be on the minds of our owners but I have not heard of any such plans. As it is I must plan whatever I can on my own to keep increasing sales and profits. Think, Bill.

Remember my story about the Bicentennial Red White and Blue Driver we introduced in 1976 to celebrate our Country's 200 birthday? We made a lot of money on that promotion because all the materials we used were items that had been discarded as defective or outdated. That inventory had already been written off so our costs to manufacture those clubs were very low. Yes that gave us a boost but that was a one time shot. What's next, expansion? Unbeknown to me our owners were planning on something in the near future which I will tell you about later as it happened. We are in the present however when something did happen to increase our sales volume. It was the introduction of graphite shafts.

Toney was on the ball with this and had been experimenting with some Graftek shafts by Exxon. Toney had samples provided by the Exxon people and they were just getting into the business of producing these new shafts. There were several companies entering the graphite shaft business and Toney felt at that time the Exxon shaft was the best. These shafts were a game changer due to the fact they were much lighter in weight than steel. They were much more expensive as well. The thing about increasing sales volume was price. It did not take anymore time to produce a club with a graphite shaft then it did with a steel shaft. Our costs went up so we had to price these clubs at a much higher price as well while making sure our profit per club increase accordingly. This will generate more sales dollars while providing a very good profit margin.

There was much to do to accomplish all of this however. The shaft manufactures had to get the word out to the consumer and the club companies started their individual advertising campaigns as well touting all of the positive reasons why graphite shaft were superior for the majority of golfers. Reduced overall weight would increase swing speeds increasing distance, less torque producing straighter shots, less vibration softer feel less shock to hands and arms, all kinds of reasons to improve the consumer's game and even reduce the chance of "Tennis elbow" and other health benefits due to all the things listed above. It is very hard to come up with something different in golf clubs to entice the consumer to change clubs however this was one big exciting change to come along in a very long time.

Toney also found that most companies were not increasing the swing weight of their new graphite offerings. For example, most companies were designing a driver using the same flex stiffness in graphite with the same swing weight as their steel shafted driver. I am not talking about clubs weighing pounds, I am talking about ounces. If the weight of a club is reduced too much it can become to light. Take a broom and swing it, then reverse the broom by holding the broom end and swinging the handle, you will get the idea of a club being to light, there is no "Punch." When reducing the overall weight using graphite Toney felt you must put some of that reduced weight back in the head of the club by at least one to two swing weights. A D1 became a D2 or D3 in a medium shaft and a D2 became a D3 or D4 in a stiff shaft. Toney really had the best playable graphite shafted wood on the market in its early stages. The other companies finally caught up but Toney had it all figured out early on.

We really had a head start with the proper designed graphite club but being the small company we were we had to rely on the loyal Penna accounts around the country to push our new graphite line of woods. We simply didn't have an advertising budget to advertise in all the golf magazines. So what did we do to promote ourselves? I was a small opportunity we could afford, a demonstrator program.

GRAPHITE DEMONSTRATORS #151

*T*HIS WAS THE BEGINNING OF the end of my fairly good relationship with Toney Penna. As I have stated many times before anything new had to be his idea, or at least make it look like it was his idea. I had to move fast on this project that my small in house group helped me come up with, a demonstrator program. If anything had to do with a discounted price Toney would not have anything to do with it. For instance, every company that I knew offered a 25% discount from the wholesale price to golf professionals if they were going to play their golf clubs. Not Toney, no sir, "If they want to play my clubs they pay the regular wholesale price, no discount!" Just like the touring pros, they did not get Penna driver free or even the 25% personal use discount. They paid the regular wholesale price and were happy to do so. Toney knew that.

I had worked out a promotional dollar budget with top management that was not very large, but I did have some money to work with. Toney just did not understand that promotional dollars could be advertising dollars and they also could be used by putting together a promotional tool such as a demonstrator program. By using a discounted price to the golf professional for such a program, all designed to generate sales. Making these clubs available for people to actually hit these clubs is better than just reading all kinds of advertising words. A potential customer can't hit words like he can clubs!

I wanted to put these "Demos" in the golf shops of our most loyal Penna supporters around the country. Each of our independent reps would receive a few demos to be placed within heavy populated golf areas golf pro shops for the best exposure. I polled the reps and asked them to send in the names of a few of their customers they felt would buy into the Demo program and do the best job of promoting these new exciting graphite shafted woods.

This was a very big undertaking for such a small company and timing was very important. We needed to get the demos out their fast before all the other companies got rolling. I could not wait any longer to get Toney's blessing and I knew that when I put this in motion without his approval I would no longer have any kind of a relationship with him. But business is business and I had to bite the bullet, I had a job to do. One thing for sure is that he could not fire me. Toney was the President of the Toney Penna Co, but he did not own the company, ATO, Inc. did. I did not report to Toney, I reported to Evan Baker the President of the parent company. I had gone over everything with Evan and he was aware of the Demo Program and what my problems were with Toney's personality. He was 100% behind me and when I, Evan Baker included, could not convince Toney that this program was a good idea, Evan gave me the OK to move forward with the program knowing full well what Toney's reaction would be towards me and towards Evan as well. We would be outcasts as far as Toney was concerned.

Evan told me not to worry about it, but I was the one who had to face Toney everyday, Evan was based in Ohio. This was a sad day because I really liked Toney, I did not want to go against his wishes, I had no choice, business is business, I had a job to do.

Demo Program Outline #152

*T*HE ONLY WAY TO EXPLAIN this promotion is to recreate my letter to the golf pros who have agreed to accept this program; I hope you non golfers find this interesting as I believe you golfers will as well. The letter and letter head follows.

Toney Penna Co.
.ADVISORY BOARD
.Bob Hope
.Perry Como
. Tom LaPresti
March 24, 1975

<u>IMPORTANT NOTICE REGARDING
GRAPHITE DRIVER DEMONSTRATORS</u>

You will be receiving your five graphite demonstrator drivers along with a display stand soon. The package consists of the following:

<u>LENGTH MODEL Degree Loft SHAFT S/W FINISH</u>
421/2" 4A 12 Lady C-8 Amber Cloud.
43" 12A 12 (2 hook) R D-2 Amber Cloud.
43" 2A 11 R D-3 Black.
43" 65A 11 S D-4 Amber Cloud.
431/2" 1A 10 XS D-5 Black.

Prober fitting of prospective customers is very important and I'm sure you will agree with me that a potential customer should have the opportunity to try several flexes to find the right one for him. We believe the shaft we are using, Graftek by Exxon, is not only the best but also the easiest to fit as the flexes offered are the same flex patterns as the dynamic steel shaft. If a golfer has been successfully using a medium flex steel shaft, then that golfer should be able to use a medium ("R") flex in Graftek.

The demonstrator program has been offered on a very limited basis and is designed as a promotional selling aid. If used correctly, graphite sales should be highly successful. If you sell any of the demonstrators, your promotion will end right there. The opportunity is gone for your prospective customers to try one, and for you to capitalize on increased sales and profits.

We are building a back- up stock of drivers, using the exact same specifications as outlined above for immediate shipment. So, if at all possible, sell what you are showing in the display unit for fast delivery to your new graphite user. We will be happy to make up any other specifications you ask for, but the delivery time will be anywhere between eight to twelve weeks, depending on our in-house orders at that time.

I believe this program to be a valuable fitting and selling aid, and you must also or you wouldn't have invested in it. The profit you receive from the five drivers is nothing, promote its use and watch your profits grow. I'm sure you will find satisfied users of the driver soon ordering fairway woods to match, so the sale is not over with just one club.

I don't need to wish a good merchandiser "Good Luck" but I will wish you good luck in putting the display together!

Respectfully yours,
TONEY PENNA CO.

William H. Faulhaber
Vice President, Sales

A Division of A-T-O Inc. Toney Penna Drive,
Jupiter, Fl. 33458 Telephone 305-746-5147

I did not do this by memory; I still had a copy of the original letter in my files. The display cost was wholesale less 25 percent. After the promotion reached its usefulness the used drivers could be sold so the golf pro would easily get his original investment back, plus all the profit from whatever sales were generated. Next … Graphite Demo results …

GRAPHITE DEMO RESULTS #153

$\mathcal{T}$HE GRAPHITE DEMONSTRATION UNITS WERE a pretty darn good success. Since it was the first type of promotion the Penna Company ever participated in there was no others to judge the numbers. A first is a first. When the orders started to come in Toney's attitude changed. He tried not to show it but you could tell he was impressed. He even started to talk to me again. Things were not quite the same because I went around him but he seemed to get over that somewhat. He was madder at the big boss, Evan Baker, than he was me, or so he let on. I kept treading on shifting sand.

Backspin here a little bit. I forgot to mention Toney had a younger brother, Charles, who was the head golf professional for many years at the Beverly Country Club in the Chicago area. "Charlie" was a lot bigger than Toney as Toney was about 5 foot 7 inches and slim. Charlie was maybe three inches taller and a lot heavier. Charlie would visit the plant in the winter when he came down from the ice covered north. He was a really nice guy and had a very good sense of humor. Charlie had a stuttering problem which he controlled most of the time, except when he got a little excited. He was not nearly as vain as Toney; he was balding but didn't try to hide it. He loved to tell the story about his older brother Toney trying his best to hide his age. When he told this story he could not help stuttering, he would say;

TTT Toney uuuuu used tttt to bbbb be mmmm my oooo older bbbb brother nnnnnn now hhhh he's mmm my yyy you you younger bbb bro bro brother.

Translation, "Toney used to be my older brother now he's my younger brother." You had to be there. The way he told it you could not help but laugh, not at this stuttering of course but his big wide smile while making fun of his older brother.

Business was going very well and the parent company seemed happy with the progress we were making. We did not have national sales meetings because our sales guys were all on their own. My communication with them was in writing and phone calls and personal visits with some. I encouraged them to meet with me at the PGA show and spend as much time in our booth as they could and meet with their customers. That way I got to spend valuable time with them, answering any questions and bringing them up to date on anything new, which was not much as our line of clubs stayed pretty constant with no real changes from year to year. The product was good so as the saying goes "Don't fix what is not broken."

In the meantime my family is getting adjusted to South East Florida; they love it and our home and they have made new friends. Our friends from Ohio who lived across Rt. 306 in Tanglewood CC development, Ed and Lorraine Flaherty came to visit on their way home from several years working in South America. Ed worked for Ford but in S.A. he worked for Philco, a division of the Ford Company. Ed was retiring at an early age, I think about 54. They were going to relocate in Delray Beach, Fl., about 40 minuets south of North Palm Beach. We will be spending some time together and later on, they will move up this way and Ed will end up working for me, so will my brother.

I am enjoying my membership at the JDM Country club and will remain a member there for nineteen years. Golf in the south is so much different than the north; there is a big adjustment as I never played anywhere but the north. What's the difference? Wind, grass, sea level, the soil is sandy not clay, water everywhere, palm trees grab your ball and won't let go. In the north I hit the ball very high, that is no good in constant windy conditions, grass on the greens were not bent, they are slower here with a lot of grain. At sea level the air is thicker and the humidity makes it heaver, the ball will not roll on softer sandy terrain like it does on harder clay so the ball does not travel as far. Water everywhere and rough has grass like wire. My handicap shot up from about a three to nine real fast and I could never get it lower than a five. My handicap finally settled in at about a seven. But I was becoming a better player and I learned to hit it much lower and much straighter.

Backspin over, time for some over spin, what's next? Penna Demo Irons?

*T*HE GRAPHITE SHAFT DEMO DRIVERS was a success and Toney was now a little more open to my suggestions. Toney's own idea of the Bicentennial red white and blue driver was also a sell out. We used all the written off materials and the orders were still coming in so we kept making them using current materials as long as we kept getting orders. You know what? I completely forgot to keep one of those red white and blue Bicentennial drivers for myself!

The profit margin was acceptable. We have been concentrating on woods and have spent little time promoting the "Super Blade" irons featuring that very short, almost no hosel, the "Ounce that Counts." I had a plan for 5 iron demonstrators approved by top management, by Evan Baker. I presented my plan to Toney and he agreed! Can you imagine? These demos would go to the golf professionals who supported out graphite demonstrator program. Below is the letter I sent to these account explaining the program. The same Toney Penna letterhead was used:

IMPORTANT NOTICE REGARDING #5 IRON DEMONSTRATORS

You will be receiving your two #5 iron demonstrators soon. One will feature a dynamic steel medium flex shaft and the other a dynamic steel stiff shaft which are being provided to you **no charge.**

Naturally, we feel we have the finest playing iron in the history of the game. We also know that anytime a golfer hits a few balls with a Penna iron, that person becomes interested in them because of the SOLID FEEL AND TOTAL PLAYABILITY.

SOLID FEEL stems from the fact that the Penna iron **has no hosel** which eliminates **one ounce** of weight that never did lend anything to the playability of an iron. Actually, one ounce of hosel weight acts as a counter-balance. Putting that ounce back into the head, where it belongs, provides the SOLID FEEL and, correctly distributed, achieves perfect balance and TOTAL PLAYABILITY.

Let your prospective customers try them and compare them with their own irons. I think they will find the Penna iron out-performing their own, in playability and distance.

I am confident that we both will soon be enjoying newly found Toney Penna iron sales.

It's "THE OUNCE THAT COUNTS"

Respectfully yours,
TONEY PENNA COMPANY

William H. Faulhaber
Vice President, Sales

While all this is happening I am getting a feeling that something is going on, I'm getting vibes of some sort of expansion but have no idea of what is about to happen. We now are entering our third year with the Penna Company with a pretty strong showing. Where do we go from here?

WHERE DO WE GO FROM HERE? #155

*T*o HEBRON, OHIO THAT'S WHERE! Hebron is located near Newark Ohio which is approximately 35 miles east of Columbus Ohio. What happened? I can't explain it any better than the news release that appeared in the June, 1976 issue of The Sporting Goods Dealer, and other sporting goods and golf magazines.

A-T-O Sets Up Rawlings Golf under Jay Farish

Formation of **Rawlings Golf** as a separate operating entity in the sporting goods network of A-T-O Inc., Willoughby, Ohio was announced in May. Jay P. Farish, former senior management member of the Fuqua Industries sorting goods group of Atlanta has been named Rawlings Golf President, reporting to President Evan H. Baker of A-T-O's Rawlings Inc., subsidiary. The new golf set-up is a result of A-T-O's recent acquisition of **Omega balls and clubs**, **Lee Trevino clubs** and **Parker golf gloves**. All of those formerly were a part of the Faultless Sports Division of Globetrotter Communications Inc. Lee Trevino continues as head of the advisory staff for Rawlings Golf. **Toney Penna** and his custom-built woods and irons remain "Flagship" of the line, according to A-T-O. Except for Penna, still In Jupiter, Fla., all Rawlings Golf operations **and management** will be in modern new facilities at Hebron, Ohio. There, both clubs and balls soon will be manufactured under one roof. Ralph Maltby, club designer formerly with **Faultless,** steps up to Rawlings Golf marketing Vice President. He is author of the encyclopedic "Golf club Design, Fitting, Alterations and Repair." Golf industry veteran Bill Faulhaber former Toney Penna sales chief moves up to **Rawlings Golf sales Vice President.** Joe Altomente, previously in sales at Faultless, becomes director of retail sales for Rawlings Golf. Promotions in the financial area include Craig Mankowski, previously controller at **Texace,** San Antonio sports hat affiliate of A-T-O, now Rawlings controller and Joe Werstak, who was head of accounting at Toney Penna, advancing to assistant controller of the new organization.

Manufactures representatives and sales organizations of Toney Penna and Faultless have been consolidated to cover the professional market and deliver a comprehensive merchandise program. A-T-O also is parent of **Rawlings Sporting Goods**, which dates to 1898 for its baseball, basketball, football, tennis and other sports products. Other A-T-O affiliates include **Adirondack,** involved in baseball, hockey and toboggan products; **Oliver** of Australia and **Fred Perry Sportswear** in tennis as well as **Texace** sports hats. end

Wow, that's a mouthful. I have indicated the different companies in **bold** so as to identify all the various companies involved. Where do we go from here? To my thoughts, etc.

My Thoughts, Etc. #156

I KNEW SOMETHING WAS IN THE works but really was caught off guard with all this. I was informed of the change and told of my new position. A-T-O wanted all management to be located in Hebron, Ohio. The Penna Co. would remain in Jupiter, Fl., as a manufacturing facility only, no sales room for customers to visit and buy product. Can you imagine, the Golf Capital of the World where so many people in the golf industry congregate in the winter and no sales personnel in the Penna facility? What the hell am I supposed to do in Hebron a small town next to cows and sheep, but not much else?

My family and I love it in Florida, we were just going into our third year there and now I either accept this new position, put our house up for sale, move our family back north to an area that I would prefer not to live! I feel very unconformable about all of this but if I want a job I have no choice at this time. Big deal, I now have another Vice President title, Vice President of Sales, Rawlings Golf. I will later finally have the title of President but that will be with my own company, it will be "William Faulhaber Enterprises, Inc." and I will call the shots. Had to form my own company to get that title but more about that later, hard way to get the title of President isn't it?

So what did I do? I discussed this with my family; they agreed we had to do what we had to do. In the meantime I will be commuting back and forth. All of these expenses were paid including a rental car at the Ohio location and I also rented an apartment. Daughter Cindy was just beginning college so she decided to enter Ohio State which had a branch in nearby Newark, where I rented the apartment. She moved up to Ohio and we shared the apartment. I was not commuting every week, most of the time every other week. Very unsettled times, each time I would return with more clothing and small items since it looked like we would indeed be moving eventually.

The long range plan is to compete with all the big boys in the golf business. First of all the Faultless Golf Ball Company was a small manufacture with most of their business making logo balls for promotional give a way's by other companies. Faultless was the first company to create a non wound golf ball, it was a molded one piece ball which was not very playable. Spalding was the first to introduce a two piece ball, Top-Flite, the forerunner of all two and three piece solid non wound balls. The brand name **Omega** was a Faultless product mane for its new two piece golf ball, their top of the line. We signed Lee Trevino to a contract, which I still have a copy, to play the Faultless Omega balls and clubs.

Can you see the product line growing for the Golf Professional market, Penna clubs, Omega golf ball, Parker golf gloves, Texace head wear and a small golf bag line? For the retail, or store line, Lee Trevino clubs made by Faultless, a line of retail balls, golf bags, Fred Perry tennis sportswear, golf gloves, all headed up by Joe Altomente, Director of Retail Sales. Both Joe and I report to our new President, Jay Farish. I have a new boss, I no longer report directly to Evan Baker, I was uncomfortable with this arrangement.

The present set up looks a little top heavy to me for what is still a growing small company. Two different sales managers, Joe, who lives in the area and me and we had to divide up two different sets of Sales Reps as well. There were many cross over's involved here, or at least that is what it appeared to me.

The product line to the Golf Professional trade was all under the name of Rawlings Golf with its product line of Penna clubs, Omega golf balls, Parker golf gloves, Texace head wear, and a limited line of golf bags.

I had to blend all of this together so we could compete with the big boys. How do I get the Omega ball to match up with the number one company, Titleist, then Spalding's great Top-Flite ball, the Maxfli by

Dunlop and others? I had to go to Arizona and do product testing, I will explain that later. I almost did not get to do anything in my new position because I damn near got killed on one of the A-T-O private jets while attempting to visit the Texace factory in San Antonio, Texas. Almost no Tomorrow is next.

Almost No Tomorrow #157

*T*HE TEXACE HEADWEAR COMPANY LOCATED in San Antonio, Texas was a fairly new acquisition so top management made arrangements for five of us to fly there for a meeting and we would create a product line for the Rawlings Golf Professional division. I would be flying on one of the A-T-O company planes with three of their executives, including the controller and one other plus Evan Baker, myself and Jay Farish, the President of Rawlings Golf. The plane was a Saberliner, a small six passenger two engine jet.

The flight plan was that those three executives would fly to Newark from Cleveland, pick up Jay Farish and myself and fly non stop to San Antonio, returning the same day. We got as far as Columbus Ohio, thirty five miles from Newark and thank God Columbus was that close or I most likely would not be writing this story.

The Saberliner Jet landed in Newark which had a very small airport with a run way just long enough for a small jet to land. The crew of two and their three passengers step out of the plane as we greeted them, introductions all around and I remember the pilot's name which I have never forgotten and never will. He was introduced to me as Captain Blodgett, a veteran pilot who appeared to be in his sixties. Obviously a very experienced pilot, kind of like what I liked to pick out as taxi drivers, older and graying, proof they have survived working many years in their trade. As you read on what I have just said will take on more meaning. Off we go, it is often said the most dangerous part of flying are the landings and the take offs, with take offs being the most dangerous.

The layout, or sitting arrangements in this small jet are quite cramped, the pilot in the left front seat, the copilot, who appeared to be in his mid twenties, in the right seat. The cockpit is open between the two pilots and the six passenger's seats with a partition at the pilot's backs. With this opening you can see what they are doing and where we are going, a view straight out of the front of the plane. There are two seats directly in back of the pilot and copilot facing the rear of the plane and the other four passengers facing forward. There were five of us for six seats; I sat in the seat directly behind the pilot, facing the rear of the plane and the other four with one seat behind the copilot unoccupied. I could turn my head to the left and see the copilot and the controls and part of the right front window, but could not see the pilot, Captain Blodgett.

We taxi to the very end of the short runway using it all for takeoff and off we roll faster and faster, lift off. The small jet takeoff angle after liftoff becomes very steep, not a gradual assent, it seems like it is almost straight up. Just as we were starting to level off somewhat, but still climbing upwards it happened. A very loud **BANG** occurred

The planed shook violently and began to shake and wobble from side to side and we lost altitude quickly. There were no words spoken by anyone, not a sound from us or the pilot and co pilot. Then I could hear Captain Blodgett calmly say to his co pilot as he was getting the plane under control somewhat, "Radio the Columbus airport, tell them who we are, where we are, that we have blown an engine on takeoff and prepare a runway for an emergency landing." I looked over at the young copilot, his hands were shaking and I swear his facial skin color was green.

While all of this was happening in a very few seconds, it seemed to be in slow motion to me, not one word was or will be spoken by any of the five of us. I must tell you that I had no doubt that we were going down, even after Captain Blodgett got the plane under control, flying a small jet loaded with passengers on one engine is hardly enough speed to create enough lift to keep us in the air and the bad engine was smoking, would it catch fire and explode? My family flashed before me and my thoughts were, am I going to ever see them again?

I never had before, or have ever since that moment, during that entire event the feeling my body was going through. It is hard to explain. Naturally there was hardly a doubt in my mind we were not going to make it, although the Captain had the plane under some kind of control it was traveling very slowly and the plane was still shaking. Strong tingling pains were going through the insides of both of my arms into my armpits and seemingly into my chest, my heart was pounding and I swear I could hear it. I was facing the other four and I can not describe the fear in their eyes nor have I ever forgotten their expressions.

I could only slightly hear the muffled voice of Captain Blodgett speaking into the radio acknowledging whatever directions and instructions he was receiving from the control tower of the Columbus Airport. There was no other conversation in the aircraft, none. I don't know the exact miles we had to travel, the approximate distance between Newark and Columbus was about 35 road miles. Between the airports and where we were in the air at the time of the blow up of the engine I can only estimate it may have been 30 miles.

I did not know what our air speed was but I bet it was not much more than 100 miles an hour, whatever the speed it was just enough to keep us in the air and I was praying the Captain could maintain that speed and whatever control of the aircraft he had until we reached the airstrip. I think it took about 15 minutes but it seemed like eternity. I was also sweating pretty freely, as I looked at the others I was not alone, I could see they were having the same feelings as I. There were no words spoken between the five of us. What in the world would one say to each other in a situation like that? Well folks, I can tell you from experience, **absolutely nothing.**

Now I could tell by what I could hear, Captain Blodgett voice very calmly acknowledging final landing instructions. He was extremely calm throughout this entire ordeal. The young copilot was visibly shaken. As we approached the runway for a landing, remember the second most dangerous thing is landings, even when the aircraft is in no trouble; I strained to look out the front window and saw the runway. What I saw frightened me all the more, on each side of the runway I could see many emergency vehicles, about four or five on each side of the runway sitting there pointed in the same direction that our plane was heading. We have a long way to go yet for a safe landing. It appeared to me that all this was happening in slow motion. I am quite sure silent prayers were being said by all.

Finally touchdown, however it was not over yet. As I looked out the side widow right before touch down all those emergency vehicles were racing down the runway attempting to keep up with the plane as it was landing and continuing on down the runway. The biggest part of the breaking system to bring an aircraft to a stop before running out of runway is reversing the thrust of the engines. But we only had one that was not smoking, reversing just one would that be enough to stop us and would having only one engine in reverse throw our plane into a spin? Not over yet folks, or all those emergency vehicles would not be racing along side of us expecting a possible crash, or fire from that bad engine?

Captain Blodgett did a masterful job, a safe landing and he has brought the aircraft to a complete stop. But this ordeal is not over yet! As we are taxiing after the landing Captain Blodgett tells us that we are being directed to a spot which is the farthest point from the Airport Terminal and when we come to a stop he will release the door, it will open, the steps will automatically come down and we are to exit the plane in an orderly fashion as fast as possible and walk quickly to a safe distance from the aircraft. Meanwhile all these emergency vehicles are following us. Is a fire or explosion possible? The aircraft comes to a stop and we do exactly as we are told. The smoking engine is being extinguished and I finally realize we made it and we are safe. Thank God and also thanks to one hell of a calm veteran pilot, Captain Blodgett. Thank you again sir, where ever you are. I would assume your now flying in heaven.

There is a Conclusion of this San Antonio trip, next.

CONCLUSION OF SAN ANTONIO TRIP #158

*W*HAT A DAY, WE ALL looked at each other and tried our best to compose ourselves. We were given a ride to the airport terminal, and we had a meeting of what we were going to do next. The three from A-T-O said they were going to continue to San Antonio by commercial air lines as the financial people had to get some things settled. I made a decision that I had enough flight time for the day and I declined to continue as did my new boss, Jay Farish.

I had something else I wanted do so I rented a car. It was Tuesday and Jack Nicklaus was hosting his very first Memorial tournament in nearby Dublin which I wanted to attend anyway. That very first Memorial tournament was won by Roger Maltbie, no relation to Ralph Maltby our new VP of Marketing for Rawlings Golf. Tuesday was a practice round day and I needed to get in touch with Lee Trevino to discuss Lee's new five year contract with Faultless. Lee's original contract was singed in 1972 and concluded in 1976, which is the current year I am writing about. I still have a copy of that contract between Lee Trevino Enterprises, Inc., and Faultless Golf Products Division of Abbott Laboratories. Lee's trademark was "Super Mex" using a sombrero as his trademark. What I needed to find out if Lee had any concerns about his Faultless contract being updated as a Rawlings Golf contract.

Detour, before I forget a little forward spin is needed here. Dee and I made a trip to Rome with another couple, Frank and Joy Steinitz in the late seventies. They lived about three blocks from us on our street in North Palm Beach. Frank and Joy became close friends and Frank and I became partners in some real estate holdings which I'll write about later. Frank was an executive with a large real estate developer whose main office was in the East. If you have never been to Rome you have no idea how bad and dangerous the traffic is. Almost all their cars were small, just big enough to squeeze three in the back and two in the front. All the taxis I saw were of that size as well. It seems nobody stops for red lights, cars even drive up on side walks, and those people drive by eye contact. At intersections the driver will watch the other car and if the driver looks towards his car, then he will take the right of way. If not, he will let the other car go. Hard to explain but in those days it was a real scary experience if your not used to it.

So to the point, we had just finished visiting the Vatican and needed to take a taxi back to our hotel. Right outside the Vatican was a large area where taxis parked waiting for customers. There must have been at least thirty taxis and all the drivers were standing beside their vehicles conversing with one another. Frank said to me which one should we take. I looked at Frank and said, "Frank, you see that older man with grey hair over there, we need to ride with him." Frank wanted to know why I would pick an old man with grey hair, I replied, "Because, Frank, he has lived to survive all this crazy traffic long enough to get grey hair. I want to ride with him!" And we did. Reminded me of the grey hair Captain Blodgett had back in 1976.

Back to Jack Nicklaus, his Memorial tournament and Lee Trevino. I parked my rental car in the preferred parking lot and with my PGA Tour Money Clip, my official credentials. Its strange how things work out sometimes, I am still on shaky ground somewhat from my flight experience a couple of hours ago and then the and very first person I ran into was the person I came here to see, Lee Trevino! I knew Lee a little bit, he recognized me as I was approaching him, our eyes made contact and we greeted each other shaking hands. He looked at me and asked if I was feeling well, it was summer time and I looked pale. I had not intended to say anything about what had just happened but since he asked me that, I told him what I had just been through. He just shook his head in wonderment while offering me his best wishes.

We had a very nice visit and he did sign another contract with Rawlings Golf. Lee eventually left the Rawlings organization when it started to crumble and signed a contract with Spalding where he remained as a staff consultant for the rest of his playing career.

After the meeting with Lee, I headed back to Newark to start a new tomorrow that I almost didn't have. That pretty much wraps up the San Antonio trip and brings us to some interesting golf ball tests.

GOLF BALL TESTS #159

I AM NOT THE ONLY ONE commuting back and forth, Jay Farish our new President of Rawlings Golf and my new boss lives in Atlanta. I am getting to know him pretty well because my commute from West Palm Beach to Columbus Ohio, has one stop, Atlanta. Jay makes his schedule to catch this same flight, he gets on and we sit together from Atlanta to our designation and take the same flight together going home for the weekend every couple of weeks.

Jay is a nice enough guy, I am getting the impression he is not too happy about moving from the great city of Atlanta to a small Ohio town located next to nowhere either. He is a native southern as well, a fish out of water seems to fit his situation. Jay is confirming what I had suspected, A-T-O's CEO. Harry Figgie is a very aggressive hard pushing business man with a large body and larger ego whose intention is to challenge the big giants of the business. Faultess makes golf balls, the Omega ball is a two piece ball and he expects us to take this product and challenge the Spalding's very popular two piece Top-Flite balls. The average golfer loves the Top-Flite ball, and the Titleist people are coming on strong with their own two piece ball. Spalding has come a long way with a two piece range ball as well and are on their way to dominating the range ball business that the U.S. Rubber company used to enjoy. Faultless has a range ball as well but struggling to gain a foothold.

How do I accomplish all of this? I know down deep, I can't, not over night, perhaps never. I discuss all of this with Jay Farish, explaining to him what the golf ball business is all about because Jay is not a golf oriented person; he is familiar with the general sporting goods business. He is a very understanding person however and a good listener. I ask him as President how he expects to accomplish all this. What are our promotional and advertising dollars going to be and we have to come up with some claims of why a consumer should switch to the unknown Omega ball from the Top-Flite or whatever ball the consumer is satisfied with. We have to come up with some damn good reasons and claims. Is our ball equal or better than the Top-Flite? What kind of field testing has Faultless done, if any?

Has any comparative testing by machine been done with the Omega ball against its intended competition? Faultless does not have the sophisticated "Iron Byron" robot that is capable of testing balls and clubs. I am explaining all of this to Jay and he is starting to think I may know a little bit of what I am talking about. I can tell he is now thinking his job, and mine, is not going to be a cake walk. Harry Figgie wants results, not excuses.

I explained to Jay that the major ball manufactures own their own Iron Byron's. That name came from the fact the robot's golf swing programmed into its computers brain was the golf swing of the great Hall of Fame golfer Byron Nelson. Jay had little knowledge of all this. I explained that machine testing was great while developing a product and once that was done that product must be taken to the public for testing by humans, golfers of all handicaps is ideal, however this takes time, months?, No, sometimes years of development. Do we have that kind of time, I doubt it.

Since Faultless testing methods were antiquated I also informed Jay that the True Temper people, the manufacture of steel golf shafts, had an Iron Byron. It was available for a pretty healthy fee for testing if we were interested. A very good reliable tool but expensive because it took a team of people to run it, program it's computer for the data needed in the testing of the product, balls, and shafts and clubs. It is a very expensive tool, old Byron is. One good thing, True Temper was located near Cleveland so they were accessible if we wanted to go that route. I can report that Rawlings Golf did not.

I can see the costs of all this is just beginning to pile up, including what Jay and I are costing the company commuting, renting of apartments, renting cars, and moving expenses. I beginning to realize I'm starting to dig a hole for myself. Putting those thought aside, I now have to deal with golf ball testing/

Golf Ball Tests Inconclusive #160

*M*Y EXPERIENCE WITH GOLF BALL testing had been pretty extensive with Spalding, first with the Dot and then with the development of two piece non wound balls which evolved and created the Top-Flite, Tour Edition, Molitor and Range ball products. This was all discussed in meetings with Jay Farish and Ralph Maltby the VP of Marketing. After providing all the details about Spalding's testing which led to their advertising claims of superior distance it was decided Rawlings Golf should follow the same method of testing because the Omega had to compete with the Spalding Top-Flite.

For any claims in advertising the tests must be done by independent testing companies. The type of test can be set by the manufacture but the actual tests can not be done by company personal, they can be on site and assist but the testing people record all the data of the tests and then put their seal on what the results are. Our plan was to do the exact same test that Spalding did a couple of years previously and use the same independent test company as well. To make it really competitive we would also do the test in the same area so the climate and soil conditions were the same and we actually used the same exact test site in Phoenix, Arizona.

Spalding used a combination of two clubs for a total distance claim. The real reason for this is, well, I am not going into that, there are such things as trade secrets, I don't think I should be getting too technical so will just generalize and let it go at that. When we tested the Omega ball we have each player hit 15 drives and 15 five irons and added the distance of each together for a total distance and compared those statistics against our competitors golf balls.

I am going to cut this off because all that is involved would be difficult to explain and might be confusing plus boring so I will conclude with one fact, our tests did not prove the Omega ball had any advantages over it's competition so we could not start an advertising campaign that our ball was superior. We could only advertise that the Omega ball by Rawlings golf was a very good playable two piece ball. The Omega golf ball was just exactly what the golf pro didn't need in their shops, another ball to take up space in their all ready crowded golf ball display case. This is going to be a tough job for independent reps to sell another ball that really wasn't going to excite anyone.

A lot of money spent with no positive results. It did tell our management one thing; this was not going to be easy getting a foot hold in the professional golf ball market. But breaking into a market dominated by Acushnet's Titlist, Spalding and Dunlop Maxfli products was not to be, Rawlings Golf never penetrated that market.

Meanwhile I miss my family and Florida. Frankly, I am not happy with what is going on, or not going on. I do not have a good feeling in general, and what happened next, I am not surprised.

I Am Not Surprised #161

*T*HERE IS NOT MORE I can write about building a successful Rawlings Golf professional only product line of golf balls, gloves, hast and Penna clubs because it didn't happen. There are no such products on the market now or even after a year or so back in 1976/77. I will conclude this part of my stories by condensing the short few months as quickly as I can. My position with Rawlings Golf started about March, 1976. My duties with Penna were included of course and I started to commute in April. After reshuffling the independent reps to meld with the other Faultless products with the retail line of products, which included Lee Trevino clubs, Joe Altomente, our retail sales manager and I worked very hard trying our best of bringing everything together.

The problems we had to address of testing the Omega ball and confirming we could not make any claims of superiority was leading us nowhere. The whole idea of a Pro only Rawlings Golf line of Penna clubs, Omega balls, Parker gloves, Texace head wear was not competitive, our expenses were very high and sales of Penna remained fair but not much else was selling. For about five or six months I kept bringing things to the apartment. I drove back and forth a few times, each time loading the station wagon with personal belongings. We had not really pushed to sell our beautiful home in Florida or look seriously for a new home in Newark either. Deep down I had a gut feeling this was not going to work out and in a way I was hoping it wouldn't either. I really did not want to relocate my family. But, I had to make a paycheck as I had no other options at the time.

It was about mid November when my flight made its usual stop in Atlanta. Jay Farish had not relocated to Ohio yet either, I don't know it he ever did. He got on the flight as usual which was never crowded so we never had a problem sitting together. Jay sat down and was unusually quite before and during takeoff. That gut feeling I had been experiencing came over me. I guess I am a mind reader as I would have bet anyone I knew what he was about to say to me after we were in the air. My thoughts were correct, Jay turned to me and said, "Bill, there is something I have got to talk to you about." I don't know why I didn't let him continue, what the heck I'm used to talking when I should be listening and I interrupted and said to Jay, "Jay, you're going to tell me things aren't working out as planned and I am not going to be part of this company anymore, right?" He replied, "Bill, your intuition is rather amazing, I'm sorry, you are correct." **I'm not surprised.**

We sat there without saying anything for what seemed a very long time. I admit I was a little numb, I've just been fired. I was the one who was usually firing people, now I really know how it feels to be on the other end. The stewardess came and we ordered a couple of drinks. Might as well fly while being high!

I really felt about as low as whale dung at the bottom of the ocean.

If there was any consolation, in our discussions later that day it wasn't that I was not doing a good job. The realization of this whole idea working out was becoming a reality since the golf ball tests were so bad. There was a sale manager in place for the retail division and it looked like the only product that was going to sell in the golf shops was the Penna clubs, so they didn't need two high priced guys and the expense involved in relocating me and my family. I was given a formal notice and I would be receiving a paycheck for three months.

The timing concerning my daughter Cindy's 1st quarter was workable, it was mid December. We planned to leave Newark when her quarter was complete. We moved so much personal stuff to Newark we had to rent a small U-Haul truck to get all of our belongings and ourselves back to good old Florida. Joe Altomente and his wife insisted on throwing a farewell dinner for Cindy and me with a few of the Rawlings Golf people as quests. I did not feel real comfortable with that but could not turn down such a nice gesture.

Cindy and I packed the U-Haul and we planned to start for Florida that evening after we left the dinner at Joe's home. The dinner was very nice and we said our goodbyes, and then headed home. I think we both felt relieved we were not moving and we wanted to get home as quickly as we could.

RAWLINGS GOLF CO. CONCLUSION #162

*T*HE FIRST THING I NOTICED when Cindy and I pulled into our driveway after our long drive was Dee had removed the house for sale sign from the front lawn. Good work Dee. With mixed emotions I'm home where I really wanted to be but I had no job.

But first a little forward spin; let's look at what happened to Rawlings Golf Professional golf products and their hopes for penetrating that market. They didn't. For a while Rawlings Golf retail store division survived with the Lee Trevino line of clubs however after a couple of years Lee left Rawlings and signed a contract with Spalding where he remained the rest of his playing career.

A-T-O the parent company sold the Toney Penna Co. to Bing Crosby's youngest son, Nathanial, who was a very good player and he was runner up in the U. S. Amateur one year. I met with Nathan a couple of times; he was really a very nice young man. He was asking me quite a few questions as he had no experience in the golf business whatsoever. I advised him to hire someone to help him run the company, but not me. I knew the business was going to fail for several reasons. I will only talk about one of those reasons, Metal woods were beginning to show up. There was no way Penna was going to get into that market; it was just not going to happen. The Penna Co. went out of business. Jack Nicklaus bought most of the club making equipment as Jack had his own golf club company located in nearby Riviera Beach producing mostly mid price clubs under the Golden Bear name for the retail stores.

The conclusion is there is no Toney Penna Co., and no Rawlings Golf Co., I am not a mind reader and I don't read palms but somehow I knew this whole thing was going to come to a dead end. How fortunate I was that I never moved my family to Newark, Ohio because it I did

I would have been out of a job there eventually. At least in Florida we would not freeze to death and I knew something would develop.

I also knew I had enough reserves to last about a year. Wife, four kids, two in college, a rather large mortgage in an expensive area to live was not ideal. This is the third time in my adult life I was in some degree of difficulty, either being broke or the possibility of being broke. I did not like that feeling and vowed that I would never ever be in that position again, ever. I am going to make sure that what happens in the future my family is going to be financially sound. Some way some how I am going to make that happen, one year passes fast so one year of reserve to me is a dangerous position to find myself.

I have now been in the Sporting goods business 20 years with most of those years in the golf business. I am 45 years old with one heck of a lot of selling and management experience. A good salesman can find something to sell to make a better than average living. I thought why not take a shot at being an independent rep myself; I have had it with middle and upper management. Just find something and take care of myself and my family. I want to be my own boss with no one to answer to but the good Lord and my family. I have to get busy and get rid of this hollow feeling and stop feeling sorry for myself.

An old friend called me when he heard the news, Don Rosi. Don was with Spalding many years ago. His career took him to being a top executive with the Ridell Co., the famous football helmet manufacturer and related athletic protective equipment. After a successful career at the Ridell Co. Don became the top man at the National Golf Foundation. Ironic, the National Golf Foundation decided to move its headquarters from Chicago to where the Golf Capital of the World was, the Palm Beaches, smart, where the action is. A-T-O decided to move their golf operation from the Golf Capital of the World to where there was no action, Hebron, Ohio. Sour grapes, I could not help that. Am I sorry for that remark? No, I am not. All that was a bitter pill to swallow.

Don called me and said, "Bill, I have an office, a desk and a phone for you here at the National Golf Foundation for your use until you find another position." The NGF was located in Lake Park, about one quarter of a mile from my house in NPB. He also offered to help me in any way that he could, personal recommendation included. I replied, "Don, you are a true friend and I appreciate the offer. I have an office in my home where I intend to set up shop, but thank you very much for the offer." How nice was that? The golf business used to be a close nit group; a lot of the top executive knew each other pretty well and would socialize with each other. Middle management was like that as well. At one time it was not a cut throat business, some things do change and not always for the better.

What Would I Do? #163

I DECIDED THAT I NO LONGER was interested in pursuing any sales management positions with any company for two reasons. Number one I did not want to relocate again. Number two I was fed up with all the politics and what these positions paid compared to what salesman can earn, it was not worth the difference. I have had it with management positions, period. Only if it were my own company, and in a few years I would indeed have a small company of my own, Wm. Faulhaber Enterprises, Inc., more about this later.

So I set out to see what I could do as an independent rep myself. I put out feelers through the grape vine what my intentions were, I was looking for golf product lines to sell to the golf professional trade in South East Florida. In the meantime I had been contacted by a couple of gentlemen located in southern Illinois. They had been given my name from someone that I was in between opportunities. Seems they wanted to get into the custom wood business, ala Penna. This one young man had a special block of solid wood which was not persimmon he thought was better than persimmon and laminated wood. Frankly I don't remember what kind of wood it was. The other gentleman involved was the financial backer. They contacted me and wanted to discuss a consultant contract as they needed advise from someone with my background.

They asked me what what it would take to bring me aboard as a consultant on a short term contract. They offered me a number close to what I had been making plus expenses and I agreed to a short term deal. I could do this with a couple of personal visits and the rest through phone conversations, answering questions and of course giving them advice and direction. I visited them and they only had a workshop and a dream. After my personal visit they agreed to pay me a two month retainer in advance for my services. To bring this to a conclusion quickly that is exactly what I did for them. When I was done relating to them what all they thought could be done with this new unproved wood head, what was involved to bring a product to the market, they realized they bit off more than they could chew. They appreciated my honesty, as I was not going to string them along just to receive a pay check. That two month pay and the three month severance I received from Rawlings Golf helped finance me for nearly a half a year while I was putting together a few items, including a line of unknown brand of shirts and sweaters.

I did hit on one good item that I thought I could build on; it was a single club which was fairly popular. It was called the "Ginty" the creation of Stan Thompson. A friend of mine and a former Spalding salesman, Jack Julian had the rights to sell this club in the South Eastern states, including Florida. You remember Jack? Remember my story about Jack Stanton and Jack Julian back in Chicago at dinner one night, Jack Julian was wearing sun glasses and people thought he was blind? Same guy, he contacted me and asked if I would like to take over the responsibility for the Ginty in those southern states as he was getting involved with something else. We made the arrangements with Stan Thompson and I had the Ginty exclusively for the south eastern states.

It Ginty was the forerunner of today's specialty clubs, the Hybrid's as we know them today, a high lofted wood designed to replace the two, three and four irons. The Ginty had the loft of a seven wood with the length of a three wood. The sole plate had two metal runners running from front to back which was designed to cut through high grass more easily than any five wood or 2, 3, or 4 irons could. It was a very easy club to hit. A great club for the average golfer to high handicap and was available in men's right and left hand and ladies.

Now I'm thinking of starting a rep organization to cover these six or seven states where I have the Ginty as an exclusive. I started to contact some reps in those areas with the idea of using them as sub reps selling the Ginty for me and possibly other product lines I was attempting to obtain.

Just about the time I thought I had something going, something happened to negate all of this groundwork and my plans change, what happened?

WHAT HAPPENED, MY PLANS CHANGED #164

*Y*OU KNOW, THE GAME OF golf is kind of like life itself, when you're playing well, it seems so easy. But when you're playing badly, the game seems impossible.

Here I am between opportunities trying to create one, not making much money, dipping into my reserves. However things are beginning to look up having acquired the "Ginty" for the south eastern states. That could be the backbone of building a business. And then I received a phone call that would shock me somewhat, a call which required that I must make a decision fairly quickly, which business decision I should take.

The call was from my favorite company, Spalding. I don't know exactly how this call came about. Backspin a little here, when I was still with Penna I had another phone call which surprised me. Spalding was having a meeting in this area. The caller indentifies himself as Richard Geisler, the current President of Spalding. Richard asks how I am doing and informs me that he is in the area and would love to drop in and personally say hello. I said certainly come on over to my house. "Dick" Geisler became President of Spalding after the guy I said I could not out last, was fired. He was the Vice President of Spalding when I left and I always thought he was a good man.

How about that, the President of Spalding just wanted to say hello because he was in the area and wanted to know how my family and I were doing. We had a nice visit, I showed him around the property, the river out back and where I was putting in a dock. We did not discuss business; it was just a nice cordial visit of about an hour. He wished me luck, we shook hands, and he left.

That visit was about a year before the call from Spalding. I have no idea if Dick Geisler's visit had anything to do with this call. I briefly outlined to the caller what I was doing and planning. After a nice conversation the caller said he wanted to ask me a question, I replied, fire away.

The caller continued, "Bill, knowing your background, working your way up the ladder from being a Golf Professional salesman, a Dealer Salesman, through middle management and then National Sales Manger with us and then other positions in top management in the industry, I do not want to insult you with my question. First of all, let me explain what I am leading up to. We are going to have an opening in your area very soon. I would like to know if you would have any interest in coming back to Spalding in a lower position than you have been accustomed. It may seem like a step back for someone with your background and qualifications. The position I am talking about is calling on the Golf Professionals in South East Florida as a salesman. We would very much like to have you back with Spalding if you're interested."

This is the very same job I had when I started my career in the sporting goods industry. I was without words for a few seconds. I asked the caller to give me a few details, approximately what the compensation plan was these days. And then I told him I would like a few days to consider this offer with the opportunity to call him back in a day or two because I'm sure I would have a few more questions to ask. He said to take all the time I needed, the caller realized I needed a little time for all of this to sink in.

First of all I had already made a decision I no longer was interested in a management position unless it was my own company. So, that was a yes. Was I insulted because I would be back in a job where I started twenty years ago, No, I have an ego but I don't think it is that big? I liked the idea of becoming an independent rep, but if what I was working that solid of a deal? No, it would be a struggle, but what isn't.

When I left Spalding after seventeen years I was fully vested in the retirement program and I also a member of a 401K program the company had recently offered to salaried employees as well. Would building on these existing programs make sense, Yes, and the 401K program I really liked because I could put into the plan up to ten percent of my income and Spalding would match up to six percent of that. That is a very good way to Invest for the future.

When I returned the call with questions I was told that the company could "Bridge the gap" of the retirement program and the 401K, the three years I would have not been with Spalding by just changing the date I was originally hired from 1957 to 1960 so my employment would appear continuous. I am not quite sure I understood all of that but if that was to my advantage, and the employee's department head, Vaughn Rist assured me it was. It seemed everyone I talked to at Spalding was doing everything they could to help me make the decision a positive one, come on back Bill.

And finally, the compensation plan had been improved since I left the company three years ago. The territory I was being asked to consider was one of the better volume producers. I would be getting a company station wagon, expenses, and the salary and commission plan was not that much lower than my last Vice Presidents job was paying, and with much better incentives, the retirement and 401K programs and the very important health insurance program for my family. I think I would be wrong in not accepting because of the security for my family by becoming an independent rep was risky. I accepted, I was about to return to the company I truly loved.

Don't ever burn the bridges you've left behind. This is the second time I have gone back to a company I had left; the other was Massey Buick back in Pittsburgh in 1953. So, welcome back home.

Welcome Home Letters #165

*B*efore I get to the subject title, although top management offered this new position to me, there was one stipulation. A new Sales Region had just been created six months before all of this and was located right here in Hollywood, Fl., just north of Ft. Lauderdale, including a mini warehouse. The new Regional Sales Manger Jack Lacey was located there as well.

The stipulation was that the final word about my being hired had to come from Jack, since that is who I would be reporting. Jack and I had a meeting and he gave the thumbs up. I was officially back on board, and what a bonus, I had a warehouse right in the middle of my new territory. Jack sent the following announcement letter to all of the Golf Professionals in my new territory:

Spalding

July 7, 1977

Dear Golf Professional:

Jack Mxxxxx has tendered his resignation to Spalding effective June 30, 1977. Effective July 1st we are happy to announce that Bill Faulhaber will be rejoining Spalding after a three year absence. Bill accrued some 17 years with Spalding in capacities ranging from pro golf salesman to Director of Pro Golf which is the position he held when he left us in 1974. Bill will be around to see you during the next four to six weeks. If we can do anything in the interim, please do not hesitate to call Bill's home, 561-848-7416.

I want to thank you for your cooperation and business during the past six months that I have been here and I look forward with Bill to a more mutually profitable relationship during the balance of 1977. My best wishes for a good summer and hope to see you at the Florida P.G.A. Show in October.

Sincerely,
Jack E. Lacey
Regional Sales Director
Region III - Southeast

I resigned effective June 30, 1974 and was hired back July 1, 1977, exactly three years to the day. After the news was announced in the various golf publications of my rejoining Spalding the phone calls started to pour in. Then the letters started to come. I still have them in my files, in addition to the many from within Spalding the letters from within the golf industry were truly touching.

I must tell you all of this was quite humbling to say the least. People really cared. I am also determined if at all possible of becoming debt free as soon as possible. I also do not ever want to find myself "In between opportunities" again unless it is my sole decision. To do that I have to become solvent, so to speak, part of that would be the retirement and 401K plans plus personal investments. The stock market was part of my plans plus some property investments. The opportunity to create the "Wm. Faulhaber Enterprises, Inc." was about to become a reality as well, but more about that later.

Spalding Customer Trips, Spain First #166

*B*ACKSPIN TIME AGAIN. I AM happy being back with Spalding and we are where we want to live. And again I have a pretty sensible employment position. All I have to do is take care of my territory and no one is going to bother me.

Spalding has for several years offered customer trip contests which also included salesmen and regional managers, the national sales manager made these trips automatically. These were first class trips designed to create closer relationship with our important customers. It was set us so participating customers who fell short of winning but had large increases in purchases still won consolation prizes so not winning the trip would not turn them off. These kinds of promotions can backfire if customers think they were fooled into buying more products with little chance of winning.

I made two of these trips as national sales manager. After I returned to Spalding in 1977, I won a trip as a salesman in, I believe, 1978 or 79. The first trip was to Madrid, Spain, boy was that a wonderful time. On the chartered flight I got to visit many of our customers coming and going. I was all over the airplane visiting with all our guests and their wives. Everyday there were group trips to various sites. Breakfast, lunch, cocktail parties and dinner each day was enjoyed by including entertainment every evening.

The highlight on our last evening in Madrid was a medieval 14th Century banquet. The hotel where we were staying had a large room permanently decorated for this event which they obviously put on every week for groups like ourselves. There were two large dressing rooms, one ladies and one man's; housing all these "Costumes" that people wore in that era. On the morning of this event we all had to visit these dressing rooms and pick out what we were to wear that evening.

The ladies outfits did not include hats, but headwear with lots of plumes and feathers were part of the men's attire. The banquet room was beautifully decorated with a head table elevated so the important people of that era were sitting a little higher looking down upon all the common people. I have no idea what our banquet titles were, but since I was national sales manager Dee and I were sitting in the middle of the head table, we were the "Big cheese."

The wine was flowing like water, as you can imagine in Spain, wine is like water. The waiters were also dressed in these ancient costumes and were serving everyone, but not before the head waiter would come to Dee and I sitting at the head table first. Then Dee and I were to sample each item, and then give the signal of our approval or disapproval. And then we would wave to the waiters it was OK to serve the rest of the people. The main course was presented to us and it was a large pig, head and all, with an apple in it's mouth. I almost didn't give my approval and I stood up and looked at the poor pig in disgust. I hesitated, then tore off a piece, tasted it, and gave my approval. I receive a loud clapping approval from the common people. You had to be there, it was the best banquet I had ever attended. Everyone loved it, what a blast; the banquet was the highlight of a great trip.

Test tasting all that food was not easy for me because, for some reason, I could not eat the food in Spain. Something they used in cooking, or something they fed the animals gave the food a taste I actually disliked. I am a little bit of a picky eater but not really bad. I survived by eating bread, butter and cheese. And wine, of course. I was never a wine drinker but during lunch and dinner the table was always set up with four different wine classes at each place setting. Each of these classes were there for sampling different types of wines that were offered, just a sip of each, and then finding the one I liked the best, then that glass would be filled up with my personal choice. At home as a kid the only wine mom served was really a sweet red wine I did not like. In Spain I found a fondness for dry tasting wines, preferably red.

Getting back to the food, one morning Dee and I were having room service for breakfast. I looked at the menu, turned to Dee and said, "I've got it, I am going to order soft boiled eggs in the shell. They can't put something on the egg to spoil the taste if it's still in the shell!" Breakfast arrived and I stared at those two eggs like they were the finest steaks in the world. I cracked one open, tasted it, and almost hit the ground. How can this be, no way did it taste good. The only thing I could conclude is the chickens are fed different grain than what we feed ours in the states. Back to my cheese, bread and butter diet.

We made a side trip to Alicante which was located on the coast. It was a beautiful little town with palm tress and colorful tile sidewalks. Four of us flew there from Madrid, the reason was that Spalding purchased our leather golf gloves from a factory there and we wanted to take this opportunity to visit that facility. When we arrived it was siesta time, everything was closed for about an hour or so. We wander around a bit, finally a restaurant opened and we went in for a late lunch. Behold, on the menu there it was, "American style cheeseburger." I could not believe it, "Medium rare please!" I couldn't wait for it to be served. And when it was served I took one bite. Well, the dry red wine was excellent anyway.

BLACK LEATHER COAT #167

I RARELY GO INTO A STORE to shop, but Dee dragged me into a shop that featured leather goods. While there I spotted a coat and fell in love with it at first sight. It was a black leather overcoat finger tip length. It was beautiful and I bought it. I still have the sales slip; Dee and I are really pack rats. Anyway the shops name was Cardinale, House of Suede, Madrid, Paid $125.00. I would guess that coat would have cost me a least twice that much in the US. Some of my friends told me when I was wearing it I looked like I was climbing out of a German tank. That coat was really good looking and I wore it everyday in the winter for two years before moving to Florida, where it hung unused in a closet for many years. Dee finally gave it to a young man we knew who was going to college in Montana.

Madrid was a very large city with no crime back in the early seventies. Women could walk alone at night anywhere without fear. The government then was a dictatorship with very strict laws that carried instant justice. If someone was caught stealing the police would chop off your hand or hands on the spot with no trial. I don't want to go there about a rape case. The city was really safe and there didn't seem to be the poverty and slums we have in the States either. The people were overall very small in stature and were very well dressed. Dinner for most was not until at least 8 PM. After dinner the night life started, it seemed all the men dressed in coats and ties and the ladies wore beautiful modest dresses or skits and blouses. The Spanish people were a very impressive good looking bunch indeed.

It was also in Spain I realize there was more to see than just nightclubs. In the States while traveling I really never took the time to look around and see the sights that were available. I just kind of took everything for granted until one day we traveled to the small town of Segovia. It was there I was absolutely shocked into reality of how small I felt in this big wonderful and beautiful world full of wonders. What got my attention was an object I saw from a distance at the entrance to Segovia, a gate of some kind?

It was a very tall stone structure with arches that appeared to be around 100 feet high. What was I looking at?

An ancient Aqueduct built over one thousand years ago!

I had to find out more about this wonderful awesome looking structure. I learned it was still being used and at the very top was a trough that carried water to this small town from the hills nearby. Think of this, over one thousand years ago the people built this using granite stones hand carved and placed together without mortar of any kind. Stones fitted on top of each other with a series of arches for strength and a gradual angle of decent of something like one inch per mile to carry water at a very slow pace. Unbelievable!

We also visited many beautiful churches and the castles were something to behold as well. Looking at pictures of these great structures does not come close to actually seeing them in person. The suits of armor worn by soldiers or knights were everywhere in these castles. The sizes of these suits of armor are very small, what is surprising is they were made for grown men of their time. Only small children would fit into them in today's world. People were really small, it's amazing how much the human race has grown in height and size compared to the size of those tin suits.

One of the things that struck me traveling around Europe and the United Kingdom is there are not a lot of new buildings. So many of those buildings are hundreds of years old, granted, they were built with granite. No pun intended. These buildings were built to stand for centuries and in the States we are use to seeing one hundred, even fifty year old buildings being torn down and replaced. Spain was a wonderful trip and next we visited Ireland.

IRELAND #168

O N ALL OF THESE CUSTOMER trips everyone was asked to wear a name tag so others would know who you were, this created a more friendly atmosphere making it easier for strangers to feel more comfortable starting a conversation with someone you have just met. Very much like Dee and I asked all of our quests to wear a name tag at our New Years Eve parties.

In 1973 the customer trip was to Ireland with a twist, we visited three other countries as well. These are only seven day trips, when everyone arrives in New York for our flight to Europe or the United Kingdom, it takes a full day to get there and a full day to return. So that really only leave five days for all the other activities. These trips can become a little rushed and the Ireland trip, as great as it was, was almost impossible to catch your breath. You will see why as I continue my story of this fun trip. Remember, five full days for the following activities, and I know I will not remember everything we did, including a scavenger hunt. But I did remember that because Dee reminded me. We were paired up in teams of six, given a bunch of clues, an automobile and a local driver. Things were hidden all over the country side, it was fun and prizes were given out to the winning teams at dinner that evening.

Hey, I made it to "Dirty Nellie's Pub" too. Great little place with dirt floors, people tipping a couple of pints and singing. Yes, they really do that in Ireland at the pubs, lots of singing and people having a good time together.

Again, I am all over the plane greeting people the whole trip, but being careful not to wake anyone catching a nap. As we approached the airport in Shannon I could see why Ireland is noted for the color of green. There were all different shades of green, beautiful.

We were staying at the very old Dromoland Castle in Clare, wonderful and quaint accommodations. The first side trip we took was a charter fight to London where we had lunch and spent most of the day shopping and sightseeing. We saw Big Ben and the Palace guards and we had a great private lunch at some famous restaurant. Counting flying time and lunch there was not much time to get back to Ireland for dinner, is was a very fast trip for one afternoon.

Another day we flew to Amsterdam in Holland for lunch at a famous grillroom, "The Five Flies". Then sightseeing as time allowed. Did you know prostitution is legal in Amsterdam? Just a little important trivia to know it you visit there someday, after all guys, you don't want to miss all the sights!

Next there was a chartered flight to Paris and we had lunch in the Eiffel Tower. We also visited Norte Dame. We stayed overnight and returned to Ireland the next day. I may step on some toes with what I am about to write. My personal thoughts, Paris is one beautiful city with some of the ugliest people I have ever encountered. Many French people, waitress, waiters, clerks, seem to hate Americans. One day we got a glimpse of the American cemetery where so many of our young boys died fighting to free France from German occupation during World War II, and World War I as well. Thousands of them buried in France, can you imagine why they feel that way about us? We left so many of our brave young men buried in France fighting for their freedom as well as ours. Short memories, I don't appreciate their attitude. My opinion.

We had a couple of French Canadians' with us who spoke French, and they were embarrassed overhearing the uncomplimentary remarks. I do understand one thing however; we do have quite a few Americans who do not know how to act when in another country. They are embarrassing and don't represent us well and unfortunately make us all look bad.

I have seen this with some of our own group of customers and on several other trips. Some are overbearing, demanding jerks who give the rest of us a bad reputation, so I do understand why we do get slammed somewhat, but in Paris it was ridicules, and I have never had a desire to return. You can have France but the rest of Europe I found very friendly. We must understand while traveling to other countries we are their guests and we should remember to respect these people and their customs. When in Rome do as the Romains do is a saying which makes a lot of sense to me.

The Irish people were also great and very friendly and I will continue with our trip there.

HURLING MATCH #169

*T*HERE WERE MANY HIGHLIGHTS ON this tripl. One thing I would have loved to do was play at least one round of golf on an Irish seaside golf course. We are a group of golf people but did not play one round of golf, what a shame. I have to admit there was no time, this trip had too many things going on and it was very tiring, even for the young.

Between all these side trips we squeezed in the main banquet which was held at the Bunratty Castle, again Dee and I were in the middle of the head table but no costumes like we had in Spain. I did not have to taste all the food before it was served either, thank goodness since the main meal was some kind of a lamb dish. I can't stand to be near lamp of any kind, but the bread, butter, cheese and the wine was excellent so I survived the dinner again, thank you.

My real highlight was a Hurling match a few of us was lucky enough to get tickets. This was a national semi finals match between Limerick and Killarney; it was sold out so our travel agency was only able to get about eight tickets. I wasn't even aware of what Hurling was and most of you I am sure don't know the sport either. It is a very exciting game I really enjoyed and I will set the stage and explain everything that I can remember about the game.

This game was played in Limerick in a very old stadium and if I were to guess how many people were there it would be about 30,000, something like the entire population of Limerick itself. The whole town was there. Hurling is played on a very large field, 100 yards wide and 150 yards long and at each end was a netted goal similar to something you would see in soccer but larger. In addition that goal also had two goal posts rising above the netted goal, like the goal posts we have for football.

There are 15 men on each team, all of them carried a bat like stick and the very end of this bat was a curved out depression similar to a long spoon. The game is played with a hard ball much like a baseball and looked to be about the same size. There are seven offense and seven defense players plus a goalie. I think there were four quarters but I don't recall. It also seems there were no time out's, the play was continues until a score. In a way it is a combination of basketball, baseball, hockey and football because the ball is batted back and forth between players and when they advance the ball they "Dribble", or bounce the ball on the end of this curved end of the bat while running.

When attempting to score a player will bounce the ball off his bat into the air and when it is on the way down he positions himself like a baseball player about to hit a pitch. He swings at the ball and if there is another player nearby he had better duck or he is going to be hit by the follow-through, which happens quite frequently. This gets to be a bloody game sometimes; no one wears any type of protective equipment like a helmet. If the ball gets by the goalie and into the net it is, I believe, two points. If the ball goes higher than the net but between the goal posts like an extra point or field goal in football it is one point. I think into the goal it is three points, not two, a better reward than just hitting it through the goal for one point.

A football field is 100 yards long, again, this field is 100 yards wide and 150 yards long, that is a lot of area and these guys are on the move constantly. I believe you have to be pronounced dead before they allow substitutes, or at least it seemed like that. A great game with constant things happening, it was really exciting to watch. I think the game ended up with a score of 22 to 19, something like that and I don't remember who won, hey, this was forty two years ago! If you have the opportunity to watch a Hurling match it is worth your time, I guarantee that you will really enjoy the game.

Another thing that people seemed to like to watch in this stadium is, well, let me explain. We were sitting in about the middle of the field so each goal was about the same distance apart from us. There were venders through out the stands selling beer and of course when in Ireland do as the Irish do so we were being good tourists, we were drinking beer. That kind of creates other things a person has to do sooner or later, sometimes sooner. I was having one of those moments and asked some citizens nearby where the men's room might be located in this ancient stadium. I was informed the rest rooms, or whatever they call them, were located on each end of the stadium behind those goal posts, quite a long walk for someone in my delicate conditions, so I took off to see it I could make it before embarrassing myself in a strange and distant land.

I made it. These "Rest rooms" were added to the stadium long after the original stadium was built, the walls were built with concrete blocks, and it had an open entrance with no doors. Upon entering I see a line of men standing with their backs to me facing a blank wall with a trough at the bottom of the wall. No stalls, no privacy, no ceiling either. I am standing there tending to business and I look up and see hundreds of people cheering, at first I thought the cheers were for me, but soon realized they were cheering for the guy who just scored a goal. The people in the stands could look straight down and observe everything that was going on below in that men's room. When in Roam, do as … oh, well. Let's see what they do in Hawaii.

Hawaii and More #170

*J*UMPING FORWARD FROM 1972 IN Spain and 1973 in Ireland, we now move on to 1977 when I have rejoined Spalding after my three year absence and darn if I don't win a Customer trip as a salesman, this one is to Hawaii. It's a nine hour flight with a layover in LA where we ran into Loren Green (Ben Cartwright) of the very popular Bonanza TV series which I mentioned before sometime ago. That meeting was a trip highlight as he was such a nice guy and joining us in conversation like an old friend.

My new boss Jack Lacey and his wife won a trip as well we got to know each other better after spending a fair amount of time with them Dee and I spent most of our time entertaining one of my customers who also won a trip, Jerry Gunderson and his wife Judy. You may remember I wrote about Jerry before about being the "The King" of the water ball retrieving business. He and Judy also operated several golf retail outlets in Florida and Hilton Head. Over the years we became pretty close friends and socialized often.

There is not much I can tell you about Hawaii, we saw and did what you see in all those commercials tempting you to come visit the 50th State. It was very nice, Hawaii is like Florida with hills and volcanoes but the temperature is cooler with lower humidity. We did get to see their famous singer, Don Ho, perform. There were lots of Hula dancers and a roast pig cook out, what do you call them? Lou what?

We did play golf on this trip, twice. We toured Pearl Harbor and the Arizona memorial and that brought back sad memories. I'll never forget December 7th, I was ten years old. Hawaii was a very relaxing trip, no rush to do things and I was not the big cheese so Dee and I had more time to ourselves.

We were very fortunate to have gone on these Spalding trips as they would have cost a small fortune on our own. But we did make other trips, since I am on the subject will I touch on where we were fortunate enough to visit outside the United States. Dee's favorite place to visit was Fatima in Portugal, she made five trips, and I made one. On one of Dee's trips to Fatima she purchased a beautiful 4 foot tall wooden carved statue of our Blessed Mother Mary, which she donated to St. Clare Catholic Church in North Palm Beach.

We also made a trip to Mexico City where we visited the shrine of Our Lady of Guadalupe. I was told there is something like 33 million people living in and around the city. During the week the city is very smoggy because of the heavy traffic and on the weekends the air starts to clear about noon Saturday and Sunday it is also free of smog but by noon Monday it was all smoggy again. I did not drink the water, but the beer and wine was safe to drink, thank you. Did you know there are Pyramids in Mexico? We visited them as well, fantastic experience.

I had mention before about going to Rome in 1984 and visiting the Vatican, what a thrill that was. The Vatican is beautiful and so full of history. Pope John Paul ll waved to us one day from his window when we and thousands were in the square. He was so far away when he waved to the crowd from his window we could hardly see him. Rome is simply fascinating; we were staying in the Cavalieri Hilton hotel and they threw a Toga party one evening, and yeah, we had to wear costumes. Mine Toga felt very drafty. There is so much to see, not because of my toga either! There are so many structures built hundreds of years ago, and to this day engineers can not explain how some of these structures were built. There is so much to see, The Coliseum, Roman Forum, Pantheon, Sistine Chapel, St. Paul Basilica and so much more. I threw three coins into that fountain a song was written about. Pennies of course, don't call me cheap, just frugal, a coin is a coin.

We also made a side trip to Florence; it was a rainy day so did not get to tour much of the city. However the highlight was, we got to see Michelangelo's famous statue of David. The statue was very impressive, standing tall on a pedestal; David's naked body seemed perfect except Michelangelo was a little stingy in one area where he might have done better using a fig leaf.

It's not a perfect world is it? So let's go visit the sights in Germany, Switzerland & Austria.

Germany, Switzerland & Austria #171

*T*HIS IS NOT A SPALDING trip, Dee set this up with a travel agency there was a couple also on this trip we really didn't know but recognized them as they attended the same Mass at our church. They were Albert and Helen Fenza, a delightful couple. Al joined the Knights of Columbus after we returned from this two week trip. Al lived to be 100 years old and to the day he passed away his mind was sharp as a young kid.

Being of German decent, both sides of my family came to the United States in the early 1830's, so I was looking forward to our visit to these three countries. I have no idea what part of Germany my ancestors came from, after all that's almost 200 years ago and I have never attempted a family search. There was a famous priest who became a Bishop and then a Cardinal with the name of Faulhaber. He was a thorn in Hitler's side during World War II. Our recent German Pope, Ratzinger was his given name, was ordained a Priest by then Bishop Faulhaber. I have no way of knowing if we are related. Dee and I saw a portrait of Cardinal Von Faulhaber in a Boston museum one year, why it was there I have no idea. He was very well known in the thirties and forties.

This was a two week trip and when I looked at our itinerary of where we would be visiting I took a deep breath. Wow, we are going to be busy, here is where were going; **Frankfurt, Wiesbaden, Rhine Valley cruise, Heidelberg, Baden-Baden, Black Forest, Engelberg, Lucerne, Liechtenstein, Arlberg Pass, Innsbruck, Vienna, Oberammergau, Neuschwanstein, Koenigsee cruise, Berchtesgaden, Salzburg and Munich.** We also visited **Freiburg** which was not on our itinerary but we talked our tour guide into a little detour. Freiburg is where Dee's step dad Oscar Koechling grew up and she wanted to see his home town. Oscar was in the army in World War One, the German army.

When we arrived in Frankfurt on our first day, we started our tour with this greeting, "My name is Willie Flicker; I will be your tour guide for your entire trip!" Willie was a delightful young man who spoke excellent English; he really made our visit enjoyable and informative.

We visited so many Castles and Churches and each one seemed better than the last one, beautiful and historic. When driving into Heidelberg in our tour bus one day someone yelled out, look at that sign over there. It was one word, **FAULHABER** in bold white letters on a red background. It turned out to be a Hi Fi Stereo store. Later we spotted another sign; this one was in the same block letters, **FAULHABER** in bold white letters on a blue background, but no other identification. Must have been a second store, a little smaller than the first one we saw. I guess the Faulhaber name is not that rare after all.

Another thing before I forget, the MacDonald's we went into we found out they sold beer. Germany is beer country; MacDonald's would not have survived if they didn't sell beer. Working people drink beer with their lunch, it's there way of life, beer or wine. Most of Europe is like that.

Backspin here a little, I remember when I was in Fatima back in the eighties I asked a bartender what the legal drinking age was when I saw two very young teenagers drinking wine. He replied, "There isn't any age limit for beer and wine." He didn't say if there was one for liquor. In most of Europe kids grow up drinking wine with their meals like we do with milk and water. I think I like there way better than ours.

These three countries are beautiful, colorful flower boxes under windows of homes and businesses, murals on their walls, no trash on the ground anywhere, everything is very clean. People don't throw things on the ground, they put trash in containers as they are proud of where they live. There really are no slums as we know them, even the poorer sections are trash free. One thing I found back in those years in most of Europe their public rest rooms, stink. I didn't need to ask directions, all I had to do was just follow my "In stinks."

I had no problem with the food in any of these countries either. I finally had something to go with the beer and the wine besides bread, butter and cheese. There were many highlights during this trip but the big one was the "Passion Play" in Oberammergau.

The "Passion" Play in Oberammergau #172

NOT EVERYONE WILL BE FAMILIAR with Oberammergau Germany and its history so I will attempt to bring you up to date. Talk about a highlight to a wonderful two week tour of Germany Switzerland and Austria, this was outstanding.

In 1634 the Black Plague hit and wiped out one third of the population in Germany and much of Europe. In this little town near the Alps the people prayed and asked God if they were spared of the Plague the townspeople would forever do something special in remembrance. The town was spared; the Black Plague did not affect their town and its people. The townspeople decided to stage the first "Passion Play" which they have done every 10 years since then. This year is 1990 and I will attempt to describe the setting, the play, its people and the beautiful small town which is also a very popular ski resort.

We arrived in Oberammergau on a Sunday afternoon and all of us were assigned to private homes where we would spend two nights with breakfast included. This year the play began on May 28th through September 30th. The play runs five days a week so that is roughly eighty shows!

We spent most of the first day touring the town, having lunch and then dinner and visiting the many shops. The men working or who own and run the shops and restaurants all have long hair and beards as they are all in the play during the week. Only native townspeople are allowed to participate in the play. The men start growing their hair and beards months before the opening play. I am told also that the people playing the main parts must have a couple of back ups due to the fact the show is held out doors with no cover and does not stop for bad weather, they continue right through thunder and lighting storms, which we actually witnessed. The chance of some of these people getting sick is always a problem so that is why all the back ups are needed. The show must go on.

While the show is in the open with no weather protection all the patrons are under a covered pavilion that holds 5,200. The day we were attending was Monday June 25th. The play starts at 9 AM and concludes at 5:30 PM with a break for lunch, the total time for the Play is seven hours! Can you imagine sitting still for that amount of time? On stage there could be up to a thousand people at one time with all sorts of animals as well. The entire play is done in German and we are given a book to follow all the words, on the left page is German and the right page is English throughout the book, making it easy to follow was being said. We still have that book.

It is unbelievable how fast the time passed by. There was hardly any sound coming from some 5 thousand people, no coughing, no commotion, it was strangely quiet. Just about the time when the two thieves were "Strapped" to their cross and then lifted upright the clouds started to roll in with thunder in the background. Then Jesus was being nailed, or so it looked, they were pounding big spikes but were "Strapping" him to the cross and all the while the thunder grew louder and louder and it became darker and darker. When the cross with Jesus was being raise all "Heck" broke loose, louder thunder and lighting all over the place. You would have thought it was part of the play and this storm came right on cue. Wow, what an effect, it was almost alarming. All the people in the play did not flinch one bit with all the noise and lightning flashing all around them. What a performance by so many and what an ending to the Greatest Story Ever Told. What a highlight!

I find it hard to believe that was twenty five years ago this year, almost to the day. Back to the good ol' States, visiting all of these countries was very informative and educational. Meeting many of the people was very nice as well. We felt very welcome in all the countries we have visited; people seem to like most Americans, except in Paris. At the end of every trip it really feels good arriving back in the States, it is a special feeling for me.

In conclusion and as a side note, for many years there was a "Passion

Play" performed in Lake Wales, Florida. Dee and I attended it once a few years after we witnessed the one in Germany. It was about three hours long, a condensed version. It was pretty good but nothing like what we saw in 1990. I don't believe that production in Lake Wales is active any longer.

Next, a few more trips outside the U.S. we were fortunate to have to have participated in.

A Few More Trips #173

*J*UST GOING TO MENTION QUICKLY a few more trips and then return to my second go round working for Spalding. We are not world travelers by any means but were fortunate to have been to some countries in the Western World. I would have loved to have gone to Australia and New Zeeland but have no desire what-so-ever to travel anywhere in the Far East.

Most of our other trips were three and four day excursions. Bermuda twice, Virgin Islands twice. The first time we went to the Virgin Islands we were living in Ohio. We made that trip with a bunch of neighbors, we visited St. Croix, a beautiful island where they make a lot of Rum. Played golf at the Carambola County Club, the most beautiful course I have ever seen. A very nice resort course with flowers everywhere, it was so pretty the scenery made it difficult to concentrate on golf, it was just lovely.

An interesting story, there were little animals running all over the course, they were Mongoose. These little guys love to kill snakes and as the story goes years ago St. Croix was overrun with snakes so several Mongoose were imported to control the snake population. There are no more snakes, the Mongoose having multiplied and now they are the problem, they are everywhere. They don't bother humans but are a real pest.

The other time Dee and I visited the Virgin Islands we were on a cruise and stopped for several hours in St. Thomas. These Islands are duty free so buying liquor is a good deal. Also jewelry, I slipped away from Dee for a short time and visited a jewelry shop and bought her a Pearl necklace. A lady shopping there overheard me talking to the man behind the counter telling him I wanted a certain type of Pearl, I can't think of the name right now, and the clerk showed me this lovely necklace which a price tag of $1,000.00 and I said fine, I would take them as I wanted to surprise my wife. This lady having heard all of this, came over to me and said, "You lovely man, that is so nice what you are doing." I have never ever had that kind of a complement before, or come to think of it, since. I guess I need to buy more jewelry?

While there I visited the Mahogany Run Golf Club because I knew the Golf Pro and wanted to ways hello. He asked me if I wanted to play the course and told me how beautiful some of the holes were overlooking the ocean. I had to decline because we would have to get back to the ship soon, but I did have enough time to get in a cart with him and he drove us out on the course and showed me some absolutely beautiful golf holes. We had a nice visit and I returned to the ship with the necklace I would present to Dee when we got back home.

That's about the extent of our trips out of the United States. Except one more, I did make a trip to Venezuela some years ago with my son Jim and some of his friends for a deep sea fishing trip. I am not a fisherman by any means and only went because my son asked me. We chartered a pretty large fishing boat and ventured out some twenty five miles into the ocean. The waves were enormous; I had to hang on the whole time. We fished for sailfish, caught some, not me though. We unhooked the ones that were caught and returned them to the sea unharmed.

It was interesting but I would never do it again. Venezuela is a big producer of oil and gas and when I was there they still did not have unleaded gas for their own use, just the old leaded gas and they were still using many old cars that would still run on unleaded gas, and the exhaust fumes were really bad. We also had an ugly American among the group; a big mouth that could not help let everyone know how important he was. We are in a strange country that does not have all the modern things we have in our country and this guy kept telling everyone he came in contact with how we do things in the United States.

One night we were told there was a club we might be interested in going to because it was called the American Club. What a mistake, they had two thugs at the door and more sinister looking guys in various places just hanging around. The waitresses were thinly clad and it was a come on type of operation. Our waitress was constantly asking us to buy her drinks and she would sit at the table with us. Watered down drinks for her with no alcohol in them, I am sure. Ridicules prices and the big mouth is puffing his chest up like a big man from the US playing up to these girls.

I am telling my son Jim we need to get the hell out of this clip joint before his big mouth friend of his gets us in trouble. There are all these sinister guys watching our every move as they obviously are part of this operation, bouncers and what ever. Jim finally convinces big mouth to shut up and we finish our drink and slowly exit the place, all eyes were on us. We were careful exiting the door watching that no one was out there waiting to hit us on the head. I think there were six of us so there was some safety in numbers.

Enough said about this trip, again I was really glad to get back home and get back to work, my second go around with Spalding.

SPALDING 2ND TIME AROUND #174

A Good Salesman Is Like A Well-Made Car ...

He Starts In Any Kind of Weather

He Establishes A Basic Design and then Sticks to it

*He Takes Modifications Only To Refine The
Already Successful Marketing Procedures*

He Gets Mileage When He's in High Gear

*He Seem To Have an Engine Which Motivates Him
From One Place to Another*

He Doesn't Freeze Up Even When the Reception Is Cool

He Is Comfortable To Be With, But Not Too Comfortable

*Oddly Enough, He Isn't As Interested In Passing
Someone Else As He Is In Just Getting*

To His Destinations Safely and <u>With Time to Spare</u>

He Takes <u>The Bumps</u> In His Business Life Amazingly Well

*Just When You Think He Might Run Out Of Gas,
He calls On His <u>Reserve Tank</u> to Get Him There.*

*Some people are more deserving than others when it comes to a second chance,
But in truth, everyone gets one. It's called ... ...*
Tomorrow

Tomorrow #175

*I*T IS NOW TODAY, TIME to start a new chapter with Spalding after one of the biggest backspins one may ever encounter. I have traveled a pretty big circle; a circle ends up where it began. You might think that it is the end but to me it is the beginning which I am determined to write my own ending. I know what is expected of me and I know how to accomplish just that.

I am a good salesman and I know it. That is not being cocky, that is being confident, something that may take more time with some than others. Some never find that level, I almost didn't. There have been some very bad times when depression can and did set in. But I can't let that take me down, God gave me a brain, I have got to figure things out myself.

I think I did that a long, long time ago the first time I overcame the resistance I received in Pittsburgh when I started to call of the golf professionals. I was an outsider, but while they were not looking I snuck inside and earned their respect. The only way one earns respect is, you have to earn it, respect is not a given. I became a complete salesman because I realized a customer is not someone that is just going to put money in my pocket, I have to put money in their pocket before I am entitled to mine, or the company I represent gets theirs. In my mind, the customer is first, I am second, my company is third, but my family is really what comes first no matter what, they just have to wait until I accomplish these other little tasks. Does that make sense?

I look at my customer as being their partner, or he/she my partner. I must look out for their interests by not overselling, or not caring what I sell just to get a sale. What I convince my customer to purchase my products they must be the correct product mix, and that product must sell through. Then and only then will we both win. I will gain a customer who trusts me, my judgment and my product. A good salesman will always do what he says he will do, answer all questions honestly. If he can't answer a question he must be honest about that, and if he says he will find out what the customers wants to know, he must do that without delay and get back to the customer with the answers to those questions. That builds trust and a good relationship. Never ignore a question or leave a question unanswered.

Beginning a new chapter in my sales career in my new south east Florida territory I do have a little head start as I already know most of my new customers because so many of them visited the Toney Penna showroom. I also attended a lot of local tournaments as well. So I was not a stranger.

The business is not the same as it was twenty years ago, it is changing. The so called "Pro Only" line of clubs and balls that for so many years could only be found in golf shops at golf courses and sold only through the golf professional is not what it used to be. To explain all that is happening will take a few paragraphs so I will begin to explain the changing pro only golf business, next.

THE CHANGING PRO ONLY
GOLF BUSINESS #176

*I*N 1977 THERE WERE THREE salesmen covering the state of Florida, myself the south east, Monty Chamberlin the north and north east, and Colin Collier the west coast. Shortly after I came aboard there was an event in the Port St. Lucie area, the three of us played a round of golf together, I don't remember who our fourth was but who ever that may have been he wasn't in the parking lot with the three of us and I keep getting reminded by Colin about how good a referee I am. Colin and Monty were agreeing to disagree about something I won't go into. So about the first thing I accomplished when I returned to Spalding was break up a fight when those two warriors were about to slug it out. I stepped in and separated them and almost got hit myself. Boys will be boys. I'm thankful I was bigger than they were or I might have caught one. Just another little detour so now I will get back to the subject title.

I will explain what the "Pro only" term means concerning the golf business. For many years all the major golf club and ball manufacturers produced a line of equipment to be sold only in litigate golf course "Pro shops." As an example my own company Spalding "Pro only" club products were Top-Flite men's & ladies, Executive men's & ladies and Tour Edition. Golf balls were the Dot, Top-Flite, Molitor, Tour Edition, Strata and Flying Lady. Another top of the line clubs and balls were offered for sale in retail stores usually the same price category, as an example Robert T. Jones, Jr. and Marylyn Smith clubs, the Air-Flite and Kro-Flite balls. All the other companies had pretty much the same offerings, one line of clubs and balls to the pro Shops only and another line for the retail stores.

The consumer who wanted the "Pro only" so called superior products they had to purchase them in these shops at the golf courses, where retail prices were seldom discounted. In the 40's, through the 70's most all of these shops were owned and operated by golf professionals, not by the golf clubs. In most cases the golf pro didn't pay rent for their shops but paid for all of their help, the assistant professional and general shop help. The golf professional was paid a salary and responsible for running all the golf operations, the profit generated by sales of golf equipment was his plus his lesson fees. In some cases when golf carts became popular the golf pro had that concession as well, or a part of it for overseeing its operation. There are very few of these shops owned and operated by golf professionals today, they may be paid to oversee the operations but the golf clubs usually own and operate their own now because of how the "Pro only business" changed.

Here is what and how the change came about, starting in the 60's and escalating to a complete change in the late 60's and 70's. As the golf business started to grow there was a change in the way many retailers started to look at the golf retail business, a few started to "Bootleg" these pro only products into their stores. Where did they get these items? Not from the companies but from some pro shops who's operators saw a quick way to make some extra money by selling these products to these retailers for a small profit. This "Side business" continued to grow, more and more pro only merchandise was being sold through these retail outlets at discounted prices which in turn started to hurt the sales and profits of the legitimate golf professionals who were not involved with this new bootlegging situation.

Many salesmen turned a blind eye to their growing sales to pro shops knowing full well all of a sudden a customer is buying many times over the amount he could possible sell to his members. In truth, the companies liked this increase in business as well so nothing was done to put a stop to the bootlegging. As a matter of fact, some were beginning to encourage this practice. I did not say that, it is something someone told me, Ha!

Then some very good business people started to open up specialty golf shops located off course. There were many ways the pro only merchandise was becoming available to them but they could not buy direct from the golf companies, yet. It had become a simple fact that these types of golf shops were here to stay so reluctantly the golf companies took a good hard look at their pro only policies and a very big change was abut to take place. Stopping the bootlegging was almost impossible, legally once the product was in the hands of our customers the companies could not dictated to whom those products could or could not be sold.

Policies were changed, if an off course retailer sold nothing but golf and tennis, and was not a full line sporting goods dealer, if they met that criteria companies began to sell these stores directly cutting out the bootleggers. All of this changed the golf business forever.

Pro Only Golf Changed Forever #177

*G*ETTING ADJUSTED TO MY NEW/OLD job of calling on the golf professionals was not as easy as it was up north. The reason, almost all of the courses in this area are in gated communities. Not so in the north, when making daily calls there I just drove into the parking lot, parked and went to the pro shop unannounced. I only needed appointments when presenting next years line in the north. Follow up calls were just a matter of dropping in to see if everything was OK and take care of anything that wasn't, plus obtaining fill in orders. If the pro was available for a few minuets, fine, if not I talked to the people in the shop, took care of business, and moved on. Working an area each day that way I could make six to ten calls, depending on how many courses in the area. Here in S.E. Florida I can not get past the gate without and appointment.

I was not used to that and It sure slowed me down, it is a job in itself making phone calls and appointments in a given area so the amount of calls per day was way less than I was used to making personally. That resulted in more phone contacts with my customers to find out if there was something I needed to take care of and taking fill in orders that was a lot more impersonal. I like to see my customers face to face, not over the phone. I have always disliked talking on the telephone and to this day I don't even own a cell phone. I know, I'm just an old foggy, whatever that is.

Things have changed, but that was only the beginning of change. The big change was the new breed of customers I now had, the growing amount of retail off course golf shops that were popping up all over the place. When I started to work this territory there were only a hand full, maybe less than five off course pro shop stores, however, they were doing a pretty healthy volume of business.

I will use new terms to separate the two kinds of customers I now have. They are the golf pro shops at golf courses, the terms are "On course", or "Green grass" golf shops, and the retail shops are "Off course" shops. These off course shops are a real threat to the on course shops because any golfer can shop there, they did not have to be a member of some club. And the selection of equipment plus clothing was much greater with much more attractive discounted prices. Now that these shops were buying direct from the companies that eliminated the middle man, the bootlegger, who got his little cut of the profit, and there were quantity buys that many of the on course buyers could not afford to purchase because the quantity was more than they could use.

Up north the private club golf professional had more of a loyalty among his more affluent members, most would support their golf pro by continuing purchasing equipment from him knowing that is how he made his living. In the south the private clubs had more of a transit part time membership, most coming from the north. Their loyalty to the golf professional here was not as strong as it was to their northern golf professional, or so it seemed. Plus more shops were being taken over by the club and paying the golf professional a salary and maybe a commission to run the shop. The loyalty of buying at the club became weaker and the off course shop business was growing.

When there are a lot of on Course customers which are more difficult to call on because an appointment was needed, plus their volume was shrinking, a salesman starts to change priorities. I could call on off course shops without going through a security gate and the volume per call was much greater, where do you think the salesman is going to spend his time and effort? Bingo, you got it. The off course accounts, of course.

Pro Only Golf Oversight #178

*W*HERE DO YOU THINK A salesman is going to spend most of his time calling on his accounts, the off course shops, that's where. I could make one call a day and get as much business as I could all week calling on the on course shops. But to have a complete territory every account needed some attention so it became a little difficult to keep calling for appointments with the golf pros when most did not really care anyway because he no longer was the shop owner. The ones that did care were not so friendly any more either because he knew I was selling his so called pro only golf clubs and balls to non golf professionals, to the off course shops, and in many cases at a better price than he could afford. We, as a company, are not making friends and our job in the field is becoming more difficult and pushing us more and more towards where the big bucks are.

On top of that there are now some large chain stores doing some bootlegging of their own. Pro only products are starting to show up and these chain stores are now adding to the on course problems but now they are also competing with the off course shops as well.

On top of all this, or at the bottom, which ever way you may want to look at it, the retail golf lines sold to sporting goods stores and department stores are hardly competitive in the golf business at all or at least in the top of the line equipment. Now these retail stores are not too friendly with our retail sales guys who sell the other sporting goods products, footballs, baseballs, etc. Their golf business has gone straight down the tubes except for medium and low price clubs and balls. We have achieved in getting every one mad at us for selling the "Pro Only" line of equipment almost anywhere.

While all of this is happening the "Mystic of Golf Pro only" equipment is being destroyed. It is now everywhere so what is so special about it now? At one time only the golf pro could sell it, but no longer, so it really isn't special anymore is it? The Mystic is gone. The glamour is no longer connected with the term "Pro Only." A unique product line is no longer just that. What was once a very strong marketing tool has been reduced to just another discounted product available almost anywhere. What a shame.

All this can be explained by looking at the time tested food chain, which will never change, the bigger fish eat the smaller fish, until there is no longer any fish, except the bigger fat ones, and the beat goes on and on.

There is no doubt the on course accounts are being neglected in many territories where there are mutable off course accounts. That is not healthy because there is still a lot of business to be had from the on course market. The salesman or companies who continue to contact these accounts are going to get the business. Buyers buy from sales people that call on them. Out of sight, out of mind, I don't care how strong a companies advertising and pull through of the product is, that product has to be in place for the customer is able to find it. If the product is not there, the consumer will most likely purchase their second choice if it is available.

As the overall business grows, some territories become too large for one salesman to do an effective job because he has too many accounts which he can't call on regularly, many of the smaller accounts become ignored. In large populated areas where two such territories exist it makes sense in most cases to split those two into three territories adding an additional sales person so all accounts receive the necessary attention required to grow the business within these territories.

Wouldn't you know it; management has decided Florida had a need to add another salesman due to the fast growth within the state. At the present time there are three of us, plus the western panhandle was being covered out of Alabama. This happened without consulting the salesmen and a split was made and it was a very large mistake. And I will explain why I said that.

I have had a lot of experience of my own making territory splits and this one was wrong from the start because the golf business has changed over the years. I personally fought management concerning this territory split and I will explain why I fought it and how I thought our company should realign our sales force.

Florida Territory Split #179

*T*HIS FIASCO HAPPENED SEVERAL YEARS after my return, Colin Collier was no longer the salesman on the West Coast of Florida, he transferred to the great state of Washington in the Pacific North West where the sun doesn't shine much and the weather is cooler. He was replaced in the Sarasota area by Chuck Jefferies. I don't remember who dreamed up this split but it sure got my attention as it greatly affected my territory. When splits are properly done they should not have a negative affect on the existing territories, at least not for more than a year, if at all. I bitterly contested this change, the following is how it was structured and then what I proposed how to undue it and restructure it the correct way. I won, by the way, so you don't have to wait until the end to find out, but I will outline what was to become a complete restructure of the national sales force in the coming years.

The golf business has changed considerably and we needed to change our approach of how to cover all accounts properly due to these changes. This territory split did not even take into consideration the changing golf business environment. As I have mentioned many of the on course accounts were being neglected due to the growing amount of off course accounts producing large volume purchases.

Backspin, here is the split. The goal was to add one salesman so Florida would go from three to four. Keep in mind that Florida is a very long state from north to south and southern Florida's east and west coasts are separated by the Everglades. From Miami to Naples on the east coast there is a direct route called Alligator Alley with nothing in-between. North of Alligator Alley in the middle of the state there is nothing but the Everglade swamps filled with all kinds of creatures you would not like to spend the night with. There is not another road going east to west until the top of the Everglades. The availability to travel east and west in south Florida is very limited as the next east to west road is from West Palm Beach to Ft. Meyers

It was decided to take from my territory Dade County which includes Miami and the Keys. In return they were adding three very small counties to my north. Those three counties population was a drop in the bucket compared to Dade County and the volume I was loosing was about one third of my total volume and would take forever to recovered.

Chuck Jeffries was the salesman for the west coast and he was given my Miami Dade County and the Keys. He lived in Sarasota and for him to cover Miami it would take him three and one half to four hours just to drive there, and then he would have to spend about a week to cover all the accounts in that area. I was fifty minuets away from Miami and I did not have to spend money on a motel and meals. He was not thrilled about that at all and he agreed with me this arrangement just to add a salesman north of us did not make any sense.

So I made a very strong plea. Because of my past reputation and experience with territory splits and my stubborn German blood line it was agreed to give me time to come up with a better plan that I insisted they let me develop and present. I had something in mind anyway and this was my chance to map out my theory of how to solve the growing problem of many of our salesmen neglecting the on course accounts in favor of off course lager volume producers. I felt I had the answer to that problem and was determined to prove my theory that so far no one else has even thought of.

MY TERRITORY SPLIT PLAN #180

*M*Y THEORY WAS SIMPLE, THERE are two different kinds of business developing so where needed there should be two different kinds of a sales force to adjust to the changing business conditions. A salesman who is calling on the On Course buyer and that buyer knows the salesman calling on him is selling the Pro Only line of equipment to his biggest competitor, the Off Course discount retail store. That On Course buyer is not a happy camper with this arrangement. Plus, the On Course accounts are being neglected because of the reason I have mentioned before, simply sales dollar volumes, a salesman is going to go where the volume is.

Two different businesses need two different sales people calling on them. I proposed creating an On Course sales group and an Off Course sales group where ever the opportunity to do so dictated a need, large populated areas where multiple Off Course retail golf stores were operating and the volume of these stores was exceeding the volume of the On Course accounts.

I wanted to do a split within one territory by adding an additional salesman in almost the same existing territory and leave the others as they are for the time being. I had to present sales numbers to prove this possible and create new volume to support two in the same area.

So I got busy with my spread sheets and I would be taking back the Miami Dade county and the Keys and keeping the three small counties to the north of Palm Beach county which had a number of On Course accounts but only a couple of Off Course accounts

I came up with the number of On Course accounts and their present sales volume and compared the present year with the previous year, the volume had dropped, not increased, as I had expected. Sales were going downward.

I came up with the number of Off Course accounts and the same figures, the present years volume compared to the previous year and their was a large increase, sales were on the upswing.

My theory was if we had a salesman calling on nothing but the On Course accounts, having no Off Course accounts with large volume to call on, he would have no choice but to call on all of those On Course accounts on a regular basis. Those buyers would be dealing with a salesman who was not calling on the stores so that salesman didn't have to defend himself.

The Off Course salesman would be spending all of his time taking care of the large volume accounts which did require a lot of his attention because the problems and responsibilities were much greater. He would not have to avoid calling on the On Course buyers who were upset with him anyway.

My figures looked good and bad. The bad was the declining sales of the On Course accounts but that was good for my presentation because I predicted that if we put my plan into action we would not only stop the declining sales, my prediction was a sales increase of a minimum 15 to 20% in the first year.

My prediction for Off Course would be a minimum of 15%. The company was always looking for an increase of 7 to 10% each year, regardless of business conditions, if they were not good you were expected to take it away from your competition. That's management thinking, but that is exactly what the competition is demanding of their salesmen as well!

I wanted a year to prove my plan was much better than theirs, not only for this area but for other areas of the country also. I had presented to top management a new idea for the future of our sales force and how we should handle the changing golf business. Do I get the chance to prove it?

Tomorrow is another day, another opportunity and tomorrow is always another gift. So what was the decision? A new sales force is born.

A New Sales Force Is Born #181

$\mathcal{P}$ART OF MY PLAN WAS that I had a young man in mind to become the new salesman. I had talked to him about the possibility of things to come and asked him if he would be interested, he said he definitely was. His name was and is, Tim Boudreau. Tim was working for a Pro Golf Discount store in West Palm Beach. Tim was single in his late twenties and had played some mini tour golf, an excellent player himself who knew what the game of golf was all about. He could relate to the golf pros he would be calling on if hired.

Since I had hired many sales people in my past management positions, plus had personally outlined other territory splits which were successful, my recommendations were accepted. The territory split plan and the salesman, everything I asked for.

I personally trained Tim and was nearby anytime he needed help. Tim had no other accounts to call on but the golf professionals on course accounts and he was making headway getting acquainted with his customers. Tim became an excellent salesman and it was a tremendous opportunity and a big jump from being a floor salesman for a discount golf store to a major company. There was a future for him and he knew it. I let him know what my expectations were for his territory, something beyond normal increases. I let Tim know he was a partner with me to prove something to the company about my theory of the sales force of the future. Tim responded.

I miscalculated in my estimates of sales increases. I predicted a sales increase for my Off Course territory of 15% and missed it by 2%, over, not under; my increase was a plus 17 %.

The new On Course percentage was off somewhat as well; I predicted as increase of 15 to 20% and missed it by a little. Tim came through with an increase of a plus 23%.

The company agreed I proved my point and from that time on the change in the sales force began in areas of the country that would support that kind of coverage. There remained dual salesman in many areas with light population but those areas had less Off Course accounts.

I don't remember what year that was, must have been 1985 or 86. Doesn't matter, it sure made my life a lot easier, I was left with something like 30 accounts to deal with, some of these accounts had more than one store and I visited all even though the buying was done by the main store, these satellite stores needed attention too.

During these early years upon my return I was approached twice by management about my interest in a change. The first one was by the International group; they were looking for a man to cover all the Islands. Sounds exotic, traveling to all of these beautiful resort islands, hopping from one to another by small commuter planes, staying in great Hotels, what a deal? I was offered a compensation package that was about the same as I was making, and I didn't have to do all that traveling month after month. There was no reason to take such an offer and I turned it down. The next, would I be interested in retuning to the mid west as the Regional Sales Manger working out of Chicago? The same area of the country I had worked before, but I was located In Cleveland then.

My answer was an immediate resounding **NO.** First of all I was through with management unless it was my own company. They countered with, "But Bill, we haven't discussed the compensation package!" I replied, "I appreciate being considered but there is no way in the world the money would entice me to move my family again. We are staying in Florida, why would I want to move to Chicago?" I continued, "Why don't you give the job to Charlie Simon, he's your Dealer Sales Manager in the Mid West and he is already in the Chicago office, I know for a fact he would love to make the switch, offer the job to him." And they did and he did! Was he ever happy, the pro golf job was just a much better position for Charlie.

Of course that ended any future offers of advancement for me, which was just fine as I was getting more and more involved with my new partners here in this territory. What, my new partners? Yes, my customers.

My New Partners #182

*A*s I HAVE WRITTEN BEFORE about my view of the importance of how a salesperson should feel about his customers. The customer comes first, the salesman second, the companies the salesman represents third, but the salesperson's family is really number one. If the salesperson is successful then the family is provided for because that formula worked for my family, my customers, me and my company.

Now that my proposed territory spilt worked out as I knew it would the new alignment of customers provided more time for me to spend with a lot less accounts to deal with, my new partners. If I can help them in anyway to a successful profitable business everyone wins. First of all I must establish a trusting and respectful relationship with every customer I can. One thing a successful salesperson must do is earn the customers respect, it is not a given. How does one accomplish all of this? Do what you say you are going to do and never promise anything you can't deliver or accomplish. Be honest in all business dealings with your new "Partners." If you don't know the answer to any questions, let your partner know you will find out and get back to them with the answer. And do just that with out delay. Take a sincere interest in your partner's conversations and their concerns.

A successful salesperson really doesn't sell anything. I must qualify each customer as to what their needs are. Also pay attention to personalities, no two are exactly alike and each person needs to be treated differently. Get to know their likes and dislikes, which can be found out pretty easily during normal conversations, that is when a person's personality comes through. Listen to them, let them speak; you can learn more when listening than when you yourself are talking. Talking to much disconnects the brain.

When presenting a product or program, do they fit into these customers needs? If I sell the wrong product or program and it fails, I fail and I have a customer who will never really trust me. I have taken the wind right out of my sails and become dead in the water, going nowhere. If my product and program is right for the customer I will reach my port easily with my sails full of the all important things I need to get there. My customer is now becoming my partner as he needs people he can trust to help his business be a success.

The more I can help my customer make his job easier the more my job will be easier as well. As the old saying goes, "One hand washes the other" is true as can be. Another thing to remember is there will almost always be one or more customers that will never be my partner due to conflicts in personalities. Human nature, not everyone is going to like each other for one reason or another. I had to learn that and how to accept that and work around those problems as best I could. Another old saying, "You can't win them all." Just don't get caught up in trying too, just do the best you can, and move on. I think everyone would like to be liked, but in real life, that is not how it plays out. It hurts sometimes but I just have to shake it off and try my best not to let it bother me. It happens and in most cases there is just nothing I can do about it. I learned to look at it as it's the other person's loss. They are not going to get the best out of me either, because they won't let that happen. Move on; treasure the good relationships, they are like gold.

Now that I have done my job, I've gotten the distribution of products into my accounts stores that the company has demanded of me, the product is in place, it is now the marketing people's job to create the consumer pull through. The product itself has to perform as well. I did my part, and did it damn well. How did they do?

There will be no particular story about that, the answer will come in bits and pieces in the days ahead as I continue these old stories, both successful and some not so successful. I always try go the extra mile.

Go the Extra Mile #183

REALIZING THE SALESPEOPLE WORKING IN these retail discount golf stores are doing the best they can it is very difficult for them to gain knowledge of all the different products they are dealing with. As a salesman I have to know as much as I can about my product and have as much general knowledge about the technical workings of my own golf clubs and balls. Knowing my own company's product line is a big job in itself and then keeping up with a the changes and improvements each year is a must, but how in the world are salespeople in these stores going to know all about all of the different manufacturers golf clubs and balls? They can't but the consumer expects them to answer all sorts of questions. These people can only do the best they can, but I saw a way to help them, and myself, by spending a lot of time having conversations with them.

These salespeople needed knowledge and if I can help them then my "Partner", their boss, may appreciate what I am doing to help his people become more knowledgeable as well. So if I can pass on general things to help the chances they will think of me and my product maybe more than my competition.

The same can be said of the owner, he can't possibly know much about each and every different golf club and the many different golf balls he must purchase for his operation. That is one big job he has, taking the time to listen to every salesman's presentation of a product line and programs that may be tied to mutable purchases. That is a lot to deal with, and then he has to decide if those different programs will be beneficial to him. What to buy and in what quantities. What is his past track record with those products, so many different choices, so many companies looking for his business?

Here is where I become his partner; I want to help him by doing most of his work for him. As I have said before, a good salesman really doesn't sell anything. If he presents himself, his product and company properly and has qualified his customer correctly then that customer wants to buy what you are presenting. I present, he has a need, and he buys. Of course during any presentation I ask my "Partner" as many questions I can, questions that are presented in such a way as I receive a bunch of yes's which puts him in a mood to say yes when the presentation is over, closing the sale, its buying time.

At this time I present my partner with a completely pre written order for all the products he has been buying from me, explaining I have taken his inventory before hand. This recommended order takes into consideration what he has bought in the past year, what inventory is left, if any, and what I am recommending for the coming year. Plus any new items just presented and whatever programs built into all of this I have also discussed. I am doing his buying for him that is what I have just done. In addition, as he knows I have done this in the past, if his inventory gets out of balance I will adjust it so he will not get stuck with an item or items that are not selling as well as anticipated. He already knows my word is good and I do what I say I will do for him. I have earned his trust in the past and most of my customers have given me the green light to write these purchases for them.

This saves me and my partner one heck of a lot of time. It also gives me the opportunity to add a new item or two that is new or he has not bought before, or an item the company has informed us we must obtain a certain percentage of distribution that is also tied into our compensation plans. I have always managed to get 100 % distribution of any product I was assigned. If that item or items didn't sell, I would pick them up and move them to a different location.

What did I do to be able to move merchandise around? Where did I store items until I could find another place for them? I had my own mini warehouse.

My Own Warehouse #184

*T*HINGS WERE NOT ALWAYS AS smooth as I would have liked as business has it's ups and downs. Long before we split my territory I found a need to have my own mini warehouse because I did not have enough room in my garage, which was also my office. I had to be in a position to keep an inventory of golf balls needed to service my accounts. I also had quite a few accounts that did not have a good credit standing with our credit department.

I felt very strongly that our credit department was becoming more and more difficult to deal with and some of our credit people who were responsible for certain territories were more difficult to deal with than others. I had one of those guys. As time went on it seemed I spent more time in battle with my credit guy than time spent calling on my customers. That was not true, of course, but it seemed like it. Credit people and sales people get along just fine, they mix together just like oil and water. That is the real world and it was not a good situation because the more I complained the worse it seemed to get.

I am going to skip over a few years, the last several years was really hard. Business conditions were not healthy, more and more of my accounts were having a hard time meeting their financial obligations on time. More and more of my accounts were being put on credit hold and quite a few were closed entirely, no more credit and I could no longer sell them anything. My warehouse grew and grew. I rented a storage unit that was 12 feet wide and 30 feet deep, pretty good size to pile up stacks and stacks of golf balls, clubs and putters.

I became my own credit man and was taking some risk; I was selling to many of these stores our credit people had shut down. I was collecting cash upon delivery and I really did not have any problems and never got stuck for any large amount of money. I was taking good care of the credit healthy accounts I had but almost all were struggling now as the so called "Pro only" merchandise was showing up in the big box stores, even Costco was selling Top-Flite X-Out balls.

As a matter of fact when one of my good customers told me Costco was retailing those X-outs for about what it cost him to buy them, he was really ticked off. It happened to be the Costco where Dee and I shopped. I checked it out and there was a large stack of about 600 dozen with a price of less than my customer could purchase them. I went home and got my check book, went back and bought the entire stock. I figured Costco makes one time purchase on some products and when they are sold those items are not replaced. It cost me something like $3,450.00, I put them in my warehouse and sold them eventually for 6.00 dozen, $3,600.00, got my money back but lost out on that amount of sales as well because I am not selling them additional product, but the product I bought. But, I stopped many consumers from buying these balls for less than my customers could purchase them. And I was right, Costco did not replace that inventory.

How was I handling all of this and not getting in trouble with my company. I had quotas to meet, distribution figures to meet to make my bonus money. I did it the hard way; the only way as far as I was concerned my own company became one of my worst competitors!

When some former Spalding management people read this may or may not agree with what I am saying or what I was doing. I could care less because they were not out here in the trenches going through what I had to do to make my quota numbers. Management was chasing their own numbers and deals were being made all over the place. Just call Rich F., "It's lets make a deal time" at the end of each month. There were deals all over the place.

Before moving on I did have one little scare when one of my Miami customers paid me cash for a delivery of golf balls, which was an ongoing thing with him. He gave me fifteen one hundred dollar bills, $1.500.00. I took those to my bank for deposit and the teller informed me that eleven of those bills were counterfeit and promptly confiscated them; I am out $1,100.00 just like that. I was asked where I got them;

I did not want to get in trouble with the law so gave them the name of my customer.

I immediately called my customer and told him what had happened and that I had to give his store name as to where I got them. He was cool and I trusted him, he was a good guy. He said that was OK that I gave the bank that information because that is the law and he did not want me to get into trouble. He also said he knew exactly who gave those bills to him, one of his South American customers, who he said would make them good. Then my customer told me he would give me the $1,100.00 the next day, and he did. Taking chances is what we were doing out here in the trenches to get out sales numbers, can you imagine?

WHAT WAS I DOING #185

*T*YING TO MAKE MY QUOTAS anyway I could, this business had gotten out of hand. There was not much loyalty anymore. There always seemed to be a better price and I was being told so by my unhappy customers. At this point I have jumped ahead of myself by several years so a little backspin is in order here. I will finish this, what I consider a sad story, later. I was working harder than ever to make my numbers. And trying to keep my income from declining, let alone thinking my income would increase every year to keep up with inflation.

I haven't even touched on my side business yet, later. As promised, if a customer was out of balance with golf ball inventory I would adjust his inventory by taking some back and replacing those items with what was selling. I was buying bulk deals from my own company and taking all the discounts available. I could not do that direct so I made arrangements with a couple of my pet accounts to buy through them. I would pay them the discounted price and they would in turn pay Spalding. They were getting what they needed for their operations from my purchases at the lower volume prices. Golf balls were the bulk of all this business, easy to move around and not much risk of getting stuck with any unwanted inventory. Golf Clubs and putters was a different story. They were harder to move and I had to be a lot more patient about reselling these items.

When I sold merchandise to my "Bad credit customers" it was the price listed in our regular wholesale price list, so I was not "Gouging" them on price. I kept the difference between that price and my net price, wholesale less volume pricing and less early payment discounts. So those customers who were operating on a COD payment basis with other companies were getting a fair price from me and they knew it.

I had more loyalty with them than some of my so called good paying customers.

So I was more than covering my expense of the warehouse, I was making a few bucks on the side. I needed to do this as I had quite a few dollars invested that I could have been investing in stocks, or other investments at that time when investing was paying some rather good returns.

At one time I thought I was the only salesman doing this on a pretty large scale. Not so, there were quite a few having the same difficulties as I, I was not alone. Sad, we were forced into all of this; it was not of our own making. We were survivors. We were good, we competed with our own company, the big box stores, the national accounts, ourselves. This was not the good old Spalding I knew for so many years.

Changing gears, a new business, *Wm. Faulhaber Enterprises, Inc.*

WM. FAULHABER ENTERPRISES, INC. #186

I FINALLY GOT BACK INTO MANAGEMENT with a great title, President. No more of that Vice President crap! Before I explain how and why I formed this company there were several investments that Dee and I were making which eventually led us into this venture. As I have mentioned several times I did not like the feeling of being broke, or any prospect of being threatened with that possibility. I wanted to insure my family would be secure and I was determined to be in a position of my own destiny, independent, that is where I was headed. Not rich, but no more financial worries if possible. I am happy to report, we are there, Dee and I are both living a lot longer than we ever dreamed of, but I don't think we are going to run out of money, just time.

So again, its backspin time and precedes the story about *Wm. Faulhaber Enterprises, Inc.* I did not accomplish all of this myself; I have another partner who agreed with my decisions. It is my wife of sixty years as of next February, 2016. It is none other than the famous Dee, short for Dolores. So I will try and use the word "We" instead of "I" but if I slip up by saying "I" please excuse me, "I made a mistake once, but, "I" may have been mistaken about that."

By the way, "I" was not only President, I was also the Treasurer. Dee was Vice President and Secretary. That makes all of this "We!" Wow. We made our second real estate purchase about 1982, a second home which is still in our family and occupied by family. Then we made a third purchase, a Town House located in the PGA complex in Palm Beach Gardens for investment purposes. There is much to tell about this unit so "I" will sidetrack a little here with some interesting facts connected with that Town House, a three bedroom, two bath, kitchen, living room and den. We put this property in the PGA rental pool, furnished the unit completely and rented it and what we were receiving in rent more than paid for the mortgage payment. Plus there are tax write offs allowed if set up properly. We now have our name on three mortgages at one time, there will eventually be six, those stories are yet to unfold but do lead to why we formed our Wm. Faulhaber Enterprise corporation.

Even Spalding was involved for a few years with our Town House unit, and this leads to another story. Remember the stories about golf ball and club testing using a robot nicknamed the "Iron Bryon?" Spalding owned one of these wonderful machines and it was located in Chicopee, Mass. Our R & D people decided to move this unit to Florida so they could have 12 months of good weather for testing purposes and asked me if I could help them find a location. So Spalding ended up having two new homes, one for Iron Bryon and a home away from home for the test team.

Two New Homes for Spalding #187

*F*INDING A LOCATION FOR OUR test robot was not difficult as it turned out. My first choice became its location for a number of years, the Frenchman's Creek Country Club in Palm Beach Gardens, a new two course complex and the owner developer was none other than John D. MacArthur.

Incidentally, the course architect for Frenchman's Creek was my friend and touring pro Gardner Dickinson. I believe these were the only two courses he ever designed, they were good too. One course was really different back then, Instead of 18 tees and greens this course had 18 tees and 22 greens. Each nine holes had two holes with two greens. You had a choice before teeing it up which of these holes you were going to play. Keep in mind these courses were built with a lot of tress and foliage so most fairways were pretty narrow. The choice was the normal green was straight away, the second green was a dogleg and if you chose the dog leg your tee shot had to be placed in a position so that the opening to that dog leg was in the right spot, a more difficult tee shot that made the dog leg hole more demanding. Pretty unique, but these extra holes have been eliminated. I suppose that decision was reached because of the additional maintenance cost of four additional greens.

Back to the robot, Frenchman Creek had a very large practice area and it was unusually wide. There was more than enough space to place a shed on one end where a portion of that range could be used for testing and there was more than enough room for members to practice without anyone interfering with the other. A grid could be mapped out for the test area that would not be unsightly or be problem. I compiled all the data I thought was necessary for a presentation to the "Old man" as John D. Mac was called. The test area would not be used constantly;

our team would only be there for a few couple of weeks each month, if that much.

I was asked by management to proceed with negotiations. I contacted John D. MacArthur, he was a very busy guy as you can imagine, but I had met him before and he was very approachable. I am a good salesman, remember. I look and listen. I look into your eyes and listen to what those eyes are telling me, interested or not, and body language. I explained our needs knowing full well he didn't need us; we were not going to put a lot of money in his pocket, what the heck, he owned most of Northern Palm Beach County at that time anyway. He had no need for my product; the need was all ours, so I played on his inner love for the game. I suggested the members might find our testing interesting, watching this robot hit golf balls was really interesting to watch.

So after presenting all of our needs and laying out all the facts that I had, I proceeded to close the sale by asking John if he would be interested in helping us and in turn we would provide Frenchman Creek with all the range balls they needed no charge for as long as we were permitted us to use that space on his range. He agreed and I almost fainted.

That's all it cost us, range balls. Can you imagine! Spalding has now gotten their first of two new homes. Now the test team needed a home away from home.

Spalding's Second New Home #188

REMEMBER THE TOWN HOUSE WE purchased in the PGA complex that we placed in their rental pool? Back then this area was really seasonal so renting a unit like mine was usually for a month or two and up to five or six months in season. It was usually empty during the summer months but the rent money for the season was more than enough to cover the mortgage payment and return of a fair profit for the entire year. The price I paid for the unit was steadily increasing in value as well so the investment was a solid one.

Spalding built a rather good looking shed on the range of Frenchman Creek CC, so it blended well and did not stick out like a sore thumb and then moved our robot into it. Our test team would be commuting back and forth form Chicopee to paradise. This team was usually no more than four people, when more help was needed like chasing down the balls hit into the grid and recording where the ball landed and the distance, carry and roll, local young people were hired for all the grunt work.

Now that the robot is located in Florida and the team lives in Mass., the cost of round trip air fare, motel, meals and miscellaneous costs for up to four people consisting of one or two weeks each month was very expensive. After the first winter season was over I thought I had a solution to save the company a lot of money plus make things a lot easier for the traveling team. Offer my PGA Town House for a yearly rental fee, not the rent we charge for in season rental. I figured out a monthly fee that would be equal to what I was receiving on the seasonal fee, it was empty in the summer anyway so I would be receiving the same money for twelve months that I was receiving for six months. Also the cost would be much less than the overall expense it was costing Spalding for Motels and meals.

What were the advantages for Spalding and it traveling team of four besides a large savings in expenses? The team would have a second home away from home, no strange expensive motel rooms. They would not have to lug so much with them each trip; they could leave a lot of clothes and personal items in the Town House. They could make coffee and fix their own breakfast, saving money and time. They could purchase all they needed to make sandwiches for their lunch, saving them time by not having to shut down the operation to find a restaurant. They could even prepare some of their own dinner meals; have their own cocktail hour without spending all that money on cocktails in a restaurant. They could sit and relax with their cocktails, watch whatever they wanted on TV. They had a place to do all their paper work. They could leave their calculators, typewriters, and all the office equipment they needed in the Town House rather than lugging it around the country each trip. A home away from home, traveling like they were was not fun; it was rough enough being away from their families. And the test site was less than three miles away from the Town House.

The test team was excited about my proposal and convinced management to rent the Town House. The guys loved it. How good was that idea? It lasted only a year! There must have been someone in management that disliked the fact I was making money with this arrangement, or just disliked me. I could never figure out any reasoning for management to change their mind and the team had to revert back to motel living! The test team was devastated. Can you imagine? Head Worms.

No skin off my nose, I just cleaned up the place and put it back in the rental pool for the time being. I owned that place for about twenty years and there were maybe ten years I rented it to our close friends from the Chagrin Falls, Ohio area who were now living in Delray Beach, Ed and Lorraine Flaherty. Ed also ended up working for me with my "Wm. Faulhaber Enterprises Inc.", but that is another story, later.

As time went on I was becoming more and more distant with the company that I loved. I still loved the old Spalding but there was management issues becoming more troublesome. I felt I was giving more to the company than I was receiving, this is no longer a two way street. Decisions being made were not what I expected, but what the hell do I know, they are smarter than me. No, I really don't think so. But, I have to look out for Bill; the decision to not rent my Town House told me that. I will end this story with another story about another proposal I made which was also turned down, and I almost lost my job over it as well.

In the past I always felt any ideas I might come up with that would benefit the company those ideas were given freely. At this point I was loosing a certain amount of loyalty because there was not much loyalty in return coming our way out here in the trenches, we were competing with our own company with all the golf equipment showing up everywhere at strange prices and strange retail outlets.

I had an idea which I presented to the Spalding Marketing Department under the name of Wm. Faulhaber Enterprises, Inc. Talk about stirring up a hornets nest. Maybe I am not as smart as I thought I was. What ever, I know I did not have, head worms.

My Proposal to Spalding #189

*T*HIS PROPOSAL HAS BEEN IN my files for 36 years and it is in two parts. The first is the "Teaser" which I sent and the second part was the actual detailed proposal which was never sent because I was turned down and was told my ideas were theirs since I was an employee, there would not be any additional compensation if they used by idea's. In addition the company wanted to know about my corporation and wanted to know if it was a distraction or conflict of interest from my Spalding employment duties. I had to explain the corporation was in existence before I returned to Spalding, that it was set up for my possible entrance into the business as a independent sales organization. They bought that part of it but not my proposal, so I never sent the second part. I did not give my favorite company my ideas because I felt I had given them enough already and would continue doing what I was being paid to do, but at this point in my career, nothing more since I did not feel they owned any part of me, I am not a piece of furniture.

As for this proposal I could not begin to explain it in a couple of paragraphs and naturally since it was mine I thought it was pretty good. So I have decided to print it out exactly as I had written it 36 years ago when the golf ball market was completely different than now, plus Spalding went bankrupt in 2003 and is no longer the same company so this would not apply now anyway. Many of you may find this boring as it is about golf, and business. I am sure my old Spalding friends receiving this will find it interesting as it happened before some of them were with Spalding. I will break this up into two or three parts and it will still be quite long, so if you want to read it, that's up to you. If you take the time to read it you just might see a side of me you did not know existed! Maybe, here we go, hold on.

Wm. Faulhaber Enterprises, Inc.
P.O. Box 12004
Lake Park, Fl. 33403
(305) 842-1987

June 7, 1979

Mr. Ralph C.
V.P. Marketing
Spalding
425 Meadow St.
Chicopee, MA. 01013

Dear Ralph:

As a follow up to our two previous telephone conversations, the following is being presented to you, the Vice President of Marketing for Spalding, by Wm. Faulhaber Enterprises, Inc., a consulting firm established in March, 1977.

I have prepared a Marketing Concept Proposal which I would like to present to Spalding that I believe will solve several very definite serious problems which now exist within the golf ball product area. Namely, the wound, surlyn cover golf balls, the Dot 90 and Dot 100, and the Flying Lady, which is a two piece golf ball.

My proposal is a marketing concept only; I am not proposing that these products be developed. The products in their present state can be utilized. However, I do suggest that the Flying Lady ball be changed to feel like a lady's ball, a softer feel by using the XL Top-Flite construction and dimple pattern. I would assume that this is already under consideration.

I believe you will agree with me that it is common knowledge that Spalding and its people are not happy with the sales of the Dot golf balls. Many have openly said, and in some cases it has been in writing, that if there is not immediate significant sales improvement, Spalding will seriously consider discontinuing manufacturing the Dot balls and drop out of the wound golf ball business and concentrate on the two piece golf ball only. It has been expressed that the present volume does not warrant the expenses of maintaining a department, its equipment and people at the present level of sales being achieved. Obviously, the return profit wise as the present volume is unacceptable.

Last ditch efforts have been and are underway to save the Dot. The consumer is being offered four balls for the price of three and the salesmen are receiving a "Spiff" commission of $2.00 for each six dozen counter units sold during May. A fairly heavy advertising program is, and has been underway. There also was the question of not listing the Dot balls in next years catalog.

In view of all these facts, it appears that Spalding is out of ideas as to how to market a wound ball (Dot) successfully, and are about to give up on this large wound ball market. It there were more ideas, a different marketing approach, and then I'm certain Spalding would have implemented them by now, or why the discussions of dropping wound balls.

I don't know the annual domestic sales volume of the Dot, but would estimate it to be less than one million dollars, and most likely about half of that amount. There is a very large wound ball business that Spalding should not give up on. I also believe that the balata wound ball business will possibly shrink, and the wound surlyn ball business will grow larger. The Dot is designed and positioned in the market to compete in this portion of the golf ball business which will continue for an undetermined number of years, because we all know there are a great number of golfers who will not play a two piece non wound ball.

My proposal would give Spalding an excellent opportunity to gain a good share of the wound ball market. I firmly believe my market concept will produce sales in the multimillion dollar category in the domestic market alone. By dropping the product there is no opportunity for any sales, let alone incremental sales, profits and increasing Spalding's total market share of golf ball sales.

Incremental sales produce profit, if the product can actually be produced and marketed at a profit. Spalding must feel that a wound surlyn ball will generate profit. If not, then the product would have been discontinued long ago.

Respectfully submitted,

Wm. H. Faulhaber
Wm. H. Faulhaber
President

The proposal next

*I*NCREMENTAL SALES PRODUCE PROFIT, IF the product can actually be produced and marketed at a profit. Spalding must feel that a wound surlyn ball will generate profit. If not, then the product would have been discontinued long ago.

Assuming this to be logical and correct, then this Proposed Marketing Concept, if accepted and used, and incremental sales that would not have been realized without this proposal, I submit the following consulting fees and royalties to be paid to Wm. Faulhaber Enterprises, Inc. for said proposal:

1) $10,000.00 consulting fee for this original marketing concept proposal for use in the United States of America.

2) $5,000.00 consulting fee tor this original marketing concept proposal for use in all other areas of the World.

3) Royalty percentage commissions (Outlined in Part 7 of this proposal) on incremental gross sales of products outlined and suggested in this proposal, based on gross sales dollars reported to Internal Revenue Service. Royalties to commence on date of product's actual introduction to the marketplace, comparing incremental gross dollar sales against the previous year's gross dollar sales on the products which may have undergone a different identity. Also including any balata wound ball that me be developed and introduced to the marketplace at any future date, as a result of the suggestions in the proposal itself.

4) Wm. Faulhaber Enterprises, Inc. has the right to inspect Spalding's books concerning actual gross sales of these products for accuracy as reported to the Internal Revenue Service for tax purposes.

5) Royalties to be paid to Wm. Faulhaber Enterprises Inc. for as long as these products are produced and marketed to the general public.

6) Royalties earned are to be paid annually no later than the 28th of February of the following year of January 1 through December 31, Spalding's fiscal sales year.

7) Royalty schedule is as follows: Since I do not know Spalding's actual gross dollar sales on these products for any given fiscal sales year or any part thereof the following royalty schedule is for example only and would be adjusted to actual gross sales as reported by Spalding to the Internal Revenue Service for tax purposes. The examples are to be applied to each individual product used as outlined in this proposal.

7A) In the first full fiscal year, or if introduced during a fiscal year, then for any part of a particular year and the following full fiscal year, 2% of incremental sales.

   1) Example: Partial year using the 4th quarter base sales for that quarter acquired in the precious year of $200,000. Sales of $250,000, obtained with new product produces incremental sales of $50,000. x 2% = $1,000. Royalty.

   2) Using the same previous year's actual sales the first 3 quarters acquired sales ($500,000.) plus 4th quarter sales acquired ($200,000.) for a total of $700,000. would be the base sales acquired on the previous product for the first full year's sales base and then royalty would be paid on incremental sales over the $700.000. base sales for the first full year of the new product. New products produce sales of $1,000,000., $300,000. x 2% = $6,000. royalty.

7B) Example: 2nd full year. 1% royalty of incremental sales over original base of $700,000. 3% of incremental sales over previous year's total sales ($1,000,000.).

Total sales $1, 250,000.

1) 1% of $300,000. = $3,000. royalty
2) 3% of $250,000. = $7,500. royalty
3) $10,500. royalty

7C) Example: 3rd full year. 1% royalty over original base sales ($700,000.) to actual sales of previous year of $1,250,000. and 3% royalty over $1,250,000. (Actual sales #1.500,000.)

1) 1% of $550,000. = $5,500. royalty
2) 3% of $250,000. = $7.500. royalty
3) $13,000. royalty

7D) Example: 4th full year 1% royalty over original base sales ($700,000.) to actual sales of previous year of $1.500,000. and 3% royalty over $1,500,000. (Actual sales $1,750,000.).

1) 1% of $800,000. = $ 8,000. royalty
2) 3% of $ 250,000. = $ 7,500. royalty
3) $15,500. royalty

7E) Royalty formula would continue on the basis of outline above for the lifetime of each individual product marketed using the original base dollar sales.

7F) The same royalty formula would apply separately for the United States of America and for all other areas of the World. All other areas of the World should be broken down by different divisions such as Canada, Australia, United Kingdom, Far East, Export, Military or however Spalding has its total business broken down into profit centers World Wide.

8. Any structural change in any of these individual products would not affect this proposal. Changes made would be for improvement in the products themselves for the purpose of holding or improving market share and/or keeping up with or

ahead of competition. Constant R&D work should always be in existence and should not have any effect of this Marketing Concept Proposal.

The program outline above and the Marketing Concept Proposal itself are being presented to Spalding only, with no intention of presenting it to any other Sporting Goods Manufacturer.

May I hear from you by return mail expressing your, and Spalding's level of interest in my complete Marketing Concept Proposal.

Respectfully Yours,
Wm. H. Faulhaber
Wm. H. Faulhaber
President

As stated before my proposal was turned down so I never sent the second part which outlined what my concept was. No one but me has ever seen it these past 36 years. However, since Spalding is no longer in business as it once was and filed for bankruptcy in 2003, the company was broken up and its name and product names were sold to other companies I no longer feel an obligation to withhold what my concept was. So, I am going to reveal the second part as originally written in my next chapter.

If you find this to be to much, not interesting to you, then don't waste your time reading what took me so long to create. I understand but I'm confident there are many of you who might appreciate and find interesting what is coming, my Marketing Concept Proposal.

MARKETING CONCEPT PROPOSAL #191

Wm. Faulhaber Enterprises, Inc.
P.O. Box 12004
Lake Park, Fl. 33403
(305) 842-1987

June, 1979

Marketing Concept Proposal
Spalding Golf Balls

*T*HIS IS A MARKETING CONCEPT proposal being presented to Spalding, a division of Questor, by Wm. Faulhaber Enterprises, Inc., a consulting firm established in March 1977.

In viewing Spalding's golf ball business I see some serious problems which this proposal is intended to correct, improving Spalding's market share overall and certain individual problem areas in particular.

Presently the Spalding Top-Flite is the number one single selling golf ball while Acushnet's Titleist balls are number one in volume due to the fact that they market numerous different Titleist's to the consumer. It's ironic that Top-Flite up until the introduction of the new XL Top-Flite has had only one "Facing" in golf pro shop showcases as opposed to competition such as Acushnet, Hogan, Wilson, and Dunlop having many. Top-Flite tends to be "Lost" among all these other products, resulting in lost sales. One or two facings do not stand out with all the competitors' brands which attract the eye of the consumer more readily, automatically adding selling strength.

The original Top-Flite and the new XL Top-Flite now give Spalding two facings in most locations but still far behind competition. There is a way to remedy the problem and solve the Dot, (and possibly the Flying Lady) problems as well.

First let's look at how competition markets their golf balls. Let's use the term "Family", a family of golf balls and packaging. Spalding's competitors use this approach. The afore mentioned Acushnet "Titleist," Wilson "Pro Staff", Dunlop "Maxfli" and Hogan all present their ball products in family packaging. Spalding is scattered - Top-Flite and XL Top-Flite are family – but Dot 90, Dot 100, Flying Lady and Molitor are not included in the "Family" concept.

Secondly, and most importantly, what are the "Names" being used by competition to tie all this family together? I've mentioned four competitors and in only one instance is the company name used in purchasing the product and that's Hogan. Let's break this down by company as follows;

All Acushnet's balls are named Titleist, the consumer does not ask for an Acushnet ball, they ask for Titleist. Titleist 100 (Black), Titleist 90 (Red), Titleist DT (Surlyn), Titleist "Pro Trac" (Pro trajectory), and Lady Titleist. When Acushnet introduce their new two piece ball you can make book on it that the ball will be called Titleist 'Something", not Acushnet. All are family names and packaging. Conclusion: Titleist sells, not Acushnet.

Dunlop's balls are named "Maxfli", or "Max". Maxfli – Blue Max, Red Max, Black Max and their two piece ball, Silver Max. Again, family names and packaging. Conclusion: Maxfli sells, not Dunlop.

Wilson is the same; the consumer sees family names and packaging and asks for various "Pro Staff" balls, not Wilson.

The trend with Hogan differs slightly, the consumer will ask for Apex 90, Apex 100 and Leader, but many times the consumer will use the company name, Hogan when asking for these products. Family packaging and names do exist however.

Spalding is a strong name but its product names are too scattered as well as packaging. I'm convinced that the name that sells is Top-Flite, with Spalding secondary, as with Acushnet, Dunlop, etc. Spalding is only family in name and packaging in Top-Flite, and again, Dot (a second family) reduced at this point to a stepchild. Flying Lady and the Molitor ball are off doing their own thing, and I believe the Molitor is the only one that should be permitted to do so as it is positioned to be different.

The biggest problems Spalding has in the golf ball area are the Dot balls. I am totally convinced that this once great name is dead, should be removed from the marketplace and put in suspended animation. The present Dots are intended to compete with other wound surly covered balls and, to some extent, with wound balata covered balls. As the balata ball market decreases, which it will, the wound surlyn market will increase. A great number of golfers will not play a two piece ball and Spalding should not give this large market away, but be in a strong position to take advantage of it.

The Dot is a good golf ball but the name is not. Although the Spalding name is very strong, the Top-Flite name is even stronger, or why wouldn't the Spalding Dot sell like Titleist DT for example?

While the Flying Lady is enjoying some success there are many ladies balls being marketed now (Lady Titleist coming on very strong). Consideration should be given to a change here, and the ball should definitely "Feel" like a lady's ball. Change to XL construction and dimple pattern.

By now you should know what direction I propose Spalding to take. Change names without any major change to the products themselves. I propose that Spalding drop the names Dot and Flying Lady at once and take advantage of the Top-Flite name by marketing five Top-Flite golf balls.

Top-Flite, Top Flite XL, Top-Flite WS-90, Top-Flite WS-100,

(WS- for Wound Surlyn) and Lady Top-Flite.
All family names and packaging.

If this marketing concept is used and is successful then balata should be considered using the same approach and should be considered a part of this proposal. (WB- for Wound Balata).

Top-Flite WB-90 Top-Flite WB-100.

My suggestion of WS-90 and WS-100 could be improved upon but the name Top-Flite is the major name of this proposal. Whatever else is added to improve the marketing concept is secondary to the actual introduction of additional Top-Flite golf balls.

Monitory advertising strength cannot be spent on a product that is not enjoying success and creating advertising dollars to further strengthen its growth. The Dot and Flying Lady to some extent falls into that category. The Top-Flite is just the opposite. By offering the Dot and Flying Lady as new Top-Flite balls, more advertising dollars should be available. "Borrowing" dollars from Top-Flite to new top-Flites is still advertising the name Top-Flite.

My proposal would give Spalding an excellent opportunity to share in the wound ball market. If dropping the product is under consideration there is no opportunity for incremental sales, profit, and increasing Spalding's total market share of golf balls. Incremental sales produces profit if the product can actually be produced and marketed at a profit. Spalding must feel that a wound surlyn ball will generate profit. If not, then the product would have been discontinued long ago.

Assuming this to be logical and correct then this proposal marketing concept, if accepted and used, and incremental sales that would not have been realized without this approach, I submit the following consulting fees and royalties be paid to Wm. Faulhaber Enterprises, Inc. for this proposal.

Stop ... here is where I repeat the consulting fees and royalty program that I stated in chapter #190. No sense in doing it again. Anyway, I tried but they insisted any ideas I had should be obligated to pass on to Spalding since I was an employee. I did not agree and did not pursue this any further, nor did they. Would it have worked, I don't know, I think some parts of it would have, we will never know. I had a blast putting this together and stirring up the pot somewhat. Got some peoples attention, that's for sure, including mine!

More about Wm. Faulhaber
Enterprises, Inc. #192

I established this Corporation in March 1977, 4 months before I returned to Spalding in July. There were several reasons why, one was I did a little consulting for a short time with another very small golf company wanting to get into the business. Also because I was in the process of establishing a south east sales rep organization and if successful a corporation would be helpful, plus, it would give me some flexibility in going into my own business, besides, I wanted to be a President! I was tired of those Vice President titles.

Detour, jumping ahead a little, remember the years interest rates jumped way up, savings accounts were paying very well as were stocks and other investments. But borrowing money came at a ridicules rate as well, around 16 to 18%? My brother Dick, Richard as his wife Bessie called him, was still living in Ohio, just south of Canton where he bought a small farm. Dick had an engineers license and a survey license, was in business for himself, the surveying business. He had a great Idea about a year or two before the interest rates went crazy. Dick came to me and wanted me to go into a partnership with him, he wanted to buy some land and build condominiums right next to a golf course and near a popular lake in Bolivar, Ohio, about 15 miles south of Canton also.

He had all these plans, the layout of the land, where and how many of these units would be built, some on the edge of a lake. Dick had blue prints of about three or four different size units; I think the plan was for about thirty units. He was going to use special heating and cooling units, which for the life of me I can't remember what it was called, had to do with using water but not steam heat.

Sounded good to me, so I said yes, I would help financially. Dick began construction on the first four units which were all under one roof. We made arrangements for a local real estate broker to handle the promotion and sales and I visited as often as I could from Florida. We needed additional financing and I am not going into a long drawn out story about all that we went through trying to acquire a construction loan. We had only one unit sold and we could not get a construction loan even at 18%. Conclusion, not every thing turns out the way you want them, we ended up loosing the whole project. It was costly to say the least, just another semester of a street college business education, so moving forward.

But not now, its backspin time again. Dee and I purchased another investment property in the PGA National complex, a two story golf villa with 3 bedrooms, 2 baths, living room, den, dining room, kitchen, screened in porch overlooking a fairway sand trap on the second hole of the Champions Course which is the same course used today for the Honda Classic held each March. We furnished the unit and put it into the rental pool. There was no problem renting these units during the season from 6 to 8 months. The income for six months more than paid for the mortgage payment and all of our expenses plus a profit on our money. In addition these units kept escalating in value so we were building our portfolio quite nicely. We now had our name on four mortgages.

How did we get that kind of a credit rating? I hate any dept except for a home or maybe an automobile. I worked very hard to build a good credit rating. When we were in our first years of marriage we would not buy anything on time unless we had the cash to back up that dept. For instance, if we purchased a new refrigerator we would make our payments for a few months then pay off the balance and that helped build our good credit rating. Then something called a credit card started to become popular. Again, we would not charge anything using credit cards unless we had the money to pay the invoice when it came in the mail. We have never ever paid one dime of interest to these credit card companies. I also paid every bill as I received them, I did not wait until the end of the month or a few days before they were due.

There are three major credit companies recording all of our

transactions as I am sure we are all aware of. I only receive a quarterly report from one of them; I don't mind telling you what our report is because we are proud of it. It is always about the same, 832 out of a possible 850. I don't know what I have to do to hit that 850, I guess I don't have enough active payments to make. What a shame. I keep preaching to our family about the importance of not paying anyone interest, except mortgages and maybe automobiles. That should be a goal for better financial security. You have to help yourself. If you are maxed out something is wrong. Backspin time for sure. You don't have to keep up with the Jones's as the saying goes. Back off; get it right, in the long run it will be the right way.

Sorry for the lecture. And now Dee and I are going to add two more mortgages.

Two More Mortgages #193

*T*HESE WILL BE IN A partnership with a friend and neighbor of ours. He is an executive with a large developer with home offices located in New Jersey. I will not use any names of the developer or the last name of my friend Frank, who unfortunately is no longer with us. But the developer is, and it is quite possible for anyone living on the east coast, north or south, you would recognize the name. Let's just use the name of "Apex" for the following stories concerning these investments. Most of the type construction Apex is involved in is medium price very affordable gated condominium developments. These are very popular second homes for our northern friends living here for the winter. Also many of these condos are purchased for investment purposes and put into a rental pool for seasonal rentals.

As I said Frank and his wife were social friends who lived near by. One evening he suggested we become partners in purchasing one of these units with the assurance it would be rented without a problem and our investment would only be the down payment. The rental fees collected will more than pay for everything with money left over. We purchase one and a short time later we bought a second unit. These two new units would also accelerate in value so Dee and I are continuing to build our portfolio and we now have our names of six mortgages.

Do you know we never even saw these units? We only knew where they were but we never even looked at them. Talk about absentee owners. We didn't have to do anything; the rental pool took care of everything for us. We just make the monthly payment, and eventually sold them after a few years and made a nice profit.

Frank came to me with another idea. He knew I had a legitimate corporation in place and suggest I consider getting involved by putting together a team of people for the purpose of completing the final finishing of the condo units Apex had under construction. When a unit is completed it really isn't because there are many contractors involved with the construction of a building. So when each is done with his part, the plumber, the electrician, the carpenter, the tile setter, the air conditioning, the painter, they really kind of mess up the place. The final operation is a team that cleans up everything needed, the finishing touches, the final caulking, touch up painting, anything little thing the contractors may have overlooked or caused. It is impossible to have every contractor come back for these small finishing touches so a fee is established per unit to put it in shape get it ready to put on the market. The official term for this kind of work is "Punch out."

That's what Frank wanted me to consider and he laid out for me exactly what I would need to do to set up such a business. I needed someone to manage people; the actual work would be done by contract to sub contractors so they were not direct employees. These sub contractors used their own trucks and tools and were really qualified technicians. These guys could fix anything. Frank also had a qualified man to head up such an operation, his first name was Marshal. So we set up a new business.

Setting Up a New Business #194

I ALREADY HAVE A FULL PLATE handling my Spalding customers and have no spare time to devote to this new business except on a limited basis so I needed someone to run the operation and get it started in the right direction. We could not go about this in a hap hazard way and slowly grow into it, we had to perform at a high level from the start or Apex would not have us around very long. We established an office in Lake Worth which was near most of the ongoing developments.

With Frank's (The executive with Apex) guidance we started this business with Marshal as my lead man, he has all the experience we need to schedule the work load and line up all the sub contractors needed but he could not do all of this alone as the "Punch Out" work load was pretty hectic from the beginning.

Enter my old friend Ed Flaherty from Chagrin Falls, Ohio who retired from Ford/Philco and now living in Delray Beach near Lake Worth. Ed has management and manufacturing capabilities and he is looking for something to do. He also wants to move a little further north as well. Guess what, I have the perfect spot for him to move to, he wants to rent, not own. My PGA Townhouse is perfect, I think so and so does Ed and Lorraine. They moved into it and lived there for quite a few years. I had a year round renter who was not going to tear up the place and long time social friends to mingle with again.

Ed and I met with Marshall and Frank and laid out a plan; both Marshall and Ed had different talents that fit together so we set up the business taking advantage of their talents to share the workload of running the Wm. Faulhaber Enterprises, Inc., all I had to do was attend a few meetings a month for updates and whatever advice I could add.

This did not take any time away from my duties of running a successful sales territory for Spalding.

This business is going to grow pretty rapidly so I will give you a preview of what my letterhead will look like as we moved full steam ahead.

Wm Faulhaber Enterprises, Inc.
4010 South 57ᵗʰ Ave-Suite 102-A   1398 Pine
Pine Ridge Circle East (F)
Lake Worth, Florida 33163   Tarpon Springs, Florida 33580
516-231-4121   813-938-7632

FAULHABER ENTERPRISES GROWTH #195

*O*UR COMPANY LETTERHEAD IS SHOWN below along with information of what our business offered as well. We soon expanded this offering as more opportunities arose and will be explained as we continue the story about this short lived business.

Wm. Faulhaber Enterprises, Inc.

**4010 South 57ᵗʰ Ave-Suite 102-A 1398 Pine Ridge Circle East (F)
Lake Worth, Florida 33163 Tarpon Springs, Florida 33580
1-1-4122   813-938-763**

**THE CONSTRUCTION INDUSTY'S
PRIMARY SUPPORTING SERVICES TEAM**

DATA PROCESSING AND RECORDS MANAGEMENT

PRE C.O. PUNCH/OUT

POST C.O. PUNCH/OUT

POST C.O. CLEANUP

PRE-OCCUPANCY INSPECTION TOUR (WALK/THRU)
CORRECTION OR WALK/THRU INSPECTION DEFECTS
THIRTY DAY (30) SQUAWK LIST
WARRANTY PERIOD SERVICE CALLS
OCCASOINAL-NON SCHEDULED SUPPORT

This all started in 1983, the above outline gives you an idea of what we offered to begin with. The Apex Developers were building on the west coast of Florida also so we had to establish a business there as well. The operation was smaller so we could handle this with one person, that person was my Son-In-Law Patrick Garcia, married to our youngest daughter, Linda. If Patrick needed assistance it was a four and one half hour drive and we would respond when ever needed. Patrick and Linda would eventually have three children, Chrissy, Cara and P.J. (Patrick also).

My brother, Richard, was now living in Lake Wales, Florida working part time for a survey firm. He came to me one day and asked if I had a place for him with my company as he wanted to work on a full time basis. At this point we needed someone to help with the heavy load of paper work, invoice billing, everything. My brother was an early computer geek and could program those early computers, so I hired my brother to handle all of this. I now have three main men in our offices here and Patrick Garcia on the West Coast of Fl., plus all the sub contractors who were willing to work with us. We didn't have anything invested in equipment except for the office. The sub contractors provided the trucks and tools needed, we paid for the materials they used. We started to upgrade our operation from the very beginning.

Upgrading Our Operation #196

*M*Y BROTHER RICHARD PURCHASED TWO computers and started programming them for what we needed, invoicing, programs, price schedules, things I just don't remember, just many things needed to cut down man hours and cut down on the paperwork, he modernized the office functions. Plus his engineering knowledge came in handy as well. I now had four people on the payroll of Faulhaber Enterprise. I also had an officer who held the title of Vice President and Secretary of the Corporation, None other than Dolores "Dee" Faulhaber, so we added her to the payroll as well; we needed to get a little class into the business for sure.

We purchased another computer and put it in my office so I could keep tabs on everything and use it for my personal use as well. This was long before personal computers became popular. They were small square boxes, looked like a TV and were limited in what they could do. No internet in those days. Everything was done using floppy discs in addition to a limited hard drive. This was 1984. Richard also bought one to use at his home so he could do some work there as well, we now owned four computers. They were not cheap in those days but I don't remember what we paid for them. We also had a lot of pencils and paperclips, some staplers; you name it, stapler removers, even desks and chairs. You would think we were serious.

While all of this is going on, things were happening; we were expanding rapidly into other service areas related to these condos. My team was a good one constantly looking into possible ways to increase our income to cover everyone's salary and make sure our operation is a profitable venture.

I will give a thump nail sketch of what was going on and quickly at that, there were opportunities my guys were telling me about that we should look into and consider adding and expanding our operation. t

Wm Faulhaber Enterprises, Inc.
4010 South 57ᵗʰ Ave-Suite 102-A 1398   Pine Ridge Circle East (F)
Lake Worth, Florida 33163   Tarpon Springs, Florida 33580
516-231-4121   813-938-763

OUR SERVICE PROGRAM RELIEVES THE
PROPERTY MANAGER
OF ALL PROPERTY MAINTANCE PEOBLEMS

DATA PROCESSING AND RECORDS MANAGEMENT

RENTAL UNIT INSPECTION AND CONDITION REPORT

FURNISHED UNIT INVENTORY

POST RENTAL REFURBISHMENT

MONTHLY MAINTENANCE SERVICE

OCCASIONAL/NON-SCHEDULED SERVICE REPORTS

*T*HE ABOVE OUTLINE IS AN example of our expansion into the property management business one step at a time. I am only showing the headings these various programs as the detailed description of these services and price structures covers three to four pages full of backup information. Below are some more services we were involved in as we continued our expansion of services, in brief.

GOOD NEWS FOR HOMEOWNERS
Introducing
An Affordable and Professional
Monthly Maintenance Program
Designed to
Protect your Real Estate Investment
Assure your Comfort and Peace of Mind
OUR FULL SERVICE PROGRAM

This program was designed for the owners who only live-in these units part time. We inspected them monthly making sure everything was in order, A/C working and set at 80-82 degrees, chemical added to drain pan to make sure they did not clog up, filter cleaning, mildew inspection, insect infestation and application of insecticide, function of all plumbing fixtures, overall property condition and repairs needed, and send a report of all the above to owner. Soon we added more service offerings.

More Service Offerings #198

*M*ARSHALL'S TITLE WAS BUSINESS DEVELOPMENT and he sure was doing a darn good job of doing just that. He, along with Ed Flaherty and my brother Richard, and with Patrick Garcia running our operation on the west coast of Florida were putting together some very interesting offerings. I have touched on a few, here are some more, again, in brief, there is much backup material involved with each and I won't bore you to death with all that detail. You might be bored enough with what I am already giving you. Read what you want, and here is a new one dreamed up by my brother Richard.

AAA DATA, INC.

DATA PROCESSING
And
RECORDS MANAGEMENT
SYSTEMS PLANNING
And CREATING CUSTOMIZED SOFTWARE
For EFFECTIVE DATA MANAGEMENT
(Full in-house staff)

GENERAL LEDGER – PAYROLL
WARRANTY RECORDS and EXPOSURE
ESCROW MANAGEMENT
AUTOMATED
MAILING LISTS and LABELS
LETTERS and INVOICESS

RECORDS MANAGEMENT
For
CONDOMINIUMS AND HOME OWNERS ASSOCIATIONS

There were several other services we offered, some I am listing below:

**HOW DO WE SERVE THE INSURANCE
ADJUSTING FUNCTION?
APPLIANCE MAINTENANCE PROGRAM
SERVICE PROGRAMS SUPPORTING
REAL ESTATE INVESTORS
PRE-PLANNED AND SCHEDULED
REFURBISHMENT PROGRAM**

And lastly in February of 1984 son Jim was entering the pressure cleaning business which he still operates to this day. So we offered the following;

WM. FAULHABER ENTERPRISES, INC.

IS NOW OFFERING A NEW AND IMPORTANT SERVICE
PRESSURE CLEANING OF OUTDOOR AREAS
UTLIZE THIS CAPABITLITY TO
REMOVE DIRT AND MILDEW

REPRESENTATIVE PRICES

POOL AREAS
DECKS … … 75.00 AWNINGS … … 15.00

SHUFFLEBOARD COURTS … … 30.00
TENNIS COURT AREAS … … 60.00

CONDO BUILDINGS
WALKWAYS (FRONT AND BACK) … … … 20.00

1ST FLOOR AWNINGS ... 20.00 - 2ND
FLOOR AWNINGS ... 25.00

The business is growing and we are doing well, but possible trouble looms ahead. What does our future business look like?

What Does the Future Look Like #199

*W*E ARE NOW INTO THIS business for about two and one half years when my friend Frank form Apex drops a bomb on me. He says that the owner of the Apex Company doesn't trust any sub contractors because of past experience. Frank says that after a couple of years the sub contractors have a tendency of becoming so well established some will start to take advantage by padding invoices for work not performed, and other types of hanky panky. So every two or three years he changes all sub contractors. Frank says he just wanted to warn me that this might happen to us as well, even though he would do his best to prevent that by conveying to the owner that Faulhaber Enterprises was at trustworthy operation.

I said to Frank, "Frank, why would you have not told me of this possibility when we first considered starting us this business. I have built up one heck of an overhead." He just shrugged his shoulders and I had to go change my underwear. What a jolt. At this point about 95% of our business was with, or connected to, Apex. Our gross income was now into the seven figures. Talk about having all your eggs in one basket, drop that basket and all the eggs are scrambled and not eatable.

I called a meeting with Marshall, Ed and my brother Richard giving them all the sordid possibilities were facing. My direction was that they had to start looking to expand our business outside of Apex. Contact other developers and see if we can make some inroads. Unfortunately I could not personally get involved spending time trying to accomplish my own request. But they were running Faulhaber Enterprises and being paid to do so, I just wanted them to know we had to do this for survival.

And then without much warning what we feared, happened. We

were being terminated in about three months. My guys had not been successful in obtaining additional customers up to that point. There was no way I was going to get caught in a dying business that would cost me a lot of money trying to keep it afloat. So I have to make some tough decisions.

Two weeks before our cut off deadline with Apex I gave my team four weeks to find other customers. In other words if we were unsuccessful in doing that there would only be two weeks left for us to remain in business. We were unsuccessful in that endeavor and I shut down the business. We didn't own any equipment other than office and I still have a lot of staplers, the computers are long gone.

Marshal and Ed Flaherty were already retired and this was a second job for both so that didn't bother them or me too much. My brother Richard had to go back working for a surveying company in Lake Wales so he was taken care of. Pat Garcia, my daughter Linda and the two girls came back to this area from Tarpon Springs and then presented us with another grandson, Patrick.

I would say we were successful even though it only lasted about three years. Shutting the business down the way I did also prevented my loosing a lot of money and it was a great experience that helped build our portfolio. I did not try and start another business; I just wanted to do what I was doing and take care of a few investment properties. Then my friend Ed Flaherty talked me into being a boater.

Our Dock and First Boat #200

As I related in an earlier story Dee and I purchased our beautiful home with the Earman River running from east to west located at the back of our property and that river empties into the "Intracoastal Water Way" which leads to the Atlantic Ocean. There are no seawalls built on natural rivers, only on man made seawalls where canals are built.

One day Ed Flaherty came to me with a proposition, Ed had an interest in buying a boat he fell in love with, a small Bay Liner cabin cruiser about 28 feet long with twin screws (Two engines and props). It was not a new boat but not very old either. He wanted me to consider going into partnership with him and o;f course I would have to build a dock to accommodate the boat. Ed talked me into it as I have now been living on water for six years and I did want to own a boat sometime, so I guess it was time.

It took about six months to get the permits and finish the dock project. In the meantime we needed a place to dock our new toy so I contacted the North Palm Beach Public Works Department about renting a dock at one of their marinas which was just up the river from us, and I spoke with the head man, Charlie Amelia, who I knew from church. I didn't know him well at the time but we became friends along the way. I explained what my problem was and asked it there was any dock space available and Charlie told me I was in luck, one just became vacant. They were hard to come by and I am sure there was a waiting list but Charlie assigned that spot for me for as long as I needed it. Remember his name; its funny how things work out because in a few years my second boat will be directly tied to Charlie. But that's another story for later.

Anyway, the dock had to extend out into the water. Our property is 14 feet above sea level so there was a fairly steep ramp built to reach the 30 foot long dock. The whole structure was a "T" design. I chose to use cement pilings rather than wood, much more expensive but worth it as they are still there 34 years later. The dock cost me about $10,000.00 and I figured that wood pilings would have had to be replaced at least once in all those years.

I ran electric and water lines down from the house, underground, which is about 150 feet. I had two overhead solar lights installed which come on at dusk and off as the sun rises. Beautiful dock and we finally had our own place to tie up our Bay Liner.

THE BAY LINER #201

*T*HIS WAS A NICE LOOKING boat and shortly after buying it the first thing I encouraged my partner Ed Flaherty to do was attend a boating class with me that was offered by the local U.S. Coast Guard Auxiliary. While In the Coast Guard reserve I had handled a 40 foot patrol boat on many occasions and was taught the rules of the road. Like out new boat, the Coast Guard 40 footer had twin engines which make handling and maneuvering of the craft so much easier. With twin engines I could turn the boat completely around in the same spot just by putting one engine in forward and the other in reverse while idling without touching the steering wheel. Docking the boat was much easier than a boat with just one screw, much easier as you could use both screws and just "walk" the craft sideways by switching the engines forwards and backwards. I felt that a brush up about boating was needed. Ed had no prior boating experience so it was important for him to attend this boating course.

So off to school we go. There are so many boaters that have no clue and they are dangerous operating a boat. I really don't know why a license is not required to operate a boat just like you have to have to operate a car. Another advantage of going through this Coast Guard boating class is we are given a certificate that I presented to the Insurance Company and I received a 10% discount on the cost of the policy covering the vessel.

There was sleeping quarters and a small head (Bathroom) and a kitchen below in the front part (Bow) of the boat. We never did use the boat for overnights, just for cruising in the ocean and the Intracoastal waters. It was a very nice craft and we had a lot of fun with it for a few years. Owing a boat is very expensive, repairs or parts that are labeled "Marine" it seemed like the price was tripled.

Keeping a boat in the water in salt water is much different than fresh water. Barnacles form quickly on the bottom and we had to take the boat out of the water every six to nine months to have the marine life removed and the bottom repainted with very expensive paint. To do all of this we have to go to a Marina where they lift the boat out and place it on dry land on blocks so the bottom can be worked on.

For some unknown reason we had engine problems constantly. Thank goodness we had two of them because it seemed like every time we went any distance one of the engines would shut down. We never knew which one nor why but we were lucky both never shut down at the same time so we could always get back with one working. Our mechanics could never figure it out either. Leave the boat sit over night and the engine that shut down would start up the next day like nothing was ever wrong. Go figure. I really think that boat was *haunted.*

We had that boat for several years and finally sold it. We really got tired of fighting the fact those engines had a mind of their own. Ed and I remained friends through all of this partnership, no small feat in it self. I am not the easiest guy to get along with and I know it so I really had to work on being a partner, it is not easy. So, I said to myself, if I ever get another boat, it will not be in a **partnership with anybody.** So let me tell you about our second boat, a House Boat and <u>my new partner!</u> This is a riot.

THE HOUSEBOAT #202

*T*HIS STORY WILL TAKE SEVERAL chapters and is some story. I joined the Knights of Columbus in 1989 and met a whole bunch of new friends. One of those new friends was a master carpenter by the name of Joe DiDia and he will become my new partner in the world of boating. Another partner, boy I am easy.

All this happened starting about 1992, Joe lived just a couple of streets away from us and he approached me one day and told me a story about a boat he was interested in. Since I had a dock he wanted to know if I would be interested in becoming a partner in this new venture and I didn't hesitated in letting Joe know I was not interested. But Joe said, "Wait a minuet Bill, you didn't even let me tell you what kind of a boat it is and what it would cost." I replied, "Joe, I don't care what kind of a boat it is or what the cost is, I am not interested in another boat for a while." Joe backed off and said nothing to me for several months.

Then one day Joe approached me again and told me the boat was a houseboat and belonged to Charlie Amealia's (Remember that name) son and it was docked behind Charlie's house and was less than half a mile away from our dock. Joe said all they wanted for the boat was about $2,000.00 because it had been sitting idle for a couple of years and would need extensive repairs. Joe said he could do all the work if I would pay for all the materials. Joe continued and said he thought he could get the price down to about a thousand dollars. Would I care to go see it? I again repeated, "Joe, I do not want to see it, I am not interested."

Then I made my big mistake, I finally said, "Joe, when they want to give the boat to us for nothing, come and see me." And then it happened they did just that and I am now a partner in a houseboat that has been given to us and I have yet to see the boat.

The next thing Joe asks me is how long my dock is, and I inform him I had it built 30 foot long to accommodate my 25 foot Bay Liner. Joe says that this houseboat is 33 feet long and we should extend the dock to 40 feet and that he would take care of that himself, which he did. My dock is growing. This is shortly after I got my first glimpse of our new acquisition. I have been putting off writing about that because to this day I still fine it hard to believe what I got myself into.

Well it's time; Joe took me over to Charlie Amelia's to see what we have just acquired. I hesitated and said, "Now?" So off we went, I had mixed feelings about all of this and was trying to prepare myself to lay my eyes on this beauty, expecting the worse. I expected it to be in bad condition and I underestimated what I was about to lay my eyes on. I'll try to explain the houseboat's condition just as soon as I gather myself.

THE HOUSEBOAT'S CONDITION #203

OFFICIALLY THIS BOAT IS A Nauta-Line 33 with a beam of 12 feet and a draft of 27" with a full hull. A full hull means its bottom is like any other boat, not a flat bottom. It was built in 1968 making it 24 years young. This is no small vessel and is powered by a single Chrysler 318, V-8 320 horse power gasoline engine with a stern drive. Which means the engine is inside the boat and has a very large stern drive and propeller fastened on the outer stern of the boat.

It could sleep 2 to 4 adults and had a small bathroom with a shower. The galley had a stainless steel sink with running water furnished by a 40 gallon tank and a small refrigerator. All of this information I found out later and I am writing about now to paint a picture of what we had acquired before I try to explain what this monstrosity really looks like.

OK, I can't delay this any longer. Upon our arrival we were taken into Charlie's Amelia's garage where we were shown a large engine completely disassembled. It was the Chrysler engine for the boat! The boat was owned by Charlie's oldest son and his younger son was a mechanic. It was he who removed the engine from the boat and took it apart so he could rebuild it. The boat did not have an engine in it! Frank, the younger son, assured us he would rebuild it at no cost to us. That was one plus, I guess.

Al right, the time has come, we exit the garage and work our way to the back of the property where the sea wall is and there it was, tied up to the sea wall in all of its splendor. Oh my goodness, I thought I was prepared for the worse, I was not. What a sight. The first observation from a distance was not too bad but as I got closer I became a little apprehensive. The windows were so dirty you could not see inside. The wooden decks looked like they were about to collapse. I looked at the stern drive and there was a small tree growing out of it. No, not weeds, a small tree, I kid you not. I was speechless.

What in the world are we doing here? Joe was just smiling and was admiring it as he could visualize how he was going to put this hunk of I don't know what, back together. I did not want to climb aboard but Joe talked me into it. We really had to be careful where we walked. We opened the back sliding door and nothing but stifling air hit us in the face. Cob webs everywhere. We worked our way along the side of the "House" to the front door next to the controls, opened it, same thing. We did not go inside, not even Joe. I was sick to my stomach; I am going to pay for all the materials to fix this thing? Do I look stupid? Yes, I sure did.

We were giving the keys to the doors and the controls and the ownership papers all signed. We now officially owned this "Thing". We now had to make arrangements to move this "Thing" somewhere for rebirth. When we relocated this "Thing" to a marina, that is when we really found out more distasteful things when it was lifted out of the water.

RELOCATING & NAMING THE BOAT #204

*J*OE AND I NEEDED TO find a boat repair place that permitted the boat owners to work on their own boat. We selected the Seminole boat yard located near the corner of PGA Blvd and the PGA drawbridge, right next door to the River House Restaurant. Now we had to make arrangements to tow this engineless "Thing" to the Boat Yard. Once we got underway it was quite a sight. People on shore must have thought we were taking it to the house boat grave yard. Should have? Maybe, I could have retired at least a year earlier. I am also going to pay the rent, now get this, for the next nine (9) months. That is how long we will be at this location. That's how long it took us working on the boat in the evenings and weekends to rebuild this beauty. **Nine months,** the rebirth of a new baby, our houseboat. I can't imagine, still can't, nine months. $$$$$$

We finally arrive at the boat yard and position the boat in the slip where they placed these large heavy straps under the boat for lifting it out of the water. A huge unit on wheels straddles the slip and the boat and begins to lift the boat out of the water. Well, you should have been there to see the look on our faces, even the people who work there looked surprised. The growth of sea life is sometimes amazing, ours qualified to be unbelievable. The bottom of the boat was completely covered with these very large barnacles which look like very large oyster, or clam shells! Stink, boy did that boat give off an awful odor once it was out of the water.

Now is was completely out of the water hanging in the air under this large lift with wheels which would then move the boat to a spot in the yard and set down on wood blocks. But before doing that, we had to go to the office and sign in and then they would assign a spot for us. Next was **"Giving the boat its new name"**.

There were three or four employees in the office; all of them seemed very interested in talking to us about this large barnacle we just pulled out of the water. Everyone seemed generally interested in what the heck we had. So now I'm talking to these nice people and providing all the information they are asking. Then this nice lady asks me what the name of the boat was?

I have to warn you at this point because my response will be exactly what I said, and I can't say it any differently, it was what it was, so don't be alarmed. Everyone seemed very interested to hear what was name the boat had and I replied, "We just acquired the boat and it doesn't have a name." She replied, "I'm sorry sir but all boats registered here must have a name." I replied, "I understand, let's just call it the **POS.**" Now it seems everyone is leaning over the counter and waiting for an answer when she asks me, "And what does **POS** stand for?"

I replied without hesitation, a **"Piece Of Shit"**. For a few seconds there was silence and then loud laughter broke the silence. Everyone was absolutely laughing uncontrollably. I can't tell you where I came up with that, it just came out with no prior thought about saying something like that at all. Some say I am fast on my feet but slow of mind. Oh, never mind, I did say that and it's my story and I am sticking to it.

After that little episode it seemed we could do no wrong with these nice people. When making repairs to boats in a boat yard such as this you are required to purchase all materials needed through them. That is expensive as all get out, everything to do with the word "Marine" is **expensive** to the point it is ridicules. These people must have felt sorry for us and although we purchased some materials from them, not much, they never questioned us about bringing our own materials onto the boat yard. They could not have been nicer and I'm convinced naming the boat **POS** did all of that for us.

Next, the continuing saga, the Boats unreal condition …

THE HOUSEBOATS SHOCKING CONDITION #205

ECEASED! THE **POS** SHOULD HAVE read **RIP.**

It turns out the only thing that was good on the boat was the hull, the rebuilt engine and the upper metal frame structure and the doors. The hull was sound and in great shape once all the oysters were removed, that turned out to be my job. The boat yard people pressured cleaned the bottom the best they could and knocked some growth off, I had to do the rest. And that took a lot of time, the growth was just like concrete, once I removed the larger pieces I had to use a sanding tool to slowly remove the rest without damaging the hull itself. Working under the boats hull was not easy. Think about this, the boat was 33 feet long and the bottom came to a slight cure and then it was 12 feet from one side to the other. That is a very large dirty job and I had to wear a mask. That was rough because I had to continually remove it so I could drink my beer. But, somebody had to do it, drink the beer that is.

The first thing Joe wanted to do was tear out all the rotten wood, and there was plenty. I made a big mistake one day and stepped on the forward hatch door. I went right through it leaving all the skin on my left shin on the hatch frame. Boy was I bleeding; first it was money now it was blood. What a good time I was having. Getting rid of the obviously bad wood would get us to the point we could start to replace it and start getting the POS back in shape. Then Joe discovered something else while ripping out the rotting wood, "Termites!"

All work came to a screeching stop. There was only one thing we could do, we had to call in the exterminator, tent the boat and get rid of those hungry little devils. Then we had to inspect other parts of the boat where we thought the wood was ok, of course from the outside much of it looked fine. Not so, much was hollow, we had to completely strip all wood out of the POS, which by this time Joe agreed that I had picked out the appropriate name for the boat.

This was a much bigger job than we thought but no use crying over spilled termites, back to work. We knew that all the beer in Palm Beach County would not last until we got this piece of something back in the water. All the wood we used had to be treated to withstand the salt water and salt air conditions so it was expensive. The decking and a lot of other wood areas had to be covered with a liquid fiber glass coating which Joe would mix up in small amounts and apply. That stuff dried up fast so only a little could be applied at a time, a dirty and tedious job indeed. Then everything had to be painted with the most expensive paint in the world, especially the hull. So, the boat repairs continued.

Houseboat Repairs #206

*T*HE HULL WAS MY BABY, all the carpentry and other delicate repairs was up to Joe and his multiple talents, mine were limited but I was a good painter having painted all our houses, inside and out. My dad taught me that painting talent; I was pretty good at that. When the hull was finally cleaned it really looked solid and it was. Had to use anti fouling Marine paint, designed to prevent the fast growth of marine life. The paint could not stop the growth, just slow it up. Expensive, you bet. If I remember correctly that paint cost me about sixty some dollars a gallon, and that's a long time ago.

I could not begin to remember how many gallons I used but I had to put two coats of primer on that bare hull and then two coats of finishing paint, four coats of paint total over that large area. $$$$$$$ When it was finished it was beautiful, things were starting to take shape. But I am a little ahead of myself here, a little back spin here.

Don't forget now, it is going to take us a full **nine months** in dry dock to put this "Thing" back in the water. Joe has to make a living and so did I. So we worked a little some evenings and as much as we can on the weekends, Sunday's after Church, where we pray we can turn this POS around into a beautiful floating masterpiece, and if we do a good job we may qualify for the **eight** wonder of the world.

Charlie Amelia's son Frank is rebuilding the engine so we don't have that in place yet. We don't have a workable stern drive and propeller either, the one on the boat with a small tree growing out of it is shot, This stern drive is no longer manufactured so we have to find another one like it or something similar that could be adapted to our situation. Joe and I went shopping; we were informed about a large Marine scrap yard featuring used parts and it was located in West Palm Beach, right next door to the Knights of Columbus Council 2075, not the Council I belong to but I have been to this facility many times so I know exactly where this place was.

Joe and I went to check it out one Sunday but it was closed. The out side of the building was accessible so we drove around winding our way through mounds of junk and we came to a loading dock. What we saw lying on the dock no one is going to believe. There is was, a stern drive just exactly like the one we needed! Our prayers have been answered. We could not believe what we saw, and it looked almost brand new. No way, we must be seeing things, this is impossible. The man upstairs must have felt badly for us for taking on the POS project and wanted to help us bring this deceased boat back to life?

As you might imagine, we were back there early Monday morning licking our chops. We met the owner and were able to purchase this unit at a very fair price. The owner was quite a character; he loved boats, was independently wealthy and ran this place as a hobby. He was a chain smoker, will never forget how he continually had a cigarette hanging from his lips, and no filters either. When the cigarette was almost going out due to the wet end, out came his pack and he lit the new one off the old. We returned to this place numerous times looking for parts and I never saw him without a cigarette. I asked a lady working there once about how many packs of cigarettes did he go through in a day and if I remember correctly she said something like twelve. And he only needed one match to light all those cigarettes, can you imagine?

HOUSEBOAT UPDATES #207

THE STERN DRIVE WAS A magnificent find and our next step was to get the rebuilt engine back in the boat and hook everything together, engine to the stern drive. That was no easy task lifting the engine up and into the engine compartment, since the boat was on blocks and the opening for the engine was about eight feet off the ground. The boat yard had a portable lift unit for doing just that and they didn't even charge us a fee for using it. Presto, the POS now had an engine. But not much else, we had to replace all the cables that controlled the engine, stern drive and steering. That included the upper deck bridge controls and the controls inside the boat. The fuel lines from the gas tanks to the engine had to be replaced as well. The boat could be operated topside (good weather) and also from inside (bad weather). That was a really big job getting everything hooked up.

Other items that needed replaced were a new propeller, two fifty five gallon gas tanks, two anchors, a forty gallon water tank for the sink, and I know I am forgetting about a lot of other small items. Oh yeah, we had to keep replacing the empty beer containers, almost a full time job in itself, very important. We had a lot of friends visit, some curious and some came to help out from time to time. They all drank beer; something about a boat yard makes one thirsty. Another thing I figured out was how to cut down on the cost for a case of beer. Buy three cases at a time, saves a lot of gas expense and time going back for more. Got to think out of the box you know.

The POS house boat is starting to look like anything but. It is really taking shape, inside and out. We are getting closer and closer to completion. I am sure I kept a record of what I spent on this free boat project but for some reason I can't find that file. I really don't remember what it finally cost me, nine months rental at the boat yard and all the materials. I suspect that down deep in my memory bank I don't want to remember. We split the cost of the beer, thank goodness as that was quite a sizable amount. So, we are ready for "Launching" of our new born baby, our beautiful houseboat.

LAUNCHING THE NEW POS #208

*T*HE TIME HAS ARRIVED, THE nine months are up and the POS has been born. It is time for the stork to arrive, put its big leather straps under the vessel, lift it off the blocks and slowly move through the boat yard to the launching area. I don't remember who was there beside Joe and I as we intended to take the boat for its inaugural short spin before taking it to my dock. Lo and behold you would have thought we were launching the Queen Mary, it seemed like every employee from the Seminole Boat yard was there plus many other boat owners who were working on their boats, was there for this big event.

As the POS was being lowered into the water they were all cheering, whistling and just having the best time. The only thing we didn't do was smash a bottle of champagne against the bow. We were afraid it would sink the darn thing. What a time, Joe and I boarded and slowing drifted off into the sunset, just as you would see in the movies. What a day, we tested all the steering and operating cables, all the moving parts were perfect, and we gave the POS it's test run heading towards home port, we docked it and gave each other a hug, and had another beer.

For all you fresh water people, when docking a boat in the Earman River, it is salt water and connected directly to the ocean, the tide in the river under normal conditions was four to four and one half feet. The changing tides requires special attention of how a boat is tied up to a dock, the lines have to have enough slack to accommodate this and cross lines are needed as well because of the incoming and outgoing currents so the vessel remains in one place. The boat can go up and down with the tide and still not bang against the dock. Three large bumpers were hung from the dock to buffer the vessels movement just in case, protecting the boat and the dock.

It is no longer a POS and we never did put an official name on the back of the boat. The next thing we have to do is have the boat "Surveyed."

HOUSEBOAT SURVEY #209

OW THAT JOE DIDIA AND I have our newly launched rebuilt POS home from the boat repair yard it is time to get the proper insurance coverage. Yes, I get a discount because of my Coast Guard certificate but we have to put a value on the boat. We also needed to get the boat inspected to make certain we were in compliance with all safety rules and regulations so we contacted "Allen's Boat Surveying & Consulting" firm located in Tequesta, Fl., right up the road a few miles from us. They conducted a "Marine Survey, Condition and Value" inspection in October of 1994. Below, in part, is their summary of their Survey;

The NAUTA-LINE 33 was surveyed with all major systems in place and operational. This houseboat has been expertly refurbished from inside and out. The vessel was found in "ABOVE AVERAGE" condition for her year construction and vintage. The vessel is virtually new except for the hull, engine and stern drive.

The Fair Market Value was based upon this surveyor's experience, the BUC RESEARCH Price Guide, vessels and equipment of like and kind, and knowledge of the local and current Marine Market Price and boat sales.

Statement of Vessel Condition: "ABOVE AVERAGE"
Fair Market Value: $20,200.00
Estimated Replacement Cost: $66,000.00

"This vessel is fit for her intended service and suitable for her intended use as an inland intracoastal and lake operated houseboat." This survey represents the true condition of the 1968 NAUTA-LINE and her current appraised market value 10/1/94.

That is a pretty darn good report. They praised the work that was done to restore this now very good looking houseboat. Next, I added a few celebrities as part of our crew.

CELEBRITIES ABOARD #210

I DON'T WANT TO GET TOO far ahead of myself but after a few years of owning the POS I came across a life size thick cardboard standup of the movie character Crocodile Dundee. Remember those movies of the Aussie backwoods adventurer? I don't remember where or how I got it, but I put it aboard the POS placing it in the front window. That was pretty neat because boaters using the Earman River were passing by my dock and they started to notice this guy standing in the front window. Boaters were taking their guests by our houseboat just to point it out and I could hear their comments of approval.

I took this one, or should a say two or three steps further. Working for Spalding Sports I was aware that we had similar stand-ups of some of our golfers and other athletes for promotional purposes, so I went to work on obtaining what I could. I was successful in getting life size stand-ups of golfers Lee Trevino and Greg Norman. Plus basketball player 7' 1" tall Shaquille "Shack" O'Neil.

I placed Lee and Greg in the two windows on the boat traffic side of the houseboat so passing boaters could view all of these three stand-ups coming and going. Can you imagine if you were in a boat headed towards the Intracoastal and all of a sudden seeing Crocodile Dundee, Greg Norman and Lee Trevino starring back at you? There was a local tour boat which took people on a couple hour cruises to see the local sights and our houseboat became one of their features, believe it or not. That tour boat started coming into the Earman River to show off this unusual sight.

What did I do with the 7'1" Shack O'Neil? He was too tall to put into the boat, so I lent it to a nearby North Palm Beach popular sports restaurant, "DeCesears, the Place for Ribs", a sports restaurant/bar where many celebrities would come for cocktails and dinner, including Arnold Palmer and many others that all of you sports fans would know. Tell you about that great restaurant later, it was a fun place for cocktails and dinner and unfortunately is now long gone. It is sorely missed by many of us old timers; we had so many great times there.

Back to the POS which could accommodate 2 to 4 adults for overnight sleeping.

POS Sleeps 2 to 4 Adults? #211

*M*Y PARTNER JOE DIDIA AND I talked repeatedly while working on the POS about how we would take our wives for overnight cruises when we got this thing in ship shape condition. He did most of the talking; I did most of the listening. First of all, to sleep 4 adults in this houseboat the four had better be really good friends. We were pretty good friends.

Secondly, my idea of camping out has always been a really good air conditioned Motel with a nice pool, restaurant and cocktail lounge. That is it, why in the world would any one want it any other way? Here's how I looked at it, for hundreds of years, actually since time began, human beings were looking for clothing and shelter. First, large leaves over poles, large leaves for toilet paper, large leaves for cloths, large leaves were very popular back then. Now people want to smoke them! After many centuries humans finally acquired actual housing, then indoor plumbing, heat, cooling, comfort, protection from big animals, small mosquito's, other humans, out-laws, in-laws. Speaking of mosquitos, I have always wondered why Noah let two of those creatures on board his Arc. Why didn't he leave them behind?

If I want to sleep under the stars I'd just go outside and look up, then go back inside with the memory of what I just saw, have a nice hot toddy, shake my wife's hand and go to sleep. Why in the world would I want to go back centuries, just to find out why all of my ancestors broke their backs to get me to this point? My parents tried their best to instill common sense into my brain, and they did. Camp out? Are you out of your common sense mind? I don't have head worms!

The time finally came, Joe told that he and his wife Alicia were planning on going north up the Intracoastal to a small lake where boaters anchored for the night, had cocktails and dinner under the stars in calm waters, listened to the night life, frogs and other scary creatures, then getting a good nights sleep and having a great breakfast, and then cruise back home. Would Dee and I be interested? I didn't even ask Dee, but told Joe I was interested all right, in how the two of them enjoyed their little venture, and wished them well. After all, what are friends for?

Off they went, smiling, Joe with a beer in one hand, steering the POS with the other. Boy did they look happy. He just knew Dee and I were going to be sorry we didn't join them for a good old time. All that sight seeing and the adventure of camping out under the stars in our newly born POS, we would miss al that fun.

Although the houseboat was brought back form the dead and outfitted with everything needed, I thought, wouldn't it have been nice if we had put screens on the windows and doors? After all, this is hot, humid Florida in the summertime; the POS does not have air conditioning, the windows and doors will have to be open for air to pass through that hot interior. On top of that in Florida there is hardly ever any breeze during the night.

Are you visualizing the portrait I am painting? I am sorry to say it a portrait of disaster. Joe and Alicia were eaten up by mosquitoes. They got absolutely no sleep and they were trapped right where they had anchored the boat. There was very little moon light and it was dark. If they wanted to pull up anchor and head back they could not see where the channel markers were. The damage was done, they could not shut the doors and windows because the little devils were already infested inside the boat, and they needed whatever little air movement there was because the temperature was in the eighties inside the boat. When they returned they could not begin to describe what a horrible time they went through. Joe really didn't want to talk about it.

There was never any more conversation about overnights ever again. We had fun for several years just touring the local waterways, having lunch and dinner aboard but back home to our dock before dusk. Eventually we tired of all the time we had to spend to keep the boat in tip top shape, sun and salt water is tough to deal with. Joe was not feeling all that good so we sold the POS to a nice young man who took it to the Carolinas somewhere. Unfortunately we lost Joe to cancer in October 2000.

Life goes on, the dock is empty again, but not for long. I thought I was done with boat partners, then my son Jim starts to plant some seeds in my cranium, something about a Pontoon boat.

Our New Pontoon Boat #212

I KNOW, I SAID NO MORE boat partners. But how can I turn my own son down? Jim had an idea about a "Family" boat, one that everyone, regardless of age or gender, could really enjoy. A pontoon boat, a long one at that, 25 footer equipped with a Honda 90HP outboard engine, so quiet while idling you can not hear it running. That is exactly what he talked me into, silver tongue kid of mine. This boat even had a potty on board in the rear, a canvas device could be raised up where a person could enter and use the portable potty in total seclusion. This is pretty neat and very important for older people who seem to have a need for access to a relief station such as this on a more regular basis than younger people.

This boat was very fast, the 90HP was more than adequate as most of these boats have a 60HP engine. Where we purchased it was kind of a story in itself. Jim shopped around and found a place in the town of Okeechobee that had the boat he wanted and the best price. This little town is located on the upper north east side of Lake Okeechobee. If you are not familiar with this large lake, take a peek at a Florida map and get an idea of the picture I am about to try to describe.

This lake is huge and supplies a large area of S. Florida with fresh water. The lake is not sea level so the water ways leading to it are not the same level. There are two locks, one on the east side and one on the west that must be used to enter and exit the lake. Jim decided that when we go to pick up the boat and trailer, rather than "Trailer" the boat all the way back home, we bring the boat back through the lake, it would be a fun trip and a way to get acquainted with the boat, then exit the lock on the east side which empties into a water way that continues east into the

Intracoastal waters in Stuart, Fl. Then head south using the Intracoastal waterway which will eventually bring us to our dock.

I agreed so we left my minivan and the boat trailer and we planned to return the next day in another car to pick up the minivan and trailer. That is a lot of extra work but Jim really wanted that long boat ride with our new 25' boat. That turned out to be quite an interesting boat ride. The lake is rather shallow so a slight breeze kicks up waves pretty quickly. The normal breeze in South East Florida comes out of the South East and that is exactly the direction we must travel, right smack into the prevailing breeze, or wind, as the case may be.

We have a cooler with some sandwiches and a liquid beverage to sustain us during this long voyage, which it turned out to be. The breeze picked up a little and so did the lake. We were headed right into the waves and the spray. No, not spray, it seemed like the lake itself was overflowing over our bow and right over us. There is no protection on a pontoon boat, just a little windshield in front of the controls, which stopped nothing. Talk about being soaking wet the entire slow trip through the lake to the lock, we had to go very slow because the waves still came spilled all over us.

Finally we reach at the lock and waited for the large doors to open on the west side of the lock. Then we entered and the doors closed behind us, then the water level started to go down as the lake level is higher than sea level. Down we go several feet, then the east doors open and off we go into the St. Lucie Waterway that takes us to Stuart and the Intracoastal, then south until we reach North Palm Beach and the Earman River where our dock is located. **Six hours,** soaking wet inside and out. What a maiden voyage, but it was fun and the boat operated great and it was very sea worthy and stable, the boat and us! This was a very strong safe boat which we found out on our first trip. It takes one hour by car to drive from Okeechobee to North Palm Beach, and as I said above it took us six hours to get our new exciting boat home.

What we decided to do next to protect our newly found entertainment center from the salt water and sea growth, why not install a boat lift alongside of the dock.

A New Boat Lift #213

I DECIDED TO HAVE A BOAT lift built so we could keep the pontoon out of the salt water. I contacted my friend who built my original dock in 1981, Bob Jandreau, of Robert Jandreau & Son to get the permits and then build it for us. Over the years Bob and I became friendly as we frequented the same watering spots. He was a good old tough guy, worked all his life on the water and in the sun. Good man and more than fair price wise, Bob always seemed to do more than what was contracted for.

The lift could not be extended into the water and had to be built on one end of the existing dock, which ran east and west. We picked the west side of the dock and the lift would run from the south, or towards the bank of the river pointing north towards the house. It had to be large enough for the 25 foot long Pontoon. Bob suggested we expand the dock as well so we had the expansion running the length of the lift which gave us large area where we could put a table and chairs on the dock. It looked like a small dance floor and the dock was no longer a "T" design. Our dock was growing rather large, as you might imagine.

During this boat lift construction one day tragedy struck the United States, it was September 11, 2001, the day the twin towers in New York were destroyed and so many people perished at the hands of the terrorists. Bob Jandreau and his crew were working on the lift when I got a phone call from son Jim who asks me if I had the TV on. I replied I did not and he excitedly told me to turn it on that something happened in New York, an airplane slammed into a building and it was on all the news channels. I had a TV on the back porch and it was the nearest to me so I turned it on. What I saw was smoke coming from a very tall building and it didn't sound like the reporters knew what had happened up to that point.

I ran down to the dock and told Bob to come quickly, something bad just happened and it's on TV on my porch, come watch this with me. He did but by the time we got to the porch the second plane had just hit; now they knew it was no accident. We sat there in shock, as all of American did, not wanting to believe what we were seeing, and then the buildings, first one, then the other started to collapsed spilling smoke and dust over the entire area. You know the rest of the story. What a terrible day, we sat there just numb. Finally after watching for what seemed eternity, Bob slowing went down to the dock, spoke to his crew, and they left for the day. It was time to mourn, time to try and make sense out of all of this, time for prayer, not time for work. The world would never be the same, and as I see it, it really isn't.

Family Fun on the Pontoon Boat #214

*N*OW WE ARE ENTERING A different experience with the family as the Pontoon boat is really a great vessel for all ages because of its versatility. We could not go out in the ocean with the houseboat but we could with the "Sun Tracker" pontoon boat if the waves are no more than a foot or two.

And it was also a fast boat with a 90 hp outboard there was little drag in the water with two large pontoons that pretty much sat on top of the water. Most boats push through the water at slow speeds. For a boat to move fast it must gain speed to get the boat on "Plane", so it is skimming along on top of the water and no longer sitting low in the water. The pontoon boat is already on top of the water so it is ready to go, it doesn't have to push through the water and gain speed to get on top of it.

As far as the number of people we could have on board the load instructions gave us the maximum amount of passengers in total pounds. That makes sense since there was a big variance in size, little kids, larger kids, big kids and big adults like me. We could take up to twelve various size people on board without much of a problem and there was plenty of seating. Sometimes we would add several portable beach chairs when we had a large gathering. We had to have life jackets for all, under all the seats there was adequate storage space. We had life rings, a flare gun and fire extinguishers, everything larger boats are required to carry, all U. S. Coast Guard approved. This is a very stable sea worthy vessel but caution should be used at to how rough the ocean is before going out into it. That rule, or common sense, covers all small craft when dealing with the Oceans and the Gulf of Mexico.

Backspin a little here, rough waters brought back a memory I had forgotten about concerning our first boat, the small cabin cruiser. One day Dee and I took my brother Dick and his wife Bessie for a cruise and we headed for the ocean. Going through an inlet can be dangerous as the currents are very strong and some days it can be worse than others. This day as I started towards the ocean and while I was going through the inlet we are almost to the ocean when I realized I should not be doing this as the waves were very high with very strong currents. But I had committed myself and I can not stop and turn around, the boat would be subject to being flipped over by the current and those incoming waves. I had no choice but to continue at a rather high speed to combat the conditions. I simply told everyone to put on a life jacket, sit down and hang on to something because we were going to bounce around petty hard. I had to get through all of this rough water and continue out into the ocean beyond all these waves and currents where the water is calmer, and then it would be safe to turn around. I am hoping that one of the engines doesn't quit on me as they do on a lot of occasions as I am going to need the power of both engines.

This is not over, now I have to maneuver the boat back through that inlet, which is more dangerous than coming out because now I am going to have all this current and high waves at my back. I am not steering into it, which is much safer going into these conditions than having them pushing the boat from the rear. The key to this is I have to go faster than the current and the waves; I can't let them catch up to my boat because it could capsize us. So again I looked at my concerned passengers and told them exactly what the situation was and what I intended to do, head back at a very high speed, it was going to be very bumpy and uncomfortable. Just hang on and say a prayer or two that I had enough ability to get us back safely. Well, I am writing about it, so all ended well. I went back to the dock and we had ourselves a couple of stiff drinks. I made an error in judgment; we were fortunate enough that nothing serious happened. Boating is dangerous, period. No one should take things for granted and one must be aware of what is going on, and what might be happening at anytime, including watching the weather, storms come up pretty darn fast, do not take chances, always take caution.

Forward spin. The pontoon was great for just cruising and going to a spot to snorkel, or swimming in shallow waters. Because the boat sat high on the water we could navigate very shallow areas by tilting the engine upwards so the prop was very near the top of the water. We could go into waters of two feet deep, with caution and at a very slow speed. That means in the inland water ways where there were channel markers indicating deeper channel water, we could go outside of those markers where other boats requiring more than two feet could not.

BOAT STORY CONCLUSION #215

ONE DAY SON JIM AND I are cruising along in our Sun Tracker 25 foot pontoon boat in the Intracoastal north and we are just south of Jupiter on a nice sunny day, we are headed south towards home and all of a sudden a **big bang** hits our ear drums and shakes us up. There is complete silence and the boat comes to a completed stop, dead in the water. We look at each other in wonderment not knowing what that sound was or why we stopped moving. What happened?

Our beautiful 90HP Honda outboard engine fell off into the Intracoastal Waterway, that's what happened! We are dead in the water and there is pretty active boat activity all around us and we have no control of where the currents are taking us, so boats are kind of dodging us. We rush to the back of the boat where the engine once was. What a feeling seeing that empty space. We did not loose the engine completely as all the control cables and gas lines were still hooked up to it, so we were dragging the engine along with where the current was taking us.

The look on Jim's face was something to behold and I am sure he saw the same forlorn look on mine. Disbelieve and anxiety along with concern, what the heck do we do now? We flagged down another boater who was more than agreeable to tow us to safety. There was a boat ramp launching area not too far from us and he got us there. We secured the boat and then dragged the engine out of the water. To save that engine since it was submerged in salt water, the engine would have to have immediate attention to remove any salt water from within the unit within 24 hours or the engine would be badly damaged.

There is no reason to go any further with that part of the story, it was Friday so it was a difficult thing to accomplish, but we got the job done. Why did it drop off? It should not have happened; it appears it was not fastened properly coupled with salt water over a period of time was the reason. Obviously, the boat was no longer under warranty. After the proper repairs Jim and I decided to sell it. No one to my knowledge ever makes any money on selling a boat. We are no exception, now that is three boats that cost my kids some of their inheritance.

I am free again. The dock and boat lift look really good, empty. No money sinking into the water and disappearing forever. A couple of years go by and then it happens again, son Jim comes to me and tells me he wants to buy another Sun Tracker Pontoon boat, this time not a party boat like we had but smaller in length, 18 foot, Bass model fitted with a couple of fishing chairs in the front, plus other benches, no potty on this one though.

Jim pop's the question, "Dad, would you go into a partnership with me on buying this boat?" My reply, "No way, I am no longer interested in being in the boat business." I continued, "Jim, my boy, you are a grown man, you on your own with this one. However, you may use my dock and the boat lift, rent free. Just take care of them."

I did it; I was no longer a partner in the boat business. My son listened to me, which he always does. That pontoon boat is still down there on the lift, and I don't have a darn thing to do with it. Oh, the joy of it all. That concludes my boat so that brings me back to the great game of golf.

GOLF, GAME OF A LIFETIME #216

SWITCHING GEARS FROM BOATS TO golf, the game of a lifetime for many, but unfortunately not everybody. I had to give it up due to a really bad left knee, which I had a total replacement finally in 2000. I played golf with that bad knee all my life but it was Arthur who finally did me in, arthritis got so bad I could not make much of a turn and some of my best drives were pathetic. I was not having any fun so I finally hung it up. Do I miss it? You bet, in my opinion golf is the best game ever because it is a lifetime game for most and also because of what golf teaches a person as a human being.

Before I get into all of that, for you non golfers what I am about to write is not just golf, it is about things in our life that I think will be interesting to all my readers, golfers or not. Some of this will be a little scattered as I write about what as it pops into my mind. That's the way it is these days, and thank God for just that! I will even touch on one little reason why golf is not growing and that has to do with caddies, but more on that later as well.

Why is golf so great? For many reasons and not all will be in this story. First I would like to start with what my impression of how individual sports compare with golf, which is what golf is, it is not a team sport. And all team sports are important too as sports have saved a lot of individuals from getting into trouble. Learning how to be a team player is very valuable in life itself. Learning to cope with playing all alone in individual sports is something else. It is just me as an individual, there are no teammates to help me or back me up, and I'm naked, all alone. I found out about myself pretty fast, am I capable? Can I compete? Do I have the desire to compete on my own? I will find that out pretty quickly through individual sports.

To me there is only one other individual sport that compares with golf, and that is bowling. Some of the other individuals sports that come to mind are tennis, ping pong, and hand ball. I'm sure I am missing a couple however the ones I have just mentioned are reaction sports, I need to react to a ball coming at me which gives me little time to think about what I have to do. I react and hit the moving object. Hitting a stationary object in my mind is much harder to accomplish! As you will note I said "In my mind" and that is exactly what makes it so difficult.

I have bowled a lot in my younger days, the normal Ten Pin game and the Rubber Band Duck pin game. All bowling alleys are the same dimension but the balls and pins vary deepening on the different type games. What does not change is you have a ball and a certain number of pins which are standing still at the end of the alley. As I get ready to bowl my mind starts to kick up all kinds of thoughts. I have to kick out the negative thoughts and concentrated on the positive and try knocking down all those pins that are just sitting there not moving. But I as an individual I am beginning to make all kinds of moves to knock something down that isn't moving. Hitting a moving ball is easier because it is a reaction with little time for bad thoughts to enter into the thinking process.

Golf is such a mind game, some of the best golfers in the world, past and present, will tell you golf is 90% mental. Bobby Jones once said, "The game of golf is played within five and one half Inches, the distance between your ears." It is just me all alone trying to hit a little golf ball. For most people just getting that stationary ball in the air is an accomplishment let alone getting the ball to go where you want it to go. I could write for hours about all the intangibles but I won't. What I am attempting to do is explain why golf and bowling as individual sports are different than other reaction sports. Can you begin to "See" the difference? The mind comes into play much more because you have time to think before you react. That makes is more difficult for a lot of reasons, it is hard to think positive all the time when so many bad things can and do happen.

There is a saying that applies here that I have used before, which is:

"If you understand this,
No explanation is necessary."
"If you don't understand this,
No explanation is possible."

More Golf is a Game of Honesty #217

THE GAME OF GOLF BUILDS character and honesty. Have any of you golfers reading this ever cheat on the golf course. Well, I have, several times. I have never cheated while playing in an event or a match but starting out as a kid I did things I should not have been doing. I can excuse those little things because I didn't know the rules very well then, if at all. That does not count because when I knew I was doing wrong does count. I can tell you honestly that the few times I rolled the ball over or moved it away from a tree, something like that, then my next one or two shots were terrible every time. Not one time that I did not follow the rules did I get away with it, I never made par or birdie, I made double bogies and triples.

I found something out about myself and the game. I knew I was doing wrong and my mind would not let me hit a good shot after an infraction. Never, so that taught me a great lesson, cheating does not pay; it penalized me in more than one way, the bad shots themselves and also my conscience I learned to take what life gives me, be thankful as it could always be worse, and do the best I can under the circumstance. That always works better for me. I can live with myself because I know I am doing the right thing. I had been taught that by my parents but sometimes you have to learn about those things on your own. But my parents taught me how to recognize my faults. We all have some and some are almost impossible to overcome, but honesty is easy, it always feels good.

Fair play is the only way. I love to see kids playing sports if they are able. It helps build quality individuals. Team sports teach a person how to be a team player; one person does not make a team. Make a team better perhaps but the term "Team" is just what it means. Then individual sports take all of that to a different level. All good stuff and I would strongly recommend encouraging your kids, grand kids to find a way to play golf. You, and they, will never regret it. I think most golfers will tell you that. Just ask one, see what they say about the sport, regardless of their ability. All golfers get something good out of the game that impacts them as a person, even if though they might not realize it.

Another thing that I learned, playing a round of golf with someone I don't know very well, if at all, It does not take long for me to recognize what that person is all about. I think it is impossible to hide someone's true personality on a golf course. It is amazing, I learned about myself too. I have tried to correct the things I didn't like about myself, little things I might do, a reaction to a shot, good or bad. I tried to be someone others would like to play a round of golf with.

When it comes to business, lunch and a round of golf with a customer can be most rewarding. It seems that a certain trust is created, a bond of some kind between the participating people. Many long time close relationships are created after a round or two of golf. It is a wonderful business tool. It can also reveal many different personalities and gives clues of the best way go about dealing with those different personalities. In sales, in any kind of business, you can not treat everybody exactly the same. I always had to figure out the best way to deal with those differences with my partners in business, my customers, and my friends as well.

Caddies and Golf Carts #218

*I*S THIS A STRANGE SUBJECT? There are a couple of different reasons for me to bring this up. One is from a personal playing history. One is for the "Good of the game". Has it disappeared?

Long before golf carts came to be when I was growing up there were caddies at the private country cubs and some at the public courses as well. Most were young kids, but in the days of tough times there were men without work trying to feed their families as well. I am going back here to the thirties and forties and into the fifties. I never caddied because I had a paper route and sold magazines to earn my spending money. I also cut grass and shoveled snow to make money. As a matter of fact my mom taught me how to save, and I bought War Bonds during World War II. I saved enough to get me all the way though high school, and beyond without my parents giving me an allowance.

A lot of kids earned their spending money and in many cases helped their family's get by as well by caddying. A lot of those caddies became golf professionals and many caddies became future golfers. Most courses were closed on Mondays back then but caddies were permitted to play golf on that day, free of charge. Most did not have golf clubs but were loaned clubs. They didn't need balls because they found their own while working their trade.

My point is, the game of golf is struggling somewhat and there are many reason why. My story is not going to deal with all of the reasons, just one little one, the caddies who came into the game as just plain golfers and also those that became golf professionals, sadly, is gone. In their place are golf carts. Golf carts do not play golf, caddies did. They were very important for the growth and future of the game. For the most part, they are gone and so are thousands of future golfers. Since golf carts thousands of kids never get introduced to the game and never enter this great sport and become the backbone of future golfers.

A large percentage of those caddies came from low income to middle class families and had very little chance to be exposed the game of golf. That opportunity is gone, and I believe has caused a very big dent in the golfing population never to be replaced. Those kids today will never get that opportunity to get off the street and find something to keep them out of trouble while learning there is something better. There are two big losses here, golf and productive young people that the game helped produce.

With regard to my personal history concerning playing with a caddy, that did not happen until I started to work for Spalding in the late fifties. My dad introduced me to the game because he was a golfer, he started playing at the age of 27 and that would have been in 1925. I was nine or ten when he gave me and my brother cut down hickory shaft clubs. When I got old enough to play a complete round of golf and through my high school days we carried our own clubs. As I said, I never had a caddy until 1957. Before that walking a course with your own bag was all that I knew and I never had a problem with that.

Then the first time I played with a caddy I felt very uncomfortable. But it was really a pleasure just walking the course with the others in the foursome, and thinking about my next shot plus conversing with the others in the group. That was really fun, kidding each other and just having a good time together. Then carts started to take over and there was less interaction within the group of four, we were separated in twos most of the time. We arrived at the location of our golf balls quickly, what I felt was lost was the walk between shots and the time during that walk I was thinking about the layout of the hole and how I wanted to play the next shot. All that was in a hurry up mode and during those years where we did use caddies it seemed like my scores were always a couple of strokes lower than when we used carts. I definitely felt I played better walking the course with a caddy and I know as a foursome we intermingled much more. It was just different. Those who never played with a caddy will never know that feeling and understand what I am saying. Walking the course with a caddy was just simply a better way to play the game of golf.

Here is a quote from Irishman Dermot Desmond: "There a three joys of golf: how you play, where you play, and whom you play with. And the first two are overrated."

I am getting closer to retirement so its time to wind down my Spalding career.

Getting Close to Retirement #219

*M*EMORIES AND MEMORY GO TOGETHER don't you think? I have been writing about things I remember, I became 84 July 22nd, and that is today, the day I am writing this, so I don't consider my memory is too bad or too good either. Many of you have been commenting on how I remember all those stories I have been writing. This is true to a point, I have been writing about things I do remember which is not too bad, but … Let me give you an example … …

In the August issue of GOLF Magazine there is an article about "The Last Duel" and I quote "It was the final time they would go head to head. Fifty years ago, Ben Hogan and Sam Snead thrilled the millions watching *Shell's Wonderful World of Golf.* The two aging legends summoned a stellar display of shot making." This dual was in 1965 and I am living in the Cleveland area.

I don't remember that program. And in my mind I should have because I have always been a fan of Sam Snead long before I went to work for Spalding. I ended up calling on Sam at the Greenbrier Resort in W. Va. as one of my customers. I even sat down one time and had a couple of beers with Sam. I was also a big fan of that early TV program because there was so little golf on TV in those years I was hoping it would create more interest in the game and create more players.

My point is I don't think I missed very many episodes of this program and because Sam was my hero in golf at the time I would have never missed that program with those two giants of the game going head to head, but, **I don't remember that program!** So I am admitting that I have memory problems, there are some things I just don't remember.

I have gotten off the subject of this story a little and it will not be the last time as things pop into my mind from time to time. Now that really sounds like 84, which is good. You know I was thinking it might not be a bad idea if you, whatever age you are, sat down and wrote your stories, you might be surprised what you come up with. Exercise the old brain, you might be surprised, and it could be fun for you to go back in time, give your kids and grandkids some of your history they don't know about. You don't have to tell everything you may remember either.

I am running out of stories about Spalding, or at least I am going to end those stories soon. But I still have several before we get to July1, 1995 my first day of retirement at age 64, which is thirty five years with Spalding over a period of 38 years. I am getting closer and closer to retirement.

Old A. G. Spalding & Bros. #220

*I*T MAY SOUND A LITTLE strange to you when I sometimes sound off about things I came to dislike about my all time favorite company, old *A. G. Spalding & Bros.* I have always loved the history of Spalding which over the years introduced so many new products and or improved products. Plus the game of golf was brought back from Scotland by a Spalding executive who was visiting that there in the late 1800's.

My problem over the last years was witnessing the demise of the first sporting goods company in the United States. 1876 was the first year that Albert G. Spalding started making baseballs. Our country was 100 years old at the time. When the United States celebrated its 200 birthday in 1976, Spalding was celebrating its 100 birthday.

Spalding filed for bankruptcy in 2003 after 127 years in business and 8 years after I retired. No, it wasn't because I retired either. I have decided not to say it was greedy owners who bled the company without regard to its future. And I won't say it was also because of some bad in house management as well. It is over so who am I to point fingers at anybody, so I have decided not to. So no, I am not going to go into all of that, what is done is done and what ever I say will not change anything. So I am not going to say those things. Who am I to judge?

You may still see the great Spalding name out there as the official ball of the National Basketball Association league is the 'Spalding Top-Flite 100" ball. The golf division of Spalding, Top-Flite, was purchased by the Calloway Golf Company so you will still see some Spalding Top-Flite golf products in the market place. The other division of Spalding, all the other sports equipment was purchased by a uniform company, Russell Southern.

We former employees have no connection to the old company,

because there is none. What a shame. No, I am not bad mouthing the old Spalding, just the one I had to put up with in the last 10 or so years before retirement. Most of my friends in sales were at least 12 years younger than I and most of them did not get to retire like I did. I was also fortunate as I had a choice when I retired, a monthly retirement check or I could take my earned retirement benefits out in one lump sum by rolling everything over into an IRA, which I did. I simply said at retirement, let me have my money, I'll take that IRA and pay myself and handle my own investments. Boy was that the right decision. I also had a 401K I had been putting money into for years so Dee and I were and are fortunate as I didn't loose any benefits when the bankruptcy happened, except a $10,000.00 life insurance policy.

In my later years the salesmen's compensation plan changed and we no longer were provided with a vehicle. I bought my own and the company paid a mileage fee. No more station wagons for me.

No More Station Wagons #221

*W*HEN I WAS NO LONGER were provided with a company station wagon I still needed a vehicle to haul around a lot of samples, plus a lot of golf balls, so my first purchase was a Ford mini van. After that van I got really fancy and I purchased a Ford custom van with the expanded top, plush upholstered seats and I even had a TV mounted above the rear view mirror that I could watch while driving. No, I didn't do that, it was more for my young kids at the time, it was an ego thing.

The biggest draw back was the gas mileages, it was terrible. It was really a good looking van, but not practical so I went in the opposite direction with my next van, it was just a plain old van which had room for five people and a big space in the back for lots of product. From ultra fancy to just a plane spacious truck.

Then I finally ended up with what I had really wanted for years. In 1990 I purchased a four door Lincoln Town Car. I figured the last years I might as well go out in style. I no longer needed to carry many samples, just a lot of golf ball stock and the trunk in that automobile was very large, I could carry 300 dozen balls in there easily.

The last five years was not easy, business conditions were not too good in the retail golf business and many of my customers had credit problems. I had a really touch credit manager to work with and naturally I thought he was too tight with the credit. But I am not going into all of that, I'm just going to wind down my last five years with that Town Car and retire early. I wanted to go out at age 63 but there was a health insurance problem. Our company policy would only carry me and Dee for something like a year and a half until we got to Medicare age of 65. So I arranged to retire shortly before I became 64. Then when that came close the company asked me to stay on and train my replacement and put me on a straight salary for three months until my 64th birthday. Mixed emotions as you might imagine. What was I going to do with all my time on my hands now? Can't play golf everyday and I don't like to fish.

In 1988 I joined the Knights of Columbus and became pretty active with them so I did have some kind of activity to keep me occupied somewhat so more about that next.

THE KNIGHTS OF COLUMBUS #222

*B*ACKSPIN A LITTLE, GOING BACK to 1988 I joined the Knights of Columbus, the Santa Maria Council 4999 located in Palm Beach Gardens, Florida. The foremost princiles of the Knights are: Charity, Unity and Fraternity, that is the three Degrees. There is a fourth Degree that was added in the early 1900's and that is the Patriotic Degree which features the Honor Guard I am sure most of you have seen, the Knights in uniform with fancy hats with plums. and they carry a sword. I am a fourth degree member but I am not a member of that elite group simply because I don't want to wear that hat. Not really, I'm just not into wearing uniforms.

It is ironic that as I just started to write about joining the Knights, the obituary of the Grand Knight (President) when I joined, Steve Borg, appeared in the paper. He was 88 and was born in Malta. RIP brother Knight.

I have never regretted joining because of the good things the Knights stand for and their charitable contributions to needy causes. The "Supreme" headquarters leaves it up to the individual councils to decide where and to whom they donate money. In recent dollar donations each year is in the neighborhood of $90,000.00 given to local charities of our choice. A couple of school tuition assistance programs, churches that need money, girl scouts, boy scouts, youth sports programs, scholarships for needy children, and Persons with Disabilities, ARC, our Tootsie Roll Program, and more.

Dee and I have made so many new friends over the 26 years I have been a member. We have a very active Ladies Auxiliary who meet once a month and have their own charitable fund raisers. They help the council in so many ways and are so very helpful in helping us set up for social activities In our large hall, such as decorating the tables and the hall itself for dances and other social events.

MORE ABOUT THE KNIGHTS #223

*O*UR COUNCIL HALL WAS BUILT in 1985 and the membership at that time worked very hard to pay off the mortgage and the bonds that were sold to a few members to fund this project. We have been debt free for quite a few years thanks to all that hard work. Our income then came in form various ways, dues is a very small part as they are only $25.00 per year and our membership is about 400.

We use to rent the all for weddings, anniversary's and other events but that was a very big undertaking, lots of man hours by our members, a lot of work to make a few dollars. After we were debt free we decided not to rent the hall anymore, it just was not worth it and we got tired of cleaning wedding cake out of our carpet. Fortunately we no longer needed that income. Why? Because we have a very successful bingo program and I will write about that later.

Our Knights of Columbus Santa Maria Council 4999 being the charitable organization it is can not own anything and can not accumulate any monies; after all of our expenses we must give the excess dollars to charity. So we have two corporations, the Knights and the Home Corporation which was established to build and operate this facility. We name it the "Columbian Building Association, Inc." It has its own officers and 15 directors. Every member of the Council is a member of the "CBA" as well. So our Council rents the facility from the CBA and that is how it is funded.

These Home Corporations are becoming fewer and fewer as our Supreme leaders are not in favor of these large facilities and would rather have a K of C Council in every Parish. I personally don't agree with that but who the heck am I to take a stand like that. It just appears to me after watching over the past 26 years that several Parishes who used to be a part of our Council broke away and established a Council of their own. I have observed that these Councils become more of a Parish men's club and do little to generate charitable endeavors, money or otherwise, like we do. Strength in numbers, you bet!

Many people really don't have any idea what the Knights of Columbus is, or does, even many Catholic gentlemen. So I decided I am going to tell you just what our council does. I have this opportunity and I am going to do just that in my next chapter.

"WHO ARE THESE MEN CALLED KNIGHTS AND WHAT DO THEY DO?

What Does Santa Maria Council 4999 Do? #224

"Who Are These Men Called Knights and What Do They Do?"

The foremost principles of the Knights of Columbus are:

CHARITY, UNITY AND FRATERNITY

*K*NIGHTS OF COLUMBUS SANTA MARIA **Council 4999** are proud of its charitable and fraternal works throughout the council year. The past year the Council has made charitable donations of **over $93,000.00** to various **Church, Family, Youth, Pro-Life and Community** activities. We also spent over **$20,000.00 in Fraternal expenses toward Council Activities.** Of course money does not tell the full story. Our Council of **400 Brothers** has **volunteered over 21,000 hours to various activities** and more than **7,500 hours** to Fraternal Services. We are in solidarity with our Priests and religious. Our support to our Catholic Faith and Church is the core of our organization.

CHURCH ACTIVITIES

Our Council volunteered over **4000 hours** to Church Activities.

An annual Religious Appreciation dinner is held in honor of Priests and religious in our area. We have a different speaker each year but our Bishop, S.K. Most Reverend Gerald M. Barbarito, D,D,, J.C.L., has attended every dinner we have held since he has been our Bishop as our Honored Guest.

Retreat for Council members at Our Lady of Florida Spiritual Center. Round table established at each of the three Parishes, St. Patrick, St. Clare & St. Francis of Assisi. The object of providing assistance to Pastors as needed. The members of the Council are involved in many of the Parishes' ministries.

In excess of **500** Bibles and Catechisms were distributed to area hospitals, nursing homes, prisons and council members.

Council supports the "Keep Christ in Christmas" program by erecting billboards at each of the four area churches and the council hall.

Support a monthly Adoration of the Eucharist as St. Clare.

A Memorial Mass is celebrated in memory of all deceased Brothers.

Members lead a weekly Scripture Study class at St. Clare.

Members lead a R.C.I A., (Right of Christian Initiation of Adults) program.

Contributed funds to Deacon Ministries.

Contributed funds to support Vocations for Priests.

Contributed funds to the State Vocation fund.

Contributed funds to sponsor 10 Seminarians.

Contributed funds to the Seminarian Burse fund.

Donation of funds given to the Poor Clare Sisters at Christ the King.

Donation of funds to St. Francis Building maintenance fund.

Donation of funds to St. Francis Choir.

Donation of funds to Our Lady of Florida Spiritual Center.

Supports St. Francis of Assisi, St. Clare and St. Patrick churches.

FAMILY & COMMUNITY ACTIVITIES will be explained in my next chapter.

FAMILY & COMMUNITY ACTIVITIES #225

"Who Are These Men Called Knights and What Do They Do?"

FAMILY ACTIVITIES

*C*OMMITTED OVER **6,000 HOURS** FOR visits to the sick and bereaved. Council host annual Christmas Party at nursing home and Council hall.

Council Ladies Auxiliary hosts a Kentucky Derby event.

Transports members to and from doctor visits and hospital therapy

Visit shut-ins and hospitalized members. House repairs for widows.

Participates in Rosary Life Chain.

Widows of deceased members are invited to participate in all functions.

Council assists widows with transportations and shopping.

Members make calls to individuals on the sick list.

Prayer cards are sent to individuals that are on the sick list.

Mass cards and special Knights of Columbus condolences sent to deceased members families.

Pallbearers supplied to any Catholic family requesting assistance.

Funeral receptions upon request are hosted at the Knights hall including lunch no charge to the deceased family.

COMMUNITY ACTIVITIES

Volunteered over **7,500 hours** to community activities.

Fund Drive for Persons with Disabilities, ARC. Tootsie Roll

Program, over 100 workers, members, wives and children, working at different locations, giving over **500 hours** and collecting over **$6,000.00**

Supports and donated funds to Special Olympics.

Supports and donated funds to "Support our Troops" including care packages.

Council holds a Super Bowl party.

Collect clothing for Saint Vincent de Paul thrift store.

Council picks up and delivers food every week for the needy.

Receive and distribute used eye glasses.

Council receives and distributes used wheelchairs, walkers, canes, crutches, etc.

Members donated 30 pints of blood.

Council subscribes to "Morality in Media" and supports the war against pornography.

Operate an Easter Love and Food Basket program.

Donates time and funds to Saint Vincent de Paul Food Program.

Council supports and funds VA Hospital Veteran Services (VAVS)

Members volunteer at the VA Hospital.

Collect clothing and distribute to the needy.

The next chapter features our **Youth & Pro-Life Activities.**

Youth & Pro-Life Activities #226

"Who Are These Men Called Knights and What Do They Do?"

Youth Activities

Volunteered over **1,000 hours** to Youth Activities.

Sponsored Scholarship Programs.
The Father William O'Shea Scholarships are presented by Fr. O'Shea and our Grand Knight to two students at St. Clare Catholic School.

Supports St. Clare Catholic School by operating booths at their Mardi Gras fund raising event.

Council sponsored and donated funds to Youth Sport Programs.

Sponsored a Basketball Free Throw contest at local schools.

Sponsored two Scout troops and donated funds to Scouting.

Members assist in CCD and other School Programs.

Donations made to the St. Clare Tuition Assistance Program.

Council sponsored scholarships at St. Clare and All Saints schools.

Sponsored scholarships for members & member's children.

Donated funds to Hope Rural School in Indiantown, Fl.

Pro-Life Activities

Volunteered over *1,500 hours* to Pro-Life activities.

Supports attendance at March for Live demonstrations in Washington, DC.

Supports and recognizes individuals active in Pro-Life activities.

Supports and recognizes women in challenging crisis pregnancies.

Distributes Pro-Life literature.

Supports Birthline/Lifeline operations

Supports the Right to Life of Palm Beach County Fair booth.

Maintains three Pro-Life memorials located in area Parishes.

Organizes and oversees the annual Pro-Life Poster Contest for High School students.

Again
The Three Principals of the Knights of Columbus

CHARITY ... UNITY ... FRATERNITY

This somewhat concludes what the Knights are all about. And again, what the last three stories were what my Council has done this past fiscal year which is July thru June. That should give you a better understanding and I will continue with more of my history of my twenty six years as a member. I think you will find it an interesting on going journey as I have so far.

My Involvement in the Knights #227

*Y*es, our Council Hall has a men's lounge with a bar. We do have a liquor license and we sell our beverages at very low prices. But I want to clear the air a bit right now because I have personally heard people say the Knights are a bunch of drinkers. I can not speak for other councils that may have there own building and liquor license like we do but I can tell you we do not have a drinking membership. First of all our bar is only open when we are having a meeting or an event. Then and only then is our council hall open. A member can not come to our hall anytime he wants and expect to get a beer, we are not open.

Our beverages prices are quite affordable; a soft drink is $1.00. A beer is $1.50. A glass of wine is $2.00 and a scotch, gin, vodka, bourbon, or a blend is $3.00. We do not make a lot of money on our beverage sales, a little, but we don't look for our income coming from beverage sales. We want our members who are active to be able to purchase a beverage at the lowest price possible because we are happy they are an active member. Unfortunately, most non profit organizations have only a small percentage of their members are actually active in participating in the organizations programs. "So few do so much" is very true statement concerning our membership and is typical of most organizations.

As a matter of fact sometimes we have a hard time trying to serve drinks no charge. Believe that? Well, let me give you an example, one night at the very end of our fiscal year we have an appreciation night for active members but ever member is invited. It is called "Knights Night Out" and is only for our male members and quests, no ladies. We have various entertainments, this year we had a magician. Our bar was an open bar, all drinks were no charge. In addition so was the meal no charge and it was a lobster tail and a filet steak with all the trimmings. With over 400 members how many would you guess would take advantage of something like that? I'll bet you are wrong. We had about sixty and the bar was not overly busy either!

Now I have to admit one thing, the average age of our membership is "Deceased!" That may be part of the reason even free drinks and a meal like that doesn't bring in more than what we had. What a wild place, you may say. Yeah, you may say that, everyone one was gone by 9 PM. We started cocktails at 5 PM, dinner at 6, entertainment at about 7:30 and the bar was open all this time.

I kid about the age of our membership but it is quite old. One reason is our location, paradise. Many of our brother Knights are from the north, they have retired and have moved to paradise and transfer their membership from their Northern Councils to ours.

I am told that almost all organizations like the Moose and Elks for are having a problem obtaining new members. One reason is the younger generation seems to be tied up more with both partners working and raising a family plus they seem to have other interests. Our council has maintained a membership level of around 400 for, I think, about the last ten years so we are holding our own even with the high rate of deaths each year, which is in the teens. We have been fortunate lately to have a few younger men join our Council and it looks like we are doing quite well considering.

I really haven't gotten into my personal involvement as yet have I? I have always felt that If I join something I have to be involved.

Join Something, Be Active #228

$\mathcal{W}$ HILE I REALIZE WE ALL have different personalities, desires, feelings, visions, degrees of responsibilities, few are leaders, many are followers, I respect everyone's individual makeup, that is what we are born with. So I don't mean to "Step on anyone's toes" with my remarks concerning this story and the subject.

Many of us are not "Joiners", I am one of them. Although throughout my life I have been involved with many different things I really am not a joiner. I really envision my self as independent, but I did join the Knights of Columbus. And I immediately became active because I don't see why anyone would join anything and then not be active in some way. Because someone talked you into it perhaps and you couldn't say no. Maybe you think by paying dues each year that helps the organization? Your dues are not what is needed, you are what is needed. If you're being ignored and not being asked to do anything, which is what we as Knights are guilty of, ask one of the active members or officers what you can do to join them and become active.

I did. First of all, I just can't sit back and do nothing, I guess I am to nosey. Any job I have ever had I wanted my boss's job next. Or, be my own boss, which I think I was in my last years with Spalding. I really think my immediate superiors just flat out ignored me and that was great because nobody bothered me. I am getting off the subject here a little so I'll back up a little.

As a new member of the Knights I was attending all the meetings and whatever events that was going on. But not one time did anyone ask me to do anything, or join any committees, yet they were always looking for help. The best way to get help is to ask someone to do something, not just ask for volunteers. So one day after a meeting a few of us were sitting at the bar having a beer, and they were offices of the council. They got into a discussion about the upcoming new fiscal year and needed to fill in a couple of positions. I am sitting there just listening. One says to the other, how about so and so for the Advocate's position, maybe he will take it if we ask him.

First let me explain there are several officers' positions one goes through and eventually end up as the Grand Knight. The Grand Knight is like being the President. The Advocate is one of those positions and is responsible for any legal matters that may arise. So there I am listening to all of this and the Brother Knight they are talking about made his First Degree with me but did not attend very many meetings. As a matter of fact he was a neighbor of the person who brought up his name. Well, when that was suggested I had all I could take of this conversation.

So very politely I spoke to them in low tones that I am known for, "What the hell do you think I am ground meat! You're going to ask a guy who doesn't even attend meetings and I have attended everything since I joined. Why don't you ask me?"

That was twenty six years ago and I haven't stopped since that day. Not too sure that makes everyone happy, but on the other hand, most of those guys in that conversation are no longer with us, RIP my Brothers. That is how I really got started as a very active Knight. And that has carried over into my retirement years, thank goodness for that. I really don't know how I could have spent all these twenty years of retirement without something worthwhile to do. Think about that if you are just sitting around doing nothing, get up and do something. You will never regret it. Some times helping others you are also helping yourself and those around you.

More Knights Activities #229

*W*HEN I BECAME ADVOCATE I was still working my butt off with Spalding. We sales guys on the road do not have 40 hour weeks. Even if not traveling overnight the hours most of us work in a week is closer to 60. Most days are like 10 hours, that's 50 hours, then paper work at night and Saturdays, plus returning all kinds of telephone calls, it can be 60 hours easily. That does not give a family man a lot of extra hours to do other things, and I always played my one round of golf per week on Saturday afternoon. But busy people find time to be busy; I still found time to be an active Knight. Yes, I even ended up being a Grand Knight, but the journey to that position is another story.

Well I might as well tell that part now. There are several officers' positions going through the "Chairs" on the journey to becoming the Grand Knight. While doing this when I became the Advocate, I was also approached and asked if I would consider becoming the Treasurer. Think of that, a sales guy becoming a Treasurer! I said, "Why not." I'm not bad with keeping records and details, my bouts with the IRS taught me that plus my mom taught me how to handle money. Most sales guys don't spend a lot of time on details. Being the Treasurer was fun, and I held that position for a total of seventeen years.

Getting back to those "Chairs", the term in office of the Grand Knight in our Council is one year, so each year officers move up through the chairs. I moved from Advocate to Warden, then to Chancellor. The next step would have been Deputy Grand Knight, then Grand Knight. All of a sudden I was only two years away from becoming the Grand Knight when I realized it would not have been fair to the council, or to me, of becoming the GK when I was still working at least 60 hours a week. I was also the Treasurer and I was working Bingo two nights a week, and that is another story.

One of the strengths of this council is having Brothers going through those officers chairs, starting as the Advocate, it takes five years, is that you learn what the heck is going on. We are not continually trying to find someone to fill in all those positions year after year. As we move up, we only have to find one brother to start at the bottom. So I did not like the idea of dropping out of the rotation, but it was the only thing to do at the time because I would not have enough quality time to take on the responsibilities it requires of being the Grand Knight.

I wrote a letter to the Grand Knight at the time and explained why I had to drop out and asked that he replace me at once so the flow of officers would not be disrupted. I kept the Treasurers job and continued to work Bingo and was also on other committees as well. I felt that when I had more time I could get back into the chairs and become the Grand Knight. As you can see, I get involved, it is just my nature, I can't sit around and let others do things and me do nothing.

The fact I never went to college made me realize without that degree to get ahead in life I had to out work the next guy. Weather that may be right or wrong, that is how I felt about it. So why not become the Grand Knight someday and if I see things that can be changed for the better, I am going to do it. But, that's another story and my main job now is being a good Treasurer.

THE TREASURERS JOB #230

*T*HE BROTHER KNIGHT WHO WAS filling in temporarily as the Treasurer until someone would volunteer to take over that responsibility was getting pretty darn despondent. And nobody was offering to do so. I would like to point out that over the years working with an organization run by volunteers that when you ask for a volunteer to fill a position it is rare that anyone steps forward. What has always worked for me if I needed help with a project that I was the chairman, I did not ask for volunteers, I picked out a few Brothers who I really wanted to work with and would go directly to them and I would ask them for their help. Nine times out of ten that Brother would say yes. That really works, people like to be asked, and it makes them feel wanted.

So the Brother who was the acting Treasurer must have know that, and he came to me and asked me if I would consider taking on the responsibility. At that time we had recently switched from a manual system to a computer system called Quicken. I told him my background was sales, not accounting, although I did keep very good records for a sales guy.

I said, "Why not." I was not near retirement at that time but I felt I could find the time to do this and learn the Quicken system, which is what I use to this day for my personal bookkeeping. Boy does that save me time when it comes to accumulating what I need for the IRS every year. I ended up being the Treasurer for seventeen years with two years out while I was the Deputy Grand Knight and then the Grand Knight. After those two positions I continued as the Treasurer for about fourteen of those seventeen years, giving up the job about three years ago after an argument with a couple of Brothers who are now my distant Brothers.

German background temper and just don't step on me without damn good cause. But, that's another story you will not be reading about. Those guys are wonderful people but not worth my ink.

I really enjoyed being the Treasurer; it was a busy job as we are a busy council with a fairly large budget of around a quarter of a million dollars. Before you ask why I would expose that dollar number let me explain, we are not a secret organization and our books are open to the public so I am not giving away any confidential information.

TREASURERS RESPONSIBILITY #231

*I*T IS MORE THAN JUST writing checks and paying the bills. First of all the K of C has done a good job in how payments are made. In other words there are cross checks to be followed for the prevention of any dishonesty. The Treasurer can not write checks without a written authorization from the Financial Secretary. It all starts with a form called "Request for Payment" which must be made out and signed by the requesting Brother, this goes to the FS for his approval and then to the Treasurer. The FS cannot sign checks and the Treasurer can not approve the Request for Payment form. It is a good safe system that I have always been more than comfortable with. The entire paper work system is very professional and all paperwork is open for anyone to view. Everything is transparent.

Each fiscal year (July thru June) a budget is prepared and presented to the officers for their input and approval. I as Treasurer would prepare the budget about six weeks before the beginning of a new fiscal year. Using past history plus any new request received by me, or any additional new expense was inserted into this proposal. Both income and outflow dollar figures would be equal, but not necessarily a must; under certain circumstances they can differ if approved by the officers. Then the next year's budget will be presented at the next business meeting for approval by the membership. This is a lot of work but after years of doing this it is really not that difficult.

Every year I used to make up a partial payment schedule of charitable donations with dates that money would be available for payment requests by the chairman of those particular donations. It is that chairmen's responsibility to fill out the request for payment form but it that is not done when the schedule date has passed the treasurer has to watch for this and get in touch with that chairman and notify them they are tardy and or what is the problem, if any. A heads up treasurer is a watch dog and he is the first in line of taking care of the council's monies.

The treasure is required to give an updated monthly report at each of the twelve business meetings. A copy of the report is given to all officers so they can follow the report as it is given by the treasurer. Believe me if there are small errors those officers seem to catch them. Most mistakes are typos and sometimes this can be embarrassing to the treasurer. As many times as I have gone over those reports before presenting them, it seems that it is hard to catch my own mistakes. So I got tired of all the bad humor coming my way when mistakes were found.

I changed by presentation by stating at the beginning of my report that I have intentionally inserted one, two or three errors for the officers to find while I was given the report. If there was any, I had already told them they were there for them to find. If they didn't find any I would simply scold them for not finding them and I was not going to tell them what they were. There were none of course but I was just going to let them keep looking. That diversion made my life easier and until they read this, they were not aware of what I was doing. Since I am no longer the treasurer I am no longer in harms way. Ha! Ha! guys, gotcha on this one, got me off the hook and you fell for it.

And now it's time to raise your hand and holler, **Bingo!**

BINGO #232

*A*FTER WE STOPPED RENTING THE hall our main income is generated from our Bingo program.

"Bingo, Raising Funds for Charity"

A little history, before our present hall was built in 1985 our council's Brother Knights was running a bingo program for St. Clare Church in their social hall. About the time our new halls construction was completed the church decided to discontinue its bingo program so the Knights no longer had the obligation of running that program. Santa Maria Council 4999 was operating a first class bingo program in our present hall for thirty years. I would like to give you a few details about our program and about some things that have happened over the 24 or 25 years that I have been a bingo worker volunteer.

Number one, I have had a blast; I really enjoy working one or two nights a week. Our charitable corporation will only let us operate twice a week, which is Monday and Friday. In this state, public bingos can operate 7 days and evenings a week, and for years we had a lot of competition in Palm Beach County, especially the Northern Palm Beach County. So before I get into the personality of ours I would like to give you an idea of how we made out over the years with all that competition.

We are still operating and almost all of our public bingo competition has disappeared over the years. Now before some of you bring up the fact that other charitable organizations still run bingo programs, yes they do but they are not in competition with ours because there is a big difference between ours and theirs. Locally, organizations' like the

Moose, Shriners and Elks run bingo once a week, usually around noon and it may last a couple of hours with prize money much smaller than ours.

To give you an idea, we open our doors at 4 PM because many bingo players like to arrive early and sit and read or just visit. We also have a food concession operation and we serve a full dinner plus sandwiches, snacks, deserts and beverages for those whishing to arrive early. We start selling game paper at 5:15 and we start playing at 6:30 with a 15 minuet break at about 8 PM, and bingo concludes at about 10 PM. And playing time is almost 4 hours. Our pay out each evening is a minimum of $3,500.00. We do run a major bingo program.

As for public bingo, they have expenses we don't have. We own our own building free and clear of debt other than normal operating costs while our competition has rent to pay and people to pay to run their operation plus all the costs of the equipment. The start up cost is substantial. All our help are volunteers so we have no one to pay salaries and our bingo computer has been paid for long ago. We have eight large TV screens located around the hall and the next number to be called is shown on those big screens. There are also two large bingo boards at each end of the hall which indicates what game is being played and how many different ways it the games can be won, plus it shows all the numbers that have been called.

Bingo Volunteers and More #233

$\mathcal{T}$WICE A WEEK SOMEONE HAS to put everything out on the selling tables that is needed to operate a night's bingo and ready the Bingo computer machine which holds numbered balls from 1 through 75. The game paper for each game must be placed by the cash drawers. Special games signs are changed each night which keep up with the changes of what their payout is. To complete all this it takes about an hour.

The cost of a starter pack $11.00 which includes 25 games. An additional 21 games are available for a total of 46 games. If a player wanted to purchase the minimum of everything offered it would cost $23.00 and that includes the $11.00 starter pack. I believe I had mentioned before our total minimum payout is $3,500.00.

Since the economy went south some years ago, it did affect bingo as you might imagine. Bingo attendance is not near what it used to be and there are reasons why so many public bingos have closed. Unfortunately the bingo community is shrinking due to the fact people grow older and it appears the younger people today have many other things to keep them occupied, so fewer people are getting involved with the game. There is very few young people playing and not many males play either; our customer base is approximately 90% females.

Our bingo attendance in season use to be 150 to 185 players a night and during the off season 110 to 150 but now It is 130 to 155 in season and 90 to 130 in the off season. That is a very sharp decline. Many of our players have played at other locations and they have told us over the years that our program is the best in Northern Palm Beach County. So we are surviving but as I see it bingo will keep declining in the future. I don't have a crystal ball but I do see ours surviving for at least 10 more years

Bingo Players like Family #234

SOME OF OUR PLAYERS HAVE been coming since we opened up 30 some years; they are very loyal to us. Unfortunately it is almost impossible to know everyone by their first name but I have managed to remember maybe 60%. We have gotten to know each over the years and we have developed many friendships. One of my jobs is selling two games, the Speedy which is played four times and a floating six pack game which is played twice. They are only .50 cents each and pay out $50.00 per game. After many years of doing this I know how many games that 90% of the players buy. They don't even ask me, most just say, "You know what I want!"

Our Bingo Chairman for the past sixteen years is Richard Guglielmo, and he has been part of our program for about 27 years. I have been working along side of Richard for 25 years and about 10 years as his cochairman. Richard really knows the game and more importantly he knows what Bingo players like and what they don't like. My knowledge of the game of bingo itself is limited as I have only played bingo once, I'm only a worker helping make our program successful.

Richard is approaching the age of 82 and shows no signs of stopping. Richard has all the special games and special events scheduled around holidays all down on paper for the next three years! If he should retire I honestly don't know who could ever replace him, I think it will take a least two people to do what he does by himself.

Some of the daily specials, a player plays for free on their birthday. If a player bingos on the date that bingo is being played then that player will receive a free bingo pack which is worth up to $16.00. there are also two drawings each month for a months free bingo and that is worth nearly $500.00. There are a few other specials but that give you an idea, Richard is always giving chances to win something extra as much as he can. He likes to give back something to the players because of their loyalty to our program which is, **"Bingo, raising funds for Charity"**

MORE ABOUT BINGO #235

I TALKED ABOUT FREE BINGO ON a player's birthday before but one of my highlights was one evening three years ago it was my 81st birthday, July 22nd. No, I did not play, I never do. It was also the same birthday for five other people that night, one of our workers and four of our lady players. So I made kind of a big deal about it by introducing each one individually then all six of us had our picture taken and that picture appeared in our monthly bulletin. I also gave a copy of that picture to each of them as well.

This story doesn't end there. I knew that another one of our players was 99 years old and she would be **100 years old in December!** After much discussion with our bingo chairman it was decided to celebrate her birthday in advance, the same evening of July 22nd.

So after all the commotion and picture taking of the six of us birthday kids, I announced that there was one more birthday that we wanted to acknowledge, even though it was not today's date. I said something like this, "I have one more birthday to announce, one that is far more important than the six of us who have ours today. This young lady has a birthday coming up in December but we decided not to wait until that date which is 5 months away. At least she was conceived 5 months prior to December and her name is Hilda Hoffmann who will be 100 years old!" "We wish to celebrate her birthday today."

It was a complete surprise to her and she was escorted up to where I was standing. I gave her a big gentle hug and then I continued, "Hilda, the K of C Santa Maria Council 4999 Bingo program is presenting to you, beginning today, **"Free Bingo Forever."**

She is very shy and a little bit embarrassed but my hug broke the ice, they always do! Ha! You noticed I said "Forever", not "Life" because to me there is on heck of a difference. She continued playing for about two years, but I have not seen her for about a year and a half. She started using a cane, then a walker and you could see her getting pretty frail. I am happy to tell you she is still with us, will be 104 this December and she is in an assisted living facility up the road in Jupiter.

In conclusion, that night we received a standing ovation for our presentation to this lovely lady and many told us what a wonderful gesture on our part. Made us feel pretty good but do you know I had several old farts that came to be and appeared a little jealous that someone was going to play free. A couple players asked me If we would do the same for them when they reached that age and I replied, "Of course we will!" Now really, come on, of course we would and be happy to do so.

Can you imagine? I did not say all of our players were gracious and kind, some are very competitive and can be a problem at times, but I guess we can be also. Thank goodness that is the exception and not the norm; they are all God's children and sometimes act like children. Growing older does that to some of us, doesn't it?

Bingo Workers #236

*I*T TAKES A LOT OF volunteers to run a successful bingo program like ours and at this time we have about 40 brothers working. We can always use more because of sickness, vacations, and other reason. I have the job of opening for both Monday and Friday evenings. I arrive around 3:30 to 3:45 and unlock the doors; there are always a couple already waiting outside. Our girls running the snack bar are sister, Shirley Green and "Snookie" Mayes, are already there preparing dinner and the snacks. I unlock all the doors and turn on the TV's which shows a bingo ball and the number of the ball is today's date. I open the safe and retrieve the bag with our money "Bank" for making change and put the proper amount in the cash drawers for the six sellers.

The floor workers start to arrive around 6 PM and we usually have four to six floor workers. Their job is to sell additional game paper that the players who wish to buy. When a player raises their hand indicating they have a bingo a floor workers will go to that person and then relay the numbers on that bingo paper. That number is entered into the computer and then the TV screens show the actual bingo.

There are normally four callers who share the duties of calling the numbers for the 46 games. Some of the callers will work the floor as well. So we are talking about six or eight volunteers who bring the total number of volunteers working a night's bingo to about 15 each evening. We have about 102 evenings of bingo a year so that adds up to a lot of volunteer hours.

Bingo ends at approximately 10 PM and after we clean up putting all the trash into our dumpster, and putting the bingo equipment back into the storage area, there is food waiting for us, prepared by our kitchen chairman Frank Bono and his assistant Ted Przybilski. So we relax with some really good food and beverage. I arrive home at about 11 PM so I have just put in close to eight hours.

Smoke Free Bingo? #237

A FEW OF OUR NEWER MEMBERS are telling us we need to upgrade our facility because they think it should look like some fancy hotel ball room. I do not disagree with that totally and I would personally support a sensible improvement program. I just wish that some of our newer members could have seen what our hall looked like a few years ago when we still allowed smoking and still had our original furnishings. I will try and paint a picture of what our main hall has looked like in the past 30 years

Do you remember when smoking was permitted almost everywhere? Well, our council hall was no exception and about 65 % of our bingo customers' were smokers. The best we could do at the time, since we could not put a divider in the middle of our hall, was to separate smokers from non smokers the best we could. Half of the hall, the east side, was the smoking area and the west side was for non smokers. Ash trays were on all the east side tables and they had to be dumped and cleaned after each night's bingo, a job in itself. That separation didn't help much because smoke travels. We had six very large "Smoke eaters" hanging from the ceiling which were designed to rotate the air around the upper ceiling blowing air from one smoke eater to the other and as the air entered these very loud monstrosities the air passed through a series of filters removing as much smoke as possible. Changing these filters periodically was also no small choir and dirty as all get out. We had large exhaust fan in the attic located in our west wall we used to pull out smoke through the ceiling tiles. This also pulled out a lot of air and our A/C's had to work harder to keep the place cool.

The cigarette smoke was really bad, some nights you could see a blue cloud hovering overhead. On top of all that, where the walls are painted white now, there was wallpaper which was not light in color. Three quarters of the walls were and still are a dark mahogany colored wood paneling. All the long tables tops at that time were also a dark brown and the plastic chairs were a dark maroon color. The dance floor was only half as big as it is now and was a dark color as well, and so was the carpet. The lights were not as bright because the glass covering was badly stained with smoke tar, and so were the white ceiling panels. Upon entering the building the stink from cigarette smoke was terrible. The whole place stunk badly and when I went home after working bingo I had to take off clothes in our garage because they smelled so badly of cigarette smoke.

My goodness this was a depressing looking place. Our newer members don't know what bad looked like, they have no idea what we were going through. We had a hard time getting our brother volunteers to work in all that smoke, so what did we do? We considered a non smoking bingo and started doing some research. In those days there were many public bingos and all allowed smoking. We searched further and found that around the country that bingo halls that eliminated smoking went out of business. We were running out of volunteers and the poor non smokers had no where to go, there were no non smoking bingo places available for them.

We decided to bite the bullet and we wanted to clean up the place but that was useless unless we got rid of the smoke. We knew we would loose many of our smokers to our competition because many of them told they would go elsewhere if they were not permitted to smoke. We took the chance that if we advertised a "Smoke Free Bingo" we may attract other non smoking players who were playing at other places and people not playing at all who would play bingo if there was a no smoking place available. What happened when we put an end to smoking is next.

WHAT HAPPENED NEXT? #238

*C*HANGE DOES NOT COME EASY and the changes we were planning were also very costly. First of all we made the announcement of our decision to end smoking in our hall. We also announced that beyond our normal 15 minute break we were going to add another break of 15 minuets during the middle of the second half which would give our smokers two breaks to go outside for a smoke. We knew that the second break would not go over to well with our non smokers so we also announced that during that break we would add an extra game that would pay $50.00 and the game would be free for anyone who wanted to skip the break. That gave the non smokers something to do and everyone seemed happy with those changes, even a lot of the smokers. We did loose some smokers but not as many as we thought and our bingo program survived.

Next, we made several changes to the hall, first we got rid of the wall paper and painted those walls an off white. We cleaned the ceiling and the light fixtures, we had bright lights again. We eventually removed those six loud smoke eaters. Can you imagine seeing those ugly large smoke eating boxes hanging from the ceiling during dinner dances? We washed down all the wood paneling. We replaced the dance floor and the carpet. We replace all the dark tables with the present light colored table tops. We replaced all the plastic chairs with heavy duty tan colored chairs at a cost of $17,000.00. I forgot what the tables cost, probably around $10,000.00. The cleaned the carpet that rises from the floor to about four feet high was dirty and smelled of smoke. We repainted all the doors, there are three double and two single doors and they were painted dark brown, they are now a light tan. We updated the area we call the waitress station, where we serve food. Now maybe our new

Brothers can visualize what our hall looked like then and what it is today in comparison? Not really that bad at all, is it? And we are not a hotel, we raise money for charity.

In addition to that, our present porch was three times as long as it is now. Two thirds of it was enclosed and a new entrance way and an office have been added. We had a double door entry and the first thing to be seen upon entering was the ladies and men's restroom signs, nice first impression.

We completely remodel our lounge, removed the old bar which was where the piano is now and built the present one. New carpet, tables and chairs were added. Pool table was where the bar is now. We made changes to the kitchen and upgraded it. Our parking lot is always in good shape because we take care of it, resurface when needed and restripe the parking areas. We want everyone to know we have not stood still these past thirty years. So my new Brothers if you are still interested in our council being further updated, let's do it, right after you join our bingo team and give us an hour or so of your time so we can make the money for all the improvements you want to make. and how about helping out with our Bingo program when you have an hour or two? That is where the money we want to spend comes from, help us earn it.

BINGO STORY NOT OVER YET #239

I STARTED OUT AS A FLOOR worker and did so for many years on both Monday and Friday before I eventually ended up handling the money and becoming a table seller, and finally a cochairman. As I have said I don't play bingo but have gained a lot of knowledge sitting beside Chairman Richard Guglielmo, one of the most dedicated people I have ever met. He actually does too much and worries too much about our success. What will be, will be, Richard. It really is up to the newer, younger members to carry on, heck your going on 83 years old. Relax a little my friend.

When I first started working bingo I started to think about the lack of security. We have a main entrance to the hall and then three other entrances into the main hall opening up to the parking lot and all doors are unlocked all night long. Players go in and out of those doors for a smoke and I started to think about the fact we have a big permanent lighted sign out front that states the hours that we have meetings and when we have bingo. We also put a sign that is on wheels out front a day or so before bingo advertising when we have bingo. I'm thinking, BINGO spells MONEY, lots of it and a all those ladies playing bingo wearing jewelry with money in their purses. We have four open doors with signs out front saying, "THERE IS A LOT OF MONEY IN HERE", and we have no security? I started to visualize that one night all four doors open at once and a couple of guys at each door with assault riffles come barging in demanding all the bingo money plus robbing everybody. Why not? The way I see it that is what we are asking for, so lets do something about that and make it safer for all of us. All of this could happen and no, I am not a negative guy, just someone who recognizes the possibility of a big problem that could very well happen.

We owed it to ourselves and our customers to do all we could to prevent something like that from happening and it was decided to hire a security guard to patrol our parking lot during bingo and then direct traffic leaving our property after bingo was over. The security guard was also responsible for checking and locking the three doors in the main hall fifteen minutes after bingo started. Players wanting to smoke had to use the main entrance. For years we used the Palm Beach County Sheriffs Department because our property is not really in Palm Beach Gardens but located in the county. So we paid for an off duty Deputy Sherriff and his vehicle, and it became more expensive each year.

Even though these Deputy's were off duty, many times they receive emergency calls and left us, leaving us without security. Not often but often enough that it was a concern. Because it was getting more expensive our officers made a decision to save that money and go without a security guard. We continued to lock the doors. It was not more than a month and we had three vehicles broken into on the same night. One was one of our bingo workers vehicles and he lost a personal computer along with other items he should not have had in his car.

So, back to a security guard and marked car with a flashing light, this time a private firm which was a lot more reasonable money wise. We are still using that firm and have had no break-ins or problems and they do traffic control as well. Security was not our only problem and I will touch on that, next.

MORE BINGO PROBLEMS #240

*T*HERE ARE MANY EXPENSES OPERATING a professional bingo program besides the facility itself. We have an outside cleaning company come in after bingo each evening to do a complete cleanup of the hall and rest rooms. One other big expense is Liability Insurance. We have to protect ourselves and the players against accidents such a people tripping and falling accidents and that insurance does not come cheap. Have we had accident problems in the past, yes we have?

One of the real dangers we have is the cement car stops we have in our parking lot. If you would like to get a few laughs someday come to our council when bingo is being played and just roam through the parking lot and see how people park their cars. First of all these elderly people like to back in so when they leave they can just pull straight out, they don't like to back out into other traffic going by in a parking lot, and I don't blame them for that, it can get ugly when there is over 100 people all trying to leave at the same time.

Unfortunately, when some back in their automobile they are not squarely in the parking spot, many times the cement car stop is exposed and dangerous if the people are not paying attention. We have many "Trip over's" happen, some just a few scrapes with some a little more serious and once we got sued. Not often but once is too many.

A couple of our exits have a very small step downwards that is troublesome at times. We have a light above each door to illuminate the exit and our lighting in the parking lot is more than adequate and is designed so we are protected insurance wise. One person many years ago sued us for quite a large sum of money claiming our parking lot was not lighted enough causing her to not see a parking cement car stop; she stumbled and did suffer some injuries. During all these allegations a light meter was used to measure our lighting and the lighting passed the test. She did not have a good case but personal injury cases that end up the court with a jury; the jury usually leans in favor of the injured.

The Insurance people are well aware of that and to prevent going to court even with a good case in their favor, feel they save more money by settling out of court, which they did in this case. And you know what happens then, yes, we soon got a notice of cancellation our insurance. It seems that insurance companies have a history of doing that, or at least upping the cost of the insurance. We had to find another insurance company and of course it would cost us more than what we had been paying. I will not tell you how much I like insurance companies. No, I won't, I don't swear much anymore.

Most of the time the people realize it is their own carelessness and do not cause a problem. Then there are the occasional "Professional fallers", people who deliberately look to make a few bucks. We had a least one that I remember. She sat near the door in the North West corner and when bingo was over all of a sudden there was a commotion, she was lying on the walk outside the door moaning like crazy while a friend of hers was screaming she could not see the small difference in the height of the pavement because of poor lighting. She had no apparent injuries and was complaining about her back, naturally. No scrapes from the sidewalk which is almost impossible. When I fall there I have always had a little blood somewhere, usually a scraped knee or a hand or elbow damage.

Two of our regular customers watch this woman kind of gently and intentionally sits down on the sidewalk and they told us what they saw. I asked them if they would be a witness in case we were sued and they said they would. We approached the women and suggested she was not hurt and might be faking her fall and that we had witness' that would support that statement. Her friend helped her up; she said we would be hearing from her lawyer, we never did and of course never saw her again.

I had a little knowledge about such incidents because by dad worked for the Pennsylvania Railroad for 45 years and was a personal injury claim agent! The stories of faked injuries he told us over the years was really amazing about what people would do to try and take the Railroad for money. Thank goodness we don't have too many of these problems but they do exist. As I have explained there is a lot of expense and other problems running a bingo program. For the most part, our operation runs very smoothly and we do have a good time with a lot of very nice customers.

More K of C Experiences #241

ECOMING A GRAND KNIGHT IS quite an experience in itself. Even going through the "Chairs", the different officers positions leading up to the "Presidents" chair I was not entirely ready for the top spot. And when I took that gavel in my hand for the first time the butterflies are there just like my first start on the basketball team, or trying to breath before my first "Tee shot" in a golf tournament. I'll never forget the first time I had to make a product presentation to a group of my peers at a sales meeting, I was wondering why I could not get enough air in my lungs and why did it feel like my legs were no longer going to hold me in an upright position. I never felt so alone in my life.

No, it wasn't that bad but when I stood in front of a group of people and conduct a meeting or a presentation for the first time in a new situation, it still was not easy. Everyone is looking at me and I started to feel undressed, and asking myself, "What the heck am I doing here and why?" What if I make a fool out of myself, what if I don't say the correct things, what if I ... ...?

I suppose everyone goes through these situations differently and those of you reading this that have had experience with something of this nature, you know how you felt about your first initial baptism under fire.

I had a script, an outline of how the Grand Knight is to run the meeting. When to I should rap the gavel, and how many times letting the audience know when to stand, sit, or whatever. I open the meeting and then ask the committee people for their reports. The only problem I had with this "Script" was that the print, the font size was perfect, if you had a magnifying glass! With glasses and bifocals, the podium the script is sitting on is two to three feet away and a microphone is three inches from my teeth, what seem to be the problems Bill?

Before my first meeting as Grand Knight I reviewed all of this and decided to rewrite the script. Not change the outline but change the size of the font so I could see and read it without a problem. Boy did that make a difference.

Instead of this … … Brothers we are abut to open this meeting in the first section … … …

To this… **Brothers were are about to open this meeting.……**

And … … **Let us stand for an opening prayer** …

I started each subject with a different color than black and separated the paragraphs by two spaces so they did not run into each other. That really worked and I never had a problem loosing my place or stumbling over the sentences. I also gave a copy of this outline to the other officers who would eventually become GK so they could follow along and become familiar with that script which will prepared them for being a future Grand Knight.

Having that script before me made my first meeting a much more relaxed nervous wreck. One thing I knew was I was going to make mistakes but show me a person who never made a mistake and I will show you that that person never did anything. So I wasn't worried about that, I'll just do the best I can. I learned that one of the most important things I must do is be prepared before the meeting starts. I talked to my officers and asked them if they were prepared to give their reports. And make sure my Deputy Grand Knight is ready to call on his different committee chairman for their reports, and did he ask his chairman if they were prepared as well. I simply wanted everyone to be prepared in advance. Then I feel confident the meeting will go smoothly.

Being the new Grand Knight I looked at the overall picture. The old saying "If it isn't broke, doesn't fix it." However there were things I felt could be improved. Standing still is like going backwards in my mind, so I set some goals with the thought of making things better than they all ready are. Why not, move ahead, there is nothing wrong with new ideas that are worthwhile pursuing to create even a better council.

My Thoughts and Goals #242

*M*Y FIRST THOUGHTS WERE, WE needed to change how we were conducting our monthly business meeting. When it came to "New Business" and "Old Business" and open discussion from the floor, our meeting was a large disaster. The only control we had at that time was a two minute time limit for anyone wanting to speak. Our council is a busy one so there are many things to discuss and decisions to be made. Some important and many not so important and during these open discussions arguments between Brother Knights was not uncommon. Some of these disagreements became almost uncontrollable and a few of these outburst pitted Brother against Brother, not a good situation. I had to fine a solution and correct this problem and our meetings were way to long, which caused some members from attending.

I know that I am only going to be as good as the people working for me, and I was fortunate to have had a very good slate of officers. This is not a one man show and to be successful, in my opinion, the best way to succeed is as a team, I must use my team, confide in them, and ask them for ideas and their input. Put my arms around them, and let them know what is going on, ask them for solutions, and never leave them on the outside looking in, that is not team work.

I had a very strong team and a very capable Deputy Grand Knight in Ed Souza. The DGK is the busiest officer of us all, I will not go into all of his duties but they are extensive. Ed today is a big part of the glue that holds this Council together. I confided in my officers and with Ed's help we decided we had to change all of this bickering during the monthly business meeting and the way to do that was hold a separated officers meeting prior to that meeting and go over any thing that needed a decision. Then report those decisions the officers made to the council members at the meeting.

I insisted that an officers meeting should not be on the same night prior to the business meeting. The main reason is I felt the officers needed to mingle with the members attending the meeting before and after the meeting, not be holed up somewhere separated from them. That is the Fraternity Degree after all. We decided to have the officers meeting, which is open to any member who wishes to attend, on the last Wednesday of the month prior to the first Tuesday, the day of our business meeting. A good thing too, because this meeting is rarely over in an hour and it usually lasts for as long as two hours. Can you imagine tying all that in one meeting? That's what we were trying to do.

That was a good start of my term as Grand Knight and I believe when accepting a position of authority I should have goals.

WHY HAVE GOALS? #243

THE TERM OF THE GRAND Knight is only one year and that passes quickly. To become a Grand Knight and just run a meeting 12 times without doing anything new, or see where things can be improved, or add something worthwhile, I think is a year wasted. I saw a lot of things that needed attention before I became Grand Knight and now I have the opportunity to do something about them. Sometimes a members voice is not heard, it should be, but sometimes it is not. The membership is supposed to listen to their Grand Knight and make changes if they make sense, and this was my time to have my voice heard.

The first thing I wanted to change is something that had always bugged me and that was the member's personal badges. All the officers wore very attractive badges, a dark blue background with white lettering similar to what I have tried to recreate below, as an example. This is what my Grand Knight's badge looks like after my term in office.

BILL FAULHABER
PAST GRAND KNIGHT
K of C Logo here
COUNCIL 4999
Palm Beach Gardens, Fl.

The members badges were awful. Before a meeting started we brought out this big case which opened up and inside were small badges with safety pin fasteners. They were small clear plastic plates with a small piece of cardboard with a members name on it which slipped into one end of the plastic, and the plastic was also yellow with age. You could hardly read the name and no one seemed to keep all this updated with new members so some didn't even have that wonderful piece of crap. After the meeting the name tag had to be put back, a member could not even take his own name tag home.

I always felt that this badge indicated the member was a second class citizen. I wanted the same kind of badge for the members just like the one the officers had but without a title, a badge the member could take home So I changed all that, I ordered new badges and I threw the old box containing all those ugly things in the dumpster.

More badges coming. We have a group of members who serve as pallbearers at funerals. At one time this was a very active group because one of our members, Bobby Fanning, was a funeral director. We performed this service for many people we did not know if we were requested, and Bobby kept us busy. But very few people really knew who we were. I started a badge program for pallbearers as well so people would see who we were. The badge was a little different as people did not need to know who we were as individuals but who we were as a group, see below.

PALLBEARER
KNIGHTS OF COLUMBUS
SANTA MARIA COUNCIL 4999
K of C logo here
Palm Beach Gardens, Fl.

Our group is still busy with our own members and family funerals but we don't do as many for people we don't know as Bobby Fanning is no longer living in Florida. We still get calls and we are happy to be of help, especially when there is hardly any family to attend these funerals. More badges and goals are yet to come.

More Badges and Goals #244

*M*Y NEXT BADGE PROJECT WAS for the bingo program, along with a change in shirts the volunteer workers wore. Actually I personally changed the shirt program before I became Grand Knight; the badges came a little later. The badge description is as below ...

RON GOMES
BINGO
k of c logo here
COUNCIL 4999
PALM BEACH GARDENS, FL.

I have always believe in name tags and badges for better communication between people who are strangers. Seeing a name makes it much easier to start a conversation. Our bingo customers did not know the names of the volunteer workers and this made the whole program much friendlier.

The bingo shirt issue was something else. Our bingo chairman in the early nineties was purchasing shirts but they were very inexpensive. He was buying them from a sporting goods store for $8.00 per shirt and they had no logo or identification. And they were all different colors so we didn't look like a team. I have always purchased all my clothes at wholesale prices since I was in the sporting goods business and I had connections with a few clothing suppliers. When we appointed a new bingo chairman, I took it upon myself to contact a local supplier; Boast and they were located nearby in Riviera Beach. Boast specialized in tennis and golf apparel and their specialty was stitching customized logos right into the shirt fabric.

I personally visited Boast and they agreed to open an account with our K of C Council so I could purchase directly from them at wholesale prices. I then took our K of C logo which was generic and I added these words around the logo, Knights of Columbus, Santa Maria Council 4999. I provided Boast with my revised logo and that logo has appeared on all of our council shirts since 1999. These were sports shirts, a three button placket with a knit color and a long tail so the shirt does not work itself out of the pants. These are very good looking shirt which I originally paid $15.00 wholesale, including the logo. Everything increases in price over time and I am now paying $25.00 per shirt. That same shirt in a golf shop with a logo would retail for around $50.00 to $60.00. I also prefer what I call "Happy colors", lighter colors as opposed to dark colors. Our team of workers is easier to see in a crowd environment and light colors do not show stains as easily, like sweat stains. Our basic shirt is white and our most recent colors beside white are gold and a pale yellow. When these three colors are mixed together they blend well and we look like a well groomed team.

As Grand Knight our team started to add new events, so just turn the page and find out what we did.

ADDED EVENTS #245

*D*URING MY TERM AS GRAND Knight we added a few events which I thought would be a strong addition to our current lineup of dances and other social events. We did not host a New Years party, so we went to work on that. Over the years most people have their own way of celebrating with friends or relatives so we didn't know how much interest would be generated. There were some members who expressed an interest but were concerned about our age group and would they be willing to stay out that late for a midnight toast. Since most of our parties never went beyond 10 PM I suggested, somewhat in jest, we could start the party at 6:30 and "Drop the ball" at 9 or 10 PM as it was midnight at that time somewhere in the world and all of our old folks might be happy with that arrangement. I was kind of kidding but also felt that that might not be a bad idea. No takers.

We did have a New Years party and with moderate success with about 40 people in attendance. It was small but everyone had a good time and we are still having a New Years Eve party to this day, but still with rather small attendance, up to 60 people. Everyone is gone by 12:05. Well, maybe a few minutes longer but not much.

We have many widows that we continue to send our monthly news letter and many continue to be active as a member of our Ladies Aux. But many have little contact with us outside or our news letter and our annual Memorial Mass which is held in honor of our deceased Brothers. This Mass is well attended and we serve light refreshments after the 7 PM mass at our Hall. Beyond that there are many widows we do not see often. While GK I sent a letter to all the widows urging them to join us at any event on our calendar, and an event like a dinner dance they were more than welcome to join us, free of charge, just as long as they would call me and let me know they were coming. Unfortunately there was not a strong response to that. But at least that was a direct contact with our widows; I did not want them to be forgotten. Then I came up with another idea, an annual Widows Luncheon. A formal invitation was mailed to all widows with a return self addressed envelope enclosed. The invitation was not only for the widow but for one guest if they wished. Why a guest? Because I realized that many widows no longer drove a car or they had a care taker, so their driver or car taker was invited as well. That made it a little easier for some to accept the invitation, and there were a few who did just that, they brought a driver and or caretaker with them.

With the help of a few brothers, George McDonough in particular as he prepared the lunch, we began our very first Annual Widows Luncheon with wine on the table as well. You might be surprise how many had a glass of wine, they really enjoyed it. And when I say table there was only one, I wanted everyone sitting together, not at separate tables. We held this in our lounge and we put many small tables together in a double row to accommodate everyone attending. If I remember correctly we had 24 people attending. Invited quests were our Chaplin Father Wm. O'Shea and Deacon Al Wesley. I was the master of ceremonies and there were no long speeches, but I wanted to keep them informed of what was going on in "Their" Council and make them feel they were still a part of it.

I wished there were more attending but the ones that did really enjoyed themselves and the event continued for about five years. Each year there were one or two less attending and I finally called it off for lack of interest. I tried something new and still consider it a success today. Maybe after all these years we ought to try it again, it would be a different group of widows unfortunately.

KNEE AND HEART PROBLEMS #246

*F*IFTEEN YEARS LATER, AM I satisfied with myself for the job I did? Not entirely but, yes, for the new things I tried and old things that I had something to do with affirmative change for the better. There were other small things we accomplished but my message is if you accept a responsible position, sit down and take a good look at what is before you, what has been going on, make notes of the good things and then make notes of whatever you see that can be approved upon. If everything is perfect, you have it made. But, everyone should have some personal goals that will be beneficial to whatever it is you are now involved.

There were two personal events that happened while I was Grand Knight. The first happened because of the second. Sound confusing? I'll try and explain what I mean by that. I have had two bad knees, both hurt playing sports, my right knee sliding into a base when I was about eleven or twelve and the left knee playing basketball when I was about fourteen. I had corrective surgery on both and I have played golf all my life with those bad knees. I am not saying that I would have been a lot better player if my knees were healthy, but I can tell you one thing, they were not an asset and most of the time I had to wear an elastic brace on my left knee for support.

Anyway, my knee Surgeon was urging me to have a complete left knee replacement as the cartilage was gone and my knee was bone on bone. I kept putting it off because I am a coward. Dee and I went on a cruise and my knee was so bad that when we hit a port, I could get off the ship but I could not walk around and sight see with Dee. I found the nearest watering place, sat down with a local beer or two and waited for Dee to come back and then we rebounded the ship.

After we returned from that cruise I contacted my knee guy and said, "OK Doc, I am ready, let's get this operation over with." The Doctor put his fingers on my ankle to measure my pulse in my lower leg. He looked at me and said, "Bill, there is something wrong here, your pulse is very week, I can hardly detect it, we need to look into this." As it turned out I had a blockage in my upper leg and a stint had to be inserted to open up the blockage. It didn't end there; I then had to take a stress test. Well, I didn't study for it very well because I failed it very quickly. The cardiologist stopped the treadmill, had me sit down, and he told me that I was to report directly to the hospital and that I could not go home first. I called Dee and informed her was going on and off the hospital I went.

I had one artery blocked 100% and one blocked 99%, that's what they told me and I still have not had anyone explain to me what difference 1% makes. Anyway I had a two way bypass operation. If I hadn't decided to have my knee done, who knows if I would by typing this right now, I was walking around about to have a massive heart attack and had no symptoms what so ever. If I had suffered a massive heart attack while on that ship I doubt if I would have survived.

That was in December 1999, I was 68 and one half years old. I sit here today as one of the luckiest people on this earth and I thank God for looking out for me as well. My brother Dick, who was 3 ½ years older, suffered a massive heart attack and passed away two months after I had my surgery. Dick had just turned 72, I got lucky and he didn't.

AFTER HEART BYPASS SURGERY #247

$\mathcal{A}$FTER THE HEART BYPASS SURGERY it took six months, June of 2000, before I was able to have my knee replacement surgery. That, if anyone one of you have had that done, especially 15 years ago, was rougher than open heart surgery as far as pain and rehab is concerned. This all happened while I was Grand Knight, I was a busy guy and so was my Deputy Grand Knight, Ed Souza. He had to cover for me a few weeks.

The end of our fiscal year ends in June and we had our Officers Installation program honoring the outgoing Grand Knight and the gavel is turned over to the new GK. I will never forget this one because it was only a couple of weeks after my knee replacement. I was still on a cane and most of this program the officers are in a standing position. I happen to sweat easily and wearing a coat and tie isn't cool for me and now I'm standing for this installation without the use of my cane. My knee is killing me and I am soaking wet with sweat. That was worse than the rehab I was going through. But all good things come to an end as did my term as Grand Knight. The title I now carry is Past Grand Knight. As the saying goes, "I am only a Grand Knight for a year, but a Past Grand Knight forever." By the way, my one year term happened to cover two different Centuries, 1999-2000.

As I have mentioned before, goals are important in life itself. The reason I have spent some time on this subject and the Knights is that there are many of our Council members who are receiving these emails. This may not mean much to a lot of my other faithful readers and I appreciated any interest you may have in all of this. I get on a soap box at times and I just hope some of what I have said will be worthwhile to my Brother Members and future Grand Knights. Goals, I will leave that subject with a challenge for future Grand Knights reading this, and all the officers as well. My challenge to you is, put some extra effort into "Membership". To me that is the most important goal, recruitment of new members.

I am not going into a long discussion about this except to say our council is trying to do a good job, but we have a long way to go. Set your goal to change how we recruit, our follow up with new members needs to improve as well. We are failing at this, and we all know it. This is not an overnight project and will take several years to correct. I challenge all of you to fix this, our present system is broken. **Now that is a Goal!**

HEART TO HEART CLUB #248

*M*Y FRIENDS AND FAMILY YOU are probably wondering when I will finally conclude these stories, You're not alone with that thought. I promise it will not be much longer as I am going to start to wind this very long winded series of stories soon. While talking about heart bypass surgery it just reminded me of two other subjects I became involved with after my surgery, the Heart to Heart Club and Cardiac Rehab.

I was first introduced to Cardiac Rehab and secondly to the Heart to Heart club. Palm Beach Gardens Medical Center where I had my surgery is well known for its "Heart" capabilities. Not all hospitals offer open heart surgery and this hospital has been at it for many years. Shortly after my surgery I was made aware of this Heart to Heart Club which is really not run by the hospital but do support this important support group, and it is run by heart patients! People like you and I who have heart disease which covers all sorts of heart problems, not just open heart surgery. Very often it is very hard to go it alone and support groups such as this is really a good thing to become involved with.

Depression is very common with heart patients and I have been fortunate as I have never had that problem, but I think I know why some go into depression. It is fear, and "Why me?" I am not qualified to diagnose any reasons why, but it has been my observation that I might be right. Help is available; and it's very worthwhile to become involved with a group that has the same problems.

The way I look at my problem or problems, I am still here to deal with them when so many are not as fortunate. I look at it as a second or third chance. I just look at the bright side, simply "Why not me", why am I still here when so many of my friends are not. I can't feel sorry for myself; I thank the good lord and my doctors, nurses and family for their supportive help. I have to be the opposite of depressed, and I am. Not everyone can do that, but by becoming involved with a support group I can see attitudes changing with many patients at each meeting because they see others with the same problems that are happy and productive. It is not the end, it is the beginning of extended life. And for some reason I've received that gift. So it should be a positive, not a negative.

What did I do when I joined the Heart to Heart club? Yes, you guessed it; I became very active.

Support Group & Cardiac Rehab #249

A s I mentioned, the Heart to Heart club is run by heart patients. It has a slate of officers and holds a meeting for members once a month. Each month there are motivational speakers, educational speakers, doctors, and pharmacy people are helping these heart patients more aware of what their problems are and how best to deal with them. The more we learn about blood pressure, how the heart works, and have medical terms explained to us, the more knowledgeable we receive, the more we understand what is going on within our body and that tends to ease our fear of the unknown.

Yes, I got involved, a Treasurer was needed because of membership dues. When I joined it was $5.00 dues a year and members received a monthly news letter. I accepted the job and held it for five or six years. The Cardiac Rehab nurses are also involved with this club; these two organizations are connected with each other. The Heart to Heart club is a non profit organization and because of this it has to have a charitable purpose. So our club donated money to an organization named Camp Boggy Creek which was located near Orlando. Young kids with heart problems attend his camp for a week and they are with other kids with the same problem. Many children can not afford the fee, so the donation from the Heart to Heart club helps to send one of those unfortunate kids to this camp each year

The subject came up of how the Heart club can generate more money because our contributions to this camp were not very much. No one seemed to want to go out and knock on doors for donations and no one came up with any kind of a money making solution. So I thought that I could solve the problem, and suggested a change with our dues being only $5.00 a year which only paid for the patient and not their spouse attending with them. The fact that we served light refreshments at the meeting the dues money did not last long. So I proposed we should consider raising the dues for the patient to $10.00 and if that patient attended with their spouse the dues for both should be $15.00 and they are both members. That would just about triple our income. We did that and no one opposed. Our contributions then jumped to about $1,500.00 per year for Camp Boggy Creek and that covered the expense of one child.

Support groups such as this are very important and I highly recommend them to anyone if they suddenly have a condition that is hard for them to deal with individually. Don't feel you can or must deal with the problem by yourself; sometimes we all need a little help. I have only touched on the subject of Cardiac Rehab rehabilitation so that will be my next subject.

Cardiac Rehab #250

$\mathcal{I}$ WROTE ABOUT THE HEART TO Heart Club but I maybe I should
have written about Cardiac Rehab first because I started rehab
first. I began cardiac rehab three weeks after my heart bypass surgery
and would you believe it, I'm still going. I am now in my 16th year and
look forward to it at 1 PM every Monday, Wednesday and Friday. If I
don't make all three in a week I get there at least two days. This rehab
is run by the hospital with a minimum of three nurses in attendance at
all times and a Cardiologist is on the duty as well.

Most medical insurances policies pay for 36 sessions for patients
that have certain heart conditions. During these 36 days a heart monitor
must be worn by the individual and their progress is closely observed
on a computer screen by one of the nurses while the patient exercises.
Before starting a nurses takes your blood pressure and everything is
recorded. Blood pressure is taken again after a full 10 minutes of activity
and then the third time after a cool down period at the end of the
session. During this hour the actual time one is supposed to be actively
exercising is about 50 minutes.

After the first 36 sessions insurance no longer covers the cost and if
you wish to continue you may do so for a fee of $8.00 per session. The
heart monitor is no longer required and is replaced with a clipboard
and an exercise sheet of paper used for recording your progress. I am
surprised that when I began in January of 2000 the price of $8.00 has
not changed. I hope they don't read this, they might raise the price.

Why am I still going there when I could belong to a health club
for a lot less money? For a couple of reasons, the nurses, the doctor
and the medical equipment available in case something happens. Yes, I
could go to a health club for a lot less money and I used to do that on

Tuesdays and Thursdays for a while, but being human, one day I said to myself, I don't think I'll go at my usual time today, and then one day I said, I think I'll skip today. Going to a health club as opposed to being regimented and committed to a certain day and time is not the same.

I enjoy and look forward to the cardiac rehab and have no reason to stop, I intend to go for as long as I am able. There are nine nurses who alternate and one nurse has been there for just about as long as I, and several others over 10 years. Same nurses for years and many of the patients have been going for years also, we are like family. The nurses address every patient by their first name, their memory is amazing. They are also active with and take turns in attending the Heart to Heart club meetings.

Most of the patients disappear after the 36 sessions but there are some who continue so some of us have know each other for a number of years. Unfortunately as time passes so do some of our cardiac rehab friends, but with this exercise I am positive it has given many of us a lot more time on this earth.

After years of observing new heart patients starting rehab, how do I describe this, is more than interesting, and maybe revealing is a better word. What I see in many of these patients' faces is confusion, depression; uncertainty and fear are words that come to mind. These nurses are wonderful the way they treat new patients by making them feel welcome with sincere tenderness and concern.

The nurses actually use me, and others who have been attending rehab for a few years, as an example of how important the rehab is as they often point us out to these new patients and ask, "Bill, how long have you been coming to cardiac rehab?" When I answer 15 years I can see the surprise look and their faces light up somewhat. What their seeing is people with problems just like theirs who are still around years later. That makes a big difference in their attitude and outlook. That makes me feel good too.

In conclusion, people who survive a heart attack, have open heart bypass surgery, or stents inserted into their veins, whatever the heart problem, we are still here when so many of our loved ones and friends have not been as fortunate. Instead of having a **negative attitude,** a question of **why me?** There is no doubt in my mind that should be a **positive attitude** and the question of, w**hy not me?**

This is **not the end**; we have been given an opportunity, an extension, **a new beginning.**

ANOTHER K OF C HIGHLIGHT #251

*T*HERE HAVE BEEN MANY HIGHLIGHTS in the past 26 years of being a member of the Knights and the one that stands out the most is about the small town of Pahokee located on the east banks of Lake Okeechobee. Pahokee is considered the poorest community in the state of Florida. Pahokee is a farming community and this story is about its migrant population, the St. Mary's Catholic Church and a priest, Father John Mericantante, and a 16th Century Icon, Our Lady of Bethlehem.

I first became acquainted with Father John in the year 2000 when there was an event hosted by his Parish. That event was called the Marion Festival. I will not go into all the details about that because that event was not about this story, just how it came about that Dee and I, and many of our Brother Knights, became involved.

The history of this Icon is, well, I can't personally describe it to you, but just maybe some of us don't even know what an Icon is. In Pahokee it is said there were mutable miracles that happened when people prayed to the Icon for help, mostly all medical conditions. Father John is somewhat of a small miracle in my mind for what he accomplished while he was Pastor there for twenty years. Before I write about that, I would like to relate the history of this Icon. So, next is some history of Our Lady Of Bethlehem Icon.

OUR LADY OF BETHLEHEM ICON #252

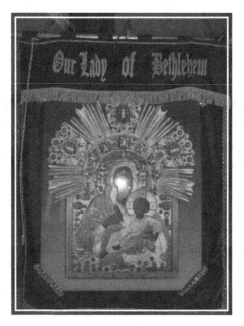

Is now located in Saint Mary Catholic Church, Pahokee,
Florida, and the message explaining its history is below.

When, Where, How and Why

*T*O UNDERSTAND THE GREAT TREASURER *before us today here in St. Mary Church, we must first look at the circumstances of the times in which it was first painted. Now somewhere in Russia, in the 16th Century a monk took to his call and began even as they do to this day the painstaking task of painting an Icon. The monk would have spent many fays in prayer and fasting before painting the images of Mary and Jesus that we see before us today.*

Don't let the beautiful solid silver fame encrusted with so many fine jewels fool you. The real value for believers is inside the precious frame on the tablet of wood and it is this small panel of wood that tells us the true age of our Icon. That it is from the 16th Century.

It was first there that the holy monk painted the image of Mary as the Mother of God and Jesus as her baby and then gave the wooden panel to a silversmith to have the frame and shield put over the simple images and to painstakingly the silversmith would cut the shield that at first hid the images that the monk had painted to reveal what we see today the face, hands and feet of the Blessed Mother and her Child Jesus.

Next a jeweler would be called in and the wealthy family for whom the Icon was made and who had commissioned the monk probably in the first place to paint the images would begin to donate sometimes all at once it they were the Czar's family itself of a noble family or sometimes over the course of years the Icon became dazzlingly decorated with precious and semi-precious stones.

Certainly the list of pearls, diamonds, emeralds, sapphires, rubies and garnets on out Icon is most impressive. But be not distracted. The real value again I say for the believer is not the jewels but the single sacred images of Mary and Jesus, looking out at us imploring us to notice them, to speak to them, to pray to them.

*Far from the 16th Century when Ivan IV (or the Terrible) as he was also called began to use for the first time the title TSAR which was the Russian translation for the Latin word for CAESAR, **this Icon was present for all the drama of Russian History.***

*And when in the 17th and 18th Century, as early as 1613 when Romanov was first chosen as Czar **our Icon was there!***

*And when at the same time under the Romanovs, Russia pushed westward taking the Ukraine and much as Poland **our Icon was there!***

*And when Peter the Great (1696-1725) sought to westernize Russian Society which lagged behind the rest of Europe **our Icon was there!***

*And when Peter the Great gained the territory on the Gulf of Finland and 1703 established St. Petersburg, **our Icon was there!***

*And when St. Petersburg became the new Capitol of Russia 1712 **our Icon was there!***

*And then later under Catherine the Great (1762-1796) Russia became the chief power of Continental Europe, **our Icon was there!***

*And when Napoleon in 1812 marched into Moscow **our Icon was there!***

*And when Russia and Austria made their Holy Alliance **our Icon was there!***

*And when in 1864 the serfs of Russia were emancipated, **our Icon was there!***

*And when the internal discontent grew and the last Tsar in the Romanov Dynasty, Nicholas II was assassinated with his entire family, **our Icon was there!***

***Yes there,** perhaps not in each event in the exact place of each historical occurrence, but yes **there in Russia** being prayed to, implored, beseeched so that through these sacred images of Mary the Mother of God and the Baby Jesus her Son, they might obtain the answers to their prayers or at least consolation and solace in their sufferings.*

Today this Holy Icon is not there in Russia but here with us. Today these Holy Images of the 16ᵗʰ Century await our prayers, our petitions, and our supplications. Now their History is mingled with ours. Now through what may be considered an act of great generosity or destiny through Mr. & Mrs. Edward Kahn, we at St. Mary Church now are to be the custodians of this precious Sacred work.

Now it is our turn to see our History as Divine watched and Guided by so Holy a Mystery where Mother and Child though in Heaven touch the earth through Sacred Objects and in return allow each one of us to turn to them and through them to touch the Face of God.

FATHER JOHN MERICANTANTE #253

OUR LADY OF BETHLEHEM ICON was acquired by Father John through Mr. & Mrs. Edward and Adele Kahn who own and operate an upscale jewelry store on famous Worth Avenue in Palm Beach. This Jewish couple and our Catholic Priest Rev. John Mericantante, of Italian decent from Boston, are close friends. At first the Icon was on loan to Fr. John as its custodian, and was to go with him wherever he might be transferred, and the Icon would go to the Holy Sepulcher Church in Jerusalem upon Fr. John's passing. Without explaining all the details, there was a change in that the Icon would remain permanently with Father John, and eventually, in the "New" Saint Mary Church in Pahokee, Florida. Father John retired at age 65 in 2013 after twenty years as Pastor of St. Mary's. Backspin time, I'm getting a little ahead of myself here. I'm just beginning my story about Father John and St. Mary's and Pahokee; forget about him retiring for a few more stories.

Fr. John and I have had many lunches together and I learned that he wanted to become a Priest since the age of six. His father wasn't so sure because he was an only son and he has three sisters. All his life Fr. John has rubbed elbows with the rich and famous but most of his priesthood has been spent serving the very poor. Fr. John will most likely be a little embarrassed when he reads all of this as he is one of my email "Buddies." Fr. John wrote a book after he retired; he never mentioned my name in that book but that is OK, he recognized the Knights of Columbus, and he is a Fourth Degree member. The name of the book is **"The Dangling Urinal: An Unconventional Catholic Priesthood,"**

I am not telling anything about Father John that he has not already written about in his book, so if he wrote it, I guess I am doing no wrong by doing the same. It is no secret that his mother and father were high up socially, his father was a District Manger for Ford and was a close friend of Lee A. Iacocca who became the President of the Ford Motor Co. His Grandfather on his mother's side owned and operated the famous Latin Quarter night club in Boston, where they became hosts and friends of famous people in all walks of life. But I don't want to rewrite his book here, just giving you a little of his background. Fr. John also studied in Rome for 4 years, and then spent several years in Chile where he eventually learned the Spanish language, which he would need when he was appointed Pastor of St. Mary's in Pahokee at the tender age of 45. By the time I first met Fr. John he had been there for six or seven years. I would be a fixture in Pahokee at least once a month for the next fourteen years.

PAHOKEE #254

$\mathcal{P}$AHOKEE IS A FARMING COMMUNITY located on the east side of Lake Okeechobee and is the home of many migrant workers and their families. There is no direct route to get there from this area because of a large area of wetlands. There is no road going east and west until about 15 miles north of where Pahokee is located. Taking that road west for 15 miles to Port Myakka at the lake then head back south for about another 15 miles to Pahokee, the trip is 55 miles. There are quite a few nurseries located in this area plus vegetables of all kinds including sweet corn. The earth is black in this area and it is called Muck", a very rich soil that is great for growing anything.

Pahokee doesn't have a movie theater, not even one fast food restaurant. As a matter of fact there are only two restaurants in the whole area and one major food market, and little else. There is little to do here for the young children, especially teen agers. Football is big here and Pahokee high school has produced some pretty good high school teams and have sent several players to the National Football League, including Antwan Bolton, an all star receiver. Pahokee built a new football stadium about five or six years ago and named it the Antwan Bolton Stadium.

There is a large black community as well as the migrants. These people have very little and the unemployment is way above the national and Florida average. When Father John arrived at the St. Mary Church he found that his parish consisted of 99% Spanish speaking members. There are seven different dialects of Spanish spoken by the migrant community, but they all do communicate with each other. It seems that most adults have limited English if any at all, but all the kids speak English. As you might imagine these poor people needs are many.

The original church was built in the 1920's and holds only 85 people and this is where the Icon was originally placed. Besides this small white church with a bell tower there is a home where Father lived. There is also a large hall beside the church where many of the church activities are held. Part of the hall was also converted into eight class rooms where children attend a Charter school that pays a small rental fee. The hall also has a kitchen at one end and at the other end there is a stage which is set up with an altar and crucifix so Mass can be held there. There are two Masses on Sunday, one in English held in the small original church with eight to twelve people attending, and the second mass in Spanish is held in the hall. Sunday's collections were only $300.00 to $350.00 per week and the Palm Beach Diocese had to subsidies the church to help pay the bills.

There was a small hospital in Pahokee but it closed down, mostly because it could not attract enough doctors, nurses and personnel needed to run the operation. No one wanted to live in Pahokee and the commute for most was too much travel time each day. So the nearest medical help is in Belle Glade, another small poor community about 15 miles away. There are no doctors or dentists located in Pahokee but Father John found a way to help with the lack of medical and dental help for his parishioners.

MEDICAL AND DENTAL HELP AND MORE #255

ONE OF THE FIRST THINGS I learned while touring the premises of St. Mary Church for the first time was an extension on the rear part of the hall. It was a medical and a dental clinic combined. Both are open one or two days a week and there are doctors and dentists who volunteer their time and talents looking after the migrant community. All this was accomplished by Fr. John Mericantante and St. Mary Church. The nearest hospital was a small one located in Belle Glade, about 15-20 miles away. These poor migrant people do not have health coverage so this clinic was very important to their medical and dental needs.

Also near by and behind the rectory are three free standing "Sheds", I can't call them buildings but they do have electricity for lighting. As I found out one was for receiving and distributing of used clothing donated by several organizations, and after discovering this our Knights of Columbus Council became another donor for the next 14 years. The clothing was inspected and unacceptable items were discarded in a large garbage dumpster. All clothing was hung neatly on hangers by volunteer parishioners and this operation was open a couple days a week for people to "Shop". Most clothing was sold for something like .10 cents to a $1.00 and much just given out with no fee whatsoever.

The second shed was used for dry good foods only, caned, bottled, boxed, etc. Again, these volunteers would distribute donated food to people they had on a list and there was a schedule when these people on that list were allowed to come on an appointed day. So it was all controlled. The third shed housed toys, small appliances and other hard good items donated, like children's car seats, strollers, etc.

At one time the water in Pahokee was unsafe and the people were warned not to use the water for drinking. Brushing teeth and bathing was not really safe either as the water was full of impurities. In recent years this has been corrected but before that there were two places that people could bring containers and acquire safe water from a purifier unit. One was located at City Hall and the other was at a small house being used for recreational purposes at St. Mary's. Can you imagine that kind of a problem in this county in these modern times, unsafe drinking water?

My Monthly Trips #256

*W*HEN I DISCOVERED THE BUILDING with all the clothing I informed Father John that people were dropping used clothing off by the garbage bag full at our council hall and we had a little problem of what to do with these items. Would he be interested if we donated what we were receiving for their project? And I would be happy to deliver this clothing from time to time. Fr. John said they would appreciate anything useful as his people had so little. So that is how I got started and we started to have lunch together. That started a fourteen year highlight for me and for many other council brothers who made the trip with me over those years.

Father John told me he looked forward to these monthly luncheons because it gave him a chance to speak English! Yes, he has a great sense of humor and is very good company. The trip takes an hour each way and was a pretty easy drive with little traffic after exiting route 710 near Indiantown, then we headed west to towards Lake Okeechobee. Over the years I took one to three other brother Knights with me, and they enjoyed the trip and having lunch with Fr. John. They learned a lot about the needs of Pahokee, Saint Mary's church, the migrants and what Father John was accomplishing.

There is really a lot to see at St. Mary's with the little church and all the other buildings, the home in which Father lived had it's own little chapel, an office, and a museum that Father put together over the years with many artifacts he has collected from many countries that he has traveled. He even had a shrunken skull! There were also seven manikins, each one depicting the seven different nationalities of his parishioners. The hall was interesting along with the medical and dental clinics, and the small soccer field, basketball court and a playground. There was also a small house used as a gathering place for young people to play games and a couple of computers for their use.

Our Brother Knights enjoyed the visit and it also paved the way for me to suggest that we put Saint Mary on our charitable list as they were in dire need of funds. We started out with a donation of about 1 or 2 thousand dollars a year but as we kept increasing our donations to other churches to 5 thousand a year we also raised our donation to St. Mary to that amount as well.

The past five years or so it became almost the same brother Knights, Frank Bono and Ron Gomes, who made the trip with me. My Van was always packed to the ceiling with clothing and sometimes small furniture, lamps, kid's car seats, all sorts of things that we were receiving at our hall. Even used computers and TV's, sometimes we received dishes, pots, pans and utensils. We took everything out there but large furniture as they had a need for almost anything.

Almost all of our trips were on a Thursday. Having lunch in Pahokee was not always easy as there was not much choice as far as restaurants were concerned. Finally a new restaurant by the name of "Jelly Rolls" opened and was owned and operated by a nice lady who was born and raised in Pahokee. The food was good and most of the time the special was meatloaf. That was generally what most of us had, except Father John. He is not a big person, and never will be because of his eating habits. We kidded him all the time about what he always ordered, black coffee and a tuna fish sandwich on white bread. Fr. John would quickly devour one half of the sandwich and wrapped the other half in his napkin and took it with him, for dinner? In 14 years I never saw Fr. John eat the entire sandwich

PAHOKEE TRIPS CONTINUED #257

*W*E LOOKED FORWARD TO THESE monthly trips and our lunch together and Father John sincerely looked forward to our visits as well. He was not a member of the Knights of Columbus and I asked him if he would consider joining and become a member of our Council, which he did. When he made that decision he was anxious to make all three of the Degrees of our council. He then asked me about the Fourth Degree, our Patriot Degree. I explained that our council was part of the Andrew Doherty Assembly of the Fourth Degree, as were about seven other Councils at that time. We made arrangements for Father John to attend the next available Degree which was held in Miami, and I attended that event with him as his sponsor.

Back to Pahokee and what was going on in his Parish. A new building was being built; it was to be an after school program facility. Father John had much to do with raising funds for the building, which if I remember correctly, the cost was $375,000. The cost was high because of "Muck", that beautiful black soil, which is very unstable to build on. There are two ways to build, either remove all the muck, which in that area can be 3 to 12 feet deep, and fill in the void with sand. Or build on cement "Pilings" which is how boat docks are constructed. That is what was used; these pilings must go many feet below to where there is solid ground. Either way of construction is expensive. Our K of C council donated $5,000.00 towards the construction of one of the rest rooms of that facility.

This facility was eventually turned over to Palm Beach Diocese Catholic Charities and they assumed the responsibilities of running this program. There now are five buildings on the Church property. This new building, the Hall with the charter school class rooms and the medical and dental clinics, the original small church, the rectory with the museum and double car garage, and the house next door used for recreational purposes. There were also those three sheds used for clothing and food. That is quite a mouthful, and all this take money for normal upkeep.

And they have no money. On top of all that, Father John mentioned at lunch one day his parishioners are urging him to build a new church. Build a new church with what? With only $300 to $400 weekly collections how is this possible? Father John says God will provide, somehow, and he intended to start investigating the possibility of such an endeavor. There was room on the property by using the small soccer field and basketball court area, more than enough room for a church and a parking lot. All of this is going to take a miracle.

MIRACLES AT ST. MARY'S #258

I HAVE ALREADY WRITTEN ABOUT THE Icon and that there was what many called prayers answered and some considered miracles. I don't know much about these claims but Father John has mentioned a few to us over the years. Things like a lady who had strange red blotches all over her body and the doctors could not identify what they were or help her. She prayed to the Icon for help and her skin conditioned cleared up. Or the young wife who wanted to become pregnant but according to the doctors that would never happen because of some sort of a medical problem, but after praying to the Icon she became pregnant and the doctors said that could not happen. There were more of course.

But now another miracle would be needed to build a new church in this very poor community. How poor, just yesterday in the Palm Beach Post newspaper (8-23/15) there was a large article in the Local Section about how bad things were in Pahokee and that their towns influential people, including a former mayor many times over, the town should file for resolution, meaning no more town, its future would be taken over by the Palm Beach County. Pahokee lost its police force some years ago and is now patrolled by the Sheriffs office. Crime rate is high, unemployment is reported at 25% and that only tells us how many are reporting they are seeking employment, so it is most likely much higher.

First of all a church can't be built without Diocese approval and everything must be run through their organization, architect, builder, everything. Any money collected must be put in a special account and controlled by the Diocese and the Diocese was not in favor of a new church at all and already subsidies the cost of running this Parish.

Their directive to Father John, collect the money first to pay for the entire project and then we will make a decision. Another question they had was if a church was built where the money would come from to support its upkeep since the weekly collections would not cover the costs.

Father John simply said if God wants a new Church at St. Mary's he will provide.

Is a New Church Possible? #259

OVER THE YEARS FATHER JOHN was fortunate enough to receive various donations from people familiar with his and St. Mary's needs. These donations kept coming on a pretty regular basis, including receiving our Knight of Columbus donation of $5.000.00 a year. I know that some of our Council Brothers donated money from time to time after they became familiar with the situation at St. Mary's, but I have no idea how many or how much over the years. Even one of my daughters, Cindy, and her husband Nick, who live in Jacksonville, made an annual contribution to St. Mary's at Christmas time, instead of giving her mom and dad Christmas gifts, this was our gift instead. Cindy and Nick, thank you.

But this undertaking of a new Church seemed almost impossible. Nothing is impossible, especially if it is meant to be, and this was. An architect draws up the plans for Father John's new church, no charge. Its design was patterned after the Spanish Churches in the South West, which makes sense since 99% of his Parish was Spanish speaking people. The word spread of Father John and his parishioners' dream of a new Church and some small donations started to show up.

Since he recently was responsible for the After School building being built for $375,000.00, Father John estimated it might be possible to build this Church for about a million dollars. And that was what he started out to collect. I am quite aware of all this because we would often discuss his plans while having lunch. He not only needed money to build the Church, he needed funds to purchase items that would be needed inside the Church. He would need an Altar; he planned to purchase about 30 statues. Fr. John was confident this church would become a reality that he began purchasing a few of these items way before he was even close to having enough money to build.

One day he received word that a gentleman by the name of Leo Albert, who lived in Palm Beach, became aware of Fr. Johns project. Mr. Albert was a very wealthy man who was a large donor of funds to the Diocese. Mr. Albert pledged $800,000.00 and arrangements were made for Mr. Albert to attend Mass one Sunday when the announcement of this large donation was going to be announced to the parishioners. During that Mass Father John explained to his flock that this gentleman was in attendance and that he had pledged this very large donation. The place erupted with applause and when things settled down a bit, Father John announced," We still have a long way to go to reach one million dollars, we have a lot of work to do."

Then Leo Albert rose from his seat and spoke, "Father John, there will be another check in the amount of $200.000.00 in the mail to you tomorrow morning." Can you imagine what response that announcement received? However, when Father John went to the Diocese with the good news, he was told that their estimate for the Church he proposed would cost a minimum of three million dollars. What a shock that was to all concerned. But their faith never wavered.

The Altar #260

N EEDING TWO MILLION DOLLARS MORE than Father John originally thought, he proceeded to campaign for more funds but in the meantime he just knew God would provide. So the good Father continued his search for items he would need to complete the new church. There was a person in Minnesota that specialized in salvaged items either being replaced or from churches being torn down. This gentleman had a very large barn where all these items were stored and displayed for sale. Father John purchased seven religious tapestries which were very large, 15' by 8' in size and about 100 years old. He also purchased a very old Altar made of wood and it was 21 feet tall and 20 feet wide. The Altar also included a confessional booth, and a communion rail which is no longer used, but it was installed in the church anyway. But the story of the Altar itself is pretty interesting to say the least. The cost was $17,000.00 and when Father spoke to our council officers about the Altar and its cost, several Brothers suggested that our Council pay for this Altar as our contribution to the new Church. And we did just that, and Father John had a bronze plaque made that would be installed in the new church near the Altar stating that the Knights of Columbus Santa Maria Council 4999 was the donor.

When I first saw this Altar after it arrived in Pahokee, it was completely dismantled of course, and It looked like there were 100 different pieces. Father John rented a deserted service station in Pahokee to store it and it needed quite a bit of work. The Altar was painted white with gold leaf trim. The white paint had turned yellow and was badly cracked. It did not make a very good appearance to say the least.

So what was his plan for restoration? And how we decided to change its appearance is interesting.

THE ALTARS NEW LOOK #261

ONE DAY FATHER JOHN TOOK us to the service station where the Altar was stored and being worked on. We were interested in the progress of its restoration. All the old paint had to be removed and carefully too since the Gold leaf covering parts of the Alter was still useable and looked good.

One of the Brother Knights with us that day was Ray Waddell, a Past Grand Knight. We were looking at the exposed wood where the paint had been removed. The plan was to repaint the Altar but Ray, looking closely at the wood, pointed out to us how beautiful the exposed wood was. The wood had a nice grain and a very pleasing color. With just a little cleaning up and minimal sanding the natural wood was really good looking. Ray said, "Father John, look at this, I think the Altar should not be repainted white and the natural beauty of this wood would look better and the present gold leaf looks great. Just remove all the white paint and polish the wood a little and we have a better looking Altar than if would repainted white."

After closer examination we all agreed and that is how the Altar will look when installed in the new church. The next problem was there was no time table in sight for the construction of a new church. When the restoration of the Altar was finally finished I happen to ask Father what he was paying for rent. My concern was the same as his, how long would he have to pay rent to store the Altar, it was adding to the cost of the whole project. We needed to eliminate that cost and I suggested to Father John, that we put it in the hall where your temporary alter is.

It was too tall to assemble all of it, but just use part of against the back wall of the stage being used for Mass services. And that is what he did; the sections he could not get on that stage were put in a small shed out back, along with several statues he had already purchased that Fr. John was having made in Mexico, at a very reasonable price I might add.

Our K of C Council is very proud to have been a small part of the new church. It is a reality now but there is more to the story of the difficult times before the church finally became a reality. It was a small miracle collecting one million dollars plus a few thousand, but how in the world is Father John going to come up with at least another two million?

MORE MONEY NEEDED #262

*W*HAT A SHOCK, FATHER JOHN Mericantante needed at least another two million dollars! And there was no guarantee the Diocese would approve the plan anyway. The Diocese main concern was, if the Church was actually built and paid for, where was the money going to come from to maintain it? Will this church ever be built? Father John's faith never wavered. ***"If God wants this Church to be built it will happen."***

It happened, but it took **six years** before final approval was given. The money had been acquired by some miracle, more miracles at St. Mary's? Father John had the money, and almost everything needed to furnish the Church as well had been acquired and paid for. Fr. John had a life size bronze statue of Leo Albert made to honor the first donor of at least one million dollars would always be present and visible at the church. Unfortunately, Leo never saw the new church as he died of cancer a couple of years before the Church was built. A very sad loss indeed, he was such a kind and caring individual and he shared his fortune with so many worthwhile endeavors.

Then another problem came up as the land had to be prepared for construction. Muck, remember that word? Large structures can not be built on that unstable land. Either pilings had to be used or the land had to be de mucked. The extra cost for either one of those two decisions was not figured in the cost of building the church. The decision was to de muck the area, a very large and expensive undertaking, another $200,000.00 and again Father John found donors to fund this project as well. The muck was three to twelve foot deep and after removal this void had to be filled in with sand.

The building contractor was chosen by the Diocese and it was none other than Marty Seriese who was a Brother Knight. I have known Marty for years even though he was a member of Council 2075 in West Palm Beach. Marty, and his father before him, had built several churches in Palm Beach County and Marty also became a Deacon of the Catholic church. Marty and his construction company did a wonderful job of creating this new beautiful Spanish looking church. And what did Father John always say? *"If God wants this Church to be built, it will be built."*

THE NEW CHURCH BUILDING #263

$\mathcal{T}$HIS IS FATHER JOHN OWN words describing his new church.

Let me attempt to take you step by step thought the new Church building. There was a great bit of time between having the money for the new Church building and the actual building of it. Well you should never leave a "Boston" Priest alone with time on his hands because he will busy himself with something! My something was planning and purchasing for the new Church over the six year period of getting the necessary permissions and permits to build. Yes six years, I had to imagine what the Church would look like and what I had to buy to make it the perfect place of worship mostly for a poor migrant family population

Since I wanted them to feel right at home, I envisioned a Mission style Church like those of Texas and California, similar to the California Mission Churches built by Father Junipero Serra. I had yet to find a definite builder but a man came to me from the West Coast of Florida and offered his services. Although he did not, in the end, build the church. He did introduce me to the architect, John Lamb, who would design and completer my Church along with a local West Palm Beach builder, Mr. Martin Serraes.

I cannot tell you how many hours I sat up designing the 9,000 square foot floor plan for the new Church. I also went on the internet to find statues of Saints which in the end were made by craftsmen in Mexico. The difference in general in the cost for a life-size statue to be purchased here in the States is $17,000.00 to a mere $450.00 to $1,600.00 in Mexico. Even with paying for a truck to come from Mexico with 10 to 20 statues, it was a lot cheaper than buying the statues here in the United States. And the statues in Mexico are so much more beautiful especially with their glass eyes that seem to look at you as you pray!

My "Ace in the hole" at this time was a young Mexican man named Vicente Torres. Somehow, someway he could always get me what I wanted from Mexico, be it a statue of a Saint or an incense burner or a four foot monstrance decorated with the four evangelists and an angel. And when the craftsmen in Mexico did not know the Saint that I wanted, all I had to do is give Vicente a holy card with the picture of the Saint in question and the master craftsmen would make the image. This was especially true of St. Teresa of Avila which the craftsmen in Mexico had never seen as a statue. I sent them the image of Bernini's "St. Teresa In Ecstasy" and not only did he copy it, but he found the exact measurements of the original and sent me the State in the exact size of Bernini's original masterpiece! It really came out so beautiful and I have never seen any other Church with an exact copy or even one in miniature. The closest I have seen is but a mere photo of the original nut never a statue of it! So you can see there are treasures at St. Mary's of Pahokee which are not seen in other Churches.

I also bought a beautiful life-size bronze of a man being swept up to heaven in the arms of a beautiful female angel playing a violin as both rise majestically toward heaven and I re-named this bronze done by the great Vietnamese artist, Tuan, "Prayer"! And we put a plaque by the statue that states: "When we pray our words become like lyrics to a song whose music is played by an angel and whose song is heard by God as our prayer". This bronze is surrounded by a beautiful round water fountain which reminds us that we have all been reborn by water and the Holy Spirit as children of God Himself!

Walking through the giant wooden arched doors made in Honduras, we enter the Church and the image of "St. Teresa of Avila in Ecstasy" is found on our left, as well as the Choir, the Confessional the painting of Mary giving Mother's milk to Jesus, her baby, and also a niche with a small copy of the famous Pieta by Michelangelo whose original is found in St. Peter's Basilica in the Vatican. On the right walking through he main doors is a statue of Divine Providence depicting the Holy Trinity and next to that Our Lady of Fatima and then the Baptismal Font and above it soars our bell tower. Next to the Baptismal Font the famous miraculous 16th Century Russian Icon to Our Lady of Bethlehem is found holding her Baby Jesus in her arms and looking gracious as a Mother upon those who could come there to be baptized and to become another "Christ". The bell hidden in the tower was a gift from another place and time which is used again at our Church of St. Mary at each Mass to call the Faithful to prayer.

Going back to the middle isle, we can see bronze plaques along the floor that go right up the middle of the aisle toward the main altar. These plaques are the Divine Praises inscribed on them both in English and in Spanish. Along both sides of the Church are niches with various Saints portrayed who were chosen because they were devotionally significant to either my people or for me, their Priest.

In the front of the Church is the Main Altar. This is a very old alter that comes from another Church which was salvaged by a man in Minnesota whose work is to go around the country and buy up things from Churches that are being closed or demolished. The ancient altar is pure wooded Gothic and towers twenty feet above the thirty foot sanctuary and at the base is another altar, that of Sacrifice and in front of the Altar of Sacrifice is a bronze plaque attached to a round piece of malachite reading: "Hic, de Virgine Maria, Jesus Christus Natus Est" which means: "Here, through the Virgin Mary, Jesus is born." Because Jesus is born every day on the Altar in the Mass, I lovingly called St. Mary in Pahokee the "Bethlehem of the Diocese."

To the left of the altar is a beautiful 16th Century Peruvian painting of Mary being crowned Queen of Heaven and Earth by the Trinity. On the right Jesus is in a painting of His Crucifixion. There are also various Saints' life-size statues in and around the altar, as well as the presidential chair and the pulpit. Going back down to the main doors of the Church above and between each Saint's side niches are the Stations of the Cross, elegantly and traditionally on tile!

Walking again through the main doors outside the Church to the right is he Baby Jesus Chapel with several memorials to those who have contributed to the building, like Leo Albert who had given us our first million dollars. There is also a monument to a little girl, Rachel Ann

Flynn, who died during the construction of the new Church and whose saintly intercession helped me personally not to despair and to continue to have hope to build the Church when all hope was almost lost!

As I had stated in a pervious chapter in the end, the Church cost us $3.7 Million to build and we had just enough, no more, no less! And to tell you the truth, I and some of my parishioners have calculated that in 20 years we had probably given out to the poor that same amount! I guess God is a good mathematician. He gave us what we had given and a lot more in Faith, Hope, and Love and as you already have been told, there is no debt on the Church! And our personal debt to the Lord can only start to be paid by welcoming all to the new Church and continuing to help others, Catholic and non-Catholic of every creed, color, and personal persuasion in His Name! It is His Will and it is our duty! And as St. Gregory Nazianzen once said: "Kindness is the only thing which does not admit of delay!"

THE NEW CHURCH DEDICATION #264

ID I HAVE MUCH TO do with the conception and completion of this new magnificent beautiful St. Mary Church? No, not really, just that Father John discussed all of this with me during our monthly lunches for six straight years. After all of that, I feel like I am part of the concrete block walls after going through all those conversations about the progress, or non progress of getting this Church built.

It's a done deal; the construction of the Church is complete. All the statues, everything Father John has purchased to furnish the new Church is in place. Now it is time to formerly dedicate the Church. I have never been to a Church Dedication before so I did not know what to expect. One thing I did know, the church has a normal seating capacity of 500 people and there are many more parishioners than that. There will be all kinds of dignitaries in attendance. Bishop Gerald M. Barbarito and his staff will be heading up this very formal dedication along with dozens of other Priests and Nuns plus the news media and a large group of our Santa Maria Council in attendance as well.

How in the world are we to get a seat? Go one and one half hours early, that's how. And that is what we did and we claimed a seat in the second row on the right side. There were a number of people already there when we arrived with the same idea. The church was beautifully decorated with flowers everywhere. There were extra portable seats along the aisles and in the rear of the church to accommodate the anticipated overflow crowd. The choir and the small Mexican Mariachi band were already in place and started to play music about an hour before the dedication. The date is September 8, 2012. Father John would retire two years later.

The church was filled to capacity half an hour before the scheduled dedication. The music passed the time quickly. It was getting near the time for the Dedication Mass to start and outside it was very hot. Pahokee is located on the shore of Lake Okeechobee, the humidity was high and the temperature was probably around 92 degrees but it felt like 100 degrees. And then fifteen minuets before the start of the dedication it happened ...

The brand new air conditioning system failed. The show must go on, the doors were opened to get air flowing through, but there was no breeze. The new football field directly behind the church was busy also, even on a Sunday, the Pahokee high school band was practicing and their music was flowing into the church competing with the Mariachi band and the choir.

I was totally soaked in sweat by this time as were hundreds of others. People were standing everywhere including a couple of hundred outside. The Church bell stated to ring signaling the beginning of the very solemn beginning of the entrance of the Bishop. The doors had to be closed again to shut out the high school bands music.

In spite of all this, the one and one half hour dedication Mass and ceremony was beautiful. Father John looked so happy and pleased during the dedication. Father John looked pretty relieved as well, his project was complete with the help of his partner, God.

I always felt that the Devil was responsible for the failure of the new air condition system because he didn't want these poor people to have a new church. Guess who won out, the people with faith that they would indeed have a new church regardless of all the pit falls. And the Devil departed, the lack of air conditioning was not going to stop this long awaited Dedication, and was this another Miracle at St. Mary's?

Parting Thoughts about St. Mary's #265

*I*TS NOW IN THE FALL of 2014 and the new Church is two years old. I have been making this monthly trip along with my Brother Knights since the year 2000. Father John Mericantante is turning 65 years and is going to retire after 20 years serving the people of Pahokee.

I decided to retire along with Fr. John and decided that my 14 year run was coming to an end. I really felt pretty good about all of this as I truly enjoyed the easy ride and knowing the items we carried in my van was going to help the needy. My association with Father John was not coming to an end however. He now resides in Palm Beach and we still have lunch about once a month. Only now, I make him drive to the North Palm Beach area ever other month. I explained to Father it was his turn to come to us for a change.

Incidentally, when Father John retired he had collected something like $400,000.00 for the upkeep of the new Church and that money is deposited in a special escrow account for that use only. Upon retirement he left everything paid for as well. Mission accomplished.

Father John has become a wonderful friend over the years. On the back cover of his book, "The Dangling Urinal," Father wrote a prayer: **"Please God, make me a good Priest!"**

God has answered two prayers of Father John's that I have observed, there is no doubt God has made Father John a good priest, the other was the completion of the new St. Mary Church that so many people thought would never happen. God bless you, Father John Mericantante, I will always be looking forward to our next lunch together.

Since I no longer travel to Pahokee, you may be wondering what we do with all the donated items we still receive at our hall. We are now giving everything to Lahaut Baptiste, a Haitian by birth and a U.S.

Citizen, has been maintaining my lawn and trimming my trees for over 30 years. There is a large community of Haitians' in this area and they are in need of almost everything. They are hard working people in need. Interestingly, Lahaut is also a Minister and has his own small church. He is a good man helping his fellow man and he and my son Jim have been friends for 35 years.

Another story popped into mind, one day Lahaut called us and asked if it would be possible for him to use our pool. He needed a place to baptize several of his church members, all adults. Why would we turn him down so Dee and I said fine, but we did not know what to expect. I believe this was on a Saturday and three cars pull up in our circular driveway and all these Haitians' dressed in white robes start piling out of their cars. It was quite a sight. We don't know if any of our neighbors saw this but if they did they never mentioned it to us. Well, they all proceeded to our pool area. Our pool is very deep, eleven foot deep in the diving area and five foot deep in the sallow end where there are entrance steps. They all entered the pool and those being baptized were submerged and the water level came up to shoulders, some were in water up to their chins. Completely soaked, they departed that way in once dry cars. That's just another story of, "You had to be there!" Lahaut only asked us to do this once and I have never had the guts to ask why only one time? Didn't they like our deep water?

Now it is backspin time, there is another story I would like to tell which goes back a few years. It is about a great restaurant and meeting place which, sadly, is no longer in existence; it is DeCesares', The Place for Ribs.

DeCesares', the Place for Ribs #266

I AM RAPIDLY COMING TO THE end of my "Stories" and here is one that I wanted to write about a long time ago but slipped through the cracks. So it's "Backspin" time again. We are all aware of "Cheers" the TV series about a local drinking establishment where everyone seems to know each other. DeCesares' was kind of like that. I will try and describe this establishment, a very popular meeting place with a spacious bar and great food.

Located in North Palm Beach, Florida on Highway U. S. 1, right next door to the U.S. Post office, it is now an empty lot. But it is not an empty place in my memory. This was originally a Banana Boat chain restaurant with the main entrance facing the road. The front part of the facility was round and the large bar was in the middle of this room. The rest of the room had booths surrounding the bar. There was a hall leading to the rear that separated two more dinning rooms and the hall led to the back door and the parking lot in rear, where I always entered. There were quite a few TV's but not like you see in sports bars today. And they were never turned up loud; this was a place where everyone communicated with each other so the sound was soft, actually I think the sound may not have been on at all.

The walls were filled with individual pictures of famous people, mostly sports figures and most were autographed. Many of those individuals had been a customer at one time or another and some were regulars' when they were in town.

The place just had a warm feeling, the drinks were more than generous and the prices were moderate. 5 to 7 PM was cocktail hour featuring two drinks for the price of one. The second drink was served with the first one and it was served in a separate little bottle placed in a small ice container. Really classy and the Manhattans were out of this world and if I drank to many that is exactly where they sent me. But Frank DeCesare and his son, Dennis, kept a pretty close eye on everyone so there never seemed to be anyone having too much to drink and getting out of hand. I frequented this popular meeting place many years and never saw anybody getting out of line.

The food was excellent, not only the ribs, everything on the menu were a quality meal and the steaks were superb as well. Before I get into the celebrities and the people I looked forward to meeting there I will always remember a time that I stopped in while I was out for my late afternoon walk. I lived just about 5 or 6 blocks away. I also played a lot of golf with Frank and Dennis so I knew them quite well. This was shortly before dinner and I was headed home, smelled the aroma of the good food, and it was cocktail hour so I darted in the back door and went to the bar. Frank was there, we greeted and I said, "Frank, I was just passing by on my walk and felt like a cocktail before dinner, but, I have no money with me." He said, "Bill, no problem, the drink is on me!" They were doubles and that was more than enough. As I was about to leave I called Frank over and said, "Frank, let me have a couple of bucks." Frank said, "What for, the drink was on me." I replied, "Frank, it's for a tip for the bartender. You don't want me to stiff her, do you?" Well, Frank was still laughing when I left. I don't think I ever paid him back either.

DeCesares Patrons #267

THIS WAS DEFINITELY A GATHERING place for sports enthusiasts, especially people involved with golf. Not only did we run into people we knew living in this area all the time, but during the winter season when the "Snow birds" arrived, I ran into people I knew from all over the east, south and the mid west that I had met over the years while traveling those areas for Spalding.

It was a fun place, everyone was always in a party mood and mixing with each other around the bar swapping stories of the past and the present. It was just a good comfortable sports atmosphere and the northerners loved it. Arnold Palmer was a regular when in the area and I saw him several times, we always spoke as Arnold remembered me from the days I called on his dad in Latrobe, Pa.

I don't remember all the names of everyone we met over the years.

Some others that come to mind whose names might be familiar to you. Quite a few of the ballplayers from the New York Yankees were regulars, like Mickey Mantel, Whitey Ford, and Roger Maris, the home run king. I had met some of these guys before because some were on the Spalding Staff. Whitey Ford and Roger Maris were, so we spoke with each other from time to time. Roger was a sad story as he died of Leukemia at an early age. As a matter of fact he was in DeCesares about six months before he died, I saw him and he looked great, you could not tell he was ill. It was a shock when he passed away shortly thereafter.

One evening Whitey Ford came in and we exchanged greetings. Then I brought the subject up about Whitey signing his first contract with Spading I said to him, "Whitey, I bet I know what your first deal was when you signed your first contract with Spalding." He said, "Ok, what do you think it was?" I replied, "It was either for a pair of shoes and two gloves, or two pair of shoes and a glove." Whitey looked surprised and said, "How did you know that? It's true, one pair of shoes and two gloves." I replied, "Whitey, our guy who signed you was Duke Zilber. He's a friend of mine and he told me that story years ago." There was another part of that contract, if Spading put his name on any equipment he would receive a royalty, and of course we did put his name on a glove soon after he signed that original contract. Can you imagine, compared to the huge deals these guys get now?

Anyway, all good things come to an end, as did this restaurant. It seems everything runs it course and we still miss it. One last story, I had acquired several life size promotional cardboard stand-ups of golfers, plus one of "Shack" O'Neil, the 7' 1" basketball player. I put some of these in the windows of my house boat, but Shack was too tall to do that, so he ended up in the hall way of DeCesares, it was placed next to many of those autographed pictures. It was quiet a sight. When I put it there on loan, Frank DeCesare bought me another Manhattan. I had my own tip money this time.

We are coming to an end of my stories, time for some rambling thoughts, next.

RAMBLING THOUGHTS CONTINUED #268

*Y*ES, MY BUSINESS LIFE WAS very interesting to me, a small town Canton, Ohio boy who struggled to graduate from High School. I know now I had a problem holding my attention to grasp the subject matter during my school years. But that doesn't really matter now; I have had a very successful business career, both in the work force and what I may have accomplished by myself. But none of this would have happened without the support of my wife Dee. And one of the things that have made our marriage work all these years is respect for each other, and the fact that I always got the last few words. They were just two simple words, "Yes dear."

And yes, I have had the privilege of meeting hundreds, no, make that thousands of interesting people, many famous and many just like you and me. And the latter have been far and away the most important to me, along with my family, of course.

To summarize just a fraction of the "Notables", I'll try and remember as far back in years as I can, a person in the sports listed below, people that I have actually met and have had at least one conversation with.

Ping Pong: I don't speak Chinese so I never met any of these great players. Nice start, huh?

Soccer: I don't speak that language either. Batting zero!

Volley Ball: Blank. How am I doing so far?

Marbles: Bill Kloss, 1937 National Marbles Champion. I was six years old then. No, I didn't know him, but he went to the same high school in Canton, Ohio, **Lehman**. So that counts.

Hockey: Dave Keon, a Canadian, Hall of Famer of Stanley Cup fame. Dave lives in this area and was part of our golf foursome for a number of years. There was no hockey played in Canton so I was never a hockey fan. I played golf with David for almost a year before I found out about his being a Hall of Fame hockey player. His many fans called him, **"Davie"**.

Tennis: Remember **Poncho Gonzales**? I can even go back further, to the great English player, **Fred Perry**. Fred has been to my home here in Florida, had coffee, not tea, on our back porch with him on one occasion. During that visit he left a personal autographed picture with us, one of the very few autographs I have. **Doris Hart** was the **lady tennis player** who also comes to mind.

Billiards/Pool: I had dinner one evening in Youngstown, Ohio with the famous **Willie Masconi**, he of steel grey eyes. We were both at a Department store; he was giving pool demonstrations' to help promote the sale of pool tables. I was with our salesman promoting the golf department and Spalding. **Willie** told me stories way back when he was very young, there were some matches with big money bet by some very shady characters that he was told if he didn't win, he may never play again. That's when he found out he had ice running thought his veins, no other player could intimidate him. He was really good company. We split the tab.

Baseball: Bob Feller, Cleveland Indians. Actually, back in the 30's and early 40's when the Boston Red sox had a minor league team in Canton, the **Canton Terriers'**, many of these players who made it to the majors lived in our neighborhood and I use to talk to them as an admiring kid baseball fan. **Kirby Farrell**, first base, **Matt Batts**, catcher, **Whitey Krowski?**, outfielder, and **Tex Houston**, Pitcher, are in my memory bank.

Football: While in Pittsburgh, the Steelers trainer **Roger McGill,** bowled "Duckpins" with him, played basketball with linebacker **George Tarasovic.** Then there was the Steelers old single wing Quarter Back **Joe Gasparella,** who was a Notre Dame QB. Joe was a neighbor, his wife was my daughter Diane's first grade teacher. There was also **Marion Motley** (from Canton), fullback for the old Cleveland Browns, and of course my golfing buddy **Bill Nelsen,** the Browns QB in the 60's. I had the pleasure of playing golf with the famous Florida coach, **Bobby Bowden.**

Basketball: Had dinner with **"Dr. J", Julius Irving** and his lovely wife. He is a golf nut and one heck of a quality person, as is his wife, wonderful people. I believe the National Basketball Association, NBA, was formed in 1948 or 1949 and prior to that these great college players played in what was then called the "Industrial League". Companies like Republic Steel had basketball teams, and the players were not considered professionals. These companies "Hired" these players as employees of some kind. But their main job was to play basketball and represent there respective companies. I remember a guy by the name of "Red", I can't remember his last name, he was the first seven footer to play in this league, and was he clumsy. But a that time, most players were a lot shorter, maybe up to six feet six or seven inches, so he towered over everyone and got most of the rebounds without jumping very high, and that's all he could do. I used to go watch those games. **I just remembered!** One year when I was a District Sales Manager working the National Sporting Goods Show in Chicago, we always had some famous athlete in our Spalding booth to greet customers. Well, one year it was **Wilt "The Stilt" Chamberlain,** all 7' 1" or 2" of the largest man I have ever met. I went up to him, looked him straight in the chest, and shook his ham, or I mean hand! I was 6' 2" and I looked like a midget. Nice guy, we had fun with him being there for one full day.

Ladies Golf: The Ladies Professional Association LPGA was formed by 13 gals in 1950. I started to attend all of their tournaments in 1957 when they played in my territory and over the years I got to know most of them. **Helen Dettweiler, Bette Danoff and Helen Hick** I did not know them well but I was on a first name basis with the rest that I met. **Alice Bower and her sister Marlene, Patty Berg, and the last two, Betty Jamison and Marilynn Smith,** were Spalding staff members.

Men's Golf: I can not go back any further than the great **Bobby Jones.** I first met Bobby in 1957, my first Spalding sales meeting. Bobby was a Vice President of Spalding and came to every sales meeting until his health stopped him. It was sad to see his decline which has been well documented. In 1957 he was vibrant, then he stated showing up with the aid of a cane, then two arm crutches and finally a wheel chair. I had the chance to have several sit down conversations with him. Probably the next oldest would be having dinner at the Masters tournament with **Gene Sarazen,** along with **Jimmy Demeret** and **Toney Penna.** I never forget having a couple of beers with **Sam Snead** who was also a customer of mine at the Greenbrier. Yes, I know **Arnold Palmer** who is about two years older than I, but he and I are considered kids compared to the others mentioned above. Remember, I have met and know hundreds of Professional golfers, I am just trying to go back in memory as far as I can.

Entertainment: When I met **Bing Crosby** he was getting up there in age, a very nice person, as was **Bob Hope** and his wife **Delores. Perry Como** was a local resident and a frequent visitor at the **Toney Penna** golf facility and they played a lot of golf together. There were others that my memory is keeping there **names a secret.**

TV, Radio & Print Media: There were so many, Golf Magazines, newspapers, national and local sports writers around the country. Radio and TV announcers and personalities, It was fun just talking to these people. I'll only name one from the past some of you may remember, **Oscar Farley,** a sports writer who I got to know at the Masters one year and we were on a first name basis. He was also famous for writing the entire TV series, **"The Untouchables"** staring Robert Stack as Elliot Ness fighting the mob during prohibition. Remember that?

Autographs: Almost **none!** I have one of **Al Geiberger,** the first to break **60** on the tour, showing off his golf ball with the number **59** on it. And I think Dee has one of **Greg Norman.** I almost forgot, **Fred Perry,** but all of these were offered to me, I did not ask. And as a famous pig once said, stuttering, "That's all folks". I always felt that being in the Sporting Goods business it was unprofessional to ask for autographs. I just could not say "Would you sign this for my kid or grand kid" kind of a thing. No, not me, can you imagine what a collection I could have had? Yes, I have been told what you may be thinking, many times I have been told that. But that is just what I believed; it would have been very unprofessional. That's my story and I'm sticking to it. Want my autograph? Sorry, at this stage in my life, it is unreadable. But, if you like straight lines!

Now that is just a few names from the past out of hundreds, a lot of name dropping isn't it? Again, my intent of the names above was trying to go back in time as far as I could remember. Not mention everyone that would not be possible, it just happened in my different career positions I found myself throughout my active working career. An interesting career to say the least so, tomorrow, I will sum this up by letting you know who are the "Most important People I've met, **YOU!**"

The Most Important People I've Met, Is You #269

*Y*ES, I HAVE BEEN VERY fortunate to have met so many notable people in my lifetime. While it was very interesting meeting them, and being on a first name basis with many, there is no one more important in my life than my **family,** and all of **you,** including all I have yet to meet.

Each and every one of you mean so much to me. All those others I've met have just passed through my life. You are in my life for ever. Sure, some of you I know better than others, some longer than others, but all of you matter to me in one way or another. That is how life works out as far as I see it.

So today I am concluding my "Stories" as I have pretty much covered the past. What a wonderful time I have had recalling all of what I have written. There was much more that have slipped from my memory but I am thankful for all that came to mind.

The past is past. The future is unknown and everything, past and future was and is in God's hands.

My next task is to edit all 269 of these email stories as I just may turn all of this into a book, not to be published for the general public, well maybe. I wonder why in the world my personal life would be of any interest to strangers. Maybe by publishing a book it would be the way I meet you.

I want a book to give to all of my family, my kids, grand kids, there wives and husbands, great grand kids, all my cousins, so they may enjoy this history of a book written by some old man who many will not remember in any other way.

706

So today I conclude my "Stories" as I have pretty much covered the past. Now I look forward to the future. May God bless all of you, and all of your loved ones?

See "Ya" all later

Printed in the United States
By Bookmasters